SOVIET-AMERICAN RELATIONS, 1917–1920

Volume I

Russia Leaves the War

SOVIET-AMERICAN
RELATIONS, 1917–1920

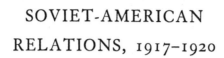

Russia
Leaves the
War

BY GEORGE F. KENNAN

PRINCETON, NEW JERSEY

PRINCETON UNIVERSITY PRESS

Published by Princeton University Press,
41 William Street, Princeton, New Jersey 08540

Library of Congress Card No. 56-8382

ISBN 0-691-00841-8, pbk.
First Princeton Paperback printing, 1989

Grateful acknowledgment is made for permission to quote from
The Magnate: William Boyce Thompson and His Time (1869-1930), by Hermann Hagedorn. Published by the John Day
Company. Copyright 1935 by Hermann Hagedorn. *A Prisoner
of Trotsky's*, by Andrew Kalpaschnikoff. Copyright 1920 by
Doubleday & Company Inc.

See page 523 ff for a complete list of acknowledgments.

Princeton University Press books are printed on acid-free paper,
and meet the guidelines for permanence and durability of the
Committee on Production Guidelines for Book Longevity of the
Council on Library Resources

10 9 8 7 6 5 4 3 2 1, pbk.

Printed in the United States of America
by Princeton University Press,
Princeton, New Jersey

This book is dedicated to
R. GORDON WASSON
in friendship
and in recognition of his selfless
and distinguished services
in the promotion of Slavic studies
in the United States

PREFACE

WHEN this study was first contemplated, the intention was not to reconstruct in detail the happenings of the initial months of the Soviet-American relationship, but rather to attempt a critical appraisal of the actions and policies of the two governments in their relations with each other over a much longer span of time. It soon became apparent, however, that despite the existence of several valuable secondary works on individual phases of Soviet-American relations in the early period, there was no general treatment of this subject, tapping all the sources available today, that could serve as adequate foundation for critical judgment. In these circumstances there was no alternative but to delve into the original source materials and to attempt to unravel, if only for one's own instruction, the tangled web of what actually occurred.

The present volume brings the first fruits of these researches, relating to the period between the November Revolution of 1917 and Russia's final departure, in March 1918, from the ranks of the warring powers. It is, admittedly, a heavily detailed account; some may think too much so. In attempting to bring together the available evidence on events at once so complex and so controversial, I have preferred to err on the side of explicitness rather than to run the risk, or invite the suspicion, of partiality in the selection of material. But beyond that: the more I saw of these records of the doings of an official generation slightly older than my own, the more it was borne in upon me that the genuine image of the diplomatic process is hardly to be recaptured in historical narrative unless the lens through which it is viewed is a sharp one and the human texture of which it consists becomes visible in considerable detail. The acts and decisions of statesmanship will seldom be found entirely intelligible if viewed apart from the immediate context of time and circumstance —information, associates, pressures, prejudices, impulses, and momentary necessities—in which they occur.

If, therefore, this narrative contains little of that broad appraisal of the initial western response to the phenomenon of communist power in Russia which many readers, perhaps, would prefer to see, it is my hope that it will at least serve as further illustration of the way the diplomacy of our century really works—of the marvelous manner in which purpose, personality, coincidence, communication, and the endless complexity of the modern world all combine to form a process beyond the full vision or comprehension of any single contemporary. It is sobering to reflect that, imperfect as this study is, there was none of the participants in the events recounted here—indeed, there was no one alive in these years of 1917 and 1918—who knew even the entirety of what is set forth in this volume.

This observation should not be taken as a questioning of the utility of the very effort of statesmanship. There is no intention here to belittle the importance of the differences that do exist in the ability of individual statesmen to comprehend or sense the trend of the times and to turn it to good account. But it is useful to be reminded that there is none who understands fully the stuff of which international affairs are made, none whose mind can embrace and calculate all its complexities, none who is not being constantly surprised by the turns it actually takes. In the end, it is only right principles, consistently applied—not the gift of prophecy or the pride of insight—that achieve the best results. These results are never wholly predictable; nor are they even easy to distinguish, when they appear. It is the tragedy of the diplomatic art that even its finest achievements are always mingled with ulterior causes and are seldom visible or intelligible to the broader public until many years have separated them from the decisions in which, in the main, they had their origin.

In offering this study to the public, I must acknowledge my indebtedness

first of all, to Robert Oppenheimer, for the inspiration and comfort he has given to a host of scholars and friends, myself included;

to the Institute for Advanced Study, for the enjoyment of its incomparable facilities for scholarly inquiry;

to the Rockefeller Foundation, for making possible the period of academic retirement in which this work could be undertaken;

to my colleagues at the Institute, Sir Llewellyn Woodward, Professor Ernst Kantorowicz, and Professor Arthur S. Link, for their generosity in reading the entire manuscript and giving me the benefit of their great experience and knowledge;

Preface

to Sir George Bailey Sansom, Professor Emeritus of Columbia University, and to Dr. Richard Pipes, of the Russian Research Center at Harvard University, for their kindness in reading, and commenting on, various portions of the work;

to the Library of the Institute for Advanced Study and the Firestone Library at Princeton University which, together, provided the great bulk of the published material used for this study and both of which gave valuable and efficient bibliographical assistance;

to the Foreign Affairs Section of the National Archives of the United States and the Manuscripts Division of the Library of Congress, in both of which I found a warm and immensely helpful reception;

to the Missouri Historical Society, for its excellent work in the preparation of the David R. Francis papers and its many personal kindnesses in connection with this inquiry;

to the Hoover Library of War and Peace at Stanford University; the Newberry Library at Chicago; the Library of the University of Chicago; the State Historical Society of Wisconsin; and the Yale University Library—in all of which I have used manuscript or special collections, and all of which have responded with unfailing courtesy and helpfulness to the demands this study has involved; and,

last but not least, to my secretary, Miss Dorothy Hessman, without whose enthusiastic and patient effort this task would have been much harder, much longer, and, unquestionably, much less adequately performed.

CONTENTS

[xi]

ILLUSTRATIONS

PLATES

MAPS

The maps were drawn by R. S. Snedeker

[xiii]

SOVIET-AMERICAN RELATIONS, 1917–1920

Volume I

Russia Leaves the War

PROLOGUE

Shine out in all your beauty,
  City of Peter, and stand
Unshakeable as Russia herself.
And may the untamed elements
  Make their peace with you.
  —*Alexander Pushkin, The Bronze Horseman*

THE city of Sankt Petersburgh—St. Petersburg, Petrograd, Leningrad, call it what you will—is one of the strangest, loveliest, most terrible, and most dramatic of the world's great urban centers. The high northern latitude, the extreme slant of the sun's rays, the flatness of the terrain, the frequent breaking of the landscape by wide, shimmering expanses of water: all these combine to accent the horizontal at the expense of the vertical and to create everywhere the sense of immense space, distance, and power. The heaven is vast, the skyline remote and extended. Cleaving the city down the center, the cold waters of the Neva move silently and swiftly, like a slab of smooth grey metal, past the granite embankments and the ponderous palaces, bringing with them the tang of the lonely wastes of forests and swamp from which they have emerged. At every hand one feels the proximity of the great wilderness of the Russian north—silent, sombre, infinitely patient.

Over this community there pass, in endless rhythm, the characteristic seasons of the north: the long winters of snow and darkness; the protracted in-between seasons of grey skies, slush, and a pervasive dampness; the white nights of the summer solstice, with their unbelievable, eerie poetry; and, finally, the brief, pathetic summers, suggestive rather than explicit, drawing to a close almost before they have begun, passionately cherished by the inhabitants for their very rareness and brevity.

In such a city the attention of man is forced inward upon himself and his own kind. Human relationships attain a strange vividness and intensity, with a touch of premonition. Under such a sky, fingers of fate seem to reach in from a great distance, like the beams of the sun, to find and shape the lives and affairs of individuals; events have a tendency to move with dramatic precision to denouements which no one devised but which everyone recognizes after the fact as inevitable and somehow faintly familiar.

The city is, and always has been, a tragic city, artificially created at great cost in human suffering, geographically misplaced, yet endowed with a haunting beauty, as though an ironic deity had meant to provide some redemption for all the cruelties and all the mistakes. For two hundred years it remained the center of a far-flung apparatus of bureaucratic power. But it was not destined to stand indefinitely, as Pushkin had hoped, against the forces of nature and the hand of change. In the twentieth century it was to endure trials and sufferings second to none in the annals of urban experience, and to lose its preeminence among the cities of Russia. The events described in this narrative have their beginning at the outset of these sufferings and this loss of preeminence.

On the evening of November 7, 1917 the life of Petrograd (as it was then called) seemed, outwardly, to be following what was almost its normal rhythm. Restaurants, movies, and night clubs were open along the Nevski Prospekt. The ballet was in progress at the Mariinsky Theatre. The streetcars moved as usual over the Troitski Bridge. The rickety droshkies that took the place of taxis still rolled quietly along the wide avenues, only the horses' hooves clattering on the paving of cobblestones and wooden blocks.

Yet only a short distance from the bright lights of the amusement center, the area around the Winter Palace was darkened and crowded with armed men; the entrances and exits to the adjoining streets were barricaded and guarded; sporadic bursts of rifle and machine gun fire rang out in the darkness over the wide expanse of the Palace Square. The sound of artillery fire reverberated from time to time across the black waters of the Neva—from the barely visible silhouette of the cruiser *Aurora,* anchored in mid-stream off the Admiralty embankment, and from the Fortress of St. Peter and St. Paul, across the river to the north.

Inside the Winter Palace, a grotesque situation existed. In the huge, ornate ballrooms, units of military cadets were quartered. Here, the air was heavy with tobacco smoke, with the smell of human bodies, with the remains of wine from bottles filched from the imperial wine cellars. In one of the innumerable great rooms on an upper floor, which was trimmed with gold, malachite, and crimson brocade, the members of the Provisional Government were sitting in proper ministerial tradition around a long green table, prolonging what had become a continuous day-and-night session. White with fatigue, smoking innumerable cigarettes, doodling frantically on the pads of white scratch paper that had been placed, with pathetic optimism, before each of them as potential repositories for a wisdom that was not there, the weary, desperate men continued to talk and wrangle through the night, drafting dramatic last-minute proclamations never to be used, dreaming up one device after another for saving the situation, while the final numbered seconds of that Russia of which they were the last custodians ticked away into history.

In a palatial residence somewhat farther up the Neva embankment, the British Ambassador, Sir George Buchanan, disconsolately watched from the windows of his drawing room the artillery activity over the river. Not far away, in a more modest building on an inside street, the American Ambassador slept the untroubled sleep of one who, though advanced in age, had never questioned the values of his youth and never attempted to peer too intently into the uncertainties of the future. In an elegant suite at the Hotel d'Europe, on the corner of the Nevsky Prospekt and the Liteiny, the two senior members of the American Red Cross Mission, William Boyce Thompson and Raymond Robins, both children of the American western frontier and nostalgic for the romance of the early mining days, whiled away the hours discussing a copper mining project in Arizona. Both were intensely interested in the Revolution, but both were helpless and bewildered in the face of the torrent of events. At 10:26 p.m. Robins retired and wrote in his pocket diary: "A great day for Russia and the world . . . War: Civil war and the Commune. What an hour. O my Father . . . Help America and Russia and the free peoples of the world."

At 2:00 a.m. Red Guards, followed by the street mob, burst into the besieged palace. Prophetically enough, it was not the direct military attack that had produced this move: the cruiser *Aurora,* contrary to legend, had fired only blanks, and the ancient artillery pieces of the Fortress had frightened those who fired them more than those against whom they were aimed. The Bolshevik capture of the Winter Palace occurred because there was much disunity and vacillation among its defenders, and someone had inadvertently left the back door open.

At 2:10 a.m. the doors of the room in which the Provisional Government was sitting were flung violently open. An individual in a pince-nez and a broad-brimmed artist's hat, looking more like the French Revolution than the Russian, burst into the room, the mob thronging the doorway behind him, and shouted: "In the name of the Military-Revolutionary Committee I declare you arrested." The ministers were then marched out under guard.

A few minutes later five Americans, drifting innocently about in the wild excitement of that night like men from another planet, stumbled upon the abandoned cabinet room, took note of the general disorder and the doodled papers, pocketed some of the unfinished drafts, then wandered farther along the endless corridors. They finally attracted the attention of the aroused mob that was busily looting the Palace, and were themselves almost lynched, being rescued only by the timely intervention of a Red Guard officer. Four of these Americans were journalists, led by the young Harvard-graduate radical, John Reed, who left an account of the night that will live long in historical literature. The fifth was that discreet but infinitely observant and well-informed figure who was to haunt the paths of Soviet-American relations for many years to come—Mr. Alexander Gumberg. Leaving the Winter Palace, the five made their way back to the Smolny Institute, where the Second Congress of Soviets, seething with passion and excitement, was receiving the news of the victories of the night and decreeing the establishment of Soviet authority. Reed concluded his classic account of the events of that night with his departure from Smolny in the early morning:

Although it was six in the morning, night was yet heavy and chill. There was only a faint unearthly pallor stealing over the silent streets, dimming the watch-fires, the shadow of a terrible dawn grey-rising over Russia . . .

The new state of affairs in Russia, ushered in by the events of that night, was destined to have the most profound effect on the relationship of the peoples of Russia to their external environment, and not least to the growing community on the North American continent known as the United States of America, whose national experience was in some ways so similar to, in other ways so different from, their own. From the moment of the Bolshevik seizure of power in Petrograd, the relationship between these two great national communities would become of increasing importance, not only for their respective peoples but for the world at large. It is to the early phases of this relationship, now fallen so largely into forgetfulness, that the present study is addressed.

CHAPTER I

THE IMMEDIATE HISTORICAL
BACKGROUND

THE seizure of power in Petrograd by the Bolsheviki on November 7–8, 1917 constitutes the formal point of departure for this narrative. But it was, of course, only the final phase of a revolutionary process which had begun with the collapse of the Tsarist system several months earlier. Before we proceed to examine the course of Soviet-American relations, it will be useful to glance briefly at the American reaction to the earlier phases of this revolutionary process.

The events that marked the fall of Tsardom in March 1917 (usually referred to, by virtue of the difference in calendar,[1] as the February Revolution) constituted one of the most amazing, least foreseen, and to this day least understood of the great political changes of history. To attempt to describe these events would surpass the purposes of this study. But there are certain features of the February Revolution worth noting here.

First of all, it was not a contrived revolution. No one planned it. No one organized it. Even the Bolsheviki, who for years had dreamed of such a day and had conceived of themselves as professionals in the art of producing revolutions, were taken wholly by surprise. The February Revolution was simply the sudden, crashing breakdown of an old dynastic-imperial system, caught between the stresses of a major modern war, for which it was inadequate, and the inertia of an imperial court that had lost its orderliness of

---

[1] For purposes of this study, the Gregorian calendar will be used throughout. The Julian calendar was retained in Russia until February 14, 1918. The difference between the two calendars was one of thirteen days, the Gregorian calendar being ahead of the Julian by that interval. Thus dates cited here for the period up to February 14, 1918 will often be mentioned in Russian sources as thirteen days earlier.

[8]

procedure, its feel for events, its contact with the people, and even the respect of the ruling bureaucracy.

A great many Russians had dreamed—like the Bolsheviki—of revolution in one form or another and to one degree or another, and had chafed under what seemed to them the interminable delay in its arrival; but from the standpoint of the ideals to which most of these people aspired, the February Revolution may be said to have come, if not prematurely, then at a most inopportune time. For one thing, the country was endeavoring to conduct a major war, involving extensive mobilization of manpower and a great strain on the entire economic and administrative system. This was an involvement which, as the Bolsheviki were later to learn to their sorrow, would not be easily liquidated and which could not fail to add to the burden of any new regime assuming power at that time. But beyond that, there was no adequate unity among the various political groups available to share in, or compete for, the inheritance of the Tsar's power. There was not, as among them, even that modicum of consensus on the terms of political competition that would have been necessary to make possible any orderly transition to some stable form of representative government. The Russian political society that had simmered under the crust of Tsarist power and had yearned for its disappearance or moderation was actually riven, itself, by tragic and scarcely reconcilable divisions. The events of the abortive revolution of 1905, and more recently the stresses of the First World War, had carried the Russian socialists to a point where their hatred and distrust of the "bourgeois" parties was extreme. Their very attachment to their country had been weakened in favor of concepts of political obligation based on class rather than on nation. The non-socialist elements, on the other hand, tended to view the socialist leaders as irresponsible demagogues, little short of traitorous. The situation was further complicated by separatist tendencies in many parts of the Russian Empire—tendencies inflamed by the unhappiness of the time and now greatly stimulated by the disappearance of the dynastic center that had been at least the symbol, and the only symbol, of political unity.

So long as the structure of Tsarist power held together, the latent antagonisms among these divergent elements were in part concealed and disguised by their common hope for a change; but, once

Tsardom was gone, there was nothing to keep the manifold antagonisms from coming out into the open, greatly accentuated by the unexpected competition for the succession into which the various elements suddenly found themselves thrust.

The situation was rendered peculiarly complicated by the fact that in the period immediately following the collapse of Tsardom neither of the two major camps of political contenders was in a position to get along, for the moment, without the other. The non-socialist parties included within their following the overwhelming portion of the political and administrative experience available in the country. They alone could muster the knowledge, the insights, and the international connections requisite to the immediate establishment of a new governmental system on the ruins of the old one. It was natural that they should take the initiative—as they did—in setting up the framework of a provisional government; and it was natural, in the circumstances, that this government should draw its legitimacy from the last Tsarist duma, or parliament, a body primarily non-socialist in its composition.

But it was the socialists, united in the various *ad hoc* "soviets of workers' and peasants' deputies," and outstandingly in the Petrograd Soviet, who commanded the confidence of the mass of industrial workers in the large cities and of the politically conscious portions of the rank and file of the armed forces. The importance of both these latter elements had been greatly heightened, from the standpoint of the struggle for political power, by the fact that the old Tsarist police force had been shattered in the process of the February Revolution, leaving the maintenance of order in the urban areas largely at the mercy of the soldier and worker elements—the only elements having disciplined young manpower and, usually, arms.

Thus it was the non-socialist parties alone who were able to provide the essential forms of the new provisional governmental power—a fact which the socialist groups, themselves not yet ready for the assumption of governmental responsibility, were fully prepared to recognize. Yet the substance of domestic power, in the sense of ultimate control over the behavior of the armed forces and ultimate domination of the city streets, rested with the socialist elements, who had their own independent organ of legislative and executive power in the form of the Petrograd Soviet and the other city soviets amenable to their influence. The Petrograd Soviet, while almost wholly socialist, was at the outset not yet Bolshevik-dominated (the Bolsheviki were still only a minority among the parties there represented), but it constituted an independent force, not really subject to the authority of the government; and many of its members held feelings of deep bitterness and suspicion toward the entire non-socialist sector of Russian society, including most of the members of the Provisional Government.

In this way there came about that dangerous duality of political authority—the so-called *dvoevlastye* [2]—which characterized the months immediately following the fall of Tsardom. The Provisional Government was permitted to function as the titular repository of state power and the external exponent of Russian interests. But internally its authority depended in many respects on the support of the Petrograd Soviet, which it could not control, which was prepared to support it only "insofar as" it served socialist purposes, and which stubbornly refused to be lured into accepting any formal responsibility commensurate with its real power. Between these two parallel governments there was no ordered relationship, no intimacy, no consensus—only distrust, hostility, and an uneasy jockeying for position.

This situation had two major implications from the standpoint of the United States. First, it meant that the chances for political stability in the new regime were small indeed. Plainly, such a state of affairs could not endure for long. The fall of Tsardom had been only the prelude to the real struggle for power. Particularly ominous was the fact that the attachment to the principles of parliamentary government was weak or non-existent in large sections of the Russian public. The common people had little conception of what political freedom meant. Many socialists were not sure that the "bourgeois" elements ought to have any share at all in the political life of the state. The monarchists were sure that the "internationalist" socialists ought not to have any such share at all. Only in limited "bourgeois-liberal" circles, soon to be left isolated and helpless by the rapid drift of power to the left, was there any real conception of parliamentary democracy in the western sense.

[2] In general the transliteration table used in this volume is that now used by the United States government. In cases where the insertion of the *y* before the *e* seemed essential to indicate pronunciation, it has been used. Family names and places have been rendered in this transliteration except where there is another version commonly in use in western literature.

Secondly, this situation meant that the prospects for Russia's continued participation in the war were very poor. The attempt to continue the war effort would have taxed the resources of even a unified and firmly entrenched regime. To suppose that such an effort could be carried out by a government lacking real authority over the troops, acting through an officers' corps which had lost face with the rank and file—this in face of the fact that the mass of the soldiers were war-weary and largely indifferent to the issues of the war, and in face of the further fact that a considerable portion of the socialists, to whom the soldiers looked for leadership, were already committed to the view that the war was an imperialist one, serving no useful purpose —to suppose this was to be optimistic indeed.

Yet the fact is that neither of these realities was widely noted in the United States; it is, indeed, not an exaggeration to say that the policy of the United States government toward the Russian Provisional Government was founded largely on ignorance of both of them and on the hope that just the opposite would be the case: that Russia would evolve rapidly, that is, in the direction of democratic stability, and that she would continue to prosecute vigorously, as a loyal and enthusiastic member of the western coalition, the war against Germany. In these misunderstandings will be found the roots not only of much of the ineffectiveness of American policy toward the Provisional Government but also of the difficulty experienced by many Americans at a later date in adjusting to the realities of Soviet power.

The misunderstandings were in no way unnatural. There was nothing in the traditional American political philosophy to make Americans aware of such virtues as the Tsarist system may have had or to cause them to doubt that the removal of this system would be followed by rapid progress in the direction of parliamentary democracy. It had never occurred to most Americans that the political principles by which they themselves lived might have been historically conditioned and might not enjoy universal validity. Interest in Russia among the American public had been confined largely to a sympathetic following of the struggle against autocracy. It had centered in two main groups. One was composed of what might be called the native-born American liberals, men whose sympathies had been captured by the sufferings of the Russian oppositionists of an earlier date. A number of American figures, including the elder George Kennan,[3] Samuel Clemens, and William Lloyd Garrison, had come

---

[3] A first cousin twice removed from the author of this study.

together in the early Nineties to set up a private organization called "The Friends of Russian Freedom," the purpose of which was to bring aid to the victims of Tsarist oppressions. This organization had endured up to the time of the Revolution. Such of the original members as were still living when the Revolution came were older people. Their impressions of the Russian revolutionary movement, based largely on observations made by Kennan in the 1860's and 1880's, related to the pre-Marxist phase of the struggle. In the period just before the Revolution, their sympathy and aid were addressed mainly to the Social-Revolutionaries who, comprising a socialist but not Marxist party, appeared to them as the spiritual heirs to the earlier populist tendencies in the Russian revolutionary movement. They had little idea of the implications of the latter-day Marxist domination of Russian revolutionary thought.

In this respect, the older liberals differed particularly from the other group of Americans, or American residents, interested in Russia. These were the newly immigrated Jews—consisting chiefly of people who had removed to this country since the 1880's in order to escape racial discrimination or political persecution, or both. In large proportion they were people affected by the Marxian doctrines that had made so profound an impression on the Jews of the Russian "pale." They were predominantly Social-Democrats, rather than Social-Revolutionaries. They differed from the American liberals in that their conception of the opposition movement in Russia was oriented toward social revolution in the sense of the shift of power to a given social class, rather than toward general political liberty in the American sense. They shared with the others only the intense desire that Tsarist absolutism should be swept away. Between them, these two groups pretty well dominated the formation of American opinion with respect to Russian matters.[4]

These circumstances would in themselves have been enough to assure an eager and unquestioning welcome of the fall of Tsardom in almost all shades of American opinion. But to them was added the close coincidence of the first Russian Revolution with America's entry into the First World War. From the standpoint of the needs of American statesmanship at that particular time, the Russian Revolu-

[4] Strangely enough, the non-Marxist Russian liberals, the Constitutional Democrats, seem to have enjoyed little sympathy or support in the United States, except in a few business and charitable circles. We have here, perhaps, another manifestation of that curious law which so often makes Americans, inveterately conservative at home, the partisans of radical change everywhere else.

[13]

tion, as generally viewed and understood in the United States, could not have come more opportunely. President Wilson, it will be recalled, was then just approaching the end of the long agony of decision involved in the determination of America's relationship to the European war. In the first weeks of 1917 the tide of events had run relentlessly in the direction of America's entry into the war on the Entente side. The German declaration of unrestricted submarine warfare, on February 1, 1917, had in fact deprived American statesmanship of the last area of maneuver, and had virtually sealed the issue. After that, it was only a question of time.

But there was still the question of the interpretation to be given officially to this tremendous departure in American policy. Technically speaking, the immediate impulse to our entry into the war lay in violations of our neutrality. But the defense of neutral rights was a confused and uninspiring issue, legalistic, involved, understood by very few. It was an issue, furthermore, on which our grievances against our future allies were only slightly less serious than our grievances against the Germans. Not only was this too narrow and technical a cause in which to lead a great people into battle, but many doubted that it was really the cause at all. There was a general consciousness among American statesmen, on the eve of the fateful step, of a need to find for this departure a loftier and more inspiring rationale than the mere defense of neutral rights, one closer to the solemnity with which Americans experienced that stirring moment, and one more directly related to the needs and ideals of men everywhere—not just to the people of the United States.

Into this questioning, the first Russian Revolution, occurring only three weeks before our entry into the war, entered with important effect because it appeared to alter the ideological composition of the coalition with which we were about to ally ourselves. At the Cabinet meeting of March 20, 1917, where it was unanimously decided to ask Congress for a declaration of war, Secretary of State Lansing (according to his own account written on the heels of the event [5]) argued for the step on the grounds that

. . . the revolution in Russia, which appeared to be successful, had removed the one objection to affirming that the European war was a war between

[5] I am indebted to Professor Edward H. Buehrig of Indiana University for drawing to my attention this account by Lansing (in the Robert Lansing MSS, Private Memoranda, Library of Congress) of the proceedings of the historic Cabinet meeting of March 20.

Democracy and Absolutism; that the only hope of a permanent peace between all nations depended upon the establishment of democratic institutions throughout the world; . . .

The moment seemed particularly propitious, Lansing added, because

. . . action by us . . . would have a great moral influence in Russia, . . . would encourage the democratic movement in Germany, . . . would put new spirit in the Allies. . . .

Wilson was at first hesitant in accepting this thesis that the Russian Revolution gave grounds for presenting America's war effort as a crusade for democracy. "The President said," Lansing's account continued,

that he did not see how he could speak of a war for Democracy or of Russia's revolution in addressing Congress. I replied that I did not perceive any objection but in any event I was sure that he could do so indirectly by attacking the character of the autocratic government of Germany as manifested by its deeds of inhumanity, by its broken promises, and by its plots and conspiracies against this country.

To this the President only answered "Possibly."

Whether the President was impressed with the idea of a general indictment of the German Government I do not know. . . .

It is interesting to note that it was Lansing and not the President who first advanced the interpretation of America's war effort as a crusade for democracy and against absolutism, and connected this interpretation with the Russian Revolution. The reasons for the President's initial reserve with regard to this concept are not clear. They probably did not rest in any lack of gratification over the Russian Revolution or doubt as to its democratic quality. More likely they reflected uncertainty whether such an interpretation of America's action was strictly accurate and also, perhaps, a lack of conviction as to the plausibility with which certain of our other future allies could be fitted into the democratic category. However this may be, Lansing's argument was not lost on the President. The view he put forward not only found reflection in the message calling for a declaration of war, but soon became the essence of the official interpretation of the purpose of America's war effort.

It is thus possible to say that while America's entry into World War I was in no wise occasioned by the Russian Revolution, this event did indeed affect the interpretation placed upon the war by the American government and public. In particular, it made it possible to construct for the American war effort an ideological rationale which, had the Russian Revolution not occurred, would have been relatively unconvincing and difficult to maintain. This was, at the time, a most welcome possibility; and one can easily understand how strong was the temptation to take advantage of it. But it implied a commitment on the part of the United States government to precisely those assumptions concerning the Russian situation which, as we have just seen, were least likely to be fulfilled: namely, that Russian political life would advance at once toward a stable parliamentary system and that Russia would continue to wage war as a member of the Allied coalition.

It was on this view of the Russian Revolution that American policy toward the Russian Provisional Government was founded; and the subsequent actions of the United States government were strictly consistent with this outlook.

The first of these actions was the prompt and enthusiastic recognition of the new regime. Here the initiative was taken by the American Ambassador at Petrograd, Mr. David R. Francis. We shall have a closer glance at Mr. Francis presently. Suffice it to note here that his relations with the Tsarist regime had been remote, unsatisfactory, and frustrating. He had found himself overshadowed, in his relation to Russian court circles, by his French and British colleagues, who were more experienced, better connected, more at home in the world of dynastic diplomacy and aristocratic social forms. Since its establishment a century earlier, the United States diplomatic mission in the Russian capital had, in fact, been generally in an inferior position as a result of the ideological disparity between the two systems and the disinclination of American envoys to attempt to rival the ponderous and expensive elegance of the great Petrograd salons.

To Francis the events that transpired between March 12–18, 1917, presaging—as they appeared to do—an area of democratic liberalism and constitutionalism, bade fair to change this entire setting. Not only was he deeply moved by the genuine idealism of the February Revolution, but wholly new vistas seemed to open up for Russian-American relations in this amazing series of events. An American Ambassador would now, for the first time since John Quincy Adams set foot ashore in Petrograd in 1809, be dealing with a political entity which had cut its ties to the institution of monarchy and was setting out along the same path of democratic government that the United States itself had taken. For such an entity, in contrast to its predecessor, the American example would surely be important, American achievements something to be studied and imitated, American help something to be coveted. Was it unreasonable to suppose that in the relations with such a country it would be the American Ambassador, rather than the British or the French, who would have the most to offer and the most to say? [6]

Accordingly, in reporting to Washington the completion of the February Revolution, Francis requested authority to recognize the Provisional Government immediately, arguing that it was "desirable from every viewpoint" that the United States be the first to accord such recognition. "This revolution," he wrote,

is the practical realization of that principle of government which we have championed and advocated. I mean government by consent of the governed. Our recognition will have a stupendous moral effect especially if given first.[7]

Washington responded favorably to this request, with the result that Francis beat the British and French ambassadors to the punch by some four hours, an achievement which gave him intense and lasting satisfaction.

When, a fortnight later, America entered the war, the official utterances of the statesmen in Washington reflected faithfully the outlook on the Russian Revolution noted above. In his message to Congress of April 2, calling for a declaration of war, the President drew

---

[6] In a letter written many years later to an American scholar (November 20, 1948, to Charles D. DeYoung), Mr. DeWitt C. Poole, one of the best American observers in Russia at that time, said: "Francis did not speak Russian and his contacts were not wide, but he was sufficiently aware of the plight of the Russian people to welcome jubilantly the overthrow of the Tsar and the coming to power of the Provisional Government . . . . with the members of the Provisional Government Francis had a bridge of understanding, and with them in power over a period of years Francis might have gone down as a pretty successful ambassador. . . ." (Poole MSS, State Historical Society of Wisconsin, Madison.)

[7] *Papers Relating to the Foreign Relations of the United States, 1918, Russia*, Vol. I, U.S. Government Printing Office, Washington, 1931, p. 6; from Telegram 1107, Francis to Secretary of State, March 18, 1917, 8 p.m.

This series of government publications, the individual volumes of which appeared at varying dates, will hereafter be referred to simply as *Foreign Relations*.

sharply the ideological issue between democracy and autocracy. He denied the possibility of any fruitful participation in international life by autocratic governments ("No autocratic government could be trusted to keep faith or observe its covenants"). He then turned, with obvious relief and pleasure, to the Russian situation, and went on to say:

Does not every American feel that assurance has been added to our hope for the future peace of the world by the wonderful and heartening things that have been happening within the last few weeks in Russia? Russia was known by those who knew it best to have been always in fact democratic at heart, in all the vital habits of her thought, in all the intimate relationships of her people that spoke their natural instinct, their habitual attitude towards life. The autocracy that crowned the summit of her political structure, long as it had stood and terrible as was the reality of its power, was not in fact Russian in origin, character, or purpose; and now it has been shaken off and the great, generous Russian people have been added in all their naïve majesty and might to the forces that are fighting for freedom in the world, for justice, and for peace. Here is a fit partner for a league of honour.[8]

This utterance was supplemented some days later by the wording of the Secretary's telegram directing Francis to apprise the Russian government of America's entry into the war. Francis was instructed to say

that the Government and people of the United States rejoice that the great Russian people have joined the powerful democracies who are struggling against autocracy . . .

and to express the hope and expectation of the United States government that

a Russia inspired by these great ideals will realize more than ever the duty which it owes to humanity and the necessity for preserving internal harmony in order that as a united and patriotic nation it may overcome the autocratic power which by force and intrigue menaces the democracy which the Russian people have proclaimed.[9]

These two passages set the tone for the approach the American government was to take toward the Provisional Government through-

[8] *Foreign Relations, 1917*, Supplement 1, *The World War* (1931), p. 200.
[9] *Foreign Relations, 1918, Russia*, Vol. 1, *op.cit.*, pp. 20–21; from Telegram 1299, April 6, 1917, 1 p.m., Secretary of State to Francis.

out the entire period of its tenure: an approach made up of a somewhat wishful and hasty welcome of Russia into the community of democratic nations; an eager desire to assist the Russian people to pursue what were assumed to be common aims of military struggle; and a benevolent but never inordinate anxiety for the ability of the new Russian regime to preserve the "internal harmony" requisite to the fulfillment of its proper role in the new community of democratic nations.

In accordance with this attitude, everything possible was done to bring assistance and encouragement to the Provisional Government. One of the principal efforts in this direction was the extension of credit. As early as April 3, even prior to our entry into the war, Francis was authorized to offer American governmental credits to the new Russian regime. In pursuance of this offer, a series of credits totaling $325 million were eventually extended at various times during the period of tenure of the Provisional Government.[10] Against these credits $187,729,750 was actually used. The amount of goods purchased and delivered to Russia before the November Revolution was of course not large in view of the shortness of time involved. The effect on Russia's contribution to the war was substantially nil.

In addition to this financial assistance, numbers of Americans were sent to Russia in 1917 in the belief that their presence there would be useful either in giving inspiration and encouragement to the Provisional Government or in helping it to cope with various technical problems thought to be associated with its war effort.

The first and most important step in this direction was the despatch of the Root Mission. Immediately after our entry into the war Washington conceived the idea of sending to Petrograd a special goodwill mission, which would welcome Russia into the democratic community and which would also manifest the American desire to be of assistance. The result was the decision, taken shortly after the middle of April, to despatch Mr. Elihu Root, distinguished Republican lawyer and elder statesman, former Secretary of State and Secretary of War, on just such a mission. He was to be accompanied by a number of other well-known American figures. The purpose of the mission, it was announced, was to manifest America's sym-

---

[10] *Foreign Relations, 1918, Russia,* Vol. III (1932), Chapter I, pp. 1–28. A further credit of $125 million was established on November 1, 1917 but was overtaken by the Revolution before any public announcement could be made of it.

pathy for the "adherence of Russia to the principle of democracy" and to confer with the Russian government about "the best ways and means to bring about effective cooperation between the two governments in the prosecution of the war." [11]

The reasons that led the President to select Root for this task are not entirely clear. A desire to demonstrate the bipartisanship of America's feeling was presumably the leading consideration; but, as Root himself sourly observed, "he never would have appointed me if I had not been 73 years of age." [12] Wilson was, as we shall see shortly, not happy in retrospect about the appointment, and there is no indication that he made it with any enthusiasm or conviction.

Worried by the fear that Root would be regarded by Russian liberals and socialists as a reactionary, the President tried to find someone to include in the mission who would counteract this impression. He turned (rather ironically, when one recalls the views of Russian socialists about the American Federation of Labor) to Samuel Gompers for advice. Gompers first recommended Mr. William English Walling, who wisely begged off.[13] The choice finally settled on Mr. James Duncan, elderly vice-president of the American Federation of Labor, and Mr. Charles Edward Russell, journalist, author, and moderate-socialist by persuasion. Other members of the mission were Mr. Charles R. Crane, who will be mentioned further in another chapter; Mr. John R. Mott, of the Young Men's Christian Association; Mr. Cyrus H. McCormick, of the International Harvester Company; and Mr. Samuel R. Bertron, New York banker. General Hugh L. Scott, only just retired from the position of Chief of Staff of the Army, was also made a member of the delegation.

Root and his party proceeded to Russia in May via Vladivostok, were transported across Siberia and European Russia in the ex-Tsar's private train, and arrived on June 13 in Petrograd, where they endured nearly a month of formalities, dinners, speeches, and excursions before returning to the United States by the same route.

In addition to the Root Mission, an Advisory Commission of Railway Experts was sent under the leadership of a well-known American

---

[11] *Foreign Relations, 1918, Russia*, Vol. I, *op.cit.*, pp. 110–111; from Telegram 1428, May 22, 1917, 5 p.m., Secretary of State to Francis.

[12] Philip C. Jessup, *Elihu Root*, Dodd, Mead & Co., New York, 1938, Vol. II, p. 358.

[13] Mr. Walling's widow kindly made available the President's letters to her husband concerning the mission. It is characteristic of Wilson's complicated feelings about the mission that he enthusiastically approved Walling's reluctance to join it and treated him thereafter with highest respect.

engineer, Mr. John F. Stevens. A number of private or semi-private American organizations likewise sent representatives or missions to Russia during the course of the summer. Of these the most prominent was the American Red Cross Commission, initially under Dr. Frank G. Billings.

It is difficult to discover any instance in which these missions had any appreciable favorable effect on the course of events in Russia during the period of the Provisional Government. The Red Cross Commission was neither needed nor particularly wanted by the Russian government, and the only influence it exerted on the situation was through the individual activities of certain of its members which, as will be seen shortly, had nothing to do with its Red Cross function. The Stevens Railway Mission, likewise the result of American—not Russian—initiative, was also not really wanted by the Russian government and was accepted only for the sake of the railway supplies which, it was hoped, would come with it. The Railway Mission spent its energies, in the summer of 1917, largely in talk and frustration, only to be overtaken by the November Revolution before it had any real chance to get down to business. (The valuable work that it was to accomplish at a later date will be discussed subsequently.)

As for the Root Mission, the most pretentious of all, its presence in the Russian capital seems to have had little effect other than to burden with a series of onerous social engagements the harried ministers of the Provisional Government, already involved in a life-and-death battle against the forces of disintegration that were soon to overtake Russia's brief experiment in republican government. Root himself, lacking not only knowledge of the Russian scene but also any deeper interest in it, was a poor choice for the task. He went without enthusiasm and did not enjoy the experience. While his public expressions were polite, his underlying attitude was smug and patronizing. "Please say to the President," he wired Lansing from Petrograd,

> that we have found here an infant class in the art of being free containing one hundred and seventy million people and they need to be supplied with kindergarten material; they are sincere, kindly, good people but confused and dazed.[14]

One seeks in vain for any indication that Root's private observations and speeches in the Russian capital had any influence on Russian

[14] *Foreign Relations, 1918, Russia*, Vol. I, *op.cit.*, p. 122; from Telegram 8, June 17, 1917, Root to Secretary of State.

political circles other than to drive home the thought that the degree of American support for the Provisional Government would depend strictly on the vigor of the latter's war effort.

Wilson's effort to give the Root Mission some sort of rapport with the Russian leftist parties by including Duncan and Russell in its membership was pathetically unsuccessful. It reflected a lack of appreciation on the President's part for the defiant bitterness of Russian radical opinion, its contempt for the moderate "reformist" philosophy of American labor, and especially its strong negative feelings toward the war. The thought that men like Duncan and Russell would have any natural intimacy with Russian socialists was indeed farfetched; and the choice became an object of derision not only for contemporaries but also for future Soviet historians.[15] Only on one occasion does any member of the mission appear to have visited the Petrograd Soviet. This was Russell. His remarks on that occasion were not warmly received, and no intimacy of contact was achieved.

It is not surprising that a mission so inauspiciously devised should have left a generally bad taste in everyone's mouth. Root himself subsequently complained:

> Wilson didn't want to accomplish anything. It was a grand-stand play. He wanted to show his sympathy for the Russian Revolution. When we delivered his message and made our speeches, he was satisfied; that's all he wanted.[16]

The President looked back on the venture with equal lack of enthusiasm: "Mr. Root?" he said to a friend in late 1918. "I sent him to Russia at the head of an important mission, and its failure was largely due to Russian distrust of Mr. Root." [17]

Root's principal recommendations to the Secretary of State, when

---

[15] In 1934 the Soviet historian I. I. Genkin ridiculed Wilson for sending "Russell (an extremely right-wing 'socialist' and an extreme partisan of the anti-German coalition), and . . . the vice-president of the A.F. of L.—a friend of Gompers—James Duncan. This was the most radical, the most 'left wing' sort of thing that the 'democrat' Wilson could dish up for the Provisional Government." (*Soedinennye Shtaty Ameriki i SSSR—Ikh Politicheskie i Ekonomicheskie Vzaimootnosheniya* [The United States of America and the U.S.S.R.—Political and Economic Relations between Them], State Social-Economic Publishing Co., Moscow-Leningrad, 1934, p. 20.)

Unless otherwise stated, translations of citations from foreign-language sources, in this work, are my own.

[16] Jessup, Vol. II, *op.cit.*, p. 356.

[17] George Creel, *Rebel at Large: Recollections of Fifty Crowded Years*, G. P. Putnam's Sons, New York, 1947, p. 253.

he returned, were first for an extensive informational program to be carried out with a view to influencing Russian public opinion, and secondly for a program to strengthen the morale of the Russian army, mainly through the introduction of recreational activities under the guidance of the Young Men's Christian Association. Neither of these recommendations bore any practical fruit. The first and most obvious explanation for this is that events were moving too rapidly and time was too short; neither could be implemented before the Provisional Government fell. But even had both recommendations been acted upon with the greatest promptness, it is not likely that their effect would have been of any importance. The Root plan for strengthening the morale of the army reflected little understanding of the depth of demoralization already reached in the Russian armed forces and of the real reasons for it. Whatever increased informational activity might have conceivably been undertaken in Russia by our government before the November crisis would surely have been rendered ineffective by those factors that have affected so many subsequent American efforts in this field: unfamiliarity with the political feelings and impulses of other peoples, lack of trained personnel, a stubborn tendency to speak subjectively in the fulsome vocabulary of American idealism rather than in terms that might have practical meaning to peoples elsewhere.

In addition to the failure of these efforts to achieve positive results, it may be questioned whether the United States government, in company with the other western Allies, did not actually hasten and facilitate the failure of the Provisional Government by insisting that Russia should continue the war effort, and by making this demand the criterion of its support. In asking the leaders of the Provisional Government simultaneously to consolidate their political power and to revive and continue participation in the war, the Allies were asking the impossible. The two tasks were mutually exclusive. Even at the time of the Revolution, both population and armed forces were already strongly affected by war-weariness. The leaders of the Petrograd Soviet, who in far higher degree than the government itself commanded the confidence of the politically active elements in the armed forces, were deeply committed to the thesis that the war aims of the Entente were imperialistic and unworthy. Obviously, this attitude opened up in the sharpest way, for the rank and file, the question as to what they were fighting for. The Revolution, furthermore, was accompanied by a tremendous weakening of the discipline of the armed forces—a process which the socialist leaders were either disinclined or too timorous to control and which they attempted to euphonize under the phrase "democratization of the army." Added to this, as the summer progressed, was the growing Bolshevik agitation for immediate land reform, an agitation which caused many of the peasant-soldiers to hope for an early redistribution of land in the villages. This anticipation served to decrease their interest in the military effort, to heighten their desire for peace on almost any terms, and to impel a great many of them—in increasing numbers as the months went on—to actual desertion.

After some initial disagreement between the Soviet and the Provisional Government over the question of war aims, the two were able to come together on a formula calling for a general "peace without annexations or indemnities" and favoring the early institution of negotiations with the other Entente powers to this end; but aiming, meanwhile, at a restoration of the fighting effectiveness of the armed forces and at least a nominal continuation of the war effort. Some members of the government and some of the more conservative leaders in the Soviet actually believed that such a program was feasible; and their optimism may have had much to do with encouraging a similar hope in the governments of the other Entente powers and in Washington. Actually, this hope was unreal. In view of the half-hearted attitude of the Petrograd Soviet toward the discipline of the armed forces, any thought of restoring fighting capacity, or even of halting the military disintegration, was a pipe dream. For the government to attempt, in these circumstances, to spur the semi-demoralized and land-hungry troops into a new war effort could only tend to force it into opposition to the rank and file, to expose its real lack of authority among the troops, and to play into the hands of the extreme, and wholly unscrupulous, Bolshevik agitation among the soldier masses. Such an effort was bound to widen the gap between government and Soviet, and to put the moderate members of the Soviet, in particular, in a precarious position.[18]

Thus the demand of the Allies, including the United States, that

[18] This danger was clearly seen by some of the Russian conservatives, as well as by certain of the foreign observers. Note, for example, the statement by Milyukov, first Foreign Minister in the Provisional Government and later historian of the events of this period: ". . . the affirmative attitude of the revolutionary regime toward the continuation of the war served . . . as the cause of its weakening. . . . The effects of the war at the front and within Russia predisposed the popular masses in advance in favor of those who . . . proved the opponents of the February revo-

Russia should renew and reinvigorate her war effort (bluntly expressed by Root in the formula "no fight, no loans") was actually in conflict with the other major aim of American policy toward the Provisional Government—namely, that the experiment in constitutional democratic government should proceed successfully.

Having once taken this attitude toward the Provisional Government, the United States government pursued it sternly to the bitter end. As the summer progressed and the situation of the Provisional Government became steadily more complicated and precarious, there were, to be sure, occasional warnings from American officials in Russia that the assumptions on which American policy rested were becoming increasingly questionable. These warnings, characteristically, came rather from the consular and military officials, who were in closer contact with the populace and the soldiery, than from the Embassy Chancery in Petrograd, whose dealings were with the Provisional Government. The Embassy officials could hardly be blamed for this. Root had borne in on them, from the lofty platform of his own prestige, that it was not their duty to question the professions or the political prospects of a regime the United States had decided to favor with its friendship and support. Nor was it easy, in that confused and unprecedented time, to perceive those political trends which are so easily identified by hindsight in the perspective of nearly forty years. The members of the Provisional Government were also partly to blame by reason of their understandable but nevertheless unfortunate reluctance to reveal to the Allied representatives in Petrograd the full measure of their real weakness. Thus the warning voices remained small and seemingly ineffectual.

Lansing, to be sure, took note of these sober voices, and followed with many misgivings the course of events in Russia. After talking with Root in August, upon the latter's return from Russia, Lansing expressed in a memorandum to the President his skepticism as to the staying power of the Provisional Government [19] and deplored the

lution. The war in that sense prepared the people for the October Revolution." (P. Milyukov, *Rossiya na Perelomye* [Russia at the Crossroads], Imprimerie d' Art Voltaire, Paris, 1927, Vol. i, p. 43.)

Similarly, in reporting the disturbances of the third and fourth of May in Petrograd, the American Consul there, Mr. North Winship, wrote: "This distrust of the allies and this feeling of being forced to continue a distasteful and irksome war which is being preached openly and [un]disguisedly by all the socialist organs and leaders, was the hidden cause of all the events of the 3d and 4th of May." (*Foreign Relations, 1918, Russia,* Vol. i, *op.cit.,* p. 50, from Despatch 300, May 8, 1917.)

[19] *War Memoirs of Robert Lansing, Secretary of State,* Bobbs-Merrill Co., New York, 1935; Memorandum of August 9, 1917, pp. 337-338.

atmosphere of optimism which the Root Mission was radiating. The President surely shared some of his uneasiness.

But there was now little to do but continue on the course that had been laid down in March and April. Unpromising as the situation appeared in the last weeks of the regime of the Provisional Government, one could never be wholly sure that things would not in some way or other work themselves out. Surely, it was reasoned, the political prospects of the Provisional Government would not be aided by last-minute switches of American policy, indicating lack of confidence in its future and vacillation with regard to the desirability of further American support.

Thus the United States government, having committed itself to a fixed and narrow line of policy, one without alternatives, had no choice but to pursue this line unchangingly as the storm clouds gathered, concealing its growing misgivings until complete catastrophe swept away the assumptions underlying that policy and created, for all the world to see, a wholly new situation.

One of the disadvantages of this situation was that it involved the extension of various forms of aid to Russia long after they could play any real part in promoting the purposes for which the respective aid programs had been designed. But far more serious was the fact that this unhappy predicament made it impossible for the Washington leaders to take the public into their confidence and to stimulate the sort of public discussion that would have been necessary if people were to be prepared for the worst eventualities.

It was, therefore, a largely unprepared American public and a government partly forewarned but still in considerable bewilderment that were startled and almost stupefied to learn, in the middle of November 1917, that the reins of power in Russia had slipped from the hands of Premier Kerensky and had been seized by a band of radical fanatics of whom one knew only that they held the most inflammatory social views and were violently opposed to the continuation of Russia's war effort.

Before we turn to the details of this painful awakening, it would be well to glance at some of the personalities most prominently involved in the forthcoming encounter between a United States at war and a Russia deep in the throes of social revolution.

CHAPTER II

PERSONALITIES

THE story of the early period of Soviet-American relations represents, like every other prolonged phase of diplomatic history, a fabric in which individual personalities appear, like threads, to bear for a time their share of the strain, only to disappear again at some point, often quite abruptly, resigning the burden to others. In general, these personalities will be introduced and examined as and when they appear on the scene. But there remains the necessity of introducing those who were already on the scene at the time this story opens; for without some knowledge of their background and the peculiarities of their approach to these problems, the account of their behavior loses much of its significance.

The persons who fall into this category consist principally of the major statesmen on both sides and the principal figures of the official American community in Russia. In normal circumstances, similar mention would have to be made of the members of the official Russian community in the United States. In this instance, however, this necessity falls away, for the Russian official community in Washington at the time of the Revolution refused, by and large, to recognize the Soviet government or to serve it, and thus failed to play a direct role in Soviet-American relations. An exception must be made here for the last ambassador of the Provisional Government, Mr. Boris Bakhmeteff, whose unusual qualities of insight and judgment commanded the confidence of many Americans and permitted him to exercise, in the role of unofficial adviser to various American statesmen, an influence by no means inconsiderable.

THE MAJOR STATESMEN

The major statesmen involved in the initial stages of Soviet-American relations—Wilson and Lansing on the American side,

Lenin and Trotsky on the Russian—need no general introduction to the reading public. Their respective reactions to the problems of Russian-American relations will best be left to reflect themselves in the happenings that make up the body of this narrative. There are, however, a few observations concerning the respective experiences and personalities of these men that might be in order at this point.

Although Woodrow Wilson has received extensive attention in American historical literature ever since his death, the full pattern of his complicated and subtle political personality is only now beginning to emerge in the light of the more intensive and detached scrutiny to which it has recently been subjected. It is the writer's hope that the glimpses of Wilson in his confrontation with the Russian problem, as they emerge in this narrative, will contribute something to the fullness and richness of this pattern.

Two points are worth bearing in mind as we observe the reactions of President Wilson to the problems posed by the Russian Revolution.

First, Wilson was a man who had never had any particular interest in, or knowledge of, Russian affairs. He had never been in Russia. There is no indication that the dark and violent history of that country had ever occupied his attention. Like many other Americans, he felt a distaste and antipathy for Tsarist autocracy as he knew it, and a sympathy for the revolutionary movement in Russia. Precisely for this reason, the rapid degeneration of the Russian Revolution into a new form of authoritarianism, animated by a violent preconceived hostility toward western liberalism, was a phenomenon for which he was as little prepared, intellectually, as a great many of his compatriots.

Secondly, while Wilson was largely his own Secretary of State insofar as the formulation of policy in major questions was concerned, he shared with many other American statesmen a disinclination to use the network of America's foreign diplomatic missions as a vital and intimate agency of policy. Nothing was further from his habit and cast of mind than to take the regular envoys into his confidence, to seek their opinions, or to use their facilities for private communication with foreign governments as a vehicle for achieving his objectives of foreign policy. Seldom did it occur to Wilson to pursue his objectives by the traditional diplomatic method of influencing the attitudes of foreign governments through private persuasion or bargaining; in the rare instances where this was done, it was mainly an irregular agent, Colonel Edward M. House, and not the permanent envoys, whose services were employed. In general, the President's taste in diplomacy ran rather to the direct appeal to foreign opinion, for which American diplomatic representatives were not required.

In these circumstances, individual diplomatic envoys, such as Ambassador Francis in Petrograd, had no sense of intimacy with the President, and no opportunity to feel that they were the special repositories of his confidence and the vehicles of his will. Like many American diplomatists who had gone before, and many who were to come after, they were left to vegetate as best as they could at their foreign stations, gleaning their understanding of the rationale of American policy from the press or from such cryptic hints as might from time to time be given them, sending their interpretative reports to a Department of State wrapped in deep and enigmatic silence, endeavoring uncomfortably to conceal from the governments to which they were accredited the full measure of their helplessness and lack of influence.

The period of time to which this volume is addressed was one in which Wilson was showing the first signs of the fatigue and strain that were to affect him increasingly in the remaining years of his presidency. House noted this as early as Christmas time, 1917.[1] Two months later, on February 27, he recorded:

The President complained of being tired. Though he looks better than upon my last visit, I can see indications of fatigue. He does not remember names as well and he does not think to do the things we decide upon. Grayson was talking of this yesterday. He said that while he gave the impression to everyone that the President was working day and night, he and I knew that eight hours work a day was about all he was equal to. . . .

It would be a mistake to conclude from this that Wilson in the winter of 1917–1918 was at all times incapable of his best work. This was not the case. In making the observations just cited, House added that he still thought the President could "do more in eight hours

[1] E. M. House MSS, Yale University Library, New Haven; Diary, December 30, 1917: "I could see some signs of weariness in him. . . ."

than any man I know." But it should be remembered that in precisely these months the strain of office was becoming crushingly great, and there were now moments when the President's energy and power of concentration were less than at other moments and less than the consistently high standard of the past. These circumstances should not be forgotten in appraising his reactions to the Russian problem in the first months of Soviet power.

✧

Of Robert Lansing it need only be said that while he, too, had experienced no special interest in Russian affairs prior to the Russian Revolution, he had had a unique preparation for the responsibilities of statesmanship in twenty-two years of practice as an international lawyer and nearly three years of grueling responsibility as Counselor and Secretary of State. Not only had he gained in this way an exceptional understanding of the diplomatic process as such, but he had acquired in high degree those qualities of thoroughness and precision that lie at the heart of the diplomatic profession. The same experiences had rendered him sensitive to the importance of international forms and amenities as reflections of the deeper realities of foreign affairs. These qualities were to stand him in good stead as he confronted the ordeals of statesmanship brought to him by the Russian Revolution and its consequences.

For his own contemporaries, Lansing's light was somewhat obscured by the contrast between his quiet, unassuming nature and the President's overriding personality. His task was not eased by the President's innate secretiveness and tendency to act on his own without consulting or informing his Secretary of State. The two men grated on each other in their official habits.[2] Foreign diplomats were quick to sense this relationship and to exploit it by taking their problems directly to the President.

In these circumstances it is not surprising that there was a tendency to underrate Lansing, and sometimes to ridicule him. George Creel charged, contemptuously, that he "worked at being dull." But this is a charge to which orderly and methodical natures must expect to be exposed in the more strident periods of history. It would be wrong

---

[2] "I find the President still antagonistic to Lansing," House recorded in his diary on December 18, 1917. "Lansing constantly does something to irritate him, and generally along the line of taking action without consultation." (House MSS, *op.cit.*)

to assume that Lansing's plodding meticulousness of method, his deficiency in showmanship, and his lack of personal color rendered unimportant the contribution he was capable of making to the formulation of America's response to Soviet power. Behind this façade of stuffy correctness and legal precision there lay powers of insight that might have been envied by the more boisterous natures with which wartime Washington then abounded.

Of Lenin we need say little by way of introduction. He had had as little interest in America as Wilson or Lansing had in Russia. Insofar as he thought about the United States at all, he probably identified it with the England he knew from his periods of exile in London. If his impression of Anglo-Saxon civilization differed from the image of continental capitalism on which his outlook of life had been formed, it was not enough to affect his thinking in any important way. It was Lenin, after all, who had corrected Marx's sloppiness and tidied up the symmetry of the doctrine by overriding Marx's admission that in the Anglo-Saxon countries the socialist revolution *might* conceivably occur by means short of revolutionary violence. In this way he had made it possible to lump all capitalist countries neatly together, and had avoided the hideous necessity of recognizing a world of relative values. For Lenin, quite obviously, America—at the time of the Bolshevik seizure of power—was just one more capitalist country, and not a very important one at that. (The Decree on Peace, drafted by Lenin himself in the fall of 1917, significantly failed to mention the United States and referred to England, France, and Germany as "the three mightiest States taking part in the present war.")

Of the four leading statesmen, Trotsky was the only one to have visited the other country concerned in the Russian-American relationship. He had been in the United States in the winter of 1917 (January 13 to March 27). He had lived in what he called a "working-class district" on New York's upper east side—162nd Street. He had worked at the editorial offices of the Russian-language socialist newspaper, the *Novy Mir,* near Union Square. Altogether, he had led, for this brief period, the peculiarly narrow and restricted life that Russian political exiles have so often tended to create for themselves in foreign capitals. As he himself put it: "My only profession in New York was the profession of a revolutionary socialist." [3]

Trotsky relates that he studied American economic life in the New York Public Library. Whatever this study amounted to, it would be a mistake to conclude that he gained from it any rich or accurate picture of the nature of the civilization he was touching on its eastern fringe. The flesh-and-blood America, with all those subtle peculiarities of spirit and custom that have done so much more than political or economic institutions to determine the values of its civilization, remained for him—fortunately for the peace of his brilliant but dogmatic mind, unfortunately for the course of Soviet-American relations—a closed book.

THE AMERICAN AMBASSADOR IN PETROGRAD

To understand the position of the American envoy in the Russian capital at the time of the Revolution, it might be well to go back a bit and to note the experiences of the Wilson administration with regard to the filling of this particular diplomatic post.

At the time of the outbreak of World War I, Russian-American relations were in a mildly troubled state. This was primarily the result of resentment by the Jewish community in the United States of the restrictions and hardships to which Jews had recently been subjected in the Russian Empire, and also of the specific problems arising out of the acquisition of American residence or citizenship by large numbers of Russian Jews. So long as the American population had contained no sizeable element of immigrants from the Russian Empire, the great traditional and philosophic differences that distinguished the political systems of Russia and America had played no appreciable part in the formal relations between the two countries. In earlier times, waves of oppression far more severe than anything known in the final decades of Tsardom had passed over the political life of Russia without unduly attracting the notice of the American public or affecting in any way the course of Russian-American relations. But in the period from the murder of the Tsar Alexander II in 1881 down to the outbreak of World War I, members of discontented Russian minorities, above all the Jews, had come to the United States in large numbers. With the addition of this

[3] Leo Trotzki, *Mein Leben*, S. Fischer Verlag, Berlin, 1930, p. 259.

element to the American population, Tsarist autocracy, precisely in the years of its decline and disintegration, became a problem for the United States, directly or indirectly, as it had never been before.

In the period just prior to 1914, dissatisfaction with the behavior of the Russian government on the part of the American Jewish community, supported by considerable sympathy in other sectors of the American population, found a lively reflection in Congressional opinion. The result was the adoption by a 300–1 vote on December 13, 1911 of a Joint Congressional Resolution charging Russia with violating the old commercial treaty of 1832, declaring the treaty terminated, and instructing President Taft to give formal notice to that effect to the Russian government. Notice of termination of the treaty was accordingly given on December 17, 1911 and became effective on December 31, 1912.[4]

The tension resulting from the termination of the commercial treaty was somewhat moderated by the labors of the patient and less emotional bureaucrats. There was a good deal of surface indignation on both sides; but the two foreign offices, in the spirit of weary and disillusioned conciliatoriness that usually marks the activity of diplomatic professionals, did what they could to hold things together. Between them they managed to prevent any inordinate disturbance of the relations between the two countries on the practical level. The cancellation of the treaty had no appreciable effect on trade between the two countries—a fact which may serve as an illustration of the exaggerated importance Americans were inclined to attach to the commercial treaty instrument as an incentive to trade. American exports to Russia, which had been running at the modest rate of about $35 million a year, began in fact to increase rapidly with the outbreak of war, due to Russian purchases of war supplies in the United States, and attained in the fiscal year ending in the summer of 1917 the formidable figure of $558.9 million. This increase in direct trade during the war was supplemented by a considerable flow of American investment to Russia, and by extensive operations in Russia by large American concerns, such as the Singer Sewing Machine Company, the International Harvester Company, some of the large American banks and insurance companies, etc. The result was that, as the war advanced, the United States found

---

[4] Thomas A. Bailey, *America Faces Russia: Russian-American Relations from Early Times to Our Day*, Cornell University Press, Ithaca, 1950, pp. 216–220.

itself, although lacking in any formal commercial treaty arrangements with Russia, more deeply engaged than ever, economically and financially, in the Russian scene. This participation led, incidentally, to the accumulation on Russian territory of a sizeable colony of American citizens engaged in business and other pursuits.

Following the denunciation of the treaty in 1911 there had ensued a period of roughly two years during which the United States was represented in Petrograd only by a chargé d'affaires. By 1914, however, the situation had settled to some extent, and the President, no doubt having in mind the rapid development of tension in Europe, decided to fill the post. He selected for this position Mr. George T. Marye, of San Francisco.

The atmosphere at that time was still decidedly cool on the Russian side. The demonstrative termination of the old treaty had not been forgotten or forgiven in the Russian capital. The Russian Ambassador in Washington took the unusual step of attempting to dissuade Marye from proceeding to his post. When the Russian Foreign Office in Petrograd was pressed for an explanation of its Ambassador's action, it replied most lukewarmly. Mr. Marye's presence, it was said, was not at all necessary, but of course he could come if he wished; the Emperor would receive him, provided he were there at that time, although this was not at all certain.[5]

Marye nevertheless proceeded to his post, was received by the Emperor, and served as ambassador at Petrograd until March 1916. He gained a strong personal attachment to the imperial family and was himself apparently much appreciated in court circles. In February 1916, however, he suddenly asked for his recall, ostensibly on grounds of health but actually, according to his own account, because "political combinations had arisen at home which affected me and . . . I felt impelled to withdraw." [6]

The real reasons for this sudden withdrawal are still obscure. Its abruptness produced a deplorable impression on the Russian government, which suspected some new species of affront. "Doesn't your Government care anything for our friendship?" Marye was asked by the Russian Foreign Minister at the time of his departure.[7] This naturally did not make things easier for his successor.

[5] George Thomas Marye, *Nearing the End in Imperial Russia*, Dorrance & Co., Philadelphia, 1929, pp. 15–22.
[6] *Ibid.*, p. 460.
[7] *Ibid.*, p. 461.

Ambassador David R. Francis

Thompson and Robins with their Social-Revolutionary beneficiaries

Seated (l to r): William Boyce Thompson, Lazarev (old Russian revolutionist), and Kathrine Bresh-kovskaya (the "Little Grandmother of the Russian Revolution"). *Standing*: N. V. Chaikovski, Frederick M. Corse (manager of the Russian division of the N.Y. Life Insurance Co.), Victor Soskice (Kerensky's personal secretary), Raymond Robins

Ambassador Francis with the members of the Root Mission
Immediately back of the Ambassador is General Judson. At the extreme right of the second row is
Stanley Washburn, and next to him, Basil Miles. Second from the left, seated, is Charles R. Crane.

Raymond Robins as chairman of the Progressive Convention in Chicago, 1916, a year before he went to Russia

John Reed

The man selected to succeed Marye was Mr. David R. Francis of St. Louis. The background of this appointment is also not clear. Francis was, of course, a good Democrat, and a prominent one. The President and the State Department were anxious that a new commercial treaty be negotiated, if possible; and Mr. Francis' extensive business experience may well have been a factor in persuading the President that he would be a suitable person to promote this undertaking. Although Francis had been offered, and had declined, an ambassadorial post (Buenos Aires) in 1914, this new offer came as a complete surprise to him. He appears to have accepted it with some reluctance, but in the belief that acceptance was a public duty, in view of the circumstances prevailing at the time.

Francis was a man of considerable prominence and distinction in his adopted state of Missouri (he was born in Kentucky), and not unknown in national affairs. In addition to a long and successful business career, embracing several fields of activity, he had served, successively, as Mayor of St. Louis (1885–1889), Governor of Missouri (1889–1893), Secretary of the Interior in the Cabinet of Grover Cleveland (1896–1897), and President of the Universal Exposition of 1904, known as the Louisiana Purchase Exposition. A survival of his political distinction was found in the fact that throughout his diplomatic career he continued to be referred to as "the Governor" and to be addressed accordingly by his associates, rather than by the customary title of "Mr. Ambassador."

When Francis went to Russia, in 1916, he was already sixty-five years of age. When the Bolshevik Revolution occurred, he had reached the age of sixty-seven. He was married and had several children. For a variety of personal reasons he left his family at home, and proceeded on his mission alone, accompanied only by his personal secretary and by his Negro valet and butler, Mr. Philip Jordan.

Philip Jordan, incidentally, was an important figure in Francis' entourage. Already in the Francis employ for many years as a personal servant, he is said to have gone along on the Russian venture out of personal concern and respect for the old gentleman, rather than for the money. His own letters from Russia [8] reveal him as a sensitive, earnest person, with a high sense of responsibility and devoted to Francis' interests. He was shocked at the violence of the

---

[8] Several of his letters to Mrs. Francis (who had taught him to write) are contained in the David R. Francis MSS, Missouri Historical Society, St. Louis.

Revolution—shocked to a point, in fact, where the United States appeared to him as "Heaven." But he was not sorry to be in Russia, where life was always interesting and never "lonely," and where he himself had an important and respected function. Throughout the entire period of Francis' stay in that country, Philip looked after the "Governor's" interests with conspicuous dignity, and with that mixture of solicitude and authority peculiar to the servants of a bygone age. He left a rich store of anecdotes about his resourcefulness, his linguistic achievements, and his ready understanding of what seemed to him to be the obvious and simple realities of the Russian Revolution.

The Ambassador took up residence in an apartment within the Embassy Chancery building on the Furshtatskaya, in a fashionable part of the city lying between its center and the Tauride district to the east. Since this latter district included the later Soviet headquarters at the Smolny Institute, as well as the Parliament building, the American Embassy found itself in the midst of some of the most dramatic and violent happenings of the revolutionary period.

Francis' taste and habits were the robust and simple ones of the American Middle West at the turn of the century. As such, they bore little affinity to the refined predilections of continental diplomatic society. Not that Francis was in any way an ascetic. On the contrary, he was so well known at home as a gourmet that he is mentioned in one of O. Henry's tales—in a scene where a cowboy, who has struck it rich and sets out to blow his unaccustomed wealth in St. Louis, appears with a companion in one of the city's most famous hostelries and says to the headwaiter: "You see the chef and order a dinner for us such as you serve to Dave Francis and the general passenger agent of the Iron Mountain when they eat here." [9] But Francis' hedonism was of a genuinely American sort. The portable cuspidor, with its clanking, foot-operated lid, may have been apocryphal; but there is no doubt that the Governor's preference for an evening's entertainment ran to good cigars,[10] good whisky, and a few good cronies around the card table, rather than to large and

[9] O. Henry, *Seats of the Haughty,* Doubleday & Co., New York, 1916. Story entitled "Heart of the West."

[10] "Smoking," Francis confessed sadly in a chatty note to the Consul at Helsingfors on December 27, 1917, "is a habit which seems to have gained more nearly control over me than any apetite [sic] I have—I don't acknowledge that I have any apetite which I cannot control." (Francis MSS, *op.cit.*)

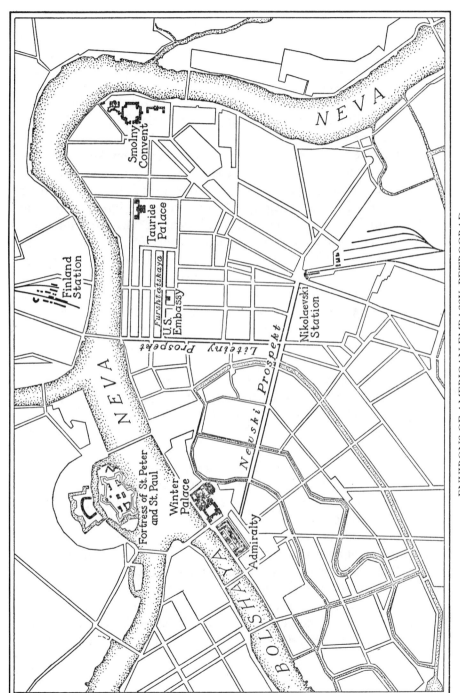

ENVIRONS OF AMERICAN EMBASSY, PETROGRAD

elegant mixed gatherings. For these reasons, as well as by reason of a certain parsimoniousness, he lived for the most part quietly in his Embassy apartment, confining his social life largely to the American colony, taking relatively little part in the social doings of high Petrograd society.

Francis kept a Ford touring car, driven as a rule by Philip Jordan. He also kept a sleigh and a team of good horses. Embassy Secretary Norman Armour recalls that the horses each had "an American flag stuck in the bridle over the outer ear which gave you the impression, when you drove with him, that you were in a merry-go-round."

Francis seems to have found no easy approach to his diplomatic colleagues. They, for their part, tended either to ignore him or to view him with amusement and condescension. His rare diplomatic dinners (marked by a squeaky gramophone playing behind a screen in the dining room, and Philip interrupting the service at table from time to time to crank it) failed to accord with the standards of diplomatic elegance then prevailing in the Russian capital. Sir George Buchanan, the British Ambassador, scarcely mentions Francis in his memoirs. The French Ambassador, Joseph Noulens, records only that Francis "parlait mal le français et se montrait peu familiarisé avec les usages diplomatiques et les principes du droit international." [11] Francis could not help but feel this lack of appreciation; and one has the impression that the self-esteem natural to a man of his years and distinction was chafed into a defensive vanity by it.

Unfortunately, something of this same awkwardness made itself felt in the Ambassador's relations with his career associates. He could not help but be aware of their greater familiarity both with diplomatic life in general and with the Petrograd scene in particular. On the other hand, it was difficult for him to seek and accept their opinions without betraying his own ignorance and forfeiting the dignity of his position. This situation (not an uncommon one in American diplomatic experience) would have been unpleasant in the best of circumstances. In this instance, it was aggravated by a further complication of a most painful sort.

On his journey to Russia in April 1916, Francis had made the acquaintance of a comely lady, reputedly about forty years of age, by the name of Matilda deCram. She had just spent six months in

[11] Joseph Noulens, *Mon Ambassade en Russie Soviétique, 1917–1919,* Librairie Plon, Paris, 1933, Vol. I, p. 185.

the United States, where her husband was residing, and was returning to Russia to join her two sons (by a former marriage), who were naval cadets. In Petrograd, Francis continued his acquaintance with her. She gave him French lessons, frequently joined him on his nocturnal walks with which he was accustomed to end his working day, and sometimes visited him in the Embassy.

Unfortunately, Madame deCram was evidently on the books of the Russian counter-intelligence as a suspected German agent. The suspicions appear to have arisen partly from the activities of her husband, who was rumored to have been associated with an insurance company owned by German and Austrian principals and to have fled Russia early in the war in order to avoid being implicated in the charges raised against the Minister of War, Sukhomlinov, on grounds of intriguing with the Germans.[12] But further suspicions rested on Madame deCram because on her voyage to America in 1915 she had travelled on the same vessel with another Russian woman, Mirolyubskaya, who was later prosecuted for revealing state secrets to the Germans. There were also reports that prior to Francis' departure from New York, Madame deCram had made inquiries about the ship on which he intended to sail and had made arrangements to be on board.

In no instance does the available record afford any reliable substantiation of any of these charges;[13] but they all came to the attention of the Allied counter-intelligence officials in Petrograd in the period following her return to Russia. These officials evidently proceeded on the principle, common in such times and situations, that the subject is to be assumed guilty unless proven innocent. They therefore viewed with high alarm and disapproval the lady's connection with the Ambassador, particularly in light of the fact that Francis' living quarters in the Embassy Chancery were in close physical proximity to the file and code room. There was also the inevitable

---

[12] The truth of this report cannot be verified. Francis said deCram had been expelled by the Russian government. It is quite possible that deCram, with his German name (evidently it was originally von Kram), was a victim of the vigorous efforts made by Russian business firms during the war to exploit war psychology in order to eliminate German influence and competition from Russian business life. These efforts appear to have involved a good deal of intrigue and reckless denunciation, much of it based on extremely flimsy evidence.

[13] Certain of the charges against Mme. deCram, appearing in documents found in the Francis MSS, *op.cit.,* emanated from sources which (although Francis did not know it) can be identified today as of doubtful veracity and reliability. This being the case, one cannot help but wonder about the seriousness of the others.

gossip and conjecture about the personal side of the relationship. One can imagine with what relish the tongues of Petrograd society, critically inclined toward Francis from the start, belabored this attractive subject.

There is, let it be said at once, nothing in the record to indicate that the Governor's associations with Madame deCram ever overstepped the boundaries suggested by his advanced age and the conventions of the day. One would like to think that such an association on the part of an elderly ambassador who had left wife and family at home and was enduring the rigors of a belated and unaccustomed bachelorhood in a strange land might—if it had to be the object of curiosity at all—have been viewed with sympathy and understanding by those around him; and such was indeed the attitude of the more sensible and experienced members of his entourage. But wartime sleuths, particularly the amateur ones, are not noted either for their sense of humor or their understanding of the lesser human foibles. The result was a deplorable atmosphere of disapproval and suspicion among some of the Ambassador's leading associates as well as the members of the Allied diplomatic missions. This situation, which was bound to lead sooner or later to denunciations in Washington, was just on the verge of coming to a head when the Bolshevik seizure of power occurred; and the major repercussions fell in the period to which this narrative is addressed.

It was easy for the members of the American community and the diplomatic corps to ridicule Francis and to deprecate his ability. An injustice had been done to him, and an undeserved one, in sending him to such a post at such a time. Only the greatest unfamiliarity with the requirements of normal diplomatic life could have explained a belief that Francis, at his age and with his experience and temperament, would have been well equipped to meet those requirements. For the further supposition that he would have been capable of penetrating intellectually the murky process of Russian political life in the wake of the February Revolution and of giving energetic and farseeing guidance in that unprecedentedly complex situation, no rational foundation is visible at all. If, in these circumstances, the President sent Francis to Russia in 1916 and kept him there as long as conditions permitted after the February Revolution, one can attribute this choice only to that unfamiliarity with the requirements and possibilities of diplomatic representation which has often characterized even the best of American statesmanship.

Personalities

One could wish for Francis' own sake that he had been withdrawn betimes to the quiet old age he deserved, and that the post had either been given to a younger man of superior education and foreign experience or left in the hands of a career chargé d'affaires. But once there, he had to "make do" with the qualities he possessed; and this, it must be acknowledged, he did—with courage and enthusiasm. It is difficult to retrace the old gentleman's adventures and activities in the first months of Soviet power—to note his stormy reactions, his vigorous opinions, his maneuverings among his impetuous associates, and even his frequent vacillations—without being moved to sympathy for him in his unexpected and unprecedented position, and to respect for the fidelity he showed to the standards and obligations he knew and for his courageous persistence in the face of much frustration and adversity.

OTHER AMERICANS

After the Ambassador, the first figure in the American official establishment to deserve mention is Brigadier General William V. Judson, who clothed simultaneously the two positions of military attaché to the Ambassador and chief of the American Military Mission to Russia. This dual position, by virtue of which the General found himself at once a subordinate and not a subordinate of the Ambassador, was a characteristic reflection of the difficulty always encountered by the United States government in finding a satisfactory relationship between military and civil authority in time of war. In his capacity as military attaché, General Judson should have reported to the United States government on political subjects only through the Ambassador, or at least with his knowledge and approval. In his capacity as chief of the Military Mission in time of war, he had a responsibility to report directly to the Secretary of War on anything he chose. He had his own channels of communication to the War Department, channels not accessible to the Ambassador—a circumstance bound eventually to be a source of confusion and misunderstanding.

General Judson was the finest type of American officer and a man of utmost integrity of character. By specialty a military engineer, he had acquitted himself with distinction of a long series of responsible and important assignments in the field of military engineering. There had, however, been one notable interlude in his career: when, in 1905, he had served for some five months as an observer on the

Russian side in the Russian-Japanese War. He had returned to Russia with the Root Mission in the summer of 1917, only to be detached from the mission there and assigned in the capacities just referred to. He had, accordingly, entered upon his new assignment only shortly before the outbreak of the Bolshevik Revolution. He was greatly interested in Russia. His military sympathies appear to have been drawn strongly to the Russian military efforts of which he was the witness in two wars. He was close to Guchkov, first Minister of War in the Provisional Government, whom he had known during the Russo-Japanese War. Conscientious in his duties and an indefatigable worker, General Judson had gained a somewhat labored knowledge of Russian politics of the time. The events of the summer and fall of 1917 were bewildering even to the most profound observers; and one has the impression that the General, like many other foreigners in Russia at that time, was hard-pressed to find any adequate connection between cause and effect in the rapid and confusing sequence of events. Nevertheless, the guidance he received from the hard-headed and pessimistic Guchkov stood him in good stead; he was one of the few American observers to note the scale and implications of the decline in military morale in the final weeks of the period of the Provisional Government and to warn Washington that the chances for Russia's continuance in the war were not bright.

It will be necessary to recount in these chapters the processes by which General Judson became, shortly after the Revolution, a strong advocate of the policy of working through, rather than against, the Soviet leaders in the effort to prevent the removal of German forces from the eastern to the western front. It should be remembered in justice to him that the implications of the Bolshevik withdrawal from the war weighed particularly heavily upon him as the senior American military officer in Russia. His position was not eased by the stubborn failure of his own government to give him any clear instructions or even to keep him abreast of its own thinking.[14] When he returned to the United States in February 1918, Judson reported in great detail to the War Department on his past actions and his views for future policy; but, like most others who tried to interpret

---

[14] The only instruction Judson ever had from the War Department in the several weeks that he remained in Russia following the Bolshevik seizure of power was a brief message forbidding him to have contact with Trotsky. Otherwise, he was left wholly on his own and could only guess at the views and desires of the Department for which he was working. (William V. Judson MSS, Newberry Library, Chicago; Report to Acting Chief of Staff, March 14, 1918.)

the Russian Revolution to the Wilson administration, he was left with the feeling of being brushed off and ignored. The President never received him or acknowledged his many reports. This lack of intimacy with the official Washington attitude confirmed him in his conviction that the wrong approach had been taken, from the beginning, to the Soviet authority. His views thus coincided closely with those later developed by General William S. Graves, the commander of the Siberian expedition. Between the two of them these officers left within a portion of the American officer corps an intellectual legacy dominated by the conviction that collaboration with the Soviet government was not only desirable but wholly possible, if sincerely and correctly sought, and deeply embittered against the State Department, whose anti-Soviet prejudice, it was felt, alone had prevented this dream from becoming a reality.

❖

Francis' first assistant on the civilian side, at the time of the Bolshevik seizure of power, was Mr. J. Butler Wright, later to become a prominent senior American diplomatist and Assistant Secretary of State. In his capacity as Counselor of Embassy, Wright had immediate charge of the Embassy Chancery, and bore the main responsibility for guiding the hand of the Ambassador through the unprecedented trials of the period. Still a relatively young officer, endowed with no special knowledge of Russian affairs, highly conscious of the importance, from the standpoint of the prosecution of the war, of the problems facing the Embassy, Wright performed his duties with great conscientiousness, but found it difficult to strike the right tone in his relation to Francis. The relations between the two men thus lacked, throughout, that intimacy which would have been necessary for a happy and fruitful collaboration. In Wright's eyes, Francis personified all the characteristic weaknesses of the political appointee in a diplomatic position. In Francis' eyes, Wright manifested the worst traits of the career officer: clannishness with other career officers, lack of frankness, undue attachment to form and protocol, a cramped stiltedness of behavior, and absence of the broad human approach in relations outside the Embassy.

❖

In the American consular, as distinct from diplomatic, establishment in Russia, the senior official and leading figure was Consul

General Maddin Summers in Moscow. As Consul General, Summers not only had immediate charge of the large and important consular establishment in Moscow—the center of much of the commercial life of the country—but also exercised supervision over the work of the American consular establishments in other Russian cities, notably Petrograd, Odessa, Tiflis, Irkutsk, and Vladivostok.

Summers was an experienced and capable officer, vigorous, conscientious, and indefatigable. He was widely respected by his colleagues and by members of the American colony in Russia for his high sense of duty, his courage, and his general integrity of character. Although lacking previous experience in Russian matters, he had the advantage of being married to a Russian lady of great charm and good sense.[15] Through her, as well as by virtue of his own qualities, he enjoyed excellent connections in business and liberal-political circles in Moscow. He took a keen interest in the development of events, and sent long and detailed reports to Washington, sometimes outpacing the Petrograd Embassy in providing the Department of State with documentary material pertaining to the progress of the Revolution.

Of all the senior American officials in Russia, Summers seems to have taken from the start the firmest and most uncompromising anti-Bolshevik attitude. This arose, perhaps, in part from his relatively conservative Russian connections,[16] but also from his own cast of mind and his disgust at the bloodshed and brutality with which in Moscow, as distinguished from Petrograd, the Bolshevik seizure of power was carried out. It must be remembered that in the period immediately following the November Revolution the personalities of the top Soviet leaders, notably Lenin and Trotsky, so impressive and fascinating to the observers in Petrograd, were not in evidence in Moscow. In general, the revolutionary pathos that characterized the November events in Petrograd—the fierce intellectual fervor, the sincere internationalism, the almost good-natured humanity—was absent, or much less in evidence, in Moscow, where events bore more the nature of a brutal outburst of social bitterness and where the Bolshevik element, reinforced by ordinary prisoners liberated from the

---

[15] Mrs. Natalia Gorainoff Summers subsequently served with distinction for many years as a member of the archival staff of the Department of State in Washington.

[16] These were "conservative" only in relation to the radical parties that dominated the scene after the summer of 1917. Before the Revolution, they would have been described as liberal.

jails, appeared rather as semi-criminal rabble-rousers than as daring intellectual idealists. Summers was thus spared those impressions that captured the imagination of Thompson and Robins and Judson and helped them to embrace the prospect of collaboration with the Bolsheviki. Throughout the brief months left to him before his untimely death, he continued to view the new rulers of Russia with unmitigated and undisguised distaste, to exaggerate the depth and significance of their relations with the Germans, and to urge uncompromising Allied resistance to their cause.

❖

Further deserving of mention, among the members of the official American community in Petrograd, are the leading figures in the representation in Russia of George Creel's Committee on Public Information—the "Office of War Information" of World War I.

It is impossible to state briefly and succinctly the function of this extraordinary child of the First World War. Although primarily set up as an agency for wartime propaganda and censorship, it had several other functions, and these were in a constant state of flux and change. Its responsibility for censorship carried it deeply into the field of internal counter-espionage, and it evidently entered also, in ways still obscure, into the forward military and political intelligence field. In their history of the activities of the Committee on Public Information, Messrs. James R. Mock and Cedric Larson state that in its foreign propaganda work

> . . . the CPI was in the closest relationship to the intelligence branches of the army and navy. . . . By the end of the war an interesting division of labor had been worked out, whereby the CPI had actual administration of propaganda into Allied and neutral countries, while the Military Intelligence Branch had executive charge for enemy countries. But in each case the non-executive agency had responsibility to help provide the information on which all propaganda must be based, and to offer suggestions.

At many of our diplomatic posts the military or naval attaché served as CPI representative during emergency periods, and in some other cases the CPI men did work which normally would have fallen to the lot of Military Intelligence. . . .[17]

[17] James R. Mock and Cedric Larson, *Words that Won the War: The Story of the Committee on Public Information, 1917–1919*, Princeton University Press, 1939, p. 237.

The man selected to head this organization was George Creel, western editor, writer, and journalist—a voluntary warrior in a hundred liberal causes. Creel's vigorous and outspoken nature, his impatience with governmental red tape, the unusual nature of his undertaking, and his understandable eagerness to get on with it: all these features were bound to place him in many respects at odds with official Washington and to guarantee him a stormy passage on the seas of wartime governmental activity. His temperament and that of the Secretary of State, in particular, were basically incompatible; and their resounding conflicts were destined to enter prominently, from time to time, into the conduct of American policy toward Russia. Creel's influence with the President, in particular, was an important check to the effectiveness of the State Department in putting through its own conception of policy toward Russia.[18]

The organization of the Committee on Public Information was whipped together in the usual chaotic fashion of wartime agencies, in April and May of 1917. Naturally, the question arose at an early date as to what could be done in the way of informational work in Russia. The recent February Revolution had given rise to high hopes that an effective program along these lines could serve not only to weld together the Russian and American peoples but also to stiffen Russia's will to carry on in the war. It was, however, by no means clear how such a program ought to be undertaken—whether through the existing State Department representation in Russia or some new field agency directly under the Committee of Public Information.

One of Creel's associates in the setting up of the committee's Washington headquarters was a man already well acquainted with Russian affairs and destined to have a good deal to do with Russian-American relations during the coming years: Arthur Bullard. Bullard was by profession a free-lance writer, both journalist and novelist, widely read and widely travelled. By conviction, he described himself as a socialist; actually, his views would today be termed liberal rather than socialistic; they accorded much more closely with

---

[18] "I have about come to the conclusion," House recorded in his diary on December 18, 1917, "that it is George Creel who is prejudicing the President against Lansing." (House MSS, *op.cit.*)

those of Woodrow Wilson than with those of the Socialist Party, of which Bullard was apparently never a member.

Bullard had been in Russia during the 1905 Revolution and had followed Russian affairs closely during subsequent years. A warm sympathizer with the Russian revolutionary opposition, he had functioned, in the years just preceding the war, as Secretary of the American Friends of Russian Freedom, the private organization (mentioned in Chapter I) of American liberals interested in the cause of political liberty in Tsarist Russia. When he arrived in Russia in 1917, Bullard had at his disposal, in this capacity, a modest sum of money which he proceeded to dole out discreetly to the Social-Revolutionary figures whom that organization befriended.

Bullard was well acquainted with, and held in high esteem by, Colonel House, with whom he maintained correspondence throughout the war years and whom he served at that time as a sort of private European observer. In 1915 and 1916 he was in England, where he followed closely the development of the local scene and of the war in general and whence he addressed a number of long reports to the Colonel, all marked by mature judgment, keen powers of observation, and excellent literary style.

There is no evidence that there was any formality in this arrangement or that Bullard was in any way remunerated for these services to House. He was a genuine idealist and his efforts were addressed strictly to the prospering of the ideals in which he believed. He lived on a modest scale, and made it a practice to earn only what he needed for the pursuit of his studies. Up to 1917 he seems to have paid his own way out of his literary earnings, even during his wartime residence abroad, and to have regarded his reports to Colonel House as a sort of voluntary wartime service.

As interest increased in a possible Russian operation of the Committee on Public Information, the idea arose of sending Bullard over first to survey the field. Bullard himself was at that time anxious to return to Russia, though not particularly for governmental purposes. He wanted to study the effects of the Russian Revolution on Russian foreign policy, particularly with relation to the Balkans. This was a matter to which he attached great importance and about which he had frequently corresponded with Colonel House.

An effort was first made by Creel to have Bullard assigned to accompany the Root Mission, with the idea that this would give him a chance to survey the situation and make recommendations as to the best way to undertake a Russian program. Creel wrote enthusiastically about this plan to President Wilson, who, prompted no doubt by Colonel House, passed on the suggestion to the Department of State as a "splendid one." Here, however, it struck a snag. Relations between Creel and Lansing were already strained. The Department, as yet unused to having its hand forced by other Washington agencies in personnel matters, resented Creel's stepping in with such suggestions, and probably considered Bullard too liberal in the bargain. It successfully resisted Bullard's appointment to the Root Mission on the grounds that another man (Stanley Washburn, who had been a war correspondent in Russia for the *London Times*), had already been named for this purpose. However, feeling that something had to be done in view of the President's letter, Lansing called Bullard in and offered him (apparently not too graciously) a job as what would today be called press attaché in the Embassy at Petrograd, at $5,000 a year with another $2,000 for "a clerk." This offer Bullard indignantly refused. Shortly thereafter arrangements were made, evidently under the encouragement of Colonel House and probably with the knowledge of the President,[19] for Bullard to go to Russia anyway, ostensibly in a private capacity, but almost certainly for purposes of interest to the Colonel as well as to Creel.

Bullard left Washington in June 1917. He was then thirty-eight years of age. His passport photo shows him as a frail, serious-featured man, with shell-rim glasses and a beard. He proceeded to Moscow

[19] Mrs. Bullard has indicated, since her husband's death in 1929, that she believed he had been in reality sent to Russia by the government. (It is possible she was somewhat misled in this conclusion by the President's enthusiastic letter of recommendation to Lansing, copies of which were in her husband's papers.) In a memorandum filed with the Arthur Bullard MSS, Firestone Library, Princeton, Mr. Ernest Poole (who accompanied Bullard on the journey to Russia) says Bullard went "not alone as a correspondent, but at the request of the President, to size up the situation and advise as to ways and means of promoting friendly relations . . . and also of helping the Kerensky Government to continue the war. I remember his showing me on the boat a letter of instructions from Colonel House." Bullard's correspondence with House, however, indicates that while his decision to go was carefully discussed with the Colonel, there was no formal arrangement. In a letter to House of June 18, 1917, Bullard wrote, "I will be going, therefore, entirely unofficially, which is from my point of view the most desirable. I will be glad to write to you from time to time, but I imagine that for the first month or two things will seem very much confused, but I hope to stay long enough to get the threads untangled."

where he spent the summer pursuing his studies of the situation, doling out his pittances to the "S-R's,"[20] and doing volunteer wartime publicity work for Summers, whom he personally liked and respected, and of whose activities in this field he thoroughly approved. Upon the opening, in November 1917, of the Petrograd office of the Committee on Public Information, Bullard was at once "drafted" for service in it; he came to Petrograd and spent the winter there for this purpose. Though nominally a subordinate of the head of the office, he was always treated with unusual respect, as a distinguished outsider whose services were in reality on a voluntary basis, and was allowed a latitude of action not normally granted to one in his position. Bullard later became head of the entire enterprise. He continued, during this period, to write directly to Colonel House. These letters were at least as important as the reports of the Ambassador, and probably much more so, in influencing the formulation of policy toward Russia in Washington.

Bullard was hampered, as an observer, by his poor linguistic ability (he was never able to achieve real fluency in Russian), his frail physical constitution, and his violent aversion to the habits and atmosphere of governmental offices.[21] But despite these handicaps, Bullard's was the best American mind observing on the spot the course of the Russian Revolution. Of all the official personalities, he alone had a background in Russian affairs, and particularly in the history of the revolutionary movement. A sensitive and quiet man, scholarly and well informed, detesting the limelight, endowed with that personal modesty which is one of the firmest foundations for intellectual penetration, he alone, of all the members of the official American community, succeeded in producing written analyses of the situation that achieved independent literary and historical distinction, not lost even after the passage of nearly forty years. His pas-

---

[20] The abbreviation, commonly used to denote the Social-Revolutionaries, will be used for purposes of brevity in this volume.

[21] Bullard wrote, in 1919, with reference to governmental work: "I loathe the atmosphere of such work. The 'very confidential,' the elaborate codes, the incessant intrigues, and undignified spying and 'diplomatic society.' It must always be a humiliation for one who has to live on his salary. The petty etiquette and formalism of it repells me. Even if I had no end of money I would hate to waste it entertaining so many uninteresting people . . . I would rather be engaged in moulding public opinion at home than in registering its decisions as a diplomat." (Bullard MSS, *op.cit.*, Box 1.)

sion for obscurity and aversion to official position was such that his name occurs relatively rarely in the course of the present narrative. But the reader should be aware that his quiet personality, strengthened by the almost universal respect he enjoyed among his colleagues, was always at work behind the scenes; and the influence he was able to exert through Colonel House, in particular, should not be underrated.

✧

After the receipt in Washington of the Root Mission's recommendations for a major propaganda campaign in Russia, the Committee on Public Information decided to open up operations in Russia on a major scale. This decision was hastened by Bullard's unfavorable reports on the rudimentary publicity work already being conducted in Petrograd and of the rivalries and feuds between various groups (particularly the Embassy and the Red Cross) then concerned with such matters.

The recommendations of the Root Commission were considerably revised and modified in Washington. But the residual program, though it called for only a fraction of the expenditure ($5,512,000) which the Root Mission had envisaged, was still an ambitious one. The man selected to head this work was another one of Creel's associates in the establishment of the committee: Mr. Edgar Sisson, who had been, at various times, city editor of the *Chicago Tribune,* managing editor of *Collier's,* and editor of *Cosmopolitan Magazine.*[22]

Sisson's appointment was made on October 23, only a fortnight before the Bolshevik seizure of power in Petrograd. After telling him of the assignment, Creel took him, that same day, to see President Wilson, who spoke to him about the assignment and outlined to him the principles by which he wished him to be guided in his work, but gave him no specific instructions. The President followed up this interview the next day with a personal note of instructions to Sisson which contained the following passage:

We want nothing for ourselves and this very unselfishness carries with it an obligation of open dealing. Wherever the fundamental principles of Russian freedom are at stake we stand ready to render such aid as lies in our power, but I want this helpfulness based upon request and not upon offer. Guard particularly against any effect of officious intrusion or med-

[22] Mock & Larson, *op.cit.,* p. 66.

dling and try to express the disinterested friendship that is our sole impulse.[23]

This brief contact with the President produced upon Sisson an effect destined to find many parallels in American official experience: namely, to convince him that he was going abroad as a personal representative of the President, endowed with the latter's very special confidence; that great things depended, in the President's view, on the completion of his mission; and that he carried with him a goodly share of the President's authority. To some extent, this impression never left him. He was to describe himself many years later, on the title page of his published memoirs, as "Special Representative of President Wilson in Russia," and to begin his narrative with the following proud passage:

President Wilson ordered me, on Tuesday, October 23, 1917, to go to Russia. I sailed from New York on Saturday, October 27, and reached Petrograd on November 25.

My letters of introduction were to Premier Kerensky and the members of his cabinet; my powers were wide and were increased by the control of funds. . . .[24]

It is, unfortunately, characteristic of American governmental practice that no comparable picture of Sisson's status and importance was ever communicated to Ambassador Francis. In apprising him of Sisson's assignment, the Department of State merely observed laconically that Sisson "represents Creel, who has been personally charged by [the] President with direction of this undertaking" (the propaganda program).[25] The Ambassador was enjoined to assist him in every way "to make his work effective and to insure sound understanding on his part of existing conditions." But the Ambassador was not told that he was being asked to receive anything in the nature of a rival or competitor to his own position. Thus the makings of trouble and confusion were implanted firmly in the situation by official Washington before Sisson ever arrived in Russia.

Sisson was a sharp, keen man, small and wiry in stature, bursting with energy and patriotic enthusiasm. He was not incapable of

[23] Edgar Sisson, *One Hundred Red Days: A Personal Chronicle of the Bolshevik Revolution,* Yale University Press, New Haven, 1931, p. 9.

[24] *Ibid.,* p. 3.

[25] *Foreign Relations, 1918, Russia,* Vol. I, *op.cit.,* p. 215; from Telegram 1808, October 29, 1917, 5 p.m., Secretary of State to Francis.

warmth or sentiment, but his nature was not outwardly warm or expansive. One of the Petrograd residents of that time has described him as "bitter and acid." His relations with those around him tended to be impersonal and distant. Journalism provided him with unlimited curiosity and a nose for the sensational, as well as with great fluency of expression and an excellent literary style. An alert, suspicious nature gave him a flair for conspiracy and intrigue. En route to Russia at the time the Bolsheviki seized power in Petrograd, he was bringing with him the ingredients for an intensive and exciting experience, from the memories of which he would long sustain himself in the prosaic post-war future. Life would have been more peaceful for the other Americans in Petrograd had he never appeared. On the other hand, the activities of that remote little American colony would have lacked an observant and indefatigable chronicler, and our knowledge of its experiences would be by far the poorer.

❖

No examination of the personalities prominently involved in the early months of Soviet-American relations would be complete without a glance at the American Red Cross Commission organized and sent to Russia in the summer of 1917 and its leading spirits—Mr. William Boyce Thompson and Mr. Raymond Robins.

William Boyce Thompson was a fabulous figure of American business in the years before the First World War. Copper magnate, stock market operator, and financial promoter, he had amassed a tremendous personal fortune and won himself a unique position in the New York financial world.

The most authoritative and revealing account of the circumstances surrounding the establishment of the Red Cross Commission and Thompson's inclusion among its members is that given in Mr. Hermann Hagedorn's excellent biography of Thompson:

. . . His [Thompson's] friends were already deep in the war as field-marshals and ambassadors. Baruch, on the Council for National Defense, was wielding dictatorial power in the economic field. Lamont was one of the most active single figures in interallied finance. Henry P. Davison, as head of the American Red Cross, was dramatizing the code of the Samaritan on an almost mythical scale. Thompson no longer found promotions and stock operations stimulating enough for his imagination.

. . . The overthrow of the Czar startled and thrilled him. Russia would be the decisive factor in the war, he said. If Russia could be held firm, Germany would be defeated. If the Russian front broke—

Thompson let it be known in Washington that he would like to go to Russia in any capacity. Davison, in the Red Cross, took him at his word. . . .[26]

. . . It was of the highest importance to have a forceful mind on guard in Petrograd in behalf of the United States. The American ambassador's, as it happened, was not that. The amiable and aging Missourian, David R. Francis, who represented his country in Russia, was filled with good intentions but no one looked to him for vision or initiative. Since it appeared impractical to supplant him, the only alternative was to send an individual such as the situation required as an unofficial envoy, to be acclaimed if he succeeded and repudiated if he failed.

How much of all this was reduced to definite instructions and how much remained a matter of hints and hopes; how much the Red Cross, the President or the State Department were involved or only certain individuals who happened to be both Thompson's friends and executives of the Red Cross, no document revealed then or thereafter. But it was made clear to Thompson that as "the representative of the United States," he would be expected "to undertake any work which," in his judgment, "was necessary or advisable in the effort to prevent the disintegration of the Russian forces." Edward N. Hurley, a member of the War Council of the Red Cross, journeyed from Washington to St. Paul to impress on Thompson the importance of "strengthening Kerensky's position with the hope that his administration would bring order out of chaos." [27]

It will be noted at once that Sisson was thus not the only person to be despatched to Russia in 1917 with the impression that he was the President's special political agent, endowed with functions similar to those normally borne by a full-fledged ambassador and overriding those of Mr. Francis, in particular.

The Red Cross Commission was organized in June and despatched to Russia in early July. It had already been arranged that Red Cross officials would, for the duration of the war, be nominally part of the armed forces establishment, and subject to the orders of the proper military authorities. They were to receive military commissions with

[26] Hermann Hagedorn, *The Magnate: William Boyce Thompson and His Time, 1869–1930,* The John Day Company, Inc., New York, 1935, p. 181.

[27] *Ibid.,* pp. 183–184. The last quotation is from a letter of Hurley to Hagedorn of May 3, 1932.

assimilated rank.[28] Thus the members of the commission to Russia were put into uniform and assigned military titles ranging from lieutenant to colonel (some of them were to retain these titles in everyday usage long after their connection with the Red Cross was ended). Thompson received the rank of colonel; his second in command, Robins, initially a major, later became a lieutenant colonel.

The commission was initially headed by Dr. Frank G. Billings, noted Chicago physician. Dr. Billings evidently accepted the assignment without fully understanding either the circumstances surrounding the mission's origin or the nature of the role Thompson expected to play in Petrograd. The expenses of the mission, even including the military uniforms of its members, were paid for out of Thompson's personal pocket;[29] and although his position in the mission at the outset was technically described as that of "business manager" it soon became evident that this was not a correct description of his own idea of his function.

It is obvious that Thompson felt himself responsible, as an individual, for the pursuit in Russia of activities having nothing to do with his Red Cross function. These activities were primarily of a political and informational nature, and had as their object the support of the Provisional Government and the stimulation of its war effort. (The mission carried, when it left Seattle, thousands of Russian translations of the President's war messages, the distribution of which it intended to begin on arrival at Vladivostok.[30]) These functions, added to the semi-military status of the Red Cross, brought the commission into close contact with the work of the Military Mission in Petrograd which naturally, in time of war, felt a keen responsibility for developments of a political nature that were affecting adversely the military contribution of one of the major Allies.

There is no evidence that the American Red Cross had, as an organization, any official cognizance of these extracurricular activities on the part of Thompson (later carried forward by his successor,

[28] Adjutant General's Order 081, Sec. 1, p. 8. War Department Files, MB879, The Pentagon.

[29] On October 19, 1918, Professor Samuel Harper of Chicago University, who was acquainted with the handling of Russian affairs in Washington, wrote to a friend in the Department of State (Jerome Landfield), that he thought it had been a great mistake to let Thompson pay the expenses of the Red Cross Commission: "I cannot understand how a man in Davison's position would agree to such an arrangement." (Samuel N. Harper MSS, Harper Memorial Library, Chicago.)

[30] National Archives, Petrograd Embassy File on Red Cross Mission; Telegram of July 6, 1917, Davison to Francis.

Robins) or that it served as a source of inspiration and instruction for them. The arrangement, from all indications, was Davison's personal doing. This was not a normal Red Cross mission: its members were not on the Red Cross payroll, nor were its expenses paid by the Red Cross. It was a hasty improvisation, concocted during the confusion of the first months of our participation in the war, and under the almost desperate consciousness of the imminent danger of Russia's departure from the ranks of the warring powers. The consequences were plainly different from what even Davison had anticipated. Within a few months, the venture was completely liquidated by the Red Cross itself; but not before it had added many a colorful page to the annals of Soviet-American relations, and had given origin to issues destined to reverberate for decades in the debates over American policy toward the Soviet Union.

The American Red Cross Commission arrived in Petrograd on August 7, 1917. By this time the Petrograd community, both Russian and American alike, was a little weary of American missions, having only recently been put to strenuous efforts to receive with due solemnity the Root Mission and the Advisory Commission of Railway Experts. To have another appear on the heels of these earlier ones, and this time with even less visible justification for its presence (the Russians were not particularly short of medical and Red Cross personnel), aroused a general sense of impatience. The result was that the Red Cross Commission began its functioning in Petrograd under somewhat inauspicious circumstances. A vivid picture of its reception in the American community there may be obtained from the following passage in the diary of Mr. George Gibbs of Milwaukee, an engineer who was a member of the Advisory Commission of Railway Experts, and at that time in Petrograd:

The American Red Cross delegation, about forty Colonels, Majors, Captains and Lieutenants, arrived yesterday. It is headed by Colonel (Doctor) Billings of Chicago, and includes Colonel William B. Thompson and many doctors and civilians, all with military titles; we dubbed the outfit the "Haytian Army" because there were no privates. They have come to fill no clearly defined mission, as far as I can find out, in fact. Gov. Francis told me some time ago that he had urged they not be allowed to come, as there were already too many missions from the various allies in Russia. Apparently, this Commission imagined there was urgent call for doctors and nurses in Russia; as a matter of fact there is at present a surplus of medical talent and nurses, native and foreign in the country and many half empty hospitals in the large cities. They do need supplies, however, and the two carloads which the Commission brought will be very useful.

This evening we were guests of Colonel Thompson at dinner at the Hotel de France. The Colonel is a very fat and yet energetic person and full of enthusiasm. We had a good dinner topped off by some excellent cigars which he had brought from the United States.[31]

Within a very short time after his arrival, Thompson had convinced himself that the problem of keeping the Kerensky government alive and Russia in the war was one of propaganda and hence of money. With enthusiasm he threw himself into the effort to remedy the situation. On his first reception by Kerensky, only two days after his arrival, he undertook to subscribe personally for a half million rubles of the new government loan. A day or two later, at a luncheon given for Kerensky and Foreign Minister Tereshchenko at the American Embassy, Thompson informed the startled Russian guests that he was sending a cable to New York "offering to be one of a syndicate of ten to purchase Russian bonds to the tune of one million rubles apiece." [32]

Kerensky himself was a Social-Revolutionary of sorts; and at his suggestion, Thompson was put into touch with Madame Breshkovskaya, the "Little Grandmother of the Revolution," who had only recently been released from a Tsarist prison by the February Revolution, and who was then living in Petrograd and participating again in party and public life. Madame Breshkovskaya and her friends were, it is true, in favor of collaboration with the Allies and continuation of the war effort. But their main concern was naturally to combat the growing influence of the Bolsheviki and to keep Kerensky in power. For all of this they needed funds, and Thompson immediately undertook to procure them. He conceived what he was doing as a move to save the morale of the Russian army from the inroads of the Bolshevik agitators and thus to prevent the disintegration of the eastern front. He was justified in his sense of military urgency and in his conviction of the gravity of the situation. But he ignored the difficulty of bringing financial assistance to any one faction in a foreign country without improving its competitive position vis-à-vis

---

[31] George Gibbs MSS, State Historical Society of Wisconsin, Madison; diary entry under date of August 9, 1917.

[32] Hagedorn, *op.cit.*, p. 192.

other factions and thus making oneself guilty of a form of intervention into domestic affairs. After a brief and unsuccessful attempt to get money for his purpose from the United States government, Thompson, an impatient man accustomed to doing things in a big way, drew on his personal account with J. P. Morgan and Company for a cool $1 million and set out to finance some of his S-R friends, whose influence he thought would be useful to the restoration of military morale. In the cynical and sophisticated political circles of the Russian capital, these donations, which soon became the subject of general gossip, were viewed with considerable amusement: the subvention of the Social-Revolutionary party by the financial barons of Wall Street.

Bullard subsequently related in a letter to Colonel House the somewhat ludicrous situation that resulted from these sudden heavy donations to the coffers of the S-R's. He had, it will be recalled, been doling out funds to some of the S-R's, quietly and in very modest amounts. He first learned of Thompson expenditures when his own friends in S-R circles came to him and began to thank him profusely for this unexpected fall of political manna. In vain he attempted to persuade them that this was not his doing and that he knew nothing about it. They accepted the explanations as evidences of his extreme refinement of method and skillful disguising of channels. Worried lest Thompson learn of the misunderstanding and resent it, Bullard went to Thompson's deputy, Robins, and tried delicately to set him right about the situation. Robins was so wrapped up in his own views and doings that he showed no disposition to listen, and Bullard, unable to muster the bluntness to penetrate Robins' ebullient self-centeredness, gave up the attempt. He suggested to the S-R's that they should themselves apprise Thompson that they had been receiving funds from other sources. But they were reluctant to reveal to outside parties anything more than they had to concerning their prior sources of funds, being always fearful of criticism on the grounds that they were the paid lackeys of capitalism. (This was a criticism which the Bolsheviki were indeed to force down their throats at a later date, but naturally on the basis of the conspicuous and well-known donations from Thompson himself.[33] The more discreet con-

---

[33] The *Pravda,* on December 7, attacked Madame Breshkovskaya bitterly over Thompson's donations, charging that this was "not Revolution but Prostitution." The reasons for this attack were strictly domestic-political. The "Wall Street" tag happened to come in handy.

tributions from Bullard never became known.) In the end, Bullard philosophically resigned himself to what seemed the inevitable, and allowed himself to bask in the undeserved gratitude that Thompson's extensive contributions brought forth.

This sudden output of American beneficence naturally could not but affect the interests and position of the American Ambassador. Fortunately for him, he was never fully informed of it, though he could scarcely fail to pick up rumors of what was going on. Thompson, together with two local American businessmen who were in on the deal, called on Francis and hinted at operations of this nature, but deliberately refrained from telling him the details, on the grounds that it might be better for him not to have official knowledge of them. (The Governor's connection with Madame deCram, viewed askance by Thompson as by others, is also said to have had something to do with this reticence.) Francis, who had opposed the despatch of the Red Cross Commission from the first but had been brusquely overruled by Washington,[34] felt himself absolved of responsibility, and accepted the resulting situation without remonstrance up to the time of the Bolshevik Revolution. Shortly thereafter, however, he found himself obliged to send to the Secretary of State a confidential personal cable, which throws a bright but melancholy light on his relations not only with the Red Cross Commission but also with the Military Mission. "Have just been asked by Judson," he wired,

. . . if I objected to allowing Red Cross use of his code, and upon my replying that he should decide himself, he told me that he had asked his department and had received authority, subject to my approval, for such use. I said I should not object. This is to inform you that I have no knowledge of contents of cables and am not familiar with what Red Cross has done. I understand that much more than a million dollars has been expended by Thompson of his personal funds, but as to methods or objects I am not informed. . . . During the last two months Thompson has seldom visited the Embassy. As Red Cross is semi-official and generally thought entirely official, I have often considered advisability of asking Thompson concerning these disbursements, as many rumors of same are current, but as I understand he is expending individual funds I did no more than advise

[34] National Archives, Petrograd Embassy File on Red Cross Mission, *op.cit.,* Francis' telegram 1443, June 27, 1917 to Secretary of State and latter's reply No. 1528, of July 3.

him through Judson with whom he is in close touch, that I hoped he would in no way reflect on our Government or country. . . . Judson said he had delivered the message but said the only reply was that Thompson said he was spending his own money and he would quit if he was not permitted to do it in the way he liked. Once subsequently he visited the Embassy but said nothing of this subject in the course of a thorough conversation.[35]

President Wilson, as will be seen, was highly displeased on learning of Thompson's disbursements. He blamed not only Thompson but apparently Francis as well for what he viewed as a reckless and flamboyant use of funds, and stored the incident away in his secretive but infinitely retentive memory. The President was evidently particularly affected by the reflection that this activity was undertaken by Thompson at a time when he, the President, had actively under advisement the whole question of the Root Mission's recommendations for the launching of a political information campaign in Russia. Thompson's action no doubt appeared to him as an unjustified and disrespectful anticipation of the presidential decision. According to Creel (whose memory was, to be sure, not always accurate in such matters), the decision to send Sisson to Russia was a reflection of this presidential displeasure over Thompson's activity.

For Dr. Billings, too, as Thompson's nominal chief, these political operations were too much. He soon gained the impression that he was being exploited as a front for activities about which he was not informed and over which he had no control. He endured the situation only a short time. As early as mid-September, "sick and disappointed," he gave up his mission and returned to the United States, leaving Thompson in formal command. "I do not know about Thompson," he wrote to a friend not long after his return; "I have very little confidence in his judgment."[36] Thompson's personal secretary, Mr. Cornelius Kelleher, was more brutal in his description of the situation. "Poor Mr. Billings," he wrote many years later,

. . . believed he was in charge of a scientific mission for the relief of Russia. . . . He was in reality nothing but a mask—the Red Cross complexion of the mission was nothing but a mask.[37]

[35] *Ibid.,* Francis' telegram 629, November 18, 1917, 12 midnight.
[36] Harper MSS, *op.cit.,* letter, Billings to Harper, April 26, 1918.
[37] William Appleman Williams, *American Russian Relations, 1781–1947,* Rinehart & Co., Inc., New York, 1952, p. 90, and footnote 166 to Chapter 3.

By the time Dr. Billings left, Thompson had become fabulous in the feverish society of revolutionary Petrograd. His immense fortune, his colorful personality, his great muscular bulk, his ubiquitous half-smoked cigars, his spectacular mode of existence—including a suite in the Hotel d'Europe, a French limousine, a wolfhound, a readiness to collect antiques (forthcoming in unlimited quantities from upperclass Russians who read the handwriting on the wall)— all made him a dramatic and conspicuous object of local attention. When he attended the opera, he was put in the imperial box and hailed ironically as "the American Tsar." [38] For obvious reasons, he was viewed by the Kerensky authorities as the "real" ambassador of the United States.

The Bolshevik seizure of power came as a great shock to Thompson. He had gone very far in identifying himself with the political fortunes of the internal-political opponents of the Bolsheviki—even to the point of supplying them liberally with funds. Being a realist, he could not fail to note the deadly efficiency with which the Bolsheviki seized power and consolidated their regime, and to be impressed with their seriousness and ruthlessness of purpose. These impressions were fortified by the reports of his second in command, Raymond Robins, whom he had sent to the provinces for the purchase of grain during the weeks just prior to the November Revolution, and who came back impressed with the power everywhere of the local soviets, as compared with other political and administrative entities. Shaken by all of this, Thompson reversed his political views under the impact of the November Revolution, and impulsively and enthusiastically embraced the idea of supporting the Bolsheviki, just as he had initially thrown himself into the support of Kerensky. He felt, however, that he was hopelessly compromised and discredited, as an individual, by the degree to which he had given his personal support to the enemies of the Bolsheviki. Robins appears to have shared this view and to have encouraged him to leave Russia.[39] Three weeks after the revolution, Thompson did leave for London and home, determined to win high level support for the idea of using the

---

[38] Sisson, *op. cit.,* p. 39.

[39] Hagedorn, *op.cit.,* p. 250. Thompson's activities may have gone further than just financing the S-R's. Judson, in his memorandum of June 18, 1919 to the Secretary of War, speaks of a "very efficient secret service organization" as having been formed by Thompson and Robins in the fall of 1917 "to combat the Bolsheviks." (Judson MSS, *op.cit.*)

Bolshevik regime as an instrument against Germany, just as he had first conceived of using Kerensky.

The effect on the Red Cross Commission of the Bolshevik seizure of power contributed further to the deplorable misunderstandings between the mission and the official American government establishment. Since Thompson had not revealed to the Ambassador and his associates the full nature of his political activities, he was evidently disinclined to explain to them the full reasons for the anxiety he felt for his own safety and for that of the members of the mission. The Embassy later guessed at the situation, but the impression produced was nonetheless unfortunate. In reporting to the Department of State on December 9, 1917, Francis said:

American Red Cross mission manifested surprising nervousness from beginning of [the] revolution, Thompson and some other members sleeping at apartment of Military Mission which had and has Bolshevik guard, and [with] which Thompson had much closer relations than with Embassy. That nervousness perhaps attributable to the disbursements . . . [recently revealed] by former secretary Breshkovskaya.[40]

In another communication Francis complained that Thompson had asked for ten places on the evacuation train and used only three. "I should not have tendered any place to a Red Cross worker," the Ambassador wrote, "as it was my understanding that they had volunteered to work under such conditions as they now seem desirous to escape." [41] A similar misunderstanding occurred in Moscow. In reporting on November 26, 1917 that the entire consular staff in that city, the Y.M.C.A., and the men connected with American enterprises would remain at their posts, Summers added that "American Red Cross members left as soon as possible after fighting began, notwithstanding my protests." [42] This obviously augured ill for the future relations between members of the Mission and the Consulate General—relations which at a somewhat later date were to assume a new and wholly unexpected importance. In this way, the concealment from the other Americans of what Thompson regarded as his "real" personal mission operated at the very outset to create misunderstandings of a most unpleasant and unfortunate nature.

[40] *Foreign Relations, 1918, Russia*, Vol. I, *op.cit.*, p. 294; Telegram 2081.
[41] Lansing MSS, *op.cit.*; Vol. 32 of Correspondence: Letter, Francis to Lansing, November 20, 1917.
[42] *Foreign Relations, 1918, Russia*, Vol. I, *op.cit.*, pp. 268–269; Telegram 89.

These circumstances all served to complicate the position of the man who was to be Thompson's successor as head of the Red Cross Mission, a figure of major importance in the first stages of Soviet-American relations: Mr. Raymond Robins.

❖

Raymond Robins, whose death occurred only in 1954, still awaits his biographer, and it is with a genuine sense of inadequacy that the following attempt is made to communicate in a few words something of his striking and colorful personality. In 1917, he was a man in the prime of life. Like Thompson, he was a product of the American West. Born in the East, but taken West as a young boy, he had worked as a miner in the Rocky Mountains, and had eventually joined in the Alaska gold rush. Not only did this venture turn out to be a financial success, but this youthful contact with the beauty and mystery of the Far North produced a profound spiritual impression, which was never to leave him.

Returning to the Middle West, Robins made Chicago the seat of his activities. Here, being both a liberal and a devout Christian, he became a cross between a political and religious evangelist, taking a prominent part in the work of the early Chicago settlement houses and in other liberal causes. Among other things, he took part in the defense of the two Russian political refugees, Rudewitz and Pouren, whose extradition the Tsar's government made intense but unsuccessful efforts to bring about in 1908.[43] Originally a Democrat, he switched in 1912 to the cause of Theodore Roosevelt and became one of the founders of the Progressive Party. He ran for Senator in Illinois in 1914 on the Republican-Progressive ticket. His inclusion on the Red Cross Commission in 1917 appears to have been the result of Theodore Roosevelt's recommendation.

When he arrived in Russia in September 1917, Robins had the advantage of a number of qualities which fitted him well for the role he was destined to play: abundant energy, considerable executive and forensic ability, some acquaintance with the labor movement in the United States, and a lively interest in the Russian revolutionary scene. He was hampered by what appears to have been a spotty and not fully balanced educational background and by a lack of those tools which might have helped him to form a more rounded judg-

[43] Williams, *American Russian Relations, op.cit.,* pp. 80–82; Bailey, *op.cit.,* p. 213.

ment of Russian events: particularly a knowledge of the Russian language and of Russian history and literature. By nature a person wholly absorbed by contemporary realities, his image of Russia in late 1917 had been gained from a few intensive but brief and recent experiences, and was lacking in historical perspective. The northern landscape and the Petrograd winter, together with his strong sense of excitement about the war and the importance of his own mission, brought back to him the most vivid associations of his youthful adventure in the Yukon and produced in him a state of mystical-religious exaltation, conducive to enthusiasm rather than to discrimination as he approached his tasks.

Robins' contribution to the analysis of Soviet realities was generally received with suspicion and rejected at home, but it was not wholly devoid of merit. He had a hatred of what he called the "indoor" absorption of knowledge. He believed in getting out and getting around, and this he did in no uncertain way. He was constantly on the move, dashing from one place to another, seeing a most extraordinary variety of people. Unquestionably, he saw more of the Soviet leaders in the early months and years of their power than any other single American. While this experience did not always lead to accurate judgments on his part, at least it enabled him to avoid a number of the erroneous impressions that fastened themselves onto the thinking of other foreigners. Thus his views about the realities of the Revolution, while spotty in their factual foundation and often vaguely expressed, were never trivial or uninteresting. They were marked, above all, by the realization that the irritating aspects of the communist personality were no reason for ignoring its impressive aspects and no reason for not giving it serious study. No American who has been long exposed to the Soviet scene can read without deep admiration and sympathy the words with which Robins endeavored, in 1919, to explain to the members of a subcommittee of the Senate Committee on the Judiciary how it was possible that an intense interest in the Soviet Union and respect for the formidable qualities of its leaders did not necessarily mean sympathy with its ideology or desire to see it succeed in its world revolutionary aspirations.

On the other hand, Robins had certain personal characteristics which made it difficult for him to fit easily into the confused pattern of responsibilities and relationships that marked the official and semi-official American community in Russia at that time. He was utterly unaccustomed to governmental procedures, and impatient of them. He had no idea of the painstaking precision that is necessary to make communication between governments effective and useful. His concept of diplomacy was a deeply personal one, in which understanding came to rest upon the fire of a glance or the firmness of a handclasp. He suffered, in his state of exalted and dedicated enthusiasm, from an inability to find with other men any normal middle ground of association between the extremes of passionate loyalty and dark suspicion. Contemporaries have described the American Indian character of his physical appearance at that time: his long black hair, his piercing eyes, his silent tread. These qualities led Thompson to dub him "The Panther." They were the counterparts of a corresponding emotional makeup: vigorous, masterful, suspicious of many, intensely loyal to a few, dramatic to the last vein. Robins was an orator, an actor, and a sentimentalist, but with it all a man of great force of character, exceptional physical and intellectual vigor, and unquestionable idealism.

All this being the case, and in view of the inauspicious circumstances under which the Red Cross Commission was introduced in the Russian situation, Robins did not find it easy to adjust his personal relations to the American community in Russia, and probably had little interest in doing so. Protected by his Red Cross status, he played a lone hand both socially and—for the most part—officially, leaving behind him when he departed in 1918 a long trail of resentments and suspicions among the members of the American official family. It is not easy, on the basis of the available record,[44] to appraise the realities under the dust of these old animosities.

Robins was a characteristic figure of the liberal movement of the Middle West in the years before World War I. As such, he shared in both the strengths and the weaknesses of that social phenomenon. He was supported by its capacity for enthusiasm, its sincerity, its robust confidence, its romanticism, and its love of action; but he suffered from its essential provincialism, the shallowness of its historical perspective, the erratic and unbalanced quality of many of its intellectual approaches. It was from this background that he derived his religious fervor and his faith in human progress; but it was also

---

[44] The Raymond Robins papers, in the State Historical Society of Wisconsin, Madison, became available to scholars generally only as this volume was in process of completion. They are extremely voluminous and have not yet been ordered.

from this background that he derived that lack of roundedness, of tolerance, and of patience with the sad necessities of man's political existence which was to make his career as a figure in Russian-American relations so stormy, so episodic, and in the end so tragic.

Robins was a man capable of commanding among his friends an admiration and loyalty no less intense than the suspicions and criticisms he provoked in others. Since it will be necessary, in the course of this narrative, to recount a number of harsh things said about him, it might be fair to terminate this reference to him with an example of the feeling his friends bore to him to the end of his eventful life. In *The Congregationalist* for October 27, 1932 there appeared the following letter from Professor Charles E. Merriam of the University of Chicago:

A powerful and picturesque figure in Chicago is that of Raymond Robins, for a quarter of a century in the storm center of the city's most tempestuous moments. Coal miner in Kentucky, seeker (and finder) of pure gold in the Klondike, both lawyer and minister by profession, settlement worker. . . . But above all, a flaming orator of marvelous power, commander of humor, satire, tenderness, emotional appeal in their finest forms, he has been a flaming sword in many a Chicago battle. With broad, democratic sympathies, incorruptible honesty and indomitable courage, his blade has been a ring of fire, and his voice a trumpet call in many a fray.[45]

No mention of Robins and his activities in Russia would be complete without a word about the alter ego who guided his steps in that country from the time of the Bolshevik Revolution, arranged his contacts with the Soviet authorities, translated for him, and served as secretary and general aide—Alexander Gumberg. Gumberg, described by Edgar Sisson as "a New York Jew with melancholy eyes, sensitive features, and a mind crammed with resources,"[46] was at that time a fairly young man. Born in Russia, taken to the United States as a boy, he had come to move in Russian-Socialist circles in New York, and had been in 1914–1915 manager of the Russian-Socialist paper, the *Novy Mir*. He had known Trotsky (a contributor to the *Novy Mir*) when the latter was there in January and February

[45] Graham Taylor MSS, Newberry Library, Chicago; letter to Fred B. Smith.
[46] Sisson, *op.cit.*, p. 94.

of 1917. After the February Revolution Gumberg had returned to Russia. He availed himself, at that time, of a Russian passport, and apparently thought of himself, in those months, as a Russian citizen. One of his brothers became a Bolshevik official, who used the party pseudonym of Zorin. He himself plainly enjoyed excellent and intimate relations with Trotsky, Radek, Peters, and other high Bolshevik officials.

Shortly after his arrival in Petrograd, Gumberg appears to have made himself useful to members of the Root Mission, and later to Mr. John F. Stevens, chairman of the American Advisory Commission of Railway Experts, as aide and interpreter. With the arrival of the Red Cross Commission, Gumberg's services were apparently transferred to Thompson and Robins. Later, for a time, he also served Sisson.

Up until the Bolshevik seizure of power, Gumberg's usefulness to the Americans in question, while considerable, had not yet achieved its full potentiality. Following the Bolshevik Revolution, his extensive acquaintance in Russian radical circles and his easy access to many Bolshevik leaders at any and all times made him an indispensable aide to Americans who had no knowledge of the Russian language and no independent means of access to the Bolshevik authorities. His usefulness to the Soviet authorities by dint of these activities was presumably not less than his usefulness to the Americans. From the time of the November Revolution until the spring of 1918 he stood in the thick of the relations between the Soviet authorities, on the one hand, and most of the American authorities, on the other, with the notable exception of the Embassy Chancery itself. He was the unofficial fixer, it might be said, for all the unofficial envoys.[47]

Gumberg, one feels, stood squarely between the two worlds in which his life revolved. He bestowed on both, with no apparent partiality, his ready understanding, his skepticism, and, in a way, his affection. With sardonic amusement he viewed their jarring impact on each other, and enjoyed attempting to soften the impact where he could. As Robins' "man Friday" and supporting genius, he no

---

[47] It should be pointed out that Gumberg was never employed by the Red Cross, who knew of him only as "presumably . . . a personal attaché of Mr. Robins." (War Department Records, The Pentagon; letter from Counsel, Department of Personnel, American Red Cross, July 19, 1918, to General Churchill, Chief of MID, War Department.)

doubt viewed his own role, despairingly and not without humor, as that of peacemaker. In a world where peacemakers are not greatly appreciated, this role was bound eventually to get him into trouble with both sides—and did. This being so, it would perhaps be well to recall in conclusion the impassioned defense of him which Robins delivered in 1919 in a Congressional committee room, when one of the investigating Senators suggested that Gumberg had been "connected with the Bolshevik Government"—a defense so resounding that it brought the sleepy spectators to their feet in a storm of applause and forced the chairman of the committee to appeal for order:

May I make the statement that the services of this Russian, Alexander Gumberg, and the character of those services, under stress and under fire, were such as to make that man, in my judgment, the most serviceable single Russian person in the most difficult days of the Russian situation? . . . I am behind him with full support and credit at all times, and ready to appear before this body or any proper body of the United States, or its courts, in defense of his patriotism, in defense of his genuine, manly service; and when, sirs, he was attacked, after I came out here, as a German agent, by lying statements that did not dare to see the light, I challenged those persons who sought to discredit him that I be called upon . . . to test the matter; and those lying, cowardly slanders ran back into the dark. It was said to me, "Robins, you are safe. You are strong, in spite of the propaganda to discredit you; . . . in spite of all said against you, you can survive; but ditch this little Jew. There is some question about him." I said, "Not in seven thousand years. I am not built on that principle. . . ."

That little Jew went through fire with me. That little Jew lay on his belly when machine-gun bullets went into the wall above us and all around us. That little Jew stood up on the fender of my automobile when we were surrounded by the pro-German anarchists, armed with bayonetted guns and magazine pistols, . . . that little Jew looked down on cocked rifles and, with a gun pushed against his belly, grinned, and said to the anarchist thieves: "You are not afraid, are you?" and I am with him to the end of the road. . . .[48]

✧

There is one other, among the American personalities prominent in Petrograd at the outset of Soviet-American relations, who deserves

[48] *Bolshevik Propaganda, Hearings before a Subcommittee of the Committee on the Judiciary, U.S. Senate, 65th Congress,* U.S. Government Printing Office, Washington, 1919, pp. 888–889.

mention. He was not a member of the official American governmental establishment—far from it. He appears only briefly and
incidentally in the sequence of events to which this narrative is
devoted. Yet his figure is so much a part of the setting, and his
reactions so intimately revealing of the realities of the age, that no
such survey of personalities seems complete without him. The reference is to that rebellious and romantic spirit who haunted the streets
and meeting halls of Petrograd in those stirring days and drank
in the impressions of the Revolution with such avid thirst and excitement: John Reed.

Actually, there is little to say here about Reed. He was, as everyone knows, a youth from the West Coast, a Harvard graduate, a
socialist, a rebel against the American society of his day, a writer—
the author, in particular, of that magnificent firsthand account of
the days of the Revolution: *Ten Days that Shook the World*.[49] In
many ways, he was childish and irritating. To the official Americans
in Petrograd, as to most Americans at home, he was provocative,
inconsiderate, intolerant, needlessly offensive. His picture of life was
fragmentary in the extreme. He could be grievously wrong about
many things (though seldom about those he saw with his own eyes).
His critical attitude toward his own country and its society had in
it all the irritating brashness of ignorant and disrespectful youth,
with no redeeming modesty, no seemly respect for age and experience. He bore his antagonism to his own society at the worst possible time: when the feelings of Americans about their own country
had been aroused to a white heat of intensity, when their own
capacity for tolerance was least.

Yet the historian cannot follow without a deep sense of sadness
John Reed's tragic and stormy passage across the scene of this inquiry. Whatever else he may have been, he was a poet of the first
order, and he had in him, awaiting only that maturity which comes
so slowly and painfully to the gifted, the makings of a great observer
of and commentator on the human scene. His view of Russia was
limited at that time to the streets of Petrograd and Moscow. For
that reason it was an inadequate one and in some respects misleading. But where his eye fell, it registered with passionate sincerity
and intensity whatever lay before it. Despite his exuberant and
uninhibited political bias, Reed's account of the events of that time

[49] Boni & Liveright, Inc., New York, 1919.

rises above every other contemporary record for its literary power, its penetration, its command of detail. It will be remembered when all the others are forgotten. And through this tale, as through the whole bizarre record of his adventures and mistakes, there runs the reflection of a blazing honesty and a purity of idealism that did unintended credit to the American society that had produced him, the merits of which he himself understood so poorly.

Perhaps it was too much to ask that the America of that time should have accepted this foolish and rebellious child and treated him with gentleness and understanding merely for the sake of his sincerity and his talents. But the impression is irresistible that the treatment actually accorded him in his home country, when he returned from Russia, was tragically unnecessary. Even his immature opinions deserved reasoned, patient argument rather than emotional indignation. And his provocative behavior would have been better met by an amused sympathy than by criminal indictments. Had such consideration been shown, a gifted nature might have been preserved for the time when its talents could mature and yield their full flower, instead of being thrust out to find a premature death in Moscow and an interment, more ironic than fitting, alongside the various revolutionary figures whose ashes repose in the Kremlin wall.

In any case, Reed was very much there, in Petrograd, when the Revolution occurred, flaming like a human torch with its contagious enthusiasm, absorbing into his youthful frame the immense, incipient antagonism that was eventually to separate two great peoples and to devastate his own life and so many others. His was *one* American way of reacting to the Revolution. It deserves to be neither forgotten nor ridiculed.

✧

All the Americans described in this chapter are now dead. They are no longer here to give to their words and actions that eloquent and impassioned defense which each, in his way, would have given. I have endeavored to bear this in mind in dealing with their persons and their affairs, and to be at all times more considerate and less dogmatic about them than they tended to be about each other. But all of them do not always appear at their best; and for this reason it is pleasant to record that, although they were all acting in bewildering and trying circumstances, there was none who sought personal gain from the situation, none (unless Reed be excepted) who forgot for an instant the interests of his country, and none who did other than to follow, with courage and conviction, the voice of honest conscience.

CHAPTER III

FIRST REACTIONS

*On last Tuesday the Bolsheviks got the city in their hands
and I want to tell you that it is something awful.
—Philip Jordan, in a letter to Mrs. David R. Francis,
November 18, 1917*

THE final Bolshevik seizure of power in Petrograd occurred November 7-8, 1917, and reached its culmination in the capture of the Winter Palace, the unseating of the Provisional Government, and the arrest of the members of the Kerensky cabinet (with the exception of Kerensky himself) during the night of November 7-8.

As indicated in the Introduction, life remained outwardly normal in many parts of the Russian capital, and the official American community was in no way physically affected by these stirring events. The Embassy played only an incidental and wholly unintentional part in the drama by providing at least a portion of the transportation for Premier Kerensky's escape on the morning of the 7th. It happened this way.

During the night of November 6–7th, the vehicles of the car pool of the Petrograd Military District, usually stationed at General Staff Headquarters and generally used as official governmental cars, were effectively sabotaged by the Bolsheviki—allegedly by the simple process of removing the magnetos. When, therefore, on the morning of the 7th, with the cruiser *Aurora* already anchored in midstream of the Neva and its guns trained on the Winter Palace, Premier Kerensky made his decision to leave Petrograd in the hope of rounding up some loyal troops with which to suppress the rebellion, he found himself without means of transportation. In the general chaos of the morning, the adjutant of the car pool, Ensign Boris Knirsha, was sent out with another officer with instructions to scare up one or two cars somewhere and somehow. Frantically, and with little real hope of success, the two men paced the Petrograd streets, searching out the homes of prominent figures known to possess private motor cars. Leaving the home of one such person, on the Morskaya Embankment, and intending as a last resort to try the British and Italian Embassies, the two men were pleased to observe, standing in front of a nearby house, a handsome Renault touring car, bearing the American flag, with a chauffeur standing by. This, as it happened, was the car of American Assistant Military Attaché Captain E. Francis Riggs. It was waiting to take Secretary of Embassy Sheldon Whitehouse to the Embassy Chancery for his day's work. Ensign Knirsha and his companion rang the doorbell and told Whitehouse's Russian brother-in-law, Baron Ramsay, that they were obliged to requisition the car because Kerensky needed it for his personal use. Whitehouse and Ramsay were skeptical, and insisted that they must have this from Kerensky himself. So all drove off together to the General Staff Headquarters, where they found Kerensky pacing dramatically up and down—the center of the growing confusion of the morning. Kerensky confirmed that he needed the car, in order—he said—to go to Luga and get loyal troops with which to put down the rabble that was threatening the security of the city. Kerensky acknowledged to Whitehouse that the Bolsheviki controlled the city and that the government, lacking reliable troops, was powerless. He thought the other members of the government would be arrested in the course of the day. He asked Whitehouse to relay to Ambassador Francis the request that he not recognize the Soviet Government, saying that he expected the uprising to be liquidated within five days.

Whitehouse saw no alternative but to yield the car. Leaving the chauffeur to stay with it and share its uncertain fate, he and Ramsay proceeded on foot to the Embassy.

Although Francis, fearful of having the Embassy involved in the political events of the day, tried to hush up the incident, it naturally became known and led to a general impression that Kerensky had escaped in an American official car, under cover of the American flag.

Actually, it was not quite this way; the details of what really occurred were marked by that bleak inconclusiveness characteristic of so many happenings in torn and chaotic times. In addition to Riggs's car, Knirsha and his companion also managed to lay hands on the Pierce-Arrow of a prominent Petrograd lawyer. On the escape from the city, Kerensky rode in the Pierce-Arrow. Knirsha himself occupied the Renault, which, driven by Riggs's Finnish chauffeur, was taken along as a reserve vehicle. As they left the General Staff building, the chauffeur of the Pierce-Arrow maneuvered the Renault into taking the lead, the purpose evidently being to give Kerensky greater protection. Since Knirsha and the Finnish chauffeur had no idea where the cortege was supposed to be going, this shift led initially to some aimless meandering in the Petrograd streets, a procedure which in the circumstances was not without its dangers. The Pierce-Arrow was eventually jockeyed back into first place, whereupon it sped out of town at a tremendous speed, the Renault in hot and bewildered pursuit. Early in the game the American flag fell off the Renault. Knirsha says he picked it up and hid it. Careening madly on the cobblestone roads, Knirsha and the Finn chased the Pierce-Arrow as far as Gatchina (some 25 miles south of town). Here the Renault was obliged to stop to get gas and to hunt for a spare inner tube. Kerensky went on ahead, leaving orders that the Renault was to follow him to Luga, 50 miles farther south. Finding gas and inner tubes in Gatchina proved to be a problem; and it was seven o'clock in the evening before Knirsha could get going again. The Renault had no proper lights. After going a short distance, according to Knirsha's laconic official report, they "ran into a rock" in the dark. In disgust, Knirsha told the chauffeur to take the car back to Petrograd; he himself went to the nearest railway station and took a train. The car, apparently little the worse for its encounter with the rock, was restored to Riggs a day or so later.[1]

Otherwise, the Petrograd Americans were in no way involved in the governmental overthrow,[2] and suffered no special inconvenience from it. In Moscow it was a different matter. There the fighting was

[1] This account of the adventures of Riggs's car is reconstructed from Knirsha's own report, included in the article "Vokrug Gatchiny" (Around Gatchina), *Krasny Arkhiv*, Vol. 9, State Publishing House, Moscow-Leningrad, 1925, pp. 171–194; also Alexander F. Kerensky, *The Catastrophe: Kerensky's Own Story of the Revolution*, D. Appleton & Co., New York, 1927, pp. 336–339; and, finally, the personal accounts of the incident kindly provided by Messrs. Norman Armour and Sheldon Whitehouse, who were residing with Riggs at the house on the Morskaya. Kerensky's account differs markedly from the others; but the latter are more circumstantial, and agree in almost all respects.

[2] Robins, speaking publicly some years later, said, "I manned a machine gun in the streets of Petrograd in the Bolshevic Revolution." (*The Herald,* Miami, December 30, 1922, War Department Records, The Pentagon.) What lay behind this statement is unclear. There was relatively little fighting in Petrograd, and no evidence that any American actually participated in it. Robins no doubt had some sort of basis for his statement, but it is not likely that it involved any actual shooting.

far more severe, and lasted for nearly a week. The Consulate General, situated on the Bryusovski Pereulok, near the center of town, found itself in the thick of the firing. A number of the personnel were caught in the office premises and obliged to spend several days there, unable to make their way to their homes. A number of others took refuge in the barracks of the French Military Mission, their own homes being too exposed for occupancy. Those who contrived to visit the office during those days, including Consul General Summers, did so only at great risk to their lives, dodging constantly into doorways and around corners, to escape the firing. Both the Consulate General and Mr. Summers' home were damaged by rifle and shell fire. Summers, remaining modestly silent about his own performance, particularly commended to the Department of State his second in command, Mr. DeWitt C. Poole, for heroism and efficiency in lending protection to the American community in circumstances of "grave danger" to himself. When the shooting ended with a Bolshevik victory, on November 14, the Americans were all physically intact, and the consular establishment resumed its normal functioning.

❖

The first act of Soviet power affecting the interests of the western powers was to call for a general cessation of the great war that was then in progress.

"Peace," it will be recalled, had been one of the major political slogans on which the Bolshevik faction had made its way to power. The promise to take Russia out of the war represented a political commitment of long standing on the part of the Soviet leaders, dating from the Zimmerwald Conference of European socialists in 1915. This was a basic tenet of Bolshevik policy. It was founded, of course, on the traditional left-socialist attitude toward "imperialist" wars; but the Bolshevik leaders were not unmindful of the fact that only by a termination of the war effort could the army be successfully destroyed as a possible focal point of armed resistance to Bolshevik power, and the support of the peasant-soldier masses for the new regime assured.

Accordingly, on November 8, the day following the initial seizure of power, in the midst of all the turbulent events of those particular days and hours, Lenin and his associates found time to have approved by the Congress of Soviets and to broadcast to the world a "Decree on Peace," proposing "to all belligerent peoples and their Governments the immediate opening of negotiations for a just and democratic peace." Such a peace they defined as an immediate one "without annexation (i.e. without the seizure of foreign territory, without the forcible incorporation of foreign nationalities), and without indemnities." [3]

In itself this was of course, from the Allied point of view, a bitterly unfriendly move. Russia was still viewed in the western countries as an ally—one of the members of the Triple Entente. No denunciation of the alliance had occurred. The Decree on Peace was adopted and broadcast to the world without prior consultation with, or warning to, the Allied governments. It clearly threatened violation of the formal obligation Russia had assumed in 1914, vis-à-vis the other Entente powers, not to make a separate peace. In 1917, when the passions of war were at their peak, the abrupt threat of Russia's defection represented not only a grievous setback to the cause of the Entente but, in the eyes of much of the western public, an act of outright perfidy and betrayal.

All this was bad enough. But in addition, the form and terms of the appeal were plainly meant to be offensive to the Allied governments. The appeal was directed not only to governments but also, over their heads, to their respective peoples. It suggested to these peoples that they should take things into their own hands and should set up "new organs," bypassing the existing governmental structures, for the purpose of defining the conditions of peace. This was, in effect, a summons to revolution. Calling for a peace based on the principle of "no annexations," the decree went on to interpret the term "annexation" as including all existing colonial relationships. The demand, therefore, was not only for a termination of hostilities but for the immediate abolition of the colonial relationship everywhere. In this way the authors of the decree burdened its primary purpose with ulterior demands of an inflammatory and propagandistic nature, bound to be offensive and unacceptable to the leading Allied nations. This was the first example in Soviet diplomacy of what was later to become known, in Soviet usage, as "demonstrative diplomacy," i.e. diplomacy designed not to promote

[3] Jane Degras, Ed., *Soviet Documents on Foreign Policy*, Oxford University Press for Royal Institute of International Affairs, London, 1951, Vol. i, p. 1.

freely accepted and mutually profitable agreement as between governments, but rather to embarrass other governments and stir up opposition among their own people.

It is difficult to believe that proposals so formulated and so presented as the Decree on Peace could have been expected to be seriously entertained by the Allied governments, unless these governments were to find themselves pressed by internal opposition to a point where they lost all independence and dignity of policy—a situation that would have been entirely acceptable from the Bolshevik standpoint. Betrayed, as they were destined to be betrayed so many times in the future, by their skepticism as to the real degree of popular support of democratic governments, Lenin and his friends were convinced that this appeal for peace would bring about "either an early peace or else a revolutionary war." [4] Actually, it produced neither.

The Decree on Peace was made available to the foreign press in Petrograd and was broadcast by wireless. Its terms were reported in some detail in the New York papers on Saturday morning, November 10. It was, however, never addressed or formally communicated to the Allied governments—a fact which of course constituted a further discourtesy, and mitigated against the likelihood of any formal reply.

The initial impact on the western countries of the overthrow of the Provisional Government by the Bolsheviki was thus one of alarm and indignation, tempered by considerable doubt that the new masters of the Russian capital would succeed in holding power for any length of time. Had the world not been in the midst of a great war, then at its crucial stage, and had the Bolsheviki not inaugurated their external relations by issuing a provocative and offensive decree announcing in effect the departure of Russia from the ranks of the anti-German coalition, there might have been more readiness in western countries to reflect on the deeper social and political realities behind the Bolshevik success and to examine from a longer range the problems of policy which this event presaged for the western governments. As it was, the revolution in Petrograd came to be regarded from the start in western countries primarily in its relationship to the fortunes of war. It could not fail, in these circumstances, to arouse feelings of bitter resentment and negation

[4] John W. Wheeler-Bennett, *The Forgotten Peace: Brest-Litovsk, March 1918,* William Morrow & Co., New York, 1939, p. 66.

in a host of Western minds, engrossed as they were with wartime emotion.

❖

In Washington, the press was ahead of the official channels in bringing to the governmental leaders and to the society of the capital news of the happenings in Petrograd. The first reports of an overthrow in the Russian capital began to come into Washington newsrooms as early as Thursday, November 8. The State Department was pressed that same day to comment on them (the first of many, many queries to be made of the State Department about American policy toward Soviet Russia), but wisely declined to do so in the absence of reports from Ambassador Francis. The following morning the front pages were dominated by the story of the Bolshevik seizure of power—the main features (Kerensky's flight, the storming of the Winter Palace, the issuance of the Decree on Peace) being reported in general quite correctly.

Later that day, according to the Washington correspondent of the *New York Times,* the Cabinet devoted all of its time to a discussion of the Russian situation. Of this—the first inner-governmental discussion of the problems of policy toward the new regime in Russia—there appears to be no official record. The Administration, according to this same press account, was "naturally concerned," but "had not lost hope in Russia remaining ·in the Allied camp." The Treasury, in particular, was worried, but inclined to continue financial aid provided the Bolsheviki did not take Russia out of the war.

About midnight, in the night from Friday to Saturday, the first official news of the coup in Petrograd was received. First, there were two messages from the Legation in Stockholm. These were followed very shortly, in the early morning hours, by several messages from the Embassy in Petrograd and from Summers in Moscow. By the opening of office hours on November 10 (Saturday) the Secretary of State had official confirmation that the Bolsheviki had at least seized power in Petrograd.

There is no indication of any further official consultations at that time. The President played golf, that Saturday morning, with his personal physician. His only official appointment for the day was with George Creel. He wrote one letter on Russian matters in the course of the day—to Charles Edward Russell, who had only recently returned from his trip to Russia as a member of the Root Mission, and "who had suggested a campaign to show the Russian people that the success of their revolution depended on the continuance of the war"—but if the news of the day had made any impression on the President, the letter did not reflect it. It did, however, contain a note of frustration that was to be found frequently thereafter in the President's references to Russian problems. He wrote:

. . . all sorts of work in Russia now is rendered extremely difficult because no one channel connects with any other, apparently.[5]

In all probability, this comment referred not to events in Russia itself, but to the complexity of American wartime governmental organization. The State Department establishment in Petrograd, the military and commercial sections attached to that mission, the Committee on Public Information, the Root Mission, the Stevens Railway Mission, the Treasury Department as representative of this government on the inter-Allied financial bodies, the American Red Cross, and the Y.M.C.A.—all, as well as the various Russian missions which had been sent to the United States, had a hand in our relations with Russia. No effective effort had been made to coordinate these various channels. The resulting confusion often came to the President's attention in bothersome ways, irritating him, and giving him a sense of frustration.

On Sunday, November 11, the President attended church in the morning, went for a drive in the afternoon, and then left for Buffalo, where he was scheduled to address the A.F. of L. The speech, delivered Monday morning, contained the first published reflection of Wilson's awareness of what had happened in Russia:

. . . it is amazing to me that any group of persons should be so ill-informed as to suppose, as some groups in Russia apparently suppose, that any reforms planned in the interest of the people can live in the presence of a Germany powerful enough to undermine or overthrow them by intrigue or force. Any body of free men that compounds with the present German Government is compounding for its own destruction. . . .[6]

In making this statement, the President attributed to the Germans ideological ambitions they did not have (the German leaders had

[5] Ray Stannard Baker, *Woodrow Wilson, Life and Letters,* Doubleday, Doran & Co., Inc., New York, 1939, Vol. VII, p. 349.
[6] *Ibid.,* p. 350.

little concern with the internal programs of Russian governments). The Bolshevik leaders could hardly be said to correspond to our idea of a "body of free men." Nor did they need any outside instruction to be persuaded that the German war aims were grasping and sinister. Bullard, then in Moscow, was quick to pick up this last point. "Mr. Wilson," Bullard observed in a memorandum prepared shortly thereafter,

. . . spoke as if he thought that the leaders of the Russian masses hoped to get decent, democratic terms of peace with the Imperial Government of Germany. . . . The Bolsheviki do not expect to get kindly terms from the Kaiser. Their one hope and their expectation is to put the Kaiser out of business. You do not have to argue to convince them of the mercilessness of the German Imperialists.[7]

The President did not return to Washington until eleven o'clock Monday evening. The following morning (Tuesday, November 13) after his usual round of golf, he spent two hours in his study. By this time a further batch of official reports had come in. They were sufficient to confirm:

1. That power in Petrograd, and probably in Moscow as well, was in the hands of the respective soviets, the Provisional Government having been deposed and most of its members arrested;

2. That the Petrograd Soviet was claiming to be the national government of Russia; that it had appointed Trotsky Commissar for Foreign Affairs; that Trotsky had officially taken over the Foreign Office;

3. That the new regime had proposed an immediate peace; and

4. That Kerensky, having made his escape, was reliably reported to be advancing on Petrograd with an anti-Bolshevik military force.

Later that day, the President wrote a personal letter to Representative Frank Clark of Florida saying that

. . . I have not lost faith in the Russian outcome by any means. Russia, like France in a past century, will no doubt have to go through deep waters but she will come out upon firm land on the other side, and her great people, for they are a great people, will in my opinion take their proper place in the world.[8]

Thereafter, nothing was heard direct from Ambassador Francis until Friday, November 16. The newspapers carried stories through-

[7] Bullard MSS, *op.cit.*, Box 13; Memorandum entitled "The Bolshevik Movement in Russia," dated simply "January 1918."
[8] Baker, Vol. VII, *op.cit.*, p. 355.

out the week about fighting between Reds and Whites. These stories were contradictory and for the most part unreliable, but they sufficed to raise serious questions as to whether the Bolsheviki would succeed in retaining power. As late as the 16th, the State Department was still complaining to correspondents that communications were so poor that it was "unable to understand what was happening in Russia." [9] It was not until Saturday, November 17, that the failure of Kerensky's attempt at counter-attack was finally confirmed on fairly reliable evidence.

One would think that at some time during that week, November 10–17, the President must have discussed further with his leading advisers the situation that had arisen in Russia, its effect upon the conduct of the war, and the attitude to be adopted toward it. But there is no indication of this in the published record. Nor is there any indication in the personal papers of the President or his Secretary of State of even any intensive preoccupation with the Russian problem.

This is less surprising than might at first appear. The information at the disposal of the United States government was still fragmentary and confusing. There was no reliable indication that the Bolsheviki were permanently installed in power. Colonel House, furthermore, had just arrived in England as special representative of the President, armed with the most far-reaching powers, to discuss with the British and other European Allies all matters relating to the common war effort—in which category the collapse of Russia was certain to be regarded as belonging. There was a natural desire to await his report before determining the American attitude toward the new situation.

❖

In the absence of any guidance from Washington, Ambassador Francis could only use his best discretion as to what to do in these unusual circumstances. His main problem, for the moment, was whether to continue to maintain the American official establishment in the Russian capital, since the government to which it was accredited had disappeared, and whether to establish communication with the new group that had usurped power. A meeting of the diplomatic corps, held on November 8, failed to give him much help or guid-

[9] *New York Times,* November 17, 1917

ance. Trotsky's move, two days later, to take possession of the old Ministry for Foreign Affairs, clearly presaged a situation in which the Bolshevik authorities would soon expect to enter into diplomatic intercourse with foreign governments. But the situation was still too confused and the durability of Bolshevik power too uncertain to permit of useful recommendations on policy toward the new regime. On the second day after the revolution, Francis wired Washington that, as a matter of course, "we should make no loans to Russia at present."[10] Beyond this he offered no advice to his government in those first days of Bolshevik power on the attitude to be adopted toward the new regime. Like everyone else in the Russian capital, he continued to watch with bated breath to see whether the Bolsheviki would be able to maintain their power against Kerensky's expected counter-attack.

While the safety of the Embassy appeared to the Ambassador to be endangered at least in such degree that he arranged to send away the unattached American women and the men with wives and children, the danger did not seem great enough to warrant, as yet, the removal of the entire establishment. Conditions were chaotic in the city, to be sure, with a small amount of incidental bloodshed; but the disorder and violence was not, as yet, directed against foreigners.[11]

On at least two occasions in the days immediately following the Bolshevik seizure of power, junior officers from the American Military Mission visited Trotsky and discussed with him the arrangements for guarding the Embassy. They were apparently assured that all foreigners, particularly American citizens, would be quite safe in the Russian capital.[12] In addition to this, the Allied military attachés, including General Judson, visited Muravyev, the Bolshevik

[10] *Foreign Relations, 1918, Russia,* Vol. I, *op.cit.,* p. 229; from Telegram 1972, November 10, 1917.

[11] Some of the foreigners clearly had exaggerated impressions of the amount of bloodshed and of the danger to their own safety. On November 30, Philip Jordan wrote to "Miss Annie Pulliam and the Francis family" (Francis MSS, *op.cit.*):

". . . Now for the Bolsheviks the first thing I must tell you is that we are all seting on a bomb. Just waiting for someone to tuch a match to it. if the Ambassador gets out of this mess with our life we will be awful lucky.

". . . you cant tell at what minute you will be killed. these crazy people are killing each other just like we swat flies at home. . . . After living in a wild country like this for 18 months it makes you feel like their is only two decent places to live one is heaven and the other is America. . . ."

[12] Judson MSS, *op.cit.,* Diary, November 14-16, 1917.

[81]

appointed military commander of the Petrograd district, besought his protection for the foreign diplomatic missions, and evidently received similar assurances from him.[13]

Not only was there thus no immediate physical necessity for the removal of the American Embassy, but there was general doubt that such a move would be politically wise. To many Americans, imbued with the characteristic American concept of diplomatic representation as a gesture of friendship to peoples rather than a channel of communication among governments, it seemed that a withdrawal of the official representatives would amount to an "abandonment" of the Russian people, or at least of those elements still favorable to the Allied cause. The Consul General in Moscow wired to Washington on November 17 that in order to counteract German espionage and propaganda

. . . as well as to lend moral support to the better elements in Russia, which will regain the upper hand, every effort must be made to maintain every American agency in Russia.[14]

Spokesmen for the ousted leaders of the Provisional Government naturally did what they could to encourage this feeling. Kerensky's private secretary, who turned up in Stockholm soon after the middle of the month and talked on November 21 with the American Minister there, gave the Bolshevik government two to four weeks of existence, at the utmost, and urged that the United States "be not impatient." The only hope was for America, he said, "not to take sides in the present struggle but to await the formation of some more stable government." [15] Similar urgings came from the Provisional Government's Ambassador, Boris Bakhmeteff, in Washington. On November 27 he left at the Department of State a communication purporting to have been drafted by the "underground Provisional Government" in Petrograd on November 22, which closed with the following words:

[13] Francis, in a letter dated November 13 to the American Minister in Sweden, said: "The Allied embassies' military attachés have visited informally the Smolny Institute, headquarters of the Bolsheviki, and have been assured that all foreigners particularly American citizens are quite safe in the capital." (*Foreign Relations, 1918, Russia*, Vol. 1, *op.cit.*, p. 235; from Stockholm telegram 1006, November 17, 1917, to the Department of State.)

[14] *Ibid.*, p. 235; from Moscow telegram 59.

[15] *Ibid.*, p. 239; from Stockholm telegram 1038, November 21, 1917, to the Department of State.

First Reactions

Rumors, which appeared in the Russian press, about the departure of the Allied representatives have an extremely unfavorable action on public opinion; any impression which might be created to the effect that the Allies are abandoning the Russian people in the present critical situation could rouse a feeling of the nation that Russia is freed from responsibility for the disrupture of the Allied action.[16]

The insistence on maintaining a diplomatic establishment in a foreign country is, of course, at variance with all diplomatic tradition and theory, unless it is accompanied by actual recognition, at least *de facto,* of the local sovereign authority. However one looks at it, the official representative in a foreign country is the guest of the local governmental authority. His privileges and facilities of residence flow only from its sufferance and favor, and are dependent upon its protection. Strictly speaking, if the United States government was not inclined to recognize the Soviet regime, it had no business asking the Soviet authorities (which by implication it did) to grant to the American official establishment in Petrograd over any considerable length of time the facilities and protection necessary to its continued residence and functioning there. The anomaly of this situation was rendered even greater by the widely held view that the very purpose of the maintenance of the American official establishment in Russia was to give encouragement to the political opponents of the Bolsheviki.

But in the days immediately following the November Revolution, the situation was too confused to admit of this logic. There had still been no formal notification to the foreign embassies of the establishment of a new regime. The Soviet authorities had yet to demonstrate, even to themselves, their ability to remain in power for any length of time. This made it difficult for the foreign representatives to arrive at any firm decision. And the Bolshevik leaders, with the uncertainties of Brest-Litovsk looming before them, could not be sure that they would not at some point have need for the representatives of the capitalist governments already situated in their capital.

Thus Francis stayed on, despite the Bolshevik seizure of power. With him stayed his staff and many of the other official or semi-official Americans in Petrograd. They continued to pursue as best they could the manifold activities, many of them wartime functions, in which they had been engaged: observing the course of events, con-

[16] *Ibid.,* p. 241.

[83]

ducting war propaganda and intelligence work, looking after American property, in some cases dispensing aid and relief to various elements of the Russian population. Francis continued to regard himself as a spokesman for the United States, addressing himself from time to time over the head of the Bolshevik regime to the peoples of the traditional Russian realm to whom, in the established American tradition, he considered himself to be accredited. But this was an anomalous situation, pregnant with danger and embarrassment to all concerned. It could not be expected to last for any great length of time.

CHAPTER IV

THE SOVIET APPROACH

TO AN ARMISTICE

War is dead in the hearts of men.—Raymond Robins,
Pocket diary, entry for October 22, 1917

THE immediate problems involved in completing the seizure of power in the major cities, as well as in the setting up of a regular government, preoccupied the communist leaders during the first fortnight following the Bolshevik coup. It was not until November 15 that the Kerensky threat was finally disposed of. By November 19, however, the most urgent problems had been dealt with, at least to the point where it was possible to give attention to other things as well. Trotsky was finally able, on that day, to establish himself in the Foreign Office and to proceed to the conduct of Soviet foreign policy.

This does not mean that Trotsky had any expectation of embarking on anything like the maintenance of normal diplomatic contact with Francis and the other envoys in the city. He mentions, in his autobiography, the statement he was reported to have made to a friend when he was asked to take over responsibility for Soviet foreign affairs:

What sort of diplomatic work will we be doing, anyway? I shall issue a few revolutionary proclamations to the peoples and then close up shop.[1]

While Trotsky says this attributed statement was an exaggeration, the fact that he quoted it is indicative of his attitude at the time.

There having been, by this time, no response to the Decree of Peace, either from the Central Powers or from the Entente govern-

[1] Trotzki, *op.cit.*, p. 327.

ments, the Soviet leaders set about, on November 20, to press with vigor and determination the effort to take Russia out of the war. Their first move, taken in the late evening of November 20, was to send a telegram to the acting commander-in-chief, General Dukhonin, directing him to propose to his German military counterpart a three months' armistice, with a view to the negotiation of peace. Dukhonin, a quiet and conscientious officer, was a man without a trace of sympathy for the communists. He had been in charge of General Staff Field Headquarters since the Kornilov fiasco in September. On November 16, not knowing the whereabouts of the last commander-in-chief, Kerensky, he had assumed command of what was left of the Russian armies. His headquarters were at Mogilev, some 450 miles south of Petrograd.

Immediately after issuance of this order to Dukhonin, the first formal communication of the Soviet government was addressed to the Allied envoys in Petrograd, including the American Ambassador.[2] This communication, drawn up in French and signed by Trotsky in his capacity as People's Commissar for Foreign Affairs, was despatched on November 21 and received by the Allied missions in the late evening. It served two purposes.

First, the communication formally advised the Allied governments that

... The National Congress of the Soviet of Workmen's and Soldiers' Deputies established on the 26th of the month of October of this year (old style) a new government of the Russian Republic in the form of a Soviet of People's Commissars.[3]

It was thus the first formal notification to the Allied governments, including the United States government, of the establishment of Soviet power. By implication, the communication constituted a claim to recognition and an invitation to the establishment of normal diplomatic intercourse. It may be said that from the moment of its receipt in Washington (on the morning of November 24) the

[2] The British, American, French, Italian, Belgian, and Serbian envoys received this communication. The lesser powers among the Allies did not.

[3] *Foreign Relations, 1918, Russia,* Vol. I, *op.cit.,* p. 244. This text is taken from Petrograd telegram 2006, November 22, 1917 to the Department of State; but the names of the Soviet institutions are here translated in the manner which later became established usage. At the time, there was considerable variation in the translation of these terms.

problem of Soviet-American relations came into being in the formal sense.

The communication then went on to call attention to "the proposal for an armistice and a democratic peace" (evidently referring to the November 8 decree), and asked the Ambassador

. . . to be good enough to regard the above-mentioned document as a formal proposal for an armistice without delay on all fronts and for the opening without delay of negotiations for peace—a proposal which the plenipotentiary government of the Russian Republic is addressing simultaneously to all belligerent nations and to their governments.

The letter closed with an assurance of "profound respect . . . for the people of the United States." The government of the United States was not mentioned.

Francis promptly put the text of this communication on the wire to the Department of State, but accompanied it with no recommendation of his own. Buchanan, the British Ambassador, in transmitting the message, urged his government to reply, by means of a statement in the House of Commons, that it would be prepared to discuss peace terms with "a legally constituted Government" in Russia, but not with one that "had broken the engagements taken by one of its predecessors under the agreement of September 5, 1914" (by which the Allies had bound themselves not to make a separate peace).[4]

At the meeting of the Central Executive Committee of the Soviet of Workers' and Peasants' Deputies, where the taking of these steps on November 20 and 21 was approved, Trotsky made a speech which stands as one of the first responsible Soviet statements on foreign policy. He began by recounting the highlights of the situation that had existed during the fortnight that had elapsed since the initial seizure of power. He discussed the reactions to the Soviet peace move, both of the enemy powers (which he found "ambiguous") and of the Allies. Britain appeared to him the most hostile of all foreign countries to Soviet power. The British *bourgeoisie,* he charged, was not unfavorable to a prolongation of the war. As for France: the war was threatening that nation with "degeneration and death." But the struggle of the French working class against the war was growing. In Italy, conditions were favorable to the Soviet initiative.

[4] George Buchanan, *My Mission to Russia and Other Diplomatic Memories,* Little, Brown & Co., Boston, 1923, Vol. II, p. 223.

The Soviet Approach to an Armistice

Turning then to the United States, Trotsky (who, it will be recalled, had been in New York earlier in the year) delivered himself of the following views:

The United States began to intervene in the war after three years, under the influence of the sober calculations of the American Stock Exchange. America could not tolerate the victory of one coalition over the other. America is interested in the weakening of both coalitions and in the consolidation of the hegemony of American capital. Apart from that, American war industry is interested in the war. During the war American exports have more than doubled and have reached a figure not reached by any other capitalist State. Exports go almost entirely to the Allied countries. When in January Germany came out for unrestricted U-boat warfare, all railway stations and harbours in the United States were overloaded with the output of the war industries. Transport was disorganized and New York witnessed food riots such as we ourselves have never seen here. Then the finance capitalists sent an ultimatum to Wilson: to secure the sale of the output of the war industries within the country. Wilson accepted the ultimatum, and hence the preparations for war and war itself. America does not aim at territorial conquests; America can be tolerant with regard to the existence of the Soviet Government, since it is satisfied with the exhaustion of the Allied countries and Germany. Apart from that America is interested in investing its capital in Russia.[5]

This speech was published in the Soviet press. The portion dealing with the United States was wired by Francis, one or two days later, to the Department of State.

The implications of this statement are worth attention. This was Trotsky, the first Soviet Foreign Minister, making in official capacity his first public observations about the United States. He was cynical about the reality of American democracy. He advanced against people and government of the United States the preposterous accusation that they desired the weakening of the Allies, with whom they were associated in the war, and that they aimed to sabotage the common war effort. The tragic solemnity of Wilson's great decision of the winter and spring of 1917 was degraded in Trotsky's view to a spineless and cynical capitulation before the "ultimatum" of the financiers. A picture was painted of disorganization and hunger in New York—"food riots such as we ourselves have never seen here." [6]

[5] Degras, Vol. 1, *op.cit.*, pp. 6–7.
[6] It is true that extensive "housewife riots," directed against the high cost of living, had taken place in the week of February 18–24, 1917, when Trotsky was in New

Finally, Trotsky's listeners were smugly encouraged to believe that America would be "tolerant with regard to the existence of the Soviet Government," because the mutual exhaustion of Germany and the Allies was sufficient to satisfy the lust of American financiers and because the Russian market would be enticing to American capitalists —in other words, one must conclude, because America had no ideals, no convictions, and no interest in international political affairs, even in the war itself, except from the standpoint of the greed of its capitalists.

Did Trotsky believe these things? To some extent, he surely did. His view of the United States was indeed a limited and distorted one, gained chiefly from within the gloomy interior of the editorial office of an obscure Russian-socialist paper in New York. On the other hand, nothing in his book of political ethics ruled out propagandistic distortion; on the contrary, his code ruled that one would be remiss in not engaging in it, if one could thereby advance the cause. Possibly a tinge of envy also entered in, and of irritation toward a country that fitted so poorly into the rigid patterns of Marxist thought. In any case, the pronouncement was plainly not conducive to a sympathetic reception in Washington of the note despatched to the United States government that same day.

On November 21, while the Soviet note was being delivered to the foreign embassies and while Trotsky was delivering his speech, the Soviet leaders waited impatiently for some response from General Dukhonin to the orders they had given him. They had no illusions about Dukhonin's political views or activities.[7] They were well

---

York. They took the form of a mass visit to the Mayor's office, together with some overturning of peddler's pushcarts. Both the Socialist Party and the I.W.W. appear to have had a hand in their origin. The shocking rise in living costs was beyond dispute; but if Trotsky thought people were suffering unduly, he was wasting his sympathy. An exhaustive investigation conducted by the Commissioner of Charities, as a result of the riots, revealed no abnormal want. On the contrary, the Commissioner of Charities came to the conclusion that "the mass of the population of New York City is in better condition than it has been for years" (*New York Herald*, February 24, 1917). Lest anyone suppose that this report was the product of reactionary bias, let it be noted that the Commissioner who issued it was none other than Mr. John A. Kingsbury, who many years later was to become chairman of the National Council for Soviet-American Friendship and in this capacity to make journeys to the "peace congresses" in Moscow in 1950 and 1951.

[7] Lenin, in a report to the Central Executive Committee on November 23, said: "It was clear to us that we were dealing here with an opponent of the people's will and an enemy of the Revolution." V. I. Lenin, *Sochineniya* (Complete Works), Second Edition, State Publishing Co., Moscow-Leningrad, 1930, Vol. XXII, p. 74.

aware that at the moment when they had sent Dukhonin the order
to seek an armistice, a number of political figures from the opposition (mostly leaders of the S-R's) were already assembling at his
headquarters, attempting to organize a rival government under his
protection. Several generals at headquarters had even issued an
appeal, on November 20, calling for the formation of a new government to replace the Bolshevik regime, and proposing the prominent
S-R leader, Chernov, as its head.[8] It must have been clear to the
Bolsheviki that these activities were taking place with the knowledge
of at least some of the Allied diplomats in Petrograd, perhaps with
their encouragement.[9] If, therefore, the Bolshevik leaders addressed
themselves to Dukhonin with orders to seek an armistice, it was not
because they trusted him or accepted him, but only because they had
not yet gotten around to replacing him with a Soviet appointee, and
did not wish to waste any time in getting on with the armistice
proposal.

During that same day of November 21, while the Soviet government was despatching its notes to the Allied missions, Dukhonin
delayed matters, hoping to gain time for the organization of a rival
government. He wired the General Staff Headquarters in Petrograd,
asking for confirmation of the authenticity of the telegram. In this
way he gained an entire day, much to Lenin's disgust. By evening
Lenin and his associates evidently decided to have no more truck
with Dukhonin and to seek other channels for the peace bid. They
therefore took two drastic measures. First, they drafted an appeal
to the troops at the front, calling upon them not to "permit counter-
revolutionary generals to destroy the great cause of peace," but rather
to take the matter of peace into their own hands and to place the
generals under arrest.[10]

Then, in the early hours of the morning of November 22, they got
through to Dukhonin's headquarters on the telephone. After some
initial sparring with the General's second-in-command, the General

[8] William Henry Chamberlin, *The Russian Revolution, 1917–1921,* The Macmillan
Co., New York, 1935, Vol. I, p. 346.
[9] Sir George Buchanan, the British Ambassador, in his account of a meeting of
November 20 with two anti-Bolshevik figures, reports that one was "to leave in the
evening for the Stavka to meet other Socialist leaders." The other was also about
to proceed to the front "where, as he told me, some twenty representative men
had already gone, for the purpose of forming a new Government and of organizing
a force strong enough to suppress the Bolsheviks." (Buchanan, Vol. II, *op. cit.,* pp.
220–223.)
[10] Lenin, Vol. XXII, *op.cit.,* pp. 72–73.

was prevailed upon to take the telephone himself. There ensued an altercation in the course of which Dukhonin declared himself unable to execute the order, explaining that "only a central governmental power supported by the Army and the country could have sufficient weight and significance for the enemy to attach to such negotiations the necessary authoritativeness. . . ." [11] Thereupon the Soviet leaders at the other end of the line delivered themselves of a solemn declaration, obviously prepared in advance, relieving him of his command on grounds of insubordination, but ordering him to carry on with his duties until the arrival of his successor, a certain "Ensign Krylenko."

The appeal to the troops, calling upon them to take matters into their own hands, was promptly made public and broadcast by radio to the front. The incident with Dukhonin was immediately reported by him to the Allied military representatives at his headquarters, and through them to their governments.

All this happened in the small hours of the morning of November 22. On the afternoon of that day the Allied chiefs-of-mission, having all now despatched telegrams to their respective governments reporting the terms of the Soviet note received the previous evening, met to discuss the matter and to define their attitude. "Agreement," Francis reported to the Department of State, "was unanimous and emphatic that no notice should be taken [of the Soviet note]. . . ." The reason for this position, he went on to explain, was that the "pretended government" was one "established by force and not recognized by [the] Russian people." The respective governments, it had been agreed, were to be asked to approve this position.[12] (Francis never had a specific reply from Washington on this point. He could infer from later instructions that this position was approved.)

At this meeting of the Allied envoys Francis learned that the British, French, and Italian ambassadors, all representatives of governments that were signatories to the 1914 agreement barring a separate peace, were instructing their respective military representatives at Dukhonin's headquarters to protest against the armistice proposal, as being in violation of the 1914 agreement. Soon after

[11] *Ibid.*, p. 71.
[12] *Foreign Relations, 1918, Russia*, Vol. I, *op.cit.*, p. 245; from Telegram 2007, November 22, 1917.

learning of this, General Judson, with the approval of the Ambassador, wired the United States representative at the headquarters, Major Monroe C. Kerth, to register a similar protest—though of course not in the name of the 1914 agreement, to which the United States was not a party. This was on November 22.[13]

It is worthy of note, from the standpoint of the reaction of the Allied governments to the Soviet note, that on the day after its delivery (November 22) Trotsky began publication of the secret agreements which had been concluded among the Allies earlier in the war and which were found by the Bolsheviki in the official files when they took over the Foreign Office. The publication of these documents was, like the peace move, a commitment of long standing on the part of the Bolshevik leaders. The world had been warned, in Trotsky's speech of the preceding day (referred to above), that this step would be taken on the 22nd. The treaties, Trotsky had said on that occasion,

. . . are even more cynical in their contents than we supposed, and we do not doubt that when the German Social Democrats obtain access to the safes in which the secret treaties are kept, they will show us that German imperialism in its cynicism and rapacity yields in nothing to the rapacity of the Allied countries.[14]

Now, in beginning the publication of the documents, he publicly contrasted the open diplomacy of the Bolsheviki with imperialism's "dark plans of conquest and its robber alliances and deals." In the statement inaugurating the publication of the documents, he wrote:

The workers' and peasants' Government abolishes secret diplomacy and its intrigues, codes, and lies. We have nothing to hide. Our programme expresses the ardent wishes of millions of workers, soldiers, and peasants. We want peace as soon as possible on the basis of decent co-existence and collaboration of the peoples. We want the rule of capital to be overthrown as soon as possible. . . .[15]

The treaties were republished almost at once in the New York press (the *New York Times* published several of them on November 25) and somewhat later (December 13) in England by the *Manchester Guardian*. Their publication caused less stir in world opinion than the Bolsheviki had anticipated. The general tenor of the agree-

[13] *Loc.cit.* Judson MSS, *op.cit.*, Diary entry for November 23, 1917: "Last night I wired Kerth . . . to act in harmony with others."
[14] Degras, Vol. I, *op.cit.*, pp. 7–8.
[15] *Ibid.*, p. 9.

ments, after all, was fairly widely known in the western countries even prior to their publication.[16] But their publication unilaterally by the Soviet government without consultation with the other powers concerned appeared, again, as an action designed to be offensive. The terms in which the publication was announced by Trotsky were clearly insulting to the western governments, and could scarcely have been chosen with a view to making it easier for them to enter into any dealings with the Bolshevik leaders. Presumably the appearance of the Soviet papers with the first of these revelations and with Trotsky's provocative statements was not without influence on the negative reactions and recommendations of the Allied chiefs-of-mission, as they assembled in Petrograd on that day to discuss the Allied reaction to the Soviet move.

On the following day, Friday, November 23, the British, French, and Italian military representatives at the headquarters on the eastern front handed their protests to General Dukhonin, as they had been instructed to do. Dukhonin's successor having not yet appeared, the General was still carrying on in accordance with his instructions. "Acting on the basis of definite instructions received from their governments," the Allied officers registered "a most energetic protest" against the violation of the 1914 agreement, and went on to warn that "any violation of the treaty by Russia will be followed by most serious consequences." [17] This was strong language, particularly coming in wartime from the military representatives of great warring powers. Since Major Kerth, the American representative at headquarters, had not yet received his instructions, and since the United States had not been a party to the 1914 agreement, the Americans were not associated with this move on the 23rd, nor do they appear to have had any advance knowledge of the wording of the protest, which was evidently left to the military representatives at headquarters to determine.

Although word of the Russian note of November 21 did not reach Washington until the 24th, London appears to have known of it

---

[16] Charles Seymour, *The Intimate Papers of Colonel House,* Houghton Mifflin Co., New York, 1928, Vol. III, p. 323: "A note in House's diary as early as the preceding August indicates that the terms of these treaties were common property, even before they were published by the Bolsheviks."

[17] Yuri V. Klyuchnikov and Andrei Sabanin, Editors, *Mezhdunarodnaya Politika Noveishego Vremeni v Dogovorakh, Notakh, i Deklaratsiyakh* (International Politics of Recent Times in Treaties, Notes and Declarations), Literary Publishing House of the People's Commissariat for Foreign Affairs, Moscow, 1925, Volume II, p. 92, Item No. 76.

on the 22nd. In any case, there took place on the 22nd a meeting of the War Cabinet in London, at which the question of recognition of the new Soviet government was discussed.[18] On the following day (November 23), Lord Robert Cecil, Minister of Blockade and member of the British War Cabinet, told the Associated Press correspondent, with relation to the Soviet armistice proposal:

. . . If it represents the real opinion of the Russian people, which I do not believe it does, it would be a direct breach of treaty obligations and Russia's alliance. Such an action, if approved and ratified by the Russian nation, would put them virtually outside the pale of civilized Europe.

"Asked whether the Allies were likely to recognize the present Russian Government," the Associated Press reported, "Lord Robert said he could not imagine such a step possible." [19]

Cecil's statement is of interest in two respects. It appears to have been the first responsible statement by any of the major western governments on the subject of recognition. Coming just at the outset of the Inter-Allied Conferences in Paris, it forecast the position the British would take in the important matter of recognition. But beyond that, it reflected an illusion from which the Allied statesmen, particularly those in Washington, would part only slowly and with greatest reluctance—the illusion that there was a significant body of Russian opinion which still "cared" about the war as a world struggle and felt an emotional stake in the purposes for which the western Allies conceived themselves to be fighting. This illusion was dangerously erroneous and stubbornly clung to, in the face of all warnings, by a portion of the Allied public and officialdom. One is moved to recall at this point the scene at the formal reception for the Root Mission in the summer of 1917 when one of the ministers of the Provisional Government, impatient over the flow of oratory about the common purposes in the war, turned to a Russian aide of the mission and said to him: "Young man, will you please tell these Americans that we are tired of this war. Explain to them that we are weary of the long and bloody struggle." [20]

❖

[18] *War Memoirs of David Lloyd George*, Ivor Nicolson & Watson, London, 1936, Vol. v, p. 2565.

[19] *New York Times*, November 24, 1917.

[20] Robert D. Warth, *The Allies and the Russian Revolution*, Duke University Press, Durham, 1954, p. 102.

The Soviet Approach to an Armistice

It might be convenient at this point to pause and recapitulate the positions in which the various parties found themselves, at the end of the week of November 17–24, a bare fortnight after the Bolshevik seizure of power. There is good reason to do this, because the following week, the last in November, was to bring a confused welter of events in the relations between the western powers and the Soviet leaders, and it is hard to reconstruct the significance of these events without a clear understanding of the basic positions of each of the parties.

In Petrograd the Soviet leaders, having abandoned the attempt to work through Dukhonin, were busy getting into communication with such of the soldiers' committees as were loyal to them, with a view to finding someone who could approach the Germans with sufficient semblance of authority to do business. They had addressed to the Allied governments an appeal for recognition and an invitation to join them in seeking a general peace, but they had not waited for any reply from the Allies before taking independent and unilateral steps to bring Russia's participation in the war to a formal end. In the appeal to the troops issued on November 22, before the Allied governments could possibly have been expected to have received and considered the Soviet approach, they had urged the soldiers to initiate negotiations spontaneously:

Let the regiments on the front immediately elect plenipotentiaries to formally initiate negotiations for an armistice with the enemy. The Soviet of People's Commissars gives you the right to do this.

Inform us of every step of the negotiations. Only the Soviet of People's Commissars has the right to sign the final convention. . . .[21]

Later, the Soviet leaders had apparently realized that the matter could not proceed with quite this engaging informality, and they took steps to arrange for a single and approved delegation to approach the Germans. This took time, but by Saturday, November 24, when the message reporting Trotsky's note was in process of being received and decoded in Washington, the arrangements were well advanced. By Saturday evening, the Bolshevik leaders were eagerly awaiting the reactions of the Allies to their approach. But they were also awaiting, probably with even greater interest and

---

[21] *Foreign Relations, 1918, Russia,* Vol. I, *op.cit.,* p. 247; quoted in Petrograd telegram 2024, November 24, 1917, to the Department of State.

impatience, the news that their military parliamentarians had finally gotten organized and had departed for the German lines.

Lenin and his associates were under the impression that they had put all the belligerents into an awkward and serious predicament by their publication of the secret treaties and their simultaneous move to end the war on a basis of no annexations or indemnities. Misled by various distorted impressions they had gained of the state of popular morale in the various warring countries and of the echo their own revolutionary actions had found abroad, they felt themselves in possession of a political lever—namely, their influence on the industrial workers and soldiers of the western countries—by means of which they could either blackmail the respective western governments into making peace on the terms they had prescribed or cause them to be crushed in a series of revolutionary upheavals. They were wholly impartial in their hatred of the belligerent governments, finding no distinctions of invidiousness as between the two warring camps; and they looked forward with eager anticipation to the effects of the political squeeze they now proposed to apply. Their principal anxieties related to their own internal situation. They viewed with particular alarm the communications addressed to Dukhonin by the Allied military officers, both because it was precisely Dukhonin, an anti-Bolshevik general, to whom these communications had been addressed, and also because of the threatening language in which they were phrased.

In the Allied embassies in Petrograd, including that of the United States, the envoys were awaiting the reaction of their governments to the Soviet peace move, the bid for recognition, and the invitation to the Allied governments to join the talks. They had made their own recommendations, and there was nothing left to do but wait. But among the personnel of the various Allied missions in Petrograd, the impact of the November Revolution, and its immediate consequences, were now beginning to be absorbed and to give rise to sharp divisions of reaction and opinion. The final exit of Russia from the ranks of the warring nations was bound to bring confusion and consternation to men whose presence and function in Petrograd were directly connected with the war effort of their respective countries. In general, the Allied foreign colonies in the Russian capital, made up of people whose lives were intimately affected by the political change that had taken place, were the first to receive and absorb the strongly divisive effect which the phenomenon of Soviet power was destined always to exert on western society.

In Western Europe, at the same moment, eyes were riveted on the forthcoming Inter-Allied Conference in Paris and on the question of the unification of the Allied war effort. The disastrous defeat of the Italians, at the end of October, had reinforced an appreciation of the need for such unification, as had the progressive disintegration of the Russian armies after Kerensky's unsuccessful attempt at a summer offensive. On November 8, the day of the Bolshevik coup, the French, British, and Italians had agreed on the establishment of a supreme war council; but the agreement was a most informal one, and a number of important organizational questions remained to be ironed out. Meanwhile, as America's war effort began for the first time to assume important military dimensions, the need for its coordination with that of the Allies was also growing apace. At the end of October, Wilson had despatched Colonel House to Europe, not only to represent him at the forthcoming Inter-Allied Conference, but to be generally available for the discussion of important political and military problems with other Allied leaders. House had arrived on November 7 in England, where he had been received with honors befitting a prime minister, if not a head of state. "Never in history," wrote the London correspondent of the *New York Times,* "has any foreigner come to Europe and found greater acceptance or wielded more power." [22] The *London Times* referred to House's conversations with the British leaders as "in effect . . . a personal meeting of Governments" and described him as "virtually the Government of the United States." [23]

On November 22, when Trotsky's first note to the Allied envoys was on the wires, House and the members of his mission were proceeding from London to Paris for the meetings of the Inter-Allied Conference (beginning November 29) and the Supreme War Council (December 1). Word of the Soviet approach was being received in the French and British governments on the very day of House's journey to Paris. The convocation of statesmen in Paris provided a convenient occasion for exchanging views on this question. It was natural that Wilson, leaning heavily as he did on House's counsel in all matters involving inter-Allied collaboration, should have

[22] Seymour, Vol. III, *op.cit.,* p. 217.
[23] *Ibid.,* p. 243.

awaited the upshot of House's discussions with other Allied leaders before arriving at any final decisions with regard to the Soviet approach.

Before we turn, however, to the deliberations of the Allied statesmen in Paris, it might be well to follow a bit further the course of events in Petrograd, where the ensuing days were to prove agitated and troublesome for the official Americans.

CHAPTER V

FIRST PROBLEMS OF "CONTACT" WITH

THE SOVIET AUTHORITIES

*Surtout, messieurs, pas trop de zêle!—Talleyrand's
advice to young diplomats*

It has already been noted that the actions of the Bolshevik leaders in seizing power and in moving to end the war caused great concern and fermentation within the American official colony. Particularly affected were the military representatives, whose function in Russia was primarily to strengthen resistance to the Germans on the eastern front and who now felt themselves faced with the complete and catastrophic failure of their basic mission. General Judson, as chief of the United States Military Mission, naturally felt the main responsibility in this respect, and it fell to him to take the lead in suggesting the course to be followed.

In the weeks after the November Revolution, Judson had come into closer touch with the members of the Red Cross Mission, particularly Raymond Robins. Robins, in turn, had been in touch with the Bolshevik leaders. Immediately after the Bolshevik seizure of power, on either the 9th or 10th of November, Robins, acting quite independently and without the knowledge of the Embassy, had paid a visit to Trotsky at the Smolny Institute [1] and had discussed with him the work of the Red Cross Commission. After a few words of frank clarification concerning the past role of the mission, Robins

[1] The Smolny Institute, an enormous structure situated at the eastern edge of central Petrograd, had served before the Revolution as an aristocratic school for girls. It was taken over in the summer of 1917 as the seat of the Petrograd Soviet. With the Bolsheviki in power, it became their headquarters, and as such the seat of the Soviet government until March 1918. The term "Smolny" was used at that time in the sense that "Kremlin" was used subsequently.

had put the question bluntly to Trotsky as to whether it was worth-while for it to stay. Trotsky had indicated that it was, and had taken certain measures on its behalf at Robins' request. (These matters related to preparations for the movement of a train of Red Cross supplies from Petrograd to Jassy, in Rumania, for the American Red Cross there, and to the removal of certain mineral supplies from the Petrograd district lest they fall into German hands.) Only three weeks earlier, Robins had referred in his diary to Trotsky as "this curse of false spirit." [2] But he, like Thompson, had reversed his views very swiftly under the impact of the November Revolution.

Robins' encounter with Trotsky and its satisfactory results con-vinced him of the possibility of dealing successfully with the Soviet authorities, at least in certain matters, and of exerting upon them —by working with them and giving them various sorts of aid—an influence which might well serve to stiffen their backs in the face of German demands and to reduce the concessions they might make to the Germans. For this reason he believed that Red Cross and other supplies should continue to be sent to Russia from the United States, and that the American officials in Petrograd should cultivate close informal relations with the Bolshevik leaders. His influence with Judson was no doubt exerted in favor of these views.

Judson himself had approached his principals in Washington, at some time prior to November 25 (probably without the Ambassa-dor's knowledge), with a suggestion that he offer to the Soviet authorities his collaboration in the preparation of the technical points of the armistice, with a view to influencing the wording in such a way as to bind the Germans not to transfer troops from the eastern to the western front. Actually, this was a futile hope. The disintegra-tion of the Russian armies was by this time a matter of fact and not of legal formality. That being the case, no scrap of paper, and par-ticularly none signed with the militarily helpless Bolshevik leaders, could possibly have deterred the Germans from a course of action regarded by them as vital to the prosecution of the war: namely, the movement of the maximum number of forces from the east to the west in strict correspondence with the development of military realities. But the situation was desperate; every possibility, however remote, had to be pursued. General Judson had accordingly made the suggestion to Washington. As of November 25 he had had no

[2] Robins MSS, *op.cit.*, Diary entry of October 21, 1917.

reply.[3] With Trotsky's note now before the Allied governments and with German-Soviet truce negotiations only a few days off, Judson's uneasiness over the course of events reached a state of acute anxiety.

On the evening of Saturday, November 24, General Dukhonin, at the Mogilev headquarters, had one of his frequent long-distance telephone conversations with General Marushevski, the chief of the General Staff in Petrograd. Both officers, it will be recalled, were carry-overs from the old military establishment, and not Bolsheviki. (Dukhonin was soon to be barbarously lynched; Marushevski, to be imprisoned.) They still had use of the military communications lines, but only under strict supervision by communist commissars who monitored their conversations.

In the course of their conversation on November 24, Dukhonin remarked incidentally that he had received "a communiqué of the Washington government giving its view on current happenings here in Russia," and asked whether Marushevski knew of it. Receiving a negative answer, he thereupon read over the telephone the communiqué to which he referred. It was apparently an item he had picked up by monitoring western radio broadcasts. Comparison reveals that it was a news item based on a story of the *New York Times* correspondent in Washington, filed November 20 and published the following day. Its tenor, as will be seen shortly, was that the American government had announced that there would be no further shipment of military supplies and provisions to Russia until the governmental situation in that country was clarified.[4]

Dukhonin requested that this document be transmitted to the Vice Minister of War, General Manikovski (also not yet replaced). Marushevski, in reply, said he would also transmit it at once by telephone to the Smolny Institute, "since our conversation is being monitored by the commissar appointed for that purpose."[5]

The next day, an aide of Marushevski, Colonel Durnovo, brought the text of the communiqué to Judson. Referring to the protest of the Allied military representatives at headquarters, Durnovo indicated (erroneously attributing the statements to Dukhonin) that

---

[3] See Sisson, *op.cit.,* p. 71.

[4] The source of this story is obscure. It was repeatedly denied by responsible officials in the ensuing days, and certainly did not represent anything resembling a considered governmental statement.

[5] See *Krasny Arkhiv,* Vol. 23, article entitled "Nakanune Peremiriya" (On the Eve of the Armistice), pp. 195–249. This article includes the verbatim record of the telephone conversation.

. . . the failure of America to protest when the others did was producing a bad effect and creating uncertainties in the minds of some which it was of the utmost importance immediately to remove.[6]

Durnovo suggested that if Judson would make a formal communication to the Soviet government along the lines of the intercepted communiqué, this would be helpful to the cause of the Russian officers at headquarters, and hence to the chances for a continuation of the war.

General Judson could, perhaps, have disposed of this suggestion by telling Durnovo of the instruction he had sent to Kerth the previous day, directing the latter to make a separate protest. But he was eager for affirmative action, and instead of doing this, he sat down and penned the following letter to "The Chief of the Russian General Staff, Petrograd":

There has been brought to my attention the following press communication from the United States:

"The American Government has announced that no shipments of military supplies and provisions to Russia will be effected until the situation of this country will be established. The government before permitting the export of American products wants to know into whose hands they will get in Russia. The exports to Russia will be resumed only after the formation of a steady government which can be recognized by the United States, but if the Bolsheviks will remain in power and will put through their program of making peace with Germany, the present embargo on exports to Russia will remain in force. The credits to the Provisional Russian Government reach to the present day 325 million dollars, of which 191 millions have already been appropriated; the larger part of this money has already been spent for the purchase of supplies, which are ready for loading. The ships allotted by America for the carrying of this freight are ready for sailing but do not receive permission to leave the ports and they will be refused coal."

It occurs to me that it is but fair to convey to your Excellency the circumstance that neither I nor the American Ambassador has as yet received from the United States of America instructions or information similar to that contained in the press report above quoted. Nevertheless, it seems but fair to express to your Excellency the opinion that the press report correctly states the attitude of the Government of the United States. We are in daily expectation of receiving information similar to that conveyed by the above mentioned press report.

[6] Judson MSS, *op.cit.,* Judson report to Chief of International Section, War Department, March 16, 1918.

Before sending you this communication I have submitted it to the American Ambassador who concurs in the expressions contained in it.

I shall avail myself of this opportunity to renew to your Excellency the assurance of my high consideration.

(Signed) W. V. Judson
Brig. Genl. U.S. Army, Amer. Military Attaché,
Chief of American Military Mission to Russia.[7]

A copy of this letter was then taken to the Ambassador by one of Judson's subordinates, and the Ambassador's approval was obtained. (The Ambassador does not appear to have sent a copy of Judson's communication to the Department of State or even to have informed the latter of its despatch and of his approval.)

In his diary, Judson had the following to say about his despatch of this letter:

We had not entirely lost hope of the success of Dukhonin and of Stavka. Such a letter, it was obvious, would immediately get us in line with our Allies. . . . General Marushevski, to whom the letter was handed by Cap't. Prince, expressed great satisfaction with its terms. . . .[8]

In this curious manner the *New York Times* correspondent in Washington became the author of the first official statement of United States policy made to the Soviet government.

The letter, after its receipt by Marushevski, was promptly passed on to Trotsky, who evidently accepted it as a full-fledged diplomatic communication to the Soviet government, and brought it at once to the attention of his colleagues. While we have only indirect evidence of the Soviet reaction, logic tells us that it must have been one of intense interest, but of mixed feelings. The letter could not be interpreted by the Bolshevik leaders in any other way than as a warning that if they persisted in their peace program, to which they were already committed in the most serious and irrevocable manner, they would be deprived of the $137.7 millions [9] of credit originally granted to the Kerensky government and not exhausted by the latter by the time it was overthrown. On the other hand, the letter cited the American Ambassador as concurring "in the expressions con-

[7] C. K. Cumming and Walter W. Pettit, Editors, *Russian-American Relations, March, 1917—March, 1920: Documents and Papers,* Harcourt, Brace & Howe, New York, 1920, pp. 47–48. Also *Foreign Relations, 1918, Russia,* Vol. I, *op.cit.,* pp. 266–267.

[8] Judson MSS, *op. cit.,* Diary, December 10, 1917.

[9] The press story, with only slight inaccuracy, implied the credit balance to be $134 million.

tained in it," and was signed by Judson in his capacity as Military Attaché as well as in his capacity as Chief of the Military Mission. Was this not a move toward the establishment of normal diplomatic contact between the American Embassy and the Soviet regime? The Soviet leaders must have asked themselves this question. And the letter may have suggested to them that the United States government was seriously alarmed by the Soviet peace move and willing to pay a price—at least $137.7 million—to forestall it.

Judson's approach was in any case too late to affect the Soviet bid for an armistice. By Sunday night, November 25, when the letter was being delivered to Trotsky, the new Soviet commander-in-chief, Krylenko, had already arrived at the front and was busy despatching a delegation of three parliamentarians to the German lines near Dvinsk. Protected by a white flag and a trumpeter, these negotiators (two of them members of a soldiers' committee) entered the German lines in the darkness of early morning on Monday, November 26. After being duly blindfolded, they were taken to the nearest German command post. From there they were despatched to the divisional headquarters of General von Hofmeister. They were received by the General at 6:20 p.m. that day. The communications system of the German army then began to function in high gear. An hour and a half later the General received authorization from Berlin to proceed with the negotiations. At 12:20 a.m. in the morning of Tuesday, November 27, the General was able to give to the Soviet emissaries a written communication to the effect that the German commander on the eastern front, General Hoffmann, had been empowered to enter into regular armistice negotiations. It was agreed that the negotiations should take place at General Hoffmann's headquarters in Brest-Litovsk. December 1st was fixed (later changed to December 2nd) as the date for the beginning of the talks. Having received this reply, Krylenko's emissaries set out on the return journey. By Tuesday afternoon, November 27, they were back within the Russian lines and the report was on its way to Petrograd that the Germans were prepared to do business.[10]

Meanwhile, the Soviet authorities, while waiting for the return of their parliamentarians, had been intensely irritated and alarmed to learn of the protest made to Dukhonin by the Allied military repre-

[10] James Bunyan and H. H. Fisher, *The Bolshevik Revolution, 1917–1918, Documents and Materials,* Stanford University Press, 1934, pp. 256–258.

sentatives on November 23. Determined to spike this contact between the Allied representatives and the officers of the old regime, and to shift the locus of such discussions to Petrograd, they took two measures. On Saturday, the 24th, they broadcast to the army (the form of address was: "To All Regimental, Divisional, Corps, and Army Committees, to All Soviets of Workers', Soldiers', and Peasants' Deputies, to All, All, All!") a new appeal, signed by Trotsky and designed to counteract the effect of the Allied note. Drawing attention to the fact that Dukhonin had circulated the note throughout the military units along the front, Trotsky pointed out that the note, while protesting against a separate armistice between Germany and Russia, had actually given no reply to the Soviet proposal for a general armistice *on all fronts*. He charged that the Allied military representatives, by addressing such a note to an officer who had been dismissed for insubordination, had committed "a flagrant interference in the domestic affairs of our country with the object of bringing about civil war." [11] He then went on to take issue, in the following words, with the charge that the Soviet government was violating Russia's treaty obligations:

As soon as it came into existence the Soviet of People's Commissars declared publicly that Russia was not bound by the old treaties which had been concluded behind the backs of the people for the benefit of the bourgeois classes of Russia and the Allied countries. Any attempt to bring pressure on the revolutionary Soviet Government by means of dead . . . treaties is bound to fail miserably. Leaving aside the threats which can not divert us from the struggle for an honest democratic peace, we should like to say that the republican government represented by the Soviet of People's Commissars proposes not a separate but a general peace, and in doing so it feels that it expresses the true interests and desires not only of the Russian masses but of all the belligerent countries.

Soldiers! Workers! Peasants! Your Soviet Government will not allow

---

[11] This reproach seems to have been unjust. Dukhonin, as we have seen, had been told to carry on until his successor arrived. There is no indication that Krylenko arrived at Dukhonin's headquarters before December 3. Nor is it clear that the Allied representatives had received any official notice of Dukhonin's dismissal when they presented their notes, although they were aware of what had occurred. A formal order was issued on November 26th by the Soviet Commissar for War, Krylenko, declaring Dukhonin an "enemy of the people" and demanding the arrest of anyone supporting him, but the order was not published until the 28th. (See Francis' telegram 2037, November 28 to Department of State, *Foreign Relations, 1918, Russia,* Vol. I, *op.cit.,* pp. 251–252.) The Military Representatives had delivered their notes on the 23rd.

the foreign bourgeoisie to wield a club over your head and drive you into the slaughter again. Do not be afraid of them. The exhausted nations of Europe are on your side. They are all asking for an immediate peace and our armistice call is like music to their ears. The peoples of Europe will not allow their imperialist governments to harm the Russian people who are guilty of no crime but the desire to have peace and to assert the brotherhood of man. Let all know that the soldiers, workers, and peasants of Russia did not overthrow the governments of the Tsar and Kerensky just to become cannon fodder for the Allied imperialists.

Soldiers, continue in your fight for an immediate armistice. Elect your delegates for the negotiations. Your Commander-in-Chief, Ensign Krylenko, starts for the front today to take charge of the armistice negotiations.

Down with the old secret treaties and diplomatic intrigue!

Hail the honest and open struggle for a universal peace! [12]

This appeal, together with the text of the notes which the French, British, and Italian military representatives had delivered to Dukhonin, was promptly published in the Petrograd press. General Judson was shocked to learn in this way, for the first time, of the threatening language of the communication his military colleagues had delivered at Dukhonin's headquarters. This was in sharp conflict with the view, to which he was rapidly inclining, that a friendly approach should be adopted toward the Bolsheviki and an attempt made to work with rather than against them in the matter of the armistice.

On Tuesday, November 27, the chiefs of the Allied military missions and the military attachés were called to the old Russian general staff headquarters at 3:00 p.m. and handed a further communication from Trotsky which they were requested to transmit to their respective ambassadors. The text of this communication, as wired to Washington by Francis without comment, was as follows:

1. As evidenced by all our steps, we are striving for general and not separate armistice. To a separate armistice we may be forced by our allies if they will close their eyes before the facts.

2. We are ready at any moment with any representatives of the Allies (translator thinks this means any of the Allies) to conduct negotiations for immediate accomplishment of an armistice.

We do not demand a parliamentary "recognition." We are recognized by the people.

We want business negotiations. We reserve the right to publish protocols for the information of all.

[12] Bunyan and Fisher, *op.cit.,* p. 246.

3. That negative attitude with which our peace initiative is being met from the side of several of the Allied Governments, cannot in the slightest change the course of our policy.

The Allies should answer: are they willing to begin negotiations for immediate armistice aiming at the conclusion of peace and democratic principles? Are they agreeable to support our initiative in this direction? Do they demand other measures? What kind?

As long as Allied Governments answer with bare "no recognition" of us and our initiative we will follow our own course appealing to the peoples after the governments. Should the results of the appeal bring separate peace, which we do not want, responsibility will fall completely upon the Allied Governments.

Trotsky.[13]

The reason for the hasty delivery of this communication to the Allied representatives on the 27th was probably a desire to anticipate the announcement of the conclusion of the preliminary arrangements with the Germans, the news of which had just reached Smolny at that time.

This communication, too, made a deep impression on Judson. He was particularly struck by the claim that the Soviet leaders were against the idea of a separate armistice.

Judson also had a long talk that same day (November 27) with Raymond Robins, who assured him (quite correctly) that the Bolsheviki were going to be in power for some time; that they alone, of all the Russian political factions, "had guts"; that in the course of time they would become more conservative; and that they were actually conducting effective anti-German propaganda.

Finally, the General received word that day (presumably deriving from this same talk between Trotsky and Robins) that his letter to Marushevski had been poorly received by the Bolsheviki and had produced, if anything, an effect quite the opposite of that for which Judson had hoped.

Disturbed by these new impressions, Judson became seriously worried lest the Soviet leaders were being needlessly frightened and estranged. "It was necessary in Russia," he later explained,

to adjust oneself quickly to changing conditions. It became apparent to me on November 27th, and not before, that the Bolsheviks were in to stay

[13] *Foreign Relations, 1918, Russia,* Vol. 1, *op.cit.,* p. 250, from Francis' telegram 2034, November 27, 1917 to Department of State. The above text is reproduced exactly as submitted to the Department of State by Francis, the insertion giving the translator's interpretation of one passage having been included in the original message.

. . . and . . . whatever we might think of them, were in a position to determine many questions that would perhaps vitally affect the outcome of
the war. . . .

The facts could not be altered. . . . The inevitable had to be faced and
the best made of it. Why . . . should we . . . play [the Germans'] game
by pursuing a policy of studied non-intercourse, aloofness and unfriendli-
ness . . . ? [14]

Having come to this view, which so strongly reflected Robins'
eloquent persuasion, Judson sat down once more, on November 27,
and penned (again, with the Ambassador's acquiescence) a second
letter to Marushevski—evidently designed to reassure the Soviet
leaders about the American attitude. It read as follows:

Referring to my letter of 12/25th November, 1917, relating to a quotation from American press reports, I desire to say that nothing therein
should be construed as indicating that my government has or may be expected to express preference for the success in Russia of any one political
party or element over another. Americans have the greatest sympathy for
the whole Russian people in the complex situation in which they find
themselves, and do not wish to interfere except helpfully in the solution
of any Russian problem. Their sympathy extends to all sections of the
Russian people. Their representatives here are now informed that no important fraction of the Russian people desires an immediate separate peace
or armistice. And it is certainly within the rights of Russia, in the position
in which she now finds herself, to bring up the question of a general peace.

There is no reason why the attitude of her Allies toward Russia or toward any important elements in Russia should be upon anything but a
most friendly foundation. . . .[15]

Judson's second communication, like the first, was immediately
sent on to Trotsky. There is no record of the Soviet reaction to it at
the time. Trotsky sent back, orally (no doubt through Gumberg and
Robins), the message that "the General was welcome to continue
communication if he desired, either by letter or in person." [16]

The Soviet leaders may well have believed, however, that there

---

[14] Judson MSS, *op.cit.*, Judson report, March 16, 1918.

[15] *Foreign Relations, 1918, Russia*, Vol. I, *op.cit.*, pp. 269–270 (also, Cumming &
Pettit, *op.cit.*, pp. 48–49). The original file copy of this letter is in the Judson MSS,
op.cit. It bears a handwritten notation by the Ambassador as follows: "No objection
to M. Attaché writing this letter in explanation of his letter of November 12/25th/17.
D.R.F." Again, no copy of this was sent to the Department of State at the time, nor
was the Department advised of its despatch.

[16] Sisson, *op.cit.*, p. 75.

was more behind this letter than was actually the case. The official history of Soviet diplomacy, published twenty-eight years later, refers to the letter as "an official declaration" and asserts that Judson was speaking "in the name of his Government." [17] The fact that Soviet historians presumably drew their conclusions from Soviet sources would suggest that Trotsky was similarly misled.

Meanwhile, Major Kerth, at field headquarters, somewhat behind the course of events, had finally addressed to Dukhonin, on the 27th, in accordance with the instructions despatched to him by Judson on the 22nd, *his* independent protest against a separate armistice. It read as follows:

In accordance with the most formal instructions from my Government, just transmitted to me by the Ambassador of the United States at Petrograd, I have the honor to inform you that since the United States of America and Russia are united in fact in a war which is essentially a struggle of democracy against autocracy, my Government protests categorically and vigorously against any form of separate armistice that might be concluded by Russia. . . .

Despite the fact that this communication represented itself as being sent pursuant to formal instructions of the United States government, Washington (which had given no such instructions) appears never even to have received an authentic text.[18]

This new communication, while not as threatening in language as the British-French-Italian note, further exacerbated Soviet feelings. Again, the fact of its presentation to Dukhonin rather than to the Soviet government aroused suspicion that its purpose was to support Dukhonin in his resistance to Soviet authority. The note was published in *Izvestiya* on December 1, together with a similar note which had been independently handed to Dukhonin by the French military representative. The publication of these two communica-

[17] *Istoriya Diplomatii* (The History of Diplomacy), by V. M. Khvostov and I. I. Mints under editorial direction of V. P. Potemkin, State Publishing House for Political Literature, Moscow, 1945, Vol. ii, p. 348.

[18] Even the War Department apparently never received a copy. At any rate, an exhaustive search of its files in 1930 failed to reveal any (letter, Secretary of War to Secretary of State, April 9, 1930; Army Records Section, The Pentagon). Cumming & Pettit (*op.cit.,* p. 53), made up in large part from Robins' files, contains a copy which is translated from the Russian text published in *Izvestiya*. The text given above is translated from the French text (itself a translation from the English original) included in the article "Nakanune Peremiriya" (On the Eve of the Armistice), *op.cit., Krasny Arkhiv,* Vol. 23, pp. 195–249. This French text came from the files of Dukhonin's headquarters.

tions was accompanied by a statement from Trotsky expressing displeasure that the two military representatives had "considered it possible to address official documents to the former Supreme Commander-in-Chief, General Dukhonin, who was removed by the Council of People's Commissaries for insubordination to the Soviet Government." Charging the military representatives with calling on Dukhonin to carry out a policy contrary to that of his government, Trotsky went on to say:

. . . Such a state of affairs cannot be tolerated. Nobody demands from the present Allied diplomats the recognition of the Soviet Government. But at the same time the Soviet Government, which is responsible for the fate of the country, cannot allow Allied diplomats and military agents for any purpose to interfere in the internal life of our country and attempt to fan civil wars. Further steps in the same direction will immediately provoke the most serious complications, the responsibility for which the Council of People's Commissaries refuses beforehand to accept.[19]

Aside from this unfortunate connotation of the Kerth letter, the matter was complicated by the fact that news of it reached Trotsky just at the time he received General Judson's second communication in Petrograd. Judson later maintained that there was no inconsistency between the two communications—the situation had merely changed between the times they were conceived. But Trotsky, determined to miss no opportunity for propaganda, professed himself puzzled to know how they fitted together. Speaking before the Petrograd Soviet later that week he observed that the Allies were "apparently in a state of the utmost confusion," and went on to say that only this could explain

the practically simultaneous appearance of the two documents, published in today's issue of *Pravda:* Colonel Kerth's letter to General Dukhonin and the letter of his chief, General Judson. If you have read them you will know that one of them completely contradicts the other.[20]

At midnight on November 27 Robins received a phone call from the Smolny Institute. The preliminary German-Soviet truce negotiations had been successful. Military operations had come to an end. Formal armistice talks would begin on December 2. "Beaten," Robins recorded in his diary; "The game is lost!" [21]

[19] Cumming & Pettit, *op.cit.,* p. 54.
[20] Degras, Vol. I, *op.cit.,* p. 13.
[21] Robins MSS, *op.cit.,* Diary, November 27, 1917.

The morning papers on Wednesday, November 28, carried the news in full, accompanying it with the text of a new appeal, signed by Lenin and Trotsky, to the proletariat of the warring countries. In this appeal, referring to the success of the preliminary negotiations and the termination of military operations on the eastern front, they went on to call once more, this time in the plainest terms, for action by the proletariat of the Allied countries against their own governments:

. . . The Government of the victorious revolution does not require recognition from the professional representatives of capitalist diplomacy, but we do ask the people: "Does reactionary diplomacy express their ideas and aspirations? Are they willing to allow the diplomats to let the great opportunity for peace offered by the Russian revolution slip through their fingers?" The answer to these questions must be given without delay, and it must be an answer in deeds and not merely in words. The Russian army and the Russian people cannot wait longer and do not wish to do so. If the Allied nations do not send their representatives we shall conduct negotiations alone with the Germans. We want a general peace, but if the bourgeoisie in the Allied countries force us to conclude a separate peace the entire responsibility will be theirs. . . .

We await your representatives! Act, do not waste a single hour! . . .[22]

In reporting to his government the issuance of this decree (he did not report its text), Francis stated—no doubt under Judson's urging —that if a separate armistice were to be concluded and to become operative, a condition of the armistice ought to be that the opposing armies should remain in *statu quo,* i.e. that there should be no transfer of German troops to the western front. He went on to say that unless he received instructions to the contrary, he proposed to request another meeting of the Allied chiefs-of-mission and to advise his colleagues to send their military attachés informally to the Soviet authorities in order to make this recommendation to those who might negotiate the armistice.[23]

The following day, Thursday, November 29, was Thanksgiving Day. The Americans in Petrograd put aside their diplomatic problems long enough to convene for the amicable purpose of celebrating the holiday. There was a ceremony at the American church. The

[22] Klyuchnikov & Sabanin, Part II, *op.cit.,* p. 92.
[23] *Foreign Relations, 1918, Russia,* Vol. I, *op.cit.,* pp. 252–253, Telegram 2039, November 28, 1917.

pastor, Reverend G. A. Simons, delivered an address on "Thy Thanksgiving in Troubled Times." In the afternoon, the Ambassador held open house for the 250 Americans still left in the city and for a few Russian guests.

While the reception was still in progress the Ambassador received a new communication from Trotsky, sent to all the Allied chiefs-of-mission and informing them—officially, this time—that the German supreme command had given its consent to the opening of negotiations for an "immediate armistice on all fronts for the purpose of concluding a democratic peace without annexations and contributions with the right of all nations to self determination." Trotsky confirmed that military operations on the Russian front had been brought to a standstill, and said that preliminary truce negotiations would begin December 2. The Soviet of People's Commissars, he wrote, continued to favor simultaneous negotiation by all the Allies. The Allied governments were requested to say whether they wished to take part in the negotiations scheduled to open at 5:00 p.m. on December 2.

This note, like the first direct approach regarding the armistice, was proper in form and unprovocative. Again, Francis put it on the wire without any recommendations of his own.[24]

❖

On the morning after Thanksgiving Day (Friday, November 30), the spirit of gratitude for blessings past yielded promptly to disagreement over the uncertainties of the future. Controversy centered around the question as to whether General Judson ought to enter into contact with the Soviet authorities with a view to influencing the terms of the treaty. The question was debated in an afternoon conference in the Ambassador's office attended by Francis himself, Counselor of Embassy Butler Wright, General Judson, Raymond Robins, and Edgar Sisson. For Sisson, who had just arrived in Petrograd, it was the first participation in this sort of deliberation.

Only two days remained before the armistice talks were scheduled to begin. Judson was impatient to visit Trotsky without delay in order to urge the Soviets to insist on the inclusion, in whatever armistice terms might be arranged, of clauses prohibiting the removal of

[24] *Ibid.*, p. 253, Telegram 2040, November 29, 1917 (sent via the American Legation in Stockholm).

troops by the Germans from the eastern front. He was reluctant, however, to make such a visit without the Ambassador's approval. The others had agreed to support him in pressing the hesitant old gentleman into giving his assent.

The atmosphere of this discussion can best be realized if one takes note of such evidence as exists of Francis' personal relations and dealings, at that particular time, with the four senior persons present at the meeting: Judson, Robins, Sisson, and Wright. The first three of these men, as we have seen, were one step removed from the Embassy Chancery itself; all took orders from agencies in Washington other than the Department of State; in no single case had Washington taken the trouble to lay down clear lines of competence and authority between them and the Ambassador.

As indicated above, General Judson bore the combined titles of Military Attaché and Chief of the American Military Mission. In the first capacity, he was certainly a subordinate of the Ambassador; in the second, it was questionable whether he was. His personal contact with the Soviet authorities had already become a painful and controversial issue between him and the Ambassador. It had arisen at some time prior to November 19 when Judson, in company with the French and British military attachés, had called on the military commandant of the Petrograd district and discussed with him the protection of the foreign diplomatic missions in the capital. "I was not aware of this," Francis wrote the Secretary of State,

until after it was done, and when informed thereof expressed my displeasure and gave orders nothing should be done . . . that could be construed as a recognition of the Lenin-Trotsky government.[25]

The matter had come up for discussion between the two men on November 19, and apparently not in a friendly manner.

Judson afterward recorded his understanding of this conversation in a stiff memorandum for the Ambassador. He understood, he said,

You do not wish me to refrain from such trivial intercourse with Smolny —on matters of telephones, guards, and the like.

Francis' equally stiff reply reveals quite clearly the tension and lack of understanding between the two men:

[25] Lansing MSS, *op.cit.,* Vol. 32 of Correspondence; Letter, Francis to Lansing, November 20, 1917.

. . . When I asked you to confer with me before having such intercourse, you said that emergencies might arise which would not give you time to confer with me. My reply was that I was in the Embassy and accessible at all times.[26]

In addition to the Ambassador's general nervousness concerning Judson's contacts with the Soviet authorities, one more unhappy circumstance must be borne in mind as affecting the relations between the two men. On November 21, the day after writing the note to Judson cited above, the Ambassador had been mortified and enraged to receive from the Department of State a telegram with regard to Madame deCram, reading as follows:

Department informed Madame Cram is employed in some capacity in Embassy. As Department has reason to suspect this woman, you are directed to take immediate steps to sever her connection with the Embassy.[27]

The message terminated with a warning that Madame deCram should not be permitted any access to classified information. The message was decoded and brought in by Wright. Francis was livid. He was sure the message was the result of denunciation somewhere in his entourage. It was most probably Judson whom he suspected (quite unjustifiably, as the record indicates). Judson, who felt very strongly about the deCram situation, had been the only one of Francis' subordinates who had had the courage to approach him to his face about it. This military bluntness may well have drawn down upon him a suspicion he did not deserve. Francis despatched to the Department on November 24 a pained and astounded reply, demanding that the Department cite the grounds for its suspicions. At the time of the November 30 meeting, no answer having as yet come in, he was still seething with resentment and suspicion. (A day or two later he received a reply from Washington telling him simply that the information "came from several sources believed to be reliable." [28])

The Ambassador's relations with Robins were scarcely less clouded than those with Judson. Thompson had left on the 27th, and Robins

[26] Judson MSS, *op.cit.*, Letter, Francis to Judson, November 20, 1917.
[27] National Archives, File 124.613/385a; Telegram, Lansing to Francis, November 14, 1917; received by Francis, November 21.
[28] National Archives, File 124.613/386; Telegram 1872, Lansing to Francis, November 30, 1917.

Le Commissaire du Peuple
aux affaires étrangeres
Petrograde.
le 7 Novembre 1917

Transmitted as Document No 3
to Despatch No. 1386, dated
July 15, 1919.

800

Received at Embassy
11 P.M. Nov. 8/21. 1917

Monsieur
l' Ambassadeur des États Unis

Avec la présente j'ai l'honneur de Vous
informer, Monsieur l'Ambassadeur, que le Cong-
res National des Conseils des Députés des
ouvriers et des soldats a établie le 26 du
mois d'octobre a.c. un nouveau gouvernement
de la République Russe sous la forme du Con-
seil des Commissaires du Peuple. Le Président
de ce gouvernement est M-r Vladimir Ilych
Lénine et la direction de la politique
extérieure fut confié à moi, en qualité
du Commissaire du Peuple des affaires ét
rangeres.

En attirant Votre attention au texte
de la proposition de l'armistice et de la
paix démocratique sans annexions ni con-
trubitions, fondée sur le droit des peuple
de disposer d'eux mêmes ,-propositionsap-
prouvés par le Congrès des Conseils des
ouvriers et des soldats,- j'ai l'honneur
de Vous prier, Monsieur l'Ambassadeur, de bien
vouloir regarder le document susmentionné
comme une proposition formelle d'une armistice sans délai sur tous les fronts et de
l'ouverture sans retard des négociations
de paix-une proposition avec laquelle le
gouvernement plénipotentaire de la République Russe s'adresse simultanément à toutes
les nations belligérantes et à leurs gou-
vernements.

Page 1 of the first communication from the Soviet Government
to the U.S. Government, signed by Trotsky

Je Vous prie, Monsieur l'Ambassadeur, de bien vou -
loir agreer l'assurance de la parfaite considération
et du respect trés profond du gouvernement des Conseils au peuple des Etats Unis qui, aussi, comme tous les
autres peuples épuisés par cette boucherie incomparable ne peut ne pas ardemment désirer la paix.

le Commissaire du Peuple aux affaires étran -
gères

Léon Trotsky

admitted Trotzky

Chargé d'affaire *Vl. Bontch-Bronévitch*

Secretaire *N. Gorbounova.*

admitted ....

was now head of the Red Cross Commission. The Ambassador, it will be recalled, had not wanted the Red Cross Mission in the first place. He was aware that he had never been treated with confidence by its leaders or fully informed of their activities.

Robins had seen Trotsky as early as the first two or three days after the Bolshevik coup and had since continued to be in touch with him through Gumberg. It was plainly he who had needled Judson into making his second communication—and for a very specific political purpose. The Ambassador had not been kept informed of these activities.

But this was not the worst. Available evidence suggests that Robins saw Trotsky at some time on the very day of the November 30 conference and conferred with him precisely on the subject of Judson's communications; yet no mention was made to the Ambassador of this meeting, despite its obvious relevance to the subject under discussion. Evidence for the meeting is to be found in the following passage from a speech delivered by Trotsky later that day before the Petrograd Soviet:

Today I had here in the Smolny Institute two Americans closely connected with American capitalist elements who assured me that the attitude of the United States is reflected correctly by Judson's letter and not Kerth's. I am inclined to believe that they are right; not, of course, because I believe in the platonic sympathy for the Russian people of which the American imperialists wish to persuade me. But the point is that after all that has taken place during the last few days the American diplomats understand that they cannot defeat the Russian revolution and therefore they want to enter into friendly relations with us, calculating that this will be an excellent means of competition with the German and in particularly with the British capitalists after the war. Anyhow, we are not in the least interested in the attitude of the Allied or enemy imperialists towards us. We shall conduct an independent class policy whatever their attitude towards us, and I mention their declarations only because I see in them a symptom of the unshakeable forces of the Russian revolution and of its Government.[29]

It is difficult to imagine who these "two Americans closely connected with American capitalist elements" could have been, if not Robins and Gumberg. If this hypothesis is correct, and if Trotsky's statement may be believed, we may note that Robins had not hesi-

[29] Degras, Vol. I, *op.cit.,* p. 13.

tated to instruct Trotsky in what was and what was not "the attitude of the United States"—a clear invasion of the Ambassador's prerogatives. It is also worth noting that Trotsky, in his public statement, recorded his skepticism about American sympathies for the Russian people, attributing the readiness of the two "Americans" to talk with him to motives of imperialistic commercial greed, and attempting to exploit the visit publicly as proof of the growing prestige of the Soviet government.

In a telegram sent to Washington the following day, after Trotsky's statement referring to the interview had appeared in the newspapers, Francis stated, rather pathetically, that he was "trying to ascertain" who the two Americans were who had presumed to speak for the United States government "when I have abstained therefrom to this moment." [30] It is difficult to believe that he could have had much question as to the identity of Trotsky's visitors, even though he could not prove his suspicions. It is also reasonable to suppose that Judson was acquainted with the circumstances of this visit. After all, the unidentified Americans had ventured to tell Trotsky which of the two military notes was authentic and which was not.

These circumstances point to a tragic state of mutual suspicion and lack of frankness within the American official community: the Military Attaché and the head of the Red Cross Mission evidently concealing from the Ambassador meetings and discussions that were taking place with the Soviet Foreign Commissar, the Ambassador having evidence that things were transpiring behind his back but being left to guess at the full reasons for them.

As for Sisson, he had arrived in Petrograd only five days before. He was, it will be recalled, the representative of the Committee on Public Information, and not an employee of the State Department. He was supposed to be in charge of all informational and propaganda activities of the United States government in Russia—a function acutely political in nature and extremely difficult to disentangle from the normal diplomatic responsibilities of the State Department. Sisson had called on the Ambassador on the day of his arrival but had not been back to see him since that, until the meeting on November 30. The touchy old gentleman had not failed to note this fact, with suspicion and disapproval. Four days later, as we shall see,

[30] *Foreign Relations, 1918, Russia*, Vol. I, *op.cit.*, p. 276, Telegram 2049, December 1, 1917.

Sisson was to make a clumsy and unsuccessful attempt, behind the Ambassador's back, to have the latter removed.

Sisson came to the meeting on November 30 already a strong partisan of Robins and Judson, with whom he had been meeting frequently. He even went so far, during the course of the meeting, as to reproach the Ambassador with inactivity and to complain that this inactivity was "driving us to perdition." This accusation, coming from a rank newcomer to the Petrograd scene, stung the Ambassador to the quick, and moved him to reply "promptly and emphatically" that "I was the Ambassador and the responsibility mine and I did not hesitate to exercise it." [31]

Wright's relations with the Ambassador had been strained and uncomfortable from the start. The relationship between Ambassador and Counselor of Embassy has tended, traditionally, to be a delicate one, the two offices being, so to speak, in tandem and concerned with the same functions and responsibilities. In this instance, the relationship was strained by everyone's awareness of Francis' unfamiliarity with the world of diplomacy. The career officers tended to hover nervously around him, revealing only too clearly their anxiety lest he do something rash, ill-informed, and likely to embarrass the government, as though *they* were the true custodians and interpreters of the government's interest and had to protect that interest against *his* inexperience. This attitude gave Francis a sense of dependence and humiliation from which he endeavored to escape, from time to time, by impulsive independent actions, dictated rather by a desire to demonstrate his authority than by the intrinsic needs of the situation, and taken in a spirit of excited glee, as by a naughty boy. On such occasions the atmosphere of the Chancery was tense and unhappy; and there would be a buzz of alarmed and indignant whispering in the wings.

Ironically enough, Wright, who had been obliged to decode the telegram about Madame deCram, to take it to Francis, and to listen respectfully to his thundering pronouncements of what he would do to the blankety-blank person who had denounced him, appears to have been himself more deeply implicated than any of the others in the denunciation.[32] (A day or two later, he asked the Department

[31] *Ibid.*, p. 295; from Francis' telegram 2081, December 9, 1917 to Department.
[32] Judson MSS, *op.cit.*, Diary entry of December 2, 1917 states that the State Department had learned about the deCram matter "thru some agency known to Wright."

for leave of absence. The request was not granted at that time and he was obliged to serve several weeks longer in his uneasy position as the Ambassador's first assistant.)

It was against this unhappy background—exemplary of the difficulties that can develop in American official communities abroad, particularly when the principals in Washington fail to work in disciplined unison—that Francis and his associates met on November 30 to discuss the problem of Judson's proposed visit to Trotsky. The Ambassador's state of mind was one of vacillating misgiving. He was not prepared to object to anything Judson wanted to do independently, in his capacity as head of the Military Mission; but he did not want him to go to Trotsky in his capacity as Military Attaché. Judson argued that the public would view the visit anyway as one by the chief of the Military Mission; but he refused to make it, even in that capacity, without the Ambassador's consent. The Ambassador conceded that the visit might be made by one of Judson's military subordinates, but Judson wanted to go in person. The discussion ended inconclusively, with no clear understanding as to what, if anything, had been decided.

The Ambassador found time, that same day, to take the question up with the other Allied ambassadors. If the others could be induced to take parallel action, his own responsibility in authorizing such a step would be less onerous. He thereupon urged upon his diplomatic colleagues that each should make an "unofficial effort" to influence the armistice terms. "My desire," he explained to the Department, was

. . . to throw safeguards around separate armistice, if inevitable, that would protect other fronts and prevent transfer thereto of German troops now confronting Russian Army; also to prevent liberation of Austrian-German prisoners and Russian prisoners. . . .[33]

But the colleagues were hesitant and unenthusiastic. They would not object to Francis' taking such a step, if he liked, on his own responsibility; but they would not join him in it, nor would they give it their blessing.

Judson also sounded out Allied feelings when he dined that evening at the British Embassy with his French and British military colleagues. The British, he reported, were vacillating and unwilling

[33] *Foreign Relations, 1918, Russia,* Vol. I, *op.cit.,* p. 279; Telegram 2050, December 1, 1917.

to commit themselves. The French were flatly opposed to such a visit.

On leaving the British Embassy (his departure was somewhat delayed because the Red Guards had indelicately made off with his car), Judson stopped at the American Embassy about midnight to report his observations to Francis. The Ambassador, after learning the reaction of Judson's military colleagues, said, "Well, what do you think about it now?" The General indicated he still thought he ought to go ahead with the visit. He understood the Ambassador to say, "Then go ahead." [34]

That night Robins concluded the entries for the day in his pocket diary with the notation: "Have closed for step with Smolny." Just what this meant is obscure, but there is every indication that the wheels were being assiduously greased, behind the Ambassador's back, and that Trotsky was kept well abreast of the discussions among the Americans.

Early the next morning, acting on the strength of what the Ambassador had said the previous evening, Judson asked Sisson ("as he had relations with Smolny") to arrange the visit for one of his subordinates, not himself. Only a day remained before the armistice talks were to begin. Judson was frantic with impatience, fearful that it might be already too late to exert any influence on the position of the Soviet negotiators. After what seemed to him an interminable time, Sisson returned, and announced that the visit was arranged for an hour later that day, but only for the General, not for a subordinate. This last proviso, he indicated, was at Trotsky's insistence. Sisson further reported that he had seen the Ambassador again and had obtained the latter's "wavering consent." [35]

On the strength of these arrangements, the General's visit to Trotsky took place the same day (December 1). It constituted the first political contact between any responsible official of the United States government and the Soviet authorities. Judson told Trotsky that he came as an individual and not in his official capacity. He emphasized, however, that the visit had the Ambassador's consent. He pointed out what he felt to be the community of interests between the Soviet and United States governments with respect to certain aspects of the armistice problem. He urged that efforts be made by the Soviet negotiators to arrange that enemy troops be held in their

[34] Judson MSS, *op.cit.,* Judson report, March 16, 1918.
[35] *Loc.cit.*

existing positions and not transferred away from the front. If this were done, he pointed out, the war would be shortened and Russia would have a better claim to speak at the peace conference. He hoped the Soviet government would not agree to any exchange of prisoners.

Judson was pleased over Trotsky's reaction to his *démarche.* "Trotsky was very responsive," Judson wrote in his official telegraphic report to the War Department:

He implied that his principles and desire for peace leave him wide latitude in armistice negotiations and stated that he would be glad to have me cable to the United States that in the negotiations he would observe and endeavor to protect the interests of Russia's allies; he further stated that the points I raised appealed to him or had already been in his mind and that armistice commission would be given instructions accordingly.[36]

The following morning the Petrograd papers appeared with a statement about the visit, put out by Trotsky:

Yesterday, 18 November [1 December], General Judson, Chief of the American Mission, visited Comrade Trotsky at Smolny. The General made it clear at the outset that at the present time he had no right to speak in the name of the American Government, as the Soviet Government was not yet recognized, but that he had come in order to start relations, to explain certain circumstances, and to clear up certain misunderstandings. General Judson inquired whether the new Government intended to end the war in conjunction with the Allies, who, according to the General, will hardly be able to take part in the negotiations on 19 November [2 December]. Comrade Trotsky briefly explained to the General the Soviet Government's policy in regard to the struggle for a general peace. The principal circumstance emphasized by the People's Commissar for Foreign Affairs was full publicity for all future negotiations. The Allies would be able to follow every stage in the development of the peace negotiations and could therefore join them at one of the later states.

General Judson asked permission to transmit his reply to his Government and in conclusion said: "The time of protests and threats addressed to the Soviet Government has passed, if indeed there ever was such a time." . . .[37]

---

[36] *Foreign Relations, 1918, Russia,* Vol. I, *op.cit.,* p. 279; from Judson's telegram to the War Department, December 1, 1917. Francis advised the State Department of Judson's despatch of this report; but the State Department never received a copy of it until it requested one in 1930 for inclusion in the *Foreign Relations* series.

[37] Degras, Vol. I, *op.cit.,* pp. 14–15.

It will be noted that in this public statement Trotsky made no reference to the main object of the visit and contrived to portray Judson's remarks in such a way as to convey the impression that Judson had apologized for the Kerth note and withdrawn it. This inaccuracy did not disturb the General. Trotsky's statement, he recorded in his diary, was

. . . less inaccurate than I apprehended it might be. It excited the Ambassador, as I knew it would, but I have urged him as insistently as I knew how to make no comment to anyone on the discrepancy.[38]

Far from being discouraged in his hope for exercising a useful influence on the Soviet authorities, Judson took occasion that same day to despatch a wire to Major Kerth instructing him to return to Petrograd. This was done, the General explained in his diary, lest Kerth's presence at the field headquarters should further irritate the Bolsheviki and embarrass his own relations with them.

The General's representations to Trotsky about the transfer of troops had little practical effect, for the transfer had actually begun even before the Bolshevik Revolution. General Hoffmann tells in his diary that the reason his troops did not press on in September, after the capture of Riga, and proceed then to take Petrograd, was that

. . . Ludendorff cannot with the best of will let us have the divisions any longer. He needs troops in the west and Austria also needs them.[39]

The Bolsheviki did actually raise the matter—quite energetically, in fact—at the truce talks, but the Germans, who had every intention of transferring to the western front as many troops as they found practicable, insisted on a formula which in effect left them complete freedom of action. General Hoffmann, who conducted the talks for the German side, had this to say in his memoirs as to the manner in which this was arranged:

The Russians laid great importance on pinning down to the eastern front the German troops stationed there and preventing us from transporting them to the west. This demand was not easy for us to meet. Even before the Brest-Litovsk negotiations began, the order had been issued for the

[38] Judson MSS, *op.cit.,* Diary, December 2, 1917.
[39] *Die Aufzeichnungen des Generalmajors Max Hoffmann,* Verlag für Kulturpolitik, Berlin, 1929, Vol. I, p. 178.

movement to the west of the main body of the eastern army. I could therefore concede to the Russians without difficulty that during the prospective
truce no German movements away from the front would take place *which
had not already been ordered or begun at that time.*[40]

The last sentence correctly describes the agreement actually arrived
at. The final armistice terms, signed on December 15, contained in
Section II this clause:

Further, the contracting parties obligate themselves not to undertake
any transfers of troops until January 14, 1918 . . . on the front between the
Black Sea and the Baltic Sea, unless such transfers had already been begun
at the moment of the signing of the armistice.[41]

There is no indication that the Germans allowed themselves to be
disturbed in the slightest, by the language of the armistice agreement, in their transfer of troops from the east to the west. The estimates were that by the spring of 1918 many hundreds of thousands
of German troops had been moved from east to west.[42]

Francis evidently felt himself embarrassed by the repercussions
of General Judson's visit, and his telegrams reflected the conflicting
feelings with which he reacted to the matter. He reported the talk
to Washington by telegram the day that it occurred, saying: "Judson
saw Trotsky today with my approval. . . ."[43] But the following day,

[40] *Ibid.,* Vol. II, p. 192. Italics added.

[41] This language is taken from the English text of the armistice agreement included in Wheeler-Bennett, *op.cit.,* p. 379. It is attributed in turn to a publication
"Texts of the Russian 'Peace,'" U.S. Department of State, 1918. It is interesting to
note that the official Soviet publication of diplomatic documents (Klyuchnikov &
Sabanin, *op.cit.*) includes only an abridged version of this armistice agreement (on
pp. 97–98) and omits the qualifying clause to the effect that transfers away from the
eastern front might be permissible if they had already begun at the moment of the
signing of the armistice. The question arises whether this could be taken as an
indication that in 1925, when the Klyuchnikov and Sabanin collection appeared, the
Soviet government was still anxious to claim credit for having attempted to help out
the Allies. The Russian text of the armistice terms, incidentally, is somewhat clearer
in that it speaks, not of transfers *on* the eastern front, but of transfers *from* this front.

[42] The Allied military authorities in the west counted on a removal of approximately 40 German divisions from eastern to western fronts during the winter (see
statements by General Tasker Bliss and General Petain, cited in Chapter IX of Seymour, Vol. III, *op. cit.*). In a memorandum to Lansing January 1, 1918, Basil Miles
(in charge of Russian affairs in the Department) said that the armistice would
"enable Germany and Austria to throw to the western front more troops than the
United States can put in France for the next eight months" (National Archives,
State Department File 861.00).

[43] *Foreign Relations, 1918, Russia,* Vol. I, *op.cit.,* p. 279; Telegram 2050, December
1, 1917.

after learning of Trotsky's public observations with regard to the visit, the Ambassador altered this version somewhat:

Judson's visit to Trotsky exciting comment, especially among Allied missions who consider it step toward recognition. Judson has insisted for some time that Soviet is *de facto* government and relations therewith should be established. After discussing matter with Allied colleagues as reported . . . I consented that Judson should send subordinate to discuss armistice provisions only and was not aware that Judson had gone himself until after visit made. . . . Judson has just shown me . . . translation [of Trotsky's published remarks]. Told by me that [he] should not have said "time for threats and protests is over"; says statement incorrect but not as much as feared.[44]

A third version of the incident was given to Washington by Francis a few days later in a long telegram reviewing the changes that had taken place and his own official reactions to them. In this telegram he said:

Judson's personal call on Trotsky was without my knowledge or approval . . . and I was compelled so to state to my colleagues at meeting of December 5 when they remarked that it was understood we should act in union and in any case Judson's visit to Trotsky was a violation of such understanding. . . .[45]

It is evident from the above that Judson's visit was regarded by Francis' Allied colleagues, particularly the British, as going beyond their understanding of what had been agreed to in the conference of November 30. The British were particularly sensitive because they were in conflict at that time with the Soviet authorities over the detention of two Russian communists—Chicherin and Petrov—in England, and Trotsky had indicated that no British subjects would be permitted to leave Russia until the Russians were released. Judson's statement seemed to them to cut the ground from under their position. It is probable that the British displeasure over Judson's visit was communicated to Washington. In sections of the neutral press, the Judson visit was interpreted as evidence of serious divisions in the Allied camp over policy toward Russia. These reactions were promptly picked up by the American press, and must also have produced a highly unfavorable impression in Washington.

[44] *Ibid.,* pp. 282–283; from Francis' telegram 2057, December 2, to Department.
[45] *Ibid.,* pp. 294–295; from Telegram 2081, December 9, 1917.

News of the Judson visit reached Washington Tuesday, December 4, through press reports in the morning papers. Francis' first telegram concerning the visit arrived that afternoon. The next day Lansing instructed Assistant Secretary William Phillips to draft a message to Francis telling him to "take no steps with Lenin or Trotsky," [46] and the Department of State issued a press statement to the effect that Judson and Kerth had both "acted without government instructions in presenting communications to the Bolshevist government. . . ." [47] The following day, December 6, the Department received Francis' message stating that the Judson visit had taken place without his consent. A telegram was then prepared and despatched to Francis referring to "press reports" [48] about the Judson visit and directing that American representatives in Russia should "withhold all direct communication with the Bolshevik government." [49] The Ambassador was directed to "so advise Judson and Kerth."

Actually, the telegram did not reflect the full seriousness with which the government in Washington viewed the incident. Lansing's desk calendar for December 6 indicates that he saw Secretary of War Baker "on Judson's recall" and further conferred with Assistant Secretary Phillips about the matter. On the following day the incident was the subject of a fifteen-minute discussion between the Secretary of State and the President.

By this time the situation had been complicated by another curious development, also flowing in part from the meeting on November 30.

After the unhappy discussion with the Ambassador, Judson had urged Sisson to use his influence in Washington to obtain White House attention for the reports which he, Judson, was sending to his military superiors,[50] and White House sanction for his policy of contact with the Soviet officials. The General evidently hoped that such intervention by Sisson would result in instructions being sent to the Ambassador, making it plain to him that routine contacts with the Bolshevik authorities would not imply recognition and were not to

---

[46] Lansing MSS, *op.cit.*, Desk Diary, December 5, 1917.

[47] *London Times*, December 6, 1917.

[48] By making reference to "press reports" rather than to Francis' telegrams, the Department appears to have saved itself the embarrassment of dealing with the contradictions involved in Francis' own reports of the matter.

[49] *Foreign Relations, 1918, Russia*, Vol. I, *op.cit.*, p. 289; Telegram 1883.

[50] Judson's reports received more presidential attention than he realized. Baker, Vol. VII, *op.cit.*, p. 373, mentions Wilson's receipt of Judson's telegram of November

be discouraged.[51] Sisson was, to say the least, nothing loath. Having been ten days in Petrograd, he was brimming with convictions and suggestions as to what the government ought to do. In addition to this, there is every evidence that he and Bullard conferred extensively with Robins, in the days following the November 30 meeting, on the subject of Francis himself, and came to the conclusion that the old gentleman must no longer be kept in Petrograd. Whether, on this occasion, Sisson recalled the President's written injunction to guard against "officious intrusion or meddling" seems doubtful. In any case, on December 4 he took pen in hand and drafted a long message to George Creel, the tenor of which was scarcely compatible with the President's instruction. He first outlined the needs with respect to the wording of the armistice agreement, following closely Judson's views. He then described the situation he had encountered in the Embassy:

Found Ambassador without policy except anger at Bolsheviks, unamenable to arguments or entreaties of his official advisers, military and civil, and General Judson very anxious to meet Trotsky for conference on terms of armistice. My own work hopelessly involved in this situation. Can hope to accomplish nothing if there is open break between the Embassy and de facto government. Risked using what pressure I could muster, helped to secure from Ambassador wavering consent to a single conference between Judson and Trotsky. Judson has reported to Washington the satisfactory results of his conference. . . . I recommend . . . instructions . . . for immediate establishment of working, informal contact with de facto power by official representatives.[52]

Having thus disposed of the problem of contact with the Soviet authorities, Sisson turned to the problem of Francis. He was reluctantly convinced, he stated,

. . . that no fruitful work can be done here by any division of our Government so long as Francis remains in charge of Embassy. Not only does he impress every one as a sick man absolutely unfitted to the strain physical

---

14 urging an effort "to state practical terms [of] peace which neither side could refuse. . . ." The Woodrow Wilson MSS, Series II (Library of Congress), reveal that Judson's letters and messages were reaching the White House through both Postmaster General Burleson and Secretary of War Baker: Wilson's notes to Burleson of November 14 and 28; note from Baker, November 23; and Wilson note to Acting Secretary of War in March 1918 ("I have been very much interested in General Judson's view of the Russian situation"). But Wilson never received Judson after his return to the United States.

[51] Sisson, *op.cit.,* Chapter VI, pp. 87 ff.
[52] *Ibid.,* p. 89.

and mental of his great post but also he has allowed himself to become subject of public gossip and of investigation by the secret police of the Allied nations because of open association with a woman suspected (?) perhaps without sufficient evidence, of espionage. . . .[53]

After discussing at length the deCram matter, and suggesting in effect that Judson and Wright be asked for their views about it, Sisson concluded with the suggestion that Francis (in order "to prevent public humiliation") be directed

. . . to hasten to Washington via Japan to report in person to the President on Russian situation and that Embassy be left with Chargé d'Affaires. Then while he is en route make inquiries. . . . It is above all important that he should leave here at once with the least possible scandal.

Since Sisson did not yet have his own code for communication with Creel, an ingenious method was devised to get the message transmitted to Creel through the Department of State, without the Department's reading it. The message was encoded with the use of the familiar Red Code book of the Department of State, with a cipher modification designed to throw the Department's cryptographers off the track. Robins, and apparently some of his associates, helped with this curious job of encoding.[54] The coded message was signed by Bullard (not Sisson) and was given to the American Consulate in Petrograd (not the Embassy) with the request that it be forwarded to the Department of State for transmission to Creel and that the latter be advised to use the Red Code in decoding it. A separate message was then sent through commercial channels to the cable censor in New York (the censors were under the Committee on Public Information) indicating the nature of the cipher modification and asking that it be brought to Creel's attention.

Sisson realized that the Department would find it undecipherable in the Red Code, but hoped that it would be passed on to Creel anyway and that the latter, knowing the key, would be able to decode it.

Sisson always believed, as indicated in his memoirs, that the Department of State was in fact unable to decode the message; and he

[53] This section of the cable is in the National Archives, Department of State File 861.00/851½, telegram from Consulate in Petrograd to State Department, December 5; received December 6, 3:22 p.m. The file copy has pencilled notation: "Paraphrased Dec. 8-J.T."

[54] Robins MSS, *op.cit.,* pocket diary entry for December 4: "Clean up and call all hands to action. We are at last driving full speed ahead. Work on coding the message that will get the Stuffed Shirt. . . ."

regretted only the delay in its transmission to Creel, who did not receive it until December 14. He thought the delay arose from the Department's bewilderment over its inability to decode the message. Actually, the Department's seasoned cryptographers made short work of this relatively elementary cryptographic problem. By Friday, December 7, they had deciphered the message and placed it in the hands of the Secretary of State.[55] Before Creel had even seen the message, the Department of State and the President had read it, had taken account of its serious implications, and—confronted with Francis' complaint about Judson and Sisson's complaint about Francis—acknowledged themselves to be faced with a decision as to whether Judson or Francis or Sisson, or all three, should be removed.[56]

The following day, December 8, the Secretary sent a telegram to Francis telling him of the receipt of the message for Creel, though not of its content, and asking him to inform Bullard that the Department could not give its code to other government offices, but would be glad to assist the Committee on Public Information by transmitting "with all possible despatch messages bearing on the business of the Committee." The message continued pointedly:

. . . In view of critical situation in Russia, however, Department feels that any information bearing on political conditions from American officials should be sent only through the Embassy. . . .[57]

A week later the Ambassador, in transmitting a formal protest from Sisson about the holding up of the telegram, reported to the Secretary of State that he had seen Sisson only once since the Judson incident and asked him whether he had credentials, written or otherwise, to the Embassy. Sisson's curt reply had been, "You have instructions; adhere [there]to." Francis then continued with the following pathetic complaint:

[55] The first thing on Lansing's desk diary for that day is a notation that he had talked to Gibson (probably one of the desk officers in the Department) "on effort of Sisson to avoid sending Petrograd news through Embassy." The Secretary then talked to Phillips about a telegram "to Creel on Francis' conduct in Petrograd." Finally, he saw Counselor Polk with regard to a "telegram re Francis." The message referred to in these terms could hardly have been any other than that which Sisson had submitted. (Lansing MSS, *op.cit.*)

[56] This impression is reinforced by the fact that on each of the first two days of the following week, the Secretary of State discussed with his associates the deCram affair. (*Ibid.*, Desk Diary, December 10 and 11.)

[57] Wilson MSS, Series II, *op.cit.*, Telegram 1888.

. . . the impression prevails here that Sisson is personal representative of President Wilson and it is reported that Sisson originated such impression. Sisson's presumption in above protest and his conduct with me indicated taking himself quite seriously but I cannot believe that [President] would send personal representative here and without your advising me thereof. . . . If Robins and Sisson represent governmental policy in establishing close relations with Bolshevik Government my position is embarrassed thereby and I am subject to suspicion by chiefs of Allied missions with whom Department has directed close relations and advised uniform action. . . .[58]

Francis' apprehensions were idle. The issue, unknown to him, had already been settled when his complaint was drafted. The Secretary had despatched to him that same day (December 15) a message to the effect that the "Department approves your present course and relies your judgment. . . ."[59] This statement reflected a carefully considered decision at the Washington end on the painful subject of "contacts." It also reflected a decision that Francis should remain and should be supported against his detractors, Madame deCram notwithstanding.

General Judson, on the other hand, received instructions a fortnight later recalling him to Washington. He arrived home in late February and, after a period of consultation in the War Department, was placed in command of the 38th Division, and somewhat later of the Port of Embarkation at New York. Although he received no special recognition at the time, he later received the Distinguished Service Medal for his service in Russia.[60]

As for Sisson, he was promptly reprimanded for his brashness, with the President's whole authority behind the reprimand. "President insists," Creel wired to Sisson on December 16, "that you avoid political entanglements and personal matters."[61] A few days later Creel confirmed to the President (by letter of December 27) that

[58] *Ibid.*, Francis' telegram 2106, December 15, 1917 to Secretary of State.

[59] *Foreign Affairs, 1918, Russia*, Vol. I, *op. cit.*, p. 316; from Telegram 1906, December 15, 1917.

[60] General Graves, at that time deputy to the Chief of Staff, General March, later assured Bullard that Judson's removal had nothing to do with his actions in Petrograd and that the State Department had not intervened in any way (Bullard MSS, *op.cit.*). The record does not bear this out, and it is doubtful whether General Graves was fully informed.

[61] Sisson, *op.cit.*, p. 90.

. . . Sisson understands he is not to touch the political situation, to avoid all personal entanglements, and that while he is not to consider himself an attaché to the Embassy, he must maintain the most friendly relations with the Ambassador.[62]

The incident thus ended with a complete victory for the Ambassador. But the echoes were to reverberate for a long time. In May 1918, by which time the relations between Sisson and Robins had developed into the sharpest sort of antagonism, Bullard cabled from Vologda back to Sisson in the United States that

. . . Robins has told Ambassador of famous cable and pretends to have opposed it. Francis cross-questioned me as to others involved. I told him nothing except truth of Robins' rôle. . . .[63]

The Ambassador's struggle over the question of "contacts" was not completed by the victories over Sisson and Judson. Robins still remained to be dealt with. On Sunday, December 9, Trotsky mentioned another American visitor to the Smolny, and this time he did the Ambassador the favor of identifying him. "The chief of the American Red Cross," Trotsky said,

came to Smolny and said straight out that in Russia there had never been any such strong government as ours and that America of course will give us all kinds of supplies except munitions which we do not require any more. The visit of the American immediately showed the People's Commissars the extreme advantages for us in the international situation.

In reporting this speech to Washington, Francis added that he supposed it was Robins to whom Trotsky referred, since Robins had been acting as head of the Red Cross Mission since Thompson's departure. He had delayed reporting the matter, he said, expecting Robins to come in and explain, but Robins had not appeared. He ended by inquiring whether members of the Red Cross Mission, wearing American military uniforms, were included in the President's directive that "American representatives withhold all direct communications with the Bolshevik Government."[64]

[62] Wilson MSS, Series II, *op.cit.*
[63] Sisson, *op.cit.*, p. 96.
[64] *Foreign Relations, 1918, Russia,* Vol. I, *op.cit.,* p. 301; from Telegram 2091, December 12, 1917, Francis to Department of State. Robins denied to Judson that he had said to Trotsky this was the strongest government Russia had had, but there is no other evidence of the misquotation. (Judson MSS, *op.cit.*)

The reply to this message confirmed the fact that Red Cross representatives were also subject to the directive and should therefore not have contact with the Soviet authorities—but that is another story. Soon, due to one of those curious turns of events which seem to have been characteristic of this period, it would be the Ambassador himself who would authorize Robins to fly in the face of the President's directive.

CHAPTER VI

ALLIED DELIBERATIONS

IN PARIS

WHILE these difficulties were being experienced by the American officials in Petrograd and their principals in Washington over the initial problems of contact with the Bolshevik authorities, the Allied governments were beginning for the first time to grapple seriously with the problems of high policy which arose out of the fact of the Bolshevik seizure of power, the ideological preconceptions of the Bolshevik leaders, and their action in taking Russia out of the war.

It was noted above that on November 22 Colonel House and his party proceeded from London to Paris for participation in the sessions of the Inter-Allied Conference and of the newly organized Supreme War Council. The first of these bodies began its meetings on November 29 in Paris. Its function was to coordinate Allied efforts with respect to such things as finance, supply, shipping, embargo, etc. Since 18 nations were represented, the plenary sessions (there were only two of them) were far too large for the transaction of any actual business. The conference was therefore broken up into subcommittees whose meetings and deliberations then extended over a considerable time. None of these subcommittees was concerned with major political matters, and there was no formal consideration of the Russian problem in any plenary session of the conference.

The Supreme War Council met only on Saturday morning, December 1, in Versailles. It had been established, after a great deal of hesitation and agonized negotiation between the major Allied powers, for the purpose of coordinating the military effort; but the extremely delicate problems of command and organization which were involved in such coordination were not yet wholly solved, and the Council was at that time still preoccupied with organizational questions. Its agenda did, to be sure, include the question of war plans for the approaching year, and it was recognized that the Council would have to ask itself within the framework of this broader question what, if anything, could be done to bring Russia back into the alliance. There is, however, no indication that this matter came up for discussion at the meeting on December 1. The first important and substantive meeting of the Council did not take place until January.

While the formal activities of these two bodies thus failed to devote any attention to the problems of policy toward the Bolshevik regime, the presence in Paris of so many leading Allied statesmen provided a favorable opportunity for informal conferences on this subject, and this opportunity appears to have been extensively utilized.

There is no evidence that Trotsky's proposal of November 21 (that the Allies join in the effort to achieve a general peace) received any serious consideration in these discussions. It seems to have been generally assumed that no direct reply could be made to so preposterous a suggestion. But there was a feeling among the British and Americans that the threatening protest filed by the Allied military representatives at Mogilev had been a serious mistake, tending to throw the Bolsheviki into the arms of the Germans.[1] For this reason they were much interested in a proposal received from Sir George Buchanan about November 27 to the effect that the Entente powers, while not going along with the move for a general peace, should voluntarily release Russia from her formal bond not to make a separate peace and thus, rather than protesting the Bolshevik action, "leave it to them to decide whether they will purchase peace on Germany's terms or fight on with the Allies."[2] In making this recommendation, Buchanan was still laboring under the impression that in some way it might be possible to bring about a continuation of the Russian war effort. "If anything could tempt Russia to make one more effort," he said in his message, "it would be the knowledge that she was perfectly free to act as she pleased, without any pressure from the Allies."

"There is evidence to show," he went on to explain,

[1] This was evidently what House was referring to when he noted in his diary, on November 29, that the British military people had "made a mess of it and conditions could not be worse." (House MSS, *op.cit.*)

[2] Buchanan, Vol. II, *op.cit.*, p. 225.

that Germany is trying to make an irreparable breach between us and Russia, so as to pave the way for the German protectorate which she hopes eventually to establish over the latter. For us to hold to our pound of flesh and to insist on Russia fulfilling her obligations, under the 1914 Agreement, is to play Germany's game. Every day that we keep Russia in the war against her will does but embitter her people against us. If we release her from those obligations, the national resentment will turn against Germany if peace is delayed or purchased on too onerous terms. . . .

I am not advocating any transaction with the Bolshevik Government. On the contrary, I believe that the adoption of the course which I have suggested will take the wind out of their sails, as they will no longer be able to reproach the Allies for driving Russian soldiers to the slaughter for their Imperialistic aims.[3]

House and the British went over the Russian situation in detail on November 29. They were favorably impressed with Buchanan's suggestion. Lloyd George tried it out the next day on the French and Italians. The reaction was violent. Clemenceau insisted that a separate peace on the part of the Russians would be a betrayal and that "if . . . all the celestial powers asked him to give Russia back her word, he would refuse." [4] Because of this Allied division, no action was ever taken by the Allies as a whole along the lines of the British Ambassador's recommendation. Balfour, after further discussion with House, did send a message to Buchanan (about December 4) for the latter's guidance, outlining the British government's position. In this message, the British government backed away from the treaty itself as a basis for British objection to the Soviet separate peace, and justified the objection by reference to "deeper principles." [5] The message was made the basis of a long press statement put out by Buchanan on December 8; [6] but it seems to have had no effect on the Soviet leaders, other than to confirm them in the belief that there was no real hope of inducing the British to join them in the peace move.

The lack of agreement on Buchanan's suggestion only highlighted the importance of the great question in which House was principally

[3] *Ibid.*, pp. 225–226.
[4] *War Memoirs of David Lloyd George*, Vol. v, *op.cit.*, p. 2571.
[5] A draft of this message was reported to Washington by House, and appears in *Foreign Relations, 1918, Russia*, Vol. I, *op.cit.*, pp. 256–257.
[6] Buchanan, Vol. II, *op.cit.*, pp. 233–237. Buchanan's statement indicates that the final message was not appreciably different from the draft shown to House.

interested: the question of war aims. If the French and Italians would not agree to release Russia from her bond, it was all the more important to see that something was done to change, in effect, the meaning of the obligation. This could be achieved by a new and more liberal formulation of Allied war aims in general—one which would implicitly stamp the old secret agreements, now so widely discredited, as outdated and subject to reconsideration at the peace conference.

On the very day that House and his party were proceeding to Paris, Trotsky, as we have seen, was beginning the publication in Petrograd of the Russian Foreign Office documents relating to the secret agreements which had bound the Tsarist government to its European allies and in which the secret war aims of the Entente were revealed. News of this move reached the statesmen in Paris as they were beginning their discussions. While knowledge of the terms of some of these agreements was (as noted above) widespread in well-informed circles even prior to their publication, the general populace in many countries was obviously less well informed, and it was plain that the ostentatious and dramatic publication of the treaties by the Bolsheviki would carry knowledge of their nature to the broad masses of the populations in the warring countries.

There was already at that time considerable uneasiness over the question of war aims. It was the darkest moment of the war. Many people in the Allied camp were becoming increasingly worried and uncertain as to whether it was desirable to attempt to fight the war to the bitter end. The Russian collapse itself had added to this feeling, causing many people in the west to question for the first time the possibility of total victory. The feeling was growing that the wartime objectives of the Allies ought also to hold out some promise of being susceptible of negotiation with the Germans. To cling to extreme annexationist aims was, as many saw it, to play directly into the hands of the military party in Germany and to make it more difficult for the German moderates to advocate a reasonable accommodation with the Allies.

What the Bolsheviki were now doing struck into the heart of these doubts and misgivings. They were, after all, connecting their announced intention to take Russia out of the war with their charge that Allied war aims were cynical and imperialistic, and were calling for a general cessation of the war on a basis of "no annexations and no indemnities." This formula, coinciding very extensively as it did with Wilson's own feelings, constituted a sharp and well-aimed challenge to the war aims of the other Entente powers, especially as embodied in the secret agreements, and an effective blow at the unity of the Allies. It led, furthermore, to the impression in some Allied circles that if only the Allies were to formulate and put forward a liberal pattern of war aims, akin to the "no annexations and no indemnities" formula, Germany's unwillingness to do business on such a basis would be exposed, and Russia might be kept in the war. An image—quite inaccurate—was conjured up in many Allied minds of a Russia anxious to fight for idealistic and democratic aims but disgusted with the cynical rapaciousness of its western Allies and therefore easily misled by German and Bolshevik propaganda into quitting the Allied camp.

This view was encouraged by circles close to Kerensky who, tending in their desperation to grasp at any straws, nurtured a faint hope that such an Allied declaration might assist them to reassert their power in Russia. On November 20 two prominent members of Kerensky's party, Chaikovski (former chairman of the Provisional Council) and Skobelev (former Minister of Labor in the Kerensky cabinet), who had remained in Petrograd in a semi-underground status and at some risk to their persons, called on both the American and British ambassadors there and urged that an Allied conference be called for the discussion and determination of a new and more liberal statement of Allied war aims.[7] They indicated that in their view any attempt to unseat the Bolsheviki and restore the morale of the army could be successful only if they could "tell the army that the Allies were prepared to discuss peace terms with a view to bringing the war to a speedy conclusion." [8] Similar suggestions were made to the Allied governments by various Kerensky representatives and supporters abroad.

It was against this background—deep anxiety for the future course of the war, an awareness that Russia's departure from the war would mean the removal of at least forty German divisions to the western

---

[7] *Foreign Relations, 1918, Russia,* Vol. I, *op.cit.,* p. 238; Francis' telegram No. 2001 to the Department. Also Buchanan, Vol. II, *op.cit.,* p. 221.

[8] Buchanan, *loc.cit.*

front before spring,[9] and a realization that the existing position of the Allies with respect to war aims was tending to strengthen German morale as it weakened that of the Entente—that the problem of war aims presented itself at Paris.

It was House who pressed for a broad and liberal concept of the purposes of the war. "I am refusing," he wired the President on November 25,

to be drawn into any of their [Allied] controversies, particularly of a territorial nature. We must, I think, hold to the broad principles you have laid down and not get mixed up in the small and selfish ones.[10]

On November 30, in the light of the French-Italian refusal to release Russia from her bond, House proposed a frontal attack on the secret treaties, with their extreme territorial demands. "I intend," he wired to Wilson,

to offer this resolution for approval of the Inter-Allied Conference:

"The Allies and the United States declare that they are not waging war for the purpose of aggression or indemnity. The sacrifices they are making are in order that militarism shall not continue to cast its shadow over the world, and that nations shall have the right to lead their lives in the way that seems to them best for the development of their general welfare."

If you have any objections please answer immediately. It is of vast importance that this be done. The British have agreed to vote for it.[11]

To this the President replied as follows (in paraphrase) on December 1:

The resolution you suggest is entirely in line with my thought and has my approbation. You will realize how desirable it is for the Conference to discuss terms of peace in a spirit conforming with my January address to the Senate. Our people and Congress will not fight for any selfish aims on the part of any belligerent, with the possible exception of Alsace-Lorraine. Territorial aspirations must be left for decision of all, at Peace Conference, especially plans for division of territory such as have been con-

---

[9] The report of General Tasker H. Bliss, American Military Adviser in the Supreme War Council, enclosed with Colonel House's report to the President in mid-December, included this significant passage: "A military crisis is to be apprehended culminating not later than the end of next spring, in which, without great assistance from the United States, the advantage will probably lie with the Central Powers. This crisis is largely due to the collapse of Russia as a military factor and to the recent disaster in Italy. . . ." (Seymour, Vol. III, *op.cit.,* p. 303.)

[10] *Ibid.,* p. 281.

[11] *Ibid.,* pp. 281–282.

templated in Asia Minor. I think it will be obvious to all that it would be a fatal mistake to cool the ardor in America.[12]

Despite the President's approval, House ran into hopeless difficulties in his attempt to get agreement to his resolution in Paris. Lloyd George, in spite of his encouraging initial reaction, gave only perfunctory support to House's proposal when it came to discussion with the other Allies. The French, House reported, were "indifferently against it, Italy actively so." [13] Various alternative proposals were examined, but none on which agreement could be obtained.

The Provisional Government's ambassador in Paris, V. Maklakov, then complicated matters by entering the discussion with a draft of his own, obviously designed to tie the problem of war aims to the internal political situation in Russia and to create a state of affairs in which the Bolsheviki would stand out before world opinion as the obstacle to a liberalization of Allied war aims, rather than as the leader in the move for such liberalization. It was also clear that his proposed language would have committed the Allied governments publicly against recognition of the new regime in Russia. This was a commitment which the United States government, at any rate, was not yet inclined to take in any formal way.

Lloyd George attempted to reconcile House's and Maklakov's suggestions by combining them in a single document, but this was unacceptable to House.

The upshot of the discussions, House reported, was only a verbal agreement

. . . that each Power should send its own answer to its Ambassador at Petrograd, the substance of each answer to be that the Allies were willing to reconsider their war aims in conjunction with Russia and as soon as she had a stable government with whom they could act.

Note, once more, the implied assumption that Russia was leaving the war *because* the aims of the Entente were greedy and selfish, and that if the western Allies would agree to something like the "no annexations" formula the Russians would turn around and resume the struggle.

House reported this decision to the President by cable on December 2. In doing so, he added the following further suggestion:

[12] *Ibid.*, p. 282.
[13] *Ibid.*, p. 285, from House cable of December 2, 1917 to the President.

The Russian Ambassador at Paris believes it of great importance that you send a message to Russia through Francis or otherwise, letting them know of the disinterested motives of the United States and of its desire to bring a disorderly world into a fraternity of nations for the good of all and for the aggrandizement of none.[14]

House had already cancelled out this suggestion, however, by a message he had sent the previous day to the President. "I hope," he had wired,

you will not think it necessary to make any statement concerning foreign affairs until I can see you. This seems to me very important.[15]

In the light of this prior recommendation, there was obviously no real desire on House's part that Maklakov's suggestion should be acted upon in Washington. House had presumably passed it on merely in order to be able to tell Maklakov that he had not failed to report the latter's views to the President.

On House's own copy of the cable of December 1, asking the President not to make any statement on foreign affairs, House made the following endorsement:

I sent this cable to the President because I had in mind his making a statement giving our war aims. I tried to get this done at Paris, but failed. The next best thing was for the President to do it.[16]

Wilson, as it happened, was not in a position to accede to House's request not to mention foreign affairs publicly before House could get home. The Annual Message to Congress, which the President was to deliver on December 4, obviously called for a passage on foreign affairs. Wilson had already planned to devote a large part of the message to foreign affairs and specifically to the question of war aims. It was, as he said in his reply to House, impossible for him to omit foreign affairs from the address, since "reticence on my part at this juncture would be misunderstood and resented and do much harm." [17] However, as will be seen below, the references to foreign affairs and war aims in this speech were largely general in nature and did not preclude or prejudice the more detailed statement House had in mind. Preparation of this latter statement was begun soon

[14] *Loc.cit.*
[15] *Ibid.,* p. 286.
[16] *Loc.cit.*
[17] Baker, Vol. VII, *op.cit.,* p. 389.

after House's return in the middle of December (he left Paris on December 6), and found its fruits in the Fourteen Points Speech of January 8.[18]

[18] The content of these passages in the December 4 speech will be discussed in the next chapter. House actually approved highly what the President said on this occasion (". . . it was practically what I should have advised if he had waited until my return . . ."). But he regretted that the passages in the two speeches, that of December 4 and that of January 8, could not have been combined. He told this to the President when he got home. Wilson, he recorded, "did not agree as to the wisdom of this, although he did not dissent." (House MSS, *op.cit.,* Diary entry of December 18, 1917.)

CHAPTER VII

WILSON AND THE

WAR AIMS

THE Paris discussions had made plain only that the Allies were *not* prepared to counter with any bold and striking approach of their own the challenge presented by the Bolshevik demand for a general peace on the basis of "no annexations or indemnities." The French and Italians, in particular, seemed determined to cling timorously and jealously to the letter of their existing agreements, and to continue to hope that a sweeping final victory would yet make possible the implementation of these arrangements. This attitude on the part of the European Allies made more urgent in American eyes the need for an independent American move in the question of war aims, designed to redeem the Paris failure, to capture world imagination, to re-enlist the enthusiasm of Russia in the Allied cause. Both Wilson and House were imbued with this conviction. House, as we have seen, would have preferred that nothing be done along these lines until he could get home and thresh the question out with the President. Wilson, for a variety of reasons, felt impelled to mention the subject in his message to Congress on December 4.

What those reasons were, we can only guess. Wilson prepared his address, as he himself stated, "without consultation with anyone"; [1] and apparently left no record of the considerations by which he was moved at that time. But the address stands as one of the few reflections of his thinking with regard to Russia in those early weeks of Soviet power; and it may be useful to recall the background against which it was prepared and delivered.

Wilson had not addressed Congress since he had appeared before it eight months earlier, on April 2, to ask for a declaration of war;

[1] Baker, Vol. VII, *op.cit.*, p. 396.

nor had he, during that period, made any public statement adding appreciably to what he had already said about America's war aims.[2] In the message calling for the declaration of war, his exposition of the objectives to which the war effort should be directed had included reference to an earlier statement, namely his address to the Senate of January 22, 1917, on the subject of the "Essential Terms of Peace in Europe." As of the end of November 1917, the record of his views on the subject of war aims therefore consisted primarily of those two statements: the one made more than two months before we entered the war and at a time when America's entry was as yet not certain; the other delivered on the occasion of the declaration of war. Interestingly enough, it appears to have been the first of these two statements that Wilson still regarded, in November 1917, as the broader and more authoritative of the two.[3]

In this first statement the President had outlined the sort of peace which, in his opinion, the United States should be prepared to join in guaranteeing. He had stressed the principles of self-determination, of free access to—and freedom of—the seas, and of reduction of armaments, as basic in any such peace. He had emphasized that it should not be a punitive peace, not one "forced upon the loser"; it was to be "a peace without victory," but one secured "by the organized major force of mankind," which the United States would join in guaranteeing.[4]

In the second address (that of April 2nd, asking for a declaration of war) Wilson had described it as the immediate purpose of the United States

. . . to exert all its power and employ all its resources to bring the government of the German Empire to terms and end the war.

[2] The message sent to the Provisional Government on May 22, 1917 on the objects of the United States in the war was basically a repetition of the views put forward in these major speeches, and there is no evidence that Wilson himself regarded it as anything more than a restatement of his stated views. (The text of this message may be found in *Foreign Relations, 1917,* Supplement 2, *The World War,* Vol. 1 [1932], pp. 71–73.)

[3] We have seen above (Chapter VI) that it was to this statement that Wilson referred in commenting on House's effort to get the Inter-Allied Conference in Paris to make a liberal statement of war aims.

[4] Albert Shaw, Editor, *The Messages and Papers of Woodrow Wilson,* George H. Doran Co., New York, 1924, Vol. 1, pp. 348–356. The commitment to support of an international organization for the preservation of the peace had already been suggested in Wilson's earlier address of May 27, 1916, in Washington, before the League to Enforce Peace.

In this connection he had recapitulated the deeper and more long-term objectives which an American victory, as he saw it, ought to serve. Here, he had introduced an ideological note which had been missing in the earlier statement. The menace to the peace and freedom of the peoples of the world was now described as lying

. . . in the existence of autocratic governments backed by organized force which is controlled wholly by their will, not by the will of the people.

The peoples of the world must be liberated from autocratic power and the world thus "made safe for democracy." For this, the United States would fight, but it had no selfish end to serve. In particular "we desire no conquest, no dominion. We seek no indemnities for ourselves . . . ." [5]

Since the delivery of that second statement a number of things had occurred which affected the United States position with regard to war aims. Very shortly after America's entry into the war the President, overriding House's misgivings, had discussed the question of war aims with the British Foreign Secretary, Arthur J. Balfour, and had been informed by Balfour of the nature of some of the secret agreements existing among the Allies. (He was subsequently supplied by Balfour with the texts of a number of these agreements.) What views he had formed on this occasion is not definitely known. Colonel House's published papers give the impression that the President recognized that there was a serious and unfortunate conflict between the sort of peace implied by these agreements and the concept of peace he had himself put forward publicly as the one for which America was striving; but that he felt that in the end the weight of grass-roots opinion throughout the world would suffice, under his leadership, to overshadow and render obsolete these older and regrettable undertakings, thus clearing the road for the type of settlement he favored. If this view is correct, we may suspect that Wilson viewed the secret agreements with disapproval, disgust, and something akin to contempt for the narrowness of the vision they appeared to him to reflect. [6]

[5] *Ibid.*, pp. 234–247. Note that the Soviet slogan "no annexations or indemnities" was only a paraphrase of these Wilsonian words. The Soviet historian, I. I. Genkin, *op.cit.*, pp. 21–25, pointed out that Wilson's Fourteen Points revealed an acquaintance with the principles of the Soviet Decree on Peace, having in mind no doubt the "no annexations or indemnities" formula. Actually, Wilson had (as seen above) long anticipated the Decree on Peace in this respect.

[6] For reasons never fully explained, Wilson was later (1919) to deny before the

Wilson and the War Aims

At approximately this same time the new Provisional Government in Russia had, after initial vacillations, come out in favor of a disassociation of Russia from the secret agreements and of a non-annexationist peace. It had, however, decided to remain faithful to Russia's formal undertaking not to make a separate peace, and had endeavored, rather unsuccessfully, to carry on the war, hoping that some new general understanding could be arrived at among the Allies about war aims. In May, apparently in connection with the despatch of the Root Mission, Wilson had addressed to the Provisional Government a message recapitulating his views on the objects of the war. But this statement had failed to receive any real support from the other Allies, had been received with some misgiving by the Provisional Government itself, and did not find any appreciable echo in the Russian or world public when it was published.[7]

Now, more recently, the Provisional Government had been supplanted by an extremist group which had not hesitated to move toward a separate peace on the basis of "no annexations or indemnities," and which was busily engaged in publishing material from the Russian official archives dealing with the secret agreements, as a deliberate affront and challenge to the other Allies.[8]

On Sunday, November 25, just when Wilson had very much in mind the preparation of his message to Congress, despatches concerning these publications began to appear in the major American newspapers, where they can hardly have escaped the President's attention.

These circumstances, together with the news of the unhelpful reaction of the French and Italian representatives at Paris, must surely have heightened Wilson's impatience with the European

---

Senate Foreign Relations Committee that he had ever had any knowledge of a number of the secret agreements. The agreements to which this denial referred included some of those submitted to him by Balfour (see Baker, Vol. VII, *op.cit.*, pp. 74–75 and Seymour, Vol. III, *op.cit.*, p. 61). The texts of those published by the Soviet government were also transmitted to Washington by the missions in Petrograd and Stockholm (*Foreign Relations, 1917*, Supp. 2, Vol. I, *op.cit.*, pp. 447, 493–507).

[7] The text of this message appears in *Foreign Relations, 1917*, Supp. 2, Vol. I, *op.cit.*, pp. 71–73. For Francis' reports of the Russian reaction and the resultant delay in its publication, see *Foreign Relations, 1918, Russia*, Vol. I, *op.cit.*, pp. 86–97.

[8] The manner in which this step was understood in Russian circles can be judged from the statement of the Provisional Government's Foreign Minister, Tereshchenko, in May, to the effect that "the immediate publication of the treaties is equivalent to a rupture with the Allies and will result in the isolation of Russia. Such an act . . . will be the beginning of a separate peace." (David R. Francis, *Russia from the American Embassy: April, 1916–November, 1918*, Charles Scribner's Sons, New York, 1921, p. 121.)

Allies. Were not the Allied governments, by their reluctance to part from a pattern of war aims which—partly because it had never been fully and frankly revealed and partly because it reflected shortsighted and selfish impulses—could scarcely command the confidence of world opinion, playing directly into the hands of both the German and Russian extremists? This view was being put forward constantly by Bakhmeteff and other representatives of the Provisional Government. Was it not justified? Was it not precisely this lack of vision on the part of the Allies that had now enabled the Bolsheviki to appropriate to themselves—cynically indeed and to no good purpose, but with perfect impunity—the very concepts and phrases which *he,* Wilson, had considered fitting and important as the basis for the Allied position? And was this not resulting in a situation whereby these concepts and phrases were not only being prejudiced in their usefulness to the Allied camp, but were even becoming exploitable in German hands? If so, this was a matter of urgency. There was no time to lose in correcting these dangerous tendencies.

The Germans, it should be noted, had not been slow to seize the opportunity offered to them by the Russian peace offer and the publication of the secret agreements. On December 2, only two days before Wilson's speech, the American papers were reporting that the German Foreign Minister, von Kühlmann, in a speech before the Main Committee of the German Reichstag, had stressed the moderation of Germany's war aims and had said:

Those in favor of war to the extreme have come out into the open, demanding victory and nothing but victory. How they intend to use this victory is shown by the secret document [sic] published by the Russian government.

To this he added the ominous statement:

The principles hitherto announced to the world by the present rulers in Petrograd appear to be entirely acceptable as a basis for reorganization of affairs in the east.[9]

This was the bitterest cut of all. Kühlmann's statement, presaging Brest-Litovsk, the loss of Russia as an ally in the war, and the transfer of great numbers of German troops from east to west, confirmed the fact that Wilson's formula of "no annexations and no indemnities,"

[9] *New York Herald,* December 2, 1917.

instead of serving as a rallying cry for world opinion in favor of Allied victory, was now actually being used to disrupt the Allied coalition.

A further event that may very well have affected Wilson's thinking in the preparation of his message to Congress was the publication on November 29 of the famous Landsdowne letter in the *London Daily Telegraph*. In this sad and impressive letter, the Marquis of Lansdowne spoke not only from the authority of his previous experience as Foreign Secretary, Viceroy of India, and Governor General of Canada, but also as one who had lost two sons in the struggle. He questioned the desirability of fighting the war to the end and urged that an effort be made to reach a compromise peace on a basis that would neither involve Germany's annihilation nor deny her her place as a great commercial nation, nor place any demands upon her with respect to her form of government. Such a settlement, he suggested, might well be guaranteed by an international organization for peace; and in this connection he referred specifically to Wilson's speech at the banquet of the League to Enforce Peace on May 27, 1916.

Lansdowne's suggestion of an immediate negotiated peace was of course in conflict with the conviction, to which Wilson had now come, that the war had to be fought to the point of military victory. Lansdowne's ostentatious avoidance of the ideological issue—his obvious reluctance to see the Allies make an issue of the German form of government—was also at variance with the current Wilsonian line. But in several respects Lansdowne's ideas were very similar to Wilson's, particularly to those that Wilson had voiced before America entered the war.[10] It can only have been embarrassing to the President to have these ideas reappear, now, in a document which was bitterly criticized in many Allied circles, including a portion of the American press, and given a relatively friendly reception in Germany. This further evidence of confusion must surely have seemed to Wilson added proof of the need for an immediate clarification of America's attitude in this entire question of war aims.

[10] Wilson's message was widely interpreted in the press as a reply to Lansdowne (see summary of editorial opinion in the *New York Times,* December 5). Nevertheless, Lansdowne himself made a public statement welcoming the message and noting "with much pleasure" that it contained "passages which completely support the views I have endeavored to express." (*New York Times,* December 6, 1917.)

It is against this background of developments that the passages dealing with war aims and with Russia in the President's message of December 4 must be judged. The President stressed in the first part of this message that the formula of "no annexations, no indemnities" was correct and deserved to be sponsored and used by the Allies. The formula had indeed been misused, he said, "by the masters of German intrigue to lead the people of Russia astray." [11] That did not mean, however, that "a right use should not be made of it." Rather, "it ought to be brought under the patronage of its real friends." The war against German autocracy had to be fought to a finish. (This was perhaps the reply to Lansdowne.) But when that had been done, peace could then be based on "generosity and justice, to the exclusion of all selfish claims to advantage even on the part of the victors." The plain people of the world would in fact insist upon this.

There then followed a passage dealing with Russia, which was apparently inserted at a late moment, after the remainder of the speech had been drafted.[12] "All these things," the President said, had "been true from the very beginning of this stupendous war," and he could not help thinking that "if they had been made plain at the very outset" then—

. . . the sympathy and enthusiasm of the Russian people might have been once for all enlisted on the side of the Allies, suspicion and distrust swept away, and a real and lasting union of purpose effected. Had they believed these things at the very moment of their revolution and had they been confirmed in that belief since, the sad reverses which have recently marked the progress of their affairs towards an ordered and stable government of free men might have been avoided. The Russian people have been poisoned by the very same falsehoods that have kept the German people in the dark, and the poison has been administered by the very same hands. The only possible antidote is the truth. It can not be uttered too plainly or too often.[13]

From this curious passage we can only conclude that Wilson shared the belief that the victory of the Bolsheviki in Russia had been made possible by the unsatisfactory pattern of Allied war

[11] The text of President Wilson's Address to the Congress, December 4, 1917 will be found in *Foreign Relations, 1917* (1926), pp. ix–xvi.

[12] An undated draft in the Wilson MSS, Series II, *op.cit.*, apparently an early one, does not contain this paragraph.

[13] *Foreign Relations, 1917, op.cit.*, p. xiii.

Colonel Edward M. House (second from left in front row), embarking for the United States after the Paris Conferences of November-December 1917. The officer on his right is believed to be General Bliss

Edgar Sisson

Boris Bakhmeteff, the last Ambassador of
the Provisional Government to the United
States

aims, as presented to the world up to that point; and that if the Allies had been sufficiently enlightened and courageous to pick up the peace concept advanced by him on January 22, 1917, and to sponsor it boldly, the Provisional Government would probably have succeeded in retaining the reins of power and guiding Russia successfully to a better future. The Allies, in other words, by refusing to follow his lead toward a broader and more inspiring concept of the purpose of the war, had produced a calamitous confusion of the whole subject of war aims; and this, in turn, had made possible the triumph of the extremists in Petrograd, the "sad reverses" in Russia's progress toward democracy, the misappropriation of the correct slogans, and the departure of Russia from the war.

This view, based on the image of an idealistic and basically united Russian populace, prepared to wage war for broad and inspiring purposes but frustrated by Allied disingenuousness and cynicism and therefore turning in misguided bitterness to domestic extremism and a separate peace, had—as we have seen—been assiduously propagated by the leaders of the Provisional Government. More than once, they had pleaded with the Allies for a liberalization of the Allied attitude on war aims, which would protect them from the charge that they were pressing an "imperialistic" war. They had been rebuffed in their desire to have this question placed on the official agenda of the Inter-Allied Conference at Paris. Even after the Bolshevik seizure of power, suggestions had been made to the Allied missions in Petrograd by prominent anti-Bolshevik political figures to the effect that the situation might yet be saved if the Allies would only call a conference and discuss peace terms.[14] This was, in early December, still the line of Kerensky's supporters.

There was, of course, some substance behind these urgings. The members of the Provisional Government had indeed found themselves hard-pressed by the left-wing extremists precisely on the issue of war aims; and their inability to make satisfactory reply had unquestionably played into the hands of the Bolsheviki and facilitated their victory. But Kerensky and his associates needed and wanted such a modification of Allied policy not in order to permit them to *carry on* the war, but precisely in order that there might be some real chance of a compromise peace which would relieve them

[14] See Francis' telegram 2001, November 20, 1917, *Foreign Relations, 1918, Russia*, Vol. I, *op.cit.*, p. 238. Also Buchanan, Vol. II, *op.cit.*, p. 221.

of the inordinate political burden involved in the endeavor to continue the military struggle, permit them to demobilize the dissatisfied troops (thus depriving the Bolsheviki of a trump political card), and so enable them to proceed without hindrance to the consolidation of their power. The Bolsheviki could not have been disarmed or halted merely by a liberal statement of Allied war aims alone; they could have been disarmed or halted only if that statement had led to a cessation of the military effort, the continuation of which involved such heavy strain on the Provisional Government. This reality may never have been made wholly clear to the western Allies by Kerensky and his associates. Perhaps they were reluctant to face up to it consciously themselves, but it followed from the entire logic of the domestic-political position. And this goal—of a compromise peace—was not at all what Wilson and the other western statesmen were thinking of at that time.

In failing to perceive this point, Wilson, like many others in the western countries, was the victim of two misapprehensions. The first was an overrating of the importance of international affairs and international issues to the average Russian peasant-soldier and citizen in comparison with the domestic issues which absorbed them in the midst of this momentous collapse of their traditional political system. The second was the failure to appreciate the savage ruthlessness of the internal political competition in Russia, as well as the profundity of Bolshevik contempt and hatred for the capitalist world. The communist leaders were prepared to stop at nothing in their effort to seize the reins of power in a confused country and to eliminate all possible sources of opposition. No modification in Allied professions with regard to war aims could, alone, have weakened this purpose or affected in any way the violent antagonism and distrust they bore toward the capitalist governments.

The vast audience of eager, simple people, all straining to the same ideals, which Wilson conceived to be present in Russia and which he pictured to himself as following, in all its "naïve majesty," his statements and those of the other Allied leaders, was simply not there. In its place was a tangle of competing political factions, locked in a desperate and merciless struggle for power. For most of these contending parties the words, actions, and importunities of the Allied governments had importance only as they affected this domestic-political struggle.

CHAPTER VIII

LANSING AND THE RECOGNITION

PROBLEM

. . . this government must continue for the present a silent witness of the internal confusion which prevails in Russia. . . . —Robert Lansing, Secretary of State, to President Wilson, Memorandum of January 6, 1918

WHEN Secretary of State Robert Lansing left Washington on Friday, November 16, for a long weekend occasioned by the death of his father-in-law, one-time Secretary of State John W. Foster,[1] it was still by no means clear that the Bolsheviki had a firm hold on the capital of Russia. When the Secretary returned to his desk on Tuesday, November 20, the papers were still full of wild and conflicting reports on the situation in Petrograd, many to the effect that armies of one sort or another were advancing on the capital to overthrow the Bolsheviki. But it was clear from the available information that Kerensky, at least, had failed in his attempt to recapture power and that the authority of the Provisional Government was completely disrupted. The Bolsheviki were definitely installed in the governmental centers. If they were to be unseated in the near future, it would plainly have to be by some new political force—Kerensky could not do it. Clearly, the time was approaching when the United States government would have to take account in some way or other of the fact that a wholly new political personality was installed in the seats of government in the Russian capital.

During the course of the week, the news from Russia received anxious attention in the State Department, particularly the press reports of the dismissal of Dukhonin and the despatch of the first Soviet parliamentarians to the German commander. At the end of

[1] Maternal grandfather of Secretary of State John Foster Dulles.

the week, the problem of what to do about the new regime in Petrograd became acute with the receipt of Francis' telegram transmitting Trotsky's first communication of November 21. On Saturday, November 24, the morning papers carried the text of the Soviet note in despatches from Petrograd, and the Department's code room produced Francis' message transmitting the official text.

The broader questions of wartime policy raised by the Soviet communication obviously would have to be considered initially by the statesmen in Paris. But there still remained the question of the attitude to be taken by the United States government toward the new regime: whether, that is, to answer or acknowledge in any way its communication; whether, in fact, to recognize its existence at all and if so, as what—as the legitimate government of Russia or as a mere *de facto* local authority. At a time when diplomatic recognition was regarded more generally as a bilateral matter, this was clearly a problem for the United States government rather than for the Allied community as a whole. And at a time when the Secretary of State was regarded rather as a legal adviser to the President than as a maker of political policy, this seemed particularly a problem for study, in the first instance, by the Department of State.

The arrival of the Soviet note was accompanied by other developments which could hardly fail to influence the nature of the Secretary's reaction.

First of all, the Provisional Government's Ambassador, Bakhmeteff, still carrying on in the absence of recognition of any other Russian government, noted the report of the Soviet communication in the morning papers and lost no time in replying to it with a communication of his own to the State Department, which he released simultaneously to the press. In this communication,[2] Bakhmeteff stated that he refused to accept the authority of the Bolsheviki, whom he termed as "anti-national and not representative of the true will of the Russian people." In the existing conditions, he pointed out, the Embassy could not "exercise in full measure the most essential of its duties and activities"; but he himself, he stated, would remain at his post and continue to do what he could for his country and his people.

The courtesy and restraint of this communication could hardly have failed to contrast with the words of an interview given by

[2] As reported in the *New York Herald*, November 25, 1917.

Trotsky to a correspondent of the Associated Press and published in the New York press that same day. Asked what the Bolsheviki would do if the Allies failed to respond to their appeal, Trotsky had said:

If the Allied governments do not support the policy of a democratic peace, the Allied peoples will support us against their own governments. Our international policy is calculated, not for capitalist diplomacy, but for the support of the working classes.[3]

There could hardly have been a clearer way of stating that the Soviet note was not addressed to the Unted States government at all, but rather to the American "working classes," in the hope that the latter would take things into their own hands and oppose their own government.

Two other reports affecting the problem of recognition reached the State Department that same Saturday morning. One was a message from Colonel House in Paris in response to a query from Lansing about the advisability of continuing to ship foodstuffs to Russia. "In Great Britain," House wired,

. . . the Russian situation is considered at the moment hopeless. There is no responsible government within sight. I would advise making no more advances at present or permitting any further contracts for purchases. . . .[4]

(He followed this wire later the same day with a further message to the effect that he had just discussed the matter with the French Prime Minister, and "he earnestly indorses my opinion."[5])

The second item was a news report of Lord Robert Cecil's statement to the Associated Press to the effect that the separate peace move would, "if approved and ratified by the Russian nation," put the new government in Petrograd "virtually outside the pale of the civilized councils of Europe."[6]

On the next day, the Sunday papers (November 25) brought the news of the appearance in the Soviet press of the first of the documents from the secret Foreign Office archives. The Sunday *New York Times* also carried a story from its Washington correspondent telling of Bakhmeteff's defiance of the Bolsheviki and adding that

[3] *New York Herald,* November 24, 1917.
[4] *Foreign Relations, 1918, Russia,* Vol. III, *op.cit.,* p. 28; unnumbered telegram from House, November 24, 1917, 1 p.m.
[5] *Loc.cit.,* unnumbered telegram from House, November 24, 1917, 3 p.m.
[6] *New York Times,* November 24, 1917.

. . . it has not yet been decided, it is understood, whether the Allied countries shall withdraw their diplomatic representatives from Petrograd, this probably depending on the course of events in the next few days.

On Monday morning the Secretary found on his desk a further message from Francis, telling of the meeting of the chiefs-of-mission in Petrograd and of the agreed recommendation that their governments should not reply to the Soviet communication. It was now necessary to decide whether to accept this recommendation. The two communications—Trotsky's note and Francis' recommendation—were therefore sent over to the White House for the President's consideration, but without as yet any supporting recommendations from the Secretary of State.

The Washington correspondent of the *New York Times* wired his paper that evening that the Russian proposal was "now in the hands of President Wilson for consideration and for such reply as he cares to make." "At the State Department," the correspondent continued,

no comment was obtainable regarding the attitude of the United States Government but there is not the slightest chance that these peace overtures will be considered in any favorable light. . . . President Wilson will himself determine the character of the decision to be reached. . . . One of the points to be carefully considered will be whether the despatch of an answer to the note is to be construed as a recognition of the Bolshevik Government. . . . It has been suggested that care and tact should be taken not to flatly ignore the Bolsheviki and drive them to further excesses, and that the German agents in Russia would seek to make the most of an American refusal to reply to the note.[7]

On Tuesday and Wednesday, the State Department received sheaves of new reports about the Russian situation, all affecting in one way or another the question of recognition. There was more news about the Soviet armistice move. Underground leaders of the Provisional Government were allegedly organizing a new government at Dukhonin's headquarters. German officers had arrived in Petrograd "to advise Lenin." Trotsky was protesting that the Allied officers had committed an impropriety in addressing their communications to Dukhonin. Finally, there was the press story of Jud-

[7] *New York Times,* November 27, 1917.

son's first letter to Trotsky. This news must have been received with some amazement in the Department, since Francis had reported nothing about it.[8] Together with the news of the unfriendly reception of the Allied military protest, it indicated clearly that the question of contact between the Allied representatives and the Soviet authorities was becoming acute, and that if something were not done soon to clarify the United States position, complications might ensue at any time.

The problem as to whether to answer Trotsky's communication was not an easy one, for the recommendations were flatly contradictory. Francis and the other Allied chiefs-of-mission in Petrograd had advised that the Bolshevik request should be unanswered. Bakhmeteff, whose influence in Washington and with Colonel House was not negligible, was urging strongly that some sort of reply be made. In a cable despatched to House on November 30, a copy of which was handed to Counselor Polk for the Department's information, Bakhmeteff said that even though the communists had come into power by violence, their armistice proposal should not be left unanswered by the Allies, because this would only strengthen them in their efforts to create anti-Allied feeling in Russia. Nor, he said, should one approach the Soviet leaders with protests or threats. One should rather try "to formulate such theses concerning the question of war and peace" as would encourage Russian opinion to favor a continuation of the war.

The President was slow in making up his mind. In giving background to the press on Wednesday afternoon, November 28, the Secretary indicated that no decision had yet been made regarding a reply to the Bolshevik proposal—the government was waiting, the correspondents gathered, for more information about the relations of the Bolshevik leaders with German army officers and about the reports that Soviet parliamentarians were crossing enemy lines to open up peace negotiations.

The following morning, Thursday, November 29, the Secretary found on his desk a cable from Colonel House in Paris, addressed to the President and himself, and reading as follows:

[8] Judson wired a copy of his letter to Trotsky to the War Department, but the latter failed to provide the Department of State with any text of it at that time. The State Department did not receive the text, in fact, until 1930, when it asked for one to include in the *Foreign Relations* series.

There have been cabled over and published here statements made by American papers to the effect that Russia should be treated as an enemy. It is exceedingly important that such criticisms should be suppressed. It will throw Russia into the lap of Germany if the Allies and ourselves express such views at this time.[9]

What House had reference to was evidently the anonymously inspired press story of the preceding week about the holding up of supplies to Russia—the one Dukhonin had picked up. But actually there was a good deal more behind House's message than just the question of supplies. It reflected, as we shall see, the first adverse reaction in the British Cabinet to the suggestion that Allied policy should be oriented exclusively to the support of the opposition to Bolshevism reported to be gaining strength in the southern districts of Russia.

At some time on Thursday or Friday, November 29 or 30, Lansing appears to have either seen the President or communicated with him in some way on problems of policy toward Russia. What transpired on this occasion is not reflected in available records; but on Saturday morning, December 1, a wire was sent to Francis telling him that he was to make no reply to the Soviet communications, and informing him cryptically that "this Government awaits further developments. The President has made no statement." [10] Clearly, Wilson and Lansing agreed that there was as yet insufficient reason either to respond to the Bolshevik peace offer or to enter into any other form of communication with the Bolshevik authorities. But no statement of this policy was made at that time to the public. Newspaper men could get nothing out of either the White House or the State Department. Counselor Polk of the Department, in wiring to House's son-in-law, Auchincloss, in Paris on Saturday, December 1, could only report

. . . no action has been taken in regard to the Russian situation. . . . Secretary feels it unwise to make any statement which would drive present Russian Government closer to Germany.[11]

It was apparently at the end of this week that Secretary Lansing sat down to clarify his own thoughts on the entire problem by put-

---

[9] *Foreign Relations, 1918, Russia,* Vol. 1, *op.cit.,* p. 271.
[10] *Ibid.,* p. 254, Telegram 1875, December 1, 1917.
[11] National Archives, State Department File 861.00/743a.

ting them down on paper.[12] This document constituted the first detailed exposé of responsible American reaction to the Bolshevik Revolution. Before we examine it, it is useful to recall one or two further facts about the background of circumstances and information against which it was written.

Lansing knew that at that very moment the armistice talks between the Russians and Germans were beginning at Brest-Litovsk. He was well aware of the danger these talks spelled for the Allies. On the other hand, the reports appearing in the press and coming in from the Department's representatives abroad emphasized the fact that the Bolsheviki controlled as yet only a portion of Russian territory and that there were other important political elements in Russia who were not identifying themselves in any way with the peace move.

Consul General Summers, in Moscow, furthermore, had just transmitted and endorsed a significant message from Arthur Bullard to George Creel, received in Washington on November 30. The message was sent through the State Department with the specific request that it be brought to the Secretary's attention. Bullard, whose special relationship to Colonel House was presumably known to Lansing, and whose views must have carried some weight, advised against recognizing the Bolsheviki, but urged that "the reasons for refusal should be clearly and publicly stated." Trotsky, he pointed out, was claiming that Entente policy was dictated by the "capitalistic fear of social revolution." This argument had contributed importantly to the demoralization of the army. The refusal to recognize the Bolsheviki should be motivated, Bullard said, "not on repugnance to their fantastic social experiments, but on sound democratic grounds." He went on to point out that the Bolshevik seizure of power was a "minority insurrection" and that their influence was limited to a few well-defined localities. They would be able to hold power only by terror. He urged a strong statement from Washington that the United States was neutral about social reforms but

---

[12] The document is published in full in *War Memoirs of Robert Lansing, op.cit.,* pp. 339–342. Lansing did not state the exact date on which the memorandum was drafted; the language used in referring to it was as follows: ". . . On December second an armistice was arranged between Russia and the Central Powers, and thereupon I made a memorandum of my views on the situation, which embodied those that I expressed to the President in our later conference" (p. 339). This would imply that the memorandum was drafted in the days between December 2 and 4.

refused to recognize an undemocratic government of violence and terror.[13]

It was in the face of these recommendations that Lansing's memorandum was drafted. The Secretary began by recognizing that the Bolshevik faction was of such a nature, politically and ideologically, that it was impossible to give it recognition. It was characterized by a

. . . lack of any sentiment of nationality and a determination, frankly avowed, to overthrow all existing governments and establish on the ruins a despotism of the proletariat in every country.

To recognize the Petrograd Bolsheviki would be to encourage their followers in other countries. One should leave them alone and have no direct dealings with them.

The fact that the Bolsheviki had remained so long in power was already, as Lansing saw it, contrary to the logic of events. They would "of course" never succeed in bringing all of Russia under their power. Russia was faced with partition, disunity, terror, and horror.

It seems to me that Russia is about to be the stage on which will be acted one of the most terrible tragedies of all history. Civil war seems certain. The cities will be the prey of mobs, thieves and murderers. Factions will struggle for mastery. Russia will fairly swim in blood, a prey to lawlessness and violence. And then to add to those horrors will come the ruthless Germans to take from this struggling mass of humanity their lands and property and to force them to obey.

I believe that the Russian "Terror" will far surpass in brutality and destruction of life and property the Terror of the French Revolution. The latter at least possessed the semblance of government and made pretense of legality. Russia possesses neither. There is no authority, no law. It is a seething caldron of anarchy and violence. I can conceive of no more frightful calamity for a people than that which seems about to fall upon Russia . . .

The only remedy, the Secretary felt, would be for a military leader —a "strong commanding personality"—to restore order and set up a new government. But none had yet shown the capability to do this. There were several candidates, but he was opposed to giving them open support:

[13] *Foreign Relations, 1918, Russia,* Vol. I, *op.cit.,* pp. 270–271; Telegram 91 of November 27, 1917.

Their enterprise seems to me too uncertain and the whole situation too chaotic to put faith in any one group or faction. . . .

To sum up: it was impossible to recognize the Bolsheviki, but it was not yet possible to put confidence in any of their opponents. What possibilities remained? None at all. The Secretary ended with the conclusion:

"Do nothing" should be our policy until the black period of terrorism comes to an end. . . .

It will be seen from the above that Lansing was ahead of his time in recognizing the significance of the revolutionary internationalism of the Soviet regime. He also forecast with accuracy and force the years of civil war, terror, and suffering that lay ahead for Russia. He showed, at that moment, a sound and healthy skepticism concerning the various military figures who might be considered potential leaders of a movement against Bolshevism. He failed, to be sure, to foresee that in the end the communists would succeed in bringing all of Russia under their power. But at that moment, he could not foresee the early breakdown of Germany and the Allied intervention, destined to confuse so seriously the issues of the Russian civil war and to assist the Bolsheviki to a position of final ascendancy in almost all of the former Russian Empire.

Lansing's recommendation, as outlined in his memorandum, was essentially for a policy of "waiting for the dust to settle." He felt, however, that some public explanation of this attitude was in order. In this, we may suppose that he was impressed with Bullard's recommendation. He may also have been moved by the fact that on the 3rd of December the *New York Times* came out with a front-page story alleging, erroneously and apparently on the basis of the Kerth protest (the text of which Lansing had never seen), that the United States had made an "energetic representation in Petrograd against the separate armistice." In any case, on December 3-4 the Secretary drafted a public declaration of policy which he thought might usefully "be transmitted to Petrograd and, through some agency other than the Embassy, be given publicity there." [14] Here he followed closely Bullard's suggestions. The legitimacy of Bolshevik authority was denied. It was asserted that there was inadequate evidence that

[14] *War Memoirs of Robert Lansing, op.cit.,* pp. 343-344, presents the "draft declaration . . . in part."

the Bolshevik leaders were "the real agents of the sovereignty of the Russian people." On the straight ideological basis of American devotion to democratic principles, individual liberty, and the supremacy of popular will, exception was taken to the "class despotism" implicit in the Bolshevik seizure of power, as something "inimical to democracy." Americans, it was said, had greeted the Provisional Government with rejoicing. In the light of the German menace, the United States government had "naturally anticipated that the Russian democracy would . . . prosecute with courage and vigor the war. . . ." Now it had watched, "with disappointment and amazement . . . the open efforts of the leaders of the Bolsheviki to withdraw from the conflict even at the expense of national honor and the future safety of democracy in Russia." The world knew that Russia was "overwhelmingly democratic in spirit and purpose." Those who were now claiming to represent it were violating treaties, abandoning Russia's faithful friends, and making common cause with "the most inveterate enemy of Russian aspirations. . . ." Such a regime, the statement inferred (though it did not specifically so state), would not be recognized.

Lansing took this draft statement to the White House and laid it before the President on the afternoon of December 4, when the President had returned from delivering his report to the Congress. Lansing had this to say in his memoirs about the President's reaction to it:

The President did not think that it was opportune to make a public declaration of this sort at the time that it was suggested. He nevertheless approved in principle the position I had taken and directed that our dealings with Russia and our treatment of the Russian situation be conducted along those lines. From that time forward the policy of non-recognition of the Bolsheviki was pursued without variation, and was at last proclaimed by Secretary Colby in the summer of 1920. . . .[15]

This statement is correct, at least as concerns the *fact* of non-recognition itself (there were to be variations in *motivation* with the course of time). The policy of non-recognition thus may be said to date from that moment—December 4, 1917—and Lansing's unused memorandum may be regarded as its first authoritative expression.

The President's rejection on December 4 of the suggestion for a

[15] *Ibid.*, p. 345.

specific statement of policy on Russia was occasioned, no doubt, by the fact that he had himself made an important public statement that same day, and also by House's request to him that he make no further statements on foreign policy until he (House) might talk to him. But it was unfortunate in that it prevented any further guidance being given to Francis and the official establishment in Russia at that time. Francis had complained, in a letter of November 20 to Lansing, that "I have not received anything from you indicating that you are aware of the situation here." [16] A brief and cryptic little message sent by the Department on November 24 in another connection was, he later complained, "the first indication received by me that Department knew of revolution in progress." [17] He had now, to be sure, received the brief message of December 1, telling him to make no reply to Trotsky's communication and advising him that the government was awaiting further developments. But this message was a very thin basis of guidance for a man confronted, as the representative of the American President, with a momentous revolution of world-wide significance in the country to which he was accredited. The belief that it was safe, or fair, to leave an ambassador in this position could only have rested on a general lack of understanding for the realities of diplomatic intercourse. But such was the effect of the President's refusal to consider Lansing's draft of a public statement of the reasons for the decision against recognition; the idea of giving Francis some sort of *confidential* guidance, going beyond the published statements, does not seem to have occurred to anyone. For a long time to come, the Ambassador would have to act with only the slenderest and most cryptic evidences of the thinking of the government whose interests he was endeavoring to represent.

[16] Lansing MSS, *op.cit.*, Vol. 32 of Correspondence.

[17] *Foreign Relations, 1918, Russia*, Vol. I, *op.cit.*, p. 293; from Francis' telegram 2081, December 9, 1917.

CHAPTER IX

THE PROBLEM OF

ANTI-BOLSHEVIK RUSSIA

. . . Local organizations appear to have sprung up in south and southeast Russia which, with encouragement and assistance, might do something to prevent Russia from falling immediately and completely under the control of Germany.—Memorandum of the British Embassy, Washington, D.C., January, 1918

As we saw in the last chapter, the decision as to the initial attitude to be adopted by the United States government toward the Bolshevik authority was taken by the second week in December. But another decision remained, or appeared at that time to remain: namely, what attitude to take toward the local non-Bolshevik centers which, according to the best reports, seemed to be developing in outlying portions of the former Russian Empire. As of the beginning of December 1917 this question pertained primarily to the Ukraine, to the Cossack country around the mouth of the Don River, and to the Transcaucasus. The decisions eventually taken were based—like so many other decisions affecting the situation in Russia in those years —on insufficient and outdated information and proved to have no concrete results. Nevertheless these decisions are worth attention, both for the light they throw on the thinking of the statesmen in Washington and as precedents for later decisions concerning the intervention.

It is impossible to understand the actions and decisions of the United States government in these matters without some sort of picture of the developments to which they were conceived as pertaining. To describe this presents a difficult task. Rarely if ever can American statesmen have had to deal with situations more complex, chaotic, fluid, and obscure than those prevailing in the Ukraine, the lower valley of the Don River, and the Transcaucasus at the end of 1917 and the beginning of 1918. Any attempt to describe these situations with full precision would represent an undertaking far out of proportion to the significance of what was involved from the American standpoint. But the American reactions cannot be understood without at least a cursory glance at this confusing background.

Let us take first the region where anti-Bolshevik resistance seemed, initially, most serious and promising: the Cossack country along the lower reaches of the Don River.

❖

Throughout the latter part of November and the first weeks of December, the pages of the American press, as well as the official reports received by the State Department, were full of items dealing with General Kaledin and his Don Cossacks, portraying them as a powerful center of resistance to Bolshevik power, in fact as the likely source of its overthrow, as well as the possible nucleus for a revived "eastern front" against Germany. These reports, by the time they reached Washington, had been filtered through many mouths and inflated by many hopes. Only this fact could account for their consistently exaggerated and over-optimistic character. But they were, for various reasons, calculated to arouse the most eager interest in Allied circles, and to be grasped at there with a wishfulness no less than that which had entered into their origin.

The general dissolution of Russian centralism following the February Revolution had led, even prior to the Bolshevik seizure of power, to the formal re-establishment of some of the colorful autonomous privileges and powers of the Cossack communities in the Don Valley. By late summer the Don region again had as its nominal head its own freely chosen "ataman"—in this instance, General A. M. Kaledin, with his seat in Novocherkassk. At the time of the Kornilov uprising, in September 1917, Kaledin, although not participating personally in the uprising, had sided publicly with Kornilov. This demonstration was sufficient to cause Kerensky to proclaim him a traitor and to order his arrest and trial. But the expiring Provisional Government was too weak to enforce its own order. Kaledin successfully defied the authority of Petrograd, and continued

SOUTHERN RUSSIA

to carry on in the Don region, as the head of a virtually independent country. He thus became the bright hope of the strongly conservative and anti-socialist element in the officer corps, who had never had any sympathy for Kerensky and who were now wholly antagonized by his temporization with the extreme Left and his suppression of the Kornilov movement. Even before the November uprising, rumors were current that Kaledin was going to march on Petrograd and liberate it from its pains and disorders.

Having successfully defied Kerensky, Kaledin naturally did not dream of recognizing the later seizure of power in distant Petrograd by the Bolsheviki, whom he regarded as even less legitimate and more disreputable than Kerensky. As, then, the process of mutiny and disaffection in the Russian armed forces reached its peak in the weeks following the Bolshevik Revolution, anti-Bolshevik officers, in danger of being lynched if they remained with their units, tended in desperation to try to make their way to the Don territory in order to join Kaledin. The saying gained currency that "from the Don there is no betrayal into the hands of the enemy," [1] i.e. once in the Don region, one could be sure that he would not be delivered up to his enemies, the Bolsheviki. In particular, many of the senior military officers who had been arrested in the liquidation of the Kornilov uprising, including General Kornilov himself, General Lukomsky, and General Denikin, succeeded in escaping in the beginning of December from their place of detention at Bykov, south of Moscow, and in making their way to General Kaledin's headquarters. General Alekseyev, the last chief of staff and former commander-in-chief of the Russian army, had already preceded them there. Together these officers endeavored to establish, alongside the specifically Cossack forces of Kaledin, the nucleus of an all-Russian armed force, the so-called Volunteer Army, which could take up the fight against Bolshevism throughout Russia as a whole.

In addition to the generals, a number of anti-Bolshevik political figures found their way to Kaledin's headquarters in the weeks following the Revolution. Most of these were representatives of the so-called "Moscow Center," a liberal-conservative political group in which the Kadet (Constitutional-Democratic) party played a prominent role. These political figures endeavored to match the formation

---

[1] In Russian: *s Donu vydachi nyet.*

[163]

of the Volunteer Army by the creation of a new all-Russian political authority which could unite the anti-Bolshevik forces throughout the country.

This gathering of famous Russian military and political figures on the Don, following Kaledin's successful defiance of the Provisional Government, naturally tended to excite the hopes and imaginations of the Allied military representatives both in Petrograd and in Jassy (the temporary Rumanian capital), who were seeking desperately for some nucleus around which renewed resistance to the Germans on the eastern front could be organized. The developments were of particular interest to the British military and diplomatic representatives in Petrograd, whose pre-revolutionary ties to the court and other conservative circles had put them into close and sympathetic contact with leading Russian military figures.

It is interesting to note that the Kornilov uprising (of which the congregation of Russian generals on the Don in December may be regarded as simply another phase) had already been the occasion of some friction and difference of opinion between the British military representatives in Petrograd and the American Red Cross Commission there. Thompson and Robins, being closely connected with the S-R's, to which Kerensky himself belonged, tended to sympathize with the moderate Left of the Russian political spectrum, and this meant—at that particular phase of the Revolution—with the Provisional Government. The British military representatives, if not the British Embassy as a whole, plainly tended to sympathize with Kornilov and his associates. On November 2, on the eve of the Revolution, Thompson had taken the extraordinary step of inviting to his hotel suite, apparently for purposes of a political-military discussion, the British, French, and American military attachés, as well as a political and a military representative of Kerensky. The meeting had developed into an acrimonious dispute. The Russian representatives walked out in high dudgeon over remarks made by the British Military Attaché, General Knox, concerning the Russian military situation. The others did no more than develop a resounding disagreement, the British and French representatives insisting that only a military dictator of the Kornilov type could save the Allied situation, Thompson and Robins (apparently with General Judson's support) arguing for support of Kerensky and—one is allowed so to infer from Robins' reminiscences—for the Bolsheviki, if worst came to worst, for anyone, in fact, but the old officers and the upper classes.

During the remainder of November and the first part of December, as the leading figures of the old officer corps began to gravitate to Kaledin, British hopes naturally followed them. The prospect that Kaledin might hold out against the Bolsheviki and the Germans was of particular interest to the British by virtue of their special interest in Near Eastern affairs and the war against Turkey. The areas adjacent to the Don on the south—the Northern Caucasus, the Caucasian Mountain range, and the Caucasian provinces to the south of the mountains—led directly to the Turkish front; and the situation in these areas, while complicated and unstable to a degree which defies description in this compass, was at least marked everywhere by evidences of autonomous or non-Bolshevik tendencies which seemed to hold out some promise that the entire area might be kept out of Bolshevik hands and retained for the Allied cause. In this case, a strong position might still be maintained both against the Turks in the Middle East and against the Germans in the Balkans. The key to the development of these possibilities seemed to lie with Kaledin.

Actually, the situation in all the areas north of the Caucasian range was far less simple and less hopeful than the reports to the outside world seemed to indicate. Once the Bolsheviki were in control in Petrograd, Allied hopes necessarily ran to the promotion of separatism. Separatist feeling did indeed exist in all these areas; but it tended to be rivalled on every hand by political impulses common to Russia as a whole, of which Bolshevism was one. In the region of the Don, traditionally known as a Cossack region, immigration of non-Cossack elements had proceeded to a point where it had left the Cossacks actually in a slight minority. The newly immigrated non-Cossack portion of the population had little interest in Cossack autonomy; it tended rather to embrace all-Russian political outlooks. In addition, practically all the rank and file of the Russian armed forces, even including some of the Cossack units, were becoming increasingly disaffected by Bolshevik influence. As the rank-and-file members of the Cossack units found their way back from the front to the Don territory around the time of the armistice, they thus became a source of weakness and disaffection rather than of strength to Kaledin.

The situation in the Ukraine was no less complex. Here, too, the

February Revolution had unleashed strong separatist tendencies, particularly among the nationalist-minded Ukrainian intelligentsia. A regional authority called the Ukrainian Central Rada had been set up at Kiev during the period of the Provisional Government, had badgered the Provisional Government mercilessly to make concessions to its demands for a semi-independent status, and had by late autumn succeeded in extorting the assurance, on paper, of a high degree of local autonomy. Actually, however, the Rada lacked many of the powers requisite to even a federal status. It was composed of a relatively small circle of intellectuals and had no effective administrative apparatus. The borders of its authority were vague. Its political appeal was diluted by a great variety of factors, including—again—the presence of large non-Ukrainian elements in the population and the tug of all-Russian as distinct from Ukrainian political tendencies. Its authority, at best, was tenuous and feeble.

Immediately after the Bolshevik Revolution, an effort was made to work out some sort of collaboration between the Bolshevik organization in the Ukraine and the Rada, most of whose leading figures regarded themselves, after all, as socialists, although their interest in nationality was far greater than their class consciousness. This effort was brief and unsuccessful. The Rada proclaimed itself, if only provisionally, the sole repository of power in several of the southern governments. While the Soviet government was prepared to recognize the theoretical right of the Ukraine to call itself independent, actual defiance was another thing. Friction between the two political centers developed rapidly. In late December, the Soviet government established a rival Communist Ukrainian regime with its seat at Kharkov and undertook, shortly thereafter, military operations against the Rada.

In Transcaucasia, a wholly different situation prevailed.[2] Here, the Bolshevik position was weakest. The dominant political impulses came from the national parties of the three main nationalities inhabiting the region: the Georgians in the north and west, the Moslem Azerbaidzhani in the east, the Armenians (many of them refugees from the recent Turkish persecutions and deportations) in

---

[2] An excellent account of the development of the situation in Transcaucasia, as in the other outlying areas, will be found in the recent work of Dr. Richard Pipes of Harvard University: *The Formation of the Soviet Union: Communism and Nationalism, 1917–1923*, Harvard University Press, Cambridge, 1954. Much of the background section of this chapter is drawn from this work.

the south and the urban centers. Up to the autumn of 1917, the Russian armed forces stationed on the Turkish front had held well, occupying lines well within Turkish territory. At about the time of the Bolshevik Revolution, however, this army, too, began to disintegrate and its demoralized rank and file to flow back into Transcaucasia. This development was viewed with great alarm by the Georgians and the Armenians, who feared not only the inroads which Russian deserters might make on the good order of the region but also the possibility of Turkish pursuit and invasion. Even the Moslems in the east, while affected by strong pro-Turkish sympathies and therefore less apprehensive of a Turkish invasion, were sufficiently interested in the preservation of order to collaborate with the others in establishing a regional authority. Elements of an autonomous regional administration, embracing all three nationalities, had existed even in the period of the Provisional Government; now, immediately after the Bolshevik seizure of power in Petrograd, these elements were strengthened and welded together into a temporary regional government called the "Zakavkazskii Komissariat." After the dissolution of the Constituent Assembly, this administrative body was reinforced by a legislative diet, in which representation was based on the results of the elections to the Constituent Assembly.

The Bolsheviki had practically no popular support in the Transcaucasus except among the deserting Russian troops; and these were, for the most part, only temporary visitors in the region. In the elections to the Constituent Assembly, the Bolsheviki had received only 4.3 percent of the votes. In December 1917 they made an unsuccessful attempt to seize power by intrigue and force. This failure further weakened their influence in the regional center of Tiflis.

These were the centrifugal tendencies that were most important to the western powers in the fall of 1917, from the standpoint of restoring resistance to the forces of the Central Powers. Let us now examine the development of Allied policy with respect to them.

❖

The British and the French were the first to interest themselves seriously in the possibilities presented by the existence of these centers of resistance to Bolshevik power in the immediate wake of the November Revolution.

The origins and exact nature of British policy with respect to

Kaledin and the Ukraine are difficult to determine in the absence of publication of the British official documents bearing on this period. The British government was apparently urged, very soon after the Revolution, by its military representatives in Petrograd and in Rumania to extend every possible support to Kaledin; although one may suppose that it must have been difficult for these representatives to suggest precisely how such help could be extended in view of the isolation of that territory from most of the Allied world. Lloyd George relates in his memoirs [3] that at some time in November the British military representatives in Rumania recommended despatch of a French-British military mission to Kaledin, together with a grant of financial support up to £10 million. This recommendation coincided with a suggestion from Colonel House to Lloyd George (on November 20) that Rumania "should be made a rallying point for Polish and Cossack troops that are willing to continue fighting." [4] The idea appears to have been further discussed with the British, French, and Italian prime ministers at the Paris conferences in the end of November, who approved in principle the despatch of military representatives from Rumania.

It is clear that the British government, while generally sympathetic to the idea of aid to Kaledin, had prominently in mind the danger of placing itself in a state of outright war against the Bolsheviki and driving the latter into unnecessary intimacy with the Germans. In what was apparently a record of a War Cabinet meeting held on November 22, just prior to the Prime Minister's departure for Paris, it was recognized that:

. . . any overt step taken against the Bolsheviks might only strengthen their determination to make peace, and might be used to inflame anti-Allied feeling in Russia, and so defeat the very object we were aiming at. Nor was anything known of the actual position that would justify us, at this juncture, in backing either Kaledin or any other leader of the party of law and order. [5]

One derives from Lloyd George's memoirs the impression that feeling in the Cabinet was not unanimous on this question, and that he himself and Mr. Balfour, the Foreign Secretary, were most reluctant to incur any drastic break with the Bolsheviki at that time. This

[3] *War Memoirs of David Lloyd George,* Vol. v, *op.cit.,* pp. 2568–2569.
[4] House MSS, *op.cit.,* Diary, November 20, 1917.
[5] *War Memoirs of David Lloyd George,* Vol. v, *op.cit.,* p. 2565.

view was stated with force and lucidity in a memorandum prepared somewhat later (December 9) by Mr. Balfour for presentation to a Cabinet meeting at which he was unable to be present. Balfour recognized, quite realistically, that nothing could be done to keep Russia in the war. What was more important was to see that Germany derived as little economic advantage as possible from the armistice. Russia would not be easily overrun. The important thing was not to force the Bolsheviki into German arms.

If we drive Russia into the hands of Germany, we shall hasten the organisation of the country by German officials on German lines. Nothing could be more fatal, it seems to me, both to the immediate conduct of the War and to our post-War relations.

. . . A mere Armistice between Russia and Germany may not for very many months promote in any important fashion the supply of German needs from German sources. It must be our business to make that period as long as possible by every means in our power, and no policy would be more fatal than to give the Russians a motive for welcoming into their midst German officials and German soldiers as friends and deliverers.[6]

As of the beginning of December, therefore, it might be permissible to say that the British Cabinet, while intensely interested in Kaledin's fortunes and inclined to receive sympathetically the urgings of their own military representatives that aid be gotten to him at once, was wary of any course so drastic that it might tend to throw the Bolsheviki prematurely or unnecessarily into the hands of the Germans. The upshot of their deliberations up to that time was that no formal recognition could be extended to Kaledin, but this decision did not preclude the informal extension of aid, as recommended from Rumania and approved by the Paris conference. Thus, on or about December 7–8, the British government secretly authorized its agents in southern Russia and Transcaucasia to extend certain financial assistance to elements in southern Russia willing to oppose the Germans or the Turks, respectively. So far as can be gathered from the cryptic records available, this amounted to an offer of £10 million, to be extended through British representatives in Rumania to whatever Russian units could be persuaded to continue resistance on the southwestern (Ukrainian and Rumanian) fronts, a similar offer of £10 million to Kaledin or Alekseyev, and the promise of unspecified sums to any of the Transcaucasian peoples who could

[6] *Ibid.*, pp. 2577–2578.

be induced to continue resistance to the Turks. This action was taken clandestinely; not even the French were told about it at the time. The United States government appears to have learned of it only on December 19. Shortly after this approval was given, British agents began to appear in the Cossack region, ostensibly for the purchase of foodstuffs.[7]

French interest was concentrated primarily, though not exclusively, on Rumania and the Ukraine. This was perhaps a natural reflection of the extensive French military interest in Rumania and the close association between the Rumanian forces and those of the Russian southwestern front. The French, as will be seen later, entertained lively hopes that encouragement of separatist tendencies in the Ukraine might operate to keep that area detached from association with the Bolshevik peace move and thus actively engaged on the side of the Entente. Their interest in the Ukraine in the winter of 1917–1918 found its motivation almost exclusively in these unrealistic, but wholly understandable, hopes. Bolshevik propagandists, always reluctant to recognize what the World War meant to the western governments, tended of course to ascribe this French interest solely to anti-Soviet prejudice of an ideological nature, and to portray it as a sinister imperialistic intrigue against the Russian Revolution.

The United States government, although lacking any direct interest in the areas concerned, also found itself pressed, on grounds of wartime necessity, to take some action on behalf of the nuclei of anti-Bolshevik opposition in southern Russia and the Caucasus. The first urgings in this direction did not come from the Petrograd Embassy, where Robins and Judson were openly hostile to the idea and the Ambassador wisely passive, but from Consul General Summers in Moscow and from Consul F. Willoughby Smith in Tiflis.

Consul Smith was the son of an American family resident in the Transcaucasus, and was therefore closely connected personally with many of the local figures prominent in political developments there. This intimacy of personal association with the local community was not conducive to the maintenance of a position of detachment with relation to local happenings. Even during the period of the Provi-

---

[7] The British Embassy in Petrograd on December 23, 1917 issued a denial that there were British officers at Novocherkassk and added: "If some British railroad experts have passed through several sectors of General Kaledin, this was exclusively for the purpose of securing the shipment of foodstuffs for the Rumanian army and the civil population of Rumania." (Francis MSS, *op.cit.,* press item in Folder, December 21–24, 1917.)

sional Government, Smith's over-eagerness and tendency to exceed his competence had worried his supervising Consul General, Summers, in Moscow, and Counselor of Embassy Wright, in Petrograd. Now, in the wake of the November Revolution, Smith began to bombard Washington with lengthy and rather confusing telegrams about political developments in Transcaucasia and in neighboring regions and with pleas for authorization to extend financial assistance both to the new Transcaucasian regime and to elements on the other side of the Caucasus Mountains.[8] These pleas were accompanied by lurid warnings that unless he was able to act immediately, resistance to Bolshevism and to the Central Powers would collapse at once.

Smith's recommendations were based on the same concept that appears to have been prevalent in British military circles interested in the Near East and southern Russia. In a telegram of November 18, he pointed to the advantages to be gained by the Allies in holding a line from the Ural Mountains to the Volga and thence north of the Don Basin to the Black Sea, which would permit command of the grain, coal, and petroleum resources of all Russia, leaving the German army to deal with the chaotic and Bolshevik-controlled areas of northern Russia, where no substantial supplies of food or raw materials would be available. The logic and appeal of this concept, from the standpoint of the prosecution of the war, were obvious; but the physical problem of getting aid to the various non-Bolshevik authorities in that region was formidable.

By the end of November, Smith's reports had built up to such a pitch of urgency that even the complacency of the Department of State was shaken. On November 26 the Department responded for the first time to his appeals, with a somewhat sour request that he explain

. . . how under circumstances you describe the financial support you propose will not tend to encourage sectionalism or disruption of Russia or civil war. Department cannot encourage tendencies in any of these directions.[9]

It was clear that Smith's suggestions had aroused in the breast of official Washington that same attachment to the cause of centralism

---

[8] The situation was at that time further confused by efforts to weld the anti-Bolshevik centers north and south of the Caucasian range into a single governmental unit.

[9] *Foreign Relations, 1918, Russia*, Vol. II (1932), p. 582, unnumbered telegram to Tiflis.

elsewhere which caused the United States government to sponsor with such deep fervor, over the course of decades, the territorial integrity of China.

The Department was, however, sufficiently moved by Smith's pleas to transmit a summary of them to Colonel House in Paris and to solicit his opinion. The Colonel talked to his British, French, and Italian colleagues and reported:

. . . The inclination of England, of France, and of Italy is to give encouragement to the Transcaucasian movement.

But he added that he personally considered this dangerous,

. . . for the reason that it is encouraging internal disturbances without our having any definite program in mind or any force with which to back up a program.

He admitted gloomily that if these people were not given money and encouragement, they might well "go to pieces." [10]

So far as the Transcaucasus was concerned, the matter was brought to a head by the Soviet approach for an armistice with the Germans on December 2, and by the corresponding suggestion made by the Turks to the Russian commander in the Transcaucasus on December 5 to the effect that an armistice be concluded there, as well. Up to that time, the army on the Caucasian front, as noted above, had held together better than any of the other Russian forces. But the effect of Bolshevik propaganda in the wake of the November uprising was severe; and when the Russian commander met on December 5 with the French and British military agents and with Smith, to tell them that he proposed to enter on the negotiations with the Turks for a truce on the basis of the military *status quo,* he warned that he would not be able to hold any number of his troops in their positions, even in the event of such a truce, unless there was a prospect of financial assistance from the Allies. Smith's report of this conversation, received in the Department on December 7, indicated that the United States government must act at once, if it were going to act at all.

Just at this time, a similar impulse came from Consul General Summers in Moscow. On December 6 he wired an interesting message telling of approaches made to him indirectly [11] by General

[10] *Ibid.,* p. 584, from unnumbered Paris telegram of December 2, 1917, 1 p.m.
[11] These approaches came through Jerome Davis, Acting Senior Y.M.C.A. Secretary in Russia, who had seen Brusilov in the hospital.

Brusilov, who was at that time in a hospital there, and by an emissary of General Alekseyev, now at Novocherkassk with Kaledin.

Alekseyev and Brusilov, both distinguished and highly regarded officers, urged American moral and financial support for the anti-Bolshevik movement in the Don Cossack country.[12] (Alekseyev, incidentally, "strongly recommended" in this connection the occupation of the Siberian Railway by the Allies.) The receipt of this telegram, on the heels of Smith's last report, and in the face of Colonel House's obvious vacillation with regard to this problem, created a question of policy which the United States government could no longer ignore.

Summers' message was received Sunday, December 9. Secretary Lansing was visited at his home that evening by Major Stanley Washburn, with whom he discussed the Russian situation at some length.[13] Washburn, a journalist and war correspondent by profession, had covered the Russo-Japanese War from the Russian side, and also the 1905 Revolution that followed it. He had functioned as a war correspondent for the *London Times* in Russia during the early years of World War I (up to 1917), covering the eastern front from the Russian side. His articles, many of which had appeared in periodical or book form in the United States during the war, were well known to the American public. He had been assigned in the spring of 1917 as an aide to the Stevens Railway Mission, which was, in fact, largely the result of his suggestion. His assignment was switched, however, to the Root Mission, which arrived in Petrograd almost simultaneously with the Stevens group. He thus functioned as an aide to the Root Mission throughout its trip. In December 1917, therefore, he was fresh from the Russian scene.

As a result of his experiences, Washburn had extensive personal acquaintance with the senior generals of the Tsarist army. He had great admiration, in particular, for General Alekseyev, at whose headquarters he had spent considerable time.[14] It may be supposed

[12] *Foreign Relations, 1918, Russia,* Vol. ii, *op.cit.,* pp. 587–588, Moscow telegram 104.

[13] Lansing mss, *op.cit.,* Desk Diary, December 9, 1917.

[14] Stanley Washburn, *Victory in Defeat: The Agony of Warsaw and the Russian Retreat,* Doubleday, Page & Co., Garden City, N.Y., 1916, Chapter 18, "General Alexieff," pp. 172 ff. Washburn had been an enthusiastic and optimistic supporter of the Provisional Government. When he saw Lansing on this occasion, he had just completed a 40-day speaking tour in the United States, undertaken at the request of the Russian Embassy in Washington.

that, as correspondent of long standing for the *London Times,* he also had a considerable acquaintance in British military circles. At any rate, he shared the keen British interest in the leaders of the Russian officer corps as a possible nucleus for resistance to Bolshevism and to the Germans.

There appears to be no record of this conversation between the Secretary and Washburn, but it is clear that Washburn spoke with some enthusiasm of Alekseyev and other military figures involved in the Don enterprise and urged the immediate extension of every possible form of aid. His words evidently made a strong impression on Lansing.

In the light of these various stimuli, Secretary Lansing took pen in hand the following day (Monday, December 10) to clarify his thoughts on this whole problem for his own benefit and that of the President. The result was another memorandum from his own pen, the text of which is to be found in the official publication of Lansing's papers.[15]

It was, one must remember, only a week since Lansing had written his long memorandum advocating a policy of "do nothing." We may suppose that during the ensuing week he had continued to search eagerly for some way out of the dilemma. Washburn's hopeful words had given what he thought might be the proper clue.

The Secretary began by listing certain conclusions he had now reached:

1. The Bolsheviki were determined to take Russia out of the war. The longer they remained in power, the worse would be the prospects for any Russian military effort.

2. Russia's defection would prolong the war by two to three years.

3. If Bolshevik domination could be broken, "the Russian armies might be reorganized and become an important factor in the war by next spring or summer."

4. The only possible nucleus of a movement capable of supplanting the Bolsheviki was Kaledin. The question was thus: what support should we give to Kaledin?

Having stated these propositions, Lansing went on to develop the extraordinary thesis that the greatest danger to the Kaledin movement lay in its probable ignorance of American policy and in its belief, instilled by German and Bolshevik agents, that the United

---

[15] *Foreign Relations, The Lansing Papers, 1914–1920* (1940), Vol. II, pp. 343–345.

States had recognized the Bolsheviki. He therefore suggested getting a message through to Kaledin "telling the true state of affairs." He then went ahead to sum up the information he had (clearly from Washburn) on the various anti-Bolshevik military personalities in Russia and to forecast that this group would "in all probability obtain the support of the Cadets and of all the *bourgeoisie* and the land-owning class." He ended by asking for an opportunity to discuss the matter with the President after the Cabinet meeting the following day.

In contemplating this memorandum, which in the light of subsequent developments contrasts most unfavorably with the one Lansing had written a week earlier, one is moved to recall that it was Washburn who had been favored over Bullard by the State Department for inclusion in the Root Mission and who enjoyed the Secretary's particular favor as a source of expert advice in Russian matters. In the matter at hand, the Secretary would have been better advised to listen to Bullard, whose views, while admittedly less pleasing and encouraging, rested on a wider basis of acquaintance with political trends in Russia as a whole.

During the interval between the presentation of this memorandum and the Secretary's requested interview with the President, pressure for some American action continued to build up. The *New York Times* appeared Tuesday morning, December 11, with startling headlines about the success of various anti-Bolshevik factions [16] and with an editorial entitled "Hope for Russia," pleading both for extension of aid to Kaledin and for American intervention at Vladivostok. Kaledin, the *Times* said, was "as certainly our ally as the Bolshevik are certainly our malignant and unscrupulous enemies." Kaledin's resistance to Bolshevism showed that "Russia is not to perish without a struggle on the part of the honorable and intelligent elements among her people to save her." If the Allies should arrange to control the terminal of the Trans-Siberian Railway, and if Kaledin were to be in control of the coal fields, "it is difficult to see how the Bolsheviki could carry out the aid and support which they are trying to give Germany." So far as Kaledin was concerned, this urging could not have checked more closely with Washburn's views and with the

---

[16] "Cossack Armies Seizing Cities; Bolsheviki Overthrown in the Province of Orenburg . . . ; Kaledines after Moscow; Siberia Cuts off Food Supplies from Petrograd. . . ." were some of the headlines.

spirit of the recommendation which the Secretary had sent to the White House the evening before. One wonders, in fact, whether the editorial was not also the result of Washburn's influence.

During the course of the morning, the Secretary heard the advice of his chief aides in the State Department. (The memorandum which they drafted for him, on the subject of "Ukrainians and Cossacks," does not seem to be available in the archives, but it may be assumed that they also supported the idea.) He then received a visit from another distinguished outsider interested in these matters, whose visit may well, in fact, have been requested by the Secretary for the purpose of getting his advice on the question at hand. The visitor was Mr. Charles R. Crane, who will be remembered by many as a wealthy businessman, traveler, and observer, with a wide range of intellectual curiosity and a particular interest in those great branches of the human family—the Chinese, the Arabs, and the Slavs—which were least known in the United States. Over the course of the years from the early 1890's to the late 1930's, he made a total of twenty-three visits to Russia.[17] He was well acquainted with many prominent academic figures in the Slavic field, notably Paul Milyukov, one-time professor of Russian history at the University of Moscow and later leader of the Constitutional-Democratic party and first Foreign Minister in the Provisional Government, and Thomas Masaryk, who needs no description. A devoted patron of Russian studies in the United States, particularly in the University of Chicago, Mr. Crane gave support and encouragement to a group of younger men (among whom Professor Samuel Harper of the University of Chicago was the outstanding figure) for whom Russia constituted a deep and abiding interest. One or two of these men served from time to time in the Department of State. (Mr. Crane's son Richard was serving there at the time of this visit to Secretary Lansing.)

When Mr. Crane came to see the Secretary on December 11, he had only recently returned from Russia. He had been one of the members of the Root Mission, and the only one—be it said to his credit—who failed to share Root's optimism over the prospects of the Provisional Government.[18] This does not mean, however, that he was necessarily pessimistic about Kaledin's fortunes. There was some suspicion among American officials then serving in Russia that

[17] Paul V. Harper, Editor, *The Russia I Believe In, The Memoirs of Samuel N. Harper, 1902–1941,* University of Chicago Press, 1945, p. 6.

[18] See Lansing's memorandum of about December 3, mentioned in the last chapter (*War Memoirs of Robert Lansing, op.cit.,* pp. 343–344).

Mr. Crane himself was at that time giving private financial support to Kaledin. However that may be, Milyukov, whom Crane knew well, was one of those conservative figures who appeared at Kaledin's headquarters in the weeks following the Revolution, and such an arrangement would have been in no way surprising. In any case, it would not be unreasonable to suppose that Crane, too, urged governmental support to the Kaledin-Alekseyev movement, closely connected as it was with Milyukov and the Kadet party.

At 8:00 o'clock in the evening of December 11 the Secretary went to the White House [19] to discuss with the President the matters presented in his memorandum of the previous day. There is no record of the discussion, but it is plain that the upshot was a decision that it was desirable to extend clandestine financial support to Kaledin. Lansing had delicately refrained from putting such a suggestion on paper; but the fact that it emerged, as a full-fledged decision, from the talk with the President indicates how far Washburn's recommendations had reached, and how deep the impression they had made on the Secretary.

Wilson and Lansing, in arriving at this decision, recognized that there was no legal authorization for the direct extension of aid by the United States government to an unrecognized political regime. This they thought could be gotten around by the simple device of loaning the money to the British or the French and letting them pass it on to Kaledin.

A telegram was accordingly despatched on December 13 to Mr. Oscar T. Crosby, delegate of the Treasury Department to the Inter-Allied Council on War Purchases and Finance.[20] Crosby was advised that

The Russian situation has been carefully considered and the conclusion has been reached that the movement in the south and southeast under the leadership of Kaledine and Korniloff offers at the present time the greatest hope for the reestablishment of a stable government and the continuance of a military force on the German and Austrian fronts. While there can be no certainty of the success of Kaledine it is not improbable that he may succeed. . . .

Any movement likely to keep Russia in the war should, it was said, be encouraged "even though its success is only a possibility." Kaledin could not be openly supported "because of the attitude it seems ad-

[19] Lansing MSS, *op.cit.;* Desk Diary.
[20] *Foreign Relations, The Lansing Papers,* Vol. II, *op.cit.,* pp. 345–346.

visable to take with the Petrograd authorities." He could not be recognized because his group had not yet "taken form." The suggestion was then made for support through the British and French; and Crosby, with strict injunctions to secrecy, was instructed to proceed accordingly.

This authorization, as it happened, led to no direct results. The British, as we have seen, had already authorized financial support to the groups in southern Russia, and Crosby felt it unnecessary to make any offer at that time.[21] Later, he was obliged to report that the turning over of any large sums involved almost insuperable exchange problems. So far as can be ascertained, no actual use was made of this authorization and no official American funds were ever placed at the disposal of any of the early centers of anti-Bolshevik activity.

The American move represented, however, a major decision of principle, one that was to constitute an important precedent for later decisions in connection with intervention. But beyond this it contributed to an even more important decision on Russian policy arrived at independently a few days later by the French and British representatives at the meeting of the Supreme War Council in Paris.

The statesmen of the two countries—Lord Alfred Milner and Lord Robert Cecil, on the British side; Clemenceau and the new French Foreign Minister, Pichon, on the other—took advantage of their common presence in Paris to discuss the question of the attitude to be adopted toward the various political groupings competing for power in Russia. These discussions took place on December 22–23. Crosby had by this time conveyed his message, and the readiness of the United States government to help financially was taken into account by the French and British statesmen in their discussions. The talks resulted in an informal agreement for the concerting of policy with regard to the portions of southern Russia not under Bolshevik control, having particular regard to the requirements of the prosecution of the war against Germany. The agreement was embodied in a memorandum prepared, apparently, by the British military representative at the Supreme War Council and approved by the respective statesmen.

This Anglo-French memorandum [22] had such importance for Allied policy in the coming period that its terms may be worth noting

[21] *Foreign Relations, 1918, Russia,* Vol. II, *op.cit.,* pp. 591–592, London telegram 7999, December 18, 1917.

[22] The full text of the memorandum is printed in *Foreign Relations, 1918, Russia,* Vol. I, *op.cit.,* pp. 330–331, in London telegram 8090 of December 29, 1917.

at this point. It provided that the two countries "should at once get into relations with the Bolsheviki through unofficial agents, each country as seems best to it." [23] The memorandum went on to repudiate the idea of direct support for a counterrevolution against the Bolsheviki but to recognize the desirability of "keeping in touch as far as we can with the Ukraine, the Cossacks, Finland, Siberia, the Caucasus, etc." With respect to war aims, it espoused the principle of self-determination, "and this includes that of no annexation or indemnities." It stressed the importance of trying to assure that Russian military supplies and the grain districts of the Ukraine should not fall into German hands, and that the Transcaucasus be guarded against the development of a Pan-Turk movement which could link Turkey to the Turkic peoples of Central Asia. It confirmed the necessity of financial support for the Cossacks and the Ukrainians and indicated the desirability of the French taking responsibility for making this support available to the Ukraine, whereas the British would take "the other southeast provinces."

The memorandum was apparently supported by "resolutions" of the Supreme War Council confirming the danger to Allied military interest of any complete Bolshevik success in Russia and expressing the view that "it is necessary for the Allies to sustain by all means in their power all the national groups which are resolved to continue the struggle." [24]

The Anglo-French memorandum put the two signatory governments, as is readily apparent, into a posture vis-à-vis the various anti-Bolshevik movements in southern Russia similar to that already adopted by Lansing and Wilson in the case of Kaledin. It went further in that it spelled out the part each power would take in the implementation of general policy.

By way of implementation of this general agreement, there was also concluded a secret bilateral convention specifically defining the geographic areas in southern Russia in which each of the two powers would take such action as might be possible—the Transcaucasus and North Caucasus being allotted for this purpose to the British; Bessarabia, the Ukraine, and the Crimea to the French.[25]

[23] This provision was probably in part the result of Colonel Thompson's influence on Lloyd George; Thompson had passed through London and had seen Lloyd George in mid-December.

[24] See Ambassador Sharp's message to the Department, *Foreign Relations, 1918, Russia*, Vol. II, *op.cit.*, pp. 596–597, Paris telegram 2942, December 23, 1917.

[25] A text of this agreement is given in Louis Fischer, *The Soviets in World Affairs*, Princeton University Press, 1951, Vol. II, p. 836. It is described as "translated from

In this agreement the groundwork was laid, in some respects, for the later British move into the Transcaucasus as well as for the position to be taken by the British with respect to the Siberian intervention. The agreement similarly laid the initial groundwork for the French intervention in the Ukraine in 1918. In both cases, however, the subsequent movement of military forces onto Russian territory represented an expansion of the original concept. The 1917 agreement envisaged the extension of various forms of aid to the anti-Bolshevik forces operating in the respective areas, but not the landing of any foreign troops.

There is no evidence that the United States government was formally consulted with regard to the conclusion of this Anglo-French convention or was even provided with a text of it at the time.[26] Washington was, however, informed through Crosby of the general nature of the agreement.

❖

While the Allied governments were in the process of making these arrangements, the senior American officials in Russia had taken the initiative of sending American observers to the areas in question. Before we pursue further the development of United States policy in Washington toward the anti-Bolshevik groupings, it might be useful to note something of the activity of these observers.

On December 16, Consul General Summers despatched one of his subordinates, Consul DeWitt C. Poole, to the Rostov area, ostensibly to examine into the question of opening an American consulate in Rostov, but actually with a view to establishing contact with Kaledin and Alekseyev. Despite chaotic travel conditions, Poole managed to arrive in Rostov within a few days' time. On December 22 he pro-

---

the French original." The French text was obtained personally by Mr. Fischer from sources known to be fully reliable and may be regarded as authentic. Winston S. Churchill, *The Aftermath*, Charles Scribner's Sons, New York, 1929, pp. 167–168, describes the Convention without citing the full text. It is also mentioned by Crosby in Paris telegram 2955, December 27, 1917 (*Foreign Relations, 1918, Russia*, Vol. II, *op.cit.*, pp. 597–598).

[26] Leonid Strakhovsky, "The Franco-British Plot to Dismember Russia," *Current History*, Vol. 33 (March, 1931), pp. 539 ff., depicted the agreement rather luridly as an expression of the most predatory British-French imperialism. Consideration of the circumstances in which the agreement was concluded would not seem to bear out so dramatic a view; and one has the feeling that Mr. Strakhovsky might have viewed it somewhat differently after completion of his subsequent valuable researches into the origins of the North Russian intervention.

ceeded to Novocherkassk, where Kaledin had his headquarters. His arrival there coincided with that of a French military representative, General Hucher, from the French Military Mission in Rumania. Immediately upon his arrival, Poole paid a courtesy call on General Kaledin, and had conferences with General Alekseyev, Milyukov, and General Hucher. The following day, he wired to Summers, warmly recommending the immediate extension of financial aid, suggesting the exact channels through which it should be sent, and indicating that this was a joint recommendation from Hucher and himself.[27] Four days later, General Hucher received a message from the French government, indicating its readiness to make available the sum of 100 million rubles; and Poole joined the French general in informing General Alekseyev of this news.[28]

While this news probably appeared to Poole as the response to his and Hucher's recommendations, it was, of course, primarily the result of the Anglo-French agreement arrived at in Paris on December 22–23. It is not clear why it fell to the French, and not to the British, to implement the agreement so far as Alekseyev and Kaledin were concerned. The wording of the agreement itself was vague with regard to the Don territory, and there may well have been confusion between the two governments as to its interpretation. When a British general appeared, a fortnight later, he told Poole (according to the latter's report) that the Cossacks came "within British sphere" in what Poole understood to be a "reorganization" for the purpose of denying to the Germans the wealth of southern Russia and for protection against the Turks (an interesting reflection of the interpretation of the Anglo-French agreement in British military circles).

The French grant was heartening, but it did not meet the demand for actual currency, which Poole had emphasized in his message to Summers. Although efforts were immediately made to overcome this difficulty, there is no evidence that any sizeable amount of currency ever reached the leaders in the Cossack country in time to be of any appreciable help to them in maintaining their position there.[29]

---

[27] National Archives, Petrograd Embassy 800 File.

[28] While Poole's participation in these dealings led to no serious consequences, it was enough to arouse the ready suspicions of the Bolsheviki. A cartoon in the *Pravda*, January 5, 1918, represented Kaledin and the Rada as monkeys performing for an organ grinder labeled "Kadet Party," while Uncle Sam, accompanied by his French and British associates, tossed in the coins.

[29] A. I. Denikin, *Ocherki Russkoi Smuty* (Sketches of the Time of Trouble in Russia), J. Povolzky & Cie., Editeurs, Paris, (1922?), Vol. II, p. 192. In the discussion of

Encouraged by the evidences of Allied support, Poole, who had intended his visit to be brief, decided to remain and watch the course of events. It was not long, however, before he began to perceive that the situation was not as rosy as he had thought. On January 6 he was already mentioning in his telegraphic despatches the danger presented by Bolshevik influence on the younger Cossacks.[30] On January 14, in a telegram to the Department of State from Rostov, he was obliged to report that "from a military point of view the position of the Don government is lamentably weak." [31] The Volunteer Army, he reported, had only something between 1,500 and 2,000 men. It had no infantry. Its artillery was practically without ammunition. The whole enterprise was threatened both by internal disaffection and by Bolshevik military action. It was out of the question, he wrote, that Kaledin's Cossacks could play any serious military role against the Germans. Nevertheless, he felt that if the Bolsheviki were to make a separate peace and the Embassies should withdraw from Petrograd (both of which hypotheses were to become a reality within the next six weeks), the United States ought to support the Don movement, as the only serious nationalist movement in the country.

Actually, Poole did not know the full measure of the weakness of the undertaking on which Generals Kaledin, Alekseyev, and Kornilov were engaged. The local Cossack population, when the pressure became real, proved largely unreliable and failed its own Cossack leaders. Relations between Generals Alekseyev and Kornilov were strained. A satisfactory division of powers between these two distinguished officers was never reached. The arrival on the scene of new civilian political figures from the anti-Bolshevik leftist parties, particularly the Social-Revolutionary Savinkov, further complicated matters, introducing old political animosities into the camp and weakening its political attractiveness for others.

Poole returned to northern Russia in mid-January. On January 26 he was in Petrograd, where he reported to the Ambassador. By reason of circumstances to be mentioned later, the Ambassador was at that time in a position to tell him that Washington had no intention of recognizing any of the anti-Bolshevik forces in Russia.

the sources of financial support for the movement in the Don region, no mention is made of any sums being received from local Allied representatives.

[30] National Archives, Petrograd Embassy 800 File, *op.cit.*

[31] *Foreign Relations, 1918, Russia*, Vol. II, *op.cit.*, p. 613, from Petrograd despatch number 1036, February 6, 1918, containing Poole's report.

The Problem of Anti-Bolshevik Russia

With United States policy thus clarified, Poole made a second journey of observation to the Don region, leaving Moscow on February 7 and traveling some of the distance in cattle cars. He arrived about February 10 at a point some 100 miles from Rostov. This was as far as he could get. By this time Kaledin was being vigorously attacked by Soviet forces operating from the Ukraine and Poole was unable to advance beyond the Bolshevik lines.

Kaledin's position had become seriously weakened, due primarily to apathy and defection within his own Cossack community. Poole spent three days with the Bolshevik forces that were assailing Kaledin's stronghold. It was on one of these three days that Kaledin, filled with despair at the faintheartedness and treachery with which he was surrounded, committed suicide. Poole, failing to get through the battle lines, returned to Moscow, arriving there February 17. A few days later the so-called Volunteer Army under General Alekseyev (a national force which had been in process of assembly under Kaledin's protection) was obliged to begin its retreat into the northern Caucasus. Novocherkassk was taken by the Bolsheviki before the end of February. With that event, the center of Cossack resistance which had sprung up on the banks of the Don in the immediate wake of the Bolshevik success in Petrograd ceased to exist effectively.

While Poole was making his first trip to the Don district, Ambassador Francis similarly sent Consul Douglas Jenkins to Kiev, to look into the opening of a consulate in that city and to report on the political situation in the Ukraine. (Jenkins had been stationed in Riga, but had been evacuated to Petrograd when Riga was captured by the Germans in late summer, and was thus available for further assignment.) Jenkins left Petrograd on December 12 and proceeded via Moscow to Kiev. Just when he arrived in Kiev is not evident from the available documentation, but it must have been roughly simultaneously with the final break between the Rada and the Bolsheviki (December 17).

Jenkins had strict instructions from the Ambassador not to do anything, in the absence of further word from Washington, that could be interpreted as recognition of the Ukrainian Rada. He leaned over backward to be faithful to this injunction. He refrained from making even any courtesy visits on the Ukrainian officials after his arrival, and simply took up residence quietly in the city, as an unofficial American observer. It was his hope that he would soon receive some sort of instruction from Washington that would clarify his status. But none ever came. Fortunately, the strict instructions Jenkins had from Francis kept him from involving himself in that unhappy situation.

When the military situation became menacing, in the latter part of January, and measures were taken to compel all foreigners to leave Kiev, Jenkins was finally obliged to call on the Ukrainian Foreign Minister, Mr. Shulgin, in order to obtain permission to remain in the city. The permission was readily granted, and no very embarrassing questions were asked.[32]

In the weeks he spent as an observer in Kiev, Jenkins was witness to the melancholy spectacle of the rapid distintegration of the independent power of the Rada and the dismal failure of tentative efforts made by Allied representatives to influence the course of events in the Ukraine. The development of the conflict between the Bolsheviki and the Rada, in the early part of December, had naturally been followed with most eager interest by the French and British, who clutched at straws in the hope of rescuing at least a portion of the eastern front from the disintegration the Bolsheviki had brought. We have seen that on December 22, in the Anglo-French agreement at Paris, the Ukraine was assigned to the French sphere of activity. Even prior to that agreement, Allied representatives, primarily French, had begun to descend on Kiev, coming both from the old Russian headquarters at Mogilev and from the military missions in Rumania. The most prominent and active of these representatives was the French general, Tabouis, who arrived from Rumania almost simultaneously with Jenkins. Tabouis at once entered into relations with the Ukrainian authorities. He was soon given the designation of "Commissioner of the French Republic to the Government of the Ukrainian Republic," in which capacity he formally presented himself to the Ukrainian Foreign Minister in early January. Under the cover of this outward activity, French agents actually turned over to the Ukrainians very sizeable sums of money, estimated to have amounted to something around 50 million rubles.[33] Never was a political subsidy more disastrously wasted. No sooner had the

[32] National Archives, Petrograd Embassy 800 File, *op.cit.,* letters of January 2, 8, and 23, 1918, from Jenkins to Francis.

[33] Sisson, *op.cit.,* footnote, p. 269. The official Soviet history of diplomacy (Khvostov & Mints, Vol. 2, *op.cit.,* p. 316) says that France offered the Rada a loan of 180 million francs "for the struggle against Soviet power."

Ukrainians accepted it than Austrian and German influence began to show itself dominant in the Ukrainian capital, leaving the Allied representatives with the feeling of having been mercilessly double-crossed.[34]

It is difficult, in retrospect, to see how the situation could have been otherwise. The military and geographic realities were such that it was the Germans who, at that time, held the real cards in the Ukrainian situation. The Rada itself, to use the words of a private American observer [35] who was in Kiev at that time, was

. . . weak, compromised by its relations with the Bolsheviki and the Austrians, lacking dependable military force, and . . . a very artificial growth without much popular support.

Order could be restored, this observer thought, only by the Entente or by the Central Powers. But the Entente had no real means of affecting the situation. That left, by process of elimination, the Germans.

From the beginning of January events proceeded to take an increasingly unfavorable course from the standpoint of the Allies. The Rada, unwilling to be represented by the Bolsheviki in the peace talks, sent its own representatives to Brest-Litovsk, when the talks were reopened there in the beginning of January. This establishment of diplomatic contact with the Central Powers was accompanied by a gradual removal of those officials in the Ukrainian government who were identified with pro-Allied tendencies. At Brest the Ukrainian delegates set about to negotiate a separate peace with the Central Powers, by virtue of which German-Austrian influence could not fail to become dominant in Kiev. While these negotiations proceeded, the Bolsheviki, who had (as noted above) set up a rival Ukrainian regime at Kharkov, mounted a military action against the Rada under the leadership of a notorious adventurer, Lieutenant Colonel Muravyev (the same who was military commandant of Petrograd in the days immediately following the Revolution). This action should not be thought of as a regular military operation comparable to those in progress on the fronts of World War I. Muravyev commanded only 600 to 800 men, and a motley band they were. But in the chaos and

---

[34] Jenkins was also approached by the Ukrainians for financial aid, but wisely refused to have anything to do with the undertaking.

[35] Mr. E. T. Heald, a representative of the Y.M.C.A. In one of his despatches, Summers cited a letter he had had from Heald (*Foreign Relations, 1918, Russia,* Vol. II, *op.cit.,* p. 660).

social dissolution that gripped the Ukraine in the beginning of 1918, that was enough. The action, launched from the Soviet stronghold at Kharkov, proceeded successfully. Severe fighting began in and around Kiev on January 29, and continued until February 8, when the resistance of the Rada was finally overcome and Bolshevik power established in the city. These events did not, however, prevent signature of the German-Ukrainian Treaty at Brest-Litovsk on the following day. The leading officials of the Rada, forced to flee from Kiev, now had no choice but to throw themselves on the mercy of the Germans and to take refuge in German-held territory.

Actually, the Bolshevik triumph at Kiev was short-lived. Less than a fortnight later, the Germans, as a result of the breakdown of the negotiations with the Bolsheviki at Brest-Litovsk, renewed the offensive on the eastern front. German troops then at once advanced on Kiev. The Allied consular officials left on February 24, at the approach of the German forces. Mr. Jenkins made his way back to Moscow, in company with his French and British colleagues. On the first day of March Kiev fell to the Germans. The Bolsheviki were expelled. The Rada was re-installed for the time being, but naturally in a position of complete dependence on the Germans.

Before his departure, Jenkins went through some difficult days. The fighting in Kiev between Ukrainians and Bolsheviki in early February was sharp and ruthless. Jenkins estimated that 2,000 to 3,000 people were killed, partly in the bloody reprisals by the Bolsheviki after the capture of the city. A shell had passed through three rooms of Jenkins' own house, but he himself was unharmed. There had been some apprehension as to what attitude the conquering Bolsheviki would take toward the representatives of the Allied powers, but it turned out to be unjustified. The Allied representatives were apparently treated with full courtesy and permitted to depart without being molested.[36]

No special American agents were sent to the Transcaucasus, since there was already a regular consular establishment there. The conclusion of the Anglo-French agreement on December 22–23 was followed almost at once by the despatch to that area of a strong British military mission under Major General Dunsterville. From that time on, the situation in the Transcaucasus became, so far as the Allies were concerned, a British responsibility. The British motives,

[36] *Ibid.*, p. 672.

in such action as they were able to take at that time, were summed up in a contemporary British official document [37] as:

1. protection of the Christian Armenians from the Turks;

2. retention of as many Turkish troops as possible on the Caucasian front, in order to relieve pressure on Mesopotamia and Palestine; and

3. checking the Pan-Islamic and Pan-Turanian propaganda, in order that it might not create unrest in Central Asia, Persia, Afghanistan, and India.

These points illustrate the extent to which the British action in the Transcaucasus was connected with Turkey's participation in the war and with protection of Britain's interests in the Middle East rather than with ideological preconceptions against the Bolsheviki or with schemes for "partitioning" Russia.

As soon as the Franco-British agreement had been concluded in December, the Department of State made it clear to Consul Smith in Tiflis that his only instructions were to keep his government informed and to maintain close contact with the British and French representatives, nothing more. He was again reminded that he was not to commit the United States government in any way.[38]

Despite this admonition, Smith's understandable concern and eager activity continued to constitute a source of anxiety to his superiors in Russia as well as to the Department of State. Wright and Summers exchanged worried letters about him. By the beginning of March, the chief of the Russian division of the State Department was reduced to a point where he sent a despairing chit to Assistant Secretary Wilbur Carr (in charge of consular affairs):

Could we intimate to Willoughby S. to keep his feet on the ground and recall say 7 times a week that he is a Consul not Lord High Executioner? [39]

But no harm was done. With the British assuming responsibility the main problem was solved, so far as United States policymakers were

---

[37] This was a report dated February 9, 1918 on "British Measures in Trans-Caucasus and Armenia," prepared by a British officer (Colonel A. Steel) and made available informally to Ambassador Page in London. National Archives, Department of State File 861.00/1277.

[38] *Foreign Relations, 1918, Russia*, Vol. II, *op.cit.*, pp. 600–601, Telegram of December 28, 1917, 2 p.m. to Tiflis.

[39] National Archives, Chit attached to State Department File 861.00/1101.

concerned. Consul Smith gradually shook down into something more resembling normal consular activity.

❖

Throughout December and January, while these developments were occurring in the Ukraine and the Cossack country, Lansing remained keenly aware of the dangers involved in any form of actual recognition of these separatist regimes in Russia. In this respect, his views evidently coincided with those of the President. But again, as in early December, the two men differed about the desirability of making a public statement of the American position. On January 8, the day of delivery of the President's Fourteen Points speech, they discussed the possibility of sending a communication to the Soviet government stating more specifically the United States position on the problem of recognition of the various Russian authorities. Lansing, after discussing the matter further with Counselor Polk, thought it better to make the United States position known to the Soviet leaders through a public statement, and he submitted to the President on January 10 a draft [40] of what he thought would be suitable for this purpose. This draft read, in part:

> Although Russia appears at the present time to be separated or to be separating into distinct political groups, each of which claims authority over a portion of the territory of the nation, the Government of the United States is convinced that the spirit of democracy continues to dominate the entire Russian nation. With that spirit the United States feels a profound sympathy and believes in the ultimate effect of its cohesive power upon the Russian people as a whole.
>
> The separate independent authorities functioning in different sections of Russia present a situation to the Government of the United States which causes it to pause before formally recognizing any one of these authorities as the *de facto* Government of the Russian nation. The evidence of the possession of a right to exercise sovereignty over all Russia by a particular group of citizens must be substantially conclusive before recognition, otherwise a foreign government might reasonably be charged with exercising through recognition an influence in favor of a group and with improperly interfering with the internal political affairs of Russia.

In the remainder of the statement, Lansing expanded on the need for a "full manifestation of the will of the Russian people" as a pre-

[40] *Foreign Relations, The Lansing Papers,* Vol. ii, *op.cit.,* pp. 349–351.

requisite for a decision on recognition, on the kindliness of America's feelings for Russia, and on the disinterested motives in its desire to render such economic aid as might be possible.

The President evidently disapproved issuance of the statement, possibly for the reason that he did not want to dilute the effect of his own Fourteen Points speech by another public statement at that time.

The Department of State was nevertheless pressed, at that very time, to state to the French government its attitude with respect, specifically, to recognition of the Ukrainian Rada. On January 9 an official note was received from the French Ambassador in Washington stating that the French government was maintaining *de facto* relations with the Rada and that

. . . the reports it has received about Austro-German activities at Kiev led it to the conclusion that it could not defer any longer taking a more clearly defined attitude toward the Ukraine.

General Tabouis, the note went on, was

. . . therefore to be instructed to notify the Ukrainian Government that the French Government is glad actually to recognize it as an independent government.

The Ambassador inquired whether the United States government "would be inclined to take a similar step. . . ." [41]

In his reply, despatched on January 11 (before he had received the President's reaction to his suggested public statement), the Secretary of State stated cautiously that

. . . this Government is giving careful consideration to the whole situation, but as yet has reached no determination as to acknowledging separate governments in Russia.[42]

Four days later, however, in reporting the French démarche to Francis, the Secretary went further and told Francis that the United States government was

. . . not disposed as yet to recognize any independent governments until the will of [the] Russian people has been more definitely expressed on this general subject.[43]

[41] *Foreign Relations, 1918, Russia*, Vol. II, *op.cit.*, p. 655 (the note was dated January 7, 1918). Apparently, this notification was never finally made to the Ukraine.
[42] *Loc.cit.* (The reply was signed by Frank L. Polk as Acting Secretary of State.)
[43] *Ibid.*, p. 657, Telegram 1992 of January 15, 1918.

Thus the policy determination made in the Ukrainian case was one of general applicability; and although it was not made public at the time, it was important as a precedent for future problems of this sort arising out of the complex circumstances of the Russian Revolution and civil war.

✧

The United States attitude toward the early centers of anti-Bolshevik political activity may be summarized as follows. For a brief period, at a time when it was by no means certain that the Bolsheviki would be able to retain power much longer, the leaders of the United States government contemplated the extension of clandestine financial aid to Kaledin through the British and the French, in the hope of restoring Russia as a military force on the eastern front. Circumstances proved to be unfavorable to the contemplated operation, and no such aid was ever extended. At no time was *de facto* recognition of any of the separatist regimes seriously contemplated in Washington.

Washington's decisions in these questions had, of necessity, to be based on information which was almost invariably ill-founded and out-of-date. In the results, one sees an excellent example of the handicaps that rest, at the crucial moments of history, upon any government which is not supported by an affective apparatus for the gathering of information about events in foreign countries. The facilities at the disposal of the United States government in late 1917 for following the confusing torrent of events unleashed by the breakdown of the Tsarist system were wholly inadequate to the needs of American policymakers. If, in these circumstances, the United States government contrived to restrict itself to limited and discreet commitments, the frustration of which caused no serious damage or embarrassment, this was due to the instinctive prudence and circumspection of the statesmen in Washington, who were aware of the unreliability of the reports available to them and refused to be panicked or frightened into impetuous action. In the light of history, their caution seems more justified than the frequent impatience of their subordinates.

CHAPTER X

THE KALPASHNIKOV AFFAIR

This Sir Francis will have to break his golden silence. . . .
—*Trotsky, in the Aleksandrovski Theater, December 21, 1917*

It will be recalled that following the Judson incident the Ambassador in Petrograd asked Washington to confirm the fact that the ban which had been placed on contacts with the Soviet authorities applied to members of the Red Cross Mission as well as to members of the regular military and informational establishments. The telegram bearing this request was despatched on December 12. The events to which this chapter is devoted will serve to describe the circumstances in which the reply to that inquiry was received and the reasons why it was, in effect, ignored.

On December 15, German-Soviet negotiations, which had actually been inaugurated in Brest-Litovsk on December 3, were finally brought to an end by the signing of an armistice agreement. This agreement provided for a cessation of hostilities up to the 14th of January, 1918, and stipulated that the two parties would immediately proceed to the inauguration of negotiations for a full-fledged peace treaty.[1]

These armistice talks had been interrupted on December 5, and the Soviet delegation brought back to Petrograd, largely because the Bolsheviki could not yet bring themselves to conclude a separate peace and wanted to see whether there were still a chance either of revolu-

---

[1] *Foreign Relations, 1918, Russia*, Vol. I, *op.cit.*, pp. 260–263, Despatch 224, December 18, 1917 to the Department of State from Consul General Summers in Moscow contains a translation of the text as published in the Moscow press. A summary of the armistice terms is given in Judah L. Magnes, *Russia and Germany at Brest-Litovsk, A Documentary History of the Peace Negotiation*, Rand School of Social Science, New York, 1919, pp. 26–28. The Russian text is printed as Item 81, Klyuchnikov & Sabanin, Vol. II, *op.cit.*, pp. 97–98.

tionary developments in the capitalist countries or of the association of the western governments with the peace move. In this connection they had published in the *Izvestiya* as early as December 7 the draft of the armistice agreement as negotiated up to that point (largely the same as the final agreement, but without the naval clauses and the section concerning fraternization between the troops). Trotsky had officially communicated these terms to the Allied governments in a note dated December 6 and delivered that same day to the American Embassy in Petrograd. In this note,[2] Trotsky included in his description of the proposed truce terms the misleading statement that the armistice was to be made conditional on the obligation that the troops should not be moved from the eastern to the western front. He pointed out that the governments of the Allied countries had by now had plenty of time to define their attitude to the peace negotiations. He called upon them to say whether they were or were not ready to join the armistice talks and, in case they were not,

. . . to state openly before all mankind, clearly, exactly, and definitely, in the name of what aims must the peoples of Europe shed their blood in the fourth year of war.[3]

There is no record that this communication was ever given any special consideration in Washington, or that it was acknowledged in any way.

In the absence of any reply from the western governments, the Soviet delegation returned to Brest and the talks were resumed on December 12. On the evening of Friday, December 14, rumors began to circulate in Petrograd of the signing of the agreement. The terms were, as explained above, already widely known. The agreement was actually signed the following day, but the news was not officially released in Petrograd until Sunday, December 16.

Sisson, who appears to have been the first to get a copy of the final armistice agreement, came to General Judson's quarters after midnight Sunday and wakened him in order to show him the text. The General recognized at once that the clause on transfer of troops was meaningless. "The Russians have been tricked," he exclaimed, "as I told Trotsky they would be."[4] Sisson, already more skeptical about

[2] A poor translation of this note will be found in *Foreign Relations, 1918, Russia,* Vol. i, *op.cit.,* p. 258, Telegram 2072, December 6, 1917 from Francis to the Department of State. A better translation is given in Degras, Vol. i, *op.cit.,* pp. 17–18.

[3] Degras, *op.cit.,* p. 18.

[4] Sisson, *op.cit.,* p. 136.

Soviet diplomatic ethics, was not so sure whether it had been the Germans or Trotsky who had done the tricking, and suspected that the General himself had been the victim. He contented himself with observing drily in his memoirs, "There was trickery somewhere."

From that time on, the General's hopes were placed on the possibility of what he called a "failure" of the armistice agreement. He had recommended as early as December 6 that he be authorized in advance, for the event of such a "failure," to express "friendly appreciation" for the Soviet position and to promise to the Soviet authorities "all the U.S. troops the Trans-Siberian Railroad could transport," plus a "real" railroad adviser (apparently not Mr. Stevens), and "assistance on a large scale of every other character." [5]

What General Judson meant by a "failure" of the agreement is not clear. As early as December 23, i.e. even before the final German peace terms were revealed, he was to come to the conclusion that the psychological moment was already at hand for just this sort of approach to the Soviet authorities. But in any case, he was now barred by the President's instructions from having any direct contacts himself with the Soviet authorities. Despite renewed requests on his part to the War Department for a reversal of the ruling (once on December 15 and later at the end of the month), he was never to receive authorization to resume his contacts at the Smolny. The burden of contact with the Soviet authorities thus continued, as we shall see, to rest on Robins' willing shoulders.

On Sunday evening, December 16, as the news of the armistice was spreading throughout Petrograd, Robins had another of his frequent meetings with Trotsky. Trotsky assured him that if the armistice continued for any length of time there would be a continued ban on the transfer of troops (Robins seems to have failed to understand that the wording of the agreement left a practically unlimited loophole for the Germans in this respect); that there was no danger of any immediate commercial intercourse with the Germans; and that the joint commission provided for in the armistice agreement would not authorize any shipments of war materiel to the Germans.

These supplementary assertions on the part of the Soviet Foreign Minister were naturally of considerable importance to the Allied governments from the standpoint of the meaning of the armistice. Robins at once reported them to General Judson,[6] who presumably

[5] Judson MSS, *op.cit.*, report of March 16, 1918.
[6] *Ibid.*, Judson Diary, December 17, 1917.

passed them on to the War Department. There seems to be no evidence that they were ever brought to the attention of the Ambassador or the State Department.

The refusal of the Allies to join in the armistice negotiations, coupled with the continued failure of the proletariat of the western countries to overthrow their governments in the expected manner, confronted the Soviet leaders with the necessity of preparing alone— an isolated, inexperienced, precariously situated regime, with a disintegrating army—to face the formidable representatives of Imperial Germany at Brest-Litovsk. This constituted the first serious reversal of Soviet diplomacy, and it was followed by evidences of sharpest resentment on Trotsky's part, directed against the Allied representatives in Petrograd. One has the impression that once the decision was made to proceed independently with the peace talks, the men in the Smolny Institute saw no reason why they should continue to observe any particular restraint with regard to the Allied representatives. Both the British and French Embassies experienced at that time severe difficulties and embarrassments at the hands of the Soviet authorities.

So far as the Americans were concerned, Trotsky found the opportunity he was looking for in a curious incident which arose just at this time in connection with the Red Cross Mission. This was the so-called "Kalpashnikov affair"—as murky and confused a series of events, in the light of available written record, as any which the course of Soviet-American relations has to offer. The historian might have preferred to leave unchronicled this complicated incident, the substance of which was of no particular importance; but its implications for the play of personalities on the Petrograd scene and the light it sheds on conditions of the time are such that he has no choice but to attempt to unravel its tangled skeins, to the extent this can be accomplished after the lapse of nearly forty years' time and in the face of the continued unavailability of a portion of the evidence.

❖

Kalpashnikov [7] (referred to in the Soviet press as Kalpashnikov-Kama) was a Russian official who had been an attaché of the Tsarist Embassy in Washington for two years before the war. According to

[7] In his book, published in this country, Kalpashnikov used the somewhat unusual spelling of Kalpaschnikoff. In the sources used for this chapter the name was spelled in various ways. I have used the transliteration system employed generally in this volume.

Francis, he had at one time been secretary of the Cabinet of Ministers in Russia. When war broke out, being at the time in Petrograd on leave from his post in Washington, Kalpashnikov resigned his diplomatic status and volunteered for medical service with the First Siberian Corps. In November 1916 he was made commissioner general of the "Siberian Regiments, American Ambulance Society," which was connected with the Russian Red Cross, and sent to the United States to give lectures and to raise money for the purchase of ambulances for the Siberian regiments. He succeeded in raising a certain sum of money, with which he purchased 72 Ford ambulances and 8 light Talbot trucks.[8] These he managed to ship, semi-assembled, to Petrograd in 1917. He himself returned to Petrograd to supervise the assembling and distribution of these units. As it happened, he sailed from New York on the same steamer with Trotsky. At Halifax the Trotsky family was taken off the boat by the British authorities, separated, and held in confinement for some time.[9] Kalpashnikov allowed himself to be used by the British security officers on this occasion as an interpreter in Trotsky's interrogation—a fact which Trotsky understandably resented and found it difficult to forget or forgive.[10]

The personal overtones of this incident were peculiarly painful. Trotsky had the impression that his arrest and detention, in circumstances which he found both humiliating and onerous, were the result of denunciation on the part of other passengers on board. He cannot have failed to suspect Kalpashnikov of being at least one of the sources of this denunciation. This, incidentally, Kalpashnikov subsequently denied. In a memorandum written from prison in 1918, he maintained that he served as interpreter merely because he was the only person on the steamer *Christiania* who spoke both English and Russian well. His services, he claimed, were rendered in the general cabin of the second class, where "I acted as interpreter for forty persons, among them Mr. Trotsky whom before then I had not even seen in my dreams."[11]

Upon arrival in Petrograd, Kalpashnikov served for some time as

[8] National Archives, Petrograd Embassy File on Red Cross Commission, *op.cit.* Certificate issued by Embassy, December 14, 1917 for despatch of train to Jassy.

[9] Trotzki, *op.cit.*, pp. 268–275.

[10] The *Izvestiya*, on December 25, 1917, stated "Colonel Kalpashnikov courteously offered his services to these gendarmes and helped them to interrogate Comrade Trotsky."

[11] National Archives, Petrograd Embassy 800 File, *op.cit.*, undated memorandum marked "Rec'd, Jan. 10th, '18," obviously written by Kalpashnikov.

an interpreter for the American Red Cross Commission and apparently, on occasion, for the Ambassador. His ambulances presumably arrived in late summer, and he set up facilities in Petrograd for their assembly. Then, for reasons still unclear, he proceeded, still technically a representative of the Russian Red Cross, to Jassy, which was at that time the headquarters not only of the Rumanian government but also of the American Red Cross Commission in Rumania. He arrived in Rumania in September and remained there until after the November Revolution. His ambulances were meanwhile in the process of assembly at Petrograd.

It should be noted that the American Red Cross Commission in Rumania, under the command of Colonel H. W. Anderson, was at that time cut off from all access to the western world except through Russia. The American Red Cross Commission in Petrograd therefore served as its supply base. The situation had already, prior to the November Revolution, led to considerable friction between the two commissions.

The news of the overthrow of the Kerensky government, with the likelihood of Russia's early exit from the war, apparently suggested to Colonel Anderson and Kalpashnikov that the ambulances might well be used in Rumania rather than left in Russia, where there obviously would be no further need of them. In any case, Kalpashnikov, after a "conference with the Queen of Rumania," [12] the significance of which is obscure,[13] left Jassy hastily on November 8 and arrived in Petrograd, after an adventurous and hazardous journey, some ten days later. He brought with him a letter to Francis from Anderson asking the Embassy's help in getting the vehicles to Jassy. About the beginning of December Anderson wired Davison in Washington for permission to have the entire batch of vehicles

. . . transferred to this Mission . . . to be operated by Kalpashnikoff under my orders as long as we desire. He is to be attached to my staff. . . . Government here anxious for arrangement made.[14]

To understand the rest of the story, we must turn for a moment to the situation in Jassy. When Bucharest was occupied by the Central

---

[12] Andrew Kalpaschnikoff, *A Prisoner of Trotsky's,* Doubleday, Page & Co., Garden City, N.Y., 1920, p. 5.

[13] The Queen took a very active interest in Rumanian military hospitals and in the care of the wounded; this may have been the reason for the interview.

[14] National Archives, Petrograd Embassy File on Red Cross Commission, *op.cit.,* message forwarded to Washington by Francis on December 5, 1917.

Powers on December 6, 1916, the Rumanian government and court retired to Jassy in the province of Moldavia. There, under the protection of the Russian army, efforts were made to reorganize and stiffen the Rumanian army. The events of the year 1917 in Russia— the political revolution and the disintegration of the Russian armed forces—were disastrous for the Rumanian government. They left Rumania isolated and helpless in the face of the military pressure exerted by the Central Powers. The ignominious position of the Rumanian government and court in the autumn of 1917, pressed between the Germans and the Bolsheviki, was particularly excruciating for the Rumanian queen, Marie. She was a granddaughter of Queen Victoria as well as of Tsar Alexander II, and the leader of the pro-Allied party in the court. When the news of the Soviet approach to the Germans for an armistice reached Bucharest in the beginning of December, the effect produced on the Queen and her entourage was initially one of utter panic and despair. On December 3 and 4, immediately after the receipt of the news of the despatch of the Soviet parliamentarians, frantic conferences took place between the Queen and the Allied representatives in Jassy, and among the latter—conferences in which various schemes were discussed for the evacuation of the Rumanian royal family, together with a portion of the Rumanian army, through the south of Russia to the Caucasus. The Queen herself, it was envisaged, might eventually be removed to British-held territory in Mesopotamia. The Rumanian army units could remain in the Don country and join Kaledin in the reconstitution of a center of military resistance to the Germans on the eastern front.[15]

A deeply interested and sympathetic participant in these discussions was Colonel Anderson. The Colonel was a Virginia gentleman, with his full share of both the charm and the chivalry associated with that distinguished origin. No man of his background and temperament could have failed to be affected by a situation so dramatic and by the plight of a lady so beautiful, a lady who was, in addition, a queen. Miss Ellen Glasgow, in her recently published memoirs, has

---

[15] The Military Attaché at Jassy, Yates, wired to Washington on December 2: "Present plan is to withdraw Rumanian army if [necessary] to Caucasus and join Don Cossacks." He later reported: "On December 4, plan of withdrawal of Rumanian army was personally presented to prominent officials, Rumanian and Allied, and argument was made that there was still hope for success in South Russia." (National Archives, War Department Files, Chronological file of telegrams from Military Attaché, Jassy, 1917–1918.)

described with acid and delightful pen her own attachment for a Colonel S, who could be none other than Anderson, prior to his departure for Rumania, and the subsequent rumors of his devotion to the Queen and his schemes for her rescue.

The Colonel was suffering, they whispered bitterly, from delusions of grandeur. He had organized the whole unit on a military basis. . . . Tales were told of . . . Oh well, tales were told. . . .

. . . One insinuation hinted that more than a liberal share of the Red Cross money was given to Rumania. Another correspondent reported, indefinitely, that it was whispered that the gallant Colonel S- had attempted to rescue the Queen from both the Germans and the Bolsheviks. . . .[16]

To this it can only be said that the plight of the Rumanian court was indeed a bitter one, the Queen's distress acute and unfeigned. As for the Colonel's feelings toward the Queen, they were certainly romantic, and characterized by a devotion which ignored neither her sex nor her charm. But one cannot help but feel that had Miss Glasgow been able, at the time, to see the entries in the Queen's own diary concerning Colonel Anderson, her anxieties would have been less. The Queen's feelings toward him seem to have been confined to an amused appreciation of his chivalrous attentions. She relates with obvious enjoyment the degree to which she was able to wear him down by taking him along on her rounds of royal visits and of functions of protocol, and his own amazement at the fortitude of royalty in the face of social fatigue. On the other hand, she speaks with genuine appreciation of his friendship in a really desperate time, and confirms the wild plans worked out with him and with other Allied representatives for flight through the south of Russia. On December 3 the diary reads:

We had Vopicka, the American Minister, and Captain Walton, the American Military Attaché, to lunch and of course the situation was gone through with its chances for remedy, for existence, for flight, for defense; . . . we are so entirely in the dark, we can make no plans, take no decisions; . . .[17]

The following day, she wrote:

. . . The *gâchis* is complete and poor little Roumania is caught in the cruellest of traps. . . .

[16] Ellen Glasgow, *The Woman Within,* Harcourt, Brace & Co., New York, 1954, pp. 221–232.

[17] Marie, Queen of Roumania, *Ordeal: The Story of My Life,* Charles Scribner's Sons, New York, 1935, p. 269.

... finally, my friend, Colonel Anderson, appeared, who is entirely with me as to *resistance à outrance.*

The plan would be that with part of our army we should cut our way through the south of Russia towards the land of the still faithful Cossacks. It is only thus that I see our escape. . . .[18]

In these anxious circumstances, Anderson hit upon the idea of having Kalpashnikov's ambulances shipped, not to Jassy, where they would probably arrive much too late to do any good, but to Rostov. Just what he had in mind for the future use of these vehicles is not entirely clear. In a later letter to Francis, Anderson stated:

... I ordered these cars to Rostov as a matter of precaution, so that we might go out south if it was deemed necessary.[19]

He certainly had in mind the possibility that the vehicles might be of use for the evacuation of his own staff. It seems highly probable that he thought they might also be of help in moving the Queen and her entourage to the Middle East; but there is nothing to prove this. There is no indication whatsoever that he intended they should be used for any military purpose by Kaledin.

In any case, having concluded that he wanted the vehicles delivered to Rostov, Anderson despatched to Petrograd on December 5 two telegrams which were destined to have a fateful effect for Kalpashnikov, and very nearly for the American Embassy. One of these was a message for Kalpashnikov himself, sent through the Embassy at Petrograd. It read as follows:

... Provide for the possibility of dispatching all automobiles assembled or non-assembled to Rostov-on-Don with the first available train. Try to convoy them to Rostov personally. . . . I shall have ready for you further instructions in Rostov, or shall meet you there. (Signed) Anderson.[20]

The second message was to the Embassy at Petrograd itself. It invited attention to the message for Kalpashnikov and added:

... Please supply him for the purposes stated therein necessary funds up to 100,000 rubles. . . . It is most urgent that this matter be done at once so please assist Kalpashnikov in the matter in every way. . . .[21]

Later that week, Colonel Anderson addressed to Francis two letters explaining his desire to have the ambulances sent to Rostov. In one

[18] *Ibid.*, pp. 270–271.
[19] National Archives, Petrograd Embassy 800 File, *op.cit.;* letter, January 3, 1918, to Ambassador Francis.
[20] Sisson, *op.cit.*, p. 150.
[21] *Loc.cit.*

of these he gave as his motive for wanting the cars sent there his anxiety lest they "fall into the hands of the enemy in the event of further invasion of this territory." He said that Major Perkins, of his own staff, who was to bring the letters, "will explain more fully the plans of this commission." [22]

Since Rostov was the most important city of the area then under the control of Kaledin, it is easy to understand how this suggestion could readily appear to the suspicious Soviet mind as part of a move to get the vehicles into the hands of the anti-Bolshevik forces in the Don Cossack region, with a view to their being used in operations against the Bolsheviki.

Actually, by the time Perkins left for Petrograd on December 10, the situation in Rumania was greatly changed. The Queen's plans had been overruled. The Rumanians had themselves decided to seek an armistice with the Central Powers. Parliamentarians, representing both the Rumanians and the non-Bolshevik Russian command, were sent to deal with the German-Austrian command on December 6. From that time on, there were no further hostilities on that section of the front. By December 10 it was clear that there would be no flight of the court to the Middle East, and this evidently meant no immediate evacuation of the Red Cross Mission. Perkins left that night (December 10) with a last-minute oral message from Anderson that the machines were *not* to be sent to Rostov. The following morning (December 11) Anderson confirmed this by despatching to the Embassy at Petrograd a further telegram:

In view changed conditions here, disregard my 569 Dec. 5. Have motors ready for shipment on arrival Perkins who carries instructions. . . .[23]

❖

With this background of events in Rumania, let us now return to Petrograd and see what was occurring there. Colonel Anderson's first messages to Petrograd for the shipment of the vehicles to Rostov had, as we have seen, been sent on Wednesday, December 5. They appear to have been sent either in clear text or in a non-confidential code (since true copies, Sisson says, were later furnished to Robins for the

[22] *Foreign Relations, 1918, Russia,* Vol. I, *op.cit.,* p. 328, from Petrograd telegram 2144, December 26, 1917, to Department of State.

[23] Sisson, *op.cit.,* pp. 150–151. Anderson's 569 was the earlier message to Kalpashnikov.

Soviets). Just when they reached Petrograd is not entirely clear. They were received in the Embassy on December 7,[24] and we must assume that by that same date the Soviet authorities, who also controlled the telegraph office, had knowledge of their contents.

The Embassy at Petrograd failed to turn the messages over to Kalpashnikov or to the Petrograd Red Cross Commission, nor does anything appear to have been said to either of these parties about them. Thus the messages continued, for the moment, to repose peacefully in the Embassy safes. Why the Embassy held up their transmission remains a mystery. Was it just inefficiency and dilatoriness? Or was there some backstairs collusion with Robins which prevented their delivery? Nothing in the records indicates the answer.

Kalpashnikov, still blissfully unaware of the scheme to send his vehicles to Rostov, continued his efforts to despatch them to Jassy. In this undertaking, he was obliged to turn to Robins and his associates for assistance. The American Red Cross Commission in Petrograd was at that time preparing the despatch of a trainload of Red Cross supplies—clothing, footwear, etc.—for the Red Cross Commission in Rumania. The question was broached as to whether Kalpashnikov's vehicles, loaded on 35 flat cars, could not be included with this same train. Kalpashnikov took the matter up with the American Red Cross office in Petrograd on December 6, and received a most unfriendly reception. He relates that on the following day (December 7) he was questioned by Robins' assistant, Mr. Allen Wardwell, "as though I was some criminal capable of embarking on all kinds of questionable things." He was told, in particular, that Robins suspected him "of the desire of joining, with the automobiles, troops fighting against the Maximalists." [25] In particular, the members of the Petrograd Red Cross Mission endeavored, according to

---

[24] *Foreign Relations, 1918, Russia,* Vol. i, *op.cit.,* p. 321, Telegram 2132, December 22, 1917, Francis to Secretary of State.

[25] Sisson, *op.cit.,* Appendix, pp. 449–451; Kalpashnikov's letter to Colonel Anderson, December 19, 1917. Kalpashnikov's side of this story is told with great feeling and vehemence in his book, *op.cit.,* which includes a foreword by Ambassador Francis, written presumably early in 1920 after both men had returned to the United States. The foreword is sympathetic to Kalpashnikov but seriously inaccurate in important points. The most detailed and objective account of the incident is given in Sisson, *op.cit.* Sisson, at that time a relatively detached observer, later collected materials on the case with amazing thoroughness and brought them together in his book; he was, however, not fully informed on the Rumanian side of the story. William Hard, *Raymond Robins' Own Story,* Harper & Brothers, New York, 1920, includes some colorful but characteristically vague and anecdotal passages concerning the incident. Francis makes reference to it in his own memoirs, *Russia from the American Embassy, op.cit.*

Kalpashnikov, to learn from him "the names and general description of my chauffeurs," a circumstance which he evidently took as evidence that the mission was serving as an outpost of Soviet intelligence.

Since the Red Cross Commission had not yet received the texts of the telegrams from the Embassy, it is difficult to imagine where Robins could have derived his suspicions about the vehicles being sent to Rostov if not from the Soviet authorities or through some informant in the Embassy Chancery. He had been to Smolny on both the 5th and the 7th. On the latter occasion he had discussed with Trotsky the matter of the shipment of the trainload of supplies to Rumania.[26] Later in the day he recorded in his pocket diary: "The wires from Anderson are confused and confusing." What wires? Where had he seen them?

Trotsky claimed, in a subsequent public speech, that the news reached him only at a later date.

On Tuesday, December 11, Robins referred again, in his pocket diary, to a "cable from Anderson that looks bad." Surely Robins by this time had *some* knowledge of the messages concerning the ambulances.

On Friday, December 14, the Embassy, having by this time received Anderson's third message cancelling the Rostov arrangements, delivered all three messages to the Red Cross Commission and issued a certificate for the Soviet authorities requesting permission for despatch of the train to Jassy, to include the ambulances. The following morning, December 15, the Red Cross Mission transmitted copies of the telegrams to Kalpashnikov, who learned in this way, for the first time, of the now-cancelled plan to send the vehicles to Rostov.

The next morning, Sunday, December 16, Major Roger Perkins of Anderson's staff arrived in Petrograd on his way to the United States, with instructions to arrange for the final shipment of the vehicles to Jassy. He was accompanied by a Russian assistant of Colonel Anderson's, one Verblunsky. On arrival in Petrograd, Perkins immediately called at the Red Cross office in the Hotel d'Europe. There ensued three days of tense, heated, and confused conferences between Perkins and the chiefs of the Red Cross Commission, before Perkins left

---

[26] In his speech delivered December 21, Trotsky said: "Colonel Robins came to me two weeks ago to make arrangements that a Red Cross train for Jassy should proceed without any obstacles being placed in its way. . . ." (Sisson, *op.cit.,* p. 152.)

again, via Siberia, on his way home. As to what took place in these conferences, there is only the report of the Petrograd Red Cross Commission.[27] (To judge by the remaining available documentation on the case, Perkins' own account might have been somewhat different.) There was now no longer any question of sending the vehicles to Rostov. Perkins was uncertain whether, in view of the situation in Rumania, the trainload of supplies for Jassy ought to be despatched at all. Robins, however, favored its despatch, and Perkins finally agreed. He wished then, however, to include in the shipment twelve of the ambulances, which he thought Anderson might need at any time for the evacuation of his own mission. This Robins opposed, on the grounds that in view of the likelihood of an immediate outbreak of civil war between the Bolsheviki and the Ukrainian Rada, "he regarded it as impossible to ship with the other supplies any motor cars whatsoever." Evidently, the same suspicions which had previously attached to the despatch of the cars to the Kaledin country now arose in connection with their despatch across the disaffected Ukraine to Rumania.

On Monday evening, December 17, a resounding disagreement developed between Perkins and Robins, the latter insisting that the other supplies could go forward, but that the motor cars must not be moved. The meeting ended with Robins walking out in a huff. It had been, he recorded in his diary, an "ugly and awkward day." Both he and Perkins had lost their tempers.

On Tuesday, according to the Red Cross report:

. . . Col. Robins had an interview with the representatives of the Russian de facto government as the result of which he received written instructions authorizing the dispatch of the train of cars containing clothing and other materials for civilian relief, but that no motor cars could be transported.

(The "written instructions" were in the form of a letter from Trotsky himself.) This dictum was communicated to Perkins, who had no choice but to accept the situation.

In the course of these conferences, Wardwell and Thacher, representing Robins, appeared to place considerable importance on the question as to whether Kalpashnikov and Verblunsky were to accompany the train personally. At one time, according to Kalpashnikov,

[27] *Ibid.*, pp. 452–455, Appendix, "Memorandum of Interviews with Major Perkins" compiled, according to Sisson, by the American Red Cross Staff at Petrograd, December 18, 1917.

they even went so far as to indicate that if these men would refrain from going, there would be no difficulty about the release of the vehicles. (Even this was later overruled by Robins.) Finally, they hinted to Perkins that Verblunsky was in danger of arrest, and that Kalpashnikov's situation might not be much better.[28] They did not, however, indicate to Perkins the source of their information. Perkins and Kalpashnikov found it difficult to judge whether the difficulties they were encountering really reflected the attitude of the Soviet authorities alone or whether it was the result of the hostility and suspicion borne them by Robins himself.

Perkins, frustrated and much disturbed, left Petrograd on Tuesday evening, December 18, after writing a long letter to Anderson reporting all his difficulties and leaving it with Kalpashnikov to despatch. He also warned both Kalpashnikov and Verblunsky that they were in danger of arrest. Verblunsky, in the light of this warning, left that same evening for parts unknown, thus disappointing both the Soviet secret police and his partner, whom he failed to tell of his plans. Kalpashnikov remained to await his uncertain fate. In view of his personal part in the interrogation of Trotsky at Halifax, he obviously had no reason to expect benevolence at Trotsky's hands.

By Thursday, December 20, Kalpashnikov, seriously alarmed over the warning he had received from Perkins, had apparently come to the conclusion that the only thing for him to do was to bypass the local American Red Cross Commission, get a separate train for his vehicles, and move them all, himself as well, out of Petrograd as rapidly as possible. Requiring for this further cooperation from the Embassy, he went to the American Naval Attaché, Captain Walter S. Crosley, and told him his tale. What Captain Crosley's relation to the matter was, if any other than that of a sympathetic listener, is not clear; but in any case, he took Kalpashnikov to see the Ambassador.

They found the Ambassador "smoking a cigar in the company of General Judson." The two men were in a gloomy mood. The recent suppression by the Bolsheviki of the first efforts of the delegates to the Constituent Assembly to convene in Petrograd (more will be told of this later) had begun to blast the last hopes in Allied circles that Soviet power might be brought to an end by orderly processes. The previous evening Francis had wired the Secretary of State:

[28] *Ibid.*, pp. 156–159, Perkins' letter to Anderson of December 17. Also Kalpaschnikoff, *op.cit.*

The Kalpashkov Affair

Yesterday for the first time I began to feel disgust and despair because for six weeks Russia had permitted the bolcheviks to remain in control, and I did not, therefore, send any cable.[29]

On top of this discouragement, the morning papers had brought another fiery appeal from Trotsky, calling on the workers and soldiers of the warring countries

. . . to wrest the issue of war and peace from the criminal hands of the bourgeoisie. . . . This is the only road to salvation for you and us. Consolidate your ranks, proletarians of the world, under the banner of peace and social revolution.[30]

Kalpashnikov told the Ambassador of Perkins' experiences, and of the latter's warning that he himself was in danger of arrest. The remainder of the conversation, as related by Kalpashnikov, was as follows. The Ambassador said:

"What does Robins want?"

"To create a scandal," I answered, "and discredit you so that if the Bolsheviki get strong enough to be recognized he could take your place." I told him this was not only my private opinion, but that of many other Russians in political and military circles in Petrograd.

"Whatever his sympathies for the Bolsheviki are," continued Ambassador Francis, "I shall never recognize them nor have anything to do with these murderers. If ever the United States recognizes this anti-democratic party, as Robins seems to think, probably it will only be after I have resigned."

. . . I declared I was ready to rough anything for a just cause. General Judson was more of a pessimist and so full of apprehensions that he already saw the possibility of the arrest of everyone and he finished by saying: "What will we do if they arrest us all? There is nothing funny in sitting in a cold fortress while the Bolsheviki are dancing a jig with the Germans over our heads."

When I arose to go away the Ambassador promised to look into the matter and expressed again his disapproval of Colonel Robins's conduct toward me, and finished by saying that the Red Cross men had not been sent over to Russia for that kind of work.[31]

[29] National Archives, Petrograd Embassy 800 File, *op.cit.*, Francis' telegram 2117, December 19, 1917, 9 p.m.

[30] Klyuchnikov & Sabanin, Vol. II, *op.cit.*, pp. 100–102. (Degras, Vol. I, *op.cit.*, pp. 18–21, contains an English translation of the appeal from the Russian text given in Klyuchnikov & Sabanin.)

[31] Kalpaschnikoff, *op.cit.*, pp. 29, 31–32.

The Ambassador, according to his own account, also gave Kalpashnikov a letter "stating that he was in charge of motor ambulances for the use of the American Red Cross Mission to Rumania" and

. . . bade him goodbye, cautioning him, however, not to attempt to move his automobiles and ambulances out of Petrograd without a permit from the Soviet Government. . . .

Kalpashnikov assured him, the Ambassador stated, that he had secured such a permit. The Ambassador's record continues:

I met him the same afternoon at a tea in the apartment of Mrs. Crosley. . . . He told me that he would start his special train containing all of the ambulances and motors loaded thereon for Jassy the next morning at eight o'clock.[32]

A few hours later, shortly after midnight on the night of December 20–21, Kalpashnikov was arrested in his own apartment. The arrest was carried out by a detachment of Lettish Red Guards under the personal supervision of the commandant of the city (Petrograd was under martial law), Blagonravov. It is clear from this circumstance that the Soviet government attached considerable importance to the case. Kalpashnikov relates that Blagonravov boasted to him on the way to the prison about his illustrious revolutionary deeds:

. . . Do you know who I am? . . . I am the famous Blagonravov. You certainly have heard about me. . . . I am the one who has given victory to the Bolsheviki in the streets of Petrograd. I am the one who arrested the Provisional Government. . . . Though I have never had even the time to finish my schooling, the whole world must know about the great deeds of Blagonravov.[33]

Kalpashnikov's room was searched, and his papers taken. Among these papers were copies of the letters he and Major Perkins had written to Colonel Anderson in the matter of the cars. Kalpashnikov himself was hauled off to the Fortress of St. Peter and St. Paul for a period of extremely unpleasant confinement, destined to endure several months—until May 3, 1918.

Friday, December 21, opened, as Robins recorded in his diary, with excitement. His chauffeur, Alexei, appeared at breakfast time with the news that Kalpashnikov was imprisoned in the fortress and that

[32] *Ibid.*, Foreword, p. ix.
[33] *Ibid.*, p. 50.

his apartment had been searched. Gumberg was at once summoned to verify the report, and did so. Robins then rushed off to tell the Ambassador. The Ambassador asked why this had been done. Robins, according to the Ambassador's account, replied that he did not know.[34] According to Sisson—a more reliable source—Robins indicated that the charges against Kalpashnikov had been based on the communication forwarded to him by the Embassy (i.e. the first telegram from Anderson) and upon the letters he and Major Perkins had written to Colonel Anderson at Jassy. (These letters were later published in full in the official *Izvestiya,* to support the charges against Kalpashnikov.)

Sisson's account continues:

. . . Of the contents of the letters the Embassy knew nothing. Its own actions seemed so incapable of distortion that the Ambassador and Counselor Butler Wright decided upon a course of frankness—to seek to demonstrate to Trotsky privately and at once that there was no basis to any charge against the Embassy, and so prevent a public accusation. News of Kalpashnikov's arrest had not yet been printed and was not during the day.

Means for unofficial communication existed in Robins' access to Trotsky for Red Cross purposes. Accordingly it was decided to supply Trotsky with true copies of Colonel Anderson's trio of messages to the Embassy to explain any purported or partial messages he might have. . . .

Robins was accordingly provided with a letter, signed by Butler Wright, enclosing copies of the messages and authorizing him

. . . to speak for the American Embassy in this connection in order to correct any misapprehension that may have arisen . . . you will recall that you heard at the Embassy this morning that no money whatever had ever been advanced to Colonel Kalpaschnikoff for this or any other purpose. . . .[35]

To send Robins to the Soviet authorities involved a departure by the Ambassador from the very policy of "no contact" which he himself had recommended to Washington; but in the heat of the moment, and in the face of the lively apprehensions which he and the others were experiencing for their own safety, this aspect of the matter evidently appeared to have lost its importance.

---

[34] Kalpaschnikoff, *op.cit.,* Foreword, p. ix.
[35] Sisson, *op.cit.,* pp. 148–149.

Robins saw Trotsky in the course of the afternoon. (He may also have tried to see Lenin.) Just what transpired in this interview it is difficult to judge, for the evidence is conflicting. The Ambassador reported later to the Department of State that Trotsky had refused to listen to Robin's explanations. This, Francis explained, was "because Robins could not state [he] was sent by me," [36] an extraordinary statement in view of the letter given to Robins by Wright that morning, specifically empowering him to say he was "authorized to speak for the American Embassy. . . ." Robins presumably handed to Trotsky, in any case, the texts of the three telegrams which he had been told to submit. These messages were already well known to Trotsky, and Robins was aware of this fact, but the submission of the messages by the Embassy gave the Soviet authorities official cognizance of them.

That evening (Friday, December 21) Trotsky broke the entire story in a public speech delivered in the Aleksandrovski Theater. A good portion of the speech was devoted to the Kalpashnikov incident. Robins plainly had forewarning of this, for he sent to the meeting a "stenographer" whose record was preserved by Sisson and published in his reminiscences.[37]

In his speech Trotsky exonerated Robins, who, he stated, "has been loyal and correct with regard to us in all his dealings," [38] and was not implicated in any way in the affair. But he bitterly attacked Kalpashnikov, accusing him of plotting to take the automobiles to the headquarters of General Kaledin, and supporting this charge by citing from Colonel Anderson's telegrams of December 5 asking that the vehicles be sent to Rostov-on-Don. He failed to mention in any way the later message cancelling the order.

Having thus given his audience the impression that Kalpashnikov had been engaged in an attempt to assist Kaledin against the Bolsheviki, Trotsky then turned his attention to the American Embassy, and in a voice which, according to Sisson, "gradually swelled with indignation," delivered the following indictment:

. . . There are here threads uncovered going from Kalpashnikov to Anderson, and probably quite by chance—[with a falsetto voice]—from

[36] *Foreign Relations, 1918, Russia,* Vol. I, *op.cit.,* p. 321, from Telegram 2132, December 22, 1917.

[37] The Alexander Gumberg papers (State Historical Society of Wisconsin, Madison) include a special pass for the theater, written out for Gumberg by Trotsky himself.

[38] Sisson, *op.cit.,* p. 152.

Anderson to Francis! This Sir Francis will have to break his golden silence which has remained unbroken since the Revolution. He has written that silence is golden and evidently belongs to the diplomatic school of Bismarck, but these documents will force him to unloose his eloquence against the calumnies which are being set up against him. They think that we are so weak that we must swallow all such affronts. For us, revolutionary dignity is of foremost importance. We have taught this to the British Embassy and we shall prove it to all who think they can tread with impunity on our toes. Such things as a donation of two million dollars to Breshko-Breshkovskaya for the propagation of ultra-patriotic literature—as the bribing of a Russian Colonel to help Kaledin—shall not repeat themselves! Let them understand that from the moment that they interfere in our internal strife they cease to be diplomatic representatives —they are private counter-Revolutionist adventurers and the heavy hand of the Revolution will fall upon their heads! [*Applause.*]

The *bourgeoisie* cannot accomplish everything with dollars. We shall either perish or maintain our honor against German and Allied Imperialists. The Russian soldiers will know henceforth that among Kaledin's supporters are men who are hirelings of the United States militarism. The *bourgeois* conscience compels them to line themselves with those who are up in arms against the proletariat! But as long as we live; as long as red revolutionary blood flows in our veins we shall not tolerate that our revolutionary dignity be impugned from any quarter! [39]

In reporting this speech to the Department of State, Francis also quoted Trotsky as saying that an Ambassador who behaved in this way

... is no more an Ambassador but an adventurer and the heavy hand of the revolution will deal with him.[40]

A third version of Trotsky's remarks concerning Francis in the speech at the Aleksandrovski Theater appears in Kalpashnikov's book and reads as follows:

Ambassador Francis has been until now silent and has worked in the dark, giving money, rapid-fire guns and other war materials to the counter-revolutionists of the south. But now that everything is discovered, that his principal agent is locked up in the Fortress of St. Peter and St. Paul, and that we hold important letters and telegrams proving that through his agents he had been in communication with General Kaledin

[39] *Ibid.,* p. 155.
[40] *Foreign Relations, 1918, Russia,* Vol. I, *op.cit.,* p. 321, from Telegram 2132, December 22, 1917.

and all the Rostov gang, the time has come for him to give explanations and tell us what he and his government mean by working against the Russian people. I shall see this thing through to the bitter end, and if I do not get satisfaction I shall not hesitate to take extreme measures and wipe out all the Americans and foreigners who dare to plot anything against the liberties so dearly bought by us for our country.[41]

Whichever of these versions may have been correct, there appears to have been no doubt that Trotsky, in his speech at the theater, said things highly hostile and threatening with regard to the American Ambassador. According to Hard (who apparently had all his information from Robins), the crowd replied to this rabble-rousing with shouts of "Arrest Francis! Hang him! Shoot him!"[42] One is obliged to note, moreover, that Trotsky's statement, including a number of wholly false charges against the Ambassador, was delivered on the heels of an interview he had had with Robins and—surely—Gumberg. In his pocket diary, Robins noted only that Trotsky "was fair to me." He added, most aptly, "Extraordinary the whole affair."

The following morning (Saturday, December 22) a further agitated conference took place in the Embassy. The Ambassador was by this time highly concerned for his own personal safety, and with good cause. Trotsky could scarcely have made such statements and aroused a mob to this sort of feeling unless he seriously envisaged physical violence against the Ambassador, probably not by the Soviet authorities themselves but by mob action under Soviet encouragement. The precedent was already there. It was less than three weeks, after all, since the Commander-in-Chief, General Dukhonin, had been beaten to death by a mob of sailors at the steps of his private railway car, while his Soviet successor, Krylenko, looked on; and the General's "barbarously profaned" body had been kicked around the town of Mogilev for days afterwards. Thus the Ambassador had no reason to suppose that Trotsky's menacing statements were a bluff. (Apparently by coincidence, a meeting of Petrograd anarchists the following day also demanded that Francis should "answer with his skin" for the detention by the United States authorities of certain American radicals, and averred that they had the wherewithal and the will to enforce this requirement. This could hardly have contributed to the old gentleman's sense of security.[43])

[41] Kalpaschnikoff, *op.cit.*, p. 75.
[42] Hard, *op.cit.*, p. 118.
[43] *Foreign Relations, 1918, Russia,* Vol. I, *op.cit.*, pp. 322–323; from Telegram 2133, December 23, 1917, Francis to Secretary of State.

In the face of this situation, the Ambassador decided to publish a refutation of Trotsky's charges, and one was prepared the same day (December 22). It was a well-prepared document, giving the texts of the other two telegrams—the two that Trotsky failed to mention— and of the two letters Colonel Anderson had addressed to Ambassador Francis on December 8, explaining that his thought of sending the ambulances to Rostov was occasioned by a concern lest they fall into the hands of the Germans. "Instructions from my government," the Ambassador stated,

are very definite and positive prohibiting any interference by any American representative in Russia in the internal affairs of this country. I have observed these instructions scrupulously and, so far as my authority extends, have directed their strict observance by all connected with the American Embassy or under its control. The charge or insinuation that I was aiding Kaledin or any other of the numerous and varied factions in Russia is absolutely without foundation and my statement to this effect should be sufficient to convince all of its truth and correctness.[44]

At the conference on the morning of December 22, it was also apparently decided to send Robins to the Smolny once more to give explanations about the affair and to try to effect Kalpashnikov's release.

As luck would have it, Washington's reply to the Ambassador's query of December 12 (whether members of the Red Cross were explicitly barred from contact with the Soviet authorities) came in on this very morning. It read:

. . . Red Cross members in uniform certainly included in instructions Department's 1883, December 6. Red Cross is so advising Robins.[45]

This meant that Robins was *not* to have contact with the Soviet authorities. The source of this dictum, it must be remembered, was a Presidential directive.

Robins also appears to have received his own similar admonition from the Red Cross headquarters in Washington on the same morning. He was now able, however, to confront the Ambassador with a difficult choice. If the Ambassador proposed to abide by the instruction then he, Robins, could no longer be of any service to him in attempting to straighten out the Kalpashnikov affair and thus in

---

[44] *Ibid.*, pp. 326–327; from Telegram 2144, December 26, 1917, Francis to the Secretary of State.
[45] *Ibid.*, p. 319, Telegram 1917, December 20, 1917.

mitigating the very real personal danger with which the Ambassador was confronted. Did the Ambassador, in these circumstances, wish him to refrain from contact with the Smolny, or were they to disregard the order? Robins' biographer, William Hard, quotes the Ambassador as saying,

Pay no attention to it. . . . I'll take the responsibility. . . . You keep on going to Smolny. Tear the order up.[46]

Francis himself, testifying before the Senatorial investigating committee in 1919, confirmed this statement in somewhat less dramatic terms. He said that on receipt of the telegram prohibiting Red Cross "contacts," he told Robins:

. . . I think it unwise for you to sever your relations abruptly and absolutely; that is, I mean to cease your visits up there. Furthermore, I want to know what they are doing, and I will stand between you and the fire. . . .[47]

The Ambassador told the Senators that he had cabled the government to this effect but had received no reply.[48] He added, "So Col. Robins continued to hold communication with Smolny. . . ." [49]

In this remarkable manner, Robins succeeded in escaping at the last moment from the operation of Washington's ban on contacts with the Soviet authorities. From that time on he proceeded vigorously with the pursuit of a series of associations with the Soviet leaders which appeared to him both necessary and desirable.

As to what transpired in Robins' further efforts to straighten out the Kalpashnikov case in conversations with Trotsky, we have only indirect reflections of Robins' own reports. The circumstances do not permit the assumption that these reports were necessarily complete, nor their reflections accurate. Francis' reports indicate that Trotsky "repulsed" Robins on the first two occasions. Hard describes as follows an alleged attempt on Robins' part to discuss the matter with

[46] Hard, *op.cit.*, p. 119.
[47] *Bolshevik Propaganda, Hearings . . . , op.cit.*, p. 956.
[48] This was not strictly correct. The Ambassador transmitted Robins' appeal on December 27; a reply was sent to him on December 29 (*Foreign Relations, 1918, Russia,* Vol. III, *op. cit.,* p. 106), but its wording, as will be seen in another chapter, was ambiguous and unsatisfactory.
[49] Sisson (*op.cit.*, p. 149) observed that the Ambassador's use of Robins as an intermediary on this occasion was important to the latter "for it legitimized conference relations with Trotsky."

Lenin (he does not indicate the date, but one must conclude it was about December 21):

He had been accustomed to going through Lenin's door into Lenin's room, on a pass, without question. This time two soldiers crossed their bayonets in front of him. He sat down. He decided to go away. He rose and approached an outer door. There two other soldiers crossed their bayonets in front of him. He sat down again. After a while he got a really successful idea. He went to a side door, and so into a little private corridor; and he walked along that corridor till he came to a door at the end of it. This door he contemplated for a moment. Then he swung it open. It was the back-exit-door to Lenin's room.

Lenin looked up from his documents and his eyes were narrowed. He looked, and said nothing. Robins said something fast.

"I admit this Rostov affair looks bad," he said. "But I can explain it. I ask you simply, before you attack the American embassy or the American Red Cross give me a chance to make the explanation."

Lenin still looked at Robins and still said nothing; and the way of his looking was as if he wished to resume the reading on his table. Robins turned and left Smolny. He thought he had probably seen Smolny for the last time.[50]

Hard further indicates that only the discovery of Perkins' and Kalpashnikov's letters to Anderson saved Robins himself from falling into serious disfavor with the Soviet authorities over the Kalpashnikov incident. It is interesting, incidentally, to note that Hard's account, which was presumably derived from the single source of Robins' own statements to Hard, paralleled Trotsky's speech in mentioning only the telegram concerning the shipment of the vehicles to Rostov and in ignoring the later telegram cancelling the first message. Hard further states that Ambassador Francis *did* supply to Kalpashnikov the 100,000 rubles requested in one of Anderson's telegrams, although Francis stated in his report to the Department of State that Kalpashnikov never applied for any money,[51] confirmed in the Embassy's letter to Robins that no money had passed, and said in his public statement that

. . . I have never paid Colonel Kalpashnikov a kopek for this purpose or for any other, nor has he ever applied to me for any funds whatever.[52]

[50] Hard, *op.cit.*, pp. 115–116.
[51] *Foreign Relations, 1918, Russia*, Vol. I, *op.cit.*, p. 321, Telegram 2132, December 22, 1917.
[52] *Ibid.*, p. 327, from Telegram 2144, December 26, 1917.

Apparently basing his opinion on these omissions and errors, Hard then went on to state:

. . . The American Red Cross Mission to Russia, and its chief, Colonel Robins, were unexpectedly proved by the documents to be innocent. But the chief of the American Red Cross to Rumania was proved by the documents to be guilty. And so was the American ambassador to Russia.[53]

If this was indeed the version of the story given by Robins to Hard in 1920, we are entitled to assume that Robins could scarcely have been an effective advocate either for Kalpashnikov, or for the Rumanian Red Cross Commission, or for Ambassador Francis, in his interviews with Trotsky.

On the evening of the 23rd, Blagonravov and some of his henchmen visited the Red Cross headquarters itself, where Robins and his aides were assembled, and announced that Robins' freight train, from which the cars bearing the ambulances had now apparently been detached, had been officially "arrested." To make this announcement was ostensibly the only purpose of Blagonravov's visit. He did not threaten the members of the mission or carry out any search.

This train, it will be recalled, carried supplies for the Red Cross Mission in Rumania which Robins had been endeavoring to despatch independently. Robins was now worried about the loss of his own train. He pleaded with Blagonravov for a day's delay so that he could appeal once more to Trotsky. After a certain amount of good-natured banter, Blagonravov was prevailed upon to agree that he would take no further steps until he received new orders. The train was finally released on Christmas Eve.

On Christmas morning the Soviet papers published the Ambassador's statement and followed it, according to the Ambassador's report, by a "number of impertinent questions indicating doubt" as to its truth.[54] By this time a further telegram had been received from Anderson explaining why he had wanted the vehicles sent to Rostov and why he had then cancelled the order. On Christmas Day Robins took this telegram, too, to Trotsky, but reported Trotsky as being still incredulous.

Meanwhile, Kalpashnikov, in the Fortress of St. Peter and St. Paul,

[53] Hard, *op.cit.*, p. 118.
[54] *Foreign Relations, 1918, Russia,* Vol. I, *op.cit.*, p. 329, Telegram 2154, December 28, 1917. See also the *Izvestiya,* No. 249, December 25, 1917.

was first confronted with a fantastic set of accusations, bearing practically no relation to the matter of the ambulances. It was charged that he had handed over to Kaledin $3 million of American gold; that he had organized "in his flat" the headquarters of a conspiracy against the government; that he had in his flat a portrait of the ex-Emperor and other high Tsarist personalities; and finally, not unflatteringly, that he had been intimate with the Queen of Rumania and by his influence had forced her to oblige the King to declare war on the Bolsheviki. It was intimated to him that he had three days in which to make his confession that if he failed to do this, things would go badly with him. At the end of three days, however, nothing happened; and he continued for many weeks to taste the peculiar anguish of a complete uncertainty with regard to his own status and fate.

On January 4, Francis reported to the American Legation at Jassy that he had learned that Kalpashnikov's release could be secured for 50,000 rubles' bail. He thought the Petrograd Embassy ought not to provide this, and added that because of

... present delicate situation the Red Cross is unwilling to assume the liability but if you wish to authorize and arrange remittance the object can be affected in all probability.[55]

There seems to be no evidence that the bail was ever put up. In any case, Kalpashnikov remained in prison several months longer.

At the end of February 1918, Kalpashnikov's case was complicated by the fact that he, together with a fellow prisoner, a well-known Russian monarchist, made a spectacular and very nearly successful attempt to escape from the fortress by an underground tunnel they had discovered. Kalpashnikov was probably saved from being shot only by the fact that the Soviet government was at that moment in the throes of moving to Moscow. After this incident he was moved to a peculiarly unpleasant prison in another part of Petrograd. On April 18 he was examined in person by Dzerzhinski, the first head of the Soviet secret police. Dzerzhinski, according to Kalpashnikov's own account, told him that the Soviet of People's Commissars had given serious attention to his case; that endless reports and investigations had been conducted with regard to it; and that it was "the big-

[55] National Archives, Petrograd Embassy 800 File, *op.cit.,* telegram from Francis to Jassy, No. 291, January 4, 1918, 3 p.m.

gest international case we have had to handle." The further course of this conversation is recounted by Kalpashnikov as follows:

Dzerzhinski: . . . You were associated with all the enemies of the proletariat who will not recognize our Soviet Government.

Kalpashnikov: But I worked in relief work with the Americans.

D.: All the foreigners and Americans were against us except Raymond Robins. Do you know him well?

K.: I should think I do.

D.: What do you think of him?

K.: He had no business to mix in politics instead of doing the relief work for which he was sent.

D.: But he was the only true and faithful friend we had among the foreigners and he was the only one who understood our aims and fully sympathized with us and was ready to support our government, and we value him greatly. The complete contempt which the other Americans and foreigners showed us exasperated us and caused big complications which nearly brought a great crisis.

K.: This crisis, which I understand was the reason for my arrest, oc- curred four months ago and I am still in prison.

D.: You are right. Our relations are getting much better. Raymond Robins expects to leave soon for America to explain to the American people that it is useless to fight us any longer and I personally think there is no reason why we should not release you.[56]

A few days later Kalpashnikov was interrogated by Uritsky, then Commissar for Justice. While the interrogation was in progress, Blagonravov came into Uritsky's office and was astonished to see that Kalpashnikov was still a prisoner. Blagonravov, Kalpashnikov re- lates,

. . . plainly said that at the time the Bolsheviki arrested me it was for the definite purpose of creating a scandal with the American Embassy and the principal objective was not me but Ambassador Francis. . . .[57]

Uritsky told him that

. . . there must be someone especially keen to have you kept in prison because the definite inquiry in Moscow concerning your case is held back on purpose. I inquired about you recently and no one knows anything definite. I asked for the documents of your case and they don't know

[56] Kalpaschnikoff, *op.cit.,* p. 226.
[57] *Ibid.,* p. 237.

where they are, but you are still filed as the hostage of the Americans at the disposition of the Council. . . .[58]

Ten days later Kalpashnikov was released, apparently by Uritsky, on his personal responsibility. On this occasion, Uritsky is said to have told him:

. . . if the Government had listened to me, all the Americans with whom you worked would have been arrested and shot.[59]

Kalpashnikov narrowly avoided being re-arrested after the assassination of Uritsky himself, an event which occurred somewhat later. He escaped only by fleeing the country under false papers.

Kalpashnikov always attributed his long imprisonment to Robins' influence, and this imputation received implicit support from Governor Francis in the foreword he later wrote for Kalpashnikov's book, in which he said:

. . . I requested Raymond Robins time and again to secure the release of Kalpaschnikoff, and his invariable reply was to the effect that he was doing all he could to effect his release.[60]

Kalpashnikov's account of his imprisonment and of his other experiences is studded with instances in which he claims that other Russian figures made statements to him indicating that Robins was a Soviet agent. He was scarcely an impartial witness, and these allegations must be taken in light of this fact.

In general, the evidence surrounding the entire Kalpashnikov affair is inadequate and in some respects curiously conflicting. Neither of the two sides appears to have been able to recall the affair in retrospect with any degree of accuracy. The Ambassador, in the foreword to Kalpashnikov's book, made the extraordinary error of accusing Robins of having leaked Colonel Anderson's telegram to Trotsky—apparently forgetting that he himself had sent copies of the telegram, together with the others, to Trotsky on the 21st. Robins' later testimony was, as we have seen, no less confusing.

The incident stands as evidence that there was a moment in the middle of December 1917 when the American representatives in

---

[58] *Loc.cit.*
[59] *Ibid.,* p. 244.
[60] *Ibid.,* Foreword, p. x.

Petrograd stood in acute danger of arrest and persecution, if not worse, at the hands of the Soviet authorities. But it stands also as a further revelation of the unhappy relations prevailing among the Americans stationed in Petrograd at that time, and of the dangers that invariably reside in any division, within official American communities abroad, of the power to deal with the local governmental authority.

CHAPTER XI

THE FIRST BREST-LITOVSK
CRISIS

*If truthfulness be the first essential for the ideal diplomatist,
the second essential is precision.—Harold Nicolson* [1]

THE alarums and excursions of the Kalpashnikov affair proved so absorbing to the principal American personalities in Petrograd during the days just before Christmas 1917 that they somewhat eclipsed, in the attention of these gentlemen, the beginning of the German-Russian peace negotiations at Brest-Litovsk.

It will be recalled that the armistice terms, signed on December 15, 1917, had provided for a month's cessation of hostilities and had stipulated that the two parties would immediately proceed to the inauguration of negotiations for a full-fledged peace treaty. Accordingly, the Soviet delegation and the delegations of the Central Powers (Germany, Austria-Hungary, Bulgaria, and Turkey) assembled again in Brest-Litovsk on December 20. The Soviet delegation was led by Joffe, assisted by Kamenev, Sokolnikov, and Karakhan. (It is interesting to reflect that Joffe died by his own hand; Kamenev, Sokolnikov, and Karakhan all appeared on the docket in the great purge trials of the Thirties.) The German delegation was headed by the Foreign Secretary, Baron von Kühlmann, assisted by Messrs. von Rosenberg and von Hoesch of the German Foreign Office. Major General Max Hoffmann, Chief of Staff to the Commander-in-Chief of the Eastern Front, sat at Kühlmann's elbow, armed with the immense authority of the High Command. Although Hoffmann's influence was of course great, Kühlmann, contrary to a widespread impression abroad, bore formal responsibility for the conduct of the talks.

---

[1] Harold Nicolson, *Diplomacy,* Harcourt, Brace & Co., New York, 1939, p. 112.

The First Brest-Litovsk Crisis

The first plenary session of the conference was held on the afternoon of December 22. Joffe set forth the Soviet position in a statement which, in view of the wide attention it was to receive in western countries, must be noted here. After reiterating the demand for a general "democratic" peace, based on the "Decree of Peace," Joffe went on to list the following points as a basis for negotiation:

1. Not to allow any forcible annexation of territory seized during the war. Troops occupying these territories to be withdrawn in the shortest possible time.
2. To restore in full the political independence of those nations deprived of their independence during the present war.
3. National groups not enjoying political independence before the war to be guaranteed an opportunity to decide freely by means of a referendum whether to adhere to any given State or to be an independent State. This referendum to be so organized as to guarantee complete freedom of voting for the entire population of the given territory, not excluding emigrants and refugees.
4. In regard to territories inhabited by several nationalities, the right of minorities to be protected by special laws, guaranteeing them cultural national independence, and, as far as is practicable, administrative autonomy.
5. None of the belligerent countries to be bound to pay other countries so-called 'war costs'; indemnities already paid to be returned. Private individuals who have incurred losses owing to the war to be compensated from a special fund, raised by proportional levies on all the belligerent countries.
6. Colonial questions to be decided on the lines laid down in points 1, 2, 3, and 4.

The Six Points were followed by a proposal for renunciation of various means of international pressure short of war, such as boycott, blockade, economic restrictions, etc.[2]

This statement, it will be noted, embodied the familiar principle of "no annexations or indemnities," prescribed complete political independence for those nationalities which had been so deprived since the beginning of the war, and stipulated that "national groups not enjoying political independence before the war," including colonial peoples, should determine their own fate by referendum. (This position was, of course, somewhat disingenuous. In speaking of political

---

[2] Degras, Vol. 1, *op.cit.*, pp. 21–22. This document can be found in the original Russian in Klyuchnikov & Sabanin, Part 11, *op.cit.*, pp. 102–104, Item No. 84.

independence, and of such things as "referenda," the Soviet leaders had in mind actually only the political rights of a given class, the proletariat; experience was to prove that even with respect to this class Soviet understanding of popular representation differed radically from the western conception of that term.)

On Christmas Day, after a good deal of internal disagreement among the four delegations of the Central Powers and within the German delegation itself, the reply of the Central Powers was completed and formally placed before the conference by the Austrian Foreign Minister, Count Czernin. In general, it appeared to accept the Soviet tenets as a basis of discussion. An exception was made in the case of the provision concerning national groups which had not enjoyed independence before the war. (The Germans recognized the far-reaching, propagandistic nature of this stipulation, and were not prepared to risk being bound to anything of this sort.) The German reply included, however, the highly significant proviso that the other Allies must also agree to this sort of settlement—otherwise the Germans would not be bound to it. This proviso reflected Kühlmann's decision to take the calculated risk (it was not a great one) that the Allies would never agree to negotiate on such a basis. If his calculation were correct, Germany did not need to fear that she herself would ever be held to the agreement.

In giving their reply, the Germans, whether by accident or design, contrived to suggest to Joffe and his associates that their vague and general agreement to the "no annexations" formula meant that they were prepared, upon ratification of a separate German-Soviet peace treaty, to withdraw their forces at once from those areas of the former Russian Empire—notably the major portion of the Baltic countries and of Poland—which had come under German military occupation during the war. Joffe jubilantly relayed this news to Petrograd. The impression he had received was of course wholly erroneous. The Germans had not the faintest intention of withdrawing their forces from these areas prior to the end of the war—that is, prior to the end of hostilities with the western powers as well as with Russia. Even at that time the German military leaders were determined to establish in the east a permanent protective belt, embracing portions of this territory, which would at least limit in favor of Germany the political independence of the inhabitants. They had no intention of restoring these areas in their entirety to Russia.

The First Brest-Litovsk Crisis

When the Germans became aware of the manner in which their disingenuous reply was being interpreted by the Soviet delegation, General Hoffmann was alarmed at the seriousness of this misunderstanding and insisted that the Russians must not be left under such a misapprehension. Accordingly, he undertook to explain the matter personally to Joffe. He chose for this purpose the occasion of luncheon on December 27. Sitting next to Joffe at table, he indicated that the Germans considered that Russian Poland and the provinces of Kurland and Lithuania had already expressed their will to be separated from Russia, and that their future should be determined in direct conversations between the representatives of the inhabitants and the governments of the Central Powers. Such a disposition of the territories would not, he maintained, be in conflict with the "no annexations" formula, as the Germans understood it.[3]

This revelation struck Joffe like a thunderbolt.[4] He feared that he had seriously misled his principals. The remainder of the afternoon was taken up in agitated discussions. The conference was called back into formal session again at five p.m. and the Russians, in order to clear themselves and to make the German position a matter of record, hastily introduced a draft for the first article of a possible peace treaty, involving a specific German promise indicating readiness to withdraw their forces at once from Poland, Lithuania, and Kurland. The Germans countered with a version which would have had the Russians recognize that the inhabitants of these territories had already demanded "full state independence and separation from the Russian Federation" [5] and thus made the obligation of withdrawal of German forces inapplicable in those territories. The deadlock, so far as the instructions of the two delegations went, was complete. The German counter-proposal was telegraphed by the Soviet delegation immediately, that same evening, to Petrograd. The following evening (Friday, December 28), the conference adjourned until January 9. But the adjournment took place not, strictly speaking, as a result of this disagreement, but rather in order to give the other Allies a final opportunity to associate themselves with the peace negotiations.

At what time Trotsky actually received the news of the clarifica-

---

[3] *Die Aufzeichnungen des Generalmajors Max Hoffmann*, Vol. ii, *op.cit.*, p. 201.
[4] *Ibid.*, p. 203. The incident is graphically described in Wheeler-Bennett's excellent account of the Brest-Litovsk negotiations, *The Forgotten Peace*, *op.cit.*, p. 125.
[5] Bunyan & Fisher, *op.cit.*, p. 484.

tion of the German attitude is uncertain, but it was almost certainly on December 29, or during the preceding night. For him, too, it must have been seriously upsetting, though not so much as for Joffe. It is doubtful that Lenin and Trotsky had placed any inordinate confidence in the rather vague and ambiguous German reply of December 25. But the position of the Soviet leaders was then in many ways a precarious and desperate one, and they were prepared to grasp at straws. In a report delivered to the Central Executive Committee on the evening of December 27 (the same evening that the German counter-proposal was put on the wire to Smolny), Trotsky had therefore given an optimistic view of the course of the negotiations. Referring to the German acceptance in principle of the Soviet proposals, he said:

. . . Even our enemies, who only recently predicted that the Germans would not even talk to us . . . must now admit that our diplomacy has met with great success.[6]

This statement became the guiding line for the tone of the Soviet press in the ensuing days. On the 29th, just as the telegram from Brest was presumably coming in, Trotsky was engaged in issuing a further and "last" appeal to the peoples and governments of the Allied countries, inviting them to take part in the further negotiations and "thus to assure themselves against the consequences of a separate peace between Russia and the enemy nations." In this document he interpreted the German position at Brest-Litovsk as meaning that the Central Powers were "prepared to evacuate in accordance with the peace treaty the occupied territories of Poland, Lithuania, and Kurland," as well as the territories occupied by the Germans in Belgium, France, Serbia, and Montenegro. Pointing out that it was now impossible to maintain that the war was being fought for the recovery of these areas, he again called on the Allied powers to associate themselves with the peace move. He conceded that a separate peace would be a blow to France and Italy. But

. . . if the Allied governments, in the blind stubbornness characteristic of declining and perishing classes, again refuse to participate in the negotiations, then the working class will be faced with the iron necessity of wresting power from the hands of those who either cannot or will not give peace to the peoples of the world.[7]

[6] *Loc.cit.*
[7] Klyuchnikov & Sabanin, Part II, *op.cit.*, pp. 104–107, Item No. 85.

Whether this appeal, with its optimistic and erroneous picture of German intentions, was despatched before the receipt of the news from Brest, or whether it was too late to stop it after the news came in, is not clear.[8] In any case, it went out to the world public on the 29th, confirming the optimistic view of the negotiations which had been put forward up to that time.

In the face of this rosy and triumphant position on the part of the Soviet government, the receipt of the news of Hoffmann's explanations can only have been worrisome and embarrassing in the extreme. In particular, it presented them with a difficult problem of presentation to the public.

For two days after receiving word of Hoffmann's clarifications, the Soviet leaders kept the bad news entirely to themselves. They had planned for Sunday, December 30, a massive peace demonstration by the Petrograd proletariat, ostensibly to celebrate the success achieved by the Soviet delegation at Brest. Apparently they did not dare release the news prior to the demonstration. On Sunday morning, the day of the demonstration, the *Pravda* published Trotsky's appeal to the peoples and governments of the Allied countries, with all its cheerful implications, but it also ran an editorial on the subject of the peace negotiations which, when examined carefully in retrospect, plainly indicates an awareness on the part of the writers of what had occurred at Brest. Due, no doubt, to this awareness, the editorial also revealed the desire to give to the mass demonstration less the aspect of a victory celebration than that of a militant expression of enthusiasm for the Soviet government and a warning to the "German imperialists." [9]

The *Pravda,* incidentally, on this occasion noted that "our guests, the Generals and diplomats of Wilhelm," would watch the parade, and described in detail the reactions these German representatives would undoubtedly experience on witnessing it. The reference here was to the members of the German technical delegation, consisting of naval and economic missions, headed by Baron Keyserling and

---

[8] The Soviet delegates could scarcely have reached Petrograd and delivered their personal report before the evening of December 29.

[9] This editorial, as available on microfilm, is partially illegible, but the following sentence is clear: "The fate of Poland, Lithuania, and Kurland will be decided by the popular masses of those areas." The editorial goes on to say that if the rulers of Germany and Austria try to decide unilaterally the fate of these east European peoples they may jeopardize the entire military gains they have made in the war on the eastern front. The *Pravda,* No. 216/147, December 29, 1917.

Count Mirbach respectively. This delegation had arrived in Petrograd two days before. Its presence in the capital had given rise to the wildest rumors and conjectures, both in Allied circles and in Russian circles hostile to the Soviet government.[10] The tone of the *Pravda* editorial reflected the strong desire that these Germans, the first representatives of the German government to arrive in the Russian capital since the beginning of the war, should get an impression of the desperate revolutionary resolve and fighting spirit of both the Petrograd workers and the soldiers of the Petrograd garrison.

Once the demonstration of December 30 was over, the Soviet leaders faced the question of releasing the bad news that the Germans were insisting on remaining in occupation of Poland and the Baltic territories. They could not conceal the news entirely. Furthermore, they felt themselves under the necessity of producing some show of unfavorable popular reaction which might impress the Germans and soften them up for purposes of further negotiation. On the other hand, they did not wish to emphasize a development that could only be regarded by their own adherents, in the light of the optimistic version they had put forward up to that time, as a distinct setback.

The deliberations as to how to release the news were of course only incidental to the examination of the wider questions as to how to proceed generally in the whole question of the termination of hostilities. The Soviet leaders felt that they could not publicly sanction the German retention of these occupied areas. They therefore did not see how they could settle on such a basis at Brest. They knew the Germans, in their present mood, would be immovable on this point. On the other hand, the Bolsheviki could not risk a renewal of hostilities on the eastern front, for which they were in no way prepared.[11]

Hopeless as the military prospects were, the Soviet leaders were still convinced that they would eventually be supported by the world

[10] Allegations appeared in the anti-Bolshevik press to the effect that their numbers ran into the hundreds. Trotsky was obliged to explain on January 1st that there were only thirty of them, accompanied, as he added contemptuously, by another thirty orderlies and personal servants.

[11] There is some evidence to suggest that serious thought was given in those last days of 1917 to a renewal of hostilities. The official Soviet edition of *Lenin's Complete Works* contains a curious undated document (almost certainly from about December 28, 1917) setting forth a list of questions (evidently to be addressed to the military delegates at the Demobilization Congress) about this possibility. In any case, a renewal of hostilities at that time was out of the question. The Germans knew this, and it cannot have taken Lenin long to find it out. (Lenin, Vol. XXII, *op.cit.,* p. 152.)

proletariat. They attributed the stiff position of the Germans at Brest to the fact that no real knowledge of the negotiations had become available to the German workers. They therefore arrived (probably on December 29 or 30) at two major policy determinations. First, since they were unable to fight, there was no alternative to continuing the negotiations with the Germans until such time as revolutionary pressure on the German government could weaken its hand. This meant that while negotiations would have to be resumed, the purpose of the Soviet delegation from this point on could be only to stall for time. To this end, it was decided that the delegation would now be headed by Trotsky, who, it was assumed, would be superior in the arts of stalling.[12] Secondly, the Soviet government would ask for the transfer of the negotiations to Stockholm, where it would be easier to assure that the inflammatory and propagandistic statements made by the Soviet delegation would be transmitted to Germany and made available to the German masses. These decisions, it must be emphasized, were arrived at by December 30 at the latest.

In the light of these determinations, it was evidently decided to play down, for the Russian public, the news of Hoffmann's demands, while at the same time to put on, for the Germans, a show of militant and revolutionary ferocity, not only threatening early revolution in Germany but also hinting at the possible resumption of hostilities by a fanatically aroused and determined Russian proletariat. To the Allied governments, always to be had on the basis of an appeal to hatred of Germany, it would be explained that Hoffmann's explanations reflected a bit of German trickery.[13]

It was apparently in accordance with this plan that the news of

[12] "In order to delay negotiations," Lenin explained, "you have to have a delayer" —and this was to be Trotsky. (Trotzki, *op.cit.,* p. 348.)

[13] The suggestion that the Soviet leaders had been "tricked" by the Germans in this respect may have rested on something more than just Kühlmann's original position at Brest. There is some evidence that when arrangements were being made in the spring of 1917 for Lenin's return to Russia through Germany, he was given to understand by German secret intelligence agents that in the event of a separate peace between Russia and Germany, the entire German-occupied territory in the east would be restored to Russia. (See papers on the "Chester incident," in the file on the Sisson Documents, National Archives.) A similar impression was communicated to Swiss circles interested in promoting a German-Russian peace. (Olga Hess Gankin & H. H. Fisher, *The Bolsheviks and the World War: The Origin of the Third International,* Stanford University Press, 1940, pp. 613–622.) While it seems unlikely that the Bolsheviki should have placed any inordinate faith in such suggestions, this may have had something to do with the violence of Trotsky's reaction to Hoffmann's revelation of the true German position.

Hoffmann's position was privately imparted to Allied circles on the afternoon of Monday, December 31. It was imparted, as we shall observe presently, in a distorted form and with misleading overtones. Some hours later, in the middle of the night, the press bureau of the Commissariat for Foreign Affairs released the news generally, in a communiqué to the press. The following morning (January 1, 1918), *Pravda* carried the communiqué inconspicuously, at the bottom of an inside page, but dwelt on its contents editorially. The editors were obviously concerned to control and steer popular reaction.

That evening a combined meeting of the Central Executive Committee and the Petrograd Soviet took place, to receive the report of the Soviet delegation which had returned from Brest. This was obviously the occasion chosen by the Soviet leaders for explaining the bad news to the influential circle of their own immediate supporters and assistants. Kamenev reported on the Brest talks, setting forth correctly General Hoffmann's position and not denying its seriousness, but maintaining, in a bit of face-saving, that the Soviet delegation had not really been deceived by the earlier and more encouraging German statement of Christmas Day.[14] The meeting then heard the statements of a number of soldier-delegates from the various armies, or what was left of them, on the European front. (These were men attending the All-Army Congress on the Demobilization of the Army, then in progress in Petrograd.) The reports of foreigners present indicate that these military delegates gave a heart-rending picture of the distress, demoralization, and helplessness of the remaining military units at the front. (The *Pravda* reported these statements the following day as ringing professions of confidence in Soviet power and of a readiness to fight for the inspiring purposes of the Soviet regime.) Trotsky then spoke, directing his remarks mostly to correcting the inaccurate rumors about the German delegation then in the city. Of the negotiations he said only that they would continue, but that they would henceforth take place in a neutral country. The meeting then approved the text (drafted in advance by the communist leaders) of a new appeal to the proletariat of the Central Powers, calling upon them to rise up and force the hands of their governments.

The following day, January 2, Trotsky gave an interview to the press, declaring that the German-Soviet peace negotiations would

[14] *Pravda*, No. 219, January 2, 1918.

[227]

continue "on the basis of the principles proclaimed by the Russian revolution." The basic policy determinations at which the communist leaders had arrived, namely to string the Germans along while trying to foment revolution behind their backs, were clearly hinted at in the last sentences of Trotsky's statement, as follows:

. . . We shall do all we can to bring the results of these negotiations to the notice of the popular masses of all European countries, despite the truly humiliating censorship which the European Governments have imposed on military and diplomatic communications. We do not doubt that the negotiations themselves will make us stronger, and the imperialist Governments of all countries weaker.[15]

At the same time Trotsky despatched, through Joffe, a telegram to the Central Powers upholding the Soviet delegation's rejection of Hoffmann's position and demanding the transfer of the negotiations to Stockholm.

The Germans came back the following day with a flat refusal to shift the talks of Stockholm. They had not been in the slightest degree moved or impressed with the Russian threats and hints of the reopening of hostilities. General Hoffmann wrote in his memoirs:

. . . The Russian masses yearned for peace, the army had disintegrated and consisted only of undisciplined armed bands, the only possibility for the Bolsheviki remaining in power was to make peace. They had to accept the conditions of the Central Powers, no matter how severe they might be.[16]

Kühlmann's oral comment, made at the time, was more colorful:

The only choice they have is as to what sort of sauce they shall be eaten with.

To which the Austrian Foreign Minister, Czernin, observed sadly, "Just like ourselves." [17]

The talks were resumed at Brest-Litovsk on January 8 to 9.

❖

This summary of the course of the first crisis in the Brest negotiations has been included because, without an understanding of the

---

[15] Degras, Vol. I, *op.cit.*, p. 28.
[16] *Die Aufzeichnungen des Generalmajors Max Hoffmann*, Vol. II, *op.cit.*, p. 202.
[17] Wheeler-Bennett, *op.cit.*, pp. 155–156, cites this passage from Count Ottakar Czernin, *In the World War*, London, 1919, pp. 232–233.

development of the Soviet attitude and the motivation of Soviet actions with respect to the negotiations in the final days of 1917, it is impossible to understand the reactions which these events produced among the leading American representatives in Petrograd and in governmental circles in Washington.

When the Soviet and German delegations reconvened at Brest-Litovsk on December 21, Francis, Robins, and Sisson were in the midst of the alarums occasioned by Kalpashnikov's imprisonment, which had taken place during the preceding night. It was not until Christmas Eve that the Red Cross train was finally released and the excitement of the Kalpashnikov affair began to die down.

According to the custom of Americans abroad, the Petrograd Americans had a festive and social Christmas, despite the Revolution and Kalpashnikov. The Ambassador kept open house on Christmas Day. Sisson entertained in the afternoon in his room in the Hotel d'Europe, with a little Christmas tree and a collection of Russian toys to give the appropriate atmosphere. In the evening the acting manager of the local branch of the National City Bank gave a dinner and dance in his apartment, serving such unheard-of delicacies as white bread, cake, and pie. The Ambassador had provided the white flour and sugar to make possible this miracle, but made up for it by attending the party and proving himself "as a forager . . . the equal of any." [18]

The fact is that the stresses of the Kalpashnikov affair had served to bring closer together the senior American figures in Petrograd, hitherto divided by such tragic suspicions. Bullard, returning in early January from a visit to Moscow, was amazed to note the improvement in the atmosphere, and correctly spotted the reason for it. "There was never a more surprised man than I," he wrote to Summers,

> when I reached Petrograd this time and found such intense harmony prevailing among those who when I saw them last were at swords point. The incident of the motor trucks had caused the miracle. [19]

Even after Christmas Day, when the newspapers were carrying triumphant accounts of the initial German reply at Brest (*Pravda* on December 27 headlined its editorial, "Our Victory"), the news of

[18] Sisson, *op.cit.,* p. 170.
[19] Bullard MSS, *op.cit.,* Box 13, Letter of January 24, 1918.

the negotiations was again somewhat overshadowed in the eyes of the local Americans by the Soviet nationalization of banks and the sequestration of safety-deposit boxes, which took place on December 27. This act obviously caused acute immediate problems for the American business community, not to mention its long-term effect on American feelings toward the Soviet regime.

On Friday night, December 28, when the Smolny Institute was about to receive the news of Hoffmann's remarks to Joffe, the American colony was similarly preoccupied by the public showing of an American war propaganda film. This was a sequence which Sisson and his associates had contrived to piece together and which they exhibited in one of the theaters on the Nevski Prospekt, with a specially hired Russian orchestra to play "The Star Spangled Banner" to produce the proper atmosphere, and with the Ambassador and the members of the Military Mission, in uniform, attending.

All these events tended to preoccupy the leaders of the American colony, and perhaps to overshadow the incomplete and confusing reports about the peace negotiations.

Meanwhile, however, Robins and Judson had not relaxed their pressure on the Ambassador to authorize some sort of regular contact with the Soviet authorities, with a view to influencing the terms of peace and preventing exploitation by Germany of Russia's military weakness. As we have seen, Francis had been shaken by the Kalpashnikov incident—to a point where he had defied instructions from Washington and had, on his own responsibility, told Robins to continue to visit Smolny. This had put Francis under the necessity of seeking Washington's *ex post facto* approval for his action. But beyond this, the steady pressure from Judson and Robins, plus the news from Brest and the failure of the various anti-Soviet factions, was causing him to waver in his own views about the attitude he and his government should adopt toward the Soviet authorities.

On the evening of December 22, the Ambassador was General Judson's guest. The old gentleman was tired and shaken. This had been, for him, the crucial day of the Kalpashnikov affair. On the previous evening Trotsky had publicly threatened him, and the mob had called for his blood. In the course of the day, he had been forced to authorize Robins to continue his contacts with the Soviet authorities. Now Judson approached him once more on the general subject of political relations with the Soviet authorities and presented him with a written memorandum which he and Major Kerth had jointly composed. The gist of this memorandum was that one should enter into "helpful, friendly, and sympathetic relations" with all the existing *de facto* governments in Russia, including the Bolshevik government; one should pour oil on the troubled waters and discourage civil war; finally, one should recognize the impossibility of Russia's waging war and try to stiffen her hands for the peace she would inevitably have to conclude.[20]

This argument seems to have had a decisive effect. The following evening—Christmas Eve—Francis despatched to Washington a telegram obviously drafted in great turmoil and anguish of spirit. His previous recommendations against any form of recognition of Bolshevik authority had, he explained, been occasioned by his belief that the Soviet government would not last long. Now, however, it had run about seven weeks, "during which period Germany has made great progress toward again establishing her influence here." There was general agreement that Russia could not resume hostilities. He was therefore willing "to swallow pride, sacrifice dignity, and with discretion do all that is necessary to prevent Russia's becoming an ally of Germany." It was just possible, he thought, that by

... establishing relations with the Soviet Government [the] Allied representatives could influence terms of peace and thus preserve Russian neutrality, thereby preventing Germany's acquiring munitions of war stored in Russia; also preventing immense Russian resources becoming available by Germany for conflict with Allies. ...

He added that he had not discussed this suggestion as yet with his colleagues, and would highly appreciate the Secretary's views on the course he had outlined.[21]

Two days later, on December 26, Francis had a long and friendly talk with Robins. He learned for the first time that Robins had been visiting Trotsky regularly "at times nearly every day." [22] Robins assured him that the work of the Red Cross could not be carried on without such contacts and warned that it would cause offense to the Soviet government if such visits were abruptly terminated. In wiring Washington of this conversation, Francis concluded:

[20] Judson MSS, *op.cit.*, Diary, December 23, 1917.
[21] *Foreign Relations, 1918, Russia*, Vol. I, *op.cit.*, pp. 324–326, Telegram 2138, December 24, 1917.
[22] National Archives, Petrograd Embassy 800 File, *op.cit.*, Francis' telegram 2148, December 27, 1917, 9 p.m.

. . . I have therefore given my consent. If you do not approve, please instruct by wire.

Robins, also, after his talk with Francis, wired Henry P. Davison, through the Embassy, asking him to "urge upon the President the necessity of our continued intercourse with the Bolshevik Government." (By "our" he meant the Red Cross Commission.) To Davison, Robins said nothing about the wider political purposes the Ambassador had in mind. Intercourse by the Red Cross representative with the government, he explained, would make it possible for him to "arrange for transportation and distribution of supplies, particularly milk." The Ambassador, he added, approved his request and had advised the State Department to that effect.[23]

The following day (Thursday, December 27) Judson noted in his diary the progress that was being made:

. . . enemy peace terms have been revealed. . . . Amb. has at last cabled home for authority to have intercourse . . . and has authorized Robins . . . to go to Trotsky . . . now . . . perhaps too late.

Lansing's reply to the Ambassador's inquiry about Robins was despatched from Washington on December 29. It delicately bypassed the question of Robins' contacts with the Soviet authorities, and merely emphasized that the Department wished the Red Cross work to go forward and was unwilling that it should be interrupted just because Robins was in uniform. Robins, the Secretary wired, was

. . . to understand explicitly that he acts for and represents Red Cross and not Embassy, Red Cross being an organization maintained by private subscription and not by United States Government. Robins may therefore continue measures to distribute supplies, specially as supplies continuing to come forward.[24]

A few days later, on January 6, Davison wired Robins that "State Department has cabled approval your unnumbered December 26." [25] This, it may be noted, was not strictly accurate. The Department had not committed itself about contacts.[26] But for Robins, who had Davison's explanatory message, the year 1918 began with what he

---

[23] *Foreign Relations, 1918, Russia,* Vol. III, *op.cit.,* p. 106, Telegram 2141, December 27, 1917.
[24] *Loc.cit.,* Telegram 1948, December 29, 1917, 7 p.m.
[25] Cumming & Pettit, *op.cit.,* p. 60.
[26] This may have been the cause of Francis' impression, stated to the investigating Senators in 1919, that he had never received any reply to his inquiry.

took to be formal authorization to continue his dealings with the Soviet authorities, though only on Red Cross business.

To return to the sequence of events in Petrograd: it will be recalled that the popular demonstration, initially arranged to celebrate the successes of Soviet diplomacy, was to be held on Sunday, December 30. Sisson decided to attend, and sent to Trotsky's office to obtain passes for his automobile. The messenger brought back word that Trotsky's secretary, Shalyapina, wanted to see the parade without getting her feet wet and would like to ride along with him. Fortified by the presence of this distinguished passenger, whose prestige thawed all police cordons, Sisson, with two or three other Americans, drove for hours among the throngs of demonstrators. There were only three vehicles on the streets of Petrograd through which the parade moved that day. One of these was Sisson's. A second, significantly, bore the leaders of the German naval and economic missions, whom the *Pravda* was so concerned to impress.[27] There could be no doubt for whom the parade was intended.

The following day, December 31, it will be recalled, was the day on which the Soviet authorities decided to release the news of Hoffmann's demands regarding the eastern European territories. It was to be late that night that the communiqué would be issued by the press bureau. However, whether at Soviet initiative or otherwise, Robins was received in late afternoon by Trotsky and the Commissar for War, Krylenko. We have only indirect reflections of what was said on this occasion. It was evident that Robins derived from the conversation (conducted, of course, through an interpreter) the impression that the Bolshevik leaders had discovered the Germans to be guilty of some sort of a "conspiracy" in connection with the Brest-Litovsk talks, as a result of which they were about to break off the negotiations and resume hostilities. It seems quite clear from the context of events that what Robins understood as a "conspiracy" had reference, actually, to the revelation by Hoffmann that the Germans intended to retain the eastern European territories under their occupation. There is no evidence that Robins understood this at all, either then or afterwards. The impression he did derive, however, was enough to send him rushing back to his American colleagues, agog with excitement and convinced that the moment for American ac-

---

[27] Sisson, *op.cit.,* Chapter XII, pp. 184–196. Sisson did not explain who was in the third vehicle.

tion was at last at hand. His first point of call was Judson's office. "Today at about 3:30," Judson recorded in his diary,

. . . Robins arrived directly from Smolny, with news that the peace negotiations were about to be broken off, that [Trotsky] has discovered a German plot; that Red Guards were already en route to the north front; that Trotsky and Krilenko were already in excited conference over defense measures; and that Tr. [Trotsky] had asked what America would do if a break came. We hastened to the Embassy. After a short conference the Amb. agreed that R. [Robins] should go to Tr. and inform him that we would render all assistance possible. . . .

The Ambassador gave a similar account. He reported to the Department the following day:

Robins entered Embassy yesterday afternoon most excited, saying had just left Trotsky and Krylenko enraged because [they] claimed to have discovered "conspiracy" of Germans and had decided to sever all negotiations. Robins wished authority to tell Trotsky I would recommend prompt effective assistance in such event, which I readily granted. . . .[28]

Robins' message, so inaccurate but so encouraging, set a number of wheels in motion. Not only did the Ambassador, as we have just seen, authorize him verbally to go back to Trotsky and assure him of American support in the event of a break in the negotiations, but Francis also went at once to see his British and French colleagues to apprise them of the news.

Sisson, meanwhile, rushed over to see Karl Radek, in the hopes of getting further information. Radek was at that time simultaneously (as head of the Soviet propaganda bureau) feeding subversive propaganda to the German armed forces and (as negotiator) participating in the official talks with the German naval and economic missions in Petrograd. Sisson had contact with him by virtue of their common interest in anti-German propaganda activities. Sisson found him that evening,

. . . walking on air, breathing war of arms and propaganda. The Bolsheviks would fight, he said, because they would perish if they did not.[29]

In this way Radek confirmed the Americans in their misunderstanding of the Soviet position.

[28] *Foreign Relations, 1918, Russia*, Vol. I, *op.cit.*, p. 418; Telegram 2172, January 1, 1918.
[29] Sisson, *op.cit.*, p. 189.

The First Brest-Litovsk Crisis

All this, it will be recalled, took place on the last day of 1917. Returning from his talk with Radek in the evening, Sisson joined some of his friends to see the old year out. He recalled in his memoirs:

We watched the scarred year of 1917 go out and greeted, according to our temperaments, the untried, undoubtedly fateful year of 1918. We were far from home, in a dark and riven land. In that moment of thoughtful pause I was not lighthearted.[30]

The morning light comes very late to Petrograd in the beginning of January, and the gray dawn of New Year's Day had hardly crept over the immense streets of the snowbound capital when Robins, Judson, and Sisson were again in the Chancery, eager to pursue with the Ambassador the exciting possibilities which the close of the old year had brought. Robins, according to his diary, had awakened "with a purpose," and was not to be put off. Once again, as on many other occasions, Philip Jordan grumbled at having to wake the Governor at the behest of his subordinates.[31] On this morning, however—the first of the year 1918—Francis was as eager as the others to get down to business, and he received his impatient visitors before leaving his bed. Their mistaken impression of the state of the negotiations now fortified by Radek's fiery observations of the previous evening, Francis and his associates continued, quite erroneously, to believe that the Soviet government was about to announce a "break" in the negotiations. They were anxious to prepare an American program of immediate assistance to the Soviet government in the event of a resumption of hostilities.

Although the morning papers had carried, in somewhat inconspicuous form, the news of Hoffmann's demands, it still did not occur to the little group of Americans that this disagreement was actually what had been meant by the talk of a "break." The Ambassador, in reporting to the Department later in the day, confessed himself bewildered as to what the "conspiracy" was that Trotsky had talked about to Robins:

[30] *Ibid.,* p. 190.
[31] "He never goes to bed these terrible times until 2 or 3 oclock in the morning," Philip reported to the family at home. "I always leave him sleep until he is ready to get up . . . this man and that secretary will come to the door wanting to see the Ambassador on business. I will tell them no I am very sorry you can't see the Ambassador right now because he is sleeping. I know but this is very important. I cannot help that please have this chair and as soon as he is awake I will give him your card. If I did not do that they would have him up at 8 a.m." (Francis MSS, *op.cit.,* letter of November 30, 1917 to "Miss Annie Pulliam and the Francis Family.")

. . . Cannot imagine . . . any fit application of such term unless it be that Trotsky and Krylenko suspect Germans also dickering with Russian reactionaries or possibly with Ukraine Rada.[32]

The Ambassador and his advisers therefore continued to speculate on the consequences that a rupture of the talks could have for American policy. Would the Germans capture the city, and should they all plan to leave? This question was decided in the negative. How, then, should America act to support the Soviet government? Sisson relates:

Like most men of action, the Ambassador was exhilarated by the prospect of having something positive to do. He began to plan a request for the movement of supplies to what he trusted would become again a fighting Russia . . .[33]

In the course of the discussion, Francis agreed to prepare a cable "recommending prompt assistance" and assured Robins that he would send this cable later when he heard that the rupture had been consummated. "Meanwhile," he reported to the Department, in a message drafted after the meeting,

suppose Robins will tell Trotsky of my agreement and latter will use same for securing better terms from Germans. . . . Shall take any step think necessary to prevent separate peace. . . .[34]

The Ambassador received his New Year's Day callers that afternoon. He was, Sisson relates, in "fine fettle," obviously bucked up by the excitement of the morning.

After the Embassy reception, Sisson went off to attend the Central Executive Committee meeting at which Kamenev was to report on the Brest negotiations. The meeting struck Sisson as the most moving that he attended in Russia.

. . . The hue of the gathering was gray, unrelieved. Perhaps eight hundred persons were present in the dreary, ill-lit hall. The rostrum was low, probably a school teacher's platform in other days. Soldiers in long uniform coats and sailors in jackets were grouped in front of it and at the sides. . . .

[32] *Foreign Relations, 1918, Russia*, Vol. 1, *op.cit.*, p. 418, Telegram 2172, January 1, 1918. It was true that in addition to the dispute over the eastern European territories, the Soviet leaders were at that moment much upset over the action of the Ukrainian nationalist authority, the so-called Rada, in defying Bolshevik authority and insisting on the right to deal separately with the Germans about peace terms.

[33] Sisson, *op.cit.*, p. 191.

[34] *Foreign Relations, 1918, Russia*, Vol. 1, *op.cit.*, p. 418, from Telegram 2172.

Lenin was not present. With Trotsky sat Kamenev, summoned from Brest-Litovsk to speak for the Peace Delegation. With his well-trimmed brown beard and eyeglasses, Kamenev had the look of a teacher or a doctor rather than an agitator and politician. . . .[35]

Leaning back in his chair with his eyes closed, the indispensable Gumberg pouring translation into one ear and a second interpreter doing likewise into the other, Sisson listened to the speeches of Kamenev and the military delegates and to Trotsky's final words. He left before the meeting was over, in order to return to the Embassy and to rejoin the discussion which was being continued that evening between the Ambassador and his senior advisers. Reports vary as to what news Sisson brought from the meeting. He recorded:

I returned from the meeting to report at the Embassy that war feeling was being born, whatever Trotsky intended to do with it, but that there was no imminence of a drastic course apt to induce Germany to denounce the armistice, nor any intent on Russia's part to denounce it. The outlook, I said, was for much talk and delayed action. . . .[36]

Judson got a different impression from Sisson's words, namely, that the speeches "all indicated a spirit of readiness to resume the war if the Germans did not yield."

Whatever the burden of Sisson's report, the remainder of the evening was devoted to a continued exploration of the steps that might be taken to stiffen the back of the Soviet leaders in their showdown with the Germans. Two drafts were worked over:

. . . one designed to indicate how far Robins could go in promising to Trotsky the Amb's recommendation of support . . . the other a proposed cable to the Dept. recommending approval.[37]

This eventful New Year's Day was further marked by the receipt, that evening, of a message recalling Judson from his duties in Russia and ordering him to report to the War Department in Washington.[38] This recall was presumably the delayed result of displeasure, in high Washington circles, with the General's communication to Trotsky and his visit of December 1. The decision had, though Judson can scarcely have known it, the President's personal approval.

When discussions were resumed at the Embassy the next day

---

[35] Sisson, *op.cit.*, p. 192.
[36] *Ibid.*, p. 196.
[37] Judson MSS, *op.cit.*, Diary, January 1, 1918.
[38] Williams, *American Russian Relations, op.cit.*, p. 122.

(Wednesday, January 2), circumstances had changed in important respects.

First of all, during the night a reply had come in from the Department to Francis' telegram of Christmas Eve in which he had suggested a change in his attitude toward the Soviet authorities. The reply said:

. . . Department desires you to continue the course you have pursued in the past and which it has approved. Department relies on your good judgment to persevere in difficult situation.[39]

This was the plainest disapproval of the Robins-Judson line.

The news of Judson's recall, furthermore, can only have impressed upon the Ambassador the fact that the question of "contacts" with the Soviet authorities was a highly delicate one in Washington, not to be treated lightly.

Finally, the morning papers carried Kamenev's full account of the disagreement at Brest over Poland and the Baltic provinces. For some reason or other, the Ambassador got the impression that it was the Germans, not the Soviets, who would yield on this point.[40] In this way he arrived by a wholly erroneous process of deduction at the correct assumption that the talks would not be broken off at that juncture, after all. This assumption probably cautioned him to make conditional upon an actual resumption of hostilities any assurances of support for the Soviet government he might recommend to Washington.

Robins, on the other hand, no doubt worried by this vacillation, felt it more urgent than ever to pin the old gentleman down in writing. In any case, he reworked personally, during the course of the day, the two draft documents that had been discussed the previous day, and brought them to the Ambassador that evening, insisting that they be formally approved. One, as noted above, was the draft of a cable to the Department of State. In it, the Ambassador was to say that he had instructed General Judson to tell the Soviet authorities informally that if they resumed hostilities he, the Ambassador, would recommend that the United States government give them

[39] *Foreign Relations, 1918, Russia,* Vol. I, *op.cit.,* p. 330, Telegram 1946, December 29, 1917.

[40] "Germany will yield this point, but with reluctance, I think," he wrote in a telegram despatched to the Department on the evening of January 2. (*Ibid.,* pp. 421–422, from Telegram 2180.)

aid and assistance. The second was a draft of a communication to the Soviet Commissar for Foreign Affairs, apparently for Francis' signature, confirming the message General Judson would be instructed to communicate. (The full text of each of these drafts is included in the Appendix.)

The upshot of the evening's discussion was that the Ambassador wrote in his own hand on the margin of the first draft:

To Col. Robins: This is substance of cable I shall send to Dept. on being advised by you that peace negotiations terminated and soviet government decided to prosecute war against Germany and Austro-Hungary. D.R.F. 1/2/18 [41]

At the bottom of the second draft the Ambassador noted:

O.K., D.R.F. Subject to change by Dept., of which Col. Robins will be promptly informed. 1/2/18 [42]

By consequence, Robins' pocket diary received that evening the triumphant entry: "The Governor and Showdown. Win! Agreement for cooperation."

It is plain that in both cases the Ambassador approved the drafts provisionally, for use only in the event that hostilities should be resumed. It also seems clear that the communication to the Soviet government was intended to be used only after prior clearance by Washington. This is borne out by the fact that in the telegram which the Ambassador despatched to Washington that same evening, he said nothing about the two drafts, but only angled rather desperately for some confirmation that the Department would look with favor on such a procedure.

Despite the purely tentative nature of the Ambassador's approval, these two documents were destined to live in history and to be the subject of varied interpretations. Robins regarded them as formal confirmation of the Ambassador's agreement to his course, and as authorization to continue it. When, in 1919, Robins got the impression from the press that Francis had told the investigating Senators that he, Robins, had continued his visits to the Soviet authorities on his own responsibility and in defiance of Washington's instructions, he demanded another hearing with the Senators (he had already been heard at length prior to Mr. Francis' appearance) and trium-

[41] *Bolshevik Propaganda, Hearings* . . . , *op.cit.*, p. 1010.
[42] *Ibid.*, p. 1009.

phantly produced these two drafts in refutation of the Ambassador's statements. With particular reference to the draft communication to Trotsky, he explained to the Senators:

> For some days I had been working under the verbal instructions of the ambassador of the United States in conferences with Lenine and Trotsky and other officers of the soviet government seeking to prevent the signing of a German peace at Brest-Litovsk. To provide against the possibility of error in statement and subsequent refutation of my authorization to represent the ambassador in the manner indicated by his verbal instructions, this document was prepared by me and submitted to him as a correct statement of his verbal instructions to me, and was O.K'd by him. . . .[43]

The other document, he said, was approved by the Ambassador "for the same reasons and purposes. . . ." [44]

Robins' version found some currency among other chroniclers of the epoch.[45] But there is no evidence that the Ambassador conceived that by initialing the documents he had performed an act of any such significance as Robins supposed. Not only do his notations make it clear that he did not mean to be committed to them except in the contingency of a renewal of hostilities, and then only after obtaining authority from the Department, but it is significant that he did not mention them in his subsequent memoirs or in the account of his activities which he gave to the investigating Senators in 1919. Sisson, too, who was an enthralled participant in most of the conferences at the Embassy in those hectic days, fails to mention the drafts in his memoirs. Had the Ambassador attached to their initialing the same significance which Robins did, it is unlikely that this fact would have escaped Sisson's keen and ubiquitous attention.

Robins presumably took the documents to Smolny and showed them to Trotsky, as written confirmation of the verbal message which the Ambassador had already permitted him to transmit. Trotsky must have had them in mind when he left, three days later, to head the Soviet delegation in the further discussions at Brest. They can scarcely have failed to persuade him of a potential American

[43] *Loc.cit.*

[44] This understanding on Robins' part was repeated in the story of his experiences which he communicated to William Hard. The document, Hard said of the draft note to Trotsky, was not for immediate presentation "but it was definitely for authority and guidance to Robins in his line of conduct at Smolny and for his full protection against any later denial of his right to have pursued that line." (Hard, *op.cit.*, p. 122.)

[45] Williams, *American Russian Relations, op.cit.*, p. 122.

support which actually had no reality except in the minds of Robins and Judson. What effect, if any, this had on Trotsky's subsequent behavior at Brest it is impossible to judge—probably not much. Yet it was a serious matter that the Soviet authorities should have been permitted to rest under a misapprehension of such gravity at this crucial moment in the development of their relations with the western world. It was not the last time such confusion would flow from Robins' ambiguous position and his eagerness to be useful.

CHAPTER XII

THE FOURTEEN POINTS

The Russian people . . . call to us to say what it is that we desire, in what, if in anything, our purpose and our spirit differ from theirs; and I believe the people of the United States would wish me to respond, with utter simplicity and frankness.—Woodrow Wilson, before the Congress of the United States, January 8, 1918

SINCE the Americans involved in the events in Petrograd were, as we have seen, themselves the victims of no small confusion, and since most of the reports reaching the Department of State came from Francis, who was perhaps the most confused of all, it is small wonder that official Washington gained only a dim and not wholly intelligible impression of what was transpiring in the relations between the Petrograd Embassy and the Smolny Institute. Nor were the statesmen in Washington any more helpful in keeping Francis informed. True, they sent him a word of encouragement and sympathy when, on December 27, they learned of the threats to his personal safety. A day or so later, when they got the message about his change of heart regarding contact with the Soviet authorities, they sent him a brief message to steady him down. But that was as far as they went. Francis remained even more in the dark about their affairs than they were about his.

It should not be thought that Francis' experience in this respect was unique. The assumption that the Ambassador abroad has no need to be fully informed of the thoughts and aims of his superiors at home is, after all, a frequent feature of American statesmanship. Posterity will never know how much confusion has been occasioned, how much effort wasted, as a result of this complacent assumption. The annals of American diplomacy are studded with mistakes and lost opportunities—some major, some minor—over the memory of which might well be placed the epitaph: "The Ambassador doesn't need to know."

While Francis was thus being left to look after himself, the Russian problem continued none the less to engage the attention of official Washington. With regard to the Soviet government itself, there seemed to be nothing to do, as the year 1917 drew to a close, but hold to the policy of non-recognition and watchful waiting which the President had already approved. With respect to the anti-Bolshevik centers elsewhere in Russia, the action taken in extending covert financial aid through the British and French seemed, again, about all that could be done for the moment. In these circumstances, the only possibility that presented itself to the President for influencing the course of events in Russia was the issuance of a ringing and detailed statement of America's war aims, calculated to rally the support of liberal opinion throughout the world and to restore the fighting enthusiasm of the Russians even as it weakened that of the Germans.

Colonel House, as we have seen, had returned to Washington in mid-December, convinced of the need for just such a statement. Under the influence of Bakhmeteff, and congenitally suspicious of contrary trends in French and British thought, House had come to the conclusion that the essence of American policy should be, not to "treat Russia as an enemy," but rather to manifest sympathy for her efforts "to weld herself into a virile democracy, and to proffer our financial, industrial, and moral support in every way possible." [1] This view differed little, if at all, from Lansing's, so far as the Russian people were concerned; but it took no account of the ideology and ambitions of the Bolsheviki. Since this latter factor struck Lansing as of great importance, the two men were never able to see completely eye to eye on Russian policy in the ensuing months.

Immediately on arrival in Washington on December 18, House took up with the President the question of a statement on war aims. No time was lost in discussion of the idea in principle, for the President was no less persuaded than House that the time was ripe for such a move. It should be a statement, they felt, which would (as the editor of House's papers put it) give

to the demand of the Bolsheviks for an explanation of the objects of the

[1] Seymour, Vol. III, *op.cit.*, p. 389.

war, such an answer as might persuade Russia to stand by the Allies in their defense of democratic and liberal principles.[2]

It was clear to both men that the statement would, by its very nature, have to be addressed, over the head of the Soviet government, primarily to the Russian people. They were aware that an attempt to by-pass the Bolshevik leaders, with a view to inducing the Russian people to fight on, was the counterpart of Lenin's hope that by appealing to the peoples of the Central Powers over the heads of their governments he could induce them to stop fighting. The difference was that in one case the appeal was founded on a sincere desire to see the democratic process take its course in the country to which the appeal was addressed, whereas in the other it was combined with a summons to violent revolution.

In both cases, the principals overrated the effects of their words. Wilson appealed to what he believed to be the democratic idealism of the Russian people—their yearning for civil liberties and for self-determination within the framework of a parliamentary system. Lenin appealed to what he believed to be the Marxist-revolutionary enthusiasm of the German proletariat. Both miscalculated. In the case of the Russian people, war weariness, land hunger, ignorance, and bewilderment, plus the harsh reality of Bolshevik power, proved far more powerful than any attachment to democratic ideals. In the case of Germany, patriotism, the habit of obedience, and an attachment to the orderly processes of government were stronger than any revolutionary enthusiasm. Both Wilson and Lenin had made the mistake of attempting to project *their* respective ideological images onto the world at large and to bespeak an international validity for principles that were actually the product of their own specific environmental and educational backgrounds.

To provide background material for the contemplated statement on war aims, Wilson requested House to enlist the services of the semi-official research and advisory unit known as "The Inquiry." This was a group of private experts and authorities brought together by House, with the President's approval and encouragement, in the early fall of 1917, to study the problems of the coming peace settlement. Centered in New York, headed by President Sidney Edward Mezes of the College of the City of New York, the group included

[2] *Ibid.*, p. 322.

such eminent figures as Dr. Isaiah Bowman, Professor Charles Seymour, Mr. Walter Lippmann, Professor James T. Shotwell, and Mr. David Hunter Miller. By mid-December the members of the Inquiry were already well launched on their study of the problems of the future peace conference. Following House's discussion with the President on December 18, they were now asked to prepare specific recommendations for the points to be incorporated into the contemplated statement on war aims, particularly with respect to the tangled territorial problems that so preoccupied the European Allies.

Over the Christmas season, while the members of the Inquiry were busy with this task, pressures were exerted on the President from an astonishing variety of quarters, urging very much the sort of statement he already had in mind to make. One of the most important sources of such pressure, and one destined to play a considerable part in the discussion of Russian affairs in Washington in the coming months, was the person and entourage of William Boyce Thompson.

After leaving Petrograd on November 28, Thompson had proceeded to London. There, with the enthusiastic backing of Mr. Thomas Lamont, he had had conferences with Lloyd George and other British figures. Lloyd George had been visibly impressed with Thompson's views[3] and had urged that they be presented as soon as possible to President Wilson. Thompson and Lamont had accordingly sailed at once for New York, full of the importance of Thompson's experience, of his outlook on the Russian problem, and of the impression he had made on Lloyd George. They arrived in New York on Christmas morning, after an eventful wartime crossing. Proceeding directly to Washington, they at once got in touch with George Creel, with a view to arranging through him an appointment with the President. They were sure the President would be eager, as Lloyd George had been, to hear what Thompson had to say. But this, Lamont recorded,

. . . was not to be. Mr. Wilson refused to see us. He was reported to us as saying he did not want to talk with anyone who would throw away a million dollars, alluding to Colonel Thompson's generous and heroic

[3] Hagedorn, *op.cit.,* p. 257; also Thomas W. Lamont, *Across World Frontiers,* Harcourt, Brace & Co., New York, 1951, p. 87.

attempt, as his Red Cross associates thought it was, to try to keep Kerensky in power and Russia in the war as our ally. We went the rounds of Washington and at every point met sympathetic ears. . . .

But no: President Wilson felt that he had made his gesture toward Russia in the various public communications that he had uttered, urging upon the Russian people the joys of democratic action.

Thompson and Lamont were dumfounded at their inability to get to the President. They could, as Lamont expressed it,

. . . hardly believe that Mr. Wilson would listen neither to Thompson, coming almost direct from Petrograd, nor to the urgent views of the British Prime Minister.[4]

Faut de mieux, they set forth Thompson's views in a memorandum, which Creel was asked to place in the President's hands. The memorandum may be seen in the Wilson papers. It can be taken as an expression of what Thompson wanted to say personally to the President, and of what he did say to Lansing, with whom he had an interview on December 31. Characteristically, in the light of Thompson's shrewd intelligence but brief and superficial experience with Russian matters, the document embraced a number of penetrating insights and a number of grievous errors. Thompson denied (correctly) that the Bolsheviki were "the wild-eyed rabble that most of us consider them," but described them (anything but correctly) as

. . . kindly, earnest men, heartily desiring to live at peace with their fellow men and being absolutely unwilling to fight each other or to enter into any form of civil war.

He criticized the Allies, particularly the British, for having supported Kornilov and for adopting an unfriendly attitude toward the Bolsheviki. He held out hope that Russian resistance to the Germans could yet be stimulated. For this, he maintained that "recognition of the Bolsheviks is not essential; *contact* is." He advocated the establishment of an informal committee, consisting possibly only of representatives of the President and Prime Minister, to sit in Petrograd and to assure the delivery of food and other relief to the Russian people through the Red Cross. He expressed confidence that the Russians, "if given any intelligent aid or support in the negotiations," would not submit to a German peace and that

[4] Lamont, *op. cit.,* pp. 90–91.

. . . it is possible, even now, to take entire charge of the Russian situation, bringing it around to our point of view absolutely.[5]

This last was certainly a rash and grievous over-statement of the possibilities of the situation, reflecting no doubt the fact that Thompson was already five weeks out of date with respect to a rapidly moving situation. If there had been any hope at the end of November that hostilities might be resumed on the eastern front, such expectations certainly no longer existed by the end of December; and the winds of interest and passion that had by this time been released from the Pandora's box of Russian political feeling were not such that anyone, least of all foreigners unversed in Russian ways, could have "taken entire charge" of them.

While Thompson's recommendations went further than Wilson and Lansing were yet inclined to go in the matter of "contacts," they were in other respects not too far from official American thinking, and particularly from that of the President and Colonel House. One has the impression that Wilson's refusal to receive Thompson resulted less from what he knew of Thompson's views than from his displeasure over Thompson's independent use of personal funds to support the Kerensky government.

One passage in Thompson's memorandum, in particular, coincided aptly with the President's own feelings, and may well have engaged his attention. Thompson expressed the belief

. . . that the President can speak to the Russian people almost as well through a message to the American Congress as by a formal communication to those representing the Russian government.

He went on to recommend that

. . . America should now declare herself in agreement with certain of the basic Russian peace terms as quoted, such as no punitive indemnities, etc.

What Thompson failed to understand was that such a recommendation merely strengthened the President in his tendency to feel that words would be enough, if they were the right words, and that any further development of "contacts" with the Bolshevik authorities was secondary, if not superfluous.

On January 1, 1918, Lansing received from Francis the text of

[5] Wilson MSS, Series II, *op.cit.*

Trotsky's appeal to the Allied peoples and governments of December 29. The Secretary was by this time keenly conscious of the importance of the ideological element in Soviet statements, and this latest document engaged his eager attention. He pondered it and discussed it with others over the 2nd. That day he penned a long letter to the President with his comments.[6] The tenor of this letter is worthy of note.

Lansing began by acknowledging the adroitness of the unknown author of the Soviet appeal. He noted that the appeal was addressed only to a given class of society everywhere, and observed quite correctly that this was "of course a direct threat at existing social order in all countries." Very astutely he then went on to point out the contradiction between the professed orientation toward a single social class and the demagogic demand for recognition of the rights of nationalities (each of which presumably embraced several classes). Thus at a very early date he put his finger on a theoretical question that was to bedevil Soviet publicists and statesmen for decades to come: namely, how to reconcile a theoretical emphasis on class as opposed to nationality with the fact that *national* feeling was the strongest political emotion of the age.

Lansing then went on to deal with the principle of self-determination, as expounded in the Soviet appeal, and to point out the horrendous implications which such a principle, if carried too far, could have from the standpoint of western political institutions. He noted that the United States had denied the right of the South to determine its own political allegiance in 1861. He observed correctly that there was a great difference between the application of the principle of self-determination to regions which lay between the territory of two established nations and to territories already embraced within the sovereignty of an established state. He pointed out what the rigid application of this principle would mean to the colonial powers. (The relevance of these observations to Wilson's own attachment to the principle of self-determination is inescapable.)

Lansing ended by questioning the authority of the Bolsheviki to speak for the Russian people. As for the American reaction, he preferred that the appeal should remain unanswered "in view of the threat against existing governments and the promised aid to revolutionists. . . ." He was convinced that nothing could be said

[6] *Foreign Relations, The Lansing Papers*, Vol. ii, *op.cit.*, pp. 346–349.

which would gain the favor of Lenin and Trotsky or render them amenable to reason. "I feel," he said in conclusion,

that to make any sort of reply would be contrary to the dignity of the United States and offer opportunity for further insult and threats, although I do not mean that it may not be expedient at some time in the near future to state our peace terms in more detail than has yet been done.

The President, too, was much interested in the Soviet appeal. On January 3 (presumably with Lansing's comment of the previous day before him), he mentioned the appeal to the retiring British Ambassador, Sir Cecil Spring Rice, who had come in to inform him of his recall. Spring Rice subsequently sent to Balfour the following account of what the President had said on this occasion:

. . . He himself [i.e., the President] with the full consent of the American people and with their express approval had made an appeal to the German people behind the back of the German Government. The Bolsheviki in Russia were now adopting the same policy. They had issued an appeal to all the nations of the world, to the peoples and not to the governments. He was without information at present, or at least without certain information, as to what reception had been given to this appeal. But there was evidence at hand that certainly in Italy and probably also in England and France, the appeal had not been without its effect. In the United States active agitation was proceeding. It was too early yet to say with positive certainty how successful this agitation had been. But it was evident that if the appeal of the Bolsheviki was allowed to remain unanswered, if nothing were done to counteract it, the effect would be great and would increase. . . .

The President had then gone on to describe the principle of self-determination embodied in the appeal and to say:

. . . In point of . . . pure logic, this principle which was good in itself would lead to the complete independence of various small nationalities now forming part of various Empires. Pushed to its extreme, the principle would mean the disruption of existing governments, to an undefinable extent. . . .[7]

From these last words one may surmise that the logic of Lansing's observations about self-determination was not wholly lost on the President.

[7] Stephen Gwynn, Editor, *The Letters and Friendships of Sir Ceil Spring Rice: A Record,* Houghton Mifflin Co., Boston, 1929, Vol. II, pp. 423–424.

While the Soviet appeal of December 29 came to Wilson's attention long after the decision to make his Fourteen Points speech had been taken and even at a time when work was well advanced on the text, it evidently did reinforce in his mind the need for just such a public statement as he was about to make. In particular, it confirmed him in the belief that it was urgently necessary to say something that could counter the continued demagogic appropriation by the Bolsheviki of his own slogans.

Further support for the idea of such a statement came in recommendations submitted from Petrograd by both Francis and Sisson in precisely those days when the preparation of the speech, without the knowledge of either of these gentlemen, was approaching completion. These recommendations, as it happened, could not have fitted more neatly with what the President already had in mind to do.

Anticipating the issuance of the Soviet appeal of December 29 (issued some hours later), Francis recommended on that day that the President, while declining the renewed invitation to participate in the peace talks, should

. . . address a communication to the Russian people explaining the declination in order to prevent Russia's falling into the arms of Germany as ally and thus induce Russian benevolent neutrality and transfer to Central Empires responsibility for continuance of war.[8]

Four days later, the Ambassador spelled this recommendation out in greater detail in a message received in Washington just two days prior to the delivery of the President's speech.[9] He requested that the President

. . . reiterate in some public manner the noble expressions of your address to the United States Senate of January 22 last. . . .

. . . Failure to reiterate these sentiments may possibly cause Russia to take a step which will . . . sacrifice the gains of the revolution. . . . The tired people of this country will not fight for territory . . . for commercial advantage . . . for treaties made by governments they had overturned, but they possibly will struggle for a democratic peace, for the fruits of the revolution, if appealed to by a country whose unselfish motives they recognize. . . .

---

[8] *Foreign Relations, 1918, Russia,* Vol. I, *op.cit.,* p. 405, Telegram 2166, December 29, 1917, 11 p.m.

[9] *Ibid.,* pp. 422–424, from Telegram 2187, January 3, 1918, midnight, "For the President."

... The only hope for Russia remaining in the war is from the failure of the separate peace. ... Such a communication as you ... can make, ... will make a deep impression on the heart of Russia. ...

In this message, which strongly reflects the influence Robins and Judson had brought to bear on him over the Christmas season, Francis made the error of overrating (for the reasons seen in the last chapter) the probability of a break in Soviet-German negotiations and the possibility of continued Russian resistance to Germany. He also failed, as we have seen, to recognize the indifference to world affairs of those portions of Russian society (notably the disintegrating army) on which the Soviet leaders were basing their power. The liberal and conservative classes had had greater interest in the war, but they were now helpless and voiceless.

The Ambassador's message arrived almost simultaneously with a similar recommendation from Sisson. Through a rather amazing relationship with Radek's press bureau (by virtue of which Sisson supplied the funds for payment of the Soviet propaganda workers when the Soviet nationalization of the banks interfered with the Soviet government's own financial procedures), Sisson had been promised Bolshevik help in infiltrating American propaganda through the German lines. He therefore wired to Washington on January 3:

If President will re-state anti-imperialistic war aims and democratic peace requisites of America thousand words or less, short almost placard paragraphs, short sentences, I can get it fed into Germany in great quanties in German translation, and can utilize Russian version potently in army and everywhere.[10]

In the light of the content of these recommendations from the Ambassador and Sisson, it is understandable that both were amazed and delighted when, a few days later, the President's speech, reading like a direct response to their requests, began to come in over the wires to Petrograd. In this way both added themselves, erroneously but understandably, to the long list of people who ascribed Wilson's Fourteen Points speech to their particular inspiration.[11]

[10] Sisson, *op.cit.*, p. 205.

[11] On January 24, Bullard wrote from Petrograd to Summers in Moscow that ". . . everybody is claiming the exclusive honor for having influenced the President to deliver [the speech]. The Governor has at least ten times told me the exact hour on which he filed his despatch urging the President to such action and, according to

Meanwhile, the work of the members of the Inquiry—the most important single source of the Fourteen Points speech—had been proceeding intensively in New York. The fruits of this effort were brought to Washington by House on January 4 and laid before the President on that day. The two men immediately entered on a detailed examination and discussion of this material, lasting late into the night and through the following morning.

With regard to Russia, the members of the Inquiry had not suggested any specific language for the address. They had restricted themselves to interpretive comment. The military situation in Russia they of course recognized as a tremendous liability to the Allied cause. But they set off against it certain factors that operated against German domination: the anti-capitalist ideology of the new regime; the power of the Russian Orthodox faith (so incompatible with German Protestantism); and the strong nationalist feelings by which the moderate elements were still dominated. "Toward Russia," the members of the Inquiry concluded,

our best success will lie: 1) in showing that we are not unwilling to state war aims; 2) in a hearty propaganda of the idea of a league of nations; and 3) in a demonstration to them that the diplomatic offensive is in progress, and that the Allies are not relying totally upon force.[12]

It was with these recommendations on the Russian question that the President, with House's help, whipped his speech into shape for delivery on the 8th.

Although Lansing, in his letter of January 2, had hinted at the expediency of an early statement on war aims, and probably suspected that something of the sort was in the wind, he was not taken into confidence about the President's intention to give such a speech or consulted on its wording until the afternoon before its delivery. House recorded that Lansing "accepted it in toto, although he made several suggestions as to words which the President adopted." [13] One

---

his theory, W.W. at once locked himself in with his typewriter and went to it. The Governor modestly hints that the President lifted some of his very phrases. General Judson has much the same story. So has Robins, a long cable from him to [Davison] arrived in Washington at the same time as Col. Thompson, a few days before the Message was delivered. Sisson had cabled at length also in time to claim some credit. And—poor little me—well a long report of mine to Col. House ought to have been in the dossier about the First of January. So you see we can all claim credit for it and look down patronizingly on the other ginks who think that they did it." (Bullard MSS, *op.cit.*, Box 13.)

[12] Wilson MSS, Series II, *op.cit.*

[13] House MSS, *op.cit.*, Diary, January 9, 1918.

wonders whether Lansing's "acceptance" was not largely a matter of resignation, in view of the late date at which he had been admitted to the discussion.

The other Cabinet members, at the President's insistence, were not forewarned at all. House endeavored in vain to persuade Wilson to be more communicative with the members of his official family.

In view of the extent to which the introductory passages of the Fourteen Points speech were concerned with the Russian problem, it is perhaps worthwhile to examine these passages in detail, interrupting them from time to time at those points where they seem to deserve comment.

The President began [14] with a reference to the Brest-Litovsk parleys:

Once more, as repeatedly before, the spokesmen of the Central Empires have indicated their desire to discuss the objects of the war and the possible bases of a general peace. Parleys have been in progress at Brest-Litovsk between Russian representatives and representatives of the Central Powers to which the attention of all the belligerents has been invited for the purpose of ascertaining whether it may be possible to extend these parleys into a general conference with regard to terms of peace and settlement. The Russian representatives presented not only a perfectly definite statement of the principles upon which they would be willing to conclude peace but also an equally definite program of the concrete application of those principles.

Wilson was evidently referring here to the six-point program put forward by the Soviet delegation on December 22. Just what he meant by the "definite program of the concrete application of those principles" is obscure.

The representatives of the Central Powers, on their part, presented an outline of settlement which, if much less definite, seemed susceptible of liberal interpretation until their specific program of practical terms was added.

The President was plainly aware of the sequence of events at Brest-Litovsk, specifically of Hoffmann's later clarification of the original German statement.

That program proposed no concessions at all either to the sovereignty of Russia or to the preferences of the populations with whose fortunes

[14] *Foreign Relations, 1918*, Supplement 1, *The World War*, Vol. 1 (1933), pp. 12–17.

it dealt, but meant, in a word, that the Central Empires were to keep every foot of territory their armed forces had occupied,—every province, every city, every point of vantage,—as a permanent addition to their territories and their power. It is a reasonable conjecture that the general principles of settlement which they at first suggested originated with the more liberal statesmen of Germany and Austria, the men who have begun to feel the force of their own people's thought and purpose, while the concrete terms of actual settlement came from the military leaders who had no thought but to keep what they have got. The negotiations have been broken off. The Russian representatives were sincere and in earnest. They cannot entertain such proposals of conquest and domination.

Where the President had gotten the erroneous impression that the talks had been broken off is not apparent. It was quite possibly from Francis' telegram of January 1, in which he reported the highly misleading impression Robins had carried away from his talk of the preceding day with Trotsky. Francis had sent a further message the next day, apparently intended to correct this impression and to make it plain that the talks were supposed to be resumed on January 8, but the wording was somewhat obscure and Wilson may not have fully grasped its significance. The United States press, carrying stories from Petrograd which mirrored the same misconceptions under which Robins and the Ambassador were suffering, may also have contributed to Wilson's bewilderment. On January 3, for example, the *New York Times* had a front-page headline: "Negotiations Said to be Broken Off."

Most striking, in these passages of the speech, is the unqualified approval and sympathy with which the President treats Soviet diplomacy in the Brest-Litovsk talks. His expressions are so unequivocal in this respect that one is constrained to wonder whether he had read carefully Trotsky's appeal of December 29, with its provocative language and its final threat that ". . . if the Allied governments, in the blind stubbornness characteristic of declining and perishing classes, again refuse to participate in the negotiations, then the working class will be faced with the iron necessity of wresting power from the hands of those who either cannot or will not give peace to the peoples of the world." Since the United States government had no intention of participating in the negotiations, it presumably fell into the category of those from whose hands power was to be wrested. But there is no hint, in the text of Wilson's speech, that he appreciated this fact.

The Fourteen Points

The note of sympathy and approval for Soviet diplomacy is struck again in the succeeding paragraph:

... The Russian representatives have insisted, very justly, very wisely, and in the true spirit of modern democracy, that the conferences they have been holding with the Teutonic and Turkish statesmen should be held within open, not closed, doors, and all the world has been audience, as was desired. ...

After then stressing the general reasons why, in his opinion, recent German statements of war aims, at Brest-Litovsk and elsewhere, should "be responded to, and responded to with the utmost candor," the President added the following highly significant considerations:

There is, moreover, a voice calling for these definitions of principle and of purpose which is, it seems to me, more thrilling and more compelling than any of the many moving voices with which the troubled air of the world is filled. It is the voice of the Russian people. They are prostrate and all but helpless, it would seem, before the grim power of Germany, which has hitherto known no relenting and no pity. Their power, apparently, is shattered. And yet their soul is not subservient. They will not yield either in principle or in action. Their conception of what is right, of what it is humane and honorable for them to accept, has been stated with a frankness, a largeness of view, a generosity of spirit, and a universal human sympathy which must challenge the admiration of every friend of mankind; and they have refused to compound their ideals or desert others that they themselves may be safe. They call to us to say what it is that we desire, in what, if in anything, our purpose and our spirit differ from theirs; and I believe that the people of the United States would wish me to respond, with utter simplicity and frankness. Whether their present leaders believe it or not, it is our heartfelt desire and hope that some way may be opened whereby we may be privileged to assist the people of Russia to attain their utmost hope of liberty and ordered peace. ...

This passage, treating at one and the same time the motives of the Soviet spokesmen at Brest-Litovsk and the state of mind of the Russian people, was, despite its eloquence, inaccurate and unrealistic. The President, it will be noted, identified the statements of the Soviet negotiators at Brest-Litovsk with the voice of the Russian people. Actually, the Bolshevik regime had no mandate from the people. It had, in fact, been repudiated by the majority of the people in elections which had been held only six weeks earlier. The instructions given to the Soviet delegation at Brest-Litovsk reflected faithfully the political interests of the Bolshevik faction at a particularly desperate moment in its history, and nothing else. This was a faction which never had been supported by the majority of the Russian people, and never would be so supported, in the western understanding of that word. Its leaders had a profound contempt for what they called bourgeois parliamentarianism, and professed to understand better than the Russian people themselves what their true interests were.

In addition to identifying these two voices, the President somewhat misinterpreted both of them. The Russian people were represented here as a people preoccupied with national humiliation at the hands of the enemy, united in their resentment of what was being done to them by a foreign power. Actually, as we have seen, great portions of them, and particularly those portions on which the Bolsheviki relied most heavily, were preoccupied primarily with the internal dissensions and passions of the time. As for the Soviet leaders, whose views had been expressed by the spokesmen at Brest-Litovsk, their conception of what it was "right" for them to accept at the hands of the Germans was not at all connected with the feelings of what might have been "humane and honorable"—both of these concepts, when applied to the political process, being repudiated by them as the earmarks of "rotten liberalism." Nor was it correct to say that their outlook was marked by a largeness of view or a generosity of spirit. Surely the Bolshevik outlook, whatever virtues it may be conceived to have, has always been one of the most narrowly and intolerantly exclusive of all political ideologies. Far from being distinguished by "a universal human sympathy which must challenge the admiration of every friend of mankind," it pitilessly consigned by concept to "the ash heap of history," i.e. to suffering and ruin, great sections of the Russian and world population, namely the *bourgeoisie* and the non-Marxist intelligentsia, though these were, even in the Marxist book, not the conscious architects of their own behavior but the helpless victims of "objective" historical forces.

The President's words "whether their present leaders believe it or not" indicated a realization of the fact that the Bolshevik leaders would be skeptical of his statements. These words would later be cited as proof that he entertained no illusions about the Bolshevik attitude. But in the same sentence he suggested that the Bolshevik leaders shared with the Russian people "the utmost hope of liberty and ordered peace." Also, his expressed desire that Americans might someday "be privileged to assist the people of Russia" to attain these blessings reflected either an attempt to appeal to the people over the heads of the regime, or a deep misunderstanding of Bolshevik psychology, in which the thought of capitalist governments helping anybody to any positive goal, except by accident or blind folly, was preposterous.

The next specific reference to Russia in the speech was Point vi of the Fourteen Points, which read as follows:

vi. The evacuation of all Russian territory and such a settlement of all questions affecting Russia as will secure the best and freest cooperation of the other nations of the world in obtaining for her an unhampered and unembarrassed opportunity for the independent determination of her own political development and national policy and assure her of a sincere welcome into the society of free nations under institutions of her own choosing; and, more than a welcome, assistance also of every kind that she may need and may herself desire. The treatment accorded Russia by her sister nations in the months to come will be the acid test of their good will, of their comprehension of her needs as distinguished from their own interests, and of their intelligent and unselfish sympathy.

This passage was not drafted by the President. It had apparently been prepared, at least in part, by House and submitted to Bakhmeteff for his approval before its presentation to the President.[15] House's own words about the passage and the President's reaction to it were as follows:

I read him a sentence that I had prepared regarding Russia. . . . I said that it did not make any difference how much the President resented Russia's action, the part of wisdom was to segregate her, as far as we were able, from Germany, and that it could only be done by the broadest and friendliest expressions of sympathy and a promise of more substantial help. There was no argument about this because our minds ran parallel. . . .[16]

[15] On December 22, according to his diary, House had conferred with Bakhmeteff and had "asked him to make a memorandum of the position this country should take" with a view to incorporation into the forthcoming speech. Possibly Point vi was derived at least in part from Bakhmeteff's response. But House records that he saw Bakhmeteff again on December 31, and "got nothing new from him worth while . . . I had in mind to advise the President almost along the exact lines he urged upon me" (House MSS, *op.cit.*).

[16] Seymour, Vol. iii, *op.cit.*, p. 331.

Aside from the extremely cumbersome wording, which must have greatly reduced the effectiveness of the article when translated into Russian, this passage was on its face unexceptionable and mildly agreeable, from the Russian standpoint.[17] The meaning of the phrase "evacuation of all Russian territory" depended of course on what you conceived "Russian territory" to be. The operation of the strong separatist tendencies unleashed by the Russian Revolution had already drawn a question mark over this concept, and bade fair to modify it still more in the future. This fact was recognized, by implication, in the thirteenth of the Fourteen Points, which envisaged an independent Poland, to include "the territories inhabited by indisputably Polish populations"—an arrangement which would have encroached significantly on the boundaries of the pre-World War Russian Empire. It was precisely this point, unclarified in the President's formula, which was at that time the bone of contention between the Bolsheviki and the Germans. The latter had, after all, accepted the principle that the occupying armies be withdrawn from everyone's territory "as soon as possible." The argument was over the question: what constituted Russian territory?

As for the remaining portions of this article, they must, from the Soviet point of view, have fallen squarely into the compartment of meaningless politeness and bourgeois hypocrisy. It is inconceivable that any of these friendly references should have been taken by the Soviet leaders as evidence of any sincere idealism or of any real possibility of genuinely helpful and sympathetic treatment at the hands of any capitalist government in the postwar era.

When the text of the President's speech began to come over the wires in Petrograd, on Thursday, January 10, there was great excitement and feverish activity in Sisson's department. Translation into Russian was begun at once. By 6:00 p.m., as much of the speech as had come in that day was ready for initial distribution. Sisson took several sets and rushed off, with Gumberg, to the Smolny Institute, determined to get the speech transmitted, if possible, to the Soviet delegation at Brest-Litovsk. Lenin and Trotsky were both away, and the central offices at Smolny were almost deserted. It became neces-

---

[17] The Soviet commentator, Genkin, *op.cit.*, pp. 20–25, refers to this passage as "distinguished not only by ponderous awkwardness but by hypocrisy."

sary to hunt out some junior officials, who were not enthusiastic over the proposal. "They smiled at me," Sisson recounts, "and asked what new caper of the Imperialistic American Government was this." [18]

Sisson had his suspicions as to what Gumberg really told the Smolny officials on this occasion. He doubted that Gumberg said what he had been asked to say—namely, that the officials should stop acting "like a lot of children." But he gave Gumberg high marks for performance and effectiveness; within an hour the material was despatched to Trotsky by courier.

It was late the following afternoon before the remainder of the text had been received, translated, and prepared for distribution. Sisson started off again for Smolny, this time accompanied by Robins. Lenin was now back. Sisson had never met him; [19] he wanted very much to do so, and was delighted when Gumberg succeeded in wangling admittance for the three of them to Lenin's office.

Lenin saw at once that the document might be useful to the Soviet negotiators at Brest. "It did not take one minute," Sisson records,

to convince him that the full message should go to Trotsky by direct wire. He grabbed the copy and sprinted for the telegraph office himself.

On Sisson, Lenin made the impression of one who might be

. . . the *bourgeois* mayor of a French town—short, sparsely bearded, a bronze man in hair and whiskers, small, shrewd eyes, round of face, smiling and genial when he desires to be. And this time he did.

As to Lenin's reaction to the content of the speech, we may let Sisson describe this, too, in his own words:

He welcomed the message as an unexpected but not undeserved staff, but he did not let us forget for a moment that he regarded it as coming not from a fellow thinker but from a just and tolerant class opponent. . . .

But on the specific matter of general peace Lenin saw the potency of the speech and accepted its help. "It is a great step ahead toward the

---

[18] Sisson, *op.cit.* This and following citations dealing with the visits to Smolny on January 10–11 are taken from pp. 207–209.

[19] Sisson thought it necessary, in his memoirs, to comment on the fact that this was his first meeting with Lenin. He explained that while up to that time he had had "channels running to every seat of power," he had nevertheless "camouflaged as a newspaper man" and had kept out of situations that smacked of recognition. Sisson says it was also Robins' first meeting with Lenin. This is, of course, at variance with Hard's account of the Kalpashnikov affair (see above, Chapter X), which implied that Robins already knew Lenin at that time. But Sisson is by far the more reliable source.

peace of the world," he said—and in English, which he speaks very well. He was as joyous as a boy over the President's humanly understanding words to Russia, and his recognition of the honesty of Bolshevik purpose.

"Yet I have been called a German spy," he said, and smiled and threw up the palms of his hands.

His only criticism was on the colonial clause, which is the only weak clause in the message. When he went unerringly for it, I knew that he had the gift for finding the cracks in any armor. But he wasn't fanatic and took the practical view that the word "equitable" could be turned in Bolshevik direction no less than in an Imperial direction.

Yet at the last he ran true to Bolshevik form (Bolshevik means more), for he said, "This is all very well as far as it goes, but why not formal recognition, and when?" That is the Bolshevik idea—ask more and more until you get it all.

It is difficult to believe that Sisson correctly gauged Lenin's reaction. Lenin may have been mildly pleased with the appearance of the speech, from the standpoint of its momentary effect on the Germans and on world opinion. But there is no evidence that he took it seriously as an expression in good faith of American policy, or that it changed anything in his view of the motives of the United States government. Only nine days later, in a document prepared for private use within the party at a most solemn moment,[20] he made it plain that his scorn for the purposes of the Allied governments as well as for those of the Central Powers remained unaltered. "The war with England and America," he wrote,

will go on for a long time; the aggressive imperialism of both groups has unmasked itself finally and completely. Under such conditions a Socialist Soviet Republic in Russia will be a model for all other peoples and excellent material for propaganda purposes. On the one side there will be the bourgeois system engaged in a strife between two coalitions of confessed plunderers, and on the other side a Socialist Soviet Republic living in peace.

Of particular interest as an indication of Wilson's incorrect understanding of Soviet motives is the evidence in this same document of Lenin's feelings with regard to the relative importance of the principle of self-determination, on the one hand, and of the prospects

[20] Bunyan & Fisher, *op.cit.*, Lenin's "Argument for Peace," pp. 500–505. This "argument" contained twenty-one points; the citations which follow in the text are from points 19 and 21. Also printed in Wheeler-Bennett, *op.cit.*, pp. 385–391, and Degras, Vol. I, *op.cit.*, pp. 34–39. (Originally published in *Pravda*, No. 34, February 24, 1918.)

for the international socialist revolution on the other. Wilson, in drawing up his Fourteen Points, was evidently under the impression that the main issue, in Soviet eyes, was the principle of self-determination. On January 20, Lenin, pointing out that to try to fight a revolutionary war at that time would be in reality to fight "for the liberation of Poland, Lithuania, and Courland," continued as follows:

. . . There is not a single Marxist who, while adhering to the foundations of Marxism and socialism, would not say that the interests of socialism are above the right of nations to self-determination. Our Socialist Republic has done and is doing everything possible to give real self-determination to Finland, the Ukraine, etc. But if the concrete circumstances are such that the safety of the Socialist Republic is being endangered in order to [prevent] the violation of the right of self-determination of a few nations . . . , there is no question but that the interests of the Socialist Republic must predominate.

Nor do the Fourteen Points appear to have made any more favorable impression on Trotsky. It never occurred to him, any more than to Lenin, to credit Wilson with any good faith in the expression of these sentiments. Just before the speech was delivered, on the eve of his own departure for Brest-Litovsk, Trotsky had expressed to two foreigners (one was the British journalist, Arthur Ransome) the cynical view that the Allies were anxious to see the Germans succeed in imposing an onerous and punitive peace on Russia, since this would ease their own problem in arriving at a peace with Germany at Russia's expense.[21] Surely nothing could have been more contrary to this view than Wilson's outright denunciation of the German terms as "proposals for conquest and domination" and his friendly support for the Bolshevik position. Yet only a fortnight after he had received the text of Wilson's statements, Trotsky took occasion to reiterate publicly, in even more incisive and provocative form, his charge that the western Allies stood behind the German terms. Speaking at the Third Congress of Soviets in Petrograd on January 26 (during the intermission in the Brest talks), he stated flatly that the Allied governments were "responsible" for the German peace terms, and added:

[21] *Foreign Relations, 1918, Russia,* Vol. I, *op.cit.,* p. 425, Telegram 2204, January 6, 1918, 5 p.m., Francis to Secretary of State; also Ransome's despatch in the *New York Times,* January 9, 1918.

. . . London gave its tacit approval of Kühlmann's terms; I declare this most emphatically. England is ready to compromise with Germany at the expense of Russia. The peace terms which Germany offers us are also the terms of America, France, and England; they [these terms] are the account which the imperialists of the world are making with the Russian Revolution. . . .[22]

Thus, whatever effect the Fourteen Points may have had on Trotsky, they certainly did not decrease his cynicism about American motives or convince him that her purposes had anything in common with those of the Soviet leadership.

The treatment of the speech in the Soviet press showed a marked variation as between the governmental and party organs. The governmental *Izvestiya,* for reasons obscure, carried the entire speech, and accompanied it with an editorial comment which, while reserved and somewhat equivocal, was at least not hostile. "The conditions laid down by President Wilson represent," the *Izvestiya* said,

a great victory in the great struggle for a democratic peace; and we may hope to find in the American people an actual ally in that struggle.[23]

The reader will note here the reference to the American people rather than to the American government, and the care taken to avoid specifically crediting Wilson with good faith or constructive statesmanship. With regard to the President's motives, the paper carefully refrained from comment.

The *Pravda,* on the other hand, as the authoritative voice of the party, pulled no punches. It had, in fact, already anticipated the President's address with publication, on January 4, of an editorial article (from the pen of Stuchka [24]) so sweeping in its qualification of the President's utterances generally as to render further comment on this particular speech almost superfluous. In this article, Stuchka had written:

. . . The American President Wilson, in the tones of a Quaker preacher, proclaims to the peoples of the world the teaching of highest governmental morality. But the peoples know the reasons for the entry of the United States into the war. The peoples know that behind this intervention stood not a concern for the interests of right and justice, but the cynical interests of the New York stock market. The American *bourgeoisie* in the course

[22] Bunyan & Fisher, *op.cit.,* p. 506.
[23] *New York Times,* January 14, 1918, despatch from Ransome.
[24] Previously, and again subsequently, Commissar for Justice, and an influential Bolshevik.

of the first three years of the war fattened on the blood of the peoples of unhappy Europe. . . . The war industry, in its turn, subordinated to itself the power of the government and forced the government to intervene in the war. Mr. Wilson serves American war industry just as Kaiser Wilhelm serves the iron and steel industry of Germany. One gives his speeches in the style of a Quaker Republican—the other wraps himself in the mists of Prussian-Protestant-Absolutist phraseology; but at bottom it is all the same. . . . This will, of course, . . . not stop the American Minister from tomorrow abetting the participation of agents of the American Mission in counter-revolutionary plots against Soviet power.[25]

To this, Sisson says he prepared a public reply, which the *Pravda* published. A search of the *Pravda* files for those days fails to reveal any such item. In any case, *Pravda's* editors plainly remained unconvinced. When the first news of the speech was received in a despatch from Stockholm, it was published by the *Pravda* under the headline: "Wilson under the Mask of an Internationalist." The subsequent editorial comment (January 12) showed no diminution of the sharpness of the communist attitude. The passages friendly to Russian purposes were given the standard propaganda twist which portrays anything favorable said by the adversary as something which the latter was "forced to admit" by the unanswerable force of circumstances. "Of course," the *Pravda* went on,

we are not for a moment in doubt about the real significance of the compliments of this representative of the American stock market. . . . We know that Wilson is the representative of the American imperialistic dictatorship, chastising its own workers and poor people with prisons, forced labor, and death sentences. . . .[26]

As a result of Sisson's heroic efforts, within a few days after the text was received in Petrograd, Wilson's Fourteen Points speech was reproduced in Russian in poster copies running into the hundreds of thousands. Three days after the receipt of the text, 30,000 copies were on the walls of Petrograd alone. A half a million copies eventually reached the eastern front, presumably falling into the hands of German soldiers.

It is impossible to assess the effect of this prodigious effort. It is the fate of many efforts of statesmanship in the international field that their effects can never be reliably measured. The speech presumably made some sort of an impression on many Russian minds.

[25] *Pravda*, No. 221, Friday, January 4, 1918.
[26] *Pravda*, No. 226, Saturday, January 12, 1918.

Possibly some of the predisposition toward America and Americans which could be observed later in the official Soviet attitude prior to the Allied intervention, as well as the enduring general friendliness of individual Russians toward Americans in years to come, may have been attributable to this stimulus.

But the Soviet leaders had remained skeptical and scornful, and had realistically noted that the message was not accompanied by recognition, the main thing for them, so far as Russian-American relations were concerned.

All in all, it is difficult to conceive that the subsequent course of events at Brest-Litovsk would have been appreciably different had the Fourteen Points speech never been made. The gap in understanding was greater, the measure of tragedy more profound, and the hour later, than Wilson suspected. Pleasant words from a prosperous, well-meaning, and idealistic people, in whose mental world the profile of genuine human evil and passion had passed halfway into forgetfulness, could not penetrate the seething maelstrom of Russia, where the fabric of society had now been broken and the accumulated resentments of seven centuries of oppression were finding their expression in chaos, violence, and measureless bitterness.

❖

There remains the question of what was really in the President's mind when he made these friendly and enthusiastic references to Soviet diplomacy. Did they represent his actual state of mind? Or were they a coolly calculated political formula, drawn up to serve a purpose by one who knew better but chose not to say so?

It is not only the later historian for whom this question has held interest. It also preoccupied, briefly and intensively, some of the more thoughtful and interested of contemporary observers.

On January 11, three days after the speech was delivered, Mr. Herbert Bayard Swope, co-editor and Washington correspondent of the *New York World,* filed from Washington a special signed story on this subject, which was printed by his paper the following day. There can be no doubt but that the inspiration for the story came, directly or otherwise, from Thompson,[27] and that it reflected the erroneous

---

[27] A long, direct interview with Thompson (by a different correspondent), which appeared in the *New York World* on January 13, 1918, made a number of the same points.

belief on Thompson's part not only that his memorandum had been the principal inspiration for the President's speech, but that it had worked a basic change in the entire outlook of the Administration toward Russia—a change which would soon result in the dismissal of Francis and in the *de facto* recognition of the Soviet government.

Swope described his piece as

. . . the story that is behind the way in which the words of welcome and cheer the President addressed to the Russian people came to be spoken— a story that deals with the downfall of one Ambassador and the possibility that another may go too. . . .

He then went on to make the following statements:

. . . America has expressed her willingness to align herself with the Bolshevik Government in Petrograd. . . .

The President's sympathies have long been with the Russians, but their formal expression was withheld until the fact was clearly established that no sinister German influence lay behind the Bolshevik program.

The definitive proof came when the Leninist-Trotsky Government spurned [the German peace offer] . . . the greatest blow yet delivered to German power. . . .

This action . . . is the beginning of the turning of that tide which the President visioned and which is not to be checked. . . .

The recognition Russia has received is an admission of how complete was the misrepresentation of the changes now going on in the Slav nation. How much of this misrepresentation was deliberate and how much was unintentional it is difficult to say. Reactionary influences in Britain and France, as well as in America, contributed their share. . . .

Although the President to a great extent was compelled to rely upon reports originating from these sources, he was not deceived. . . .

Enlightenment came from new and more veracious sources. It cannot be said that much help in gaining the true perspective was received from the American Ambassador at Petrograd, David R. Francis. He seems to have been uniformly antagonistic to the revolutionaries, and so the State Department, which apparently relied on his reports, accepted the belief that the Bolsheviki were moving toward a separate peace. . . .

Turning then to the recently announced recall from Petrograd of the British Ambassador, Sir George Buchanan, and ascribing it to a similar disillusionment of the British government with his allegedly biased and reactionary interpretation of Russia, Swope went on to say,

. . . There are those in Washington who believe Francis may be the next. . . .

The President has never been solely dependent on his Ambassador for his knowledge . . . other sources made up the lack. The representatives of the Committee on Public Information sent to Russia . . . helped much to remove the misunderstanding. And there were others . . . Red Cross officials and those with no public connection—who saw the truth and told what they saw when they returned to Washington.

And they brought these reports back to the President so that he too might see wherein the Russian scheme of things had spiritual kinship with those ideals he had phrased as the aspirations of America.

The recognition of this similarity . . . will give the Russians financial as well as moral support. . . .

But the recognition means still more. It means that the war has entered that final phase in which political strategy is of greater weight than military tactics. . . .[28]

Three days after the appearance of this story in the *World* (i.e. on January 14), the *New York Times* published a sharp rebuttal from the pen of a well-known liberal publicist, Mr. William English Walling. Referring specifically to Swope's article, Walling pointed out that since the President's speech of January 8 efforts had been made to interpret this statement "as indorsing the Bolsheviki and the Bolshevist peace terms." He pointed out:

. . . These strangely concerted efforts have come not alone from the Socialists, the pacifists and extremists, but also from certain sources that claim to be close to the administration. . . .[29]

He then proceeded to take issue in the most vigorous and confident fashion with Swope's interpretation of the President's remarks and to give what reads like a highly authoritative picture of what was actually in the President's mind when the speech was drafted.

The President, Walling said, had not expressed any readiness to have America align herself with the Bolsheviki—only a willingness to work with them "in so far as the Bolsheviki showed themselves in the future willing to work with us." The President realized per-

[28] *New York World,* January 12, 1918, p. 3.

[29] On January 10, the *New York Times* correspondent in Washington quoted an unidentified State Department source as saying that Russia had been told (presumably in Wilson's speech) that "there is no difference between her declared terms and those of the United States."

fectly well the depth of the anti-American prejudice among the Soviet leaders, and this realization was indicated by the phrase *"whether their present leaders believe it or not,* it is our heartfelt desire and hope . . ."[30] etc.

Mr. Walling then went on to describe in a strangely authoritative tone the background of knowledge about conditions in Russia against which the President had drafted his speech:

President Wilson is fully aware that there are half a dozen or more "Governments" throughout Russia which do not recognize the Bolsheviki in their territories. He is also aware that the Bolsheviki obtained their present position in Moscow, Petrograd, and on the northwestern army front largely by violence. He knows that the elected members of the Constitutional Assembly have shown a non-Bolshevist majority, in spite of the fact that the Bolsheviki have imprisoned representatives whom they did not like and ousted others. . . . He knows that, even as late as the Fall, nearly all the municipal elections gave anti-Bolshevist majorities, which caused Lenine and Trotzky to dissolve the municipal constitutions when they came into power. He knows that the railway union failed to recognize the Bolsheviki, until it was reorganized by Lenine and Trotzky. He knows that of the twenty important Socialist newspapers in Russia, only two support the Bolsheviki and that most of the others have been suppressed. . . .

The President also knows that all the world-famed Russian Socialist leaders except Lenine and Trotzky have either been persecuted or imprisoned so as to deprive the Russian masses of their natural and chosen leaders—some of whom have served in and out of prison for half a century. . . . The Bolsheviki are only one of three chief Socialist factions in Russia. . . . The other two factions . . . have been more friendly to the Entente than to the Germans. The Bolsheviki, on the contrary, have been steadily Germanophile and hostile to the Entente. They are not pro-German in the sense of being pro-Kaiserists, but they are pro-German in the sense of being pro-German Socialists. . . . These same Bolsheviki repudiate utterly all the representative labor organizations of Great Britain, America and France! The Bolsheviki regime has been a reign of violence, not to say a reign of terror. It is utterly impossible that it should be recognized by America or any democratic Government. . . .

Walling then voiced an urgent warning about the intrigues directed toward Francis' recall:

[30] Italics added.

The Fourteen Points

There is no time for delay. Apparently the move is already on foot to recall Ambassador Francis, who, as Mr. Swope asserts, "accepted the belief that the Bolsheviki were moving toward a separate peace which would have been a German peace." This is not a belief on the part of Ambassador Francis. It is an absolutely established fact. It is established by the separate peace negotiations of the Bolsheviki, by the assertions of their leaders, and, above all, by their declared peace program. While they were not willing to accept a German peace as far as Russia is concerned, there has been no indication whatever that they were unwilling to accept a German peace as regards those "capitalistic and imperialist nations," America, France, Great Britain, and Italy. . . .[31]

Walling went on to compare the President's Fourteen Points, one by one, with the Bolshevik demands at Brest-Litovsk and to emphasize the differences between them. The President had demanded indemnities for Belgium and other countries overrun by the Central Powers; the Bolsheviki called for no indemnities. The President had spoken of a "wrong done to France" in regard to Alsace-Lorraine; the Bolsheviki did not regard this as a wrong. The President had demanded an independent Polish state on an ethnical basis; the Bolshevik position on Poland had not envisaged the incorporation into a Polish state of German or Austrian territories inhabited by Poles. The President had demanded autonomy for the subject peoples of Austria-Hungary and Turkey; the Bolsheviki had made no such demand.

Ridiculing Swope and like-minded persons for attaching such overwhelming importance to the professed Bolshevik peace terms ("all our information about Russia, it seems, was wrong, until the refusal of the Bolsheviki to give up Russian territory to Germany shed a great white light on the situation"), Walling concluded as follows:

It is highly improbable that the Committee on Public Information has any idea of the fearful misrepresentation of Russian conditions made by its agent or agents—misrepresentations which can be explained only in the supposition that one or more of these agents is himself involved with the anarchists or Bolsheviki.

. . . It is incredible that either President Wilson or the Committee on Public Information will allow this effort to misinterpret the Government policy, however well intended this effort may be, to go uncontradicted.

[31] *New York Times,* January 14, 1918, p. 4, "Move to Recognize the Bolsheviki?"

The Fourteen Points

If this article represented only Mr. Walling's speculations and rested on no more than his own assumptions with regard to what was in the President's mind, it stands only as one more interesting voice from the cacophony of American public opinion about Russia during the winter of 1918. If, on the other hand, Walling was in any way encouraged to write this article by persons in the Administration, his article would stand as perhaps the most revealing and important single reflection of the feelings of the President with respect to the new regime in Russia during the early months of its power. The question therefore arises as to whether the article was in any way inspired or informed by the Administration.

William English Walling was a well-known publicist and traveler, of strongly liberal convictions, who had made visits to Russia before the war and had manifested a keen interest in the Russian revolutionary movement. He was a great personal admirer and friend of Samuel Gompers. At Gompers' suggestion, President Wilson had invited Walling to become a member of the Root Mission in May 1917, feeling that Walling's strong sympathies for the Revolution would help to overcome the conservatism of Mr. Root. Although Walling evaded acceptance of this invitation, his relations with the President appear to have remained not only untroubled by his refusal but even strengthened in cordiality. Walling continued to call on the President on the occasion of his own frequent visits to Washington. Whether he saw the President, or anyone in the Administration, just before writing this article, however, is not clear.

Walling had previously been on terms of intimate friendship with Bullard, the two men having been drawn together by the coincidence of their upper-class origin and education and by their liberal views, which in both cases bordered on socialism. But later events, some of them personal, had produced an estrangement, all the more painful by virtue of their previous intimacy. Walling, himself violently patriotic and anti-German, suspected Bullard of the characteristic radical-socialist indifference to the issues of the war, and broadened this suspicion into a conviction that Bullard entertained secret sympathies for the Bolshevik action in taking Russia out of the war, if not for the Bolsheviki themselves. Being apparently quite unaware of Thompson's activities, Walling jumped to the conclusion that Bullard must have been the source of the views put forward in Swope's article. It was against Bullard, in this fancied role, that Walling's polemic was directed.[32]

Nothing could have been more unjust to Bullard. It is true that Bullard had no use for Francis, and that he had connived at the intrigue to bring about his recall; but he had few illusions about the Bolsheviki. This being so, he was actually somewhat uneasy over what seemed to him to be the insincere pro-Soviet overtones in the President's speech. "I am a believer in Democracy," he wrote to Summers in precisely this connection;

I have a long line of Puritan ancestors and . . . a conviction . . . that Honesty is the best policy. . . . I am outraged at the use of force against argument. From all these points of view, I find it desperately hard to work with the Bolsheviki. They are as undemocratic, in our Western sense, as the former Tsar. They are as cold blooded in their disregard for the truth as any thugs I ever knew. And they have no more idea of tolerance toward a difference of opinion than Torquemada.

But politics . . . makes strange bedfellows. . . .[33]

It is interesting to note that Raymond Robins, just at the time when his own invitation to join the Red Cross Commission was being decided upon in Washington in June 1917, had written to Davison recommending Walling's inclusion on that commission. Robins had praised Walling highly on that occasion, as a "man of wealth, education, and high personal character," who had written a book on Russia and who had been

. . . active in support of the radical movement in that country for some years. He knows personally many of the present leaders of the revolutionary movement. . . .[34]

It is evident from this statement that Robins thought highly of Walling, and the relationship was presumably mutual. Walling would have been amazed to learn that Swope's views actually came, not from Bullard, who was largely innocent of any such thoughts, but from the immediate entourage of Robins himself.

The Walling article was supported by an editorial in the *New*

[32] For the information concerning Walling's relations with Bullard, and his correspondence with the President about the invitation to join the Root Mission, I am indebted to Mr. Walling's widow, Mrs. Anna Walling.

[33] Bullard MSS, *op.cit.,* Box 13, Letter of January 24, 1918.

[34] American National Red Cross Archives, Washington, D.C.: Letter, Robins to Davison, June 21, 1917.

York Times belaboring the Bolshevik leaders for their iniquities, and ending with the stern warning:

> . . . If there are any bureaus, agencies or individuals at Washington that are seeking to bring about a formal recognition of the Bolsheviki . . . their activities should have the immediate attention of the Secretary of State.[35]

All this drew blood from George Creel. In the course of his article, Walling had cited at length passages from Swope's article with which he particularly disagreed. In doing so, he had contrived, intentionally or otherwise, to cite only Swope's references to "representatives of the Committee on Public Information" as among the sources of his story and to neglect to mention that Swope had also referred to "Red Cross officials." The omission evoked from Creel, who knew Thompson to be the real source of the information, a fury so violent that one is moved to wonder whether Creel had not found himself the object of some Presidential reproach in connection with the Swope article. In any case, an acrimonious correspondence ensued between Creel and Walling, in the course of which Creel showered Walling with bitter charges of dishonesty and bad faith and refused to be assuaged by the latter's conciliatory replies. In some way or other, even the State Department became engaged in the affair. In the days immediately after the appearance of the article, Counselor Polk spoke both with Walling and Creel on the subject—a sign that the controversy was a matter of interest well beyond the confines of Mr. Creel's own office.

On January 17, three days after the appearance of his article in the *New York Times,* Walling carried the matter to the Secretary of the Interior, Mr. Franklin K. Lane, in a letter reading as follows:

> The pro-Bolshevik attitude of the Chairman of the Committee of Public Information is more marked and dangerous than I knew when I had my interview with you. Mr. Creel has issued orders against all further criticisms of the Bolsheviki on the part of his numerous writers —most of them, including the labor men, are strongly anti-Bolshevik. . . .
>
> I regard the President's diplomacy towards Russia as wise and correct. The policy of Mr. Creel however is suicidal. Not only Bullard, but several other of the New York correspondents are Socialists and I believe this is the source of Mr. Creel's error. If action to prevent the continua-

[35] *New York Times,* January 15, 1918.

tion of Mr. Creel's policy has not already been taken, I trust such action will be taken at the earliest moment, and I have no doubt it will be.[36]

Secretary Lane sent this letter on to Polk, who replied on January 22 with the following cryptic communication:

I have your letter of January 19, enclosing a letter from Mr. William English Walling. I have discussed this matter, both with Mr. Walling and Mr. Creel.[37]

What occasioned Polk's interest is shrouded in that mist of perfect discretion that was thrown over so many of the operations of the State Department in an earlier day. One thing, however, is clear. The Walling article did *not* shake the President's high opinion of its author, nor did the views expressed in it meet in any way with Presidential displeasure. Only two or three weeks later (February 13), the President forwarded to the Secretary of State a paper he had received from Walling in which the latter had warned that to aid the Bolsheviki "is not only playing with fire, it is almost certain to end the war before German defeat or American victory—with all the consequences that must inevitably follow such an indecisive outcome." The left-wing of the socialist movement, Walling had written, was international in character, cared nothing about the war aims of the Allies, and would play into the hands of German imperial ambitions. In a note forwarding this paper to Lansing, the President said:

I wish you would read (it deserves very careful reading) the enclosed paper by Mr. William English Walling which Mr. Gompers was kind enough to send to me. It seems to me to speak an unusual amount of truth and to furnish a very proper basis for the utmost caution in the conduct of the many troublesome affairs that we are from time to time discussing.[38]

The Secretary of State, too, noted Walling's views with high approval. He felt, he said in his reply to the President, that

. . . Mr. Walling had a keen appreciation of the forces which are menacing the present social order in nearly every European country and which may have to be reckoned with even in this country. It is really a remarkable analysis of the dangerous elements which are coming to the

[36] National Archives, State Department File 861.00/977.
[37] This note is attached to the previous letter, and is found in the same file.
[38] Wilson MSS, Series II, *op.cit.*

surface and which are in many ways more to be dreaded than autocracy; the latter is despotism but an intelligent despotism, while the former is a despotism of ignorance. One, at least has the virtue of order, while the other is productive of disorder and anarchy. It is a condition which cannot but arouse the deepest concern.

I think that Mr. Walling's views in regard to the Bolsheviks are helpful and sound, and after reading them I am more than ever convinced that our policy has been the right one and should be continued. . . .[39]

All of this fortifies the impression that William English Walling was in fairly close touch with the Administration on Russian matters during the winter of 1918. It is evident, at the very least, that his boldness in undertaking to say publicly what was in the President's mind when he spoke on January 8 did not meet with Mr. Wilson's disfavor. Had his interpretation of the President's thoughts been incorrect, the results would surely have been different.

One more detail must be added to complete the irony of this curious episode. If Walling was unwittingly in error in attributing Thompson's views to Bullard, Creel was no less in error, also unwittingly, in his violent protestations of the innocence of his own committee and its representatives.

In one of his irate letters to Walling, written on January 24, Creel wrote:

What I complained about . . . is your action in assuming and declaring that any representative of the Committee in Russia ever urged recognition of the Bolsheviki; or has sent to the President or to me, any word of any kind that would indicate an effort on their part to secure recognition for the Bolsheviki, or to urge their cause in any part.

Bullard and Sisson have but one duty, and that duty is apart from politics. . . . They have nothing whatever to do with the political situation in Russia.[40]

On that very day, as fortune would have it, Thompson, without, as yet, Creel's knowledge, was receiving a cable from Robins which ended with the following words:

. . . Cannot too strongly urge importance of prompt recognition of Bolshevik authority and immediate establishment of modus vivendi making

[39] *Foreign Relations, The Lansing Papers*, Vol. II, *op.cit.*, pp. 352–353, Letter of February 15, 1918.
[40] National Archives; Legislative, Judicial and Diplomatic Records Branch, Justice and Executive Section: Files on Committee on Public Information.

possible generous and sympathetic co-operation. Sisson approves this text and requests you show this cable to Creel. . . .[41]

With that, we must let the episode stand, not only as a reflection of the President's views concerning Russia, as evidenced in his Fourteen Points speech, but also as a testimonial to the extent to which, among hasty and opinionated men, error can become the object of passion, and passion the source of error.

[41] Cumming & Pettit, *op.cit.*, pp. 76–77.

CHAPTER XIII

SIBERIA—THE BACKGROUND

WHILE the above-described events were transpiring in European Russia, the effects of the Revolution were naturally making themselves felt in the Russian Far East and creating there a new situation which engaged in varying degrees the attention of the Allied powers, particularly Japan and the United States.

What is known of the reasons for Japan's entry into World War I on the Allied side and her subsequent adherence to the Declaration of London (by which the five major Allies agreed that they would not make a separate peace) will suffice to explain why the Japanese government followed with the most avid attention the course of the Russian war effort and the development of the internal situation in Russia during the years 1915 and 1916.

Initially, Japan's main concern, so far as Russia was concerned, was that the Russians should not make a separate peace but should continue the war on the European front to its final conclusion. A separate peace between Russia and Germany was, in the early stages of the war, the Japanese nightmare. It might well have meant a general German victory, the demise of Japan's one great ally—Britain—and the emergence of a vengeful Germany as a power in the Far East. Having gratuitously entered the war on the Entente side and having exploited this association in order to seize German possessions in Shantung, Japan had no reason to count on German benevolence in such a contingency. At best, she would have to face a powerful German bid to recover her possessions in Shantung. At worst, the Germans might appear, depending on the nature of the German-Russian relationship in the wake of a German victory, as the eager patrons of Russian aspirations in the Far East from which they too would expect to profit, or as the heirs to Russian rights and claims in that area. The Japanese had not forgotten Germany's previous encouragement of Russian expansion in the Far East, and particularly Bülow's refusal, in 1900, to concede that Manchuria was part of China and subject to such restrictions as the Chinese treaties placed on the ambitions of the other powers with respect to China. The Japanese also had in mind the precedent they themselves had established by insisting that they were the heirs, by conquest, to the entire German position in Shantung. A Germany victorious over Russia could, by the same token, lay claim to Russia's entire position in Manchuria.

To be sure, Russia's preoccupation with the war in the West held tremendous advantages for Japan, for it drained Russian strength and reduced Russia's capacity for resisting Japanese pressures on the Asiatic mainland. But this advantage, like so many others in the affairs of nations, had its limits. If it went too far, it could lead to the dangers and evils of a complete German victory. The Japanese, in contrast to some of the western peoples, were sufficiently sophisticated to realize that they would not be benefited by a total destruction of the power of their adversary.

Actually, this was the direction in which—through no fault of the Japanese—events tended to move, beginning with the year 1915. The growing evidences of the failure of the creaking Tsarist system to measure up to the strains of a prolonged modern war convinced the Japanese that if events were allowed to take their course, a separate German-Russian peace would be inevitable. To this danger, the Japanese responded, in the peculiarly dialectical fashion of the East, by a combination of military aid to Russia (for a serious price) and veiled threats of a military occupation of Russian territory in the Far East in case a German-Russian peace should become a reality. At the same time, and to some extent as a *quid pro quo* for military aid, Japan moved to take advantage of Russia's weakness and the reduced interest of the other European powers in Far Eastern affairs by expanding her own position in Manchuria at Russia's expense.

The relationship of these various elements of Japanese policy is indicated with characteristic precision and delicacy in the following passage from Viscount Ishii's memoirs:

. . . As the author now looks back upon it, he believes that the reason Russia did not make a separate peace with Germany when all the fighting spirit was gone from her front line forces was her fear of the wrath of the three Allies and particularly her fear that Japan would invade

Siberia with fresh troops. This fear was Japan's trump card. The war at this point (during the autumn and winter of 1915) was developing favorably for Germany. Utilizing her alliance with Turkey, she threatened to instigate the Persians and Afghans to attack the Indian frontier and to encircle Russia with a long ring of enemies stretching all the way from Persia, Afghanistan and Turkestan to China. Russia thus faced the prospect of being caught in a German net. If to escape it she sued for separate peace with Germany, she would only be inviting attack from Japan in the rear. Indeed Russia had to choose between the frying pan and the fire, as it were. At this point Japan on the one hand attempted to restore her fighting spirit, which had been lost owing to lack of weapons, by supplying her with munitions; and on the other prevented her from making separate peace, in the face of the German net closing in on her, by encouraging her with closer Russo-Japanese union and specially binding her not to make any treaty with a third power injurious to Japan.[1]

This last reference, prohibiting Russia from making any treaty with a third party injurious to Japanese interests, referred to the agreements concluded between Russia and Japan in July 1916. The exact nature and significance of these agreements remain to this day enigmatic. They consisted of (1) a published instrument of only two articles; (2) a secret treaty, the text of which was first brought to light by the Bolsheviki in December 1917; and (3) a secret protocol covering certain specific and immediate questions at issue. The published instrument and the secret treaty were drawn up in the veiled, almost algebraic, language of the military diplomacy of the period, to be authentically deciphered only by the initiated. We shall probably never know precisely what was meant by them, and they may have meant different things to the respective parties. The agreements had the general tenor of a contingent alliance against a specific, but unnamed, foreign power. Conceivably, this might have been Germany. But careful analysis indicates that it was more probably the United States which was envisaged: the agreement, in other words, was designed to give Japan protection against possible American opposition to contemplated changes (in Japan's favor) in the *status quo* in Manchuria, reflecting Russia's growing weakness. These changes, or certain of them, were apparently indicated in the secret protocol. They evidently included the transfer to Japan of the seventy southernmost miles of that portion of the Chinese Eastern

[1] Kikujiro Ishii, *Diplomatic Commentaries,* Johns Hopkins Press, Baltimore, 1936, p. 107.

Railway which ran south from Harbin to Changchun and connected, at the southern end, with the Japanese-owned South Manchurian Railway. The agreement to transfer this stretch of line, running through one of the richest areas of Manchuria, was an important concession to Japan. The protocol also seems to have envisaged concessions to Japan with respect to navigation rights on the Sungari River, heretofore wholly within the Russian sphere of interest. There may have been other concessions as well.[2]

Insofar as Russia received any *quid pro quo* for the concessions, it appears to have been solely in the form of deliveries of munitions. Viscount Ishii said in his memoirs that:

. . . The Japanese Government . . . delivered to Russia all available stocks of munitions, excepting, of course, those needed for Japan's own defence, and operated the Koishikawa (Tokyo) and Osaka arsenals night and day to turn out new munitions for her. According to the author's recollection, some six or seven hundred thousand old and new rifles, as well as a proportionate number of machine guns, small guns and field guns were delivered in due course. In addition, the Japanese government took over a number of private factories and operated them exclusively for the manufacture of clothing, swords, shoes and other equipment for the Russian army. The aggregate value of war equipment of all types supplied to Russia reached the high figure of Yen 300,000,000.[3]

These developments all indicate that by the summer of 1916 Japan was already moving systematically to take advantage of Russia's military preoccupation in the west and to expand her position in Manchuria at the expense of that of Russia. At the same time, she was forcing Russia to accept a portion of the responsibility for defending these changes in the *status quo* against possible opposition from the only power that would be in a position to oppose them with any real force in the post-war period—the United States of America. Plainly, if such moves were in progress by the summer of 1916, any further drastic weakening of Russia's power (such as was later actually brought about by the Revolution) could not fail to raise in most acute

[2] A detailed discussion of these agreements will be found in Ernest Batson Price, *The Russo-Japanese Treaties of 1907–1916 concerning Manchuria and Mongolia,* Johns Hopkins Press, Baltimore, 1933, Chapter VI, pp. 77–90. See also Chitoshi Yanaga, Japan since Perry, McGraw Hill Book Co., Inc., New York, 1949, p. 382; and Frederic Coleman, *Japan Moves North: The Inside Story of the Struggle for Siberia,* Cassell & Co., Ltd., London, 1918, p. 18.

[3] Ishii, *op.cit.,* p. 106.

form the question as to what further benefits Japan might expect and endeavor to reap from this unique situation, and how—again— the almost certain American opposition to such changes should be dealt with. In these realities one had the logic of the entire complex of problems involved in the subsequent Allied intervention.

Small wonder, in these circumstances, that the Japanese followed the course of the Russian Revolution with the most concentrated attention. Throughout the spring and early summer of 1917, the Japanese Embassy in Petrograd was bombarded with requests from Tokyo for information about the state of the Russian army and the advance of the revolutionary process, accompanied by admonitions to the Ambassador to bear in mind the immense importance to Japan of the developments taking place before his eyes.[4] Small wonder, too, that throughout the year 1917 and the first months of 1918 Tokyo followed, with anxious and almost fevered attention, every conceivable indication of the development of American policy toward the Manchurian and Siberian areas.

The Russian public was not slow to grasp the unhappy significance of the shift that was taking place in the balance of power in the Far East. Ever since the Russian-Japanese War, the Russians of Eastern Siberia had been acutely conscious not only of the military weakness of the Maritime Province in the face of Japanese armed power, but also of Siberia's general economic and social weakness in the face of the rapid industrialization of Japan herself and the economic advance of the neighboring areas, particularly of Manchuria. It was to counteract this weakness that the Tsar's government had established in 1910 an interdepartmental commission known as the Amur Expedition, the purpose of which was to strengthen, generally, the economic and social development of the Amur Valley and contiguous areas. This operation made a good start under the direction of an ambitious parvenu in the Tsarist governmental service, N. L. Gondatti. At the end of 1911 Gondatti became Governor General of the Pri-Amur region, in which position he continued until the February Revolution. His strong sense of Japanese danger and his vigorous efforts to prevent Japanese penetration and economic domination of the eastern Siberian area are said to have had a powerful effect in

---

[4] See intercepts of official communications between the Japanese Foreign Office and the Embassy at Petrograd, "Foreign Diplomats on the Revolution of 1917," *Krasny Arkhiv,* Vol. 24, 1927, pp. 108–163.

heightening both awareness and fear of Japan among the population of the area.[5]

As Russia's strength was drained away by the war, this fear of Japan was naturally heightened, until it began to take on the quality of a general obsession. An English journalist and war correspondent, Mr. Frederic Coleman, writing at the end of 1917 just before the intervention occurred (and therefore without benefit of hindsight), observed that:

It is astonishing how deep-rooted the anti-Japanese sentiment in Siberia has become. . . . The Japanese menace was very real to the people of the Pri-Amur. It is a country of rumour. Every day news would be spread, after the coming of the Russian Revolution, of Japanese troops having occupied Harbin or having been landed at Vladivostok. A Russian from Irkutsk told me that his wife used the threat of a Japanese invasion to quieten the children. . . .[6]

While this apprehension was less lively in European Russia than in the Russian Far East, it was shared in considerable degree by the officials and political circles of the capital. We have already noted Viscount Ishii's view that only the fear of Japan restrained the Russian government from making a separate peace with Germany at an even earlier date. It is not surprising, therefore, that as early as March 1917, immediately after the February Revolution, rumors were spread in Petrograd, and appeared in the press there, to the effect that in case Russia were really to withdraw from the war, Japan would declare war on Russia and attack Vladivostok. These rumors were apparently fostered by Russian conservatives anxious to discredit the line of policy to which the parties of the left were committed. But they were not in any way disagreeable to the Japanese Ambassador in Petrograd, who noted that the spread of these reports constituted "a useful means of pressure on the Russians."[7] Indeed, the Russian Foreign Office showed itself, during the period of the Provisional Government, very solicitous of Japanese good will and anxious to compose all outstanding differences.

Throughout the war, the French had pressed repeatedly for use of

[5] Coleman, *op.cit.*, Chapter IV, pp. 40–55.

[6] *Ibid.*, pp. 59–60.

[7] "Foreign Diplomats on the Revolution of 1917," *Krasny Arkhiv*, Vol. 24, *op.cit.* See particularly Telegram 430, April 26 (May 9), 1917, from Ambassador Uchida to the Japanese Foreign Minister, Motono.

Japanese troops somewhere on the front against Germany, either in the east or the west; but the inhibitions of the other Allies, including the Japanese themselves, had invariably vitiated all such projects. After the failure of the final Russian offensive in the summer of 1917, the French made a last effort to persuade the Russians to ask for the despatch of Japanese forces to the eastern front.[8] But the leaders of the Provisional Government were no less fearful than their predecessors had been of any entry of Japanese troops onto Russian territory, and would not hear of it.

This approach, and the Russian reaction to it, evidently remained unknown to the United States government, who in late October 1917 approached the British with a similar suggestion. Although the British government, under the shock of recent military reverses, was somewhat more inclined than it had been earlier in the war to explore the possibility of using Japanese forces on the *western* front, its reply indicated that it did not see much chance of enlisting Japanese aid in the east.

. . . The view of the British Cabinet is that the Japanese authorities would never assent to such a proposal if made. It may be that the United States administration may have some better means of knowledge, and of course if they think that the Japanese could be induced to send an expeditionary force to Russia we would support them in every way possible. . . .[9]

This discussion of the possible use of Japanese troops on the eastern front was of course overtaken by the Bolshevik seizure of power and Russia's withdrawal from the war. But it had two noteworthy effects.

First, in the minds of those in western Allied circles who overrated the intimacy between Germans and Bolsheviki and who regarded the latter as allies or agents of the former (and of such there were many), Bolshevik territory tended to be identified with enemy territory, and resistance to Bolshevism with resistance to Germany. Having accustomed themselves to the thought of possible Japanese par-

---

[8] For the history of the efforts to enlist Japanese military aid in the war against Germany in Europe, see the article "Les Projects d'Intervention Japonaise," by Albert Pingaud, *Revue des Deux Mondes*, Vol. 59, September 1, 1930, pp. 31–59. For an account of Russian reaction to the last French proposal, see Noulens, *op.cit.*, Vol. II, p. 46.

[9] *Foreign Relations, 1918, Russia*, Vol. II, *op.cit.*, p. 1, Message of the Prime Minister to the Ambassador at Washington, November 1, 1917. I have found no record of the United States communication to which this was a response.

ticipation on the old eastern front, from the Baltic to the Black Seas, these people found it even easier to envisage Japanese power being similarly engaged on the "new front," which they saw as the outer fringe of Soviet power within Russia itself. This was, in fact, an even more inviting idea, by reason of Japanese proximity to the Siberian area and the relative ease with which the Japanese could operate there.

This thought appealed particularly to the French. There is no question that of all the Allied governments it was the French which reacted most violently to Russia's departure from the war. To what degree France's extensive financial investments in Russia were a factor in determining the official French attitude is unclear. The French were also passionately concerned about the effects of the Russian Revolution on the war itself. In any case, French anger against the Bolsheviki, and suspicion of them, was so intense that any front established against Bolshevik power anywhere was identified in French eyes with a front against Germany, and found favor accordingly. This applied to Siberia, as to other parts of Russia. The fact that Vladivostok was separated from the German forces by 5,000 miles of civil chaos does not appear to have modified this feeling appreciably. By this process of reasoning and deduction, the French became the unswerving, enthusiastic, and undiscriminating partisans of any Far Eastern intervention, anywhere, by anyone, and at any time.

Secondly, the Japanese themselves could not fail to be impressed with the obvious desire of the western powers to use them in the war against Germany, and with the apparent indifference, particularly on the part of the French, to whatever ulterior consequences this might have for Russia. To the Japanese mind, the advantage to Japan of participation in the European war had always been seen largely in the prospect of putting the western Entente powers under obligation to Japan, and then exacting a price in the form of concessions to Japanese aspirations on the Asiatic mainland. The outbreak of civil war in Russia, with one faction threatening to make peace with Germany and the other professing loyalty to the Entente, now opened up a new and extremely interesting possibility, namely, the extension of Japanese influence not only into northern Manchuria but also into Siberia proper, by agreement not only with the western powers but also with important Russian political forces, claiming with some reason the right to speak for the nation as a whole.

❖

Two other factors entered prominently into the background of the events that transpired in the Russian Far East following the Bolshevik Revolution, as they affected American interests. The first of these was the presence in Siberia of large numbers of prisoners-of-war from the Central Powers. Concentrations of these prisoners were located at a number of points along the Trans-Siberian railroad, notably at Omsk, Krasnoyarsk, Irkutsk, and Blagoveshchensk. They appear to have been in overwhelming majority prisoners from the Austro-Hungarian armies, the officers including a higher proportion of Austrians, the rank and file being made up largely of Hungarians, Slovaks, etc. There were relatively few Germans. In Irkutsk, for example, out of 11,000 prisoners only a few dozen were Germans. In the Pri-Amur district, 1,000 officers and 1,500 men were Germans out of a total prisoner-of-war population of some 12,100.[10]

Of these prisoners, only a portion were actually confined. Large numbers were working in the Siberian communities under conditions not too different from those governing the employment of the free Siberian population. As will later be seen, relatively few of these prisoners were ever armed and used by the Bolsheviki. These were almost exclusively men who had embraced the communist ideology, wished to throw in their lot with the Russian Revolution, and did not want to be repatriated. Only a tiny proportion of these, if any, can have been Germans. Their influence on the course of events in Siberia following the Bolshevik coup was not great.[11] The vast majority of the prisoners had little interest in the Russian civil war, and desired only to get home.[12] Above all, there is no evidence that the German or Austrian governments had anything to do with the arming of the prisoners, or that the latter were used to promote the purposes of the Central Powers in any way.

[10] National Archives, State Department File 861.00/1711 (1918); Letter, Major Walter S. Drysdale to Consul Caldwell, March 21, 1918.

[11] See report of Captain W. L. Hicks (British) and Captain William B. Webster, April 26, 1918 in Cumming & Pettit, *op.cit.,* pp. 177–184.

[12] National Archives, State Department File 860.00/1280, Drysdale's report of February 5, 1918.

The existence of these prisoners along the Trans-Siberian railroad was a source of concern to western Allied circles from the very beginning. This apprehension was ably and successfully exploited by the anti-Bolshevik elements in Siberia, who filled the ears of the Allied representatives with lurid tales of the arming of the prisoners by the Bolsheviki and pictured a Siberia effectively taken over by the Germans through this device.

The second of the two background factors was the accumulation of military supplies in Vladivostok. The fact that the western Allies had no channel for shipment of supplies to Russia across the Atlantic except the remote ports of the Russian north, some of which were closed by ice for a large part of the year, had operated to increase greatly the significance of Vladivostok and the Trans-Siberian Railway as a route of access to Russia for military and other supplies. Just how it came about that the limitations of the handling capacity of the Trans-Siberian Railway were so little taken into account is not apparent.[13] But the fact is that from the spring of 1916 supplies were despatched to Vladivostok in such quantities that the railway became a real bottleneck. The main trouble was not at Vladivostok itself but in the Tomsk division of the railway, in central Siberia, a division which for some reason was weak and poorly operated. This weak link lessened the carrying capacity of the entire road, reduced the rate of possible removals from Vladivostok, and led to severe congestion at that port. By the end of July 1917, 662,000 tons of supplies had accumulated at Vladivostok and were awaiting removal, supplies which included railway materials, nitrate of soda, high explosives, shells, barbed wire, phosphate, metals, equipment, food, and raw materials. The most authoritative estimates at that time were that it would take the remainder of 1917 and most of 1918 merely to move the existing accumulation to the interior, even if the railway functioned normally throughout.

Existing warehouse space had long been exhausted, despite the fact that 82,000 square feet of new space had been constructed during the war. The supplies were piled up, frequently in disregard of all

[13] The fault appears to have lain primarily with the Russian government and its purchasing commissions, not with the Allies. As late as the spring of 1917, the Russian government was continuing to press the American government to ship munitions by this route, promising that pier space would be provided at Vladivostok for unloading of twenty-five ships a day from the United States, and apparently giving no warnings about the existing accumulation of freight. Frederick Palmer, *Newton D. Baker: America at War,* Dodd, Mead & Co., New York, 1931, Vol. I, p. 111.

the requirements of preservation, wherever space was to be found. They could be seen scattered all over the city and its environs: on vacant lots, in side streets, on suburban hillsides—exposed to the weather, to the effects of time, and to the curiosity or depredations of the inhabitants.[14]

In view of the difficulty that would have been involved in moving these supplies over the Trans-Siberian Railway even in normal circumstances, it is somewhat difficult to understand in retrospect the alarm shown by the western Allies, after the Bolshevik Revolution, lest the supplies fall into German hands. Within a short time after the November events, conditions in eastern Siberia had become so chaotic that operation of the railroad was thoroughly disorganized. Under these circumstances it would have taken many years, if not decades, to remove this materiel to European Russia and to make it available to the Germans, even had the will been present. Nevertheless, the safety of these supplies and, in particular, protection against the eventuality that they might be removed by the Bolsheviki and delivered up to the Germans, constituted a major preoccupation of French and British statesmanship in the period following the Bolshevik seizure of power.

❖

Closely connected with the accumulation of supplies in Vladivostok, and even in part occasioned by it, was another factor which entered into the pattern of America's interest in the Russian Far East at the time of the Bolshevik Revolution: the presence and activity in Russia of the Stevens Railway Mission, mentioned in Chapter I. The idea of sending to Russia a small group of experienced and competent American railway men, to advise the Russian government on how operation of the Trans-Siberian Railway might be improved and its carrying capacity increased, had arisen in the spring of 1917, largely from the suggestions of Mr. Stanley Washburn. A query was addressed to the Provisional Government through Francis, asking whether such a mission would be welcome. The Russian leaders were unenthusiastic about the proposal. They gave their consent to it only when they were assured that extensive shipments of rolling

[14] See the *New York Times Magazine*, Sunday, December 23, 1917; article entitled "Vladivostok's Vast Supplies in Pro-Ally Hands," by G. P. Conger (former Y.M.C.A. secretary in war prison camps in eastern Siberia). Also Coleman, *op.cit.*, Chapter IX, pp. 120–137.

stock and other railway material would be forthcoming from the United States as a corollary to the despatch of the railway mission. Mr. John F. Stevens, a distinguished American engineer well known for his work on the Panama Canal and on the construction of the Great Northern Railway, was selected to head the mission. Together with four highly qualified technical associates and a small clerical staff, he sailed from Vancouver for Vladivostok in the middle of May, arriving in Petrograd a month later.[15]

Once in Petrograd, the Stevens Mission got caught up in all the complexities of both Russian and American governmental confusion. Its functions were poorly differentiated not only from those of the Ambassador but also from those of the Root Mission. The two missions arrived in Petrograd only one day apart—thus giving rise to the most complicated problems of protocol. The situation was not aided by the fact that Root had pleaded in vain with the President to have the Stevens Mission subordinated to himself.

By mid-summer Stevens had recommended not only extensive shipments of materials to Vladivostok but also the despatch to Russia, via that port, of a large contingent of railroad engineers. Despite the difficulties of assembling such a force in wartime, Washington applied itself vigorously to the problems of recruitment and preparation. By November, at the time of the Bolshevik seizure of power, the expedition, consisting of 350 men under the direction of Mr. George Emerson, General Manager of the Great Northern Railway, was ready to sail. Like the members of the Red Cross Commission, these men were formally sworn in as members of the armed forces, and given simulated rank.

Stevens, for his part, had left Petrograd on the very eve of the revolution (approximately October 28) to inspect the line between Moscow and Omsk. He was therefore not in Petrograd or in close touch with the Ambassador at the time the Bolsheviki seized power. In Stevens' absence, Francis, sharing the general doubt that the Bolsheviki would remain long in power, recommended that the Emer-

---

[15] The view of the Stevens Mission put forward in Soviet historical material has reflected the customary cynicism about American motives. In the work of Genkin, *op.cit.*, on Soviet-American relations, the Stevens Mission is portrayed as having been despatched by the United States government for the purpose of spying on the Trans-Siberian Railway with a view to facilitating Japanese intervention at a later date. There could, of course, be no suggestion more absurd than this, or one that would have caused greater amazement to both American and Japanese statesmen of the time.

son mission be despatched anyway, notwithstanding the political upheaval. He anticipated that by the time Emerson reached Vladivostok whatever government might be in existence there would "be pleased to utilize Stevens' and Emerson's force." [16] The Emerson corps therefore set sail from San Francisco on November 19, 1917, on the transport *Thomas*. Word was sent to Stevens to proceed to Vladivostok and to meet Emerson there.

❖

One other special situation must be noted before there can be any intelligible recounting of the sequence of events in early Soviet-American relations involving the Far East: the peculiar importance of Harbin and the Chinese Eastern Railway with relation to the situation in Siberia. The complexities surrounding the Chinese Eastern Railway and the play of international interests and intrigue around the North Manchurian area defy exhaustive treatment within the scope of this narrative. It is impossible, however, fully to understand the sequence of events in Vladivostok and other points in the Russian Far East without having in mind at least the main elements of the situation in Harbin and along the Chinese Eastern Railway.

It will be recalled that Manchuria intrudes northward, as a great salient, into the territory of eastern Siberia, placing itself athwart the direct line from Vladivostok and the Maritime Province to Lake Baikal and European Russia. When, at the close of the 19th Century, the Trans-Siberian Railway was constructed to link European Russia with the port of Vladivostok on the Pacific Ocean, the decision was taken not to construct the line, in the first instance, around the northern borders of Manchuria but to project it, by arrangement with the Chinese government, directly across the North Manchurian territory, at a saving of several hundred miles in distance. This concept found its fruition in the construction of that peculiar institution known as the Chinese Eastern Railway.

The line was actually built during the years between 1897 and 1901. It consisted primarily of the east-west connection linking Chita with Vladivostok, but also included a spur from Harbin south to Changchun, where it connected with the South Manchurian Rail-

---

[16] *Foreign Relations, 1918, Russia,* Vol. III, *op.cit.,* p. 208, Telegram 1979, November 13, 1917.

EASTERN SIBERIA AND MANCHURIA

way. The administration was arranged on a basis which gave the Russian government effective control over the management of the line, though ownership was nominally international.[17]

In the main, these arrangements survived the Russian-Japanese War. Only later, on the eve of the First World War, did Russia proceed to the construction of an alternative line, the so-called Amur line, on the longer route around the north of Manchuria, entirely on Siberian territory. This second line was completed, and operating after a fashion, at the time of the Russian Revolution. But the Chinese Eastern still represented, in 1917, the shortest, most efficient, and most heavily employed route for the movement of supplies from Vladivostok to European Russia. It was of interest to the western powers from this standpoint, as well as for its great significance as the economic and political nucleus of the rapidly developing North Manchurian area.

Under the complicated international arrangements for the guarding and administration of the Chinese Eastern Railway, as they had developed by 1917, the entire railway, and the zone of territory contiguous to it, constituted a species of Russian colonial domain. Within this zone the Russian government exercised a quasi-sovereignty, which gave it a dominant position in the entire North Manchurian area. The managing director of the railway, in 1917, was General Dmitri L. Horvat.[18] He had his seat in Harbin, and also functioned as commander of the Russian forces in Northern Manchuria. He was virtually, at the time of the first revolution, in the position of military governor of a remote province, with enormous local power. Soon after the February Revolution, his power began to be undermined by fermentation among the troops and railway personnel under his control. By the time of the Bolshevik Revolution, it was seriously weakened, and he found himself in a distinctly precarious position.

This special situation in Harbin was somewhat analogous to the general trend of political events in Siberia proper following the February Revolution. It must be borne in mind that in eastern Siberia the population was largely concentrated in a few urban centers along, or near, the Trans-Siberian Railroad from Irkutsk to Vladi-

[17] A useful summary of the diplomatic origins of this project will be found in George E. Sokolsky, *The Story of the Chinese Eastern Railway*, North-China Daily News & Herald, Ltd., Shanghai, 1929.

[18] This name will be found in some sources transliterated "Horvath"; the form used here is that found in official government usage.

vostok. In addition to these last-named cities, the most important were Khabarovsk, Blagoveshchensk, and Chita. In all of these cities, the months following the February Revolution represented a period of increasing unrest and political fermentation, with the moderate democratic groups and the S-R's competing bitterly with the Bolsheviki for local control. This competition was particularly intense for the reason that it was only after the February Revolution that the local government system common to European Russia was extended to Eastern Siberia. By November 1917 the patterns of local government had had no time to settle. The Bolshevik uprising thus came at a moment when there was already a high degree of instability in all local government arrangements.

Confusion was increased by the fact that even the moderate administrative bodies, the so-called *zemstvos,* which in theory took a positive attitude toward the Provisional Government in Petrograd, proved in practice to be little amenable to its discipline. Petrograd was far away, and Siberian affairs had always been administered largely on the spot. Special political agents sent out by the Provisional Government found increasing difficulty in asserting their authority in local affairs.

Thus the general picture throughout the summer of 1917 in Siberian cities was that of the existence of three different sets of authority: the direct representatives of the Petrograd government, the moderate local government bodies, and the soviets of workers' and soldiers' deputies. In the political struggle that ensued, not only did power tend to gravitate to the last of these three entities, but power within the soviets themselves tended, especially as the autumn progressed, to move from moderate hands to those of the Bolshevik extremists.

CHAPTER XIV

SIBERIA—THE FIRST EXCHANGES

There is . . . in Japan . . . a fear of American action in the same way as in the United States there is a fear of Japanese action. . . . Japanese public opinion should be reassured as to the possibility of sole American intervention.—The Japanese Ambassador in Washington, Sato—confidentially—to Woodrow Wilson

AT the time of the November Revolution, the United States had official representatives at Vladivostok and Harbin and nowhere else in the Russian Far East. The importance of Vladivostok to the United States had been greatly enhanced during the course of 1917 by the use of that port as a channel of entry for American war supplies and as the common travel route, used by the Root Mission and by many other American visitors, between the United States and European Russia. By late summer 1917, the Consul at Vladivostok, Mr. John K. Caldwell, was thus a busy and harried man, whose responsibilities and preoccupations were growing day by day.

The socialist element in Vladivostok was made up, in the absence of any extensive number of industrial workers, largely of members of the Russian armed services, both military and naval. For the most part, up to the time of the November Revolution, these men were politically under the influence of relatively moderate leaders. Their number included, however, an extreme radical faction which became increasingly vocal and ambitious as the year 1917 ran its course. This element constituted a growing source of concern to the western consular representatives in the port; it was soon supplemented by a large number of persons who had hitherto been exiles in the United States and now, returning to Russia in the new freedom provided by the February Revolution, got as far as Vladivostok and remained there.

Between the growing influence of this extreme element and the unsettling proximity of the Japanese, Consul Caldwell followed the course of events throughout the summer and fall of 1917 with an anxious eye.

During the early months of the year Japanese naval vessels entered the port several times on regular courtesy visits. This did nothing, of course, to allay the general nervousness about Japanese intentions, to which reference was made in the last chapter.

When the *U.S.S. Buffalo* brought the Root Mission to Vladivostok in the first days of June, the high morale and good discipline of the ship's company made an excellent impression generally and had a perceptible, if temporary, favorable effect on the discipline of the Russian naval units in the port, a fact which was naturally welcomed not only by the Russian naval officers there but also by the Allied representatives in the city, and no doubt had something to do with the decision, taken shortly thereafter, to send the United States Asiatic Squadron as a whole on a courtesy visit. The assent of the Russian government to such a visit was solicited and procured in mid-summer, and the visit was scheduled to begin on August 28. For some reason, the visit was then cancelled, or postponed, but the idea remained active in the minds of the American representatives in Petrograd and Vladivostok.

In late summer, the activities of the radical element in Vladivostok began for the first time to arouse the serious concern of the Allied consular officers there. On September 20, soldiers of the 4th Artillery Regiment (a particularly disaffected unit) put out a summons to a general workers' and soldiers' meeting to discuss the introduction in Vladivostok of the "social revolution," to be accompanied by the abolition of private ownership in land, factories, and mines. This startling appeal alarmed the Consular Corps. The main Allied representatives (Japanese, British, French, and American) met to consider the situation, and decided to send a letter to the representative of the Provisional Government in Vladivostok, asking for information as to what steps the government proposed to take in the light of this challenge to its authority.

Actually, the incident had no immediate effect. The meeting of workers and soldiers took place as announced, but proved to be purely discursory. Nevertheless, Caldwell reported to Washington:

... it is generally admitted that this was partly due to the fear that the Japanese will take full and permanent charge of this district on the least sign of disorder and to the fact that the letter of the Consular Corps gave rise to a belief that warships had been asked for and that an American and Japanese fleet was lying just off the harbor ready for any emergency.[1]

The incident thus revealed clearly both Allied sensitivity to anything like a Bolshevization of Vladivostok and its environs, and the acute awareness on the part of the population of the connection between the political prospects of the Bolshevik faction and the policies of the Allied governments with respect to this area. It is noteworthy that several weeks before the November Revolution the Bolshevik movement in the Soviet Far East appeared to everyone as a direct challenge to Allied interests and prestige.

Another consequence of the incident was a renewed recommendation from Caldwell for an American naval visit to the port—"not for the purpose of quelling disorder, but with a view to making it less likely to occur." This recommendation, first made by despatch on October 4, was renewed by telegram on November 8 (i.e. the day of the Bolshevik Revolution in Petrograd). On this second occasion, Caldwell pointed out that unless something were done to keep the situation from deteriorating, disturbances could ensue which would interfere with the program of the Stevens Railway Mission. Pointing to the likelihood of Japanese naval visits, he said the Japanese fleet would be unwelcome since "all Russians . . . believe Japan desires to occupy this territory permanently."[2]

Caldwell's recommendation found favor in Washington. Admiral Austin M. Knight, Commander-in-Chief of the Asiatic Fleet, was immediately ordered to pay a visit to Vladivostok in his flagship, the *U.S.S. Brooklyn*. The visit was set to begin November 25.

It is interesting to note the interpretation given to this visit in Soviet historiography:

. . . As early as November 1917, in the heat of the election campaign for the Constituent Assembly, the American cruiser *Brooklyn* anchored in Vladivostok harbor and trained its guns on the city. This was designed,

[1] National Archives, State Department File 800.855, Vladivostok, 1917; Caldwell despatch 153, October 4, 1917, to the Department of State.

[2] National Archives, binder entitled "Confidential Correspondence and Code Telegrams received and sent, 1908 to 1917, Inclusive" and containing Vladivostok correspondence; Caldwell's telegram of November 8, 1917, 2 p.m.

as the Americans saw it, to prevent a Bolshevik victory in the elections. However, notwithstanding this overt threat, the majority of the toilers of Vladivostok cast their votes for the Bolsheviki.[3]

The American records contain nothing to substantiate any such interpretation. The visit represented, as we have seen, the execution of a project conceived earlier in the year. It flowed immediately from suggestions made by the Consul at Vladivostok before he had any knowledge of the Bolshevik seizure of power at Petrograd. Although the United States government clearly hoped that the presence of the vessel would have a stabilizing and reassuring effect on the situation, there is no indication that the timing of the visit had anything to do with the elections. Nor was there in Washington the faintest idea of using the vessel for armed action, or the threat of armed action, against the city itself; nothing, in fact, could have been farther from the thoughts of the President and the Secretary of State.

The transfer of power to the Bolsheviki in Petrograd thus found the United States government preparing to carry out a naval visit to the port of Vladivostok and to land there a large contingent of railroad engineers, whose mission was to assist the Russian authorities in improving the work of the Trans-Siberian Railway.

While news of the overturn in Petrograd naturally increased nervousness and fermentation in Vladivostok, and strengthened the extreme radical element, there was no immediate seizure of power by the local Bolsheviki. On November 23, Caldwell telegraphed that fighting was not expected in Vladivostok "due proximity Japan and expected arrival of *Brooklyn*." He added, however, the disturbing news that Japan had in Vladivostok "at least 800 soldiers and officers in civilian clothing with arms ready for distribution." [4]

The *Brooklyn* arrived at Vladivostok on November 25, on schedule, and remained in port until December 11, when she sailed for

---

[3] A. I. Melchin, *Amerikanskaya Interventsiya v 1918–1920 gg* (American Intervention, 1918–1920), Military-Naval Publishing Company, Moscow, 1951. Reliable figures on the voting in Vladivostok do not seem to be available. In the Amur District as a whole, the Social-Revolutionaries received, with 96,658 votes, an absolute majority. The Bolshevik vote was only 32,355. It is, however, in no way improbable that the Bolsheviki should have had a majority in the city of Vladivostok itself. (See Oliver Henry Radkey, *The Election to the Russian Constituent Assembly of 1917*, Harvard University Press, Cambridge, 1950, Appendix.)

[4] National Archives, "Confidential Correspondence . . ." *op.cit.;* Caldwell telegram to Department of State, November 23, 1917, noon. This assertion about disguised Japanese forces in Vladivostok was made by Caldwell quite categorically. I have found no confirmation of it from other sources.

Nagasaki and Manila. The visit was in every way successful. In his subsequent official report to the Navy Department, Admiral Knight related:

> The men of the *Brooklyn* were given liberty very freely, after a talk by the Commanding Officer in which he explained the various ways in which they could assist in forwarding the purpose of the visit. The result was excellent. Only two minor cases of disorder occurred. The bearing of the men was in all respects admirable and the example set the Russian sailors and soldiers, especially in the punctiliousness with which officers of both nations were saluted, had a marked effect on the manners of the Russians themselves.
>
> On the evening of November 30, the Russian sailors entertained the men of the *Brooklyn* at a supper followed by a theatrical entertainment, and on December 8, a return entertainment was given by the *Brooklyn's* men. The conduct of both affairs was above criticism.[5]

Caldwell confirmed in his despatches that the visit "had an excellent effect, both the officers and the men making a fine impression." [6]

The members of the ship's company—incredible as this may seem in the light of the habits and preoccupations of a later day—were specifically forbidden to engage in any form of intelligence work or to interest themselves in any information of a secret nature.

On December 4, Admiral Knight addressed a local "Russian-American Committee" which had been established to promote commercial relations. He hinted that if Russia were to leave the war American shipments to Vladivostok might well cease. This hint was taken up by the local press, which had also heard and noted with interest the premature Washington wireless report about the threatened termination of shipments.

According to one contemporary source, Admiral Knight also entertained "the most prominent and powerful Bolshevik in Vladivostok" at luncheon on the *Brooklyn* and disarmed the latter's suspicions that the visit portended the seizure of the Trans-Siberian Railway by the Americans.[7]

On December 6, at Caldwell's request, Admiral Knight met with the Allied consuls for an informal discussion of the situation. The question was raised as to whether the *Brooklyn* should not remain

---

[5] National Archives, State Department File 861.00/981, Report submitted December 14, 1917, by Admiral Knight at Nagasaki, to the Navy Department (Operations).

[6] National Archives, State Department File 800.855, Caldwell despatch 184.

[7] Coleman, *op.cit.*, p. 60.

longer. "It was the unanimous opinion of the Consuls," the Admiral reported to Washington, "that no reason existed for requesting me to postpone my departure beyond the date I had fixed (December 11)." The consuls further agreed that the excellent effect produced by the *Brooklyn's* visit "would continue to be felt after the departure of the ship." [8]

This last judgment proved to be quite incorrect, so much so that one is moved to wonder whether the motives of certain of the Allied consuls in encouraging the Admiral to leave were wholly disinterested. The situation, in fact, began to cloud up seriously before the *Brooklyn* had even cleared the port.

Stevens, be it noted, had by this time arrived in Vladivostok and joined Caldwell in his anxious study of the situation. The *Thomas,* with Mr. Emerson and his party of 350 railwaymen, was due very shortly.

On December 11, the day of the *Brooklyn's* departure, Caldwell despatched a gloomy and worried message to Washington. Things were, he wired, "still quiet here," but conditions were becoming worse. The local Soviet was interfering with the operation of the railroad, and attempting to seize the office of the state bank. He still thought the Bolsheviki too weak to take power at once, but he saw no likelihood of the situation improving. He included in his message a phrase "anticipate fighting here," which was deciphered in Washington to read "antagonists fighting here," and gave the impression that matters were approaching a decidedly crucial pass.

In the given circumstances, Caldwell continued,

. . . Stevens and all consuls consider presence foreign force desirable until Allies' attitude decided unanimously. American force is preferred but Japanese better than none despite hostility felt. . . .

Stevens, he added, agreed with him that it would be impossible for the Emerson corps to accomplish anything under these conditions, and joined him in recommending that the corps be re-routed, for the time being, to Japan. The port, he pointed out, was about to freeze. By the end of the month all incoming vessels would be at the mercy of the ice-breaker crews, "who are not dependable." [9]

This telegram created something of a stir in Washington. The

[8] National Archives, 861.00/981, Admiral Knight's report, *op.cit.*
[9] *Foreign Relations, 1918, Russia,* Vol. II, *op.cit.,* p. 6; from unnumbered telegram, December 11, 1917, 6 p.m., Caldwell to Secretary of State.

State Department was surprised to learn (as a result of the garbled passage) that fighting had actually broken out in Vladivostok, and startled at the bald recommendation by both Caldwell and Stevens for what sounded like outright military intervention. Lansing chanced to be meeting, that day, with Elihu Root, and took the occasion to discuss the Siberian situation with him. Root, as we have already noted, had resented the President's earlier refusal to make the Stevens Mission subordinate to his own. The idea of armed intervention in Russia was decidedly contrary to his cast of thought. His influence may well have been added, therefore, to the rejection of a suggestion with which, after all, Stevens had associated himself. In any case, Lansing at once despatched a reply to Caldwell, admonishing him that:

. . . it would seem wise to refrain from discussing or considering in any way the question of the advisability of presence of foreign force in Vladivostok at the present time and you may so advise your colleagues if they bring up the matter again.[10]

Despite this admonition, the Secretary took occasion, the following day, to tell the Washington correspondents of Caldwell's suggestion. From this one can only conclude that while he did not favor further discussion of intervention among the Americans in Vladivostok, he was not averse to having the Japanese know that the suggestion had been made.

It proved too late to divert the *Thomas* at sea. On December 14, the transport appeared in Vladivostok harbor with its load of railway engineers and supporting personnel. Stevens and Caldwell pondered the problem of what to do with these people; at the moment, there was no possibility for useful work. Conditions along the railroad were chaotic. No single authority had full control. Nor were there adequate accommodations for the men ashore. There was not even enough food available locally to provision the ship for any length of time. There was a danger that she might at any time become icebound in the port. The Emerson corps turned out, furthermore, to include a number of undesirable interpreters—"mischievous political agitators"[11]—who had obviously wangled the free ride to Vladi-

[10] *Ibid.*, p. 7, Lansing's telegram of December 13, 1917, 6 p.m.
[11] *Foreign Relations, 1918, Russia,* Vol. III, *op.cit.*, p. 211, Stevens' telegram of December 15, 1917, 9 a.m.; also Caldwell's messages to the Department of State of January 9 and 13, 1918, pp. 216–217.

vostok for ulterior purposes. The Allied passport control authorities were reluctant to let these men land to join the extreme radical element in the port, already bloated by the previous arrival of numerous revolutionary figures who had been in exile in the United States. If the engineers were permitted to come ashore, these agitators could not be prevented from doing likewise; once ashore, they would not easily be lured back on board again. The local Bolshevik press at once began to make an issue of their presence in the harbor and to demand their release.

In these unhappy circumstances, the engineers and supporting personnel were all kept on board, on Stevens' orders. After three days, the *Thomas* left again, with Stevens aboard, and proceeded to Japan, to await there a clarification of the situation.

❖

While the *Brooklyn* was still in Vladivostok, western opinion had been startled by press reports to the effect that a thousand Japanese troops had been landed there. These reports appeared first in the Petrograd press on December 8, and were promptly picked up by western correspondents in Petrograd and wired to the United States, where they appeared in the New York papers the following day.[12]

In Petrograd, Francis immediately queried his Japanese colleague about the rumors. The latter said he had no information, but believed them to be untrue.[13]

The Department of State, although under the impression (derived from Caldwell's earlier report) that some Japanese troops were already there, checked at once with Caldwell and with Ambassador Roland S. Morris at Tokyo.[14]

[12] The Provisional Government's Ambassador in Japan professed to believe that these reports of a Japanese landing had been put out as a trial balloon by the Japanese government itself. This was not implausible. Japanese interest in the Vladivostok situation was becoming very warm indeed; and we have already seen that the Japanese Ambassador in Petrograd, where the reports first appeared, considered that the spreading of rumors of this sort had its uses.

The report, oddly enough, appears to have been cheerfully confirmed to the correspondent of the *London Times* in Washington by a spokesman of the Japanese Embassy there, who made the astounding statement (for which there is no other evidence) that the Japanese had been "using engineer troops to manage the port and the Trans-Siberian terminus for some time," and that "the arrival of fresh troops might be described as a reinforcement." (*The Times*, London, December 12, 1917.)

[13] *Foreign Relations, 1918, Russia*, Vol. II, *op.cit.*, p. 6, Francis' telegram 2073, December 8, 9 p.m., to Department of State.

[14] *Loc.cit.*, State Department telegram to Morris, December 11, 1917, 4 p.m.; also *ibid.*, p. 7, telegram to Caldwell, December 12, 1917, 7 p.m.

Caldwell reported that no Japanese troops had landed at Vladivostok, nor did he know of any having been despatched, although he added that many people seemed to expect their coming and some even hoped for it.[15]

The Tokyo reaction was also mainly negative, but far from reassuring. To be sure, the Vice Minister for Foreign Affairs, queried by Ambassador Morris on December 14, termed the press reports "absurd and nonsensical." There were, he said, "at the present moment" no Japanese troops in Vladivostok. Nor, he added pointedly, were there any *Japanese* men-of-war in the harbor there. But the Japanese Navy Department confirmed the fact that arrangements had been made to send warships in case of emergency.[16] From other sources Morris was confidentially informed that three army divisions had been placed in a state of readiness "to leave for Harbin and, if deemed necessary, Vladivostok immediately." [17] The following day (December 15), the secretary to the Japanese Minister of War admitted to the American Military Attaché in Tokyo that "some preparations" were being made; whether troops were actually sent would depend on circumstances; at present there was no expectation that this would be necessary. In case troops should have to be sent either to Vladivostok or Harbin, he added, it would be only in numbers sufficient to protect Japanese interests.[18]

Morris might have understood better these somewhat equivocal observations on the part of the Japanese had he then been aware of a circumstance of which he was to learn much later: namely that at just this time (December 14) the British Ambassador also discussed with the Japanese Foreign Minister

. . . what action ought to be taken by the Allies in Siberia to protect stores and ammunition at Vladivostok and to control in case of emergency the Amur and Trans-Siberian Railways.[19]

British interest in the possibility of some Allied action at Vladivostok had become active almost immediately after the Bolshevik

---

[15] *Ibid.*, p. 9, Caldwell's telegram to Department, December 16, 12 p.m.

[16] The Japanese Consul at Vladivostok had told Admiral Knight on December 6 that a Japanese man-of-war was being held in readiness to proceed to Vladivostok in case its presence there should be needed. (Admiral Knight's report, *op.cit.*, National Archives, 861.00/981.)

[17] *Foreign Relations, 1918, Russia*, Vol. II, *op.cit.*, pp. 7–8, Morris' unnumbered telegram of December 14, 1917, 4 p.m.

[18] *Ibid.*, p. 8, Morris' unnumbered telegram of December 15, 1917, 4 p.m.

[19] *Ibid.*, p. 84, Morris' despatch No. 84, March 22, 1918, the Department.

seizure of power in November. Colonel John Ward, subsequently in command of the British forces in Siberia, tells in the published account of his experiences that the 25th Battalion of the Middlesex Regiment (of which he was then in command) stationed at Hongkong, received "one morning in November, 1917" instructions to hold itself in readiness to proceed to an unknown destination,[20] and he cites evidence to show that the contemplated destination was Vladivostok. (This is borne out by the wording of the War Cabinet paper of January 1, to be mentioned below.) But the final orders were not issued at that juncture, due no doubt to the realization in London, on second thought, that such a step would require careful co-ordination with the policies of the other Allies.

The possibility of some sort of intervention in Siberia, designed to protect the Trans-Siberian Railway against possible German encroachments and to keep it available to the Allies as a channel of access to the anti-Bolshevik forces in southern Russia, had come up for discussion among the senior statesmen at the Inter-Allied Conference in Paris at the beginning of December. On December 1st, Clemenceau brought the matter up with House and urged upon him the desirability of a Japanese expeditionary force. A wider conference, attended by the British, French, Italian, United States, and Japanese representatives, took place on December 3rd. A memorandum has survived, from the pen of Marshall Foch, purporting to set forth the "ideas developed" on this occasion.[21] Here, departing from a wildly exaggerated estimate of the possibilities for German expansion into Siberia and the Far East, the view was expressed that the Allies ought immediately to proceed to the occupation of the entire Trans-Siberian Railway, from Vladivostok to Moscow—the burden of the operation to be borne by Japan and the United States. This may, indeed, have represented the views of the French; but it certainly did not represent those of Balfour or House. The latter was then, as later, wholly unsympathetic to the idea of such intervention, but he

[20] John Ward, *With the "Die-Hards" in Siberia,* George H. Doran Co., New York, 1920, p. 17.
[21] For House's talk of December 1st with Clemenceau, see Seymour, Vol. III, *op.cit.,* p. 387. The Foch memorandum, one of the most interesting documents of this period, appears to be nowhere available in western archives. It is reproduced in full, in the original French text, as an appendix (pp. 19–22) in the Japanese-language work *Shiberia Shuppei no Shiteki Kenkyu* (Historical Research on the Siberian Expedition), by Chihiro Hosoya (Tokyo, Yuhikaku, 1955). I am indebted to Mr. Hosoya for bringing this document to my attention.

evidently acquiesced in the suggestion that the matter be explored further among the respective governments, with a view to seeing what possibilities existed for achieving the aims in question. Whether he reported this understanding to Washington, and if so whether it came to the knowledge of the Department of State as well as the President, remains unclear.

It seems most unlikely that the British Ambassador to Tokyo had instructions, when he visited Motono on the 14th, to advance anything in the nature of a formal proposal for military intervention in Siberia. It seems much more probable that his instructions were to sound out informally the Japanese reaction to the earlier French suggestions, particularly in the light of the *Brooklyn's* visit to Vladivostok and the rumors of independent Japanese action there. The Japanese government seems, however, to have derived an impression that the Ambassador's visit had a much more far-reaching purpose; this became, in fact, the basis for the subsequent Japanese contention that the initiative in the Siberian intervention had come not from them but from the western Allies. One is moved to suspect that Motono, who was—as will be seen shortly—a passionate proponent of the idea of intervention, permitted his own yearnings to color and distort the report he made of his conversation with another—a human weakness of which the annals of diplomacy afford innumerable examples.

Whatever the British approach consisted of, we may assume that the idea of a joint Allied landing at Vladivostok was vigorously supported in Tokyo by the French representatives. We have already noted that the French favored intervention in Siberia, actively and enthusiastically, from the very beginning. They appear to have taken advantage of every evidence of continuing deterioration of the situation in Siberia as an occasion for pressing their arguments for a Far Eastern intervention. Presumably they too approached the Japanese along these lines in December.

It is probably an understatement to say that these British and French approaches met with an intensely interested reception on the Japanese side. Coming at a time of serious complication in the Vladivostok situation, and on the heels of the visits of the *Brooklyn* and the *Thomas* to Vladivostok (which can hardly have been correctly understood in Tokyo and must have caused some uneasiness and speculation), the manifestations of French and British interest must surely have created in many Japanese minds the impression that the hour of decision could not be far away.

On the other hand, the particular suggestion to which the British were leaning at that time, namely for a *joint* expeditionary force in which at least token forces of the western Allies should be included, involved obvious disadvantages from the Japanese standpoint. It was too strongly reminiscent of the circumstances attending Japan's entry into the war against Germany in 1914 and the subsequent differences with the western Allies over Japanese policy toward China. It conjured up visions of Japan being hampered and frustrated in her Manchurian and Siberian ambitions by the same sort of unhappy sense of obligation to the western Allies that had hampered and frustrated her policy toward China as a whole in the earlier years of the war. There was the consideration as to whether the most favorable moment for intervention on the Siberian mainland had yet arrived. Finally, there was the question: what would the Americans do if the British and French suggestions were accepted? And what would they do if these suggestions were not accepted? They had just sent a warship to Vladivostok. They had just been, apparently, on the verge of taking the Trans-Siberian Railway under their effective technical control. They had not associated themselves with the British suggestions for a joint expedition. Was it possible that they were preparing to act unilaterally? If such were the case, or if there were even any serious possibility of this, would it not be better for Japan to accept the British-French suggestion at once and get there first? Or would this simply lead to a sharp and unnecessary conflict with the Americans, and bring them in, as formidable and independent competitors, where they might—given a more circumspect policy on Japan's part—have preferred to remain aloof?

It was in this maze of problems that Japanese statesmanship was obliged to wander in the middle of December 1917. Given the complexity of the pattern and the variety of conflicting considerations, it would have been a wonder if these problems had not occasioned wide differences of opinion among the Japanese statesmen. This, in any case, is what Ambassador Morris subsequently believed to be the case. The Foreign Minister, Viscount Motono, was, he reported,

. . . from the very first inclined to accede to the suggestion of the British Government and undertake some military movement in Siberia. In this he was supported by the General Staff. The Premier and Baron Goto, however, were far more cautious and doubted the wisdom of acting with England under the terms of the Anglo-Japanese alliance.[22]

This, however, was afterthought on Morris' part. At the moment, in mid-December, neither he nor, apparently, the Department of State had any definite knowledge of the British approach.

❖

While we consider the developments in the Vladivostok situation, it is well to note the events that were occurring at the same time in Harbin. There, the situation began to deteriorate immediately after the Bolshevik seizure of power in November. Pressure against Horvat on the part of the local Soviet soon became intense. There were serious threats that the entire railway administration—and with it, of course, the attendant political power—would be taken out of Horvat's hands.

In the face of these developments, the General showed himself uncertain, vacillating, and opportunistic. Instead of taking a firm stand against communist pressures, he attempted to temporize and compromise with those who were attacking the morale and discipline of his force. Only four days after the Revolution, the American Consul, Mr. Charles A. Moser, and his British colleague found it necessary to call on Horvat and to impress upon him the fact that not only the Russians and Chinese, but also the western powers, had an interest in good order in Harbin and along the railway.

. . . We stated that we were obliged to regard him as the head of the local administration and the one upon whom we had to rely for the protection of our nationals. He could inform the Bolsheviks, or whatever party might pretend to power, that his removal from his place as head of the Russian administration by any individual or body of revolutionists could not be looked upon with indifference; but that any attempt of such a nature would oblige us to ask our Governments to take such measures as they believed advisable for the protection of their nationals in Manchuria.

General Horvat promised to inform us immediately of any serious movements threatening to jeopardize our interests or to take the control of the administration from his hands. . . .[23]

[22] *Foreign Relations, 1918, Russia*, Vol. II, *op.cit.*, p. 85; from Morris' despatch 84, March 22, 1918. Baron Goto was Minister of the Interior in the Terauchi Cabinet.
[23] *Ibid.*, p. 3, from despatch of November 17, 1917 from Consul Moser at Harbin to Minister Reinsch at Peking.

The situation in the city continued nevertheless to deteriorate, and the spread of lawlessness and violence soon reached a point where the safety of the large foreign colony was seriously jeopardized. By the beginning of December the matter had begun to engage the earnest attention of the Allied ministers in Peking. There was at first some discussion of the possibility of putting Harbin and the railway zone under some form of international control. There were even suggestions that the United States should itself provide a contingent of troops for this purpose. The general consensus, however, was that the most suitable first step was to ask the Chinese to step in and take control of the situation with their own forces. At the beginning of December the Allied ministers, on their own responsibility, made this suggestion to the Chinese government. The American Minister at Peking, Mr. Paul S. Reinsch, in reporting the step to the Department of State on December 6, called attention to the possibility that an attempt on the part of the Chinese to implement this recommendation might very well lead to a state of war between China and Russia: a situation which the Germans would have greeted with glee and which they would have exploited as a further serious weakening of the Allied coalition. In this case, Reinsch pointed out, international control might be the only answer; and he asked the Department to enlighten him as to how far the American government would be inclined to go "in an eventual international administration and policing of the north Manchurian railway zone." [24]

These suggestions—for Chinese intervention or international administration at Harbin—put Washington in a most awkward position. Plainly, international administration would have to involve the Japanese. This was regarded as wholly undesirable. The idea of the Chinese restoring their authority in northern Manchuria fitted excellently, in theory, with traditional American policy. But there was an inconvenient question: what, at the moment, was "China"? The country was split between north and south, in a state of virtual civil war. The northern government was dominated by the Premier, Tuan Chi-jui, who required and accepted Japanese support for the maintenance of his position domestically, and who was extensively beholden to the Japanese. It was plain that any new military exertion on his part could take place only with further Japanese support and thus

[24] *Ibid.*, p. 5; from Reinsch's telegram of December 6, 1917, 7 p.m., to Department of State.

heighten his dependence on Japan. Was it desirable that the Bolsheviki be expelled in Harbin only in order that a Japanese puppet might be installed? Yet how could the United States say "no"? The territorial integrity of China had been the keystone of American policy for nearly twenty years. It was precisely the United States which had always refused to recognize the internal weakness of China as a valid reason why China should be treated any differently from any other power, and had insisted that China, regardless of the quality of Chinese administration, ought always to be master in her own house. Washington was now hoist with its own petard. Grudgingly, with some gnashing of teeth, the Department replied to Reinsch that in its view China was "within her right in employing troops to protect her sovereignty and territorial integrity." The United States would not, however, be disposed to encourage an armed conflict.[25]

The Chinese, armed now with Allied sanction, at once despatched 3,500 troops to Harbin. These forces proceeded, on Christmas Day and the following day, to disarm the disaffected Russian forces there. The operation proceeded without too much difficulty, although the leading communist political agents succeeded in making their escape. Horvat's authority was not formally challenged; it was, in fact, ostensibly restored. But it now rested in greater degree than before on Chinese sanction, and behind the Chinese stood the Japanese. With every day it was becoming plainer that the preoccupation of the European powers with the war in the west, together with the breakdown of Russia, could not fail to play into Japanese hands, however one tried to prevent it.

On the day after the Chinese coup, Consul Moser reported:

Today the town is seemingly quiet, though Chinese soldiers patrol the streets everywhere. The power of the Bolsheviks is destroyed, for the time being at least. It is too early, however, to forecast the outcome. With General Horwath hopelessly discredited it looks [as] if the Railway and Municipal Administrations will continue to remain the playthings of the Russian revolutionary organizations, which are without cohesion or authority. . . .[26]

The incisive action by the Chinese appears either to have gone beyond what the British government had bargained for or to have

---

[25] *Loc.cit.*, Reinsch's telegram of December 8, 1917, 4 p.m.
[26] National Archives, State Department File 861.00/1183; Moser despatch of December 27, 1917, enclosure to Peking despatch 1851, January 17, 1918.

given rise to second thoughts in London. For, while Chinese action was still in progress, London queried Washington as to whether the United States would not be disposed to join in putting a restraining hand on the Chinese.[27] The Department of State replied by repeating the rather cryptic formula it had already communicated to the Consul at Harbin: that China was "within her right in employing means to protect her sovereignty and territorial integrity." The Department went on to whistle in the dark, expressing its confident hope that the Chinese government would find it wise to be lenient in such a position, that the use of force would not be found necessary, and that circumstances would soon adjust themselves so "as to permit of an orderly and proper administration of affairs at that place." [28]

These happenings occupied the final days of December. The year 1917 thus ended with the Harbin Bolsheviki having accomplished nothing more than getting themselves expelled from Manchuria, at the price of a strengthening of nominal Chinese control, and virtual Japanese influence, in the affairs of North Manchuria. Would the same pattern be followed in Siberia?

❖

The final days of 1917 saw a new flare-up of Allied attention to the Vladivostok situation.

On December 22, Caldwell reported further on the situation in Vladivostok. The city, he stated, was still quiet but a Bolshevik attempt to seize full power was probable in the near future. This, he thought, would result in a paralysis of the port. He pointed to the prisoner-of-war danger, and expressed the belief that in the event of a separate Soviet-German peace some form of Allied control of Vladivostok and the Pri-Amur district would be necessary "to protect shipping China and Japan routes." The Trans-Siberian Railway from Irkutsk west to European Russia was, he reported, already in Bolshevik hands. The telegraphic communication was cut west of Chita.[29] (This meant, of course, that he no longer had direct communication with the Petrograd Embassy.)

---

[27] *Foreign Relations, 1918, Russia,* Vol. II, *op.cit.,* pp. 14–15; Memorandum No. 659, December 28, 1917, from British Embassy to Secretary of State.

[28] *Ibid.,* pp. 15–16; Memorandum, December 29, 1917, from Secretary of State to British Ambassador in Washington.

[29] *Ibid.,* pp. 10–11; Caldwell's telegram of December 22, 1917, to the Department of State.

The *U.S.S. Brooklyn* in Vladivostok harbor

Admiral Austin M. Knight, Commander in Chief,
U.S. Asiatic Squadron, at a social gathering in Japan

General Dmitri L. Horvat, Russian Governor and General Manager of the Chinese Eastern Railway

The American Embassy, Petrograd, 1909-1917

Caldwell followed up his report on December 27 with the news that the General Commissioner appointed by the Provisional Government to replace the Governor General of the Maritime Province had just been arrested by the Bolsheviki because he had attempted to turn over his authority to the moderate Zemstvo body. The chief of the commercial port had also been removed.[30] These acts were taken as presaging an early seizure of power by the Bolshevik element.

Two days later, incidentally, Caldwell addressed a letter to the arrested commissioner, specifically requesting that it be published. The letter referred to local press reports to the effect that he, Caldwell, had asked for the despatch of American troops to the port, and went on to say:

. . . I have not requested the despatch to Vladivostok of American troops and sincerely hope that conditions here will not make necessary the presence of any foreign troops at any time.[31]

The reason for this move was that Caldwell suspected that the press reports had been inspired by the Japanese. His reply, designed primarily to counter this misinformation, had the added advantages of keeping the Japanese in a healthy state of suspense, and of lending moral support to the unfortunate Commissioner.

Three days later, on December 30, Caldwell relayed to Washington a dramatic message from Moser in Harbin. The British Consul there, it seemed, had received a report to the effect that Irkutsk was in flames; the Bolsheviki were murdering and plundering the inhabitants and ravishing the women; the streets were covered with the corpses of murdered children; the French and British, including the French Consular Agent and two French officers, had been murdered. The Japanese, it was stated, had been informed. Help was implored.[32]

This report was, to say the least, exaggerated. At the time of the November Revolution, the French had in Irkutsk a commercial agent by the name of Jandroux who headed a colony consisting principally of about fifty governesses and tutors employed in the homes of wealthy Irkutsk citizens. He was later joined (January 22) by a regular Consul General who bore the unhappy name of Gaston Bourgois. (Although Bourgois pronounced his name with a hard

---

[30] *Ibid.*, pp. 13–14; Caldwell's telegram of December 27, 1917, 8 p.m.

[31] National Archives, binder entitled "Confidential Correspondence . . . ," *op.cit.*

[32] *Foreign Relations, 1918, Russia*, Vol. II, *op.cit.*, p. 16; Caldwell's telegram of December 30, 1917, noon, to the Department of State.

"g," its resemblance to the term "bourgeois," just then on so many tongues, was too close to avoid notice. He complained bitterly in his despatches about this unfortunate coincidence; it was, he said, as though he had served in Paris during the French Revolution and had borne the name of M. Aristocrat.)

Irkutsk had indeed been, in December, the scene of much violence. The local Soviet had made an attempt to seize power as early as the 19th of November, and had immediately come into sharp conflict with the moderate city administration. On the 8th of December the tense political situation came to a head, and violent street fighting began between the conservative forces—mostly Cossacks and military cadets—and the Bolsheviki. The disorders lasted about ten days.

According to Jandroux's reports, as published ten years later in the Soviet historical journal *Krasny Arkhiv*,[33] he himself was obliged first to hide in his own cellar and then to take refuge in another part of town. When the fighting ended on December 18 with a Bolshevik victory, he returned to his home only to find it completely wrecked. His report says that some Chinese and Greeks were killed and that hundreds of foreigners were plundered. In a letter dated December 23 and addressed "Dear Count," he included this curious passage:

. . . In Harbin the rumor got about that I had been killed and the Japanese Consul General sent a telegraphic inquiry to get confirmation of this rumor and to find out the situation in the city. We answered him with the most alarming sort of a telegram.

Actually, there is no evidence whatsoever that any French citizen was killed at that time in Irkutsk, and there is considerable evidence that no western residents were killed at all.[34] One is constrained to

[33] *Krasny Arkhiv*, No. 34, 1929; pp. 126 ff. This issue carried the purported texts, in Russian translation, of a number of reports submitted to their French superiors by Jandroux, Bourgois, and finally Major Pichon, who was sent to Siberia in the winter of 1918 by the head of the French Military Mission in Petrograd, General Niessel. *Krasny Arkhiv*, in its introductory note, said merely that these documents had been "recently" found among various materials which had accumulated in the Central Archives in the years of the Revolution. The reports of Jandroux, as given here, do not give the impression of being translations. They contain a number of Russian touches which give rise to doubt as to their complete authenticity. However, even if they are not fully authentic or involve some degree of distortion, one must assume that the main historical facts and dates mentioned therein must be substantially correct, as flagrant falsifications in this respect could easily be checked up on.

[34] Jandroux, in a further letter of January 1, said that the lives of foreigners continued to be in danger, but made no mention of any western resident having been

concede the probability that the report of the massacre in Irkutsk was in some way or other deliberately perpetrated for the specific purpose of alarming the Allied governments and inducing them to intervene.[35] Unfortunately, the report found considerable currency, and was not without its effect on Allied policy. As late as the end of January, the French Foreign Minister, in conversation with the American Ambassador in Paris, referred to the killing of three French citizens in Irkutsk by Russians. Whether he was ever disabused of this impression is not clear.

✧

Against this background of fact and fiction, the Siberian situation continued to be the object of renewed and intensive attention in a number of the Allied chanceries.

On December 21, Bakhmeteff mentioned to Lansing certain information he had received from France about the French desire for foreign intervention at Vladivostok. The information presumably came from his colleague Maklakov in Paris. It was to the following effect:

> The French Government and public opinion are deeply stirred by the fact that the important storage of munitions in Vladivostok can be seized by the Bolsheviki. It is understood that there has arisen a distinct desire of the Allies to occupy Vladivostok with Japanese troops.[36]

This was apparently the first direct hint to the American officials of the suggestions the French and British had made in Tokyo.

The concern of officials in Washington over Japanese intentions with regard to Siberia must have been somewhat heightened on December 22 when news was received, both from Francis and in press reports, of the terms of the secret treaty concluded between the

killed. Major Walter S. Drysdale, of the United States Army, who was sent from China to Irkutsk as an observer in mid-January, reported: "I could find no evidence that any foreigners in Irkutsk were killed but some were wounded accidentally as a result of the artillery, machine gun and rifle fire within the limits of the city." (National Archives, Department of State File 860.00/1280; Peking despatch no. 1884, February 7, 1918.) Drysdale did not say what the nationality of the wounded foreigners was.

[35] In later American papers, there are specific references to the biased interpretations and misleading information put out by the French consular officials in Irkutsk. The town seems, in fact, to have been the source of much of the misleading rumor about the prisoner-of-war danger.

[36] Lansing MSS, *op.cit.,* Vol. 32 of Correspondence: Letter, Bakhmeteff to Lansing, December 21, 1917.

Russians and the Japanese on July 3, 1916—terms which had just been published by the Soviet government. The agreement, as we have seen, was evidently directed primarily against the United States. The Department of State had heretofore known only that such a treaty existed, but had had no knowledge of its terms. It had entertained suspicions from the start that the edge of the agreement was pointed toward the United States. "This new treaty between Japan and Russia," Polk had written to Francis on August 18, 1916,

may mean very little; on the other hand, there are certain indications which make it necessary for us to go very carefully in our relations with these two governments until we know a bit more definitely what their attitude will be toward the United States. I do not think the alliance is an offensive or defensive alliance, but it would not have to be that in order to be of real importance to us.[37]

The language of the Treaty, as revealed to the Department on December 22, was obscure and puzzling, and it was several weeks before a careful study of it could be completed by the Department's experts.[38] But even a casual glance was enough to heighten, rather than relieve, the suspicion that the document had the nature of an agreement designed to neutralize the effects of a possible adverse American action to some new change in the *status quo* in Manchuria. The realization that only eighteen months earlier the Japanese had probably been engaged in this sort of maneuver naturally served to make the Washington statesmen only more wary of any new proposals looking toward Japanese expeditions on the Siberian mainland.

Three days later, on December 24, Stevens, who had arrived in Tokyo, was taken by Ambassador Morris to see the Japanese Foreign Minister, Viscount Motono. Stevens expounded his own views at length, warning against any sort of armed intervention "even in eastern Siberia." He dwelt on the folly of any enterprise which would serve to antagonize the proletarian element in Russia. Asked for his constructive suggestions as to what to do about the situation, Stevens expressed belief in the efficacy of a large commission of Allied personnel,

[37] Frank L. Polk MSS, Yale University Library, New Haven; Folder 15.
[38] *Ibid.*, Folder 39; Memorandum by Williams, Chief of Far Eastern Division, to Secretary of State, March 5, 1918, analyzing the treaty. This study confirmed the anti-American quality of the agreement.

. . . composed of men of well known administrative capacity who would be at least sympathetic with the progressive spirit which . . . is destined to control the future of Russia.

The Japanese Foreign Minister indicated vague sympathy, or at least understanding, for Stevens' view. Morris understood him to say that

. . . the Japanese Government is opposed to using military force even in Siberia lest such action should crystallize Russian feeling against the Allied powers.[39]

Evidently the Japanese were concerned to avoid any statements that might excite American suspicions of an early Japanese move and precipitate unilateral action on the American part.

On December 27, Lansing took occasion to speak to the Japanese Ambassador in Washington about the Vladivostok situation. His record of the conversation was as follows:

I . . . told him that the view of this Government was that it would be unwise for either the United States or Japan to send troops to Vladivostok as it would undoubtedly result in the unifying of the Russians under the Bolsheviks against foreign interference. He said to me that that was the exact view of his Government and that they had no intention of sending troops to Vladivostok for the same reason that we opposed it. He said that both Great Britain and France had made the suggestion but that the Japanese Government did not consider it wise to adopt the suggestion.[40]

This appears to be the first real confirmation to the United States government that suggestions had been made to the Japanese by the British or the French with respect to intervention in Siberia. It occasioned no great surprise in Washington. Wilson and Lansing were aware, through House's talks at Paris, of the trend of French and British official feeling.

On the same day, December 27, Lansing also saw the British Ambassador, Spring Rice, and discussed the Vladivostok situation with him. There is no record of what transpired at this meeting. The following day Spring Rice came again to the State Department, spoke with Assistant Secretary Phillips, and showed the latter a message

[39] *Foreign Relations, 1918, Russia*, Vol. ii, *op.cit.*, p. 12; Morris' telegram of December 24, 1917, 11 p.m. to Department of State.
[40] *Ibid.*, p. 13; Memorandum, December 27, 1917.

he had received indicating that the British Foreign Secretary, Mr. Balfour, had discussed Siberia with the Japanese Ambassador in London on the 26th. On that occasion Balfour had gained the impression from the Japanese Ambassador ("more from his manner than from anything the Ambassador said"):

. . . that the Japanese were planning to land a force at Vladivostok. Mr. Balfour told the Ambassador that independent action on the part of the Japanese would be most unfortunate, and urged upon the Japanese Ambassador that if action was contemplated they should consult with the United States.

Mr. Balfour has expressed the hope to Spring Rice that if the Japanese propose joint action the United States Government will not refuse.[41]

On Saturday, December 29, Spring Rice addressed to President Wilson a personal and secret letter [42] enclosing a memorandum of a conversation he had had that day with the Japanese Ambassador, Sato. The latter, Spring Rice explained, had just received orders to proceed to Japan, did not know whether he would be returning to Washington, and wished to see the President before departure. Spring Rice suggested that the President should receive him. Meanwhile, he went ahead to indicate in the letter the burden of what Sato wished to convey to the President. It was, in summary, the following:

1. Japan was content with the existing situation but could not witness with indifference the extension of German control over Russia.

2. Japan did not wish to take action *prematurely* in east Asia.

(. . . If Japan takes action before the danger has taken form she would be giving strength and new material to the German propagandists . . .)

3. Japan cared more about the German danger than about Russian public opinion, but she also suspected and feared American intentions.

(. . . It must also be remembered that there is a strong suspicion in Japan of the Allies and especially of the United States who are suspected of

[41] National Archives, State Department File 861.00/912; Memorandum of December 28, 1917, Phillips to Secretary Lansing. Actually, the impression conveyed was slightly inaccurate. It appears to have been Robert Cecil, not Balfour, who had discussed the matter with the Japanese Ambassador.

[42] The letter and its enclosure are to be found in the Wilson MSS, Series II, *op.cit.*

designs on eastern Asia. There is undoubtedly a fear of American action in the same way as in the United States there is a fear of Japanese action. . . .)

4. Japan was making military preparations to move into Siberia, if this should prove necessary.

5. Japan would like to know whether the United States was contemplating intervention.

(. . . It would be important . . . that Japanese public opinion should be reassured as to the possibility of sole American intervention. . . .)

6. Japan would like freedom of action in east Asia, and wished to be treated as an equal.

This Japanese approach appears not to have been inspired by any specific instructions from Tokyo but rather to have reflected Sato's personal initiative. Sato was, however, a well-informed man, and his carefully formulated statement represents the most interesting and revealing available indication of Japanese thought at that time. It is therefore worthwhile pausing here to note its wider implications. The following seems to flow clearly from the wording of this document:

1. The Japanese were reluctant, before getting a clearer view of United States intentions, to make any final decision on the French and British suggestion that they intervene at Vladivostok.

2. They were particularly concerned to know whether there was any possibility of the United States acting unilaterally, without prior consultation with the other Allies.

3. They themselves were making active preparations to intervene, and wanted the United States to know this in order that Washington might not suppose it could get away with any unilateral surprise move.

4. Nevertheless, they wanted the United States to know that they did not propose to take action "prematurely," so that the United States would not feel under the necessity of making a move to forestall a possible Japanese action.

5. They desired that their policy should be regarded as related to the German danger, which gave them a legitimate formal grievance, rather than to the state of Russian opinion, which they knew would be unfavorable to them.

6. They wished that the Allies would agree to grant them a free hand to intervene alone, if and when they felt the time had come.

It was by this time clear to the Japanese that the situation in Siberia presented for them an opportunity of which, sooner or later, they would, as they saw it, have to avail themselves. It was clear that at some point, and possibly very soon, it would be necessary for them to take action on the Siberian mainland. They very much hoped, however, that things would develop in such a way that they might intervene alone and not be troubled with Allied associates breathing down their necks and hampering their freedom of action. The suggestions made to them up to that time had all envisaged some form of joint intervention, and had therefore not appealed to them. Nor were they, from their own standpoint, in any hurry. The Soviet-German peace negotiations at Brest-Litovsk were only beginning. The Japanese justification for military intervention in Siberia would be stronger if they could await the actual conclusion of a separate Soviet-German peace, which would give formal grounds for the assertion that Russia had betrayed the Entente and placed herself on the side of the enemy. Furthermore, at this moment, the Bolsheviki had not yet quite completed their conquest of eastern Siberia. If the Japanese were to go in before the anti-Bolshevik elements were thoroughly crushed, they might be faced with embarrassing claims from these anti-Bolshevik elements to be recognized as friends and allies rather than enemies and treated accordingly. It was better to wait until the Bolshevik coup was complete. Finally, and most important of all, American intentions were unclear; abrupt and premature action might frighten the United States into action on its own. This was the last thing the Japanese wanted.

The only available copy of Spring Rice's letter is to be found in Wilson's private papers. There is no indication that it was ever communicated to the Secretary of State. It was sent to the President on Saturday, December 29. The following day, Sunday, the President spent quietly at home. On Monday he did, as Spring Rice had suggested, receive the Japanese Ambassador.[43] There is no evidence that he consulted with the Secretary of State before doing so, or that the Secretary was present during the conversation. There seems to be no American record of what was discussed. It is not even certain that Sato was aware, at that time, that Spring Rice had passed on his

[43] Baker, Vol. VII, *op.cit.,* p. 438.

observations in such detail. The Japanese records are said to indicate that the talk ·was mostly general, and that the Ambassador came away with the impression that the President was not actually averse to the idea of a Japanese action in Siberia. If this is so, it is most unlikely that the two men understood each other.

CHAPTER XV

JAPAN ASKS FOR A

FREE HAND

If conditions should . . . require occupation of Vladivostok . . . , Japan asks that this task be left to her alone. . . .—The Japanese Foreign Minister, Motono, to the American Ambassador in Tokyo, January 17, 1918

PRESIDENT WILSON had, it will be recalled, met with the Japanese Ambassador on the last day of 1917. As the new year began, the Siberian question, destined to absorb the attention of both President and Secretary of State more than any other problem of America's foreign relations during the coming six months, was not long in announcing its ugly presence.

On December 31, the War Cabinet in London had discussed the problem of the military supplies at Vladivostok. On New Year's Day, President Wilson was provided with a copy of a cable from Lord Robert Cecil reflecting the results of the War Cabinet session. This document, too, is in the Wilson papers. It was not published in the State Department's *Foreign Relations* series. Its content was as follows:

Jan. 1st, 1918. URGENT. VERY SECRET. War Cabinet are very uneasy about Vladivostok. There are lying at the port 648,000 tons of very valuable military stores including 136,000 tons railway material; 60,000 tons nitrate of soda; 15,000 tons explosive; 58,000 tons barbed wire; 70,000 tons shells of Russian pattern; 43,000 tons phosphate; 27,000 tons metal, including copper and aluminum, and 78,000 tons tea, rice, cotton and rubber. All accounts that we receive agree in describing the situation in Vladivostok as very uncertain. A large proportion of troops there are certainly Bolshevik and it is quite possible at any moment they may seize the stores and send them to Petrograd to be sold to the Germans. In these circumstances the British Government feel the question of landing a sufficient force to guard these stores should be reconsidered. Such a force would necessarily have to mainly Japanese, but it is important from many points of view that it should contain an element of other nationalities, lest the Bolshevik should be able to say it was an attempt to invade Russia. Unfortunately available British force in the neighborhood is very small and most we could provide would be two companies from troops now stationed at Hongkong. It seems therefore of great importance that the United States Government should send a contingent to co-operate in any military proceedings of the kind indicated.

I spoke this afternoon to the Japanese Ambassador on the subject. He did not receive the suggestion very favorably and expressed the hope that everything would be done by peaceful means such as conceding local Government in that part of Siberia, to avoid intervention. I agreed with him that it would be better to avoid intervention if we could be sure the stores would be safe, but that their amount and value seems to render it necessary not to run any risk of their being transferred to the enemy. He promised in any case to give these views to his Government. Robert Cecil.[1]

Again, there is no indication that this document was communicated to the Secretary of State and no record of what reply, if any, was given to it. Two days later Spring Rice called on the President in order to inform him of his own recall and the appointment of Lord Reading as his successor. The two men had on that occasion a long conversation, an account of which appears in the second volume of Spring Rice's papers.[2] This record does not indicate that any reference was made to the Far Eastern situation. Most likely, the British document was a telegram to Sir William Wiseman (key figure in British Intelligence in the United States and informal liaison between Wilson and the British War Cabinet) and reached the President through House.

When the Secretary returned to his desk on January 2, we do not know whether he had before him the secret messages the President had received from the Japanese and the British. We know, however, that he did have on his desk the false report from Irkutsk and another disturbing message from Caldwell. The situation in Vladivostok, Caldwell reported, was continuing to deteriorate. "Better class Russians" were still pleading for Allied intervention. The Consular Corps had agreed that foreign warships would have to be

[1] Wilson MSS, Series II, *op.cit.*
[2] Gwynn, Vol. II, *op.cit.*, pp. 422–425.

present if any order were to be preserved. The Japanese Consul was asking his government to send ships. It was "most desirable" that the others do likewise. The ships "should arrive unannounced, entering at dawn, because reign of terror is threatened if intervention announced." [3]

The following morning, January 3, the Secretary received a further telegram from Morris in Tokyo. Morris said information received in Japan indicated that conditions were improving in eastern Siberia and there was no confirmation of the massacre in Irkutsk. The Japanese Foreign Office, however, was watching conditions closely. Meanwhile, the Japanese government was "fully prepared to act promptly if intervention is deemed expedient." Motono, he said, had expressed to the Russian Ambassador his regret that there had been no exchange of views between the Allied powers in regard to the situation in Russia. He had also expressed the wish that he might know the attitude of the United States government. [4] Plainly, nothing had been said to Morris about the approach to the President.

During the course of that same day (January 3), Lansing talked with the Japanese Ambassador. His desk calendar gives the subject of this talk as the "possible necessity of protecting Siberia from German domination." No record of the talk is available. The Secretary's position could hardly have been different from that which he had made known to the Ambassador some days before. The Ambassador's statements may well have suggested, however, that the Japanese government, in response to the recommendation of its Consul in Vladivostok, was preparing to send a war vessel to that port. Later that day, in any case, Lansing addressed a note to the Secretary of the Navy saying that he had received a telegram from the Consul at Vladivostok

. . . which leads me to ask you to send a warship to that port. While I understand that the *USS Brooklyn* is under orders for Australia, I nevertheless believe it would be well to have Admiral Knight at Vladivostok. [5]

Attached to this document, in the Wilson papers, is the draft of a telegram from the Navy Department to Admiral Knight, instructing

[3] *Foreign Relations, 1918, Russia,* Vol. II, *op.cit.,* pp. 16–17, Caldwell's telegram of January 1, 1918, 1 a.m.
[4] *Ibid.,* p. 17; Morris' telegram of January 2, 1918, 4 p.m.
[5] Wilson MSS, Series II, *op.cit.*

him to proceed to Vladivostok. Written in pencil at the close of the message is the following phrase:

If possible avoid landing armed forces at Vladivostok unless necessary to preserve American lives.

The next day, January 4, the decision to send Admiral Knight back to Vladivostok was modified after a series of conferences, first between Lansing and Phillips, later between the President and the Secretaries of War and Navy.[6] It was decided to order the Admiral, then at Manila, to proceed only to Yokohama and to await further instructions there.

On January 5 the Russian Ambassador in Tokyo learned from the Minister for Foreign Affairs that the Japanese government had definitely decided to send a cruiser to Vladivostok, to arrive there about the 9th, and that the British government was doing likewise. The British cruiser, he was told, was to be sent from Hongkong. The Russian Ambassador at once relayed this news to Morris. In passing it on to the Department of State, Morris wired:

. . . I assume that these arrangements have been made in consultation between the British Government and the Japanese although British Ambassador made no mention of them in discussing the situation in Vladivostok with me today.[7]

Some days later, both the British and the Japanese governments officially communicated to the United States government the fact that they were sending war vessels to Vladivostok. The first of the Japanese vessels, the *Iwami,* arrived there on January 12. The British cruiser *Suffolk,* sent from Hongkong, reached Vladivostok January 14.

No notification was given to the Soviet government of these naval visits, as indeed none had been given of the visit of the *Brooklyn* in December. On January 19 the People's Commissariat for Foreign Affairs sent a note to the Japanese Ambassador in Petrograd, asking to be informed of the "reasons and aims of this act of the Japanese

[6] Lansing MSS, *op.cit.,* Desk Diary, Friday, January 4, 1918.
[7] *Foreign Relations, 1918, Russia,* Vol. II, *op.cit.,* pp. 19–20, Morris' telegram of January 5, 1918, 10 p.m. Actually, the Japanese records are said to indicate that the British decision was taken first, without prior consultation, and that the Japanese, feeling their hand forced, merely followed suit.

Government." [8] The Japanese evidently failed to reply. For some days there were rumors that the Japanese Ambassador would be expelled from Petrograd, but nothing of this sort occurred.

On January 17 a second Japanese vessel arrived in Vladivostok harbor. The cruiser *Asahi,* Caldwell reported at that time, was awaited the following day, and a supply ship shortly thereafter. This would make a total of four. Again, in the face of these circumstances, Caldwell pleaded for the presence of the *Brooklyn*. But this time his recommendation was countered by the Americans in Japan. After exhaustive discussions between Ambassador Morris and Admiral Knight on the one hand, and the Japanese government, as well as the French, British and Russian ambassadors on the other, Morris and Knight recommended against it. The *Brooklyn* continued to be held for the time being at Yokohama.

During the first days of January the Japanese professed to be somewhat bewildered by the British suggestions for a joint intervention, and continued to manifest a cautious and tempered reluctance to contemplate any sort of joint landing at Vladivostok. Commenting to Morris on Lord Robert Cecil's *démarche* of January 1 (which Morris thus learned of for the first time) the Japanese Vice Minister for Foreign Affairs said on January 7 that he was puzzled over the British suggestion, because only a few days earlier, on December 26, Lord Robert Cecil had urged upon the Japanese Ambassador in London "the inadvisableness of antagonizing Maximalist party now in control in Russia." The Japanese government, the Vice Minister had continued, was

. . . waiting further explanation of the apparent change of attitude of the British Government and of its immediate intentions before taking final decision.

He himself, the Vice Minister,

. . . thought it would be premature to land troops, as he understood British Foreign Office proposes, inasmuch as that might incur anti-Allied feeling.[9]

The despatch of the Japanese war vessels to Vladivostok naturally led, however, to a new spate of rumors. On January 10, Ambassador

[8] Francis MSS, *op.cit.,* Folder—January 11–22, 1918; Item from the Petrograd *Novaya Zhizn,* January 19, 1918.
[9] *Foreign Relations, 1918, Russia,* Vol. II, *op.cit.,* p. 20, Morris' telegram of January 7, 1918, 8 p.m.

Bakhmeteff, who had for some days been warning State Department officials about Japanese intentions with regard to Siberia, called on Assistant Secretary of State Breckinridge Long,[10] and read to him telegrams received from his colleagues at Tokyo, Paris, and London, all expressing the conviction "that the Japanese intended and were making preparations to effectuate an occupation at Vladivostok and Khabarovsk." Bakhmeteff urged that if any action of this sort had to be taken, it should be joint action taken by all the Allied powers, and not unilateral action by the Japanese. Bakhmeteff added that he had just been told by the British Ambassador that there was information to the effect that the Germans were sending submarine parts via the Trans-Siberian Railway to an assembly point on the Pacific Asiatic coast. Himself by training an engineer, Bakhmeteff had pointed out to his British colleague, he said, that this was a "physical, military, and naval impossibility." When Long suggested that the Japanese might be motivated by a fear of an attack against Japan by rearmed German and Austrian prisoners in Russia and Siberia, Bakhmeteff also correctly pointed out that most of these prisoners were Austrians, not Germans, and that such a move was not within the realm of possibility.[11] One cannot fail to note the contrast between Bakhmeteff's sober and unquestionably correct appraisal of these possibilities, and the wild and exaggerated fears by which a good deal of Allied policy continued to be dictated in the coming months.

Morris, on being queried from Washington about these evidences of anxiety in anti-communist Russian diplomatic circles, gave it as his impression that the Japanese government had no present intention of occupying any territory in eastern Siberia but added that

. . . the army is powerful and the general staff, I believe, would welcome and probably exaggerate any occurrence which might afford an excuse.[12]

Meanwhile, the Department of State took such measures as it could to improve the information it was receiving from the Far East. In a wise move to test the alarming reports from Irkutsk, the Department authorized Major Drysdale, then serving as American Mili-

[10] National Archives, State Department File 861.00/938½, Memorandum from Miles to Lansing, January 4, 1918.

[11] *Foreign Relations, 1918, Russia,* Vol. II, *op.cit.,* p. 23, Memorandum of Third Assistant Secretary of State Long, January 10, 1918.

[12] *Ibid.,* p. 27, Morris' telegram of January 13, 1918, 12 p.m.

tary Attaché at Peking, to proceed from Harbin to Irkutsk for an independent investigation of the situation in that part of Siberia. At the same time, the Department asked Caldwell for more specific information about the situation in Vladivostok. Caldwell responded, on January 13, with a report to the effect that while the city was still nominally under Zemstvo control, actual power lay in the hands of the local Soviet, by whose tolerance alone the Zemstvo was able to continue to function.[13] Caldwell seemed to feel that things were not as bad as they had been in December, and was actually encouraging about the possibilities for early employment of Emerson's railway engineers; but it must have been apparent to anyone reading the telegram in Washington, particularly anyone who had in mind the example of Petrograd in the last weeks of the Provisional Government, that the Vladivostok situation was highly unstable and boded nothing favorable for the future.

On January 10 the French government brought the matter of American policy to a head by addressing to the United States government the first overt and formal appeal for a full-fledged military intervention in Siberia. This appeal, embodied in a formal note delivered to Lansing on January 10 by the French Ambassador in Washington, M. Jusserand, was ostensibly based on reports the French government had received from Irkutsk. The note read as follows:

Mr. Secretary of State: Immediately upon hearing through the French Chargé d'Affaires at Peking of the events that took place at Irkutsk, the Government of the Republic decided that it should take the measures needed to secure the lives of its nationals which might again be threatened on account of the growth of anarchy in Siberia.

Consequently the immediate sending to Harbin and thence to Irkutsk of the largest possible French force, detailed from the corps of occupation in China and placed under the command of Major de la Pornarède, has been considered by the French Government which would desire the co-operation of its allies and a joint arrangement as to the final organization of a military mission in the matter of men, appropriations and supplies.

China should be treated as an ally and therefore asked to detail to the mission a part of the troops that have been operating at Harbin and all available contingents.

Besides, since the mission is to appear as being inspired by the desire of bringing the cooperation and support of the Allies to the Russian

[13] *Ibid.*, p. 25, Caldwell's telegram of January 13, 1918, 8 p.m.

elements in Siberia that have remained true to the cause of the Entente, the accession of Russian military elements should also be asked.

As is known to your excellency, the attention of the Allies was already drawn, at the last Paris conference, to the desirability of some joint action tending to protect, if possible, Siberia from Maximalist contagion, to secure the use of the Trans-Siberian and Russian railways for southern Russia to the advantage of the Allies and by isolating Vladivostok, if not too late, to protect the stocks of all kinds that are stored there. This would offer a chance to prevent German influence, which in the event of a separate peace might predominate in northern Russia, from getting a foothold in Vladivostok to the great detriment of the situation of the Allies in the Far East.

By order of my Government I have the honor to make this plan known to your excellency and to say how great a value it would attach to obtaining the adhesion and cooperation of the Federal Government in immediately carrying it out. . . .[14]

The French Foreign Minister later explained to Ambassador Sharp in Paris that this note had been prompted by the news of the killing of three French citizens in Irkutsk.[15] (A few days later a member of the Foreign Minister's staff told an American in Paris that six Frenchmen had been assassinated in Petrograd.[16] There is no evidence to confirm this; and it may be taken in all probability as one more manifestation of the misinformation about the safety of French citizens in Russia to which the Quai d'Orsay appears to have been systematically subjected.)

On January 16 the American reply was delivered to Jusserand. The American government, Lansing said, had not failed to give consideration to the French plan. He quoted recent advices from Harbin as indicating that the situation in Irkutsk was quiet as late as January 9 and that the foreign consuls were active in protecting foreigners. The earlier report through Harbin had greatly exaggerated the danger. The note concluded:

The American Government is disposed to believe that such a military mission as is proposed is not required by the present condition of affairs in Siberia. It is believed that it would be likely to offend those Russians who are now in sympathy with the aims and desires which the United States and its cobelligerents have at heart in making war and might

[14] *Ibid.*, pp. 20–21.
[15] *Ibid.*, p. 32, Paris telegram 3086, January 23, 1918, 11 p.m.
[16] House mss, *op.cit.*, letter, Arthur Hugh Frazier to House, January 29, 1918.

result in uniting all factions in Siberia against them. The American Government regrets, therefore, that it is unable to give its support to the proposals as suggested in your excellency's note. . . .[17]

This French proposal for a joint intervention, coming on the heels of similar British urgings, prompted the Japanese government to make even more open and emphatic its desire that Japan should be permitted to act alone if and when any further action became necessary. The Japanese government, it will be recalled, had already indicated this in its secret approach to the President at the turn of the year. It had made its position known privately to the French and British on several occasions. Now, evidently alarmed at the renewed suggestion for a joint intervention contained in the French note, the Japanese Foreign Minister not only reiterated this position to the French Ambassador, saying that the Japanese desired to be permitted "to meet the situation by sending their own war vessels exclusively, without the cooperation of the other governments," [18] but also made a similar statement to Morris in Tokyo. The Japanese, Motono told Morris, would not object to the presence of the *Brooklyn* at Vladivostok; but

. . . if conditions should . . . require occupation of Vladivostok and the lines of the Chinese Eastern and Amur Railways, Japan asks that this task be left to her alone. . . .

The British, Motono added, had been asked to agree to this, as a matter of confidence in Japan's good faith. The Japanese were pleased, he said in conclusion, that the United States had opposed the suggestions for a joint intervention.[19]

Morris' telegram reporting this conversation was of course sent to the President, who found the Japanese suggestion, as he observed in a note to Lansing, "very significant of possible coming events." The President's note continued:

[17] *Foreign Relations, 1918, Russia*, Vol. II, *op.cit.*, p. 29, from Lansing's note 2043 to the French Ambassador, January 16, 1918. Lansing's desk diary shows that he discussed this matter three times on January 14 and 15 with Breckinridge Long and with Williams (Chief of the Far Eastern Division). The desk diary (Lansing MSS, *op.cit.*) does not indicate that Lansing discussed the matter with Wilson at any time between receipt of the French note and despatch of the reply. The reply must, however, have been cleared with the President, if indeed it was not drafted by him.

[18] *Ibid.*, p. 32, Pichon's statement to Ambassador Sharp, contained in Paris telegram 3086, January 23, 1918, 11 p.m.

[19] *Ibid.*, pp. 29–30, Tokyo telegram, January 17, 1918, 5 p.m.

The fact that the Japanese are sending a larger naval force to Vladivostok than they at first led us to expect makes an uncomfortable impression on me, particularly in view of this latest request.

It seems to me clear that we should show very clearly in our reply that we should look upon military action in that quarter with distinct disapproval.[20]

The Secretary of State was at that time ill and confined to his home. The President, in Lansing's absence, discussed the matter further with the Secretary of the Navy, Josephus Daniels, saying that he thought something ought to be done. He suggested that Daniels get together with Polk and work out some sort of action. The two men accordingly conferred. Daniels and his associates in the Navy Department thought the Japanese should be asked to restrict themselves to the stationing of a single vessel at Vladivostok. The upshot of the conference was that Polk drafted a message to Morris which, after clearance by Lansing and the President, was sent to Tokyo on January 20. In presenting the draft of this message to the President, Polk referred to the situation as a "very delicate one . . . that presents grave possibilities." He argued for making the United States position "tactfully clear" to the Japanese "as it would be a serious matter if they should proceed to land an armed force in Vladivostok on the assumption that such a step met with our approval." [21]

The American government, Morris was asked, in this message, to tell the Japanese,

. . . feels very strongly that the common interests of all the powers at war with Germany demand from them an attitude of sympathy with the Russian people in their present unhappy struggle and that any movement looking towards the occupation of Russian territory would at once be construed as one hostile to Russia and would be likely to unite all factions in Russia against us thus aiding the German propaganda in Russia. The American Government trusts the Imperial Japanese Government will share this conviction and hopes that no unfortunate occurrence may make necessary the occupation of Vladivostok by a foreign force. The information received by this Government indicates that the situation there is quiet and is not one to cause alarm. . . . In the opinion of the American Government the presence of more than one Japanese war vessel at Vladivostok

[20] *Foreign Relations, The Lansing Papers,* Vol. II, *op.cit.,* p. 351; President Wilson's note to Secretary Lansing, January 20, 1918.

[21] National Archives, Department of State File 861.00/997–998, Letter, Polk to Wilson, January 18, 1918.

at present is likely to be misconstrued and create a feeling of mistrust as to the purposes of the Allied Governments which Japan does not desire any more than the United States.[22]

There seems to be no record of any Japanese reaction or reply to this communication.

A day or two after despatch of this message, Polk received a visit from Mr. H. Fessenden Meserve, formerly representative of the National City Bank in Moscow, who had passed through Japan and called on Motono on his way home from Russia. Motono had asked him to tell the President that he, Motono, hoped that the United States government

. . . would not send troops to Vladivostok or Harbin for the purpose of keeping order, as any such movement on our part would create a very unfavorable impression in Japan.[23]

Again Motono had asked that the preservation of order in Siberia "should be left entirely with the Japanese."

This news, too, Polk passed on to the President, raising the question as to whether it called for any further communication to the Japanese government. The President thought not, for the moment, but hoped that Morris would soon be able to throw more light on the Japanese attitude and intentions. "I do not think it will be safe or wise to leave the Japanese government in any doubt as to the impression such an attitude on their part makes on us," he observed to Polk.[24]

After despatch of the reply to the Japanese, the American representatives in Paris and London were asked to acquaint the respective governments with its contents. The French Foreign Minister, M. Pichon, expressed respect for the American view and indicated that the French government would not press the matter further.[25] The British were obviously still torn and indecisive. Balfour, hard-pressed by contrary influences in the British government, expressed to Page

---

[22] *Foreign Relations, 1918, Russia,* Vol. II, *op.cit.,* p. 31, Telegram to Morris, January 20, 1918, 6 p.m.

[23] *Foreign Relations, The Lansing Papers,* Vol. II, *op.cit.,* p. 352, Polk to Wilson, January 24, 1918.

[24] *Loc.cit.,* the President's reply of January 28.

[25] *Foreign Relations, 1918, Russia,* Vol. II, *op.cit.,* p. 32; Paris telegram 3086, January 23, 1918, 11 p.m.

his personal agreement with the American position, but added that events might at any time "create a different situation." [26]

❖

Thus ended what may be regarded as the first round of exchanges between the interested powers with regard to the situation created in eastern Siberia by the Bolshevik seizure of power in Petrograd. It carried developments roughly up to the beginning of the crucial phase of the Brest-Litovsk negotiations, at the end of January. Before we leave the subject, it might be well to review the situation as it had developed to this point.

Despite the fact that by the middle of January the Bolsheviki had not yet completed the seizure of power either in Harbin or in Vladivostok, nor had any final agreement on a peace treaty yet been reached between the Bolsheviki and the Germans, the French and British had both taken occasion, within the weeks immediately following the Bolshevik seizure of power, to suggest intervention of one sort or another in the Russian Far East.

The British had at first (rather casually, one senses) suggested the landing of a joint Allied force, mainly Japanese but to include British and American units, at Vladivostok, for the purpose of protecting the military supplies accumulated there. When the response to these suggestions revealed something of the seriousness of Japanese plans and calculations with relation to Siberia, as well as the danger of an American-Japanese conflict arising out of any hasty move, they backed off perceptibly from their original suggestion, but only— apparently—in order to be able to think the matter through a bit more carefully and to explore with greater prudence and thoroughness the possibilities for agreement among the various Allied powers. Their growing interest in the anti-Bolshevik forces in southeastern Russia—an interest which was to survive even Kaledin's suicide and the collapse of the Don Cossack resistance—was causing them to take an increasing interest in the Trans-Siberian Railway as a whole. All in all, it was evident, as the month of January drew to a close, that the British were beginning to preoccupy themselves intensively with the Siberian situation, and that the abortive suggestion of January 1 was not the last that would be heard from them on this subject.

[26] *Ibid.*, p. 33, London telegram 8388, January 24, 1918, 11 p.m.

The French had gone much further than the British and had proposed a full-scale joint military intervention into the heart of Siberia. They had done this against a background of inadequate and partially incorrect information, and with little apparent regard to consequences other than the possible effect on the European war. They had accepted without great remonstrance the rejection of this suggestion by the other Allies, but remained the undiscriminating partisans of any form of Allied action in Siberia that could conceivably make difficulties for the Germans.

The Japanese had made it clear to the other Allies that they were opposed to any joint undertaking and wished to be permitted to handle the situation alone. They had mounted a show of naval strength in Vladivostok harbor and had made preparations for a landing of troops. But they had thus far refrained from taking any violent action. They were plainly afraid of needlessly provoking the United States into taking some unilateral action of its own. In the absence of American consent to independent action on their part, they were under no necessity of taking any immediate action at all, for the situation in Siberia was still developing to their advantage. Overcoming internal disagreements and misgivings, they continued therefore to bide their time, angling meanwhile for some arrangement which would guard against an independent American action and, at the same time, give them a free hand to exploit the developing situation by their own efforts, in the light of their own interests, and at whatever time should suit them.

The United States government, for its part, had plainly and unequivocally rejected all suggestions looking toward any form of foreign intervention in Siberia. The reason given for this position was the fear of antagonizing the Russian people.

This view was wholly sincere, as far as it went. It checked with Colonel House's strong opposition to "treating Russia as an enemy." It checked with Lansing's strong belief that "the Russian people are sovereign and have the right to determine their own domestic organization without interference or influence by other nations." [27] It checked with President Wilson's insistence that Russia should be conceded "the independent determination of her own political de-

---

[27] *Foreign Relations, The Lansing Papers,* Vol. II, *op.cit.,* p. 351, from the draft statement presented to the President by Lansing on January 10, 1918 (apparently not approved by the President).

velopment and national policy" and should receive the "intelligent and unselfish sympathy" of the Allies. The available written records of prior date do not indicate that any other motive was involved on the part of American statesmen. However, reasonable assumption, together with the later history of the United States approach to this problem, would suggest that these fears were linked to a lively distrust of Japanese motives and to a feeling that once the Japanese became established in any way in Siberia, it would not be easy to induce them to withdraw.

CHAPTER XVI

THE DIAMANDI INCIDENT

It is a terrible thing! To fall from the midst of living people into the company of corpses, to breathe the smell of corpses, . . . this is something unbearable.—Lenin, January 19, 1918

THE Kalpashnikov affair, described in Chapter X, was not the only instance in which Rumania's position as a member of the Entente was to enter briefly but violently into the pattern of early Soviet-American relations.

As the German-Soviet discussions got under way again in Brest-Litovsk on January 9 and the days following, the question of Rumania's relationship to the peace talks inevitably arose. When the original Bolshevik armistice proposal was made on December 2, the Bolshevik parliamentarians were unable to speak for the southwest front, where their influence was relatively weak. On this front the fortunes of the Russian and Rumanian armies had been linked, in the immediately preceding period, in an association as intimate as it was trying for both parties: the joint presence of both armies on the Moldavian territory to which, after the fall of Bucharest, the Rumanian court and government had withdrawn. Immediately after the conclusion of the German-Soviet truce, it became necessary for the Rumanians also to sue for an armistice, since further resistance was unthinkable. On December 6 Russian and Rumanian parliamentarians approached the representatives of the Central Powers jointly. An armistice was concluded on December 12.[1]

At just about this time, however, the rank and file of the Russian forces in Moldavia were beginning to be seized by the same de-

[1] H. W. V. Temperley, Editor, *A History of the Peace Conference of Paris,* Oxford University Press, London, 1920, Vol. III, p. 5. (Noulens, Vol. I, *op.cit.,* p. 184, gives the date as December 17. There seems to be a curious dearth of direct historical record concerning these events.)

moralization and disaffection that were disintegrating the Russian armies elsewhere along the line. This process was, of course, intensively promoted by agitators sent in by the Bolsheviki. The result was the rapid transmutation of many of the Russian units on the Rumanian front from disciplined bodies into disorderly marauding hordes.

This situation naturally presented the most serious sort of danger for the Rumanians, on whose territory it was occurring. Not only was the pillaging intolerable in a country already contending desperately with famine and disease, but the morale of the Rumanian forces themselves was clearly jeopardized. As yet, the Rumanian troops were little disaffected; but they were stationed in intimate proximity to the Russian troops, the agitation was directed to them no less than to the Russians, and indiscipline, especially when backed by political agitation, could only too easily become contagious.

The Russian commander, General Shcherbachev, found himself helpless to control his troops without outside assistance. Their behavior was a danger not only to himself but to his officer corps in general. He had no choice, therefore, but to accept the help of the Rumanians in disarming his mutinous units and expelling them to neighboring Russian territory. This operation was carried out with little difficulty, in the latter part of December, by the relatively well-disciplined Rumanian forces.

The news of these happenings, colored no doubt by the excited emotions of the local communists and by the congenital Russian tendency to sweeping exaggeration in political matters, produced a violent reaction, partly of anger and partly of alarm, in Petrograd. On January 1, 1918 the papers carried sensational reports of the misdeeds of the Rumanians, including the allegation that they had lured members of the Revolutionary Committee of the troops of the southwestern front to their headquarters at Jassy and had there attempted to execute them, being prevented only by the indignant intercession of one of the Russian Cossack units. (This incident is not implausible; this was no child's play on either side.) Trotsky came out at once with a fiery public statement, calling on the Rumanian Minister in Petrograd, Count Constantine Diamandi, to communicate to the Soviet government in the course of the day all that he knew about these happenings and to state what steps the Rumanian government had taken to punish the "criminal elements in the Rumanian officers' corps and bureaucracy who had dared to raise their hand against the Russian Revolution." He went on to warn the Legation that "they"—i.e. the Soviet leaders—were the protectors not only of Russian but also of Rumanian revolutionaries. Every Rumanian soldier, worker, and peasant, he said, would have the support of the Soviet regime against the Rumanian "bureaucracy." The Minister was enjoined to inform his government that the Soviet regime would not shrink from the severest measures against the Rumanian conspirators, "the associates of Kaledin, Shcherbachev, and the Rada," no matter how lofty their position.[2]

In publishing this proclamation, the *Pravda* followed it up with an ominous notice to the effect that the Rumanian Minister had given certain explanations to the Soviet Foreign Commissar about this matter, but that they were not considered satisfactory.

During the early days of January several other items appeared in the Soviet press on this same subject, all pointing in the direction of rising Soviet anger over the Rumanian action.

On January 13 further reports were received at Smolny, indicating that the Rumanians were continuing to disarm and expel disaffected Russian units and to arrest the communist organizers and agitators among the troops. It was thereupon decided at Smolny that the time had come to bring matters to a head by issuing an ultimatum to the Rumanian government and arresting the members of the Rumanian diplomatic mission in Petrograd, for detention as hostages.[3]

Diamandi was warned of this decision in advance by Captain Jacques Sadoul of the French Military Mission, who had excellent connections at Smolny. Coming on the heels of Trotsky's earlier threats, the warning can scarcely have been a surprise to him. He confided the circumstances of his plight to his friend the French Ambassador, Noulens, who was his guest at lunch that day (January 13) and who had apparently not been taken into confidence on this matter by his own subordinate, Sadoul. The two gentlemen

[2] The *Pravda*, No. 218, January 1, 1918.
[3] Khvostov & Mints, Vol. II, *op.cit.*, p. 352. There is some evidence that Trotsky, then at Brest, in his communications with the Smolny pressed for the adoption of these measures against the Rumanian Mission; and this led to insinuations at a later date that the measures had been taken under pressure from the Germans. For this, there is no serious evidence. The attitude of the Rumanian government tended to give encouragement to the Rada and Kaledin at a moment when this was still most dangerous to the Soviet regime. Trotsky plainly wished to take some incisive and dramatic action to thwart Rumanian purposes and to bolster Soviet prestige in that area.

recognized that there was no time to be lost. The French Ambassador took custody, then and there, of the Rumanian's secret papers. The precarious state of affairs was not permitted, however, to interfere with the luncheon, which was consumed at leisure, with gaiety and enjoyment. It was late afternoon before the French Ambassador departed. The agents of the Soviet police had apparently tactfully awaited the departure of the guest before proceeding to their unpleasant task. Noulens had scarcely been home an hour when he received word that Count Diamandi, in company with four of his subordinates, had already been taken into custody and was confined in the grim and historic bastions of the Fortress of St. Peter and St. Paul.[4]

Noulens at once notified Francis, who was now, after the departure of the British Ambassador, doyen of the diplomatic corps. Buchanan, ill and frustrated, had been withdrawn by his government and had left Petrograd on January 6. As the ambassador with the longest term in Petrograd, Francis had now succeeded to Buchanan's position as doyen of the corps.

On receiving word from Noulens about Diamandi's arrest, Francis immediately made arrangements to convene the entire diplomatic corps in the American Embassy the following morning, to consider the situation.

It is easy to understand the concern with which the other diplomats, and particularly those of the Entente powers, viewed Diamandi's arrest. They had all lived under considerable concern for their own safety in the preceding weeks—and none more so than Francis himself. It was the general feeling that unless a firm stand was taken in the case of Diamandi there was little likelihood that the Bolshevik authorities would continue for long to respect the persons of the other diplomatic envoys, particularly those of the Entente powers.

The following morning the diplomatic corps met at the United States Embassy and drew up a joint note of protest to the Soviet government. It was first proposed that they should state in the note that unless Diamandi were immediately released they would all ask for their passports at once. This note of ultimatum was dropped, however, at Francis' insistence. The latter knew, Sisson explains in his memoirs, that the President "did not want the United States to

---

[4] Noulens, Vol. I, *op.cit.*, p. 184.

cut its relations with Russia" at that time.[5] When the note had been drafted, Francis sent to Smolny a request for an audience of the entire diplomatic corps with Lenin at 4:00 p.m. This was agreed to, in a personal note from Lenin, written in English in his own hand.

While the chiefs-of-mission were deliberating in the morning, the wheels, unbeknownst to most of them, were being greased at Smolny by the indispensable Gumberg. Acting, according to Sisson, with the knowledge and consent of Francis, Gumberg got word to Lenin

... that if he wished to make Russia helpless before Germany and destroy his own party all he would have to do would be to keep the Rumanian in jail, but that if he had hopes for the future the best practical politics would be to release the man.[6]

According to Francis, the news of the pending arrival of the diplomatic corps caused a certain consternation in the Smolny Institute. It was, after all, to be the first Soviet diplomatic reception. Some of the leaders felt that Lenin's battered and barnlike office was not suitable, and suggested putting in new rugs and furniture for the occasion. Lenin rejected the suggestion, but made certain concessions: chairs were provided for the comfort of the ambassadors, and a wooden bench for the ministers and chargés.[7]

The atmosphere of this visit is well recalled by the French Ambassador's account of the arrival of the diplomatic corps at the great building on the banks of the Neva, whose spacious halls for so many years had housed the sedate functions of Russia's most select and aristocratic girls' school.

I shall never forget the state of indescribable disorder in which the entrances of a building so recently aristocratic now found themselves. Military camping gear, kettles in which was prepared the soup which the Red Guards and the People's Commissars shared fraternally, wooden bowls encrusted with grease, were mingled with cannons, machine guns, and rifles, some stacked, others leaning against the walls or lying around the floor among every possible sort of debris. Nothing could better have documented the brutal and disorderly character of the revolution. In the interior of the corridors and the numerous rooms that we had to pass through in order to reach Lenin, a similar spectacle presented itself. Revolvers and cartridges were thrown pellmell into the corners of the

[5] Sisson, *op.cit.*, p. 222.
[6] *Ibid.*, p. 223.
[7] Francis, *op.cit.*, p. 216.

apartments where so recently the daughters of the nobility had lived in order and elegance.

The building was vast. We had to pass through a whole series of halls before, at the end of a corridor and under the shadow of a doorway, there appeared a little man with an enormous head and with the slanting eyes of a Tatar: it was Lenin.

The face, dominating and powerful, was indeed that of genius, but the semi-flat nose, the mouth and the chin gave him the disturbing aspect of a barbarian. The implacable severity of the doctrinaire and a sovereign contempt for humanity were stamped on that tightly closed, common face. When he saw us, the stereotyped smile that relaxed his features betrayed his satisfaction. He was triumphing at the idea of seeing these Ambassadors who, up to this time, had refused to have anything to do with him, come—to protest, to be sure, but also to request.

We entered a fairly narrow room. Chairs for the members of the diplomatic corps . . . were arranged facing a table behind which Lenin was sitting, having at his left the Under Secretary of State for Foreign Affairs, Zalkind, Doctor of Sciences of the faculty of Algiers. . . .[8]

If we may believe the official Soviet record of the meeting, Lenin and Zalkind were not the only Soviet officials present. There was a third, who took no part in the conversation. None of the diplomats appears to have noticed him. It was Stalin. For him, too, it was the first encounter with representatives of the western world. One can imagine with what interest Stalin, drawn as he was to Lenin by a relationship in which admiration vied with the consciousness of inferiority and a burning oriental envy, followed the course of this first encounter between his idol, the great communist leader, and the representatives of a hated bourgeois world. One is constrained to wonder how much of Stalin's demeanor in his later encounters with the statesmen and representatives of the western powers was patterned after the sardonic self-restraint with which, on this first occasion, Lenin masked the contempt and loathing he bore his diplomatic visitors.

The French Ambassador's account continued:

We had the impression that the partition behind Lenin's back was not a real one but simply a false façade, behind which the acolytes would be listening: which would have been in no way surprising, given the procedures of the Soviet system, where everyone spies on everyone else, where

[8] Noulens, Vol. I, *op.cit.*, pp. 185 ff.

the chiefs are controlled by the agents of the committees if not by those of the GPU.[9]

Lenin explained that while he understood some English he had difficulty in speaking it. The interview then proceeded in French. In general it passed off without too much unpleasantness. Francis, using his Secretary of Embassy, Mr. Phelps, as an interpreter, made a brief opening statement and presented the joint written message of the diplomatic corps. Lenin explained the reasons for the arrest of the Minister, basing it on the actions of the Rumanian government toward the Russian troops. The French Ambassador then spoke, arguing that the Minister's arrest was indefensible, regardless of the differences between the governments.

The Belgian Minister, who was a socialist in Belgian terms, undertook to reinforce the views of his American and French colleagues but succeeded only in drawing an unexpectedly violent reaction from Zalkind. The latter had characteristically shown nothing but courtesy toward those bourgeois representatives who made no pretense of leftist sympathies, but could not restrain himself when a professed socialist appeared on the opposite side, particularly one who frequently annoyed him with representations on behalf of Belgian investments in Russian street railway companies.

Toward the end of the interview, the Serbian Minister, who had been containing himself with increasing difficulty as the session progressed, finally lost patience. Rising abruptly from his seat, he unburdened himself of a veritable tirade of accusation and abuse against Lenin and his associates, charging them with being bandits and with dishonoring the Slavic race and ending with the announcement that he was spitting in their faces. The other diplomats were shocked at this outburst and attempted to restrain their violent colleague. But Lenin, who had followed the Serb's statements with an imperturbable, ironic smile, urged the others to relax and leave him alone. "We prefer this brutality of expression," he said, "to the language of diplomacy." [10]

Lenin ended the interview by promising to bring the diplomats' complaint to the attention of the Soviet of People's Commissars.

[9] *Ibid.*, p. 187. The Ambassador, as was sometimes the case with later western envoys, somewhat overrated the sinister quality of the arrangements. The partition was always there; it concealed nothing more menacing than Lenin's secretary and a telephone operator.

[10] *Ibid.*, p. 189.

Then, continuing to smile enigmatically, he shook the hand of each diplomat in the corridor as they left. Later that evening, he observed, ironically, to Sadoul that he was still quite shaken by the experience of meeting so much high society all at once. He only regretted that the Ambassadors,

. . . who showed such commendable initiative when it came to defending the privileges of their honorable fraternity, did not manifest a similar activity when it was a question of the interests of their governments or the blood of their soldiers.[11]

Five days later, in connection with the meeting of the Constituent Assembly, Lenin wrote an eloquent little essay expressing his revulsion at the brief contact with the bourgeois world which the Assembly had required him to endure.[12] One wonders, on reading it, whether it was really only the Constituent Assembly and, accordingly, the *Russian* bourgeoisie he had in mind, or whether he was not also thinking of his recent encounter with the diplomats in the Diamandi case. He began with a Latin quotation: "I have lost a day, and in vain, my friends." He continued as follows:

. . . After live, real, Soviet work, in the midst of workers and peasants who are occupied by real things, by the cutting of the forest and the tearing out of the roots of the landowners' and capitalist exploitation—one was suddenly obliged to be carried into a "strange world," to be brought face to face with some sort of arrivals from a new world, from the camp of the bourgeoisie and its voluntary and involuntary, conscious and unconscious servants, dependents, lackeys and defenders. From the world of the struggle of the toiling masses and their Soviet organization against the exploiters—into the world of honeyed phrases, of tongue-slick, empty declamations, promises and again promises. . . .

As though history had inadvertently or mistakenly turned the clock back and we had before us, instead of January 1918, May or June 1917! It is a terrible thing! To fall from the midst of living people into the company of corpses, to breathe the smell of corpses, . . . this is something unbearable! [13]

After the diplomats left Smolny, developments took a curious turn. A meeting of the Soviet of People's Commissars was apparently

[11] Jacques Sadoul, *Notes sur la Révolution Bolchevique,* Éditions de la Sirène, Paris, 1920, p. 196.
[12] The charge that this was the bourgeois world was Lenin's. Lenin's opponents on that day were primarily the Social-Revolutionaries, hardly a bourgeois party.
[13] *Lenin,* Vol. xxii, *op.cit.,* p. 182.

called for eight o'clock that evening, to consider the matter. In the interval before the body met, further consultations evidently took place between the Smolny Institute, on the one hand, and Gumberg, with or without Robins, on the other.

At some time in the late afternoon, Robins and Gumberg also visited Francis and discussed with him the possibility of his putting pressure on the Rumanian government to yield to Soviet desiderata in the conflicts that had arisen in Moldavia. This idea had evidently been in active discussion among the senior Americans that day. Judson had wired the War Department in the course of the day, reporting the circumstances of the Diamandi incident and adding:

If present incident does not prove fatal to all relationships, I urge as measure of extreme military importance that pressure of Allies be brought on all concerned including Ukraine and Rumania to adopt modus vivendi with Bolsheviks to save from starvation Russian troops. . . .[14]

Francis was favorably impressed with these suggestions. "In the course of conversation," he later recorded,

. . . I remarked that if the Bolsheviks released Diamandi, I would see what I could do to bring about better relations between the Roumanian Government and the Soviet. I had heard that Soviet Russian soldiers were being killed in large numbers by the Roumanians because some of those soldiers had taken property that did not belong to them and had assaulted women. I was going to advise the Roumanians not to kill Soviet soldiers. This conversation was in confidence; . . . I did not send any message nor intend that the conversation should be repeated to the Bolsheviks.[15]

With this knowledge of the trend of the Ambassador's thoughts, Robins and Gumberg disappeared again. Late that evening, both the French and American ambassadors were informally notified by Smolny that the decision had been taken in principle to release Diamandi.

---

[14] National Archives, War Department Section, 1918 Chronological file of telegrams from Military Attaché, Petrograd; Judson's cable 177, January 14, 1918 to War College Staff. Judson's diary (Judson MSS, *op.cit.*) indicates that on the following day he formally requested the Ambassador's permission to undertake personal mediation between the Bolsheviki and the Rumanians, involving first an interview with Trotsky and then a personal visit to the Rumanian front. These passages suggest that someone had given Judson a highly colored, and strongly pro-Bolshevik, picture of the sources of the difficulties between the Rumanians and the disaffected Russian troops on the southwest front.

[15] This passage will be found in a separate sheet included in the manuscript of Francis' memoirs, but omitted from the published version (Francis MSS, *op.cit.*).

Personal file

Mr.

David R. Francis

American Ambassador

Petrograd

Sir;

Being unable to connect with You by telephone at 2 o'clock as agreed, am writing in order to inform You that I shall be pleased to receive You at my office, Room 81, Smolny Institute, at 4 o'clock p. m. to day.

Respectfully Lenine

Lenin's note to Francis, agreeing to receive him in the Diamandi matter

Entrance to the Smolny Institute at the time of the Diamandi incident

The Diamandi Incident

The following morning, the *Pravda* carried two important items on the Rumanian affair. The first was an ultimatum from the Soviet government to the Rumanian government demanding the release of the members of the Revolutionary Committee of the 194th Regiment of the 49th Division, allegedly arrested and held by the Rumanian government, as well as the punishment of those who had made the arrest and a guarantee against repetition of this sort of action. The Rumanian government was given twenty-four hours to comply; if it failed, the Soviet government would take "the most energetic military measures." Following this ultimatum, in the *Pravda's* columns, was a long official statement about the Diamandi arrest, in which the various negotiations of the preceding day were described. A meeting of the Soviet of People's Commissars, it was stated, had taken place at eight o'clock in the evening. The participants had come to the conclusion that the arrest had been justifiable and correct, but they had decided nevertheless to release the Minister. Why? Because "the purpose of the arrest had already been achieved." In explanation of this last assertion, the following astonishing statement was then made:

. . . Just before the session of the Soviet of People's Commissars, at 7:40 p.m., there was received from a reliable source the following telephone communication, taken down by Comrade Zalkind: "The American Ambassador assures us that immediately upon Diamandi's release, he will go to the latter and protest to him against the attack of the Rumanians on the Russian troops and will make a corresponding statement to the Rumanian Government through the American representative in Rumania. He regards the arrest of Diamandi as a formal expression of protest by the Russian Government against the actions of the Rumanian Command. . . ."

The formal statement concluded by pointing out that since the arrest had now served its purpose (i.e. by forcing the United States to intercede with the Rumanians on Soviet behalf) and since it was now possible

. . . to leave the Rumanian Minister advantageously to the influence of the other envoys . . . it was decided to release him, notifying him that measures to release the Russian soldiers arrested by the Rumanians would have to be taken within three days.[16]

Thus, the release of the Rumanian Minister was officially based on an alleged assurance from the American Ambassador that the

16 *Pravda*, No. 1, January 15, 1918 (evening edition).

United States government would intervene, in favor of the Soviet government, in the complicated situation prevailing between the Rumanian government and the disaffected Russian troops in Moldavia. In this way, Soviet face was saved and the release of Diamandi was made to look like the by-product of a Soviet diplomatic triumph rather than a yielding to the demand of the diplomatic corps.

There can be little doubt as to the origin of this curious telephone message. The Ambassador himself later recorded in his published memoirs:

> . . . I had sent no statement and had authorized no one to make any statement for me, by telephone or otherwise, to Zalkind. . . . It was not until some time later that I learned what was behind this action. . . .[17]

In his unpublished papers, Francis was more specific:

> . . . either Robins or Gumberg revealed it to the Bolsheviks, and that gave them the basis for the published excuse about the release of Diamandi.[18]

The publication of this item was, of course, highly embarrassing to Francis. Diamandi himself was naturally outraged; Francis had to write him a soothing letter, explaining:

> . . . I have had no communication direct or indirect, nor have I sent any message to anyone connected with the Soviet Government on the subject of your arrest or your release.[19]

But for some reason, the Ambassador seems never to have reported this phase of the incident to the Department of State; and Sisson, too, ignores it in his memoirs. Perhaps all were a bit ashamed.

Actually, the Soviet ultimatum to Rumania did not lead to any immediate formal declaration of war. The Soviet government at that

---

[17] Francis, *op.cit.,* p. 219.

[18] Francis MSS, *op.cit.,* original manuscript of Francis' memoirs. Robins' pocket diary (Robins' MSS, *op.cit.*) only hints at the complicated goings-on of that day, but the entry is sufficient to confirm the intensive exchanges that were taking place between the Red Cross Mission and the Soviet authorities: "Russian New Year's Day. Rumanian Ambassador and his case in international situation. Smolny is deserted. The Ambassador and his doyenship. The great Reception and his back is stiffened. Luncheon. Smolny and the bad hour. They all file out the powers and the power politics of this western age the whole world. Zalkind and Menken and Peters and the Embassy and Europe and Sisson and General J. and Astoria." ("Europe" referred to the Hotel d'Europe, where the Red Cross offices were situated; "Astoria" to the Hotel Astoria, where some of the Allied representatives had headquarters.)

[19] Francis, *op.cit.,* p. 220.

moment was incapable of supporting any sort of serious military action in that part of the world. In the days immediately following Diamandi's arrest, relations between the Rumanians and the Bolsheviki, far from improving, were subjected to further strains, much worse than anything that had occurred up to that point. A new separatist regime in the Russian province of Bessarabia, originally believed to be sympathetic to the Soviets, was persuaded by the Rumanians to throw in its lot with them and in effect to associate that province with Rumania. The Rumanians, by "invitation" of this new entity and by agreement with the Russian commander, General Shcherbachev, then proceeded to occupy Bessarabia, whose food supplies they urgently needed. If there had previously been any hope of compromising the differences between the Rumanian government and the Soviet leaders, it was now too late. Yet what was done by the Soviet government, in the face of this new situation, was only to break relations, a step announced by the Soviet of People's Commissars on January 26. In the same statement, the final deportation of Diamandi was ordered and an order was issued for the seizure of the Rumanian gold reserve in Moscow, which was to be preserved for eventual delivery into the hands of the Rumanian people.[20] The reserve was actually seized and sealed the same day.

Diamandi had been released from the Fortress of St. Peter and St. Paul on January 15. The French Ambassador had assisted at the event, and had taken Diamandi's part in the long and acrimonious disputes with the prison commander which preceded final release. Diamandi then remained several days as the guest of the French Ambassador at the French Embassy.

On the afternoon of January 28, Diamandi was suddenly confronted with a demand that he leave Petrograd within ten hours. He asked Francis to intervene for a longer period of grace; Francis sent Robins to Zalkind on his behalf, but to no avail. At one o'clock in the morning the Minister, attended by fifteen of his Legation guards, was packed off in a special train to Finland.

Sisson has recounted in his memoirs the fantastic tale of Diamandi's further fate as he learned of it.[21] In Finland, according to this account, he first became stranded because of the civil war. He

[20] Khvostov & Mints, Vol. II, *op.cit.*, p. 355.
[21] Sisson, *op.cit.*, p. 232. The story is also appended as a note to Document 37, pp. 17–18, *The German-Bolshevik Conspiracy,* War Information Series No. 20, October 1918. This version differs in small details from the one given in Sisson's book.

was eventually obliged to abandon his Rumanian guards and to proceed alone on his journey, accompanied only by a Soviet commissar, Svetlitsky, who had been attached to him in the capacity of guard and protector. When the pair finally reached the last point in Finland, Torneo, the town had unexpectedly, on the previous day, fallen to the Finnish Whites. Diamandi and his Soviet "angel" thus came, upon arrival, into the hands of the White Finnish authorities, who proceeded to search them, and were astounded to find on Svetlitsky an order, signed by Trotsky and addressed to the local Red Commissar of Torneo (who had been forced out only the day before), calling upon him to "do away with" Diamandi at the border. With relish, the Finnish Whites executed Svetlitsky instead.

Diamandi, in any case, pushed on alone to Sweden—and freedom.

CHAPTER XVII

THE CONSTITUENT ASSEMBLY

Le Comité Central Exécutif a adopté le décret dissolvant l'Assemblée Constituante. Voila donc évanouie la dernière grande illusion des Alliés qui . . . persistaient à mettre tous leurs espoirs dans cette Assemblée.
—*Jacques Sadoul, Petrograd, January 19, 1918, to his friend Albert Thomas*

THE ten days following the arrest of the Rumanian Minister on January 13 constituted a second period of high tension in Petrograd. The first, in mid-December, had directly involved Russia's relations with the western powers and had found its reflection—so far as the Allied Embassies were concerned—in such episodes as the Kalpashnikov case. The crisis of mid-January, while not without its menacing overtones from the standpoint of the Allied diplomatic missions, was primarily of a domestic-political character, and centered about the convocation on January 18 of Russia's first and last democratically elected parliamentary body, the Constituent Assembly.

No other episode served to illustrate more strikingly the desperate quality of the Bolshevik will to power than the fate of this last and tragic effort of their opponents to steer the Russian Revolution in the direction of western parliamentarianism. When the first Russian Revolution occurred, in March 1917, one of the basic points in the political program of the first provisional ministry had been the early convening of a constitutional convention, or "constituent assembly" as it was usually called in English usage,[1] to determine the permanent form of national government. The intention to hold a constituent assembly accorded with the wishes of every major political party and faction operating in Russia during the period of the

---

[1] This translation of the Russian term for this body, "Uchreditelnoye Sobranie," will be used henceforth.

[343]

Provisional Government. It was the basis of the very expression "provisional government." The parties of the left, including the Bolsheviki, not only subscribed to the principle of holding such an assembly, but demanded it—repeatedly and insistently.

By late summer 1917, the Provisional Government, after a series of delays, finally began actual preparations for the holding of the assembly. An electoral commission was appointed to arrange for the elections, which were to take place from November 25 to 30, inclusive.

Awareness of the pending elections, and the uneasy feeling that they might turn out unfavorably from the Bolshevik standpoint unless they took place under Bolshevik control, were presumably among the factors that caused the Bolshevik leaders to choose the time they did—the beginning of November—for the seizure of power. The argument put forward publicly, however, was that *unless* the Soviets seized power, there could be no assurance that the Constituent Assembly *would* be duly held and honestly conducted. On November 1, less than a week before the uprising, Lenin, arguing in favor of a revolt, wrote in a public "letter to a Comrade":

. . . Is it so hard to understand that with power in the hands of the Soviets the holding of the Constituent Assembly is assured and its success a certainty? The Bolsheviki have said this a thousand times.[2]

The following day, Trotsky, in a public speech, reemphasized this line. The *bourgeoisie,* he said, were sabotaging the Constituent Assembly by every means. They were even perfectly capable of dissolving it by force. Bourgeois governments had done this in the past.

. . . What still remains to be done is to assure the life of the Constituent Assembly and give it the possibility of carrying its decisions into effect—and precisely for that we need decisive revolutionary instruments of power such as only the Soviets would represent. Whoever undermines the Soviets . . . undermines the Constituent Assembly. . . .[3]

In the proclamation issued by the Bolshevik Military-Revolutionary Committee on the morning of the Revolution, announcing that the Petrograd Soviet was taking upon itself the responsibility for preserving order in the city, the opponents of the Bolsheviki were again charged, in the first sentence, with the intention of disrupting

---

[2] *Rabochi Put,* No. 40, Thursday, October 19/November 1, 1917, p. 8.
[3] Speech at the All-Russian Conference of Shop Committees; *Rabochi Put,* No. 42, Saturday, October 21/November 3, 1917, p. 10.

the Constituent Assembly,[4] and the reader was allowed to infer that this was one of the dangers which necessitated the Bolshevik coup. In the announcement of the successful seizure of power, broadcast the following day to the country at large, the Military-Revolutionary Committee promised three things: that the new Soviet power would immediately propose a just peace, that it would turn the land over to the peasants, and that it would convene the Constituent Assembly.[5]

No sooner had the establishment of Bolshevik power in Petrograd and Moscow become a certainty, however, than the attitude of the Bolshevik leaders toward the Constituent Assembly began to change. Heretofore the Assembly had appeared as a form of re-insurance against the establishment of any sort of conservative or moderate dictatorship capable of suppressing the Bolshevik faction, and advocacy of its immediate convening had been a convenient means of goading and discrediting the hard-pressed Provisional Government. Now, when power was actually in Bolshevik hands, the Assembly began to appear as a potential danger and embarrassment to the Party. In the factual sense, it could not now increase the Party's power, but it might well weaken it, especially if it did anything to throw doubt on the legitimacy of the November uprising. Lenin, in particular, was full of misgivings. He warned in the gloomiest terms against holding the elections and proceeding with the convening of the Assembly. But the Party's commitment was extensive; there was not full agreement in the Bolshevik ranks as to the course to be followed; and the coalition entered into with the Left Social-Revolutionaries in the weeks immediately following the Revolution further limited the regime's freedom of action. The decision was still further complicated by the fact that many Bolsheviki believed that the Party's success in seizing power had actually served to win the political support of the majority of the population. These people felt that the elections could therefore safely be risked, particularly in view of the advantages enjoyed by the Bolshevik faction through its control of Petrograd and Moscow.

It was finally decided that the elections should be permitted to take place. But the Bolshevik attitude toward them remained marked at all times by extreme nervousness and an almost panicky determination not to permit the procedure to end in any expression of popular

[4] *Rabochi Put,* No. 45, Wednesday, October 25/November 7, 1917, p. 1.
[5] *Rabochi Put,* No. 46, Thursday, October 26/November 8, 1917, p. 1.

opinion that could weaken, or deprive them of, the power they had already seized by force of arms.[6]

The Electoral Commission, established by the Provisional Government and charged with the conduct of the elections, refused to recognize the legitimacy of the Bolshevik seizure of power, and continued to implement preparations for the election in accordance with the instructions of the defunct Provisional Government. This procedure was viewed with sharpest misgiving by the Bolshevik authorities, but they did not seriously interfere. The elections thus took place as scheduled, beginning November 25, in the great majority of the electoral districts throughout the country. They represented the first sounding of the popular will ever conducted in Russia under rules comparable to those which prevail under western parliamentary systems. That they were, in general, honestly held and that they constituted a faithful reflection of the feelings of the voters does not appear to have been seriously challenged by historians of the Revolution.

The result was highly unfavorable to the Bolsheviki. Out of a total of 707 deputies elected, 410 were Social-Revolutionaries, only 175 Bolsheviki. Even with the addition of the Left S-R's, who at that time split away from their own party and joined with the Bolsheviki, the Bolshevik faction still had the support of less than a third of the body. The Bolsheviki, as was to be expected, proved to have their strength in the big cities, where the moderate conservative parties ran them a close second. But the peasantry, by far the most numerous segment of the population, voted almost solidly for the S-R's.

As the results of the election gradually became known, the Bolshevik attitude toward the Constituent Assembly turned into one of the utmost alarm and fury. Yet, having permitted the election of the body, the Bolsheviks found it hard to prohibit its convening. After some dissension and hesitation, the decision was taken by the top leadership of the party that the Assembly should not be barred from an initial session, but that every possible discouragement should

[6] Edward Hallett Carr, *A History of Soviet Russia, The Bolshevik Revolution, 1917–1923*, The Macmillan Co., New York, 1950, Vol. I, p. 112, makes the following interesting comment: "The Bolsheviks, well versed in revolutionary history, were alive to the precedent of the French Constituent Assembly of May 1848 whose function, three months after the February revolution, had been, in a well-known phrase from Marx's *Eighteenth Brumaire*, 'to cut down the results of the revolution to a bourgeois standard' and to prepare the way for the massacre of the workers by Cavaignac."

be thrown in its path and that it should be confronted with the choice either of legitimizing the Bolshevik seizure of power and confiding supreme power in the All-Russian Congress of Soviets or of being forcibly dissolved.

From that time on, every conceivable means of harassment and intimidation was brought to bear on the members of the Electoral Commission and the anti-Bolshevik deputies to the Assembly. On December 6, Uritsky, who was later to be the first head of the Petrograd Cheka, was appointed commissar "over" the Electoral Commission. He appeared the same day, unannounced, in the room where the Commission was working—"an ordinary, middle-aged person with short legs, wearing a pincenez with a black ribbon, and wide trousers." [7] Without greeting the members, and ostentatiously keeping his hands in his pockets, he announced that the Commission could proceed with its work only in his presence and with his permission. When the members of the Commission refused to recognize him, they were at once arrested and escorted to a crowded room in the Smolny Institute, where they were detained under guard for some days.

The Provisional Government had scheduled the opening of the Assembly for December 11, and the approach of this date produced the first crisis between the Soviet authorities and the non-Bolshevik members of the Assembly. By this time only some forty-five deputies had succeeded in reaching Petrograd. On the eve of the 11th, the Soviet authorities for some reason set the Electoral Commission, as such, at liberty. But at the same time, they outlawed, in effect, the Constitutional Democratic Party, and arrested a number of its members who had been elected deputies to the Assembly. This action effectively eliminated from further participation in the Assembly the only important moderate-conservative party which had been represented there. From that time on, the control of the Assembly was in the main a battle between two strongly leftist parties: the S-R's, who had the majority in the Assembly, and the Bolsheviki, who controlled the city streets.

On December 11, when the Assembly was supposed to begin its sessions, an effort was made by the small band of anti-Bolshevik deputies then present and at liberty in Petrograd to inaugurate in-

[7] Mark Vishnyak, *Dan Proshlomu* (Tribute to the Past), Chekhov Publishing House, New York, 1954, p. 328.

formal meetings in the Tauride Palace, the seat of the former Duma, which was to serve as the home of the Constituent Assembly. These efforts were frustrated by the Soviet authorities, who locked up the building, placed it under guard, and forbade further meetings on the grounds that the Assembly could have no existence until 400 of its members (a quorum) should be present in the city. The Bolsheviki then proceeded to name their own date for the holding of the Assembly, namely, January 18. This gave more time for their own preparations.

The battle was now on. As more of the deputies began to arrive in Petrograd, the Bolsheviki neglected no steps to impress upon them the danger in which they would be placing themselves if they dared to take action not consistent with Bolshevik purposes.[8] On December 26, the *Pravda* published a set of "theses," drafted by Lenin, on the subject of the Constituent Assembly. In this document the shift of Bolshevik policy toward the Assembly was rationalized on grounds convincing only to those who shared a belief in the ultimate righteousness of the Bolshevik cause and held that this justified an unlimited policy of expediency. "The interests of this revolution," Lenin wrote, "stand over the formal rights of the Constituent Assembly." He warned brutally that a complete endorsement by the Assembly of the legitimacy and actions to date of the Soviet regime would be the only "painless solution" of the crisis that had arisen; if this course were not taken, the crisis would have to be resolved

. . . only in the revolutionary manner, only by the most energetic, swift, firm, and decisive revolutionary measures. . . .[9]

In the three weeks that ensued before the opening of the Assembly, the attitude of the regime became steadily more grim and more menacing. An order was issued for the convening of the Third All-Russian Congress of Soviets on January 21st, three days after the date set for the meeting of the Constituent Assembly. It was plainly the intention that if the Assembly were still in session and still showing

[8] *Ibid.*, Chapters VII and VIII, contains an interesting and detailed account of the actions taken by the Soviet authorities to frighten and discourage the Electoral Commission and the deputies to the Assembly. Of further interest in this connection are the memoirs of V. M. Chernov, *Pered Burei* (Before the Storm), Chekhov Publishing House, New York, 1953. See also Vishnyak's earlier work: *Vserossiskoye Uchreditelnoye Sobranie* (The All-Russian Constituent Assembly), Paris, 1932.

[9] *Lenin*, Vol. XXII, *op.cit.*, pp. 131–134.

itself recalcitrant at that time, the authority of the Congress of Soviets would be invoked as a rival force, and supported against it.

As the day of the Assembly opening approached, military measures were taken by both sides; but whereas those taken by the S-R's, who were in a semi-underground status, were pathetic and largely futile, those taken by the Bolsheviki were elaborate, and effective in the extreme. Two days before the meeting of the Assembly, the mounting of guns began around the Tauride Palace. From that time on, preparations continued with increasing intensity. All troops in the city were placed on emergency status; those which were not ordered out for street patrol were confined to barracks. Units of sailors from the Baltic Fleet and of Latvian sharpshooters (the most radical, the most devoted politically to the Bolsheviki, and the most trigger-happy of all the armed forces in the area) were brought in to patrol and defend the palace and the area around it. Bolshevik agitators, charged with whipping these units up to the proper pitch of proletarian indignation against the non-Bolshevik deputies, did such a good job that it became difficult to control them at all. The excitement was heightened by the fact that on the evening of the 15th (the day following his meeting with the diplomatic corps in the Diamandi matter), Lenin was fired at while driving in his car through the streets of Petrograd, and saved only by the presence of mind of the Swiss communist, Platten, who pressed Lenin's head down and received the bullet in his own hand. This news, coming out just prior to the convening of the Assembly, increased the Bolshevik inclination to violence.

On the eve of the convening of the Constituent Assembly, the Soviet Central Executive Committee reaffirmed that "all power in the Russian Republic belongs to the Soviets and Soviet institutions," and warned that

. . . any attempt on the part of any person or institution whatever to usurp this or that function of state power will be regarded as a counter-revolutionary act . . . and crushed by all means at the disposal of the Soviet power, including the use of armed force.[10]

When dawn came on the 18th, the entire district around the Tauride Palace had been turned into an armed camp, with the palace

[10] The *Izvestiya*, January 17, 1918; this passage is cited in Carr, Vol. I, *op.cit.*, pp. 117–118.

in the center. The surrounding streets were heavily patrolled and guarded to the distance of a mile or two in every direction; free circulation within this area was completely inhibited. Popular demonstrators in favor of the Assembly, of whom several thousands tried to get to the vicinity of the Palace, were forcibly halted, their processions broken up, and an unknown number killed or wounded (Sisson finally estimated the dead at about thirty and the wounded running into the hundreds). The deputies themselves were permitted to approach the palace and to enter only through successive cordons of armed guards. They were progressively isolated as they advanced, in such a way that when they arrived at the building they found themselves alone, without their supporters, and in effect the prisoners of the fiercely excited sailors and other Red Guards, who treated them to a steady barrage of jeers and insults. The corridors of the palace and the entrances and galleries of the hall itself were packed with these aroused, armed men, who never ceased their threatening attitude toward the deputies and who had to be restrained on several occasions from opening fire on them during the session of the Assembly.

The non-communist deputies were ready to begin the session by about 1:00 p.m., but the Bolsheviki held up the opening until about 5:00 p.m., apparently to make sure that they were definitely in command of the Petrograd streets and that there was no possibility of any successful popular demonstration against them. When the Assembly was at last opened, the Bolsheviki tried to seize control by storm. One of their members, Sverdlov, wrested the gavel from the hand of the oldest deputy, who was endeavoring to open the meeting, called on everyone to sing the Internationale, and attempted in this way to obtain domination of the proceedings. When the S-R's stood their ground and elected one of their own members, Chernov, as chairman of the Assembly, the Bolsheviki went over to a tactic of harassment and filled the hall with wild din and disorder whenever anyone was speaking who was not one of their members or followers.

Lenin himself was present, and acted as master of ceremonies for his faction. It was plain to observers that every nerve of his politically impassioned being was aroused by this supreme parliamentary contest. His face deathly pale with tenseness, his burning eyes darting constantly over the scene and absorbing every detail, he directed his cohorts like a commander in battle, whenever there was any

[350]

chance of their dominating the proceedings. When opposition speakers had the floor, he stretched out at full length on the steps leading to the podium and reinforced the harassing operations of his followers by appearing to go to sleep out of sheer boredom.

When it became evident, toward midnight, that the S-R's were prepared to drive through, on the strength of their majority in the Assembly, a whole series of independent resolutions having virtual constitutional effect, the Bolsheviki demonstratively walked out on the proceedings. They were followed a short time later by their allies, the Left-S-R's. From that moment on, the situation in the hall became very ugly. With no further visible reason for restraint, the armed sailors began to show increasing signs of truculence and impatience. The non-Bolshevik deputies, worn with fatigue and hunger (there was no food to be had in the building), were urged several times by the sailor guards to terminate the session. Repeated warnings were given to them that the command staff of the palace could no longer guarantee their safety if they persisted in remaining. In a mounting crescendo of threats and importunities, the S-R's, now practically alone on the floor of the hall, hastily adopted resolution after resolution, trying to get them all formally on record before the final blow should fall. At 4:40 a.m., the session was finally closed under mounting pressure from the sailors. To the accompaniment of a torrent of abuse and menacing shouts from their guardians, the exhausted deputies began to leave the palace. There is no question but that the safety of the entire Assembly hung, at this moment, by the slenderest thread; for the mood of the sailors was by this time such that if a single shot had been fired a massacre would unquestionably have followed. The deputies were protected, at this final juncture, only by the orders of Lenin himself and by the physical intervention of a number of their Bolshevik colleagues who, though animated by no friendly feelings toward the S-R's, realized that their position might be jeopardized by bloodshed at this point and stood between the sailors and the deputies as the latter left the hall.

In tiny groups, the harassed and exhausted deputies disappeared into the darkness of the winter morning and sought whatever places of refuge or hiding they could find in the great snowbound city. Several had already been in underground status and had taken their lives in their hands by even appearing in the Assembly. For many it was their last open appearance in Soviet-controlled territory. It remains one of the wonders of the Revolution that they got away at all.

By ten o'clock in the morning, the Soviet government had issued a decree dissolving the Assembly and had barred the doors of the great palace against any re-entry of the deputies.

Thus ended Russia's one and only constitutional convention. In the coming months and years there would be many attempts to overthrow the Bolsheviki by force of arms, but this night marked the end of the last effort to cope with Bolshevism by the processes of parliamentary democracy. From now on, there could be no really established claim to popular sanction on the part of the Soviet regime.

To Lenin the situation held no terrors. He left the Tauride Palace around midnight, satisfied of his ultimate triumph, convinced that the crisis had been surmounted, unconcerned for the abuse he had heaped on the theory of majority rule. But in the relationship to the western world, there was an element of finality in what the Bolsheviki had done during the course of that night. The more sensitive of the western observers realized this. Later in the day the young New Zealand linguist who wrote for the *New York Times*, Mr. Harold Williams, one of the most passionately interested and best informed of the western observers in Russia at the time of the Revolution, sat down and poured out his sense of horror and despair in a despatch to his paper:

. . . A snowstorm is raging full in this fiercest of all winters, and it is as though all the powers and elements of darkness were rushing and roaring in the whirlwind that enwraps this city of doom. . . . The Bolsheviki do not profess to encourage any illusions as to their real nature. They treat the bourgeoisie of all countries with equal contempt. They glory in all violence directed against the ruling classes. They despise the laws and decencies that they consider effete. They trample on the arts and refinements of life. It is nothing to them if in the throes of a great upheaval the world relapse into barbarism.[11]

❖

The United States government was not directly involved in the crisis occasioned by the convening of the Constituent Assembly; and if the history of that incident has been recounted in such detail above, it is because the reactions of the American observers at the time can

[11] *New York Times,* January 22, 1918; Petrograd dateline of January 19.

be judged only in the light of the real circumstances and atmosphere then prevailing. These events were not wholly without their repercussions in American circles.

The Constituent Assembly was the white hope of those who still sought for a genuine democratization of the Russian Revolution; and the Embassy in Petrograd naturally followed with keen interest the course of the elections and the preparations for convening that body. On Tuesday, January 15th (the day of Diamandi's release), according to one of Francis' telegrams, the Embassy had a representative at the meeting of the S-R leaders where the tactics to be followed in the coming session of the Assembly were being thrashed out.[12] There is no evidence to show who this representative was, or what was the purpose of his presence at the meeting. The discussion turned on the attitude the S-R's should adopt in the Assembly with respect to the negotiations with the Germans for a separate peace. There was some talk of voting that the Assembly, in order to steal Boshevik thunder, should make a proposal to the Allied governments for a general peace. This was the basis for the subsequent contention of Robins and others that the S-R's were actually more inclined to a separate peace with Germany than were the Bolsheviki.

That same evening, realizing that the convening of the Assembly would produce a real crisis, some of the Americans met in Sisson's room to coordinate their observation of the coming events, and to listen to a lecture by Major Kerth on the science of street fighting.[13]

On the morning of the 18th, the day the Assembly was to convene, Sisson went in person to the Foreign Office to get passes for himself and other official Americans to the Assembly. He found the great building completely deserted except for Karl Radek's wife and Trotsky's secretary Shalyapina, who had recently been his companion in watching the demonstrations of December 30. The two ladies, "huddled in furs," were having breakfast in the entrance hall to the vast but chilly apartment which had formerly served as the private suite of the Foreign Minister. But they were none the less willing to oblige. Sisson's quest for the passes was perhaps aided by the fact that he came in company with Arthur Ransome, the British correspondent who was later to marry Shalyapina.

[12] *Foreign Relations, 1918, Russia,* Vol. I, *op.cit.,* p. 350.
[13] For this and further accounts of Sisson's experiences at that time, see his memoirs, *op.cit.,* Chapter XVI.

Having obtained his passes, Sisson set out first to see what was going on in the streets. He witnessed the breaking up of some of the demonstrations on the Liteiny Prospekt, in the immediate neighborhood of the Embassy, watched the crowds taking refuge behind the huge ridges of shovelled snow, and noted the blood on the snow at many points.[14] He then called at the Embassy, which was situated in the immediate vicinity of these disorders, and tried to get the Ambassador to accompany him to the opening of the Assembly. This Francis declined to do, but only in deference to the wishes of his Allied diplomatic colleagues, with whom he had just been in consultation.

Bucked up by his success in the Diamandi incident, Francis was now enjoying to the full his new role as doyen of the diplomatic corps. Not only did this role satisfy his thirst for activity,[15] but it gave him a new importance in his own eyes, and particularly with relation to his diplomatic colleagues. One may suspect, furthermore, that his colleagues, however they might have quipped about him in more peaceful days, were not sorry to have the United States Ambassador taking the lead in the protection of the status and personal security of the diplomatic corps in a dangerous time. Thus Francis began to hold, in the American Embassy Chancery, a series of regular diplomatic meetings—sometimes calling on the whole corps, sometimes only the Allied envoys.

One of these meetings of the Allied colleagues had taken place on the morning of the 18th, to consider the question of the attitude to be taken toward the Constituent Assembly, which was scheduled to meet that day. Francis had pointed out to the Allied chiefs-of-mission the fact that the convening of the Assembly represented a crisis in Russian affairs and "seriously affected Allied interests." [16] He had favored the idea of the Allied envoys attending in a body, but had said that if this were unacceptable, he would be prepared to go alone

---

[14] The Liteiny was evidently the line beyond which the Bolsheviki were not prepared to permit the demonstrators to approach the Tauride Palace. This accounts for the bloodshed there. Philip Jordan also witnessed some of the shooting. Writing to Mrs. Francis the afternoon of the 18th, he said: "I have just returned from the street whare the firing is going on and people are running for their lives. I could count at least ten dead ones but the machine guns was turned in my direction and just about that time I had business at the Embassy. . . ." (Francis MSS, *op.cit.*, Folder, January 11–22, 1918. The letter was erroneously dated January 17.)

[15] In a letter to his son, on the 18th, describing the numerous meetings he had held, Francis said proudly: "You can see therefore how much occupied I am." (*Ibid.*)

[16] *Foreign Relations, 1918, Russia*, Vol. I, *op.cit.*, p. 351.

as their representative. There was no concurrence, however, in these suggestions, and it was decided that no one should attend on that day. (The Ambassador remained of the opinion that this decision was a mistake—that the presence of the diplomatic representatives might have had a "pacifying effect." [17] The French Ambassador shuddered, in retrospect, at the thought of their becoming involved in such a dangerous and disorderly procedure.[18])

Sisson thus went on to the Tauride Palace alone. It was then around noon. After exhibiting his passes to numerous control cordons, he found himself admitted to a diplomatic box, already occupied by several British and French military representatives in uniform. He stuck it out until eleven o'clock in the evening when, wearied and hungry, he left for home. By ten o'clock in the morning he had learned of the Soviet government's action in disbanding the Assembly.

The Allied ambassadors met again during the course of that next day (the 19th) at the American Embassy, but, as Francis put it, "did nothing." They do not seem to have realized the finality of the Bolshevik action in dissolving the Assembly.

In the evening Sisson made another trip to the Tauride Gardens, but found the streets empty except for armed patrols, and the windows of the palace dark. The city, on that evening, he said,

. . . muttered over the street killings of the preceding day and was gloomily passive. The atmosphere at Smolny was cheerful.[19]

When the Allied chiefs-of-mission met again on the 20th, they recognized that there was nothing further to be done with respect to the Assembly. As was so often to be the case in the coming months and years, communist unity, alertness, and decisiveness were met by passivity, divided counsels, and indecision on the part of communism's adversaries. Not that there *was* much to be done, at that dark moment in the winter of 1918, when every energy in the Allied camp was rivetted to the Western Front. But a milestone had been passed: the Bolsheviki had finally stamped themselves as usurpers. From this time on, they would be irrevocably separated from the western powers by that subtle barrier dividing regimes which defer in prin-

[17] Francis, *op.cit.,* p. 203.
[18] Noulens, Vol. 1, *op.cit.,* p. 161.
[19] Sisson, *op.cit.,* p. 247.

ciple to the popular will from those which do not—a barrier that does not rule out co-existence, but that defines its nature and prescribes its limitations. The aftermath of the dissolution of the Assembly was, perhaps, the moment when this fact should have been both recognized and marked in some way by the western governments.

For some days after the dissolution of the Constituent Assembly, the atmosphere of violence and terror engendered by the excitement of the Assembly continued to dominate the city. It looked for a time as though the Bolsheviki might not be able to control the dragons' teeth they had sown with their demagoguery. On the evening of the 19th, two Kadet ex-Ministers of the Provisional Government, Shingarev and Kokoshkin, who had been arrested in December (both of them deputies to the Constituent Assembly and members of its Electoral Commission), were brutally murdered in their beds in the Mariinski Hospital, to which they had just been transferred on grounds of their state of health. The murder was carried out in cold blood by the armed sailors ostensibly charged with guarding the prisoners. The hospital, on the Liteiny Prospekt, was not far from the Embassy. Horrified at the news, Francis sent a Russian servant, and later the Commercial Attaché, to view the bodies and to confirm the murder. Coming on the heels of the very recent arrest of the Rumanian Diamandi (who had been confined in the same fortress with the two ministers before their transfer to the hospital), this incident was a new shock to the Allied envoys.

Francis, as it happened, was just at that time receiving a series of ugly threats from the anarchist faction in Petrograd. These threats were mostly connected with the trial and imprisonment in the United States of the left-wing agitators, Mooney and Berkman.[20] On the very day the Kadet Ministers were murdered, the anarchist newspaper threatened that if these and other American radicals were not immediately released, Francis would be held personally responsible. Violence, the paper stated darkly, would be answered by violence, death by death.[21]

---

[20] Mooney, in a shocking miscarriage of justice, had been sentenced to death (later commuted to life imprisonment) for alleged complicity in the San Francisco bomb outrage of July 22, 1916. Berkman, an immigrant anarchist, had been arrested in New York for agitation against the draft law.

[21] *Foreign Relations, 1918, Russia*, Vol. I, *op.cit.*, pp. 353–354 reports text from the newspaper.

The Allied chiefs-of-mission met again the following morning (January 20) in the Embassy. All were deeply shocked and affected by the news of the murder of Shingarev and Kokoshkin. The anarchist threats added to the uncertainty. The Rumanian, enjoying the brief respite between his release from prison and his final expulsion from the country, urged that they all depart at once; but no one was prepared to take this step. While the meeting was in progress, a phone call was received at the Embassy from an anonymous woman who said she had information to impart but was afraid to come to the Embassy in person. The Commercial Attaché, Mr. Huntington, and the Ambassador's private secretary, Mr. Johnston, were sent to meet her at a nearby intersection. She turned out to be a Russian woman known (not too favorably) to the Embassy as the widow of a well-known American businessman. The woman told them that she had learned from one of a group of soldiers who had recently participated in a looting of the cellars of the Italian Embassy that the same group was preparing to attack the American Embassy that evening, that the building was to be burned, and the Ambassador killed.[22]

The Ambassador, as it happened, had arranged a large farewell reception that evening for General Judson, who was to leave the following day for the United States. There were two hundred guests. In view of the various threats, Judson had asked for a Bolshevik guard. The result was the arrival of some dubious and troublesome characters who were only with difficulty restrained from invading the party to tear the epaulets and insignia off certain of the guests— Russian officers who had rashly come in civilian overcoats but with full uniform underneath.

After the other guests had left, Francis, Judson, and Secretary of Embassy Norman Armour sat up disconsolately, in the wee hours of the night, waiting for the guns to go off. The situation was not a happy one. Demoralization, indiscipline, and irresponsibility were in the air. Everyone had in mind the murder of the Kadet Ministers

---

[22] Francis, *op.cit.*, p. 209. Robins maintained that this woman was "the divorced wife of Proctor, of Proctor & Gamble, of Cincinnati, and was at that particular hour in the secret service records of three of the allied nations as a German agent in Russia." (*Bolshevik Propaganda, Hearings . . .*, *op.cit.*, p. 797.) Denunciation had reached such fantastic proportions in Petrograd during the war that the circumstance cited by Robins should be judged with greatest caution.

by their own guards twenty-four hours earlier. What would this night bring? Half of the Soviet guards were loitering menacingly in the vestibule. The other half, Francis recalled later, "were playing cards in the janitor's room and betting fifty roubles each." [23]

Judson and Armour were loath to abandon the old gentleman to the threatened reprisals or to the no less menacing attentions of the guards. They finally persuaded him, at 2:30 a.m., to leave with them, and to take shelter for the night in Johnston's lodgings. It was the only time, in his two years in Petrograd, that Francis spent the night elsewhere than in his own Embassy. Fortunately, there was no attack.

"The following morning," Francis later wrote,

I sent the bolshevik guards home, giving them about thirty roubles each. They looked upon the gift contemptuously, but accepted it nevertheless. That was my only experience with bolshevik guards.[24]

After this experience, the Ambassador relied for the protection of the Embassy on some American Marine couriers, who happened to be delivering the diplomatic pouches at Petrograd. They objected strongly to being detained in Russia for this purpose, but upon being overruled performed their duty faithfully and effectively.

❖

The Constituent Assembly had its epilogue, as the Soviet leaders had planned that it should, in the Third All-Russian Congress of Soviets. The sessions took place from January 23 to 31 in the same hall where the Constituent Assembly had attempted to deliberate. The Congress, in contrast to the Assembly, was a docile body, wholly under Bolshevik domination, and prepared to take its lead without serious question from the Smolny Institute. This time there was no armed display—rather, music, singing, bright peasant costumes, and an atmosphere of fiesta, all carefully prearranged in the manner destined later to become so characteristic of twentieth century totalitarianism.

The Congress was addressed on the first day (January 23) by three persons who purported to bring greetings from the American proletariat. The first was Reinstein, who was not really an American, but

---

[23] Francis MSS, *op.cit.*, Letter of April 23, 1919, to Basil Miles.
[24] *Loc.cit.*

a returned exile like Trotsky. The next was Mr. Albert Rhys Williams, an American who, like the third, John Reed, had been helping the Commissariat for Foreign Affairs in some of its propagandistic activity, presumably of an anti-German nature.

Williams, according to the record in the files of the Petrograd Embassy, began by referring to "this sort of parliamentarianism" (referring apparently to the procedures of the Congress of Soviets as opposed to those of the Constituent Assembly). "This sort of parliamentarianism," he announced,

will also be adopted by us when the American proletariat makes up its mind to undertake a revolutionary struggle and to rise against its own bourgeoisie—for it is now clear that only by a revolution can it win its freedom. Hurrah for Revolutionary Russia! Hurrah for the International Revolution! Hurrah for the power of the Soviets! [25]

When Williams had finished, Reed was introduced by Reinstein, rather luridly, as an American socialist who had been indicted for opposing the draft law and for inciting to sedition in the army and who was now returning to America to stand trial by a bourgeois court, which would perhaps sentence him to forty years' imprisonment. In this case it was to be hoped, Reinstein said, "that some hand equal to that of Trotsky would be able to deliver him or set him at liberty." (The second and final *New Masses* trial, to which Reinstein was referring, was held in New York City at the end of September, 1918. Reed was among the defendants. The jury split—eight for acquittal, four against—and the indictment was dismissed.[26] Reed therefore did not require a "hand equal to that of Trotsky" for his liberation.)

Sisson had earnestly warned Reed not to appear at the Congress, and thought he had his assurance that he would not do so. According to Reed's biographer, the decision to speak was taken only at the last moment. Sisson thought both Reed and Williams proved them-

---

[25] National Archives, Petrograd Embassy 800 File, *op.cit.,* contains a document covering Williams' and Reed's statements. The texts given there are evidently re-translations into English of the Russian translations of the two men's remarks. Since they are extremely poor translations, ungrammatical and awkward, I have taken the liberty of revising the language slightly, to accord more closely with the English phrases Williams and Reed may be supposed to have employed; I have endeavored not to alter the sense.

[26] Granville Hicks, *John Reed: The Making of a Revolutionary,* The Macmillan Co., New York, 1936, pp. 315–320.

selves poor speakers, that they "made a sorry, stammering show of themselves." [27] Reed, like Williams, used language which clearly endorsed the Soviet brand of parliamentarianism as opposed to that of the Constituent Assembly. He reiterated Williams' confidence in the imminence of social revolution in the United States. "In returning to the conservative country of the ruling imperialists," he said,

I take great satisfaction in the knowledge that the victory of the proletariat in one of the world's most powerful countries is no longer a dream but a reality. . . . I promise you . . . that I will tell the American proletariat about all that is being done in revolutionary Russia, and I am convinced that this will evoke an answer from the oppressed and exploited masses.[28]

Such statements naturally aroused indignation among the large majority of the Petrograd Americans, whose feelings had already been outraged by the events of the past few days and who had noted with horror and dismay the contemptuous suppression of Russia's first and only constitutional convention, the brutal murder of two of the most distinguished of its deputies, and the persecution of many others. The events surrounding the episode of the Constituent Assembly served to drive still deeper the growing differences between those Americans who favored collaboration with the new Soviet regime and those who opposed it, increasing the bitterness and depth of commitment on both sides, making it harder than ever for the two parties to find a common language.

❖

The significance of the events surrounding the convening of the Constituent Assembly seems to have been only poorly and partially understood in the United States. Francis' own reports were confused, and failed to give any adequate picture of what had transpired. The press reports were better, more penetrating, and more detailed. But by this time people in the United States were surfeited with the voluminous and bewildering accounts of revolutionary events in Russia. Many had arrived at the belief that the Bolsheviki were usurpers, criminals, and probable German agents, and they were uninterested in further evidence. Preoccupation with the war was so

[27] Sisson, *op.cit.*, p. 257.
[28] See footnote 25.

great that the news of the negotiations again in progress at Brest-Litovsk tended to overshadow in public attention the accounts of internal political happenings in the Soviet capital.

Thus the reports of the dissolution of the Constituent Assembly received relatively little attention in the American press. Such comment as appeared was largely along the lines of "I told you so." Nobody had supposed, the *New York Times* said, that Lenin would permit the Constituent Assembly to function or that the delegates "would pluck up courage enough to resist the Bolsheviks." [29] (This last could not have been more unjust; few parliamentarians can ever have manifested more courage than those who sat for fifteen hours in the Tauride Palace on the night of January 18–19, 1918, under the wavering muzzles of the guns of the Kronstadt sailors.) Other papers shared this pessimism. The *New York Tribune* recognized that "the Bolsheviks have remained a usurping minority"; but its editors revealed their greater interest in the war than in the prospects for Russian democracy when they added:

> . . . Unless a military dictator appears . . . the situation will continue from the Entente point of view to be practically hopeless. . . .[30]

In general, it was widely recognized that the dissolution of the Assembly put an end to any real claim to parliamentary legitimacy on the part of the Bolsheviki. There was now, as the *Outlook* of January 30, 1918, pointed out, no longer any representative body in Russia—nothing but a "despotic committee claiming to represent the proletariat only but having no other evidence of that mandate than the bayonets of the Red Guard." To the American public, with its strong attachment to constitutionality, this was a weighty realization.

Lansing was at home ill with grippe when the news was received of the dissolution of the Constitutional Assembly. When he returned to his desk on January 28th, the event had receded into the past, and he was overwhelmed with new problems. The news of this suppression of the constitutional process in Russia can only have confirmed him in the lively abhorrence he already felt for the ideology and methodology of Bolshevism.

As for the President, his reaction was sad and passive. On January 21 he wrote to Samuel Gompers:

[29] *New York Times*, January 22, 1918.
[30] *New York Tribune*, January 22, 1918.

I liked your suggestion about a message to the Russian Constituent Assembly, but apparently the reckless Bolsheviki have already broken it up because they did not control it. It is distressing to see things so repeatedly go to pieces there.[31]

To Thomas Lamont, who had written again, urging him to see Colonel Thompson, Wilson replied on January 31:

... I have heard a great deal about Col. W. B. Thompson, and everything I have heard has attracted me. Some day I hope I shall have a deliberate talk with him, but just at present the changes taking place in Russia are so kaleidoscopic that I feel that information and advice are futile until there is something definite to plan with as well as for.[32]

Thus the effect of the dissolution of the Assembly, so far as American policy was concerned, was only to increase the sense of helplessness and hopelessness on the part of American statesmen, to convince them that events were moving too fast to be understood, and to cause them to be doubly wary of taking any action at all in matters affecting Russia.

On the British, the dissolution of the Assembly apparently had a more tangible effect, inclining them to place the anti-Bolshevik factions in Russia on an equal basis with the Bolsheviki in the implementation of their policies, and increasing their readiness to extend aid to these anti-Bolshevik elements wherever the situation seemed to warrant it. From the press reports of the time, one gains the impression that the erroneous news of the rupture of the Brest-Litovsk talks in late December, coming on the heels of Thompson's luncheon with Lloyd George, had brought the British government in the beginning of January closer, for a time, to the idea of a *de facto* recognition of the Soviet regime. This tendency was checked, however, both by the news of the resumption of the German-Soviet talks at Brest (on January 9) and by the suppression of the Constituent Assembly. Sir George Buchanan, just back from his post as Ambassador to Petrograd, was deeply shocked by the news of the dissolution of the Assembly and the murder of the two Kadet Ministers; and whereas he had previously opposed a complete rupture with the Bolsheviki, he now swung over to the consistent advocacy of a policy of armed intervention by the Allies in Russia.[33] Others in London

[31] Baker, Vol. vii, *op.cit.*, p. 486.
[32] *Ibid.*, p. 514.
[33] Buchanan, Vol. ii, *op.cit.*, p. 256.

seem to have been similarly affected. In a secret telegram of January 30 to Sir William Wiseman, for transmission to Colonel House, from some member of the British government,[34] it was stated that:

... It is not our wish to quarrel with the Bolsheviki. On the contrary we look at them with a certain degree of favour as long as they refuse to make a separate peace. But their claim to be the Government of all the Russians either *de facto* or *de jure* is not founded on fact. Their claim to this position, in particular since the forced dissolution of the Constituent Assembly, is no better than that of the autonomous body in South East Russia which it is sought to assist by the occupation of the Siberian Railway; ...

This concept of an equalization of treatment of the Bolsheviki and the rival Russian factions found further reflection in a telegram despatched about that time to the British government's agent, Mr. Bruce Lockhart, in Petrograd. In this message it was said:

... With the *de facto* Bolshevik Government at Petrograd we are prepared to enter into relations in just the same way as we have done with the *de facto* Governments of the Ukraine, Finland, and elsewhere.[35]

The dissolution of the Assembly may thus be said to have had the effect of obviating, for the time being, any inclination of the Allies to recognize the *de jure* legitimacy of the new Soviet regime, and to have increased in the eyes of Allied statesmen the legal and moral justification for the extension of aid and *de facto* recognition to the anti-Bolshevik factions in Russia. This tendency found further nourishment in the final denouement of the Brest negotiations, which followed so rapidly upon the dissolution of the Assembly.

[34] Wilson MSS, Series II, *op.cit.*, enclosure to letter from Colonel House to President Wilson of January 31, 1918. This message will be treated at greater detail in connection with the further discussion of the background of the Far Eastern intervention.
[35] *War Memoirs of David Lloyd George*, Vol. v, *op.cit.*, p. 2593.

CHAPTER XVIII

BREST-LITOVSK AND THE

AMERICANS

On the evening of January 6 the special train bearing the Soviet delegation, headed by Trotsky in person, left Petrograd once more for Brest-Litovsk, where the peace talks were to be resumed on January 9. It is not necessary to attempt, within the framework of this study, a detailed résumé of the course of the further discussions at Brest.[1] But the Brest-Litovsk negotiations stood at the center of all Allied interest in Russia and indeed of all the international relations of the Soviet government in January and February 1918. Everything else revolved around the discussions: the problems of "contact" and recognition, the relations with the non-Bolshevik elements in Russia, even—in large measure—the question of Far Eastern intervention. The United States government was, it is true, a passive and almost wholly silent bystander at the unfolding of the Brest discussions. Yet without bearing in mind the general progress and nature of the Brest talks, as the determinant background of all Russia's foreign relations at that time, we cannot understand either the process of thinking in Washington in relation to Russian matters or the actions of the Petrograd Americans in that winter of 1918—not to mention the behavior of the Soviet leaders themselves in their relations with western representatives. A brief review of the course of the Brest discussions in January and February 1918 may therefore be in order.

---

[1] The interested reader will find a lucid and highly readable account of these negotiations in the excellent study by Mr. John W. Wheeler-Bennett, *The Forgotten Peace* (*Brest-Litovsk, March 1918*), *op.cit.;* and the memoirs of Major General Max Hoffmann, of Baron v. Kühlmann, of Count Ottokar Czernin, and others will fill remaining gaps.

Brest-Litovsk and the Americans

We have seen that the events at the end of December had brought home to the Soviet leaders, for the first time, the full seriousness of their plight. With reckless desperation, intent only on winning support among the soldier-masses and on depriving their political adversaries of a potential weapon that could be used against them, they had systematically demoralized the old army and had hastened its disintegration as a fighting force. If they had thought at all about the military vacuum this action created, they had comforted themselves with the illusion that the working "masses" of the western countries would force their respective governments to join in the effort to arrive at a general peace, in which case they, the Soviet leaders, would be supported in their negotiations with the Germans by the prestige of the undefeated western powers. In any case, they hoped that the Russian Revolution would find so lively an echo in Germany that it would prove impossible for the German government, in the light of domestic public opinion there, to inflict upon the first "workers' government" a punitive and onerous peace. The events of the month of December had blasted both these hopes. The western Allies had *not* shown any disposition to join the Bolsheviki in the quest for a general peace. And, although there was growing opposition in Germany to the uncompromising annexationist policies of the German High Command, the opposition was not sufficient to modify appreciably the High Command's determination to exploit to the full, in the interests of Germany's military position generally, the enormous advantage that had suddenly accrued to Germany from the disintegration of the Russian armed forces. The Bolsheviki therefore suddenly found themselves, as of the beginning of January, alone, defenseless, and face to face with a determined, strong, and impatient adversary.

In these circumstances, as was seen above, the decision was taken at the end of December that Trotsky should return to Brest and attempt to prolong the negotiations, in the hope that meanwhile internal discontent in Germany and Austria-Hungary, fanned by Bolshevik propaganda and the example of the successful Russian Revolution, would increase to a point where the respective governments would either be overthrown or compelled to modify the strong position they had taken at Brest.

When the conference reopened, on January 9, Kühlmann first announced that since the other Entente powers had failed to accept the

Russian offers of December 25, these offers were now null and void.[2] He then demanded that the Russian representatives get down to business and negotiate a separate peace along the lines already indicated by the Germans, i.e. on the understanding that the fate of the German-occupied Russian territories would be determined in direct negotiations between the inhabitants of those areas and the German government. Trotsky still objected vigorously. He insisted that if this was to be done the arrangement be discussed in terms of outright "annexation"—to which the Germans were unwilling to agree. He put forward various schemes for modifying the German position. For two days Kühlmann, resisting the impatient demands of the Austrian Foreign Minister and the German military representatives for an immediate showdown, debated fruitlessly with Trotsky. Finally, on January 12, Kühlmann's patience being exhausted, General Hoffmann was permitted to confirm in blunt and vigorous terms the German refusal to consider the Soviet proposals.

The final crisis of the negotiations would probably have come then and there, had it not been for the presence at Brest, by this time, of a full-flung delegation from the Ukrainian Rada, empowered to negotiate independently with the Central Powers on behalf of the Ukraine. Since most of the food and natural resources in which the Germans and Austrians were interested were to be found in the south of Russia, the Germans at Brest turned to separate negotiations with the Ukrainians as a means of bypassing the obdurate and provocative Bolsheviki. Overriding the misgivings of their Austrian allies, for whom the deal with the Ukrainians held serious dangers and disadvantages, the Germans pressed ahead to negotiate a separate peace treaty with the Ukraine. To the Bolsheviki, the presence and activity of the Rada's delegation was of course dangerous and embarrassing in the extreme, since it threatened to deprive them of much of what little bargaining power they possessed. They reacted by bringing to Brest Ukrainian puppets of their own, ostensibly representing the rival Kharkov Bolshevik regime (mentioned in Chapter IX), and by pressing frantically ahead with the military offensive against Kiev, hoping to suppress the Rada before a separate German-Ukrainian

---

[2] The following recapitulation, inserted solely for the convenience of the reader in following the repercussions of the Brest negotiations on Soviet-American relations, is taken primarily, with due appreciation, from Wheeler-Bennett's excellent work, referred to above. I have also availed myself gratefully, for this purpose, of the discussion of this subject in Carr, Vol. III, *op.cit.,* Chapter XXI.

treaty could be signed. The affair developed into a race between Muravyev's forces, operating against Kiev, and the efforts of the Germans to reach an agreement with the representatives of the Rada while they could still be said to represent a flesh-and-blood regime.

The Germans exploited the Ukrainian situation ably as a means of bringing pressure on the Bolsheviki. On January 18 the German terms were restated to Trotsky in all bluntness, and he was provided with a map showing the line, in the area north of Brest, which the Germans insisted on holding. As for the territory south of Brest, this, he was told, would be dealt with in the negotiations with the Ukrainians. It was then agreed that the talks would again be suspended for ten days, to enable Trotsky to consult with the other members of the Soviet government. With this sparse harvest, Trotsky started back to Petrograd on the night of January 18, while the Constituent Assembly was experiencing its final agony in the Tauride Palace. The Germans, meanwhile, continued to press the representatives of the Rada for the conclusion of a separate German-Ukrainian peace.

The following days were taken up by agitated debates among the Bolshevik leaders over the position to be taken in the light of the uncompromising German stand. This painful question produced the first great crisis within the Soviet leadership—the most serious it was ever to face in Lenin's time. For decades thereafter, the valleys of the Communist Olympus would continue to reverberate, in moments of tension and violence, with bitter arguments and recriminations over the positions taken by individual communist figures at this difficult moment in 1918.

In the days following Trotsky's return on January 20, a bare majority of the Bolshevik leadership still favored defiance of the Germans and an attempt to conduct a revolutionary war against the Central Powers. The minority were divided almost equally into two factions, one headed by Lenin, who favored immediate conclusion of peace with the Germans on the best terms possible, and another headed by Trotsky, who advocated a flat refusal to sign the treaty on German terms, coupled with continued demobilization of the Russian armies and the issuance of a simple declaration by the Soviet government to the effect that the war, as far as Petrograd was concerned, was at an end. This last measure involved, of course, the calculated risk that the Germans might renew the offensive on the

Eastern Front, a risk which Lenin viewed more seriously than did Trotsky. Reluctantly, however, Lenin agreed to the adoption of Trotsky's position, as a compromise, if no better solution could be obtained. This decision was finally approved by the Central Committee of the party. Trotsky therefore returned to Brest at the end of January empowered to adopt the position popularly known as "no war—no peace," and break off the talks, when and if no other recourse remained.

The talks were resumed at Brest on January 30. The arguments over the Ukrainian question were good for two or three days of further delay. On February 4 and 5 negotiations were briefly suspended again to permit further consultation between the representatives of the Central Powers and their respective governments. When discussions re-opened on February 6, the first development was the completion and signature, on February 8, of the separate treaty between the Germans and the Ukrainian Rada, which the Soviet delegation refused to recognize. (This occurred, ironically, on the day that Kiev finally fell to the Bolshevik forces under Muravyev.) Then, on February 10, it being clear that a final German ultimatum was only a matter of hours, Trotsky sprang his announcement to the effect that the Soviet government would neither continue the war nor agree to a peace on German terms. With this pronouncement, the Soviet delegation abruptly broke off the talks, and left immediately for Petrograd.

Because General Hoffmann greeted Trotsky's announcement with a startled exclamation: "Unerhört" (Unprecedented), the Soviet delegates came away with the impression that they had achieved a species of diplomatic triumph. Trotsky's formula, they concluded, had taken the wind out of the Germans' sails; it had left them frustrated, disarmed, and looking very silly. In western circles this version also found some currency. Actually, there was little justification for such a view. Trotsky's gesture had changed nothing in the military realities. It had merely relieved the Germans of any obligation to respect further the armistice, the formal rationale of which had been only to make possible the conduct of peace negotiations. Even had the Central Powers, as Kühlmann and Czernin would have preferred, accepted the resulting situation and refrained from reopening hostilities, the German position in eastern Europe would have remained powerful and the Bolsheviki would not have recovered the occupied areas about which they had been arguing.

On February 13 Trotsky, back in Petrograd, reported optimistically to the Central Executive Committee about the effect of his move. For a day or so the members of the Bolshevik hierarchy congratulated themselves on having adroitly extracted themselves from a difficult situation. But the German High Command was not to be trifled with in this manner. Already deeply engaged in preparations for a major offensive on the western front in mid-March, the German military leaders could not tolerate the uncertainty in which Trotsky's position would have left the eastern front. The Germans wanted to know where they stood, and felt strong enough to insist on finding out. On February 16, word was received in the Smolny Institute from the Russian military representative at Brest to the effect that he had just been notified by General Hoffmann that on February 18 the German army would renew military operations. Lenin had been right in his apprehensions.

General Hoffmann was as good as his word. On February 18, the Germans renewed the offensive all along their eastern front, encountering no appreciable resistance and advancing eastward as rapidly as climatic conditions and transport facilities would permit.

Even in the face of the German notification that hostilities would be resumed, the Bolshevik leaders, again overriding Lenin's views, awaited confirmation of the actual beginning of hostilities on the 18th before facing up to the situation—meanwhile making frantic last-minute efforts to undermine the German command by renewed propaganda to the German troops. Late on the night of the 18th, after bitter internal wrangling, the Bolsheviki finally recognized the facts of the situation and sent off a wire to Brest-Litovsk stating their readiness to sign, under protest, the German terms. The Germans, however, anxious to reap the full fruits of their new advance, were in no hurry to settle. They delayed matters by one means and another, and increased the severity of their demands, refusing, with entire formal justification, to be held to the offers they had made at Brest. Their troops, meanwhile, continued to advance all along the front in an operation which envisaged the complete occupation of Latvia and Estonia and an advance further south considerably beyond the subsequent (1920–1939) borders of the U.S.S.R.

[369]

The new German terms, received in Petrograd on the 23rd, evoked a storm of hysterical indignation and defiance in Soviet circles. It took the immense leverage of Lenin's one and only threat of resignation to compel his hot-headed comrades to accept the terms. All through the night of the 23rd to the 24th he argued with the various bodies whose agreement was essential to so momentous a decision. Their resistance finally overcome, the Soviets made their capitulation known to the Germans in the early morning of the 24th. Lenin's realism in this, the greatest crisis of his career as ruler in Russia, had saved the Soviet regime from the destruction to which the excited bravado of his followers would almost certainly have consigned it.

Trotsky, not unnaturally, yielded his position as chief negotiator in connection with the decision, and virtually gave over the office of Commissar for Foreign Affairs. (He was not formally replaced until three weeks later.) On the evening of the 24th a new Soviet delegation, which included Sokolnikov, Karakhan, and Chicherin, left for Brest-Litovsk to sign the new terms. Delayed by wartime conditions, the delegation did not arrive until February 27. There were new last-minute demands by the Turks, for recovery of the areas lost to Russia at the Congress of Berlin in 1878. These demands having been accepted, the peace was finally signed on the afternoon of Sunday, March 3.

The final German terms to which the Soviet emissaries were forced to set their signatures, in March 1918, have frequently been represented as outrageously onerous. Considering that this settlement came after three long years of warfare for the outbreak of which the Russian government shared at least a considerable measure of responsibility, and that Russia was in effect a defeated power, and considering also that the Soviet government had proved unreceptive to earlier and milder proposals, it is difficult to find justification for so extreme a view. No actual reparations were demanded. The new border in northeastern Europe was considerably more favorable to Russia, from the standpoint of the territory left under Moscow's control, than that which was later actually established with Allied support after Germany's final defeat and which came to be regarded by the western world as normal throughout the entire period from 1920 to 1938. It is true that the Germans had no thought of conceding real self-determination to the peoples of the areas they were detaching from Russia; but neither, for that matter, did the Bol-

sheviki themselves. The requirement that the Petrograd regime recognize the separate German-Ukrainian Treaty was indeed a bitter
blow, and the subsequent German occupation of the Ukraine an even
more bitter one; but again the injustice was mitigated by the fact that
Bolshevik authority in the Ukraine had been brief and tenuous, and
the right of the Bolshevik leaders to speak for the Ukraine at all was
questionable. The requirement that the Soviet government should
cease anti-German propaganda, though the cruelest cut of all to the
communist mind, was not an unreasonable demand to be imposed
on a defeated country at the crucial moment in a great world war.
The commercial provisions, while naturally not unfavorable to Germany, do not appear unduly severe when compared with those imposed in the other peace settlements that were to follow. To this it
must be added that the Soviet government entered upon the arrangement with a total absence of good faith, determined to violate and
evade it to the absolute limit of German patience—a circumstance
of which the Germans could scarcely have been ignorant and which
they reciprocated, incidentally, with a comparable (if less ostentatious) cynicism.

The news of all these events, fortified by a stupendous volume of
rumor and speculation, had created by the end of February a state
of the highest uneasiness in Petrograd. The German advance from
February 18–24 had brought the German troops roughly to the future eastern frontier of Estonia and Latvia. Their northern outpost,
at Narva, was only a hundred miles from Petrograd. The Russian
capital could easily be occupied by the Germans within a space of
two or three days, should they decide on such a step. In the light of
these circumstances, a general flight from the city began. On March
6 the decision was taken to move the seat of the Soviet government
to Moscow. The move began at once, and the most important offices
were reopened in Moscow by the middle of March.

Meanwhile, there still remained the question of the ratification of
the treaty. For this, the Congress of Soviets, the highest governmental
body under the new structure of power, was summoned to convene
in Moscow on March 12. Its opening was delayed for two days, in
circumstances which will be discussed below. Ratification was finally
voted on March 16. German ratification ensued six days later.

❖

Brest-Litovsk and the Americans

The United States government had no occasion to react officially to the unfolding of events at Brest-Litovsk. One of the parties to the negotiations was a government with which the United States was at war. The other was a regime which the United States had not recognized. In neither case was the United States government under any obligation to concede any international validity to the actions taken, nor did it at any time do so. It had been careful not to have any part in the matter itself, and had not even replied to the appeals and communications from the Bolshevik leaders.

In his speech of January 8, the President did indeed take cognizance of the fact that German-Soviet talks had taken place (he was under the erroneous impression that they had been broken off); but he did so only to stress the insincerity of the German position and the sinisterness of German motives. After resumption of the negotiations, on January 9, the President appears to have made only two public references to the Brest talks.

The first of these was in a message delivered to Congress on February 11, by way of rebuttal to the German Premier, Hertling, and the Austrian Foreign Minister, Czernin, both of whom had made public replies to Wilson's Fourteen Points speech. Wilson himself was unhappy, in retrospect, about this message, and it has largely faded from historical memory.

In his February 11 message the President voiced discontent with the Brest talks only because of their bilateral nature, which ill fitted his own dream of a general peace settlement. The idea of making such a statement had been discussed by the President with Colonel House on January 29. "We have tentatively decided," House wrote in his diary that day,

to answer the Hertling and Czernin speeches in this way: In reply to Hertling's assertion that differences between Russia and Germany must be settled between the two, and questions between France and Germany should be settled in like manner, we will call attention to the fact that this is the old diplomacy which has brought the world into such difficulties, and if carried to its logical conclusion Germany and the rest of the world cannot object if England and the United States should conclude between themselves treaties by which the balance of the world would be excluded from their raw materials.[3]

[3] Baker, Vol. vii, *op.cit.*, p. 505. This passage seems to reflect a certain misunderstanding of the Brest settlement. There was nothing in the German terms at Brest-Litovsk which implied any monopolization of Russian raw materials by the two

Accordingly, in his message to Congress on February 11, the President charged Hertling with confirming "the unfortunate impression made by what we had learned of the Conferences at Brest-Litovsk," and went on to explain:

. . . He will discuss with no one but the representatives of Russia what disposition shall be made of the peoples and the lands of the Baltic provinces; . . .

. . . those problems . . . cannot be discussed separately and in corners. None of them constitutes a private or separate interest from which the opinion of the world may be shut out. Whatever affects the peace affects mankind, and nothing settled by armed force, if settled wrong, is settled at all. . . .[4]

The second public utterance of the President with respect to the Brest-Litovsk negotiations was embraced in the message he despatched on March 11 to the Congress of Soviets, who were assembled in Moscow to debate the ratification of the Brest-Litovsk Treaty. The circumstances of this appeal will be discussed in a later chapter. It is enough to note here that there is some question as to whether it was really the Brest-Litovsk pact that the President had mainly in mind when he despatched his message. It is true that those who first agitated in Washington for the despatch of such a message were animated by the hope that it might delay or prevent ratification of the Brest-Litovsk Treaty. It became, in fact, the official Soviet interpretation that such was the purpose of the message.[5] But House's letter to Wilson, urging him to send such a message, makes it quite clear that the aim, as *he* saw it, was to influence the French, British, and Japanese in their attitude toward the proposed Siberian intervention and that the hope of affecting ratification of the treaty, if it was present at all, was quite secondary. The message itself did not specifically mention the treaty, and referred only to

powers after the war. The commercial agreement which comprised part of the treaty applied only to the duration of the war, during which time Germany was, in any case, in a state of the sharpest and most ruthless sort of economic warfare vis-à-vis the western powers.

[4] *Foreign Relations, 1918,* Supplement 1, *The World War, op.cit.,* pp. 109–110.

[5] In a footnote to the second Soviet edition (1930) of *Lenin's Complete Works,* Vol. XXII, *op.cit.,* p. 619, the editors said: "By this message Wilson hoped to restrain Soviet Russia from a separate peace with Germany, to draw her to the side of the Entente, and to utilize the Russian army for diverting German forces from the western front."

. . . this moment when the German power has been thrust in to interrupt and turn back the whole struggle for freedom and substitute the wishes of Germany for the purposes of the people of Russia.[6]

The President never clarified his own feelings on this point. But it would seem unlikely, on the face of it, that he should have entertained any great hope that his statement would affect the proceedings of the Soviet Congress. He was painfully aware that his Fourteen Points speech, a much more powerful statement, had failed to have any appreciable effect of this sort. And his admission, in the text of the statement, that the United States was not in a position to bring aid to the Russian people can hardly have been calculated to give the Soviet delegates the feeling that they had any hopeful alternative to ratification.

Beyond this there is little to reveal the state of the President's mind with regard to the happenings at Brest-Litovsk. One finds no record of his ever having discussed the matter with anyone, beyond what has been noted above. On the day after the despatch of the message to the Soviet Congress there was a Cabinet meeting, but Secretary of the Interior Lane complained afterward that nothing had been talked of

. . . that would interest a nation, a family, or a child. No talk of Russia or Japan.[7]

The private papers of the Secretary of State are equally uninformative. The memorandum which the Secretary submitted to the President on January 2 dealt extensively with the attitude of the Bolshevik leaders toward international affairs and with the problem of recognition and communication with that regime in the light of this attitude, but contained no reference to the talks with the Germans. In the draft of a public statement which the Secretary proposed to make on Russian policy and which was submitted to the President on January 10 (the President rejected the idea), there is again no mention of the Brest-Litovsk talks. Although the Secretary's desk diary indicates many discussions of the Siberian situation with various State Department officials and foreign diplomats, as well as with Colonel House and the President over this period, it does not indicate any discussions of the Brest-Litovsk conversations as such.

[6] The text of Wilson's message to the Soviet Congress will be found in *Foreign Relations, 1918, Russia*, Vol. I, *op.cit.*, pp. 395–396.

[7] Baker, *op.cit.*, Vol. VIII, p. 20.

Some further light on the position of the United States government in this respect is shed by communications despatched by the Department of State to other governments on the day following the despatch of the President's message to the Soviet Congress. Both of these communications must surely have had the President's approval.

To the French government, which had suggested that the United States join in "an immediate and most energetic protest," by the Allied governments "against the recently concluded Russo-German peace," Acting Secretary Polk replied that

. . . owing to the present rapidly changing and uncertain conditions in Russia, the Government of the United States, although according in principle with the views outlined in the suggested protest, would prefer, for the present, to abstain from joining in the publication of the proposed declaration.[8]

To the Japanese, who had inquired informally whether, in the light of the Brest-Litovsk Treaty, Russia was now to be treated as an enemy, neutral, or pitied friend, the Acting Secretary caused the following oral reply to be made:

In the view of the Government of the United States recent events have in no way altered the relations and obligations of this Government towards Russia. It does not feel justified in regarding Russia either as a neutral or as an enemy, but continues to regard it as an ally. There is, in fact, no Russian government to deal with. The so-called Soviet government upon which Germany has just forced, or tried to force, peace was never recognized by the Government of the United States as even a government *de facto*. None of its acts, therefore, need be officially recognized by this Government; and the Government of the United States feels that it is of the utmost importance, as affecting the whole public opinion of the world and giving proof of the utter good faith of all the governments associated against Germany, that we should continue to treat the Russians as in all respects our friends and allies against the common enemy.[9]

In the light of this evidence, one can only conclude the following as to the official American attitude toward the events of January and February 1918 which led to a separate German-Soviet peace. The President, who in matters of this sort was the real source of American statesmanship, naturally viewed the whole course of developments with the greatest displeasure. This attitude arose less

[8] *Foreign Relations, 1918, Russia*, Vol. I, *op.cit.*, p. 435.
[9] *Ibid.*, p. 397.

from the specific clauses of the Brest-Litovsk settlement, which interested him little, than from the fact that the settlement represented a bilateral arrangement, anticipating the general peace conference to which he aspired. Worst of all, by sanctioning a species of German intervention into Russian affairs, the settlement provided precedent and further incentive for a similar Japanese incursion in the Russian Far East: a prospect embarrassing and displeasing to American statesmanship. A separate Russian-German treaty thus actually prejudiced the prospects for a general Wilsonian peace both in Asia and in Europe.

On the other hand, Wilson saw nothing he could do about the situation, beyond the effort he had already made to inspire the Russian people with confidence in his own altruism and good will and his attachment to the principle of a liberal and just peace, negotiated openly and multilaterally and sanctioned by the acceptance of the entire international community. If, as seemed regrettably to be the case, the Russian people failed to respond to this assurance by returning with new enthusiasm to the prosecution of the war against Germany, this was because German military might, abetted by the short-sighted Bolsheviki, was "turning back" the struggle of the Russian people for freedom and repressing the true popular will. There was therefore nothing to do but to prosecute with vigor and determination the war in the west, hoping that the defeat of Germany would at last release those liberal impulses in the Russian people to which he, Wilson, would know how to appeal. In the meantime, one would simply refuse to take official cognizance of events which, however real, were uncongenial to the purposes of American statesmanship.

There is no evidence that the President ever discussed the Brest-Litovsk situation at any length with his Secretary of State, but such evidences of his attitude as reached the State Department can scarcely have been disagreeable or surprising to Lansing. The thought of any dealings with the Bolsheviki had been repulsive to him from the start. For him, too, there was no answer but to wait. But he must, one suspects, have longed for a greater intimacy with the President in these great problems of foreign policy—an intimacy comparable, at least, to that enjoyed by Colonel House.

It was thus in a glum and frustrated silence, though not in disagreement, that the two senior American statesmen, each in his office on opposite sides of the narrow street dividing the White House from the State, War and Navy Building, privately noted—but refused officially to recognize—the final stages of that process by which the Russia of World War I was transformed from a failing ally of the Entente into a sullen and disarmed bystander, partially occupied by the enemy, ruled by a group of men who loathed both warring camps with every fiber of their fanatical and profoundly political natures.

CHAPTER XIX

WASHINGTON AND THE PROBLEM

OF "CONTACTS"

. . . all the Embassies have established some sort of backstairs contact. It is inevitable that they should. . . . One hundred and one things must be attended to. . . . Some frank working agreement ought to have been arrived at at the very start. . . .—Arthur Bullard, January 1918

As THE consolidation of the Soviet power became evident with the suppression of the Constituent Assembly and the collapse of resistance in the Ukraine and the Caucasus; as, at the same time, alarm over the trend of the Brest-Litovsk talks caused the Bolshevik leaders to take a somewhat more cautious and conciliatory attitude toward the Allied diplomats in Petrograd; as the favor of the Smolny Institute became more and more essential to the physical safety and well-being of the western residents in the capital; and as, finally, the thought gained currency in some Allied circles that a greater intimacy with the Soviet leaders might make it possible to influence their attitude and that of Russia generally vis-à-vis the Germans— as these developments took their course, the question of informal contact with the Soviet authorities took on a growing and even urgent importance. For the Americans, such informal contact was largely a question of Raymond Robins; for it was tacitly conceded that if such contact was to be encouraged at all, Robins, with his extra-governmental position, his passionate interest, and his established connections, was the most suitable channel. But the position of the Ambassador was also involved; the question became whether, in the event informal contact were to be further encouraged, he should remain at Petrograd at all: whether he was temperamentally suited to the task, whether his presence would not be an impediment to any closer relationship with the Soviet authorities.

Before we turn again, then, to the experiences of the Americans in Petrograd, it might be well to have a closer look at the development of thought in official Washington with respect to these matters, and particularly at the somewhat enigmatic position of Robins himself.

We have already noted in an earlier chapter the circumstances by which Robins, in the last days of 1917, obtained the approval of the Ambassador and his principals in the Red Cross in Washington to the continuation of his contacts with the Soviet leaders. It will be recalled that the State Department had delicately avoided committing itself on this question.

The arrival of Colonel William Boyce Thompson in England, in the middle of December, and his later appearance in Washington, had further strengthened Robins' position. Thompson had told Lloyd George that the Revolution had come to stay and that the Russians were out of the war for fair. The Allies, he had said, would have to choose, so far as Russia was concerned, between a hostile or a friendly neutral. He had favored working for a friendly one and urged the desirability of the western powers having informal contact with the Soviet leaders. Lloyd George had been impressed. In the Anglo-French discussions at Paris on December 22–23, it had accordingly been decided that each country would "at once get into relations with the Bolsheviki through unofficial agents, each country as seems best to it." (See Chapter IX.) This had resulted in a decision on the part of the British government to despatch to Petrograd an unofficial agent whose specific function it was to be to maintain informal contact with the Bolshevik authorities. The man selected for this delicate task was Mr. R. H. Bruce Lockhart, who, despite his relatively youthful age of thirty years, had been Acting British Consul General in Moscow throughout much of the earlier period of the war and had, in fact, only recently (September 1917) returned from Russia. Mr. Lockhart's new assignment, as unofficial agent in Petrograd, was made known to the Soviet authorities through unofficial Bolshevik agents then in London. As a *quid pro quo,* the leading agent, Mr. Maxim Litvinov, had his status in London regularized, in the sense that he was allowed to remain for the time and to represent the Soviet government there in a similar unofficial capacity.

[379]

Washington and the Problem of "Contacts"

Lockhart left England early in January. A British cruiser took him as far as Norway. Proceeding across Sweden and Finland, he arrived in Petrograd on Monday, January 28, just too late to call on Trotsky before his second departure for Brest-Litovsk.

The fact that the British had now made regular arrangements for the exercise in Petrograd of the sort of function Robins himself had been exercising on an *ad hoc* basis, lent a new aura of legitimacy to Robins' peculiar position and activity. He was naturally intensely interested in Lockhart's mission, though initially somewhat mistrustful. On the occasion of their first encounter he set about to clarify the situation with a bluntness and emotional fervor that must have startled the unprepared young Britisher. Robins' account of this encounter, as related to the Senatorial investigating committee a year later, is worth noting at this point:

. . . A member from the British Embassy came to me and said: "There is an Englishman here, just arrived, who has been in Russia, and comes back with some relation to the Government who wants to have you for dinner." I said: "No; I am too busy. I have wasted all of my time at the British Embassy that I expect to waste there. I know your policy; it is perfectly definite, and I won't go." Then he told me some more things about the special power that this man had, and I said, "I will go"; and I went, and we had dinner, and after dinner we separated together, and he began talking close, and I began fencing. I suppose his guard was up, and so was mine. It was a difficult situation. All sorts of criticism had run across one line and another. I did not know his purposes. Finally in the twist of the things, he showed me his credentials, and it was perfectly clear that he then represented the power of the British Government in the situation.

I said to him: "Now, I want to ask you a question, Mr. Lockhart. Are you free? You can not handle this Russian story from Downing Street or anywhere else. It is too much of an original outdoor situation that you have got to shift from day to day. No man knows it 12 hours ahead. All I am trying to do is something that is useful and right while we do it, and not prejudge the future." He said: "I am absolutely free." I then took him over to my office, and we opened up everything I had of a documentary nature, and went through the whole situation with all its light and shadow and everything else that I knew. The next morning we went out to Smolny. He had a great advantage because he speaks and knows the Russian language and had many lines of Russian contact. When we were coming back we talked together, and I said to him,

Washington and the Problem of "Contacts"

". . . I think I am right in my judgment and am acting on it. The life of the mission and my own life and supplies here are being dealt with on that basis, on the basis that this thing is an international social revolutionary situation opposed to all governments, but more opposed right now, because it is nearer to them, to the German militarists than anything else, and that we can do business with them on that basis. . . ."

Having thus put his cards on the table, Robins proceeded to warn Lockhart about the ghost of William B. Thompson that still dogged his own footsteps.

. . . "You will hear it said that I am the representative of Wall Street; that I am the servant of William B. Thompson to get Altai copper for him; that I have already got 500,000 acres of the best timber land in Russia for myself; that I have already copped off the Trans-Siberian Railway; that they have given me a monopoly of the platinum of Russia; that this explains my working with the soviet. . . . You will hear that talk. Now, I do not think it is true, Commissioner, but let us assume it is true. Let us assume that I am here to capture Russia for Wall Street and American business men. Let us assume that you are a British wolf and I am an American wolf, and that when this war is over we are going to eat each other up for the Russian market; let us do so in perfectly frank, man fashion, but let us assume at the same time that we are fairly intelligent wolves, and that we know that if we do not hunt together in this hour the German wolf will eat us both up, and then let us go to work."

Robins further recounted to the Senators how Lockhart, after checking around among other members of the diplomatic corps and the foreign colony, returned and admitted to Robins that "they sing a different song," as Robins had predicted "they" would. But, Lockhart said: "I believe your song, and I am going to work that way." Robins concluded, triumphantly:

And from that time until I left Russia, the British high commissioner and myself were in absolute agreement on every move. We ate breakfast together every morning.[1]

The French, it may be noted, already had at that time a similar channel of backdoor liaison with the Bolsheviki in the person of one of the junior officers of the French Military Mission in Petrograd, Captain Jacques Sadoul. Sadoul, a lawyer by profession and a socialist

[1] *Bolshevik Propaganda, Hearings . . . , op.cit.,* pp. 801–803.

[381]

by persuasion, enjoyed his military title and status by virtue of having been called up, as a reserve officer, to wartime military service. During the early period of the war he had functioned as an aid to Albert Thomas, the French socialist leader, then serving as Minister of Munitions in the French government. Thomas, like a number of other leading western European socialists, had visited Russia during the period of the Provisional Government, and continued to take a keen interest in the course of the Russian Revolution. It was presumably at his instance that Sadoul was despatched to Russia and assigned as a member of the French Military Mission there, in September 1917. During the ensuing year, until his own break with the French government at the time of the final withdrawal of the Allied representatives from Soviet-controlled territory in the early fall of 1918 (he eventually identified himself completely with the communist cause), Sadoul addressed to Albert Thomas and other friends in France a series of interesting letters, recounting his experiences and setting forth in great detail his interpretation of the political developments in Russia and his recommendations for French and Allied policy at that time. These letters, published in France in 1920 under the title *Notes sur la Révolution Bolchevique,* constitute one of the major primary sources on the contacts between the Bolshevik leaders and western governments, as well as western socialist circles, during the first months of Bolshevik rule.

Sadoul's position was generally analogous to the positions of both Robins and Lockhart, but it was closer to that of Robins. Sadoul, like Robins, had a passionate and sympathetic interest in the course of the Revolution; an admiration for the Soviet leaders, particularly Trotsky; a contempt for the regular diplomatic representatives of the Allies, whose position and duties he understood very poorly; and a burning disgust for the policies of the western governments vis-à-vis the new Soviet regime. Lockhart, for his part, was more cosmopolitan and tolerant in his tastes and views, and certainly less impassioned ideologically. Sadoul's peculiar position, like that of Robins, arose largely through the force of circumstances. It was not "planned," and did not have the sanction of a clear governmental decision, as did that of Lockhart. Sadoul shared with Robins the inconvenience of the presence in Petrograd of a full-fledged ambassador of his own government. Lockhart was mercifully relieved of this burden. In Sadoul's case the awkwardness of his position was aggravated by the fact that the French Ambassador, M. Joseph Noulens, former Minister of War, was a man of considerable distinction in France, whose self-esteem in no wise lagged behind his elevated public and social position. Since Sadoul's status, like that of Robins, had never been regularized by his own government, his political activities constituted a difficult problem for his Ambassador and led to jealousies and confusions within the French establishment which were no less painful than those occasioned for the Americans by Robins and his proclivities. The French Ambassador found himself torn, much as Francis was, between resentment of Sadoul's irregular diplomatic contacts and an irrepressible curiosity to hear the interesting news that Sadoul invariably brought back from his interviews with Soviet officials. Like Francis, Ambassador Noulens was also not averse to availing himself of the services of a useful intermediary when it came to protecting the security of the members of the French Mission.

Despite this similarity in their positions, Robins and Sadoul do not appear to have been drawn to each other or to have maintained any intimate sort of liaison. This may have been due in part to linguistic differences, but only in part. Each was an egoist, preoccupied with his own experiences. Each was inclined to attach to his own contacts with the Soviet authorities an overriding importance, not to be rivalled by any other.

Both Lockhart and Sadoul were naturally interested in Robins—Lockhart more, Sadoul less—and their respective descriptions of him are worth noting. Let us take Lockhart first:

. . . Robins, who was a philanthropist and a humanitarian rather than a politician, was a wonderful orator. His conversation, like Mr. Churchill's, was always a monologue, but it was never dull, and his gift of allegory was as remarkable as it was original. With his black hair and his acquiline features, he had a most striking appearance. He was an Indian chief with a Bible for his tomahawk. He had been a leading figure in Roosevelt's "Bull Moose" campaign for the American Presidency in 1912. Although a rich man himself, he was an anti-capitalist. Yet, in spite of his sympathies for the under-dog, he was a worshipper of great men. Hitherto, his two heroes had been Roosevelt and Cecil Rhodes. Now Lenin had captured his imagination. Strangely enough, Lenin was amused by the hero-worship, and of all foreigners Robins was the only man whom Lenin was always willing to see and who ever succeeded in imposing his own personality on the unemotional Bolshevik leader.

[383]

Washington and the Problem of "Contacts"

In a less official sense Robins had a similar mission to my own. He was the intermediary between the Bolsheviks and the American Government and had set himself the task of persuading President Wilson to recognize the Soviet régime. He knew no Russian and very little about Russia. But in Gumberg, a Russo-American Jew, who for years had been in close touch with the Bolshevik movement, he had an assistant who supplied him with the necessary knowledge and arguments. And Gumberg's arguments in Robins' mouth made a most convincing case for recognition. I liked Robins. For the next four months we were to be in daily and almost hourly contact.[2]

Sadoul, like Lockhart, was struck with the fact of Robins' Progressive-Republican background. "Some time ago," he wrote from Petrograd on March 13, 1918,

. . . the Americans placed in contact with Trotsky Colonel Robins, a politician well known in the United States who once ran for Vice President on the Roosevelt ticket.[3] He is, I think, a very intelligent and able man, who can be useful. Unfortunately, it seems to me that he inspires only a qualified degree of confidence in Trotsky, first of all because he represents the most imperialistic and capitalistic party in the United States, but also because he shows himself too completely the diplomat, too "slick" in his discussions with the Minister for Foreign Affairs. For some weeks now British interests have been similarly represented at the Smolny by a consular agent, Lockhart, who appears to certain of the Bolsheviks to be more serious and more open than Robins. Unfortunately, Lockhart, like Robins, is a good bourgeois. What we need are allied socialists, and left-wing socialists at that.[4]

Robins himself, in his later statements, spoke of Lockhart with respect and enthusiasm but scarcely mentioned Sadoul.

If the first effect of Colonel Thompson's return was to provide Robins with an English counterpart, the second was to strengthen the growing feeling in a number of Washington quarters that Robins' dealings with the Soviet government ought to be regularized and encouraged. We have already seen that the theme of the memorandum Thompson presented to the President was "recognition is not necessary; contact is." He surely urged this same conviction on the

[2] R. H. Bruce Lockhart, *British Agent*, G. P. Putnam's Sons, New York, 1933, p. 220.

[3] In this, Sadoul was mistaken. Robins had run for Senator in Illinois on the Progressive-Republican ticket.

[4] Sadoul, *op.cit.*, p. 262.

Secretary of State and on his many influential friends in Washington.

Whether Thompson's representations were the decisive factor in changing the Washington climate, or whether urgings from other sources also played a part, is not apparent. Bullard was at that time urging, with characteristic eloquence and realism, the same view. "The whole arrangement is absurd," he wrote,

all the Embassies have established some sort of backstairs contact. It is inevitable that they should . . . one hundred and one things must be attended to. . . . Some frank working agreement ought to have been arrived at at the very start. Instructions should be sent, telling the Embassy and the Missions to go the limit in cooperation with the present *de facto* government—short of formal recognition. I am not enough of an international lawyer to know the correct phraseology. . . . I urge this greater measure of cooperation with the Bolsheviki with my eyes wide open to the fact that they will not be grateful. We will not be able to secure any cordial treatment or any lessening of the habitual line of insults and vituperation. [But] as long as we are at war with Germany . . . we find our interests in common—some of our interests.[5]

In any case, at the beginning of the new year, just after Thompson's appearance in Washington, interest was renewed there in the subject of "contacts." On January 1, 1918, two days after Thompson's call on the Secretary, the President wrote to Lansing:

. . . I am writing to ask your opinion as to the most feasible and least objectionable way (if there is any) in which we could establish similar unofficial relations with the Bolscheviki. W.W.[6]

On the same day, apparently quite by accident, the official in charge of Russian affairs in the State Department, Mr. Basil Miles, submitted to the Secretary of State a set of recommendations which constituted in essence a complete acceptance of the Robins-Judson-Thompson line. Among these recommendations were proposals that Ambassador Francis be withdrawn, leaving the Embassy in the hands of a chargé d'affaires; that the Red Cross Mission be further developed under Robins' leadership; and that similar rapid develop-

---

[5] Bullard MSS, *op.cit.*, Box 13. While these passages were contained in a memorandum dated simply "January 1918," the paper was evidently the result of long preparation, and we must assume that Bullard was urging these ideas on Colonel House even earlier.

[6] National Archives, State Department File 861.00/936½. What the "similar" refers to is not clear from this communication.

ment be made in the Petrograd propaganda bureau of the Committee on Public Information (Sisson's shop). Finally, Miles suggested, somewhat cautiously, that full power should be given to the American Military Attaché at Petrograd.

. . . to take such measures as he deems necessary regarding the Russian situation as a purely military problem; the Military Attaché in Rumania to be under his direction. . . .

He pointed out that the withdrawal of the Ambassador would facilitate such a measure; in fact, he added, the suggestion "does not apply if Ambassador be not withdrawn." [7] Miles was evidently ignorant of the fact that an order recalling General Judson was being despatched by the War Department, with the President's personal approval, that very day—a circumstance which reveals something of the secrecy and lack of coordination with which personnel matters of this sort, engaging the President's personal attention, were handled.

The following day, Miles issued a further memorandum reporting an interview he had just had with Mr. William T. Ellis, former Petrograd correspondent for the *New York Evening Post,* who had left Russia only four days before Colonel Thompson. Ellis strongly supported Robins personally, as well as Robins' belief in the need for contact with the Soviet authorities, and criticized the Allied governments, and the American government in particular, for its irritating and provocative behavior toward the Bolsheviki. Mr. Ellis, incidentally, had called on the Secretary on December 28, and had presumably expressed similar views to him.[8]

There is no direct evidence of the reception given to these recommendations by the Secretary or of what reply was given to the President's inquiry of January 1. Both Wilson and Lansing had evidently been unfavorably affected by the tactlessness and overzealousness of Francis' unruly associates. The feelings of both had been reflected in the sharp reprimand to Sisson for his injudicious meddling and his attempt to bemuse the Department of State's code room, and in the recall of General Judson for his visit to Trotsky. The Secretary

[7] National Archives, State Department File 861.00/935½.
[8] The recommendations for Francis' removal were further supported, about this time, by Mr. William Franklin Sands, former head of the prisoner-of-war section of the Petrograd Embassy, who had had friction with Francis in that work and who also appeared in the Department of State in January.

had just despatched to the Ambassador, on December 29, a message approving the course he had followed (see Chapter XI) and telling him to carry on as before. Neither President nor Secretary was a man to reverse hastily a decision taken with all due deliberation.

Finally, so far as the recommendation for withdrawal of the Ambassador is concerned, we are at liberty to suppose that the most telling criticism Thompson had to levy against the Ambassador was the deCram affair, over which excitement was at its peak just at the time when he, Thompson, had left Petrograd. After talking with Thompson on December 31, the Secretary did, in fact, send Francis a private message, to be deciphered only by himself, pointing out that no reply had been received to his last message about Madame deCram. The Secretary expressed the hope that the Ambassador had "taken action," adding that the matter had become the subject of gossip in Washington and that there was danger of scandal. To this bait the old gentleman now rose with fiery eloquence. In a reply drafted on January 2, in the midst of the excitements of the turn of the year, Francis asserted that the Secretary's message "throws new light on the subject and reveals correctness of my suspicion that I am being attacked by professed friends." Previously, he explained, he had supposed the Secretary's anxiety was occasioned by the suspicion of espionage that rested on Madame deCram. Now that the true cause of the Secretary's fears had been revealed (this last message from the Secretary had contained no reference to the charge of espionage),

. . . permit me to say that anyone charging improper relations with party named is a willful liar and anybody who repeats such rumors after hearing of this denial by myself is also willful liar. Person named has not visited Embassy since receipt your 1844, November 14, 4 p.m. If this statement does not put an end to gossip I shall demand names of those responsible therefor. Do not be concerned about my personal reputation which needs no guardian other than myself; your interest however is appreciated. Both you and I have matters of too much import on our minds and hands to be annoyed or diverted by such personal gossip.[9]

This vigorous reply from Francis left the President and Secretary no choice but to take his word or to remove him at once; and it is clear which way the decision went. When a reply finally went to Francis, at the end of January, from Counselor Polk, oil was poured

[9] National Archives, State Department File 123F84/59b.60.

on the troubled waters. The Ambassador, Polk said, had misunderstood the reasons for the Secretary's warning. The Secretary was glad to learn that the lady's visits to the Embassy had ceased.

Thus the question of removing the Ambassador was settled. In the general question of recognition, there was also no change. The *New York Times* correspondent on January 4 reported the State Department as stating "definitely" that "no real decision" had been made on recognition; that no *de facto* recognition had been extended to the Bolsheviki; and that the United States government was maintaining "an interesting attitude of impartiality as between the contending factions." [10] But this still did not settle the delicate problem of "contacts."

After the turn of the year, in the light of Davison's approval of Red Cross contacts with the Soviet authorities and of the more favorable climate both in the Embassy and in the Department of State, Robins developed with great intensity his contacts at the Smolny Institute—particularly (but not exclusively) with Trotsky. These relations seem to have been accompanied by equally intensive relations between Gumberg and several subordinate Soviet officials.

We shall have occasion to observe in another chapter some of the substantive results of these contacts. It is enough to note at this point that while the individual visits or discussions were rarely reported to Washington in detail, the fact that they were taking place was repeatedly brought to the attention of the State Department. It will be recalled that on January 2 Francis had reported, in connection with the excitement over the first Brest-Litovsk crisis: ". . . Am using Robins in these matters. Do you understand and approve?" [11] To this question, he never received a reply, but it is interesting to note that a few days later, in apprising him of the delivery of the Fourteen Points speech and informing him that the text of the speech was being cabled to him, the Department instructed him to have this text "conveyed unofficially to Trotsky," a directive which

[10] *New York Times*, January 5, 1918. A few days later, the government's commitment to the non-recognition policy was deepened by a letter from the Secretary of the Treasury to Lansing, pointing out that recognition of "any government in Russia other than the Provisional Government" would involve thorny financial problems, due to the need for repayment of the credits which had been extended to the Provisional Government. (Francis MSS, *op.cit.*, Folder, January 11–22, 1918; Letter from McAdoo to Lansing, January 17, 1918.)

[11] *Foreign Relations, 1918, Russia*, Vol. I, *op.cit.*, p. 422.

makes it plain that the Department of State was well aware of the facilities he enjoyed for such communication.

On January 9 Francis referred again in a telegram to the Department to "Robins, who visits Smolny often. . . ." [12]

On January 23, in transmitting one of Robins' messages, Francis added:

. . . Robins, Sisson, especially former, in close relations with Smolny. Robins visits me daily, gives desired information concerning Bolshevik policies, therefore cannot refuse his requests to send cipher cables to Davison, Thompson, . . . [13]

The message to which this remark had reference was, as we shall have occasion to note in the next chapter, of a highly political nature; in fact, it was a solemn recommendation for recognition of the Soviet regime. The fact that Robins was permitted, without remonstrance from Washington, to send messages to such tenor through Embassy channels is noteworthy in itself. In other instances, this kind of activity aroused keen displeasure in Washington. Only six weeks earlier, Francis had transmitted without comment a similar message from Jerome Davis of the Y.M.C.A. to his principal, Mr. John R. Mott, General Secretary of the International Committee of that organization, setting forth views and recommendations much less far-reaching than those contained in Robins' messages of January. The Department, on this earlier occasion, transmitted the message to Mott, but did so with manifestations of disapproval so emphatic as to lead one to suspect that the President's own feelings must have been involved. Lansing wrote personally to Mr. Mott, complaining about Davis' recommendations—"so obviously at variance with the announced policy of this Government"—and stating that "any attempt by unauthorized persons to deal with diplomatic questions is fraught with grave danger." Mr. Mott was asked to "counsel your people in Russia to confine themselves to the work which has taken them to that country. . . ." [14] Francis, too, was reprimanded for even transmitting Davis' message. The Department, he was told, "prefers to have recommendations on political situation come from you." [15]

[12] *Ibid.*, p. 336.
[13] *Ibid.*, pp. 356–357.
[14] *Ibid.*, pp. 289–290, letter of December 7, 1917.
[15] *Ibid.*, p. 292, Telegram 1891 to Petrograd, December 8, 1917.

The absence of any such reaction to the transmission of Robins' cables contrasts strangely with the extreme sensitivity in the case of the Y.M.C.A., and is difficult to explain unless there had been some change of heart in Washington during the short space of time or unless Robins was recognized as occupying a very special position.

Some idea of the excellence of Robins' connections with the Smolny Institute is afforded by the fact that on February 7 he was able to write to Francis saying that Lenin had ordered he be given, for Francis' possible use, the unlisted telephone numbers of Lenin, Trotsky, Chicherin, Bonch-Bruyevich (Chief of Chancery for the Soviet of People's Commissars), Dzerzhinski (head of the secret police, from whose office, Robins explained, "all important arrests are made"), Peters (head of the Military-Revolutionary Committee and police commandant, in effect, of Petrograd), and, finally, of the Fortress of St. Peter and St. Paul, the dread place of incarceration for the most dangerous political criminals.[16] This extraordinary communication must have gone far to relieve Francis's apprehensions of personal danger, in the wake of the Constituent Assembly crisis.

In mid-January, the question of contact with the Bolshevik authorities was continuing to worry the President. Lansing sent him the text of a message received from the Chargé d'Affaires in Copenhagen suggesting that one of the Allied nations be commissioned to conduct *de facto* relations with the Bolsheviki on behalf of all of them, and that this nation be the United States. To this the President replied, on January 20,

Here is the ever-recurring question, How shall we deal with the Bolsheviki? This particular suggestion seems to me to have something in it worth considering, and I am writing to ask what your own view is.[17]

There is no record of Lansing's reply.

A day or so later the question of unofficial contact with the Soviet

---

[16] Francis MSS, *op.cit.*, folder, February 7–15, 1918, letter from Robins to Francis of February 7, 1918. Peters, incidentally, of whom Robins said that he "speaks English and is a rather special friend of mine," was later to become notorious as the leading agent of Soviet terror in the early period. The connection with Peters went, surely, through Gumberg. Peters, a Latvian by origin, had lived long years in London and had returned to Russia, like Gumberg, after the February Revolution. Two photographs of the period show him standing with Robins, Gumberg, and other persons on the occasion of some Bolshevik ceremony or demonstration.

[17] Baker, Vol. VII, *op.cit.*, p. 483.

government was again agitated by Thompson's activities, and this time quite effectively. Having failed to reach the President directly, Thompson had set about to mobilize influential support for his views both in private circles and among his acquaintances in the Senate. Aware, no doubt, that the President would not be likely to respond to stimuli from the Republican side, Thompson appears to have succeeded in interesting Senator Robert L. Owen, of Oklahoma, in his ideas.[18] Senator Owen was a Democrat, a member, in fact, of the Democratic National Committee, and also of the Banking and Currency Committee of the Senate. He was an admirer of Robins, and plainly lent a friendly ear to Thompson's views. On January 23, the Senator called on the President and presented to him a letter reading in part as follows:

After consulting with a number of gentlemen relative to the conditions in Russia, and the need for additional action looking to influencing favorable Russian opinion, particularly Mr. H. L. Carpenter, Mr. Raymond V. Ingersoll, and Mr. H. F. Meserve, I wish to suggest to you the urgent importance—

First, of recognizing the Bolsheviki Government as *de facto*, or at least establish intercourse with them whereby they may feel that the Government of the United States has a friendly and sympathetic feeling for the present *de facto* Government in Russia. I think this suggestion is the more justified because the Constitutional Assembly, through which it was hoped a stable government might succeed, has not been able to maintain itself for lack of force. . . .[19]

Further passages of the letter urged immediate relief shipments to Petrograd and the establishment of a courier service among the American establishments in Russia. Finally, reflecting the unshakeable American faith that the mere presence of large numbers of other Americans—regardless of such trivia as personal qualifications, linguistic attainment, or official function—is bound to be helpful in any troublesome foreign situation, the Senator urged the appointment of a great many consular officers to various Russian cities "as a means of contact with Russian opinion and with the Russian people."

[18] Williams, *Russian American Relations, op.cit.,* p. 128, states that Owen had broken party ranks to support Robins' candidacy for Senator in 1912. Mr. Williams, basing his view on material in the Wilson and Thompson papers, likewise indicates that Owen's approach to the President reflected Thompson's influence.

[19] National Archives, State Department File 861.00/986.

Washington and the Problem of "Contacts"

The President sent Owen's letter on to Lansing, with the comment:

Senator Owen is very earnest about the enclosed suggestions and I have promised him that I would discuss them with you. I would be very much obliged if you would consider them pending our next conference.[20]

The Secretary, however, was at that time ill with the grippe. The President's note was passed on to Miles, who again drafted a memorandum opposing *de facto* recognition but reiterating the belief that the time had come "to deal unofficially with all parties in Russia, including the Bolsheviki." [21] To Owen's other suggestions he was favorable.

This memorandum, or some reply based upon it, was evidently submitted to the President in response to his inquiry. But the reply failed to satisfy him. His mind apparently turned to the activities of Robins in Petrograd, and he went back at the Secretary, on February 4, quite understandably, with further question:

As I understand it, our official representative in Petrograd *is* keeping in touch with the Bolshevik leaders informally. Am I not right? [22]

The Secretary once more forwarded the inquiry to Miles, who returned the following day with what seems, in the light of the written record, a somewhat casuistical reply. Its tenor was summed up by Miles himself, at the outset, as follows:

The President understands "our official representative in Petrograd is keeping in touch with the Bolshevik leaders informally"; this understanding does not appear to be in keeping with the facts.[23]

In explanation of this conclusion, Miles went on to say:

The Department has steadily refused to allow the Embassy or Consulate at Petrograd to enter into any relations with the Bolshevik authorities, either formally or informally.

Recently the Ambassador has used Robins, head of the Red Cross commission, as a channel of information; also to hand Lenin copy of the President's address to Congress. To save the Roumanian Minister the Ambassador went straight to Lenine and again to the Foreign Office.

[20] *Ibid.*, 861.00/1048½.
[21] *Loc.cit.*
[22] *Ibid.*, 861.01/14½.
[23] *Loc.cit.*

[392]

Washington and the Problem of "Contacts"

All observers returning from Russia seem agreed that the unbending adherence to this policy of holding absolutely aloof has been aggravating; has even tended to throw the Bolsheviks into the hands of the Germans.

After listing various instructions sent to Francis in the matter of recognition of, and dealings with, the Soviet authorities, Miles then concluded:

The Ambassador has interpreted these instructions as barring him from establishing any understanding with the Bolshevik leaders. Even Robins is understood to have been used as a channel of information, not of communication or to keep in touch.

The Secretary's reply to the President's inquiry was not despatched until February 9. There is no record of its nature. If it was based on Miles's memo, as it appears to have been, it certainly gave the President an inadequate picture of the intensity of Robins' contacts with the Soviet authorities and the degree to which he was regarded by them as an unofficial spokesman of the United States government. After all, at the very time the reply to the President was in preparation, a message was received from Francis in which he, while still opposing full recognition, explained that he was "endeavoring to establish gradually working relations with view to influencing Soviet Government." [24]

The upshot of the exchange between the President and the Secretary was evidently favorable both to Miles's urgings and to the Ambassador's inclinations, for on February 14 the Department wired Francis that it

approves your course and desires you gradually to keep in somewhat closer and informal touch with Bolshevik authorities using such channels as will avoid any official recognition. . . . Department's previous instructions are modified to this extent.[25]

To this instruction, Francis drafted a reply which he never sent but which is none the less revealing of his thought. Its tenor will have a familiar ring for all those who have borne responsibility in later years for the cultivation of diplomatic contact with Soviet officials. "Thanks," Francis wrote,

[24] *Foreign Relations, 1918, Russia,* Vol. I, *op.cit.,* p. 369, Petrograd telegram 2336, February 5, 10 p.m.
[25] *Ibid.,* p. 381, Telegram 2065 to Petrograd, February 14, 5 p.m.

for your 2065. Am gradually establishing closer working relations with Soviet but they render such task difficult by impugning American motives and sending propagandists there while inconsistently objecting to my even seeking information concerning Russian conditions and I have told Robins to so inform Trotsky.[26]

Thus on the eve of the final Brest-Litovsk crisis, with its drastic consequences for the official American colony in Petrograd, the United States government finally relaxed its rigid formal ban on contact between the Embassy at Petrograd and the Soviet authorities and sanctioned the intercourse which, by virtue of Robins' enthusiasm and the force of circumstances, had already been instituted and actively cultivated.

While Robins was never mentioned in the Department's messages on the subject of contacts (unless the message of December 29, telling him to go forward with the Red Cross business, be taken as an exception), it is clear that both the Department of State and the President were very much aware of his position and activities in Petrograd and were consulted by the Red Cross in all matters having to do with his continued presence in Russia. At some time shortly prior to February 20 the chairman of the American National Red Cross, Mr. Henry P. Davison, hit upon the idea of calling Robins out from Russia for a conference in Paris.[27] With whom Robins was to confer in Paris and for what purpose, and whether he was later to return to Russia, is unclear. Davison first took the matter up with Counselor Polk at the State Department, who apparently did not object, and then prepared a telegram to Robins, giving him the necessary orders. Before the message could be despatched, however, Davison received a visit from General Judson, who had just arrived in Washington on his return from Petrograd and who brought to Davison a cordial letter of introduction from Robins. Judson strongly urged against removing Robins from Petrograd at that moment. Impressed with Judson's arguments, Davison decided to abandon his proposal. Again, he solicited Polk's agreement to the change in plans; and when this agreement had been received, he wrote a letter to the President

[26] Francis MSS, *op.cit.,* folder for February 16–28, 1918.

[27] Mr. Davison would have found it most difficult, in actuality, to realize this scheme; the development of the Finnish Civil War made transit through Finland extremely precarious and difficult for Americans at just this time. Few succeeded in completing the journey, and did so only with long delays.

(February 21) recounting the entire course of the matter and apprising him of the final decision. He received, the following day, a written reply from the President, in which the latter agreed that there was probably nothing better to do "for the present until things clear up in that unhappy country." [28]

This completes the résumé of the fragmentary evidence available in the written record as to Robins' position in Petrograd during the winter of 1918. This evidence, reinforced by later references in Francis' telegrams to Robins' wiring directly to the "War College" (a term generally used at that time to refer to the War College Division of the General Staff) [29] and by the impressions of other Americans who were in Russia at that time, all suggest that Robins considered himself the bearer of responsibilities, inherited from Thompson and tacitly approved by the leaders of government in Washington, that went beyond anything the official record indicates. It is plain that these responsibilities, if they existed, were never made known to Francis, who was left to guess at them from the circumstances. Whatever the arrangement may have been, however, it was no more than a "one-way" process, in the sense that Robins' reports were received and noted in Washington, but no instructions or communications of a political nature were ever sent to him nor was he used at any time by his principals in Washington as a channel of communication to the Soviet leaders in political questions. His role was evidently conceived as that of an informal listening post, providing senior statesmen in Washington with an independent source of information that could be used to supplement the regular channels of information, and maintaining for this purpose contacts which could, in case of necessity, be wholly disavowed by the United States government.

It is only too clear that Robins, in exercising this function with the energy and flamboyance peculiar to his temperament, was bound to appear in Petrograd as "the real American Ambassador" and thus to diminish Francis' prestige and his potential usefulness in the formal

---

[28] This exchange of communications between Davison and the President will be found in the Archives of the American National Red Cross in Washington, in the file of correspondence dealing with Robins. No regular file of reports from Robins to his principals in the Red Cross is available in these Washington Archives.

[29] National Archives, State Department File 123 Su61/121, 1918 (Francis' telegram 112, April 20, 1918, from Vologda).

ambassadorial position. But this was a heyday of irregular diplomacy, with Colonel House in the lead; and there is no evidence that the effect on Francis of Robins' activities caused any appreciable concern in a capital distinctly careless of the institutions of traditional diplomacy.

CHAPTER XX

COMPLICATIONS IN PETROGRAD

IN the immediately preceding chapter, we have had occasion to note the background of the curious relationship between the Red Cross Mission and the Soviet authorities. It becomes necessary in the present chapter to describe three incidents, occurring in the last part of January, that illustrate the results to which these irregular arrangements could, and did, lead.

❖

The Diamandi incident was the occasion for tense and exhaustive discussions among Bullard, Sisson, Gumberg, Robins, and Judson about American policy toward the Bolsheviki. These discussions were stimulated, at least in part, by a message Francis had sent on January 9. After some initial gossip about a visit with the French Ambassador and other subjects, he had added, as though in afterthought:

. . . Beginning to think separate peace improbable perhaps impossible and inclined to recommend simultaneous recognition of Finland, Ukraine, Siberia, perhaps Don Cossacks Province and Soviet as *de facto* government of Petrograd, Moscow and vicinity. Understand another government organizing at Archangel and comprising territory equal to England, France and Germany combined. More later.[1]

It is clear that what Francis had in mind was the idea, which gained considerable currency in Allied (particularly British) circles throughout January, of a simultaneous *de facto* recognition of all the various authorities commanding sizeable portions of Russian territory—a proposal to which the United States government, for

---

[1] *Foreign Relations, 1918, Russia*, Vol. I, *op.cit.*, p. 336, from Francis' telegram 2212, January 9, 1918.

its part, never warmed. It was also clear that he did *not* intend this rather casual remark as a deliberate and formal recommendation for recognition of the new regime in the capital to which he was accredited.

Nevertheless, shortly thereafter (about January 15) Robins delivered to the Embassy Chancery, for transmission to William B. Thompson in Washington, a message of highly political import which included the following sentence:

... The Ambassador has recommended simultaneous recognition of Bolshevik, Ukraine, and present Finnish authorities. . . .[2]

Worried by Robins' misinterpretation of his message and the possible effect in Washington, but evidently reluctant to open the issue of Robins' right to such communication with his principals in the United States, the Ambassador held up Robins' message for some days while he pondered the problem.

A few days later, on Sunday, January 20, Trotsky returned from Brest-Litovsk. Robins saw him the day after his return. They discussed, in addition to regular Red Cross business, the Rumanian affair, the position of the American Ambassador, General Judson's forthcoming departure, and also—no doubt—the general possibility of American recognition. Robins told Trotsky that General Judson was leaving in order to make arrangements for American assistance in case the Brest-Litovsk negotiations should break down.[3]

On the following evening a further conference took place between Robins, Gumberg, Sisson, and Bullard; as a result, another and much more far-reaching recommendation was drawn up, again in the form of a message to Thompson, to be signed by Robins. It began with a statement that the Soviet government was now stronger than ever before. The authority and power of the government had been enhanced, it was said, by the dissolution of the Constituent Assembly, an event which had been generally accepted throughout Russia as final, and which had not produced any important protests. Had the Assembly not been suppressed, a separate peace—it was indicated—would probably have been concluded at once by the S-R's. The Bol-

[2] National Archives, Petrograd Embassy 800 File, *op.cit.*
[3] There is a note of this visit in Robin's pocket diary (Robins MSS, *op.cit.*). Judson, in his memorandum of June 18, 1919 to the Secretary of War, told of Robins' "clever" attempt to persuade Lenin and Trotsky that his (Judson's) departure was for the purpose stated (Judson MSS, *op.cit.*).

sheviki, on the other hand, would stick by their guns and refuse to abandon their principles in their negotiations with the Germans. In these circumstances, the message concluded:

... Cannot too strongly urge importance of prompt recognition of Bolshevik authority and immediate establishment of *modus vivendi*, making possible generous and sympathetic cooperation. Sisson approves this text and requests you show this cable to Creel.[4]

An interesting light is shed on the origin of this message by a private communication which Gumberg felt called upon to send, a year or two later, to his brother, the Bolshevik Commissar Zorin. In this letter Gumberg, defending his dealings with Sisson, proudly cited Sisson's concurrence in the abovementioned message as the result of his (Gumberg's) influence during the two days before it was despatched. (Gumberg provided his brother with a text of the message to illustrate his point.[5])

This message was taken to the Embassy by Robins the following day (January 23), with a request that it be despatched to Washington through Embassy channels, like the message of the previous week. Francis agreed, rather unhappily, to this, and sent both messages—this and the earlier one—to Washington. He told the Department, in an accompanying message, that since Robins was supplying him daily with information concerning Bolshevik policies, he could not refuse his requests that he send such cables, but he trusted that the Secretary of State would not construe his transmission of them as indicating approval of their content. He went on to explain that he had held up the January 15 telegram, waiting for a chance to discuss with Robins the clause about the Ambassador's recommending recognition of the Bolsheviki—"as he misunderstood me if so thought." He had only meant, he said, to suggest the "establishment of working relations" with the various *de facto* governments. As for the second telegram, he was specifically *not* in agreement, he said, with the contention of Robins and Sisson that the Soviet government was daily growing stronger.[6]

---

[4] Cumming & Pettit, *op.cit.*, pp. 76–77.

[5] The Gumberg MSS (*op.cit.*) contains a document in Gumberg's handwriting which was evidently the first draft of this communication. It is undated, but its content shows that it was written very shortly after Gumberg learned of John Reed's testimony before the Senate Subcommittee on the Judiciary in February 1919.

[6] *Foreign Relations, 1918, Russia,* Vol. I, *op.cit.*, pp. 356–357, Francis' telegram 2274, January 23, 1918.

The Robins-Sisson recommendation of January 23 had no visible effect on the United States government. But whether the same could be said of the Soviet government is doubtful.

The Soviet authorities were of course fully informed of the recommendation. Not only was it despatched in code through Embassy channels, but Robins took the precaution of sending it independently through commercial channels as well.[7] It is not likely that the Soviet authorities, already engaged in intensive and evidently quite successful efforts to break the ciphers of the Allied missions, would miss a highly important political message of this nature, sent *en clair* through commercial channels.

On the following evening, January 24, Trotsky sent for Robins and informed him that he was leaving at once for Brest-Litovsk. He then asked, according to Robins' report to the Ambassador, whether Robins knew what the United States government proposed to do about recognition. Robins said he did not know. Trotsky asked whether the Ambassador knew. Robins "thought not but would ask." (One cannot help but wonder whether Trotsky's query was not, in reality, "Have you had any reply to the message you sent yesterday?")

Robins went to see the Ambassador the next day, January 25, and apprised him of Trotsky's departure and of his query about recognition. "I told him," Francis reported to Washington, that "I had no instructions concerning recognition and was satisfied Government would not act other than in concert with Allies."[8]

The following morning Robins learned (apparently to his genuine surprise) that Trotsky had not departed and was still carrying on in the Smolny Institute.[9] Evidently worried by the misapprehension about Trotsky's whereabouts under which Francis was now laboring, Robins reported to him that Trotsky "had returned." The Ambassador was unconvinced. "I doubt," he wired to Washington, "whether he started. Possibly this was scheme to force our hand."[10]

---

[7] It is difficult to see how, in doing this, Robins could have failed to jeopardize the official code. The message through the Embassy was evidently in confidential code, for the copy in the National Archives is a paraphrase; the text sent through the commercial channels was presumably a true reading.

[8] *Foreign Relations, 1918, Russia*, Vol. I, *op.cit.*, pp. 358–359, telegram 2292, January 26, 1918.

[9] Robins' pocket diary for January 26 begins with the entry "Trotsky still here." (Robins MSS, *op.cit.*)

[10] *Foreign Relations, 1918, Russia*, Vol. I, *op.cit.*, pp. 358–359, from Francis' telegram 2292, January 26.

Complications in Petrograd

The Ambassador's suspicion was shrewd. There is, in fact, not the slightest evidence that Trotsky left Petrograd at any time between January 23 and 25, or that he ever intended to.

The incident suggests that Trotsky deliberately deceived Robins about his own plans and movements in the hopes of panicking the Americans into a hasty gesture of recognition. He was at that time just facing the task of reporting to the Third All-Russian Congress of Soviets on the alarming course of the Brest talks. He was also engaged in bitter arguments behind the scenes over the policy to be adopted in the face of German demands, and was attempting to dissuade his colleagues, despite the obvious military danger, from accepting the German terms. In both connections, a promise—or even a semi-promise—of American recognition and assistance would have been a distinct boon to his position.

Whether the eager encouragement given Trotsky by Robins (and also by Sadoul) was an important factor in causing him to hold out stubbornly against acceptance of the German conditions is something we shall probably never know. Judson, in a letter to Robins a year later,[11] said that he would like to recommend Robins for the Distinguished Service Medal on the grounds that

... you (almost entirely *you*) with a little bit of sympathy rather than assistance from a few others, were able to delay the signing of the Brest-Litovsk Treaty . . . so long . . . that the Germans' spring drives lacked manpower and failed, by just the margin you created, to win the war for the Hun.

❖

The second incident relates to Robins' understanding of the reasons for the removal from the Soviet Foreign Office of one of its initial senior officials, Zalkind. When Trotsky left for Brest-Litovsk in the early days of January, Chicherin (who was soon to serve as his regular deputy and later to replace him) was not yet back from England, where he had been residing at the time of the Bolshevik Revolution and had then been detained by the British authorities. It was Zalkind who functioned as Trotsky's deputy until Chicherin's return at the end of the month; and it was with him, therefore, that Robins and Gumberg were obliged to deal during Trotsky's absence in the middle of the month.

Zalkind, allegedly a nephew of Trotsky, had the reputation in

[11] Gumberg MSS, *op.cit.*, Judson to Robins, March 12, 1919.

western circles of being a nervous and irrascible man, of violent anti-western sentiments. None of the foreigners appear to have been personally drawn to him in any way. In some quarters he was denounced as a likely German agent. On the other hand, a curious unsigned intelligence report, now in the Francis papers,[12] would seem to indicate that Zalkind had been, intentionally or otherwise, the main source of Allied knowledge about Soviet "black chamber" proceedings.

In any case, relations between Zalkind and Robins were not good in the latter part of January. It will be recalled that it was Zalkind who was identified in the governmental communiqué as the official who received the mysterious telephone message from the American Embassy on which the release of the Rumanian Minister, Diamandi, was justified. The authors of this message can surely not have intended it to be splashed out at once in the newspapers, as was actually done; and one is constrained to suspect that some of the friction between the Red Cross Mission and Zalkind may have arisen from this incident.[13] Even after Diamandi's release, it was with Zalkind, again, that Robins and Sadoul were obliged to negotiate in the vain effort to avert his expulsion.

It was just at this time that a decision was taken by the Bolshevik leaders to remove Zalkind from his post in the Foreign Office and to send him abroad. This decision was touched off by the receipt in Petrograd, at the end of January, of reports to the effect that serious strikes and disorders had broken out in Germany and that the country was on the verge of revolution. Tending, as they so frequently did, to overrate the seriousness of political unrest in Europe, and anxious to do everything in their power to promote such unrest, the Soviet authorities hit upon the idea of sending to western Europe a number of their top-flight political operators. Zalkind, Kamenev, Petrov, Lozovski, and Kollontai were all originally mentioned in this connection.[14] The decision to send Zalkind on such a mission

---

[12] Francis MSS, *op.cit.,* document dated February 15, 1918.

[13] It is perhaps not by chance that in the Gumberg MSS, *op.cit.,* the translation of the governmental communiqué concerning the American telephone message in the Diamandi case was clipped to a similar translation of the announcement of Zalkind's departure from the Foreign Office.

[14] See Zalkind's own account, in an article published in 1927 in the official magazine of the People's Commissariat for Foreign Affairs (*Mezhdunarodnaya Zhizn,* No. 10, 1927) entitled "NKID v 1917-om godu (The Narkomindel in 1917)": "In the middle of January 1918 [this referred to the Old Style date] the first reports

had evidently been taken by January 30 at the latest. Sadoul mentions it in a letter written that day to his friend Albert Thomas.[15]

It should be noted that Chicherin was by this time back in Russia, after his release from imprisonment in England, and was available to take over the Foreign Office during Trotsky's absence at Brest-Litovsk. He assumed his position as Trotsky's deputy, officially, on January 29. Thus Zalkind was fully available for reassignment.

Just in these same days an incident occurred which aroused particular irritation against Zalkind among the Americans. On January 11 the participants of an anarchist meeting at the Mikhailov Artillery School in Petrograd had passed a fairly violent resolution about the Mooney-Berkman cases. It was stated in this resolution that

. . . if measures are not taken to save the lives of our comrades in America, then we, the revolutionary workers and soldiers of the city of Petrograd, will take energetic measures in the line of demonstration before the American Embassy.[16]

This resolution was sent to the Soviet Foreign Office by the anarchists. On January 26 Zalkind passed this mildly menacing resolution on to the American Embassy with a simple transmitting note, in which he said nothing about taking any measures to protect the Embassy against the suggested danger, and expressed no regrets or apologies. The Ambassador, angered by what appeared to him a deliberate threat and affront on the part of the Soviet government, asked Robins to remonstrate at Smolny.

Someone, most probably Gumberg alone, saw Lenin about the matter on January 29. Robins came to the Embassy later that day and reported that Lenin, on learning of Zalkind's action, had been highly incensed, had removed Zalkind from his position, and had

---

were received of large scale unrest among workers and sailors in the countries of the Central Powers. . . . It was decided on our part to send Comrade Kamenev to France and me to Switzerland in order to confront the Entente countries with the reality of the socialist revolution in Russia."

Similarly, John Reed later recounted: "I was present in the Commissariat of Foreign Affairs one January morning at 3 o'clock when news of the great German strikes arrived. Immediately all was hilarious excitement. Commissars were to be sent all over Europe immediately." (Pamphlet by Reed about the Sisson documents, published in late 1918 by the Liberator Publishing Co., New York. A copy of this pamphlet is in the Sisson Documents File, National Archives.)

[15] Sadoul, *op.cit.*, pp. 215–216.

[16] National Archives, Petrograd Embassy 800 File, *op.cit.* A text of this resolution in the Francis MSS, *op.cit.*, shows it to be dated December 29, old style, which is January 11, new style.

appointed Chicherin in his place.[17] Robins had also evidently derived the impression that Lenin had promised to make Zalkind apologize.

An hour or so later, the Embassy received a visit from a young man (one M. Skossireff) who was not known to the Chancery but who held himself out as a representative of the Secretary of the People's Commissariat for Foreign Affairs. He told Secretary of Embassy Bailey that an anarchist demonstration against the Embassy had been planned for that evening but that the Soviet government had given orders that it be broken up. The connection with the Zalkind incident was made clear by the fact that the young man requested an acknowledgment in writing of Zalkind's earlier note transmitting the anarchist threat.

The visit was at once reported to Robins, who correctly spotted it as a shabby bit of Foreign Office face-saving. He got Bailey to make a memorandum of the incident. This memo, he later said,

. . . was taken out and laid in front of Lenin after midnight that night and we said, "This is the way your Foreign Office has followed your instructions to apologize." The next morning the *Izvestiya* carried the line that Zalkind had been removed as Assistant Commissar for Foreign Affairs.[18]

It is unlikely that Robins' intercession in the matter of the anarchist petition had any appreciable relation to Zalkind's removal, although Lenin, who was not lacking a sense of humor in such matters, may have enjoyed letting Robins conclude that it did. The decision to send Zalkind to western Europe had, as we have seen, already been taken at the time this incident occurred, and for utterly unrelated reasons. Zalkind, in his memoirs, failed to connect the two events in any way. Nor does his amused account of the anarchist incident indicate that the latter episode was taken at all seriously at the Smolny Institute. He sent the petition to the Ambassador, Zalkind relates, because he thought it necessary to warn him against any eventuality.

. . . But the old Ambassador became mortally frightened and appealed to Lenin for help. This was promised; but at the same time I caught hell about it from Vladimir Ilyich [Lenin]: "Don't go scaring the ambassadors," he said, "for nothing at all." [19]

[17] *Foreign Relations, 1918, Russia,* Vol. I, *op.cit.,* p. 363, Telegram 2310, January 31, 7 p.m.
[18] *Bolshevik Propaganda, Hearings . . . , op.cit.,* p. 822.
[19] Zalkind, "KNID v 1917-om godu (The Narkomindel in 1917)," *op.cit.*

Despite these circumstances, of which he was evidently ignorant, Robins gained the impression that Zalkind had been dropped in response to his remonstrances. He was evidently immensely impressed and heartened by this development, which he interpreted not only as a diplomatic triumph for himself but as conclusive proof of Lenin's loyalty and good faith in his dealings with those of the Allied representatives who were prepared to deal loyally with him.

❖

The third of the incidents to be noted here relates to the strange attempt by the Soviet authorities to appoint John Reed a Soviet consular representative in New York.

On January 29 Francis received from Chicherin, of whose status as a Foreign Office official he had had no previous notification, a handwritten note conveying the astonishing news "that the Russian Consul in New York, Mr. Oustinoff, has been dismissed and that Citizen John Reed has been appointed Consul of the Russian Republic in New York." [20]

In explaining the background of this appointment, Reed's biographer, Granville Hicks, writes that Reed

. . . had asked that he might be made a courier, as Louise Bryant had been, so that his notes and papers would be safe, and Trotsky had thereupon proposed the consulship. Meeting Arno Dosch-Fleurot, a newspaper man, Reed expressed his joy in the indignation the appointment would arouse. There was some serious discussion, in the course of which Dosch-Fleurot predicted that Reed would be arrested. "Perhaps it's the best thing I can do to advance the cause," Reed said. Then, with a grin, he hitched up his trousers and said, "When I am consul I suppose I shall have to marry people. I hate the marriage ceremony. I shall simply say to them, 'Proletarians of the world, unite!' " [21]

To appreciate the impact of this notification upon the official Americans, one must recall the circumstances of Reed's relations with them during those recent weeks and months. He had been closely connected with Robins and had, in fact, been on his payroll from time to time, partly, it appears, as a gatherer of information (prior to the November Revolution), and partly as a propagandist. The two men were on good personal terms and enjoyed each other's hospitality. Reed had been at Robins' rooms for Christmas dinner. Robins was

[20] National Archives, Sisson Documents File, *op.cit.*
[21] Hicks, *op.cit.*, p. 295.

one of those who occasionally gathered for long and intense discussion in Reed's cold, Bohemian diggings.

With the official Americans, however, Reed had been in poor standing. He was contemptuous of them, and did nothing to conceal his feelings. More than once, his slighting remarks had got back to their ears and poisoned their feelings toward him, which were already ruffled by his arrant radicalism and pacifism. Francis was suspicious of Reed from the start, believing him responsible for spreading in Petrograd the rumor about the forthcoming execution of Berkman in California, a rumor which Francis termed "as far-fetched a tale as has ever been made the subject of an appeal to a mob" and one which did, indeed, make serious trouble for the Embassy, even to the point of jeopardizing the personal safety of its members.[22]

Even with Gumberg, Reed's relations were not good. The two men had jarred on each other in the early days of the Revolution. They had accused each other of cowardice in connection with a trip they made together to the "front" to check on the success of Kerensky's counteroffensive. It seems likely that in later days Gumberg resented the influence of Reed and some of his liberal American friends on Robins, doubting the adequacy of their understanding of the complicated situation with which Robins was attempting to deal.

In mid-January, preparing to depart for the United States, Reed had called at the American Consulate and asked for visas on the passports of himself and Mrs. Reed (Louise Bryant) to ease their passage through the various Allied and other passport authorities on the long journey home. The Consul, Mr. Tredwell, issued the visas, but warned the government privately that he suspected the Reeds to be "carrying papers."

Shortly thereafter, on January 17, only a few days before Reed's appointment as Consul, Francis received a request from the Department of State to report on Reed's whereabouts and activities. The

[22] In this indignation, Francis was only partially justified. Berkman, it is true, was no martyr. For the serious offense of making public speeches urging young men not to comply with the draft law—this in time of war, and he himself an alien—he served one year in the penitentiary and was then deported, screaming and protesting, to Finland. The rumor that he was to be executed flowed from reports to the effect that he was to be extradited to California for trial together with Mooney—a suggestion that never materialized. But the Mooney case itself was indeed a grievous blot on the record of American justice and one for which the United States could expect to become the object of protests from many quarters.

query was referred to the Counselor of Embassy, Wright. In replying to the Ambassador, Wright enclosed a copy of Reed's remarks at the Congress of Soviets, and added:

[Reed] . . . is on payroll of Bolsheviki, placed there by Robins to write captions for the photographs of the Revolution and possibly other propaganda for use in Germany. Robins thinks good job is keeping him out of mischief (in view of the attached speech, I am not inclined to concur).

Has said nothing inimical to U.S. to Consul except that "liberty of free speech should not be curtailed" and criticized U.S. laws regarding same. To which Consul said he replied that he considered him no patriot and regretted that there were no laws that could keep him out of the U.S.[23]

Francis combined his reply to the Department's inquiry about Reed with the news that Reed had been designated Soviet Consul in New York. In the course of this report, he stated:

[Reed] . . . has been employed by Robins in propaganda work among enemy armies as has Rheinstein also. These two together with Albert Williams, all Americans, stood guard at the Soviet Foreign Office one night at least, when attack was expected, do not know from whom, but think by Social Revolutionaries; no attack was made. The appointee very intimate at Smolny.[24]

Francis added that he understood that the Soviets had tried to make a similar appointment of a British subject, one John McLean, as Consul to Glasgow.

Naturally, the communication about Reed's appointment was received by the Americans, both in Petrograd and in Washington, as a deliberate and frivolous affront. Reed, though referred to in the Soviet note as "Citizen John Reed," was not a Soviet but an American citizen. He was travelling on an American passport and bespeaking the protection of the United States government for his movements. The Soviet authorities were well aware that he was in bad odor with his own government and under indictment by an American court. To accredit such a man as consul to a city in his own country, and that without so much as the courtesy of a prior consultation with United States officials, was an act of such flagrant

[23] National Archives, Petrograd Embassy 800 File, *op.cit.*, Memorandum of January 24, Wright to Francis.
[24] *Ibid.*, Francis telegram 2302, January 30, 1918, 10 p.m.

discourtesy as to indicate that the motives were not serious, as indeed they were not.

This action by the Soviet authorities came, it should be noted, on the day prior to the forwarding of the anarchist threat. Both actions emanated from Trotsky's office. It may very well be that Zalkind was involved in the second, as well as in the first.[25]

Francis and Sisson both, by their own confession, made efforts to bring about the revocation of Reed's appointment. Francis says he acted through Robins. Robins, in turn, indicates that he used Gumberg. Sisson also claims to have used Gumberg for this purpose. Gumberg's representations were successful; the appointment was cancelled at once. All three Americans were happy about the result, and convinced that it was the result of their own individual representations.

Let us note, however, Gumberg's own account, as privately communicated, a little over a year later, to his brother in Russia:

In January 1918 Trotsky appointed Reed Consul General of the Soviet Government in New York. I had grounds for considering this appointment undesirable and told this to Vladimir Il'ich [Lenin]. . . .[26]

In support of his opinion, Gumberg related, he laid before Lenin two documents he had in his possession—both of them written by Reed. One was a proposal Reed had made to Sisson for the publication of an official American Russian-language newspaper in Petrograd. The other was a report by Reed about certain negotiations he had conducted with various Soviet officials concerning future Russian-American commercial relations.[27] Gumberg's account to his brother continued as follows:

Upon reading these documents, V.I. [Lenin] sent them on to Chicherin, who asked Reed about them. Reed confessed that he was their author. The result was that Chicherin told him that he could not become consul of the Soviet Government. (Whether I did well in preventing Reed from becoming Consul, you may judge for yourself or ask other well informed people.)

[25] Robins' pocket diary (Robins MSS, *op.cit.*) for January 30 contains the entry: "Begin war on Z and R . . ."—presumably Zalkind and Reed.
[26] Gumberg MSS, *op.cit.*
[27] *Ibid.*, contains copies of both these documents.

Gumberg said nothing to his brother about the feelings of Francis and Robins.

The two documents Gumberg laid before Lenin were indeed curious ones to flow from the pen of John Reed. The newspaper he was proposing would have had as its purpose the promotion of American private business in Russia, an undertaking for which one would hardly have supposed that Reed would entertain any particular enthusiasm. The second document was addressed to a similar purpose. The content of the documents indicates clearly why they were shocking to Lenin. It was indicated in the first that Reed had reliable information to the effect that the Soviet of People's Commissars would welcome the founding of such a newspaper—an assertion for which it was most unlikely that he had any adequate basis. In the second document, after recounting his negotiations with a number of Bolshevik and Left S-R personalities, Reed stated that

... the Russian Government is prepared to recognize the necessity for the establishment of a restricted capitalistic state within the bounds of the Socialist state. . . .

This, too, must have made Lenin jump.

In the little circle of American leftists in Petrograd to which Reed belonged, Sisson was unquestionably identified from the beginning as an important American intelligence agent, probably with lines leading to very high circles in Washington. Possibly Reed's curious proposals were designed, with tongue in cheek, as a device with which to whet the appetites of American financiers and persuade them that American business had a future in Russia even under Bolshevik power. Whatever the motivation, the effort was clumsy and childish. In this instance, the utter unfamiliarity with governmental realities which burdened Reed's relationships with the representatives of his own country got him in trouble with the Soviet authorities whom he so much admired.

On February 6 Reed left for Sweden and the United States—heartbroken, according to Francis, over the cancellation of his appointment as Consul. The story remains cloudy to the end. Just prior to his departure, Reed paid a farewell call on Sisson, and reproached him with being a cause of his misfortune. Gumberg, on the other hand, told his brother a year later:

. . . Reed knew that I was guilty of his exclusion, as I told him about it myself.

Sisson, like the Ambassador, noted that Reed departed "in a supposedly dejected state of mind." Being less trusting than the Ambassador, however, he looked for the hidden motive. He believed that Reed, by this show of dejection, was trying to lead the Americans into believing that he had lost all facilities for carrying suspect papers out of Russia, and in this way to disarm their suspicions that he was going as a communist courier.

It was indeed a tangled web in which these various children of America, each with the most selfless of convictions, had enmeshed themselves.

A year later, under questioning by the members of a subcommittee of the Committee on the Judiciary of the Senate, Reed was asked what persons he had found in Russia who had formerly been residents of the United States. In answering, he referred among others to "Alexander Gumberg, the man who got the Sisson documents for Sisson." [28] What the Sisson documents were will be related in another chapter. To be identified as the person who delivered them to American officialdom was not calculated to endear anyone to the Soviet authorities. When Reed's assertion was published, it hit Gumberg like a bolt of lightning. It was the direct cause of the long bill of defense he addressed to his Bolshevik brother from which some of the information in this chapter is derived. Reed's statement, Gumberg told his brother, was the result of his intercession with Lenin to spike the consular appointment:

. . . As a revenge . . . he dreamed up about me the fairy tale that I supplied Sisson with his famous documents.

❖

These three incidents have been described not because of their effect on the subsequent course of Soviet-American relations (none of them left any appreciable traces there) but rather for the manner in which they illustrate the infinite possibilities for misunderstanding, confusion, intrigue, and malevolent exploitation that are always present when inexperienced people, whose status is unclarified, are permitted to dabble in the transactions between governments. It was by

[28] *Bolshevik Propaganda, Hearings . . . , op.cit.,* p. 572.

just such dabbling that the initial stages of American-Soviet relations were dominated, and from this that they received their muddy complexity. Out of the resulting confusion grew, in large part, the many myths and controversies by which their memory has been followed.

CHAPTER XXI

THE BREAKUP IN PETROGRAD

FROM the end of January, when the last American diplomatic courier visited Petrograd, travel and communication between Petrograd and the western countries via Finland and Europe became precarious and almost impossible, due to the development of the Finnish civil war. Subsequent to February 1, the Embassy received no further mails via Europe; general telegraphic correspondence was erratic and subject to incalculable delays. Americans who left Petrograd after the end of January, hoping to make their way through Finland to Sweden, found themselves held up in the portion of southern Finland controlled by the Reds, and reached Sweden, after many adventures, only at the end of March. Efforts were made by the Embassy and the State Department to keep in some sort of touch with regard to the torrent of events and the various problems arising out of them, but these efforts were perforce feeble and largely fruitless. From the latter part of January the official American colony in the Russian capital was virtually on its own.

❖

The divergent reactions of Sisson and Robins to Lenin's personality and behavior, on the occasion of their joint visit to Lenin on January 11, seem to have constituted the first serious difference between these two Americans, who had theretofore worked together in apparent intimacy and harmony. Sisson, it will be recalled, recounted in his memoirs how Lenin at one point in the interview referred (smiling and throwing up the palms of his hands to indicate the absurdity of the charge) to the fact that he had been called a German spy. Robins was duly impressed, and accepted the disclaimer as a reference to the obvious. Not so, Sisson. "As I turned over the incidents of the session with Lenin," he recorded in his memoirs,

. . . a lower stratum of my mind began to send its message upward. When it broke through I found myself repeating Lenin's sentence, "Yet I have been called a German spy!" Without incentive from us he had spoken from inner compulsion. We had heard the voice of his brooding. The subject was one he hugged to himself, however unwillingly. . . .

If ever a man had a hard shell it was Lenin. I could not conceive a tenderness of covering. I could imagine, instead, that as a dictator he felt his prestige subject to injury from imputations of servile dealings and that, confronted by two innocents like Robins and me, he had used the chance to get us to proclaim a denial for him. Where Robins saw a sensitive person I saw a calculating one.[1]

Thus Sisson came away from the interview with the suspicion that "the lady had protested too much": that Lenin was perhaps really a German spy after all. This suspicion had much to do with Sisson's later reaction to other experiences that will be recounted below.

Robins, on the other hand, came away from the encounter with a personal admiration for Lenin that he was never to lose. Sisson was quick to note this. "On Robins," he wrote,

. . . the effect was different. Some fire in him was lighted. Lenin, too, must have observed something malleable in him. Mischief came of the contact between the two.[2]

The incident led to altercation and bad feeling. "In a day's time," Sisson wrote, "we were acridly debating Lenin." The day after the interview was recorded in Sisson's diary as the day of the "Robins' grouch." In the weeks that followed, this difference multiplied itself in the interpretations that the two men gave, respectively, to the course of events. The resultant personal strain grew with each new crisis.

On February 2 Robins brought to Sisson a set of documents which had come to him from a source he was unwilling to reveal. These consisted mostly of English translations of what purported to be circulars of the German General Staff, the German Ministry of Finance, the Reichsbank, and other German governmental offices dating from the earlier years of the war (two of them even pre-dating the war). The general tendency of these circulars, if you credited their au-

[1] Sisson, *op.cit.,* p. 214.
[2] *Ibid.,* p. 213.

thenticity at all, was to indicate that the German government had begun even prior to the outbreak of war in 1914 with the implementation of elaborate plans for sabotage and subversion in the Allied countries and that the Bolshevik leaders had served them as paid agents in the implementation of these efforts. There were also a few letters of later date (mostly spring and summer of 1917) between various persons, chiefly people residing in Scandinavia, suggesting (the implications were not very clear) that the Germans had extended financial aid to Lenin and other Soviet leaders in the period just after their return to Russia in 1917. The circulars, it may be said at this point, were rather obvious and clumsy forgeries, the authenticity of which no one seriously attempted to maintain in subsequent years. The letters were more plausible, though not very conclusive.

Robins was inclined to discredit the material, and felt that no further attention should be paid it. Sisson suspected, in fact, that the only reason Robins had produced it at all was a fear that he might be subject to criticism if he withheld it from the attention of the official American representatives. Sisson himself, however, was immediately interested in the documents and felt that by submission to further study either their authenticity or their falseness would be established.

Robins indicated that he had made a tentative appointment that evening to meet the mysterious source of the documents. It was decided that he should keep the appointment, apparently with a view to getting more information about the papers. Whoever the person was, it must have been someone of whom Robins was deeply suspicious. Sisson recounts that some hours later, before leaving to keep the appointment, Robins came dramatically to Sisson's rooms "leaving his keys with me in the contingency that he did not return."[3] He came back for the keys at one o'clock in the morning, Sisson says, "safe and tight-lipped." He had seen his man, he intimated, but had gotten nothing and knew of nothing more to do.[4] According to Sisson's further account, Robins gave him no additional assistance in the study of the documents.

As events were to prove, Robins had no need to be so cautious and mysterious about this affair. Within a day or two the documents were

[3] *Ibid.*, p. 292.
[4] Evidence on Robins' strange expedition is conflicting. His pocket diary for February 3 has the entry: "J.O. at 6 a.m. Curious return and a deep sleep thereafter." (Robins MSS, *op.cit.*)

in wide circulation in Petrograd. A copy, again in English, was delivered on February 4 to Sisson's office on the Gorokhovaya Ulitsa. A Russian copy was found about that time to be in the possession of the dragoman of the American Embassy. Copies soon reached other diplomatic missions. Lockhart mentions that Trotsky had a bundle of them on his desk in Smolny when Lockhart called on him there on February 24. They had been published, earlier that winter, by a Kadet newspaper in the anti-Bolshevik Cossack country, the *Pri-Azovski Krai*. (They may have represented some of the evidence prepared by agents of Pereverzev, Minister of Justice of the Provisional Government, for use against the Bolsheviki at the time of the July disorders, in 1917, but only partially used at that time.)

On the evening of Monday, February 4, Ambassador Francis received a visit from a Russian journalist known to Allied circles as Eugene Semenov. (His real name was Kohn.) He was a correspondent and one of the signing editors of a somewhat lurid evening paper, regarded by many as a scandal sheet: the *Vechernaya Vremya*.[5] Sisson described him as a large man with a black beard and the extreme pallor often seen among Russian urban types. He was presumably either casually acquainted with the Ambassador or known to him through members of the Ambassador's staff.

Semenov produced for the Ambassador's edification a photostat of a document which he claimed had been filched from the files of the Soviet government in the Smolny Institute. It purported to have been written, at Brest-Litovsk, by Joffe, who, it will be recalled, was head of the Soviet delegation in the first stage of the negotiations there and accompanied Trotsky as assistant when the latter went to head the delegation in early January. The letter was dated December 31—presumably the old calendar, which would make it January 13 in the new. The letter, which was fairly long, was addressed primarily, and almost entirely, to the Rumanian situation; but it concluded with a reference to the fact that a certain Wolf Vonigel, who had been

[5] One of the two papers owned by the well-known conservative publicist, Suvorin. The other was the *Novoye Vremya*. The latter was extensively supported by subsidies from the Tsar's government in the last months of its power. Both papers were violently anti-Semitic and anti-German, and took the lead in whipping up anti-German hysteria during the war. For this they evidently received some support from the Russian competitors of German business interests in Russia. Semenov, in addition to his journalistic activities, had been functioning as an agent of the "Provisional Government of the North Caucasus," trying vainly to drum up Allied financial support for that brief and tenuous undertaking.

charged with the command of the Soviet-German agents who were to be sent to the Rumanian front, was also to have responsibility for spying on the "military agents" of the Allied countries. The final sentence read:

... As regards the English and American diplomatic representatives, General Hoffmann has expressed the agreement of the German staff to the measures adopted by Comr. Trotsky and Comr. Lazimiroff with regard to watching over their activity.[6]

Semenov left a copy of this photostat with the Ambassador. The main purpose of his visit was ostensibly to interest the Ambassador in the possibility of obtaining further information of the same sort from the same source. It was of course explained that this was a risky and expensive undertaking and would cost money.

Whether this was Semenov's first visit to Francis and whether this was the only document he showed him on this occasion, is uncertain. In the Francis papers there is a copy of another Russian document, purporting to come from the Soviet files, which suggests, among other things, that Madame deCram was receiving visits from some of the senior officials of the German armistice delegations that were in Petrograd from the end of December to the end of February. Since this document does not appear among the series of documents later sent to Washington, it seems possible that Francis, in order to avoid further embarrassment to the lady and to himself, may have suppressed it and never shown it to anyone. There is, it may be added, every reason to believe that it was spurious, and no reason to believe that Madame deCram ever received any of the German officers.

On the morning after Semenov's visit, the Ambassador summoned Sisson and appealed to him for advice as to what to do with the photostat of the alleged Joffe letter. He appears not to have consulted either the Counselor of Embassy, Mr. Butler Wright, a wise and experienced career officer, or the military officers still available on the Military Mission. Nor did he mention the matter to Robins.

Alone, Sisson and the Ambassador pondered Semenov's document. If genuine, they thought, it was of high importance. After all, General Hoffmann was quoted as having twice hinted to Trotsky of "the necessity of immediately beginning . . . operative actions on the

---

[6] *German-Bolshevik Conspiracy, op.cit.,* p. 20, Document 37a.

western front on a very large scale." The Bolsheviki, furthermore, were shown as collaborating actively in Germany's war effort.

The Ambassador asked Sisson to undertake an investigation of the authenticity of the document, "saying that he was without facilities." [7] Sisson then (not before) told him about the circulars Robins had recently brought him. They decided that all these documents, the circulars and the letter, should be wired to Washington as soon as possible. Some days were apparently required to prepare the voluminous material for transmission. The telegram was finally despatched in sections over a period of three days, from February 10 to 13. This unusual flow of messages must surely have aroused the attention of the Soviet cryptographers, who were engaged at that time, apparently with reasonable success, on the breaking of the rather primitive diplomatic ciphers then in use by the Allied diplomatic missions. We must assume that they had little difficulty in ascertaining, or guessing, the nature of this series of messages.

Francis accompanied the material with a further message saying that he proposed to draw $25,000.00, to use "for objects which I cannot trust to cables." [8] A copy of this telegram was sent in the routine way to the President, who had apparently not yet seen the text of the documents themselves, which were then still in process of transmission. His feelings still smarting from the recollection of Thompson's flamboyant expenditures, Wilson at once remonstrated against such an allotment. Francis' telegram, he wrote to the Secretary of State on February 16,

. . . makes me exceedingly uneasy. Our views and Francis's have not in the least agreed as to the use that should be made of money in Russia and I hope that you will let him know that we cannot (under the terms under which moneys are put at our disposal) accept drafts of this kind. It may be necessary to accept this one (I leave that to your judgment) but this should not be repeated, of that I am clear.[9]

But when the nature of the need was explained to the President, he professed himself satisfied, and the money was granted.

Sisson, meanwhile, had thrown himself with such fervor into in-

[7] Sisson, *op.cit.,* p. 293.

[8] National Archives, Sisson Documents File, *op.cit.;* Telegram 2359, of February 11, 12 p.m.

[9] *Ibid.,* Wilson to Lansing, February 16, 1918. Apparently the President held Francis responsible, quite unjustly, for Thompson's liberal use of his own funds for political purposes.

vestigating the authenticity of the documents that he effectively abandoned, then and there, all connection with his regular propaganda work, never—in fact—to resume it. He immediately got in touch with the heads of the British Secret Service in Petrograd. After overcoming a certain amount of natural initial suspicion on their part, he was able to gain their confidence sufficiently to learn from them that they were in touch with a Russian group who had actually succeeded in tapping the direct telegraph wire between the Soviet delegation at Brest-Litovsk and the Bolshevik headquarters in the Smolny Institute, and were receiving the proceeds of this extraordinary operation. Sisson was shown some of the resulting intercepts. He could not make much out of them, most of them being in code and decipherable only in part, with many confusing garbles; but what he saw was sufficient to convince him of their genuineness (all present evidence would seem to confirm that they were indeed quite genuine). Since the British told Sisson they had the impression that Semenov was connected in some way or other with this same group (later to be known in official documents as the "wire group"), Sisson was naturally confirmed in the impression that Semenov was a reliable person and that his documents were probably genuine. Semenov, for his part, further whetted Sisson's appetite, in the days immediately following the first visit to the Ambassador, by producing two or three other fascinating documents purporting to come from the Smolny files. When, therefore, the Secretary of State, after receiving the first set of documents, replied to Francis on February 18 that he had read them with great interest and trusted that the Ambassador would "make every endeavor to obtain further evidence not only of German intrigue with Bolsheviki but also with members of former government," [10] Sisson's enthusiasm was more than redoubled. He was by this time convinced that he had stumbled on something of vital importance to the American and Allied war effort. From that time on, no other purpose existed for him than to lay his hands on all available documents from this source and to get them to Washington as soon as possible. This was an enthusiasm, it may be noted, which tapped to the deepest roots not only his unquestionable and fiery patriotism, but also his anti-German feelings (violent to the point of blindness), his innate suspiciousness, and his congenital

[10] *Foreign Relations, 1918, Russia,* Vol. I, *op.cit.,* p. 381, from telegram 2074, February 18, 4 p.m.

eagerness, as a good professional journalist, to unearth and bring to public knowledge an important and sensational story.

For the first days after Semenov's initial call at the Embassy, Sisson, still not convinced of Semenov's good faith, remained in the background and let the Ambassador be the point of contact—a curious reversal of the roles more common to governmental usage. From about February 10, however, he began to see Semenov himself and to acquire from him a regular flow of copies of documents supposedly residing in the Smolny files.

The documents were ostensibly of varied sources. The most numerous purported to originate from a special bureau, situated in Petrograd, of the intelligence section of the German "Great General Staff." [11] This agency went by the name of the "Nachrichten-Bureau." The content of these documents consisted for the most part of rather peremptory orders to the Soviet government from a certain "R. Bauer," the ostensible head of the Nachrichten-Bureau.

Another series, not quite so numerous, purported to emanate directly from "Section M/R of the Central Division of the Great General Staff." They were signed by "O. Rausch," who called himself "Chief of the Russian Section of the German General Staff." There was no indication at what geographic point Section M/R and Herr Rausch were supposed to be functioning. In the circumstances, they could hardly have been supposed to be elsewhere than in Petrograd itself. (The stationery on which these letters were printed had Berlin on the letterhead, but in all but one of them this had been crossed out and no other place of origin was given.) These letters, like the one from the purported German intelligence office in the Smolny Institute, bristled with unceremonious orders to the Soviet of People's Commissars and other Soviet authorities to do various things agreeable to German interests.

All of these communications were drawn up and typed in the most excellent Russian. Rausch and his adjutant, as well as Bauer's adjutant, even signed their names in Russian characters. Bauer himself used Latin characters.

Other series of documents purported to emanate from Soviet counter-intelligence agencies at the army headquarters, which was

---

[11] Actually, there was at that time, in the German military organization, no *Grossergeneralstab*. There had been such an entity, prior to the outbreak of the war, and would be one again; but at that time there was not.

still being maintained on the eastern front, or from the Soviet "Commissariat for Combatting the Counter-Revolution and Pogroms."

The general tendency of all the documents was to reveal the Soviet leaders in the Smolny Institute as the paid agents and subordinates of the German General Staff, performing, in particular, various services injurious to Allied interests.

Stimulated by a generous use of American funds, photostats of the documents soon began to flow in a steady stream. Sisson's new preoccupation with their procurement was bound to put further strain on his relations with Robins. It compelled him to be secretive and mysterious about his movements. He apparently abandoned the use of Gumberg as aide and interpreter. All in all, Robins can hardly have failed to become aware that he had been cut off in some way from the confidence of Sisson and the Ambassador. Sisson, on the other hand, resented Robins' refusal to participate in the investigation of the authenticity of the first set of circulars (nothing seems to have been said to Robins about the further documents), and suspected the motives for this lack of interest.

Beyond these personal issues, there was growing disagreement between the two men over the wider questions of policy involved. As Sisson's enthusiasm for the documents increased, together with the depth of his personal commitment to the thesis of their authenticity, his suspicion of the Soviet leaders became highly inflamed. Robins, on the other hand, was utterly incredulous of the authenticity of the documents. ("There were more forged papers . . . in Russia than ever before in human history. . . . I could prove anything by all the documents you want." [12]) He still strongly believed that the best way to get resistance to the Germans in eastern Europe was to treat the Bolsheviki with consideration and hold out to them the promise of aid in case of a breakdown of their negotiations and a resumption of hostilities. Believing this, he considered that to trifle with dubious documents of this nature was simply to play Germany's game. Thus the difference between the two men soon attained that unfortunate combination of the personal and ideological which so often produces the most violent of human antagonisms.

In the late evening of Thursday, February 7, two days after his first meeting with the Ambassador on the Semenov documents, Sisson, according to his own account, made an effort to talk out the growing

[12] *Bolshevik Propaganda, Hearings . . . , op.cit.,* pp. 802–803.

tension with Robins in the intimacy of his own hotel room and in the presence of the philosophic and conciliatory Bullard. Robins, according to this same account (the only one available), responded by walking out abruptly on the conversation. He came in and apologized the following morning for his rudeness, but declined to renew the conversation. The incident had affected him deeply. He described the issue at hand, in his diary, as the "final showdown of power and faith—a crisis in the deeper reaches of our task." [13]

The next days were ones of extreme tension and excitement over the course of the Brest-Litovsk negotiations. It was, it will be recalled, on February 10 that Trotsky made his dramatic announcement of "no war—no peace" and started back to Petrograd. The news of this announcement reached Allied circles in Petrograd on Monday, February 11, and brought to the highest intensity the varying views among the Allied diplomats as to the proper course to be followed toward the Soviet authorities in these difficult and unprecedented conditions. Sadoul and Robins, in particular, had developed a feeling that the entire future of the Russian attitude toward the war, if not the final outcome of the war itself, was at stake. Both men experienced a frantic sense of the urgency of some gesture of understanding and support from the Allied governments. It must not be forgotten that this was the darkest and most crucial winter of the war, when anxieties and the sense of wartime obligation were at their highest pitch, nerves and energies drawn to the utmost level of endurance.

On that Monday, February 11, while Allied circles in Petrograd were buzzing with excitement over Trotsky's defiant gesture and the breaking off of negotiations, Robins, Sisson, Bullard, and Robins' assistant, Thacher, met late at night in Sisson's rooms, together with some of the American correspondents, and hotly debated the significance of this last development. When the correspondents had left, Sisson, in the presence of the other three, made an effort to resume the private discussion to which Robins had recently reacted so violently. Robins "angrily refused." [14] Sisson (we are accepting, throughout, his own account) then said that he would not accept that attitude on Robins' part. At this, Robins, ordering Thacher to accompany him, again rose and left the room.

[13] Robins MSS, *op.cit.*, pocket diary entry for February 7.
[14] Sisson, *op.cit.*, p. 308.

When he had gone, Sisson wrote him a curious little note, facetious, schoolboyish, grotesquely out of accord with what was the genuine tragedy of the occasion, but meant to be conciliatory. "Colonel," it began, "how's your mad?" Robins did not respond. He came to breakfast the following morning (the two men had been accustomed to take their meals in common), but refused to speak. It was the last meal the two men shared. From the moment when that silent breakfast party disbanded, Robins and Sisson never spoke to each other again, either in Petrograd or anywhere else.

There can be no question—everything we know of Robins would support this—that Robins was profoundly stirred by this break with Sisson, not only from the personal standpoint, but also and more importantly from the standpoint of the tremendous issues of policy he felt to be involved. He devoted the remainder of the morning to the elaboration of the schemes for Allied aid which, he was sure, would follow naturally from Trotsky's defiance of the Germans. The work included another visit to Smolny—apparently to Lenin himself.

Lockhart, as it happened, was giving a house-warming luncheon that same day; Robins was to be the chief guest. Lockhart has left us a brilliant word-picture of Robins as he appeared at that luncheon party, three or four hours after his last breakfast with Sisson. Despite its length, this passage is too striking and illuminating not to be included:

During luncheon Robins spoke little, but afterwards, when we were assembled in the smoking-room, his tongue was loosed. Standing by the mantelpiece, his black hair smoothed back with characteristic gesture, he made a moving appeal for Allied support of the Bolsheviks. He began quietly, analysing the various Allied arguments against recognition and demolishing the ridiculous Allied theory that the Bolsheviks were working for a German victory. He drew a touching picture of a helpless people facing with courage and without arms the greatest military machine in history. We had nothing to hope from the demoralised Russian bourgeoisie, who were actually relying on German aid for the restoration of their rights and property. Then he began his eulogy of Trotsky. The Red Leader was "a four kind son of a bitch, but the greatest Jew since Christ. If the German General Staff bought Trotsky, they bought a lemon." As he worked up to his peroration, he became almost indignant over the folly of the Allies in "playing the German game in Russia." Then he stopped dramatically and took a piece of paper from the flap pocket of his uniform. I can see him now. Consciously or not, he had provided himself with an almost perfect setting. Before him a semicircle of stolid Englishmen. Behind him the roaring log-fire, its tongues of flame reflected in weird shadows on the yellow-papered walls. Outside, through the window, the glorious view of the slender spire of Peter and Paul with the great fire-ball of the setting sun casting rays of blood on the snow-clad waters of the Neva. Once again he pushed his hair back with his hand and shook his head like a lion. "Have any of you read this?" he asked. "I found it this morning in one of your newspapers." Then in a low voice, quivering with emotion, he read Major McCrae's poem:

> We are the Dead. Short days ago
> We lived, felt dawn, saw sunset glow,
> Loved and were loved, and now we lie
>   In Flanders Fields.
> Take up our quarrel with the foe:
> To you from failing hands we throw
> The Torch; be yours to hold it high.
> If ye break faith with us who die
> We shall not sleep, though Poppies grow
>   In Flanders Fields.

When he had finished, there was an almost deathly silence. For what seemed an eternity Robins himself turned away and looked out of the window. When, squaring his shoulders, he came back at us. "Boys!" he said. "I guess we're all here for one purpose—to see that the German General Staff don't win this war."

Three quick strides, and he was by my side. He wrung my hand. "Goodbye, Lockhart," he said. Four more strides, and he was gone.

As a dramatic performance Robins' effort was immense. Today, it sounds like emotional hysteria. Doubtless, too, he had rehearsed all his effects before his shaving glass in the morning. But at the moment his words made a deep impression on every one who heard him. There was not a laugh or a smile. . . .[15]

All this took place, as will be recalled, on Tuesday, February 12, the day after the news of the breakdown of the Brest-Litovsk negotiations reached Petrograd. The following morning, Robins went again to see Lenin. Trotsky, still on his way back from Brest-Litovsk, had not yet arrived in the capital. The Germans had not yet reacted to Trotsky's move. Lenin was conscious that Trotsky's dramatic gesture at Brest (to which he had consented only with great re-

---

[15] Lockhart, *op.cit.*, pp. 222-223. For permission to include this remarkable passage, I am indebted to Mr. Lockhart and to his publisher, G. P. Putnam's Sons.

luctance) would bring new and bitter problems of policy. He did not yet know how bitter those problems were to be. He was presumaably eager to explore the extent of Allied readiness to aid, in the event that some sort of resistance to the Germans should become unavoidable.

This was of course by no means the first time the possibility of Allied aid had been discussed with western representatives. We have already noted the exchanges that took place between Robins and Trotsky at the time of the first rumored break in the negotiations, around the beginning of the year. On January 20 Sadoul had written to Thomas:

. . . For almost two months not a week has passed that the Bolsheviki have not requested through me—unofficially, it is true, but sincerely—Allied military aid.[16]

On January 24, Trotsky had intimated to Sadoul, with unparalleled impudence, that the Allies, by their refusal to give aid, would be responsible if Russia were forced to sign a separate peace.[17] "The moment has come," Sadoul quotes Trotsky as saying on that occasion, "for the Allies to make up their minds." The Bolsheviki were reluctant, Sadoul explained in another letter on January 29, to make a formal request in the absence of some encouragement from the Allies, but

. . . on the morrow of the day I give Trotsky official assurance that we are disposed to aid the Soviet Government in the work of military reorganization against Germany and that we will undertake solemnly to refrain from interference in Soviet internal affairs, I shall bring to the Quai Français a request signed by Trotsky, in the name of the People's Commissars.[18]

Similar intimations must have been made to Robins on many occasions.

Prior to mid-February two forms of aid had been envisaged: military assistance in the re-establishment of some sort of regular Russian armed forces, and technical aid in, and supply for, the rehabilitation of the transportation system. For the first, the Soviet leaders looked

[16] Sadoul, *op.cit.,* p. 202.
[17] According to Sadoul (*Ibid.,* p. 204), Trotsky said: "Nous ne voulons pas signer cette paix la, mais que faire? La guerre sainte? Oui, nous la décréterons, mais à quel résultat arriverons-nous? Le moment est venu pour les Alliés de se decider!"
[18] *Ibid.,* p. 212.

primarily to the French, who had a large military mission in Russia. For the second, their thoughts naturally turned to the United States, which not only had the broader productive basis but was also less suspected (and with some reason) of ulterior commercial motives in projects of this sort.

It was apparently this last field which was discussed by Lenin with Robins on February 13. After the discussion Robins at once prepared another long message to Thompson, apparently despatched by the Embassy on the 15th. This message gives a good picture of his thinking as of that date.

He began with an observation which was actually an oblique reference to Sisson's quest for secret documents and which, viewed in retrospect, could not have been more true:

Am convinced by daily consideration and reconsideration of facts and events as they have occurred since you left Russia that Trotsky's astounding answer to Germany at Brest-Litovsk was uninfluenced by any consideration other than the purpose of international Socialism striving for world revolution. Every act of Bolshevik government is consistent with and supports this theory. Contrary theory of German control and influence no longer tenable. . . .[19]

From this, Robins went on to assert that it was to Allied advantage that Bolshevik authority should continue as long as possible. He thought that the Soviet government would not accept peace on German terms, and that the Germans would not press the issue if satisfactory trade relations could be established. The second of these propositions was to be disproved the following day; the first, a fortnight later. In general, the ensuing weeks were to bring the most drastic alterations in the entire situation, but none of these reversals would shake Robins' faith in the recommendations for American aid to which the remainder of the message was addressed.

The Bolshevik authorities had expressed willingness, he went on to say, to deliver to the United States whatever surplus they might have of "metals, oil and other raw material vitally necessary to Germany's continued prosecution of the war" (thus preventing them from falling into German hands) in return for "commodities and supplies of non-military character." In addition, they desired "American assistance and cooperation in railway reorganization." By entering on

[19] Cumming & Pettit, *op.cit.*, pp. 79–80.

such arrangements and giving the Russians assistance and technical advice on economic reorganization, Robins thought the United States might "entirely exclude German commerce during balance of war." He recommended specifically that funds be placed at the disposal of the Commercial Attaché for the purchase of raw materials.[20]

Actually, Francis had already asked for money for preclusive buying, in order to keep surplus supplies from falling into German hands. On February 14, the day before Robins' message was sent, the Department had confirmed in a message to Francis that $1 million had been put at the disposal of the Military Attaché in Petrograd for this purpose. So no reply was called for on this score.

As for the alleged Soviet "request" for American assistance and cooperation in railway reorganization—to which much importance was later attached by Robins and his associates—it was plain that if there were to be any United States assistance in reorganizing the railways, the proper agency would be the Stevens Mission, then waiting in Japan. Stevens was, so far as the Department knew, already busily exploring every practical possibility for cooperation with the Soviet authorities at the Siberian end. But both Stevens and the Consul at Harbin were reporting[21] that collaboration with the Bolshevik authorities was not possible and that any operations going beyond the Chinese Eastern Railway would require a large armed force for the protection of the line. This meant, of course, that the question of technical railway assistance in Siberia proper immediately became caught up with the question of Allied intervention in Siberia and specifically with the British proposal, to be discussed in a later chapter, that the Japanese be requested to occupy the Trans-Siberian Railroad as mandatory for the other Allies. The suggestion wired by Robins was therefore not susceptible of treatment except within the larger and extremely delicate problem of "intervention."

❖

In the ensuing days and weeks, Bolshevik desperation mounted, with the revelation of the implacable determination of the German High Command and the growing evidence that Germany was, as Lenin put it, only "pregnant" with revolution and that parturition

[20] The text of this telegram can also be found in *Bolshevik Propaganda, Hearings . . .* , *op.cit.*, pp. 808–810, with explanations interjected by Robins.

[21] *Foreign Relations, 1918, Russia,* Vol. III, *op.cit.*, pp. 218–221; Harbin telegrams of February 1, 3, and 10, 1918.

was not imminent. As this desperation grew, so did the seriousness with which the Bolshevik leaders were inclined to contemplate the humiliating and distasteful alternative of Allied aid. As the evidences of this seriousness impressed themselves, in their turn, on Robins' consciousness, his own excitement grew: excitement at the thought that here was a real and important opportunity, perhaps even vital to the war effort, and that he, Robins, struggling to overcome the shortsightedness (the "indoor minds," as he put it) of the men around him, was the unique agent through which that historic opportunity would have to be realized if it were to be realized at all. From this time on, he threw himself into the cause of "Allied aid for Russia" with an ardor no less intense than that which Sisson was devoting to the procurement of his documents.

In this way the unfortunate Ambassador found his two most active and high-powered political aides going off in diametrically opposite directions: Sisson convinced that the Bolsheviki were German agents and frantically gathering material with which to prove this to a waiting world; Robins seeing in the Bolshevik leaders the only likely potential source of resistance to Germany and pleading for the Allied aid he was sure would release that potentiality. Between these divergent pressures, on the part of men far younger, more active, better informed, and intellectually more agile than himself, the old Governor vacillated uncomfortably, swayed first by one argument, then by the other, seeing merits in each, yet suspicious—and properly so— of both. Of Robins' telegram of February 15 he said, in a comment to the Department of State:

While I hesitate to endorse unreservedly, it largely coincides with my views, which however likely to change with any alteration of Bolshevik policy.[22]

With respect to Sisson's documents, Francis was equally undecided and unenthusiastic. The documents had been wired to Washington, he explained, at Sisson's instigation, to prove a relationship "which I thought existed from the beginning of the last revolution until my conviction shaken by Robins."[23] He was now satisfied that Lenin and Trotsky had accepted German money; on the other hand, he thought they "may possibly not have been German agents con-

[22] National Archives, State Department File 861.00/1108; Telegram 2371.
[23] *Foreign Relations, 1918, Russia,* Vol. I, *op.cit.,* p. 380; Telegram 2365, February 13, 11 p.m.

tinuously." [24] Thus he continued to maneuver between his two assistants, not daring (as on previous occasions) to restrain either of them, finding it easier to give each his head so far as circumstances permitted, yet endeavoring not to commit himself fully to either's position. His position was summed up in a passage of a message wired to the Department on February 24: "Robins, Sisson estranged, not speaking to each other, but both confidential with me." [25] This message, garbled in transmission, was decoded in Washington to read: ". . . both *condescending* with me"—a Freudian slip of the telegraphic process that could not, in actuality, have been more apt.

In these strained circumstances, it was of particular importance to Robins to gain and retain Lockhart's sympathy and support. Lockhart, so far as can be ascertained, was the first of the British representatives to take an interest in him and to treat him with both personal kindness and deference for his views. Robins was anxious to demonstrate to this new and sympathetic witness that collaboration with the Soviet leaders, based on a reasonable amount of reciprocal good will, was indeed possible. But beyond this, Robins appears to have experienced a real need for a sympathetic and admiring ally. Mere subordinates, apparently, would not do. He had had Judson, but Judson had left. He had had Sisson, but Sisson had become disaffected. It was Lockhart to whom, in this moment of bitter disappointment and concern over Sisson's defection, Robins turned for support and approval. The subconscious connection between the two relationships becomes clear if we recall, first, that the final seal of the break with Sisson was Robins' silence at the breakfast table and his failure to appear for further of these common repasts, and then note the final words of Robins' account to the Senators of his relations with Lockhart:

. . . and from that time in January until I left Russia, the British high commissioner and I were in absolute agreement on every move. *We had breakfast together every morning.*[26]

[24] *Ibid.*, p. 384; Telegram 2400, February 21, 4 p.m.

[25] *Ibid.*, p. 387, presents an abridged text of this telegram (no. 2410) which omits this passage. The full text, as received by the Department, will be found in the Breckinridge Long MSS, Library of Congress. The full text, as drafted by Francis, is in the Francis MSS, *op. cit.*

[26] Italics added. There is no evidence that this statement was literally true—a circumstance which only accentuates its symbolic quality.

This new dependence on Lockhart is, conceivably, the explanation of an otherwise unaccountable incident which took place on that same February 15. On that day Lockhart received, he says in his memoirs, an urgent request from Robins to come to see him. He repaired immediately to Robins' room. Again, we will let him tell the rest of the story:

> ... I found him in a state of great agitation. He had been in conflict with Saalkind, a nephew of Trotsky and then Assistant Commissar for Foreign Affairs. Saalkind had been rude, and the American, who had a promise from Lenin that, whatever happened, a train would always be ready for him at an hour's notice, was determined to exact an apology or to leave the country. When I arrived, he had just finished telephoning to Lenin. He had delivered his ultimatum, and Lenin had promised to give a reply within ten minutes. I waited, while Robins fumed. Then the telephone rang and Robins picked up the receiver. Lenin had capitulated. Saalkind was dismissed from his post. But he was an old member of the Party. Would Robins have any objection if Lenin sent him as a Bolshevik emissary to Berne? Robins smiled grimly. "Thank you, Mr. Lenin," he said. "As I can't send the son of a bitch to hell, 'burn' is the next best thing you can do for him." [27]

The historian can only confess his helplessness before the apparent discrepancy suggested by this account. The incident as described by Lockhart resembles closely, as will readily be seen, Robins' understanding of what, in essence, had actually occurred a fortnight earlier, in the Zalkind incident. While mystery still surrounds Zalkind's movements in the first ten days of February, there is no reason to suppose that he was still in the Foreign Office, or that the question of his removal was still under discussion as late as February 15.[28]

In the light of these facts, one is drawn to the conclusion either that Lockhart made an error in the date (but he draws it from a specific and detailed passage in his diary, including other happenings of that day) or that the phone call was in some way staged for Lockhart's benefit. Robins spoke almost no Russian, so the telephone con-

[27] Lockhart, *op.cit.*, pp. 225–226.
[28] Francis reported on February 4 that Zalkind had "started for Switzerland" (*Foreign Relations, 1918, Russia*, Vol. I, *op.cit.*, p. 368). The Petrograd *Nash Vek* reported, February 5, that "the train with which Zalkind and other members of the delegation left for abroad has not arrived in Torneo." On February 8 Sisson had called at the Foreign Office and had asked Petrov, one of Chicherin's assistants, where Zalkind was and what he was doing. Petrov had been evasive.

versation must certainly have been in English. Yet Lenin had declined, at the time of the Diamandi incident, to use English when
speaking with the diplomatic corps, citing his poor speaking knowledge of the language. Since telephone conversation in an unfamiliar
tongue is notoriously more difficult than face-to-face discussion, it
would seem most implausible that Lenin should have been actually
speaking English with Robins.

Is it conceivable that Robins' conscience might not have objected
to the re-enactment, for Lockhart's benefit, of a scene which had, in
effect, actually taken place somewhat earlier? This would not have
been seriously reprehensible. Such a re-enactment would have been
only in minor degree a deception, since the episode *had,* after all, really
occurred. It must be remembered that only three days before, Robins,
a great showman with an intense love for drama and effect, had produced a deep and unforgettable impression on a startled audience of
phlegmatic Englishmen. Sincere though he was, he cannot have been
unaware of this effect. He was under great emotional stress, after his
break with Sisson, and there must have been a real temptation to
drive home to his British friend the reasons for his confidence in his
own position.

But all of this leads only to conjecture and not to proof. The historian can only leave this curious incident shrouded in the same cur-
tain of doubt and bewilderment that continues to cover so many
other incidents in the lives of the Petrograd Americans through these
stormy winter months.

❖

From the 15th of February, things moved, for the American Embassy in Petrograd, to a rapid and drastic conclusion. It was on Saturday, February 16, that news was received in the Smolny Institute
of the decision of the Germans to resume hostilities. While this shat-
tering development did not become generally known to the public
and to the Allied Embassies until Monday afternoon, the 18th, some
inklings had evidently filtered out to better informed people somewhat earlier.

Sisson recounts that he spent Sunday evening playing bridge with
Governor Francis, the Chinese Ambassador, and Colonel Ruggles.[29]

---

[29] Colonel James A. Ruggles, who became Military Attaché on Judson's departure
in late January.

The Governor, betrayed by his enthusiasm for poker, was a rash bidder, but, as Sisson says, "we let [him] pay in food and drink." (The food shortage was by now really acute in Petrograd, and the days of mid-February represented one of the most difficult periods from this standpoint.) When the bridge game was over, the Chinese Ambassador observed casually that he expected to leave Petrograd soon: telegraphic communication was getting difficult, and he would like to make his report in person. The others did not fail to note the quiet hint. "His lone remark," Sisson says, "left us thoughtful, indeed." [30]

When the news of the German decision was released the following day, it was at once apparent to the Allied diplomats that they were in immediate danger. The Germans, already in Estonia and in Finland, were only a short distance away. They had resumed their advance. Since they were confronted with no serious military opposition, they might easily be in Petrograd within the week. For Allied nationals, departure through Finland had become extremely precarious; Francis, in contrast to some of his Allied colleagues, did not consider it possible at all. Nor was it certain that it was desirable for the Allied representatives to leave Russia entirely. The reaction of the Soviet government to the German attack had still to be tested. In a message despatched late Monday evening Francis indicated that the government might move to Moscow, and he said he thought he would also go there if possible. [31]

The following day, Tuesday, February 19, there were agitated conferences among the members of the official American colony. The Ambassador called at Sisson's rooms and talked with him and his associates about the situation. Later, Sisson went to the Embassy and urged the members of the Ambassador's staff to get the old gentleman away under any circumstances, even if the Bolsheviki were to knuckle under and accept the German terms. These urgings apparently bore fruit. On the next day, Wednesday, when it became known that the Soviet government was going to attempt to meet the German terms, Francis wired to Washington:

Soviet government demoralized, nearly stampeded. Germans reported 70 versts from Dvinsk toward Petrograd. Regardless whether Soviet proposals accepted think I should leave with staff but not fully decided. Ger-

[30] Sisson, *op.cit.*, p. 332.
[31] *Foreign Relations, 1918, Russia*, Vol. 1, *op.cit.*, p. 382; telegram 2387, February 18, 10 p.m.

mans could control city within forty-eight hours. If depart, planning go eastward but all arrangements indefinite. More later. If leave I shall confide interests to Norwegian Minister, my most sympathetic neutral colleague, who represents no other power.[32]

Sadoul, meanwhile, was conducting frantic negotiations with Trotsky about the possibility of Allied aid. He had not yet received the long-awaited clearance from his government, but on Wednesday (February 20) he decided to take a long and desperate chance, and proceeded, quite on his own, to offer Trotsky the support of the French Military Mission in any operations designed to slow up the German advance and to sabotage facilities which the Germans might use. Trotsky, however, was suspicious of Sadoul's exuberant enthusiasm, and wormed it out of him that he had no authority for such an offer. He demanded that Sadoul bring confirmation from his Ambassador, and Sadoul left the Smolny Institute determined to do just that. He confessed disingenuously to Thomas, in a letter written the following day, that he attempted to escape from his embarrassing predicament by representing to his Ambassador that it was Trotsky who had made the original suggestion.[33]

Fortunately for Sadoul, his audacious initiative occurred almost simultaneously with a decision of his own government precisely along the lines he was recommending. He did not know that while he was speaking with Trotsky on Wednesday, the French government had already put on the wire an instruction to the Ambassador in Petrograd, M. Noulens,

... to inform Chicherin ... indirectly that if the Bolsheviki resist the German menace and defend Russia against the German aggression, France is ready to give the Bolsheviki help in money and material.

This French decision, incidentally, was communicated to Assistant Secretary of State Phillips in Washington on February 19, with a query as to whether the United States would give similar instructions to Francis.[34] On the original of the memorandum of the conversation, which Phillips drew up, the Secretary of State later that day made the following significant notation:

[32] *Ibid.*, p. 383; Telegram 2395, February 20, 3 p.m.
[33] Sadoul, *op.cit.*, pp. 241–243.
[34] *Foreign Relations, 1918, Russia*, Vol. 1, *op.cit.*, p. 383; Memorandum from Phillips to Secretary of State, February 19.

This is out of the question. Submitted to Pres't who says the same thing. R.L. 2/19/18.

The French were presumably advised accordingly, but there is no evidence that anyone thought to tell Francis of this important decision.

In Petrograd, the French Ambassador, Noulens, being suspicious of Sadoul, evidently failed to tell him of the telegram from Paris; but he "understood at last," as Sadoul put it, and agreed to give the desired assurance. "At my request and in my presence," Sadoul reported happily to Albert Thomas,

the Ambassador telephoned to Trotsky and said, "In your resistance to Germany you may count on the military and financial support of France."

But despite his joy, Sadoul, remembering past experiences, was still skeptical:

. . . These are beautiful words, splendid promises. We will see whether our representatives are prepared to pass from words to actions.[35]

Actually, the French assurance failed to alter anything in the Soviet government's decision to yield to the German terms. But there were, as was seen in an earlier chapter, various delays with respect to the capitulation. Thus the Germans continued to advance, and the diplomats continued to be faced with the probability of an early arrival of German troops in Petrograd.

On Thursday morning, February 21, therefore, the five Allied ambassadors met once more, and agreed that they had no choice but to prepare for departure from Petrograd on short notice. The British Chargé proposed, for his own part and that of his mission, to leave Russia entirely. He thought he would attempt to make his way out via Murmansk or Finland. The Japanese and Chinese ambassadors also made up their minds to leave the country, but proposed, quite naturally, to leave via Vladivostok. The French and Italians were undecided.

In Francis' case, the decision was more difficult. We have already noted the somewhat unorthodox concept of diplomatic representation that animated both the United States government and its Ambassador in Petrograd: the idea, namely, that the Ambassador was accredited to the Russian people rather than to the Russian govern-

[35] Sadoul, *op.cit.*, p. 243.

[433]

ment, and that his function in Russia was not so much to provide a channel of inter-governmental communication as to express America's enduring interest in the Russian people and her moral support in their struggle for freedom. It was from this concept of the ambassadorial function that so many Americans derived the feeling that the Ambassador's complete withdrawal would be a form of "abandonment" of the Russian people. The alternative to this "abandonment" was, as people then put it, "to keep the flag flying." The fact that the Ambassador had no means of influencing the actual course of events or of saving the Russian people from the harsh necessity of accommodation to Soviet rule did not seem, to the Americans of the time, to weaken in any way the power of the argument.

Francis, none too firm in his understanding of diplomatic tradition, frustrated in his representative capacity by the triumph of communist power, and naturally eager to find some significance for his presence in Russia, embraced this outlook with enthusiasm. He felt, as one of his subordinates of that time put it, that

... so long as the war with Germany continued, it was his duty and an important contribution to the war effort, for him to remain in Russia and try to keep up some semblance of a front there.[36]

Francis confirmed, in a telegram despatched to the Department of State on the day of the meeting, that he was "unwilling to absolutely abandon Russia to [the] Germans." [37] He was strongly supported in this feeling by the other Americans in Russia, especially those whose Russian friends, being anti-communist, were becoming increasingly apprehensive of what might befall them if Allied influence disappeared entirely.

It should be noted in justice to Francis that he did not see the value of his remaining exclusively in terms of moral support for the Russian people. He also thought that his staying might have some slight effect on the Germans and on their policy with respect to the transfer of troops to the western front. "If only," as his subordinate put it,

the Germans could be kept guessing and sufficiently uncertain as to Russian or Bolshevik intentions as not to feel they could safely transfer too many of their divisions from the Eastern to the Western Fronts, as they

[36] From a private letter by the one-time Secretary of Embassy in Petrograd, Mr. Norman Armour, to the author.

[37] *Foreign Relations, 1918, Russia,* Vol. i, *op.cit.,* p. 384; Telegram 2400, February 21, 4 p.m.

had already begun to do, that would be a very great help to the Allied cause.

Thus Francis decided not to leave Russia entirely unless actually forced out by physical compulsion. According to his own account, he explained his decision to his colleagues on the morning of February 21:

> I said to them: "I am not going out of Russia."
> "Where are you going?" one of them asked.
> "I am going to Vologda," I said.
> "What do you know about Vologda?"
> "Not a thing except that it is the junction of the Trans-Siberian Railway and the Moscow-Archangel Railway and that it is 350 miles further away from the Germans."
> "Well, if it is unsafe there, what are you going to do?"
> "I am going east to Viatka, which is 500 miles east, and if it is unsafe there I am going to Perm. If it is unsafe at Perm, I am going to Irkutsk, and if it is still unsafe, I am going to Chita, and if necessary from there I am going to Vladivostok, where I will be protected by an American man-of-war, the *Brooklyn,* under Admiral Knight." [38]

A more detailed picture of the rationale of this plan was given by Robins in his testimony before the Senatorial Subcommittee in 1919:

> . . . the question of American interests remaining in Russia was of real concern to the Ambassador and myself. We wanted to stay there and play the hand out and rewin it if it was possible. We did not see any gain in abandoning it and running away. . . . Vologda was selected because transportation was good, opening to Archangel and Petrograd and Moscow and Siberia and Vladivostok and Finland; communication was good, telegraph to Archangel, wireless to Murmansk, and the English controlled the cable to London; and if we lost the Finnish cable, and if we lost Vladivostok, connections were still open. Vologda was far enough north, at least, to be out of range of any expected German advance. Petrograd could fall and Moscow could fall and Vologda would still be free. We investigated thoroughly and found it a small rural timber-working community, where there had been very little riot or effect of revolution.[39]

Robins further related that he himself went to Lenin and obtained the latter's agreement to make railway accommodations available for the official party.

❖

[38] Francis, *op.cit.,* p. 234.
[39] *Bolshevik Propaganda, Hearings* . . . . *op.cit.,* p. 799.

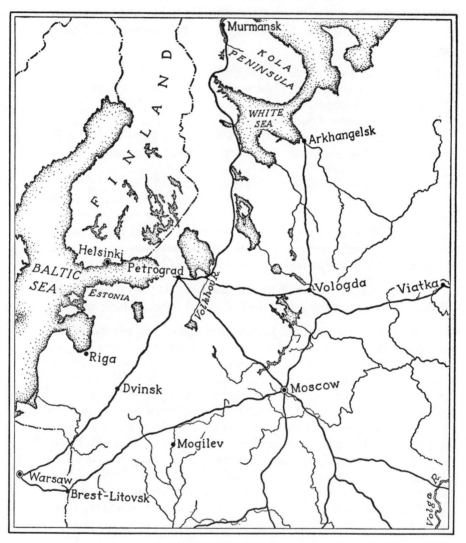

NORTHERN RUSSIA

The remainder of the week was taken up with the confusion of departure. Events were tangled and torrential. Neither records nor memories reconstruct them in any accuracy of detail. It was decided that the bulk of the Embassy staff should proceed in advance of the Ambassador, sharing a train with the staffs of the Chinese and Japanese Embassies. The Ambassador, attended by Counselor Butler Wright, Secretary of Embassy Norman Armour, Colonel Ruggles, Captains Riggs and Prince, his private secretary, Mr. Earl Johnston, Philip Jordan, and the unfortunate Marine couriers, would follow shortly after, on another special train. He was to be accompanied on this train by the Japanese, Chinese, Siamese, and Brazilian chiefs-of-mission, and also by a number of the members of the American Red Cross Mission. Robins himself proposed to remain behind in Petrograd. Sisson, too, planned to stay long enough to round up the last of his documents, then to make a try for escape through Finland. The Embassy building on the Furshtatskaya, where Francis had spent every night but one since his arrival nearly two years before, was to be placed under the protection of the Norwegian Minister. (An illustration in Sisson's memoirs shows the old building after departure of the Americans, brooding, empty and disconsolate, over the deserted, snowcovered street, the Norwegian flag flying benevolently above it.)

The first train, bearing twenty-three members of the Embassy staff, got off on Sunday, February 24. The British and French missions left the same day, heading for Finland. (The British mission, led only by a chargé d'affaires, eventually got through. The numerous and high-powered French group, led by Ambassador Noulens, got hopelessly stranded and finally, many weeks later, had to abandon its plan and join Francis in Vologda. Noulens never got over his bitterness over this incident, feeling that his British colleagues had abandoned him.)

On February 25, the day following the departure of the French and British, Francis wrote a letter to his son that gives a good idea of the mood of the moment. He had outwaited the French and British, he indicated, because as doyen of the diplomatic corps he did not want to be the first to leave. The Soviet government, he thought, was doomed. He was proud, now, that he had never recommended recognition. The Germans were expected in Petrograd "tomorrow or next day." He would have to make his getaway very soon, now. He looked back with satisfaction on his performance as Ambassador:

... I have attended closely to my trust, & have recd. commendation from the Dept., but never a word or expression from Pres. Wilson. His hands & mind are full & thoroughly occupied & he has risen to the full heighth of his responsibility.[40]

The future was indeed uncertain, and the President's silence painful. But Francis could still find compensations that might have escaped a more complicated personality. "Tell Dave," he wrote in the same letter to his son,

[that I] rec'd Feb. 22 the two bottles bourbon he sent me by Joe Miller, were 4½ months on route but highly appreciated. . . .

The next morning (Tuesday, the 26th) it was decided that departure could be delayed no longer. The train was to leave that evening. The day was spent in final packing, tidying up, clearing out papers. The confidential files for the preceding ten years were burned. The earlier files (long shelves of dusty, bound volumes of correspondence, handwritten and in faded yellow ink) were left to the care of the Norwegians.[41] Francis hoped eventually to return, but there could be no certainty about this.

By evening all was ready. In the Embassy building the last bags were dragged out, the last doors slammed. The Ford had had to be abandoned, temporarily, to the uncertainties of the time (it later turned up in Vologda). Thus the Ambassador made his departure in the sleigh, behind the horses with the American flags at their ears. The Russian servants stood stolidly in the entryway, waving good-by, their feelings buried under that impenetrable blankness of expression that had become, with the ages, the protective coloration

[40] Francis MSS, *op.cit.;* folder for February 16–28, 1918.

[41] The Norwegians eventually sent some of these to Washington. In 1934, Mr. Angus D. Ward, then serving as Secretary of the American Embassy in Moscow, paid a visit to the former Embassy building in Petrograd, and was shown around the premises. Glancing into the stables at the rear of the courtyard, he happened to see something white looming on top of what appeared to be a pile of rubbish, and found it to be a bust of George Washington. Looking further, he discovered practically the entire correspondence of the Petrograd Mission with the Department of State from 1818 to 1908, quite unscathed. The volumes were removed, with the consent of the Soviet government, and sent to Washington, where they now repose in the National Archives.

of the Russian peasant masses. The sleigh, presided over by the vast bundled figure of the coachman Andrei, moved off briskly and quietly into the darkened streets, down the straight line of the Liteiny, rimmed with enormous snowbanks, left onto the wide expanses of the Nevsky Prospekt, and so to the Nikolayev Station.

Russian railway stations are always crowded caravansaries, but on this night, with the German seizure of the city believed imminent, crowds thicker than usual were milling about, trying to board the trains for Moscow. With white-aproned porters and other factotums breaking the way, the Ambassador and the members of his party filed through the dense throngs to the platform.

The train appeared to be the regular Vladivostok express, commandeered for the use of the diplomatic party. A bitter battle of protocol had been waged through the day. The train had both blue and red upholstered cars. American Secretary of Embassy Armour, in distributing the space, had assigned the blue to the Japanese party, the red to the Chinese. The Chinese insisted that red, in railway usage, was an inferior color, denoting something almost as degrading as second class. If the Japanese had blue, the Celestial Empire should have it, too. Station masters and experts on railway protocol were summoned, Armour relates, to testify that the colors had equal prestige value. No one remembers how the dispute was settled.

Another hitch occurred at the last minute. Trainmen suddenly divulged that they had orders that the train was not to go. Robins, always the last recourse in emergency, was summoned to the rescue. The orders, he found, had come from the Security Committee of the City of Petrograd, now taking over with a heavy hand in the face of the threatened seizure of the city by the Germans. He was told the reason: the seizure of the city appeared less imminent than it had twenty-four hours earlier; the departure of the American Embassy, it was thought, might increase the panic, might lead to disorders, even to counterrevolution—who could tell?

Robins rushed off to Smolny to see Lenin. He found him hunched over his office desk. His world was crashing around him. Many of his followers were close to open revolt. All was trouble and uncertainty.

The weight of supreme responsibility pressing on his shoulders, Lenin listened patiently to Robins' dramatic argument:

. . . I know there is a certain danger in the city . . . but Commissioner, it is worse to keep that train there than to send it out. You know better than I do that the old control in the barracks has passed . . . and if they go down there and loot the American Embassy or want to kill the American Ambassador, you may not be able to protect it or him, and then there would be a blot on the soviet in Russia from which it would never recover.[42]

Lenin yielded. Robins tore back to the station and, to make sure that nothing more went wrong, changed his plans and boarded the train himself.

At two a.m., on Wednesday, February 27, 1918, the special train bearing Ambassador David R. Francis, his reduced staff, and a few of his diplomatic colleagues, pulled out of the Nikolayev Station, southbound on the arrow-straight line that runs to Moscow. The conspicuously marked American Red Cross car brought up the rear. A few miles out of town, the train took a switch to the east, leading off the main Moscow route, and moved out, in the winter darkness, onto the single-tracked line that stretched away in the direction of Vladivostok, some 5,470 miles beyond.

The train moved at the leisurely gait of all Russian trains. The clacking of the wheels was muffled by the deep snow. Inside the big wooden cars, warmly heated by birchwood fires, it was almost silent except for the rhythmic creaking of the woodwork and a faint rumble of the trucks. Skirting the southern bend of the Neva River, the train chugged its patient way eastward, through the hours of darkness, along the lonely wooded strip between Lake Ladoga and the swamps to the south. Toward morning, but still in the winter darkness, it crossed the bridge over the icebound waters of the broad Volkhov, and rolled on into the limitless forests on the other side. As the Petrograd area thus receded into the wintry night, the days of America's diplomatic representation in Peter's new city on the banks of the Neva—days that stretched back in unbroken continuity over some 108 years to the arrival of John Quincy Adams in 1809— came to an abrupt, and seemingly final, termination.

[42] *Bolshevik Propaganda, Hearings . . . , op.cit.,* pp. 799–800.

CHAPTER XXII

~~~~~~

THE SISSON PAPERS

The Bolsheviki accepted money from the German Government, whom
they hated, . . . with the full intention of betraying their benefactors at
first—and every—opportunity.—*Arthur Bullard* [1]

~~~~~~

WE HAVE NOTED, in the last chapter, the beginning of Sisson's efforts
to procure, through the curious clandestine channels available to
him, documents said to emanate from the official files of the Soviet
government and purporting to prove that the Bolshevik leaders were
in a position of subservience to the German government and taking
orders from various German governmental authorities, notably the
Russian Division of the German General Staff and a subordinate
office of that General Staff situated in Petrograd. We have seen that
Sisson was enormously impressed with the significance of these documents, and that he threw himself with single-minded intensity into
amassing all that he could in a brief time, removing them from
Russia, and placing them in the hands of the United States government. His sense of urgency was heightened by the precipitous events
in the latter part of February: the possibility of early German capture of Petrograd, the general departure of the Allied representatives,
and the talk of the forthcoming move of the Soviet government to
Moscow. As it happened, Sisson had planned to leave Russia anyway
around the end of February, turning over the propaganda work to
his subordinates who, he felt, were fully capable of conducting it
on their own. The development of the situation in mid-February
only confirmed him in this intention, but at the same time it increased in his mind the urgency of accumulating as many as possible
of the documents prior to his departure.

---

[1] Arthur Bullard, *The Russian Pendulum: Autocracy—Democracy—Bolshevism*,
The Macmillan Co., New York, 1919, p. 102.

The Sisson Papers

During the latter part of February, Sisson continued to receive from Semenov photostats of various documents in this series. He was anxious, however, to obtain the originals, feeling that only these would be conclusive proof of the state of affairs to which the documents pointed. After the departure of the Embassy, knowing that his own continued presence in Petrograd would be only a matter of days, he made intense efforts to complete his collection of the documents, and particularly to obtain originals of those which he had thus far seen only in photostat form. An understanding was accordingly arrived at between Sisson, Semenov, and the head of the so-called "wire group," Colonel Samsonov, that the Russian agents should stage a raid on the Smolny files at the time of the Soviet government's move to Moscow, with a view to procuring the originals of the documents.

Although Sisson did not see the actual raid, he was given to understand that it took place during the night of March 2–3, the eve of his own departure from Russia. When he called at the Smolny Institute on the morning of Sunday, March 3, to say his good-by, he saw several large pine boxes of document files, with their sides broken, lying on the snow in the courtyard. It was his belief that these were the files that had been rifled.

Sisson and Bullard met secretly, later that day, with some of the Russians understood to be members of Semenov's group, to receive the booty derived from the escapade. Seven or eight Russians were present. "For two hours," Sisson relates in his memoirs,

. . . we sat around a long table, listing, checking, and reading. Everyone was exuberant and some of the members of the Russian party were inclined to eloquence. One wanted a pause to toast the "historical occasion." I thought history could take care of itself and that we had best do the same for ourselves. When the detail work was done, Bullard and I clasped each man by the hand, thanked him, and wished him safety and whatever good luck there could be in a clouded land. It was farewell. No man of this band ever was taken by the Bolsheviks.[2]

Having a keen sense of the importance of his documents, Sisson had an equally lively consciousness of what he believed to be the extreme personal danger these operations involved not only for him-

---

[2] Sisson, *op.cit.,* p. 363. Actually, only 14 of the originals were obtained; for the rest, Sisson had to content himself with photostats.

self and the others directly implicated but for the entire official American group in Russia. The Ambassador, in his last talk with Sisson prior to departure, had said he had been asked to warn Sisson that Trotsky was aware of the inquiry and to advise him to halt it. The Ambassador was not inclined, he had said, to sponsor the advice, but he wanted to tell Sisson that he was concerned over the warning. "I asked him," Sisson records, "to name his informant and he did so. I considered the warning a bluff, designed to frighten me. Trotsky could have no knowledge except through persons I did not believe would care to put me in peril." [3] Nevertheless, the seed of apprehension had been planted in Sisson's mind. From this time on, he felt that his activity involved mortal danger; that his own life, the lives of everyone associated with him in the enterprise, indeed the security of the whole American establishment in Russia, were at stake in the preservation of secrecy about the procurement of the documents. Thus the question of their removal across the frontier was a serious and worrisome one.

By a stroke of good fortune, he succeeded in planting the documents on a wholly innocent Norwegian courier, who was starting out for Norway at roughly the time of his own departure. Sisson's idea was to stick as closely as possible to the courier and recover the documents at some point beyond the reach of the Soviet secret police.

By late Sunday afternoon, March 3, everything was in readiness for departure. The last conspiratorial farewell call was paid on Colonel Samsonov, who rashly donned his Tsarist officer's uniform for the occasion. Sisson then set out across the river for the Finland Station.

The sun was setting and the spires of Peter and Paul and the Admiralty agleam as we drove toward the Finland station across the Neva. Miserable Petrograd was roofed with beauty for a passing hour, its final scene for me. [4]

Sisson was not a warm person, and he did not often inspire warmth in others; but he deserves to have it recorded that it was with real

---

[3] *Ibid.*, p. 356. The draft of a telegram, never sent, dated February 18 and initialed by Francis, indicates that Trotsky had observed to Robins that if the Ambassador did not know the tales of Soviet subservience to the Germans were untrue he was "badly mistaken." Francis professed himself bewildered to know where Trotsky could have learned of this. He noted that Sisson had told Robins about his telegram submitting the first batch of documents (Francis MSS, *op.cit.*). Of course telegraphic intercepts might also have been the source of Trotsky's information.

[4] Sisson, *op.cit.*, p. 399.

feeling and appreciation that he took leave of his closest associates when he left Russia. It had been an eventful and trying winter, producing that crystallization of human relationships into strong antagonism or firm friendship which has been the invariable effect of the Russian atmosphere on Americans fated to live within it. Sisson tells of the final farewells in the train compartment:

. . . We talked lightly, but my heart was heavy. From Bullard particularly I hated to part. The winter had welded us close, and I feared, too, what Russia might yet hold for him. Yet I had reliance, too. He was careful, reflective, and wise, and a man of action, withal.[5]

❖

This completes the account of Sisson's experiences in Russia. But in order that the reader may have a clear understanding of the significance of these documents and the part they played in the mutual relationships of the Americans involved, as well as in the subsequent affairs of the United States government, it may be useful at this point to jump ahead of the narrative and to follow Sisson and his documents into the more distant future.

The journey through Finland proved to be adventurous. Like everyone else who had tried to leave Russia by that route at that particular time, Sisson got temporarily bogged down in Finland, as a result of the difficulty involved in crossing the battle line. It was not until the end of March that he and a few other stranded Americans finally succeeded in crossing the line. They were transported by the Reds to the middle of a frozen lake and left there on the ice with all their baggage, a forlorn and helpless little group clutching an American flag, until the Whites came out and rescued them.

All the way across Finland and Scandinavia, Sisson hovered nervously around the Norwegian courier, showering him with attentions and concerning himself no less anxiously for the security of the courier's passage than for his own. At Helsinki he succeeded in attaching the Norwegian to the American party and thus bringing him in safety all the way to Stockholm. The Norwegian, Sisson relates, was somewhat bewildered but not displeased with these attentions.

Sisson recovered his precious materials in Oslo. There he examined the documents carefully for the first time, though what he could

[5] *Loc.cit.*

make of them, in view of the language barrier, is unclear. As soon as circumstances permitted, he proceeded to London, where he had expected to show the documents to the British government, according to arrangements made with his British colleagues in Petrograd. To Sisson's embarrassment, however, the Ambassador in London, Mr. Walter Hines Page, received a telegram from the Secretary of State to "instruct Mr. Sisson to report to the Secretary of State and until that time to discuss the Russian situation with no one." [6] The instruction was sent at Wilson's direction; the record reveals nothing of the President's motive. The order was a pity, for it meant that Sisson failed to learn at first hand the British estimate of the authenticity of the documents. The British were well familiar with them, not only having seen the ones Sisson had obtained, but having received others from the same source and having themselves, by all appearances, worked closely with Colonel Samsonov.

Believing that his documents would be triumphantly exposed by the United States government to an astounded world the moment he arrived home and delivered them, Sisson wired from London on April 25, before sailing for New York, urging that orders be issued for all representatives of the Committee on Public Information and the Red Cross to be out of Russia within a fortnight. His thought was of course that the Soviet leaders would be so enraged by the revelation of their conspiracy with the Germans that they would immediately arrest the remaining Americans in Russia.

Sisson reached New York on May 6 and proceeded at once to Washington. He reported to Creel, and then called on the Secretary of State. The Secretary passed him on to the Counselor of the Department, Frank Polk. Polk has recorded this visit as follows:

. . . He seemed to expect that the Department would publish the documents immediately. I asked him to let me have his opinion on the documents, which he seemed loath to do stating that they spoke for themselves, that he had nothing more to add to what was contained in his memorandum accompanying the documents and that he was very interested in seeing how an Executive Department of the Government would handle this information. Making every allowance for Mr. Sisson's unfortunate manner, he seemed rather critical and annoyed that the Department had not been

[6] National Archives, Sisson Documents File, *op.cit.;* the above language is cited in a memorandum of September 20, 1918 prepared by the Counselor of the Department of State.

more impressed than it had with the importance of the disclosures revealed by him and had not promptly rushed into print. His attitude was rather one of a newspaper man who had secured what he thought was the greatest scoop in history and which was not being made use of by his superiors. . . .[7]

Polk went on, in this memorandum, to explain why the Department was in no hurry to publish the documents:

It was understood that Mr. Grew was to be consulted before the documents should be published, the reason for this being that it would be best to withhold them until the psychological moment had arrived. In other words, that the effect in Germany would be greater if the contents of the documents became known at a time when things were going badly for Germany and not when they were having military successes which was the case at the time the documents were submitted by Mr. Sisson.

Whether this was the real reason for the Department's lack of enthusiasm or whether it simply thought it superfluous to raise the question of the authenticity of the documents, the record does not show.

The original of Sisson's report was delivered into the hands of President Wilson, presumably by Creel, on the night of May 9, 1918.

Sisson, as indicated in Polk's memorandum, was dumfounded at the unwillingness of the State Department to use his documents immediately. But the Department stuck to its guns, and for the time being nothing was done. The copies of Sisson's report and of the documents, which had been placed in the hands of the Secretary of State, were put away by Polk in his confidential files for such time as a final decision might be made about their publication.

Sisson, however, was not to be put off lightly. Four months later, through processes that have never been fully revealed, the President was persuaded—behind the back of the Department of State—to release the documents to the public. On September 13 or 14 Secretary Lansing learned, to his amazement, that the publication of the documents had been arranged by the Committee on Public Information, to begin on September 15. The action, Creel says in his memoirs, had been "ordered" by the President.[8]

---

[7] *Loc.cit.*

[8] Creel, *op.cit.*, p. 183. Mr. Polk said, in the memorandum referred to above: "All these papers have been held in my confidential file and no intimation whatsoever was given me by Mr. Sisson that they were to be published. The first I heard of such action on the part of the Committee on Public Information was received from Mr. Miles and Mr. Patchin." (The reference is to Basil Miles, in charge of Russian affairs

It was, of course, shocking that such a step should have been taken without prior discussion with the Department of State. The official corps of Americans remaining in Russia were, as it happened, just at that time in a particularly delicate and precarious position—especially Consul DeWitt Poole in Moscow. It was clear that any offensive gesture toward the Bolsheviki could easily bring about their arrest and imprisonment—possibly even worse.

Lansing, obviously much agitated on learning of the Committee's intention, at once (in Creel's absence) wrote to Sisson, who was by this time General Director of the Foreign Section of the Committee, and begged him to refrain from publication. He pointed out in considerable detail the danger involved for Poole and the other Americans in Russia. In these circumstances, he was "unwilling to share responsibility for the consequences which may result from the publication of these documents." [9] He concluded by pointing out that the British had been advised in April that the United States government was against publication until after further consultation between the two governments. He assumed, therefore, that the British were being kept informed.

Sisson's reply was curt and uncooperative. Four months earlier, when he had first contemplated publication of the documents, he had peremptorily and without explanation insisted on ordering out the personnel of his own office in Russia, though the situation was then not nearly so tense. Now, when only State Department and Red Cross personnel were involved and when the situation was genuinely explosive, he experienced no comparable anxiety. "I would suggest," he replied to Lansing,

... that Mr. Poole be instructed to place himself in the keeping of the Swedish Consul, and to have Mr. Wardwell and Mr. Andrews do the same, provided he and they cannot get out of the Bolshevick area.

That publication will add anything to their present peril is difficult to conceive.

You will put them in actual danger of being connected with the exposure (in which they have no part whatever) by pointing them out as your reason for urging an abnormal action.

A story that has been in the newspaper offices of the country for 24 hours cannot be suppressed by normal means.

in the Department, and to Philip Patchin, Chief of the Division of Intelligence and Information.)

[9] *Foreign Relations, The Lansing Papers*, Vol. II, *op.cit.*, pp. 384-385.

My knowledge of London-Washington conference is confined to the fact that I asked permission to turn over to the British Government the part of my material it lacked, and that by your order to Ambassador Page and to me, I was not permitted to do so.[10]

A copy of the Secretary's letter to Sisson had been sent to the President. The same was presumably done with Sisson's reply. Yet there was no intervention on the President's part. The fact that the Secretary of State was permitted to go unsupported by the White House in the face of this defiant reply from Sisson, a subordinate official of another agency of government, on a matter definitely in the area of foreign affairs, speaks for itself.

Release of the documents to the press began, in defiance of the Secretary's wishes, on September 15. The British were given no forewarning. Fortunately, the release did not have the effect on Poole that the Secretary had feared. But the facts bear out Lansing's view that the situation at that moment was incalculable; anything might have happened.

The documents were released in installments, and appeared in the American press over the course of the week following September 15. They consisted of the set of documents purporting to emanate from the Smolny files, plus the circulars and letters which Sisson had obtained initially through Robins, plus one single document which appears actually to have represented an intercepted telegraph message from the Soviet delegation in Brest-Litovsk to the Soviet leaders in the Smolny Institute. (The series supposed to be from the Smolny files was later supplemented in the government archives by a number of documents of the same nature, and obviously of the same origin, purchased by Vice Consul Imbrie in Petrograd after the Embassy's departure, and by two more items sold to Consul DeWitt Poole in Moscow by some Poles in that city; but these were not published.) The release of the documents was made officially, in a United States government publication, under the imprimatur of the Committee on Public Information; and there could be no question that the government backed the authenticity and significance of the material.

The State Department, it will be recalled, had never been consulted and had never given an opinion on the authenticity of the material.

Most of the newspapers appear to have taken the documents at

[10] *Ibid.*, p. 385.

face value, but a considerable stir was occasioned by vigorous attacks launched on their authenticity by the *New York Evening Post,* which had taken pains to check with Robins and others who were on the pro-Bolshevik side of the fence.

Further question as to the authenticity of the documents came from the British government. Ambassador Page communicated to the Department on September 19 from London that:

... the War Office, the Foreign Office, the Postal Censor and the Admiralty examined the material carefully and in a general way reached the decision that the documents which appeared to be genuine were old and not of any particular value, and those which had propaganda value were of a doubtful character. . . .[11]

Page quoted a British Intelligence officer as saying that careful tests made by the Postal Censor had shown that documents purporting to come from different sources had been typed on the same machine; from this and certain of the characteristics of the handwriting the British inferred that most of the documents were forgeries.

This questioning was sufficient to persuade the Committee on Public Information that something had to be done to give substantiation to the authenticity of the documents. In releasing the documents serially to the press, the Committee had promised that when the serial release was ended it would publish the entire collection in a single governmental pamphlet, which would include facsimiles of some of the more important documents. The committee now decided that before this pamphlet was issued steps should be taken, for the first time, to obtain expert opinion to substantiate the documents. Creel therefore requested the National Board for Historical Research to appoint "an authoritative committee, small in numbers"[12] to assemble at once in Washington, to consider carefully the authenticity of the documents in the light of the charges raised against them, and to render an opinion which could be published together with the pamphlet edition. The Board agreed to do this.

Dr. J. Franklin Jameson, editor of the *American Historical Review* and Director of the Department of Historical Research of the Carnegie Institution of Washington, and Dr. Samuel N. Harper, Professor of Russian Language and Institutions in the University of Chi-

[11] Mock & Larson, *op.cit.,* p. 319; paraphrase of London telegram 2044, September 19, 1918, communicated to Creel by Philip Patchin in letter dated September 20.
[12] *German-Bolshevik Conspiracy, op.cit.,* p. 29.

cago, accepted appointment by the Board for this purpose. Professor Archibald Coolidge also appears to have been asked to participate in this inquiry, but, as Harper cryptically put it, he "did not formally participate in the work." [13] In any case, the report was signed by only the first two named.

In the amazing period of precisely one week, Professors Harper and Jameson studied the 68 documents produced by Sisson (plus one appendix) and drew up and presented to Creel a 2,300-word report of their findings. Of the first group of documents (the early circulars and letters) they concluded that while they saw nothing in the texts "that positively excludes the notion of their being genuine, little in any of them that makes it doubtful," they had insufficient means of testing their genuineness and could make no confident declaration. With regard to two of the circulars for which, in contrast to the remainder, the German originals were available, they said that while they did not consider these to be "simply forgeries" they did not think them to be "in their present shape, documents on whose entire text historians or publicists can safely rely as genuine." Of the remaining 53 documents, which constituted the bulk of the collection and consisted almost exclusively of the documents purporting to come from the Smolny files, they said,

. . . we have no hesitation in declaring that we see no reason to doubt the genuineness or authenticity of these fifty-three documents.[14]

Harper, in his published memoirs, described the pressure put upon Jameson and himself, in the name of wartime necessity, to give their opinion that the documents proved Lenin to be a German agent:

. . . With his country at war, the academic man, when called upon by his government to use his academic talents for a war purpose, often faces a problem of duty in two directions and finds difficulty in properly protecting himself.[15]

A further passage in the original draft of these memoirs, excised in publication, elaborated on this unhappy subject:

My experience with the Sisson documents showed clearly the pressure to which University men are subjected in time of war. My position was particularly difficult because my area of study was under the control of a new

[13] Harper, *op.cit.*, p. 112.
[14] *German-Bolshevik Conspiracy, op.cit.*, pp. 29–30; from the report of the Special Committee to Mr. Creel.
[15] Harper, *op.cit.*, p. 112.

group which was talking peace, and I felt it was my academic duty to explain why the Bolsheviks were working against a continuation of the war, not only on the part of Russia but in general. Thanks to the support of Professor Jameson I was able to hold out to a certain degree against a complete abandonment of the rules of the student but it was impossible for a University man not to make a contribution to the development of the war spirit, even if this involved the making of statements of a distinctly biased character.[16]

It should be said in justice to Professor Harper that his subsequent unhappiness about this report was heightened by the fact that he later had access to a good deal of evidence with regard to the documents which was not available at the time he and Professor Jameson viewed them so hurriedly in 1918.

The appearance of the governmental pamphlet, with the full collection of documents and the Harper-Jameson opinion, fell within a few days of the termination of the war in November 1918, and the public reaction was largely smothered in the excitement of that great moment.

For roughly a year and a half thereafter, the whole question of the documents and their authenticity lay dormant. The originals of the documents themselves were turned over to President Wilson when Harper and Jameson had finished with them, and were placed by the President in his personal files in the White House.

The matter might well have passed then and there into history had not Sisson himself, now back in New York as an editor for *McClure's Magazine,* apparently been stung by the skepticism which, despite the Harper-Jameson opinion, continued to be manifested in many quarters with regard to the genuineness of the material. He came to the conclusion that this skepticism existed only because inadequate study had been given to the documents. Further research into the circumstances of their origin and the conditions suggested by their content would, he felt, confirm their authenticity and emphasize to the public their great historical significance. He therefore set about, in the spring of 1920, to prod the Department of State into launching a more careful and exhaustive inquiry into the authenticity of the documents. In this inquiry, he was aided by Mr. Allen Carter, then acting chief of the Russian Division in the Department of State, who never doubted that the documents were authentic, and by Harper, who continued to manifest a lively interest in the subject.

[16] Harper MSS, *op.cit.*

In the spring of 1920 the Department of State, under Sisson's constant urgings and needling, made efforts in a number of directions to obtain information which would throw greater light on the authenticity of the documents.

These efforts extended throughout most of the year 1920, taking on many forms. Circular instructions were sent to various missions in the field, asking them to follow up various leads. Queries were addressed to the British Foreign Office and the British Secret Service. People were interviewed. Publications were studied. Documents of various sorts were assembled. Throughout all of this activity, Sisson looked over the government's shoulder: suggesting, commenting, querying, explaining. All those involved in the work of investigation were, or professed to be, fully persuaded of the genuineness of the documents; the task was to assemble conclusive proof to support this hypothesis.

Among these various measures, an attempt was made to recover the originals for further study. They were, it will be recalled, in the President's files. Creel, who had evidently been the person to hand them over to the President, was asked to recover them for the use of the Department. He paid a visit to the White House for this purpose around the end of July 1920, but for some reason met with no success. A few days later (August 9), Arthur Bullard assumed charge of the Russian Division of the State Department. He immediately took up with White House Secretary Joseph P. Tumulty the question of obtaining a loan of the originals, only to receive, on August 18, a sharp rebuff in the form of the following reply:

I have brought to the attention of the President your desire for the return of the Sisson papers, and he has asked me to explain to you that just now he has not time to lay his hand on these papers, but when he does he will make the proper disposition of them.[17]

Creel had another try at the White House in December of that year. He did everything in his power, he reported afterward to Sisson, to get the documents, but:

. . . The situation is hopeless. The President will not let anybody go into his files and insists that he will look up the documents himself. I have put the matter in the hands of Mrs. Wilson and will keep up the search.[18]

[17] National Archives, Sisson Documents File, *op.cit.;* letter from Tumulty to Arthur Bullard, August 18, 1920.
[18] *Ibid.,* letter from Sisson to Bullard, December 20, 1920.

By this time, Harding had been elected and Wilson's term of office was about to end. The Department therefore waited until May 1921, by which time President Harding had taken over, and then renewed the effort to find the originals. But the new White House Secretary, Mr. Rudolph Forster, reported that the documents were not in the White House files; President Wilson must have removed them when he relinquished his office.

In view of the impossibility of obtaining the originals, the inquiry into the authenticity of the documents was dropped. The extensive file of correspondence that had been built up in the course of the inquiry was deposited, together with the photographs of the documents, in a large cardboard carton. The carton remained for many years in the premises of the old Eastern European Division in the Department of State, until such time, in fact, as that division was abruptly and inexplicably abolished in 1937. While many of the division's files were destroyed or dispersed on orders from on high, the cardboard carton, with its valuable but voluminous accumulation of evidence relating to the Sisson documents, survived and passed into the bored hands of the European Division, which had inherited the Eastern European Division safes. The European Division, not knowing what to do with the carton, sent it to the Division of Communications and Records.

On January 10, 1940, some nineteen years after the last substantive attention had been given the documents, someone in the Division of Communications and Records discovered the box and brought it to the attention of the chief of the division, under cover of the following chit:

> Here are some very old documents known as "Sisson Documents" which were turned over to DCR a long time ago by EU. They have been kept in the file in Room 476, but it seems to me they are lost in here and should be kept in the safe or in the European Section.[19]

Exactly what happened to the carton after that is swallowed up in the mysteries of governmental files. But by the autumn of 1954 it had found its devious way to Room 2410, State Annex 3, in the Historical Division of the Department of State. And finally, on the afternoon of January 7, 1955, it made its appearance at the Foreign Affairs Section of the National Archives in Washington, where it

[19] *Ibid.*, Chit to Mr. Salmon from "A.L.C." January 10, 1940.

obviously belongs, and where its contents are now available for the satisfaction of scholarly curiosity.

As for the originals: on December 19, 1952, as President Truman was preparing to leave the White House, an envelope containing the original documents, together with Sisson's report, was found in a White House safe. Those who found it had not the faintest idea what the material pertained to. Wearily they sent it over to the Justice and Executive Section of the Legislative, Judicial and Diplomatic Records Branch of the National Archives. There it now reposes near —but still not together with—the supporting material.

✧

The above account has been included in this narrative in order that the reader may have some idea of what was at stake in the dispute between Robins and Sisson over the question of the acquisition and interpretation of the documents. It will also explain why the question of their authenticity was never adequately resolved within the official American family.

An examination of the evidence available with regard to the source and authenticity of these documents would in itself constitute a scholarly exercise of major proportions and would far surpass the scope of this inquiry, to which it is only incidentally related. Suffice it to note, for purposes of this narrative, that with the possible exception of a few relatively unimportant items, these documents were unquestionably forgeries from beginning to end.[20] The evidence for this is to be found in a number of their characteristics: in their historical implausibility, in their implausibility from the standpoint of governmental usage, and in a whole series of glaring technical weaknesses (handwriting, dating, language, form, etc.). For the probable identity and motives of the author of the documents there is formidable evidence.

There were at least three serious reasons why the spuriousness of the Sisson documents was not established at an earlier date. First of all, as has been seen, no proper governmental inquiry was ever made into their authenticity. The examination by Harper and Jameson was hasty, and conducted under circumstances not conducive to the elucidation of the full facts. The later examination in the

[20] See article entitled *The Sisson Documents,* by George F. Kennan, in *The Journal of Modern History,* Vol. xxviii, No. 2, June, 1956.

Department of State was hampered by lack of access to the original documents, as well as by the fact that several of the people concerned had already committed themselves fairly extensively to the thesis of their authenticity.

Secondly, the person or persons who produced the documents were actually well-informed on what was going on in the Smolny Institute (they clearly had some connection with those who were tapping the Brest-Smolny telegraphic channel) and were able to weave fact and fiction together in an unusually skillful and baffling manner. There is, of course, no reason why forgeries may not contain much correct information.

Thirdly, there was just enough truth behind the general thesis that the Bolsheviki had "accepted German gold" to throw many people off the track and, apparently, to cause the Bolsheviki themselves to refrain from any attempt to refute the documents.

With regard to this last point, it is clear that Lenin and a number of his associates, in returning to Russia in the spring of 1917 through Germany, operated on the basis of some sort of agreement with the German authorities. There is even some evidence of political understanding, in the sense that hints were thrown out by the German intelligence agents that Germany would be willing, if the Bolsheviki were successful in Russia, to terminate the war on a basis of no annexations and no indemnities. That Lenin and his associates were really naïve enough to attach any great importance to any such assurances seems hardly likely, though Trotsky's reaction to the German demands, in late December 1917, raises some question about this.

It is entirely possible that the Bolsheviki, in pursuance to these arrangements, received clandestine subsidies from German sources during the summer and early autumn of 1917. The Germans, anxious to see the war on the eastern front brought to an end, had every reason to subsidize the Russian faction which was most deeply committed to the achievement of an early peace. There was nothing in the code of Bolshevik ethics to inhibit the acceptance of such subsidies, and nothing that would have caused the Bolshevik leaders to feel the slightest sense of moral obligation to the Germans by virtue of having accepted them. It is entirely possible, therefore, that behind some of the letters from the summer of 1917, published among the Sisson documents, there may have been some real substance, and that some German money passed, through intermediaries in Scandinavia, into Bolshevik hands during the summer of 1917.

There is, however, no reason to believe that any German money passed to the Bolsheviki after the November Revolution, or that the Bolshevik leaders were in any position of clandestine subservience to the Germans in the winter of 1917–1918. After the November Revolution, the Germans had no need to subsidize the Bolsheviki, for the German objective—the disintegration of the Russian armed forces—was now an accomplished fact. The Bolsheviki had no reason to draw on German funds, for they were now in possession of governmental power in Russia and had at their disposal the assets of the state treasury as well as the nationalized banks. The agony of decision that marked Soviet policy toward the Germans throughout the course of the Brest-Litovsk negotiations was only too genuine; and it plainly reflected the true nature of the Bolshevik relationship to the German government. To suggest, as the Sisson documents did, that this was all a bluff of cosmic proportions, that Lenin and Trotsky were in reality wholly beholden to German masters throughout, and that the violent and dramatic debates within the Bolshevik family over Soviet policy in the Brest-Litovsk negotiations were a form of deceit practiced by the Bolshevik leaders on the mass of their associates, is to move into the realm of historical absurdity.

In this instance it was Robins, the vague and exalted enthusiast, whose understanding was closest to the truth, and Sisson, the sharp and zealous war-worker, who lost himself in a forest of delusion. This was unfortunate in two respects. It served, in later years, to increase the bitterness of Robins and many others who shared his outlook, for it confirmed them in the belief that their opponents must be either ill-informed, blind, or dishonest. But beyond this, Sisson's belief in the authenticity of the documents later communicated itself quite extensively to State Department officialdom, and added an unnecessary burden of suspicion to the formation of their judgment about the Bolsheviki—a task which involved plenty of real questions, without the addition of any false ones.

Had the processes of the United States government been more orderly, had the State Department been brought into the picture at the start, had the British been duly consulted and respectfully heard, and had the authenticity of the documents been properly examined and clarified, the United States government might have been spared one of the most shocking and indefensible of public commitments, and the official American view on the phenomenon of Bolshevism in coming years might have been slightly more sober and realistic than it actually was—less concerned with fancied evils in the pattern of Bolshevik behavior and more concerned with the real evils, which, as it happened, were fully sufficient to the day at hand.

CHAPTER XXIII

SIBERIA AND THE

FINAL BREST-LITOVSK CRISIS

The Government of the United States . . . has . . . the utmost confidence in the Japanese Government. . . . But it is bound in frankness to say that the wisdom of intervention seems to it most questionable.—*Message transmitted orally to the Japanese Foreign Minister by the United States Ambassador, March 7, 1918*

THE movement of the Brest-Litovsk negotiations toward the final climax could not fail to agitate the simmering question of a possible Allied intervention in the Russian Far East. If, as was commonly feared in the west, Germany was about to reduce Russia to the status of a satellite, was it not urgent that the Allies should at least take under their control—and thus deny to German domination—that portion of the former Russian Empire to which they had easy strategic access, namely, Siberia? In the agitated days of late January and February, while Francis and his associates approached the end of their experience in Petrograd, this question pressed itself on many minds, and the Siberian pot began to boil briskly.

The situation on the spot, to be sure, remained without significant change. The Bolsheviki effectively controlled the entire Trans-Siberian Railway line, all the way to Vladivostok. In this port they held the real levers of power, although they permitted the city administration to remain nominally in the hands of moderate socialist elements, possibly hoping in this way to avoid giving provocation for foreign intervention. British and Japanese warships continued to lie in the harbor and to dominate it with their guns. The sailors from the British cruiser *Suffolk* were given frequent shore leave and moved about the city without friction. The Japanese were generally kept on shipboard to avoid incidents, in view of the strong anti-Japanese feeling among the Russian population. Through passenger traffic continued to move over the Trans-Siberian Railway more or less normally, but a freight block near Omsk still impeded the movement of freight. Thus the great accumulation of war supplies continued to lie scattered throughout the vicinity of Vladivostok, exposed to the rigors of the Siberian winter.

While the Bolshevik element in Vladivostok was violently averse to any form of intervention, the moderate elements looked with hope to the possibility of some sort of joint Allied action which would serve to keep the port out of Bolshevik hands. "None of the people," Consul Caldwell reported on February 1,

would welcome action here by Japan alone. It is possible that conditions may yet become such that Japan would feel compelled to take active steps here to protect her interests, owing to her proximity; for her to take such steps alone would arouse the hostility of all the population, whereas if others of the Allies, particularly America, took part there would be little or no hostility or opposition, except from the elements represented by the "Red Guard." [1]

By February, a new complication had arisen in the Siberian situation by virtue of the plans and ambitions of a Russian Cossack officer in command of Russian forces in western Manchuria, Captain Grigori Semenov. Semenov's forces were stationed around the western end of the Chinese Eastern Railway. He had been able to keep his men removed from Bolshevik influence and available as an effective fighting unit. It was, to be sure, only a tiny force, numbering but 750 men, infantry and cavalry, including no artillery. Three hundred of the men were Mongols, the remainder being made up of officers, cadet officers, and Cossacks. But in the chaotic conditions then prevailing in Siberia a small, compact force could accomplish wonders. Semenov was eager to cross the Manchurian border into Siberia and capture the section of the Siberian railroad between Krasnoyarsk and Irkutsk. For this he turned to the Allied representatives in Manchuria for assistance. The British, preoccupied with the chimera of a German seizure of the Trans-Siberian, and thinking Semenov's action might serve to forestall such an outcome, were

[1] National Archives, Petrograd Embassy 800 File, *op.cit.;* Despatch from Caldwell to Department of State, February 1, 1918. The general information about conditions in Vladivostok is also taken largely from this source.

favorably inclined to the suggestion. The Japanese had their own reasons for wishing to support Semenov, but no particular desire to consult with others about their plans in this respect.

At a later date, Semenov was to become a Japanese puppet, and the source of considerable trouble and annoyance to the other Allies. In the winter of 1918 he appeared to many western observers as one of the few sources of hope for a healthy reaction to the Bolshevik challenge in Siberia, and one that gave promise of keeping Siberia out of German hands.

❖

After the American rejection in January of the French suggestion for an Allied-White Russian intervention from the Chinese side, the wheels of international diplomacy in the Siberian problem, far from slackening their tempo, had begun to move at an even faster pace.

It was noted earlier (Chapter XV) that as the month of January drew to a close the British were beginning to preoccupy themselves intensively with the Siberian situation. Balfour had acquiesced, on January 24, in the American rejection of the French proposal, but had added, significantly, that events might at any time "create a different situation."

Events, as it seemed, were not long in doing just that. Four days later, the British government returned to the charge with a memorandum presented to the Department of State by the British Embassy in Washington, suggesting that Japan be asked, as mandatory for the Allies, to occupy the entire Trans-Siberian Railway.[2] The reason cited for the timing of this new proposal was that whereas some weeks before all Russia had presented a spectacle of unredeemed chaos, now "local organizations"—Cossacks to the north of the Caucasian range, Armenians to the south—had sprung up "which, with encouragement and assistance, might do something to prevent Russia from falling immediately and completely under the control of Germany." The question was how to reach them. To this question, the Allied occupation of the Trans-Siberian Railway was the only suitable answer.

The actual basis for this argument is obscure. The situation in the south of Russia does not seem, in fact, to have improved significantly

---

[2] *Foreign Relations, 1918, Russia,* Vol. II, *op.cit.,* pp. 35–36; Memorandum 112, January 28, 1918, British Ambassador to the Department of State.

in the period immediately preceding the despatch of this note (in the Cossack country it was actually deteriorating rapidly).[3] One may perhaps be forgiven, therefore, for suspecting that a more important reason for the timing of the new proposal was that the British government had by now had time to weigh the Japanese disapproval of the initial proposal for *joint* intervention, to take soundings in Tokyo, and to gain the impression (probably from Motono) that the Japanese government might not object to entering Siberia as the mandatory of the other Allies, provided she could act alone, and provided the request came from the others and had the approval of the United States.

In advancing this proposal to the State Department, the British took note of the objection they knew would be raised in American circles—namely that an intervention by the Japanese alone would be intensely unpopular in Russia and would tend to throw the Russians into the arms of the Germans—and they attempted to deal with it in advance by denying the premise. Their information indicated, it was said, that the Russians

. . . would welcome some form of intervention in their affairs, and that it would be more welcome in the form of the Japanese, engaged as mandatories of the Allies with no thought of annexation or future control, than in the shape of the Germans. . . .

To back up this proposal, a cable was sent to Colonel House through Sir William Wiseman—apparently from Balfour (the copy in the Wilson MSS is unsigned). Here two further points were stressed. First, the British government, while it had no wish to quarrel with the Bolsheviki, could not (especially since the suppression of the Constituent Assembly) regard the latter as "the Government of all the Russians." Secondly, so far as the Japanese were con-

[3] In a letter to Balfour of January 8, 1918, Lord Robert Cecil (then acting as Balfour's deputy in the Foreign Office) had written: "The Russians appear determined not to fight with anyone except one another. Even that they do in a half-hearted way. . . . As for the Caucasus, the position is absolutely chaotic. . . . We are engaged in trying to find money to help the Armenians, and at the same time to persuade the Georgians and the Tartars to reserve their massacring temper for the Turks. . . . The position north of Tiflis is even more mysterious. About 50% of our telegrams describe Kaledin as hopeless and useless with an infinitesimal following. The other 50% represent Kaledin and Alexieff as being at the head of a large organization embodying all the Cossack tribes from Siberia to the Black Sea, in a Federation of growing importance and power. . . ." (Blanche E. C. Dugdale, *Arthur James Balfour, First Earl of Balfour, K.G., O.M., F.R.S.,* Hutchinson & Co., Ltd., London, 1936, Vol. II, pp. 254-255.)

cerned, it was privately admitted that, notwithstanding contrary language in the memorandum presented to the State Department, it might indeed prove impossible to get the Japanese to leave the Maritime Provinces of Siberia once they had entered them; but, it was argued, the Japanese would intervene sooner or later in any case; to bring them in as the mandatory of the Allies would at least serve to embroil them more seriously with the Germans.

This last argument reflected once more the Allies' mis-estimation of German interest and ambitions in Siberia. The Germans were well aware that the Russian collapse would bring Allied influence into eastern Siberia in one form or another, but they were apparently quite reconciled to this prospect and had no intention of becoming "embroiled" with the Japanese over it. They knew that whereas a Japanese intervention would not be likely to affect anything they coveted for themselves (the Japanese at no time contemplated advancing much beyond Manchuria), it could hardly fail to excite jealousies and suspicions among the powers of the Entente coalition.[4]

The inspiration for the British proposal seems almost certainly to have come from British military circles, and particularly those officers stationed with the Supreme War Council in Paris. General Spears, the senior of these officers, had himself been stationed for three years in Japan. At some time in January, Spears drafted a paper advocating Japanese occupation of the entire stretch of the Trans-Siberian Railroad from Vladivostok to Chelyabinsk in the Urals, on the grounds that this would consolidate national feeling in Russia, inhibit further transfer of German troops to the western front, and possibly even save Rumania. This paper evidently found favor with the British War Office, for it was officially submitted by them to the French General Staff for consideration.[5] The reasoning in this later paper

[4] An indication of the German attitude in this question is to be found in the basis for the Brest-Litovsk talks proposed to the German government by Ludendorff on December 3, 1917. Ludendorff suggested that the Russians be assured, if necessary, that if the Japanese were to react to a separate German-Russian peace by attacking Siberia and the Russians were to defend themselves, Germany would not exploit the situation by attacking Russia from behind. (Captured German Foreign Office Documents, National Archives, Reel No. 1123.) This is, of course, a far cry from any intention of seizing Siberia.

[5] This document is referred to and summarized in a telegram from Frazier, American Diplomatic Liaison Officer at the Supreme War Council, sent through the Paris Embassy on February 10 at 10 p.m. The full text, used for the above summary, will be found in the Wilson MSS, Series II, *op.cit.* As presented to the French War Office, it was dated February 15, but it had no doubt been the subject of discussion in British circles prior to that date.

is so close to that of the British démarche of January 28, and particularly of Balfour's letter to House, as to suggest strongly that the impetus for the British action came from the same quarter.

This suggestion is strengthened by the fact that in urging on Lansing consideration of the British proposal, the British Chargé d'Affaires suggested that the Secretary consult the views of General Bliss, the American Military Advisor in the Supreme War Council at Paris, on the military merits of the proposal.

In relaying to House these British urgings for a Japanese action, Wiseman, who was better informed than any other foreign representative as to what was in the minds of House and the President, had no illusions that the suggestion would be favorably received. House had already told Wiseman that the President feared such action would play into the hands of the Germans, and doubted its military advantage.[6] "Unless Bliss . . . cables strongly in favour," Wiseman telegraphed to London, "I think the President will reject the proposal."

This pessimism was fully justified. House was wholly unimpressed with the reasoning of the British communication. He passed it on to the President, as he had been asked to do, and suggested to Wilson that he also talk to Wiseman. But he added, in this connection:

I have never changed my opinion that it would be a great political mistake to send Japanese troops to Siberia. There is no military advantage I can think of that would offset the harm. Leaving out the ill-feeling which it would create in the Bolsheviki Government, it would arouse the Slavs throughout Europe because of the race question.[7]

The President did see Wiseman (February 3), as House had suggested, and threw further cold water on the British approach.[8]

The following day (February 4), House received from Balfour a further message which revealed little real enthusiasm for the British proposal.[9] Balfour, it may be noted, had never been fully persuaded of the desirability, on balance, of intervention.[10] The initiative in the formulation of policy toward Russia in London appears to have

[6] Sir Arthur Willert, *The Road to Safety, A Study in Anglo-American Relations,* Derek Verschoyle, London, 1952, p. 147.

[7] Wilson mss, Series II, *op.cit.;* House to Wilson, February 2, 1918.

[8] *Ibid.,* House to Wilson, February 3, 1918.

[9] National Archives, State Department File 861.00/1049½.

[10] For Balfour's personal attitude in the intervention problem, see his cable to House of March 6, 1918, Seymour, Vol. III, *op.cit.,* p. 397.

been somewhat divided, in the winter of 1918, between the Foreign Office, on the one hand, and the so-called Russian Committee, on the other. The latter was a body designed, nominally, to reconcile Foreign Office and War Office opinion on Russian matters, particularly the problems presented by the centers of non-Bolshevik power in the outlying regions of the former Russian Empire. But the Foreign Office evidently viewed the Russian Committee, as foreign offices are apt to do in such situations, with distinctly mixed feelings, clung tightly to the theory of its own prerogative in matters of foreign policy, and permitted the committee to carry on without senior Foreign Office representation.[11] The result was that the views of War Office and Foreign Office were not always actually reconciled, and London sometimes spoke with two voices when it came to matters affecting Russia.

In the message received by House on February 4, Balfour responded cordially to House's misgivings about the British proposal, and agreed with alacrity "to the necessity for caution in dealing with a situation of very great inherent difficulty." He added that the British had "meantime" received news that Semenov was making progress in Siberia and said that another telegram would be sent to Washington suggesting that the question of Japanese occupation of the Siberian railroad be deferred "till we know how Semenov fares."

Such a telegram was indeed sent, describing the hopes the British were placing on Semenov; but Balfour was evidently overruled on his desire for a deferment of the proposal concerning the Japanese, for this message, delivered in Washington on February 6, suggested precisely the opposite and urged that Semenov's success *not* be allowed to defer consideration of the earlier proposal.[12]

The United States government, pursuant to the British request, had solicited on February 2 the views of General Bliss in Paris. But, finding itself thus pressed by the British, it set about, without awaiting the General's answer, to prepare a formal reply to the British démarche. There could be no question as to its tenor. The President had already expressed to Lansing, in a note written February 4, his

[11] See Lord Robert Cecil's letter of January 8, 1918, to Balfour; Dugdale, Vol. II, *op.cit.,* p. 255.
[12] *Foreign Relations, 1918, Russia,* Vol. II, *op.cit.,* pp. 38–41.

strong disapproval of the British proposal. "I am clearly of the judgment," he had written on that occasion,

that there is nothing wise or practicable in this scheme and that we ought very respectfully to decline to take part in its execution. . . .[13]

The wording of the State Department's reply to the British, despatched on February 8, was therefore stark and uncompromising:

The information at the disposal of the American Government does not lead it to share the opinion of His Britannic Majesty's Government that any form of foreign intervention in the affairs of Russia would be welcomed by the people of that country. It is believed on the contrary by the Government of the United States that any foreign intervention in Russian affairs would, at the present time, be most inopportune.

The United States government, it was added, had not despaired of the possibility of a change for the better in Russia "without foreign intervention." In any case, if intervention were unfortunately to become necessary, it should, the Department felt, be "undertaken by international cooperation and not by any one power acting as the mandatory of the others." [14]

If it was Secretary Lansing's hope that this reply would dispose of the Siberian problem for a time, he was to be disappointed. The following morning the problem was back on his desk in the form of a message from Morris in Tokyo, which raised the whole question again. It seemed that Stevens, now in Harbin, had wired Morris:

The situation in my opinion grave. The Allies should act vigorously or they may later on be at war to hold north [route] across the Pacific.

Stevens' opinion carried considerable weight in Washington. But, more important still, Morris reported that the Japanese Foreign Minister had spoken to him again, this time favoring a unilateral Japanese intervention, saying that he was consulting with the British and French about it, and asking for the views of the American

---

[13] National Archives, State Department File 861.00/1097. What Wilson had in mind here was only the wisdom of approaching the Japanese. He was under the impression that the Japanese would refuse such a proposal at that time; but he "felt it unwise to make a request which would in itself give the Japanese a certain moral advantage with respect to any ultimate desires or purposes she might have with regard to the Eastern Provinces of Siberia."

[14] *Foreign Relations, 1918, Russia*, Vol. II, *op.cit.*, pp. 41–42.

government.[15] Delicately, he had voiced his understanding of the fact that the position of the United States government was somewhat different from that of the other Allies, inasmuch as the United States was not a party to the 1914 Declaration barring a separate peace, which—one could infer—would be invoked to justify the contemplated action. (In other words: "We don't need your formal assent, and you really have no right to stop us; but we would like to be sure you will not interfere.")

Motono, like Stevens, had pointed to the threat of the spread of German influence in Asia via Siberia as the main reason for an early intervention.

The Japanese démarche set the discussion off once more. It apparently came as a shock to the President because of his belief, up to that time, that the Japanese were averse to taking any action whatsoever. Colonel House dropped in on Lansing the afternoon Morris' message was received, and the whole matter was gone over once more.[16] It was evidently decided that in light of this ominous evidence of Japanese interest, the earlier reply to the British was not strong enough—that a new statement of the American position, addressed to the Allied community as a whole, was now in order. Work was therefore put in hand on the drafting of a new communication and proceeded over the weekend of February 9-10. On February 12 the new draft was laid before the President and received his approval. On February 13 it was despatched, in identic terms, to the Japanese, British, French, and Chinese governments.

This last statement left nothing to be desired in forthrightness. The United States government considered, it was said, that the Japanese request (to the effect that Japan be given a free hand in Siberia) "if acceded to, might prove embarrassing to the cause of the powers at war with Germany." Four considerations were cited in connection with this view:

1. Intervention would antagonize the Russian people.

2. There was no immediate necessity for intervention.

3. If such necessity should arise, then the intervention should be joint, not unilateral.

4. In any case, the United States might find it necessary to insist that if there were to be any occupation of the Chinese Eastern Rail-

[15] *Ibid.*, pp. 42-43.
[16] Lansing MSS, *op.cit.*, Desk Diary, February 9, 1918.

Ambassador Francis with visitors in the Embassy Chancery

Ambassador Francis (third from left); John F. Stevens (second from left), Chief of the Advisory Commission of Railway Experts; and other members of the Commission

Robins and Gumberg with Russian and American acquaintances

In front row, l to r, are Raymond Robins, police chief Peters, unknown Russian (possibly Karakhan), Russian boy mascot of the Red Cross Commission, Alexander Gumberg, and Charles Stephenson Smith, Associated Press correspondent

way, as part of an occupation of the Trans-Siberian Railway, this be done by China rather than by the Japanese.

. . . Circumstances do not seem to warrant at this time a decision to take steps in Siberia which would . . . have the effect of arousing Russian opposition and resentment.[17]

After despatch of this communication to the respective Allied capitals, including Tokyo, the Department of State took occasion to reinforce it by oral discussions with the western Allied representatives in Washington. For the Japanese, however, Lansing conceived of an additional and even more forceful expedient which, he thought, might have the added virtue of increasing Washington's knowledge of what was taking place in eastern Siberia. The *Brooklyn*, it will be recalled, was still being held in readiness at Yokohama. Ever since the arrival of the Japanese and British ships at Vladivostok, Caldwell had continued to plead for another visit of the vessel to that port. The Secretary of State now solicited the President's consent (on February 13 and 15) for such a visit. On February 16 he was able to write to the Secretary of the Navy:

The President informs me that he desires Admiral Knight to return with the *Brooklyn* to Vladivostok for a visit in order to observe conditions at that port. I shall be glad to have the Admiral's views of the situation, which is somewhat complex. . . .[18]

The Secretary particularly requested that Admiral Knight make a study of the question of the accumulation of war supplies and of what was needed to keep them out of German hands.

The *Brooklyn*, as a result of this decision, re-entered Vladivostok harbor on March 1, and the Admiral proceeded at once to an examination of the situation, even including an inland visit to Harbin.

On February 16 Lansing called in the Washington correspondents and gave them—apparently for the first time—background information on what was taking place in Siberia. The Japanese were already putting out one statement after the other, warning the world that they felt themselves uniquely responsible for the preservation of peace in the Far East and that they might be obliged to take action if the situation were to develop to the detriment of Japanese in-

[17] *Foreign Relations, 1918, Russia*, Vol. II, *op.cit.*, pp. 45–46; telegram from Lansing to Ambassador Page in London, February 13, 1918, 7 p.m.

[18] *Ibid.*, pp. 46–47.

terests.[19] The Secretary was evidently concerned to have the American press prepared in the event of some sudden and unexpected development.

All in all, it was evident that the United States government was now seriously aroused over the possibility of some Japanese action in Siberia and that, while highly reluctant to see anything of this sort take place, it was insisting (and this was precisely what the Japanese did not want) on retaining its own freedom of action, including the possibility of sending forces itself, if an attempt were made to force its hand.

Again, as in the case of the earlier reply to the British, if the Washington statesmen hoped that this firm expression of disapproval by the United States government would put an end to the discussion, they were doomed to disappointment. With the rapid approach of the climax in the Soviet-German peace talks, the Siberian question was becoming more agitated than ever. The ensuing days brought a series of confusing and alarming messages.

On February 18 a message came in from Major Drysdale of the United States Army, who had been sent from China to Irkutsk in mid-January to observe conditions in Siberia. Drysdale supported the thesis that there was serious danger to Siberia from German intrigues, and he advised financial assistance not only to Semenov but to a similar leader, Kalmykov, who commanded the Ussuri Cossacks. These two forces, he thought, could control the entire Chinese Eastern Railroad from Vladivostok to Karimskaya. He cited the American, British, and French consuls at both Vladivostok and Harbin as agreeing with him in this recommendation.

The following day brought a rather confusing message from London. The British government, Balfour had assured Ambassador Page, had not committed itself to any policy or action with regard to Siberia; it had not even approached the Japanese government. All

[19] The chief Japanese "spokesman" in the United States, Dr. T. Iyenaga, addressing the Lawyers' Club in New York on the same day Lansing received the correspondents, called attention to a statement of Terauchi, the Japanese Premier, in the Diet to the effect that if peace should be endangered to the detriment of Japanese interests "the Japanese Government will not hesitate to take the proper measures." This was characteristic of Japanese statements at the time. Iyenaga went on to explain that the situation with respect to Russia's departure from the war was not yet wholly clear, and that for the moment "caution and best endeavors should be our watchwords"; but he made it plain that the situation might change at any moment. (*New York Times,* February 17, 1918.) This was, it should be remembered, the very day on which the Germans announced the renewal of the offensive on the eastern front, although that was not known as yet in New York or Washington.

it had done, according to Balfour, was to make preliminary inquiries through its representatives at Washington and Tokyo; the plan to ask Japan to occupy the railroad had been abandoned. Balfour, Page concluded, was

. . . now trying to get his Government to formulate some sort of Siberian policy to be discussed with the American Government and his [the] Allies; but . . . the Cabinet has not yet taken the subject up.[20]

Two days later, another telegram was received from Morris, relaying a number of disquieting reports about developments in Vladivostok (again, from French sources) and about increased Japanese military activity.[21]

Finally, the government at long last received from General Bliss his views on the British proposal. These opinions had been solicited (on British suggestion) on February 2, but had been delayed by confusion in the handling of telegraphic messages. General Bliss reported that on February 18 and 19 the permanent Military Advisors to the Supreme War Council, of whom he was one, had considered the question of Japanese intervention, had concluded that "the occupation of the Siberian Railroad from Vladivostok to Harbin . . . presents military advantages that outweigh any possible political disadvantages," and had recommended occupation by a Japanese force, on the basis of some guarantee as to Japanese purposes, and with provision for a joint Allied commission to supervise Japanese actions. The question of occupation of further stretches of the Trans-Siberian Railway was to be left to future determination in the light of circumstances.

In commenting on this resolution of the Military Advisors, however, General Bliss somewhat weakened its force. He thought that to bring the Japanese into Siberia involved grave danger and that the resulting military advantages would be small. He considered, in fact, that "all the purely military advantage that can be secured will be obtained by the occupation of Vladivostok." [22] But he agreed with his British and French colleagues that some chance must be taken.

There can be no question but that both Wilson and Lansing, anxious to defer to military opinion wherever the interests of the

---

[20] *Foreign Relations, 1918, Russia,* Vol. II, *op.cit.,* p. 48; London telegram 8723.
[21] *Ibid.,* p. 50, Tokyo telegram of February 19, 11 p.m.
[22] Wilson MSS, Series II, *op.cit.*

war effort were genuinely concerned, had awaited General Bliss's views with eagerness and attached considerable importance to them. But his message did not introduce any new element of importance into their calculation. General Bliss saw possible military advantage only in a Japanese occupation of Vladivostok, and only for the purpose of protecting the supplies. Even this advantage, he thought, would be small; and he felt that such a step would be attended by "possible grave danger." The concern which he expressed for the security of the military supplies was met by the fact that Admiral Knight had just been instructed, four days earlier, to proceed to Vladivostok and to make a study of this whole question. Thus General Bliss's reply, despite the resolution of the Military Advisors to which it was appended, afforded no grounds for modifying the position already taken with respect to the British proposal.

Just at this time, it might be noted, Stevens had succeeded in making arrangements to take his idle engineers, who had been waiting in Yokohama ("eating their heads off," as Robins contemptuously observed to Trotsky), and put them to work on the restoration of efficient operation on the Chinese Eastern Railroad, working from Harbin both east, toward Vladivostok, and west toward the junction with the Trans-Siberian. It was his hope that this operation could later be extended to Irkutsk, and that the entire network from Vladivostok to Irkutsk, including the Amur line, could eventually be taken under American technical control.

Everyone felt relieved that some employment had at last been found for the railway corps. Even the President voiced his pleasure over this fact in a note to Lansing on February 20.[23] In approving this arrangement, the government was careful to impress on the ambassadors in Tokyo and Petrograd, as well as on Stevens, that nothing was changed in "the friendly attitude toward Russia which has been manifested consistently by this Government." But in sanctioning the introduction of the engineers into Manchuria, the United States government was bringing itself one step closer to the acceptance of responsibility for the state of affairs in the troubled Siberian area.

❖

[23] *Ibid.* The first batch of these men were moved from Nagasaki to Harbin in the first days of March (National Archives, State Dept. File 861.00/1148). The remainder could not, as it turned out, be used at that time, and were obliged to cool their heels in Japan for another six months. (Roland S. Morris mss, Library of Congress, Box 7).

Siberia and the Final Brest-Litovsk Crisis

By the time the American note of February 12 had been read and digested in the various Allied chanceries, the situation had been complicated by the news of the renewal of the German offensive in Russia. This further inflamed Allied fears of a German domination of all Russia and Siberia, and provided an atmosphere anything but favorable to the reception of the American communication. In the last days of February, therefore, as panic and confusion increased in Petrograd, the pressures for intervention mounted rather than declined.

The Allied chanceries, furthermore, were by now beginning to pick up evidences of the growing Soviet interest in the possibility of Allied aid—evidences assiduously gleaned, wistfully exaggerated, and eagerly transmitted by Robins, Lockhart, and Sadoul. These evidences led to the hasty conclusion that perhaps the Soviet leaders were moving toward a frame of mind in which they would actually welcome Allied intervention. For this desperate hope there was little real foundation, particularly as concerns the Far East. The significant expressions of Soviet opinion in the party press (to which the Allied representatives paid too little attention) continued to reveal a wholly impartial loathing and suspicion of both warring "imperialist" camps. But the idea of a possible Soviet acquiescence in Allied intervention took root rapidly in the somewhat fevered Allied thinking of the moment, and this consideration was of course at once added to the arguments used to shake the American statesmen from their stubborn opposition to Siberian action.

Thus, in the final days of February, official Washington found itself subjected to a veritable barrage of pressures and suggestions, most of them based on premises which today stand out clearly as unsound, and about which the Washington statesmen were only too justified in their intuitive skepticism, but which it was not then possible to challenge with complete certainty. The French Foreign Minister, for example, told Ambassador Sharp in Paris that the situation was one of great gravity and begged that the United States government "not defer action until it was too late to remedy the evil threatened by German occupation and pacification of Russia." [24] He stressed that

. . . it was only contemplated to have Japan enter Siberia . . . after an amicable understanding had first been made with the Russian authorities.

[24] *Foreign Relations, 1918, Russia*, Vol. II, *op.cit.*, p. 51; Paris telegram 3221.

From Irkutsk, Harbin, and Peking came further reports about Semenov's promising activities, about the mobilization of German prisoners-of-war at Irkutsk, about the alleged desire of the Russian population for intervention, about Japanese military preparations. From Summers, in Moscow, came a renewed, earnest appeal for intervention, in which connection he forwarded verbatim a similar strongly worded recommendation from Poole (for a *joint* occupation of the Siberian railroad, not by Japan alone). Even Francis, in the throes of planning his departure from Petrograd and obviously influenced by the Allied diplomatic colleagues with whom he was meeting daily, climbed on the bandwagon with a series of recommendations along the same line. Russia, he wired on February 21, was in a fair way to become a German province with a monarchic form, in the light of which danger "I earnestly urge that we assume control Vladivostok and the British and French control Murmansk and Arkhangel in order to prevent supplies . . . falling into German hands."[25] He renewed this recommendation in terms of great urgency three days later. Finally, Morris wired from Tokyo on the 24th that Stevens had become convinced that the German influence in Siberia was growing steadily more serious "and will have to be met by force in the near future." Stevens felt that the Japanese government was about to take action. "He is now inclined to believe," the Ambassador reported, "that such action by Japan is necessary if Siberia is to be saved from German control."[26]

A particularly disturbing report reached Washington on February 23 from Peking. The Minister there had been confidentially informed

. . . that the Japanese Government has proposed to the Chinese Government cooperation between Japan and China in restoring order in Siberia. President Feng has expressed his approval of the principle and has so instructed Chinese Minister at Tokyo. In strict confidence China asks the advice of the American Government. The Japanese have not yet given to China any details as to the form which the action proposed shall take.[27]

This news had worrisome implications. It confirmed the fact that Japanese diplomacy was becoming active. But beyond that, if the Chinese were to join forces with the Japanese in this venture, the United States would find itself faced with the unanimous opposition

[25] *Foreign Relations, 1918, Russia,* Vol. I, *op.cit.,* p. 384.
[26] National Archives, State Department File 861.00/1148.
[27] *Foreign Relations, 1918, Russia,* Vol. II, *op.cit.,* p. 55.

of all the other powers involved in the area. This development hit, in fact, at the heart of traditional American policy in the Far East, which was to support the great land powers, Russia and China, against the Japanese and the European naval powers. That China, supposedly interested in preservation of the *status quo,* should join the Japanese alone in a venture into Siberia, was a most unsettling prospect, which simply did not fit into the established American concept of what was involved in the problems of the Far East.[28]

To the Chinese request for advice, Lansing replied guardedly on February 23 by directing the American Minister at Peking simply to communicate orally to the Chinese Foreign Office the views contained in the recent communication to the Allied governments about intervention.[29]

On February 24, Morris reported that the French were talking to the Japanese about the possible purchase by Japan of the supplies accumulated at Vladivostok. The Japanese Foreign Minister, he wired, had told the French Ambassador that he deplored the failure of the Allies to sanction Japanese intervention, that all preparations had been completed, and that the need for action became every day more imperative. As for Japan, she was willing, Motono had indicated, to act without American assent, provided the French and British would agree.[30]

On Tuesday, February 26, while Francis was in the throes of departure from Petrograd, Lansing went to the White House and had a long conference with the President on the Siberian question. The conversation was evidently occasioned primarily by the disturbing prospect of a Chinese involvement in the Japanese plans, a subject which the two men had not had occasion to discuss personally since the exchange with the Chinese government three days before. But the talk apparently ranged further; and on this occasion, for the first time, some sort of modification of the American position may have

[28] The Chinese indicated to the State Department three days later that the reason for their concern, and the reason why they were contemplating accepting the Japanese proposal, was that they feared that a unilateral Japanese occupation of the line west of Manchuria would enable the Japanese to secure a permanent hold on Outer Mongolia.

[29] In this response to the Chinese request, merely informing the Chinese of what had already been said to other governments, one has a clear example of the traditional American aversion to bilateral discussion with individual foreign governments, and the corresponding preference for speaking either to the world at large or to other nations as a group.

[30] *Foreign Relations, 1918, Russia,* Vol. II, *op.cit.,* p. 56.

been envisaged. While the Secretary was speaking with the President, a representative of the French Embassy approached Basil Miles, the chief of the Russian Division, with a renewed French appeal for a change in the American attitude on intervention. Miles's memorandum about this conversation was on the Secretary's desk when he returned from the White House. The Secretary forwarded it at once to the President with a chit saying, "I do not see that it changes our *proposed* policy. . . ." [31] One would think from the use of the word "proposed" that *some* new departure in American policy must have been under discussion.

The following day, Wednesday, February 27, was practically monopolized by the Siberian question, so far as the Washington statesmen were concerned. The British, in the first place, now introduced their big guns. Lord Reading, the new British Ambassador, called on the President and handed him the text of a long telegram he had received from Mr. Balfour, dated February 26. It began with a solemn statement that recent events in Russia rendered "in the considered opinion of the British Cabinet" the adoption of the policy outlined by the British government "a matter of great urgency." The message went on to define the most important Allied interests in Siberia as being,

. . . one, the preservation of the military stores now lying at Vladivostok . . . and, two, the denial to the enemy of the vast agricultural resources available to the west of Lake Baikal.

As for the first of these interests, His Majesty's Government had no doubt that the military stores would be effectively dealt with by Japan "with or without our consent." But the Japanese, acting independently, would not be apt to penetrate beyond the junction of the Amur and Siberian railroads, and their action would thus not meet the second of the two requirements. To induce the Japanese to go farther, it would probably be necessary to ask them to act as mandatory and to give them financial assistance. The Japanese, however, could be induced to act only if they could take action alone, unencumbered by the military presence of the other Allies. If the United States would not agree, then obviously a common approach would be impossible; Japan, in this case, would act on her own; but Japa-

---

[31] Wilson MSS, Series II, *op.cit.* (italics added).

nese action would then be insufficient to serve the real Allied purpose, and would be devoid of those safeguards by which it might otherwise be surrounded. The British government renewed its appeal that the United States join Great Britain, France, and Italy "in immediately inviting Japan to occupy the Siberian railroad"—the occupation to extend at least as far as Omsk and to be accompanied by declarations designed to reassure the Russian people.[32]

The Ambassador also gave the President a further message saying that the British government had learned that enemy prisoners in Siberia were being organized with a view to cutting the Siberian railroad. Could not instructions be sent to Mr. Stevens to see what he could do for the protection of the line, "with or without the assistance of General Semenov"?

It was clear from the wording of this approach that the British and French now expected the Japanese to intervene in the very near future, whether or not the United States associated itself with the request that they do so. What was at stake in the American attitude, if this view was correct, was only the question as to how far the Japanese should go, and how much good their intervention would do the Allied cause.

As though these powerful representations from the British were not enough, the Secretary received on the same afternoon a call from the French Ambassador, who brought him a copy of a telegram received from his colleague at Tokyo, which read as follows:

Immediate consent to the Japanese arrangement concerning Siberia is indispensable. Mr. Motono has seen the French Ambassador and has shown himself ready to promise disinterestedness and even to say so publicly. He also declared that he was ready to pledge his country to act so far as the Ural Mountains.[33]

This reference to Japan's readiness to declare her disinterestedness and to advance as far as the Urals, coming on top of the British approach, made a deep impression on Lansing, who was already shaken by the formidable body of opinion building up in opposition to the American position. For months he had held stoutly, against all attacks, to the view of the President and Colonel House that any form of intervention must be resolutely opposed. Now, for the first

---

[32] *Ibid.* Reading made a similar communication to Lansing the same day.
[33] *Ibid.*

time, under the almost universal pressure of the Allies and United States representatives abroad, he wavered.[34] He sat down the same afternoon and addressed a note to the President, telling of his conversation with the Ambassadors and indicating his own change of heart. In describing the new information he had received, he told the President that the telegram from the French Ambassador in Tokyo "is to me of especial interest in view of the avowal of Motono to declare publicly the disinterestedness of Japan and also the pledge to carry on military activities as far as the Ural Mountains—that is, to the confines of Asia." He then went on to say:

Since we talked over this matter yesterday I do not know as the conditions have materially changed, but certainly the French telegram has thrown a new light upon it and I think we should carefully consider whether or not we should urge the Allied Governments not to make Japan their mandatory.

My own belief is that Japan intends to go into Siberia anyway and that it might be a restraint upon her if she should make a declaration such as Motono proposed. So far as this government is concerned I think all that would be required would be a practical assurance that we would not make protest to Japan in taking this step.

As the whole matter is of vital importance and requires immediate action if any is to be taken I would be grateful if you would give me your views and guidance at the earliest possible moment.[35]

The following day, Thursday, February 28, while the President pondered this change of heart on the part of his Secretary of State, the Secretary's time continued to be taken up solidly with the alarums and excursions surrounding the Siberian problem. General Judson was now back, and his friend the Postmaster General was phoning in an effort to get attention for the General's recommendation that the United States itself move in and take over operation of all the Russian railroads, in addition to sending 50,000 men through Vladivostok to a line somewhere west of the Urals.[36] There were negotiations with Chandler P. Anderson, of the War Industries Board Council, about "50,000 tons of nitrate at Vladi." The Japanese Chargé came

---

[34] The messages from Stevens seem also to have played a prominent part in wearing down Lansing's resistance to the pressures of the other Allies.

[35] *Foreign Relations, The Lansing Papers*, Vol. ii, *op.cit.*, pp. 353–355.

[36] Lansing had received the General on February 20, but made no record of this visit other than to observe, rather unenthusiastically, that he had "carried only little information." (Lansing MSS, *op.cit.*, Desk Diary, February 20.)

in on a fishing expedition. (The Secretary, still awaiting the President's reaction to his change of heart, put him off with a request for more information about the situation.) Subordinate State Department officials, alarmed by the unceasing rumors from Irkutsk about German prisoners being armed and concluding (since the Brest peace was not yet signed) that Francis would be leaving the country for good, came in with a desperate recommendation for sending a regiment from Tientsin to Irkutsk to meet Francis on his way out through Siberia.[37] House shuttled between White House and State Department, talking Siberia in both places.

A message from Tokyo, received that same day, quoted an official public announcement of the Japanese government to the effect that while Japan was "not yet in a position to commence military activities" the situation was being carefully considered. The statement ended, however, with the observation that it might be "some time" before decision would be taken:

... The views of the Allied powers must be ascertained and the fullest understanding reached before a final decision can be made.[38]

In this guarded language there was a hint of deeper realities, and one that might have spared the United States government some of the anguish of decision, but it apparently went unnoted in the general turmoil of the moment.

On Friday morning, March 1, the President phoned Lansing asking him to come to the White House at noon. By this time, the Secretary must have received some indication that his change of heart was approved by the President; for when Lord Reading called, later that morning but before the Secretary had been to the White House, Lansing said that the United States could not join in requesting the Japanese to take action in Siberia, but would "doubtless raise no objection."[39] In explanation of the American unwillingness to join in the request, he pointed out again, as he had on the 27th,

... such an agreement as was proposed would amount to a treaty and that would have to be submitted to the Senate, where there were several strongly anti-Japanese Senators who would oppose it.[40]

[37] *Ibid.*, Desk Diary, February 28. Francis, in a moment of despair over his prospects for remaining in Russia, had requested such assistance.
[38] *Foreign Relations, 1918, Russia*, Vol. II, *op.cit.*, pp. 60–61.
[39] Lansing MSS, *op.cit.*, Desk Diary, March 1, 1918.
[40] *Foreign Relations, The Lansing Papers*, Vol. II, *op.cit.*, p. 354.

At noon the Secretary went to see the President, who handed him the draft (composed by the President himself) of a message for transmission to the Japanese government. Whatever Lansing may have been told before, this message made it absolutely plain that the President, like the Secretary, had now been swayed to a point where he dared no longer oppose the action urged by the other Allies, although he did not feel in a position to give it specific sanction. The message, as drafted personally by the President, was as follows:

The Government of the United States is made constantly aware at every turn of events that it is the desire of the people of the United States that, while cooperating with all its energy with its associates in the war in every direct enterprise of the war in which it is possible for it to take part, it should leave itself diplomatically free wherever it can do so without injustice to its associates. It is for this reason that the Government of the United States has not thought it wise to join the governments of the Entente in asking the Japanese government to act in Siberia. It has no objection to that request being made, and it wishes to assure the Japanese government that it has entire confidence that in putting an armed force into Siberia it is doing so as an ally of Russia, with no purpose but to save Siberia from the invasion of the armies and intrigues of Germany and with entire willingness to leave the determination of all questions that may affect the permanent fortunes of Siberia to the Council of Peace.[41]

Colonel House, who had been in Washington earlier in the week, had evidently discussed this change of attitude with the President. Whether he had actually seen the text of the proposed message prior to its transmission to Lansing, is not clear; but he had evidently indicated in some form acquiescence in the general course it embodied. No sooner had he returned to New York than he was troubled with great misgivings about what had been decided. The burdens of wartime statesmanship were now growing too heavy and multitudinous for even the strongest shoulders. "The truth of the matter is," he later recorded in his diary,

. . . I was not well while in Washington and was not able to give the matter as clear thought as it deserved. The President, too, was tired. . . . Neither of us, I think, was altogether fit last week to properly solve the problems which confronted us. There was never a more critical week in our

---

[41] *Ibid.*, p. 355. The original draft of this message, plainly typed in the White House and probably by Wilson himself, is in the National Archives, File 861.00/1246.

history and the fact that it found us both at a rather low ebb was unfortunate to say the least.[42]

Although the message was drawn up primarily for communication to the Japanese government, it was the President's wish that it should first be made known to the British, French, and Italians. Lansing, who was leaving for a much-needed vacation immediately after his White House appointment, charged Counselor Frank Polk, who was to take charge of the Department in his absence, with the task of showing it to the Allied envoys. Polk at once invited the envoys to the Department for this purpose. Just before receiving the first of them (the French Ambassador, M. Jusserand), Polk showed the message to Mr. William C. Bullitt, then serving (with office in the State Department) as adviser to both the White House and the Secretary of State on developments in the enemy countries. Bullitt strongly deplored the change of heart which the message reflected. He at once recognized that it did not faithfully reflect House's views, and shrewdly surmised that it would not remain unchanged if House were given an opportunity to reconsider. Accordingly, he urged Polk to hold up communication to the Allied envoys and not to show the message to anyone at that point. It was sure, he said, to be reversed; Polk would be sorry if he transmitted it. But Polk did not feel at liberty to ignore the President's instruction. The argument was still in progress when the French Ambassador's arrival was announced. Telling Bullitt, "Now get out, Bill, and forget about it," Polk proceeded to carry out his instructions, showing the message to the French and British that afternoon and to the Italians the following morning.

The Japanese Chargé, who had evidently gotten wind of the situation from some quarter, also appeared in Polk's office on Saturday morning and asked if there were any communication for him; but Polk fortunately put him off and revealed nothing to him of what had been decided.[43]

Meanwhile, Bullitt had not been idle. After his representations to Polk on Friday afternoon he had returned to his own office and

[42] House MSS, *op.cit.*

[43] "I told him," Polk reported to Lansing on March 15, "I would let him know, and took good care not to commit myself as to whether we had made up our mind or as to our attitude." *Foreign Relations, 1918, Russia*, Vol. II, *op.cit.*, p. 68.

had drawn up a vigorous memorandum of protest about the step that was being taken, warning in particular about the loss of moral position it would involve. "We cannot stand aside," he wrote in the conclusion of this paper;

we cannot wash our hands of this matter. Unless we oppose, we assent. Pontius Pilate washed his hands. The world has never forgiven him.[44]

When the memorandum was finished, Bullitt phoned House in New York, told him of the tenor of the message to the Japanese, and read his own memo over the phone. He then took a copy of his memorandum and left it, with House's approval, at the White House.

House was shocked to realize, apparently for the first time, the full nature and finality of the step that was being taken. He had not known, he confided to his diary, that the President was going to act so quickly.

House talked the next day with both Elihu Root and the Russian Ambassador, Bakhmeteff. Both shared Bullitt's apprehensions, and considered that Japanese intervention would tend to throw Russia into the arms of Germany.[45] In the light of these urgings and his own misgivings, House despatched that same evening an urgent note to the President, telling him of his talks with Root and Bakhmeteff and continuing as follows:

We are treading upon exceedingly delicate and dangerous ground, and are likely to lose that fine moral position you have given the Entente cause. The whole structure which you have built up so carefully may be destroyed over night, and our position will be no better than that of the Germans.

I cannot understand the . . . determination of the British and French to urge the Japanese to take such a step. Leaving out the loss of moral advantage, it is doubtful whether there will be any material gain. . . .[46]

The following day, Sunday, March 3, before receiving House's letter, the President summoned Polk for a further discussion of the Siberian situation and showed himself anxious that the message to the Japanese government should be despatched promptly the next morning. When House's letter reached him, however, on Monday

[44] Wilson MSS, Series II, *op.cit.;* also, National Archives, State Department File 861.00/1290½.
[45] The Russian Ambassador also saw to it that his views were made known in detail on Saturday morning to the Department of State by one of his subordinates.
[46] Seymour, Vol. III, *op.cit.,* pp. 393-394.

morning, the President at once made inquiry through House's son-in-law, Auchincloss, as to whether House had seen the text of the message before he framed his note. House confirmed to Auchincloss over the telephone that he had seen the message, and went on to warn once more of the "loss of our moral position" and the "dulling of the high enthusiasm of our people for a righteous cause . . . in exchange for a vague and nebulous military advantage." [47] He urged the President to warn the other Allies of the possible effect of Japanese action and to insist that the Japanese make a public statement of the reason for their intervention and of their policies with regard to Siberia.

These arguments were sufficient to sway the President from his purpose. He at once phoned Polk and instructed him to hold up transmission of the message to Tokyo. The following morning (Tuesday, March 5) he summoned Polk to the White House and handed to him the text of a substitute for the earlier communication. It was a message designed to be read to the Japanese Foreign Minister by the Ambassador in Japan (though the Ambassador was not to leave a copy unless requested to do so). Its tenor was as follows:

The Government of the United States has been giving the most careful and anxious consideration to the conditions now prevailing in Siberia and their possible remedy. It realizes the extreme danger of anarchy to which the Siberian provinces are exposed and the imminent risk also of German invasion and domination. It shares with the governments of the Entente the view that, if intervention is deemed wise, the Government of Japan is in the best situation to undertake it and could accomplish it most efficiently. It has, moreover, the utmost confidence in the Japanese Government and would be entirely willing, so far as its own feelings toward that Government are concerned, to intrust the enterprise to it. But it is bound in frankness to say that the wisdom of intervention seems to it most questionable. If it were undertaken the Government of the United States assumes that the most explicit assurances would be given that it was undertaken by Japan as an ally of Russia, in Russia's interest, and with the sole view of holding it safe against Germany and at the absolute disposal of the final peace conference. Otherwise the Central powers could and would make it appear that Japan was doing in the East exactly what Germany is doing in the West and so seek to counter the condemnation which all the world must pronounce against Germany's invasion of Russia, which she attempts to justify on the pretext of restoring order. And it is the judgment of the

[47] *Ibid.*, p. 395.

Government of the United States, uttered with the utmost respect, that, even with such assurances given, they could in the same way be discredited by those whose interest it was to discredit them; that a hot resentment would be generated in Russia itself, and that the whole action might play into the hands of the enemies of Russia, and particularly of the enemies of the Russian revolution, for which the Government of the United States entertains the greatest sympathy, in spite of all the unhappiness and misfortune which has for the time being sprung out of it. The Government of the United States begs once more to express to the Government of Japan its warmest friendship and confidence and once more begs it to accept these expressions of judgment as uttered only in the frankness of friendship.[48]

In his subsequent official report to the Secretary of State, Polk stated that "certain changes were made" in the earlier communication. This was certainly an understatement. A glance at the two documents will show that the second represented a quite different approach. The crucial statement that the United States had no objection to the request being made by the other Allies was omitted, as was, in fact, every reference to the question of the formal United States relationship to the proposal for Japanese intervention. All that remained of the earlier draft was the note of confidence in the proper and reasonable intentions of the Japanese and the passing reference to the eventual role of the peace conference in deciding the permanent fate of Siberia. In the new draft, the United States maintained its uncompromising opposition to the idea of intervention in general, merely observing that if its views were to be overridden by the others, then it would be desirable that the Japanese give explicit assurances concerning the nature of their intentions. It emphasized that even such assurances could easily be discredited "by those whose interest it was to discredit them," and that the entire action might easily play into the hands of the enemy.[49]

---

[48] *Foreign Relations, 1918, Russia,* Vol. ii, *op.cit.,* pp. 67–68; contained in Washington telegram of March 5, 1918, 4 p.m. to Tokyo. Original White House draft is in the National Archives, State Department File 861.00/1246, with Polk's notation: "Handed me by President March 5, 1918."

[49] It is of interest to note the treatment given this incident by the official Soviet history, *Mezhdunarodnye Otnosheniya na Dalnem Vostoke, 1870–1945* (International Relations in the Far East, 1870–1945), edited by Ye. M. Zhukov, State Publishing House for Political Literature, 1951, p. 272. Stating that on February 27 Lansing had written to Wilson that he "considered it possible to permit Japan to take action on the condition that she should advance her forces as far as the Urals," the Soviet historian went on to say: "Wilson approved the proposal of Lansing with the single reservation, that the question of Siberia should be finally decided at the Peace Con-

Siberia and the Final Brest-Litovsk Crisis

It was evidently now the expectation of House and the President, in the light of Motono's statements in Tokyo, that Japan would take action anyway, despite the failure of the United States government to approve the Allied request. The British, and no doubt also the French, continued, even after the terms of the American note had been made known to them, to urge the Japanese to do just that, and did not conceal this from Washington.

As it turned out, however, the Japanese government, to everyone's surprise, continued to refrain from intervening, basing their position formally on the grounds that the success of the undertaking depended on the wholehearted support of all the great powers associated in the war against Germany and that it could not be launched without such support. They were unwilling, they stated in their reply to the American communication (handed to the American Ambassador in Tokyo on March 19), to take

. . . any action on which due understanding has not been reached between the United States and the other great powers of the Entente.[50]

But now, it being clear that no unanimous approval of the other Allies was to be expected, they began also to stress a new note, one which would make it possible for them, if they so wished, to act wholly on their own responsibility, without raising any question of Allied approval. They referred pointedly to the possibility that the situation in Siberia might develop in such a way as to jeopardize Japan's national security and vital interest and that in this case Japan might be "compelled to resort to prompt and efficient measures of self-protection" for which she would count on friendly support and understanding from the other Allies.

The vacillation by which both Wilson and Lansing were seized, at the turn of the month from February to March, in their attitude toward the Siberian problem was brought on not only by weariness and pressure of duty (although these, too, played their part) but also by the evidence they saw of a growing Japanese impatience to act in Siberia, and especially by the impression they gained in the

---

ference." The Soviet historian apparently drew his statement here from the memorandum which was not sent, ignoring the one which was.

[50] *Foreign Relations, 1918, Russia,* Vol. II, *op.cit.,* pp. 81–82.

last days of February—that the Japanese were preparing to take action, if need be, by agreement with the British and French alone, disregarding the absence of American consent. This impression was conveyed to them in several ways, but particularly by Morris' report of the latest French-Japanese discussions and by the British approach of February 27. The impression seems to have rested, in each case, primarily on statements made by Foreign Minister Motono, in Tokyo.

Actually, it seems most doubtful that this was a correct reflection of the position of the Japanese government. To be sure, the course of events in German-Soviet relations—the breakdown of the Brest-Litovsk negotiations, the renewal of hostilities, and finally the Russian capitulation—must have tended to strengthen the position of Motono and the other proponents of intervention. It must have enabled them to argue with considerable persuasiveness that the golden moment for intervention had arrived—that if the Soviet government continued to resist Germany it would be compelled to invoke and accept Allied support, whereas if it yielded to German terms, Russia would be finally and formally out of the war and the Allies would then be justified in any action they found it necessary to take in protection of their own interests. These were weighty arguments; and it must be assumed that, supported by the vigorous urgings of the British and French, they placed considerable strain on the position the Japanese government had adopted.

But there seems to be no evidence, aside from the impression which the British and French representatives derived from Motono's statements, that the position of the Japanese government—namely, that Japan would not intervene unless the United States accepted its share of the responsibility for the decision—was ever really altered at any time throughout this period. All other evidence points to the conclusion that important, and in fact decisive, forces in Tokyo continued to oppose firmly any change in policy. These forces included the Premier himself, Baron Goto, several influential senior statesmen, and a large and important segment of parliamentary opinion. Many influential Japanese feared that if Japan consented to intervene in Siberia while America remained uncommitted, she would risk engaging her strength in a costly and not easily terminable continental involvement, while America stood aside, conserved her own forces in the Pacific, and waited for the moment of Japan's maximum exhaustion to throw her own weight into the balance. Thus the weight of opinion in the authoritative Advisory Council seems to have remained at all times adverse to any extensive Japanese action without American concurrence.

If a contrary impression was conveyed to Wilson and Lansing, this must be attributed to a certain wishful distortion of the real situation all along the line, but particularly in the contacts between Motono and the Entente envoys in Tokyo. Here was an instance where better information could certainly have eased the strains of American statesmanship, which is not to imply that this information would have been easy to acquire. It is, in any case, to the credit of the American statesmen and their closer advisers, that they were better informed at this juncture by their own instincts and convictions than by the reports that reached them across a world so torn, so confused, so full of desperation and impatience.

CHAPTER XXIV

ROBINS AND RATIFICATION

... the Anglo-French bourgeoisie are laying a trap for us: "Just come along, my little dears, and go to war *right now*. . . . We will profit magnificently from it. Germany will strip you bare, . . . and will give us better terms in the west, and incidentally Soviet power will go to the devil. . . . Come on and fight, dear 'allied' Bolsheviks, we will help you."

—*Lenin*

WHEN Ambassador Francis and the members of his entourage awoke on Thursday, February 28, 1918, their train was in the station at Vologda, having arrived there in the depths of the night. To his great irritation, the Ambassador learned that the first train, under charge of Secretary of Embassy Bailey, had not remained at Vologda, as Bailey had been specifically ordered to have it do, but had continued on toward Siberia.[1] Telegraphic inquiry up the line brought the information that the train had gotten as far as Viatka (now Kirov), 395 miles east of Vologda, and had just left that point on its way toward the Urals and Siberia. On the Ambassador's orders, it was finally stopped at a little station called Vereshchagino, between Viatka and Perm, where it was detained for some days until arrangements could be made to sort out the staff and bring back to Vologda those whose services were wanted there, the remainder being permitted to continue on to Vladivostok and home.

Francis remained at Vologda, as he had determined to do if it

---

[1] Bailey had written instructions from Francis to stop at Vologda and await the second train. The reason for his failure to do so is still obscure. He blamed the railway officials at Vologda, and claimed that the train had in effect been forced through. In the entourage of the Ambassador there were of course suspicions that the American officials in charge of the first train had been animated by fear of the German advance and wanted to get out as rapidly as possible.

should prove in any way possible.[2] At the outset he and his party lived on the train. He was not unduly uncomfortable, although his staff lived in conditions that were unavoidably somewhat cramped. Mr. Norman Armour, one of the two diplomatic officers accompanying the Ambassador, has described these days in a letter to me:

. . . The railway station restaurant or food counter was of course the favorite haunt—particularly while there was still a fair assortment of food to offer: big jars of dill pickles, chorney kleb [black bread], kvass [a non-alcoholic beer], and hard boiled eggs were among the favorites, as I remember, although by February 1918 the supply had dwindled sadly. The above, incidentally, was to be my diet for the first two-three weeks, for on arrival in Vologda until I found a room in a house in town, I lived in my compartment in the train. [I had the] upper berth in a small compartment, with Butler Wright in the lower berth (until he left Vologda for Vladivostok on his way home), and my dog . . . under the lower berth. He, in fact, also came to like even the dill pickles, although I don't think he ever took to kvass!

The Chinese and Japanese chiefs-of-mission, anxious to get back to their respective countries before the expected Siberian intervention began, spent only two days in Vologda and continued their journey on the regular Trans-Siberian Express, leaving chargés d'affaires with the group in Vologda. Francis gave them a farewell dinner on his train on the evening of their departure, and Philip Jordan showed his inimitable resourcefulness by producing, even in those strained circumstances, "chicken creamed on toast, excellent soup, fish and ham, canned fruit and champagne, as well as tea and cigarettes and cigars." [3]

On Sunday, March 3, Francis received a visit from the Mayor of Vologda, who tendered his compliments and offered his assistance in arranging for the Ambassador's residence in that city. This assist-

[2] According to Lockhart, *op.cit.*, p. 235, Robins stated over the telephone from Vologda, on the day following arrival of the train, that Francis was contemplating proceeding to Siberia and would probably leave the next day unless Lockhart could elicit from Lenin some statement that would encourage Francis to remain. This is a curious statement, for there is no other evidence that Francis contemplated going farther, and everything in his own private and official correspondence indicates the opposite. Some members of Francis' entourage suspected Robins of encouraging the Ambassador to continue in order that he, Robins, might not be further encumbered in his relations with the Soviet authorities by the presence of the official representative.

[3] Francis MSS, *op.cit.*, from a personal letter written on March 4 by the Ambassador's personal secretary, Mr. Earl Johnston, to a relative at home.

ance the Ambassador gratefully accepted. The result was perhaps most authoritatively and accurately described by Philip Jordan, in a letter written to Mrs. Francis on March 9:

. . . the Mayor told him if he had the time to spare that he would like to show him a large club house that was not in use at present. The Ambassador went with him and oh my what a dandy house he gave the Ambassador. It is all furnished. All rooms are as large as the pink room and as clean as it can be . . . we are now keeping house and living in grand style. Now Mrs. Francis after trying to describe [this] to you I want to ask you if you don't think that was awful nice the way the Mayor has treated the American ambassador. Of course you must take into consideration that the U.S. does not recognize these people or have any thing to do with them. The Mayor of New York City could not have done any more than this poor Bolshevik Mayor did.[4]

On Tuesday, March 5, the Ambassador moved to the club, in company with the Brazilian Chargé and the Siamese Minister (accompanied by a three-year-old boy and a nurse) who were also to occupy the building. They were later joined by the Japanese Chargé. In the course of time life naturally became a bit confining; Armour has described the comic monotony of conversation on the long summer evenings when the little group had been together for some time. But the physical comforts left little to be desired. Food, in particular, was undoubtedly better than in Petrograd. All in all, there can be no question but that Vologda was a well-chosen point of residence; and the local authorities, as Philip Jordan observed, did all in their power to make the diplomats comfortable.

Some four weeks after Francis' arrival, the group at Vologda was joined by the large party from the French Embassy, led by Ambassador Noulens, who had tried in vain to get out of Russia through Finland. After a similar period of waiting in their train, quarters were found for them in an abandoned school building not far from the club house.

Before long the British Chargé, Mr. Lindley, who (to the indignation of the French colleagues he left behind) had succeeded in getting out through Finland, was also sent back to Vologda via Archangel to represent the British government.

In this way, Vologda became for a time a curious sort of diplomatic center. Francis himself described it to the Mayor as the "dip-

[4] *Ibid.*

lomatic capital of Russia," [5] and was pleased at the Mayor's appreciation of this compliment. But the effort of these diplomatic figures to perform their official functions in a remote provincial town had its ludicrous as well as its practical side. It was only natural that the little diplomatic colony in Vologda should become the butt of many witticisms, not only on the part of those westerners who followed the Soviet government to Moscow, but also on the part of the Bolsheviki themselves, to whom the habits and reactions of all western diplomats, not only those in Vologda, would never cease to be a source of amusement and head-shaking.

Once again, as in so many other instances in the history of international relations, the locus of diplomatic activity had its effect on the spirit by which it was animated. Remote Vologda soon developed its own political atmosphere, quite different from that which prevailed in the new Soviet capital. Lockhart, especially, was sensitive to this, and scornful of the little diplomatic society there. It was, he wrote,

... as if three foreign Ambassadors were trying to advise their governments on an English Cabinet crisis from a village in the Hebrides.[6]

The Vologda diplomats, he claimed, "lived on the wildest anti-Bolshevik rumors," and moved the representatives in Moscow to a mixture of amusement and despair by their frequent requests for confirmation of these absurdities. He even quotes his Italian colleague in Moscow, General Romei, as saying with reference to Vologda:

If we had put all the Allied representatives in a cauldron and stirred them up, not one drop of common sense would have come out of the whole boiling.[7]

There was, to be sure, a certain detachment and otherworldliness about the little Vologda colony, and mistakes were doubtless made by virtue of this quality. But the atmosphere of Moscow was also not without its misleading and distorting sides; and from the perspective of nearly forty years, the Vologda atmosphere seems no more unreal than any other.

❖

[5] Francis, *op.cit.*, p. 237.
[6] Lockhart, *op.cit.*, p. 246.
[7] *Ibid.*, pp. 246–247.

The added confusion bound to flow from the dispersal of the Allied staffs—some going to Vologda and others accompanying the Soviet government to Moscow—was not long in making itself felt in the handling of political matters. The first days following the departure of the diplomatic missions produced a regular comedy of errors—or tragedy of errors, as Robins would more likely have termed it—in the efforts of the American representatives, in particular, to effect some sort of communication between the Soviet leaders and their own government.

Robins was not a man to endure for long the forced inactivity of life in a railway car in the station of a remote Russian provincial town. In the days immediately following arrival in Vologda, he remained in close contact with events in Petrograd. He had frequent telephonic and telegraphic communication with Lockhart. Gumberg and Arthur Ransome (who had accompanied the party to Vologda) were in similar contact with Trotsky's secretary, Shalyapina. On arrival at Vologda, Robins even wired Lenin directly, asking for information on a whole series of questions about the signing of the peace treaty and other matters. He received a brief reply, signed by Lenin, reporting that the peace treaty was not yet signed, but politely referring him to Petrov, of the Foreign Office, for further information along these lines.

In Petrograd, Sadoul and Lockhart remained in daily personal contact with Trotsky and continued to discuss with him the possibilities of Allied assistance. Lockhart, who had intended to follow Robins shortly to Vologda, found these talks so interesting that he changed his plans and decided to remain for some days in Petrograd and then to follow the Soviet government to Moscow. Something of the tenor of the conversations with Trotsky was no doubt divulged to Robins over the telephone, but scarcely all; and the knowledge that such discussions were proceeding heightened Robins' impatience over his own isolation and inactivity. He stuck it out over Saturday, March 2, but only apparently by reason of a curious side effect of the celebrated misunderstanding of the Soviet government with respect to Karakhan's telegram from Brest-Litovsk.

Karakhan, it will be recalled, was a member of the Soviet delegation sent to Brest-Litovsk to sign the final German terms. Having arrived in Brest on the afternoon of February 28, Karakhan and his associates had their first discussion of substance with the Germans on March 1. They found themselves confronted with a rigid ultimatum and concluded that it was useless to attempt to argue the matter any further. "In view of this," Karakhan wired on March 2 to the government at Petrograd,

and owing to the fact that the Germans have refused to stop war activities until the treaty signed, we have decided to sign without discussion and leave at once. We have asked for a train, expecting to sign and leave tomorrow.[8]

In connection with this request for return transportation, however, Karakhan had already—prior to the despatch of this message—sent an earlier telegram to the Soviet government, saying: "Send us a train to Toroshino near Pskov with an adequate number of guards. . . ." This message, arriving in advance of the other, was taken by Lenin and his associates to mean that for some reason negotiations had been broken off; that no signature would take place; and that hostilities would be resumed.

Under the impact of this alarming impression, believing the German advance on Petrograd to be imminent and Allied assistance to be of vital importance, Lenin despatched a telegram to the "American Embassy, Vologda, attention Gumberg and Ransome," transmitting the complete text of Karakhan's message and adding:

In all probability this telegram signifies that the peace negotiations have been broken off by the Germans. One must be prepared for an immediate offensive of the Germans against Petrograd, and for a general offensive on all fronts. It is necessary to rouse everybody and to take necessary measures for protection and defense.[9]

This message was accompanied by one from Shalyapina to her future husband, Ransome, in which she said:

As Lenin's telegram means war, and consequently your immediate going further, I am sending my best wishes for a happy journey.[10]

It was probably only in the light of these messages, received Friday evening, that Robins remained in Vologda as long as he did. When the misunderstanding was cleared up and the news came through, on Sunday, that the peace treaty had been signed after all,

[8] Bunyan & Fisher, *op.cit.*, p. 522.
[9] Francis MSS, *op.cit.*
[10] *Ibid.*

he got his car attached to a train of "14 cars of rifles and sailors" bound for Petrograd,[11] and departed abruptly, leaving a note for Francis to explain the suddenness of his departure and his failure to say good-by.

En route to Petrograd, Robins' train passed one on which Sadoul was proceeding to Vologda. Had Robins known of this, and of the nature of Sadoul's mission, he would probably have delayed his departure, for Sadoul was coming on business which interested Robins intimately. We will let Sadoul tell of it in his own words, written on Saturday, March 2:

> To inaugurate the era of diplomacy without diplomats, Trotsky and Lenin proposed to me yesterday that I go to Vologda to see the Ambassador of the United States in order to inform him of the difficult situation created for the Allies by the danger of Japanese intervention in Siberia and in order to ask him, first, whether his government is in agreement with the Japanese Government and, secondly, if there is no such agreement, what his government expects to do to forestall an action obviously hostile to Russia and contrary to Allied interests.[12]

It might be mentioned at this point that the news of the possible imminence of Japanese intervention had become generally known to the world public in the last two or three days of February. The *New York Times,* whose columns can serve here as a good sample of what was reaching public attention, carried on February 26 a front-page story from Harbin, under the headline "As Russia Yields, Japan May Move Army into Siberia." The story indicated that the Japanese expected to take action at an early date. This appears to have been the first clear indication to the American public of the nature and seriousness of the discussions then in progress. The next day the paper carried strong hints from London along the same lines. On February 28 its Washington correspondent confirmed that Japan had directed inquiries to the Entente powers with regard to intervention.

Similar reports were of course reaching Petrograd. Although the Soviet press, obviously concerned not to add to the public anxiety, did not print any of them until after signature of the Brest-Litovsk Treaty, they were no doubt available to Trotsky by the first day of

[11] Robins MSS, *op.cit.,* pocket diary, March 3, 1918.
[12] Sadoul, *op.cit.,* p. 251.

the month. They must have created great perturbation in the minds of the Soviet leaders, who still had prominently in mind the possibility that they might be driven out of western Russia by the Germans and who now saw themselves being squeezed between a Japanese occupation of Siberia and a German occupation of Russia proper. They were, of course, astute enough to realize that Allied eagerness for the adoption of an anti-German attitude on their part gave them a certain bargaining power. They therefore began at once to fill the ears of the unofficial Allied representatives in Petrograd with hints that if the Allies would only refrain from intervening in the Far East, the likelihood of Soviet resistance to German designs, treaty or no treaty, might be heightened, whereas if the Far Eastern intervention were to materialize, they would have no choice but to throw themselves on the mercy of the Germans.

Sadoul believed that the Soviet leaders could actually be persuaded to permit a certain cession of territory to the Japanese in the Far East, if the Allies would help them militarily in Russia proper. He was confident that once they regained some military strength, they would immediately challenge the validity of the Brest-Litovsk Treaty, the conditions of which he regarded as obviously "unacceptable and inapplicable." He therefore threw himself with enthusiasm into his new role as Soviet representative, trying to prevent Japanese intervention, and persuaded his chief, General Niessel, after some initial argument, to let him proceed to Vologda and transmit the Soviet statements and questions to Francis. The General gave him a letter to Francis, explaining the circumstances, prudently requesting that any reply be communicated "through your own agents." [13] Sadoul arrived in Vologda on Monday evening, March 4. He had interviews late that night and the following morning with Francis, whom he afterwards described to his friend Albert Thomas as "respectable vieillard, d'intelligence un peu lente et visiblement fatigué par la vie qu'il mène en gare de Vologda, dans le wagon diplomatique." [14]

What transpired in the talks between the two men is not wholly clear, particularly insofar as the Japanese question is concerned. Sadoul came away very pleased with the talk, and reported later that the Bolshevik leaders had been "enchantés" with the results. Francis

[13] Francis MSS, *op.cit.*
[14] Sadoul, *op.cit.*, p. 254.

had agreed, he wrote Thomas, that the Japanese intervention in Siberia should be modified and limited and should lose all anti-Russian character; also that there should be a parallel American action which would reassure Russia and protect the interests of the Entente generally.

Francis of course had no authority to promise anything of the sort, and was well aware of this. One is moved by Sadoul's enthusiastic reaction to suspect that his knowledge of governmental procedure was not much firmer than that of Robins.

Actually, Francis had been much exercised about the Siberian problem. Not only did he believe, for some reason, that intervention was already decided and imminent, but he had also somehow gained the idea that an anti-Bolshevik government was about to be established at Irkutsk. Two days before Sadoul's arrival, he had already written to the Commercial Attaché, Mr. Chapin Huntington, who was on the first train, directing him to stop off at Irkutsk and to function there until further notice as a liaison officer with "the Russian authorities." In this letter to Huntington, he wrote:

. . . I have many reasons to believe that the predominant Far Eastern power looks upon the present situation with contempt—and that events of great importance may be impending. May I urge you, therefore, to pay particular attention to this phase of the situation, to give it your unfailing scrutiny and to advise me of any developments of this nature that may arise.[15]

Francis and Sadoul obviously spoke about Siberia, and especially about the possibility of the Stevens Railway Mission being used to assist the Bolsheviki in their possible resistance to Germany. One result of the talk was Francis' decision to send the Embassy Counselor, Butler Wright, on to Harbin, to find out and report what had become of the Stevens Mission, and then to continue on to Washington and advise the government about the Siberian question generally. Sadoul reported it as agreed between him and the Ambassador that the Stevens Mission would be placed at the disposal of the Bolsheviki as soon as possible.

[15] Francis MSS, *op.cit.,* letter, Francis to Huntington, March 3, 1918. What Francis had heard of must surely have been the abortive attempt of certain partisans of Siberian autonomy to set up, on February 22, an underground "Provisional Government of Siberia" at Tomsk. The attempt amounted, in view of Soviet control of the territory, to no more than a gesture. The leading participants fled immediately afterward to Harbin.

Francis, however, did not mention any talk of Siberia in his report to Washington of Sadoul's visit. He merely said, in a message sent March 5:

... Trotsky sent French officer here to ask me what moral and material assistance Allies could render if peace not ratified at Moscow Conference March 12. I am sending Military Attaché and Riggs to Petrograd tonight to confer with Soviet Government which realizes its helplessness if peace not ratified as Lenin, Trotsky both think will be the case and I concur. ... I have instructed Military Attaché to assure Soviet Government that I will recommend moral and material cooperation provided organized resistance is sincerely established which will give promise of retarding German advance and engaging attention of troops who would otherwise be sent western front.[16]

(It will be noted that Francis was precisely back in the position he had adopted at the end of December on the occasion of the first crisis in the Brest-Litovsk negotiations.)

But in the light of what Sadoul told him, the Ambassador now withdrew his recommendation for intervention in Vladivostok and the northern ports; "their capture," he wired, "now would be unwise." He also told Washington of his sending Wright eastward to Harbin to "keep close touch with eastern conditions, observe corps movements, inform Stevens concerning railroad situation," but he did not specifically relate this to his talk with Sadoul.

The Military Attaché, Colonel Ruggles, left that same night, March 5, for Petrograd with his assistant, Captain Riggs, as indicated in Francis' telegram. They were armed with an instruction from Francis directing them to confer

... with the Soviet Government or its Military Attachés concerning military preparations for resistance to the German advance in the event the separate peace may not be ratified by the Moscow Conference or in the possibility that the German advance may be resumed before the Moscow Conference is held.[17]

The reference to the "Moscow Conference" had relation to the Fourth Special All-Russian Congress of Soviets scheduled to convene in Moscow within a few days to consider ratification of the Brest-Litovsk Treaty. It will be noted that neither of the contingencies envisaged by Francis materialized.

[16] *Foreign Relations, 1918, Russia,* Vol. 1, *op.cit.,* p. 392.
[17] Francis mss, *op.cit.,* letter, Francis to Ruggles, March 5, 1918.

In the same communication, Francis repeated his promise to recommend American assistance as indicated above. "This letter," he concluded, "is not for exhibition to the Soviet Government but for your instruction and guidance. . . ."

Upon their arrival in Petrograd, Ruggles and Riggs found that their task had already been largely accomplished by Robins. He had arrived in Petrograd early in the morning of Tuesday, March 5, had at once gone out to the Smolny Institute, and had talked with Trotsky and Radek. They had spoken of the Far Eastern situation, and Trotsky, according to Robins, had brought up the question of American assistance by asking him, "Do you want to prevent the Brest peace from being ratified?"

From that point, according to Robins, the dialogue continued as follows:

Robins: There is nothing that I want to do so much as that.

Trotsky: You can do it.

Robins: You have always been against the Brest peace, but Lenin is the other way; and frankly, Commissioner, Lenin is running this show.

Trotsky: You are mistaken. Lenin realizes that the threat of the German advance is so great that if he can get economic cooperation and military support from the Allies he will refuse the Brest peace, retire, if necessary, from both Petrograd and Moscow to Ekaterinberg, re-establish the front in the Urals, and fight with allied support against the Germans.

Robins: Commissioner, that is the most important statement that has been made to me in this situation. Will you put that in writing?

Trotsky: You want me to give you my life, don't you?

Robins: No; but I want something specific. I do not ask you to sign it. You make a written statement of your specific inquiry, interrogatories to the American Government, and that with affirmative response these things will take place, and after writing arrange that Lenin will see me and that he will agree to this, which is counter to what I have had in mind as Lenin's position, arrange that a fourth person, my confidential Russian secretary, whom you know and I know, Mr. Alexander Gumberg, shall be with me, and I will act on that.[18]

Robins left Trotsky to prepare the statement. He returned at 4:00 p.m. Trotsky handed him the document. Together, accompanied by Gumberg, they repaired to Lenin's office and joined him in his

[18] *Bolshevik Propaganda, Hearings* . . . , *op.cit.*, pp. 800–801.

frugal afternoon repast. The document was translated, and its terms explained, for Robins' benefit. Not only did it satisfy him, but he accepted it as a statement of highest significance. Pleased and excited, he rushed off to show it to Lockhart and to wire it to Francis.

The language of the document is worth noting. It may be taken as representing just about the limit to which the Soviet leaders were willing to go, at the moment of their greatest extremity, in exploring collaboration with the United States and Great Britain. It was a piece of paper to which, ever after, Robins would attach an importance no whit less than that ascribed by Sisson to his sensational secret papers. The text was as follows:

In case (a) the All-Russian congress of the Soviets will refuse to ratify the peace treaty with Germany, or (b) if the German government, breaking the peace treaty, will renew the offensive in order to continue its robbers' raid, or (c) if the Soviet government will be forced by the actions of Germany to renounce the peace treaty—before or after its ratification—and to renew hostilities—

In all these cases it is very important for the military and political plans of the Soviet power for replies to be given to the following questions:

1. Can the Soviet government rely on the support of the United States of North America, Great Britain, and France in its struggle against Germany?

2. What kind of support could be furnished in the nearest future, and on what conditions—military equipment, transportation supplies, living necessities?

3. What kind of support would be furnished particularly and especially by the United States?

Should Japan—in consequence of an open or tacit understanding with Germany or without such an understanding—attempt to seize Vladivostok and the Eastern-Siberian Railway, which would threaten to cut off Russia from the Pacific Ocean and would greatly impede the concentration of Soviet troops toward the East about the Urals—in such case what steps would be taken by the other allies, particularly and especially by the United States, to prevent a Japanese landing on our Far East, and to insure uninterrupted communications with Russia through the Siberian route?

In the opinion of the Government of the United States, to what extent—under the above-mentioned circumstances—would aid be assured from Great Britain through Murmansk and Archangel? What steps could the Government of Great Britain undertake in order to assure this aid and thereby to undermine the foundation of the rumors of the hostile plans against Russia on the part of Great Britain in the nearest future?

All these questions are conditioned with the self-understood assumption that the internal and foreign policies of the Soviet government will continue to be directed in accord with the principles of international socialism and that the Soviet government retains its complete independence of all non-socialist governments.[19]

It is important to note certain things about this communication. In the first place, it committed the Soviet government to nothing. It constituted merely a query as to what aid would be forthcoming in certain contingencies. It did not even say definitely that the Soviet government would accept such aid if it were forthcoming. Moreover, none of the three contingencies envisaged in the communication materialized. The query was actually out of date within two weeks after it was made. To hold it out, therefore, as Robins did, as proof of Soviet willingness to collaborate with the Allies, was stretching a point to a degree which only the general extremism of wartime psychology could explain.

A clearer picture of Soviet views on that crucial day was contained in Lockhart's report of his own conversation with Trotsky of the same date. Trotsky, Lockhart indicated, was still under the impression that the Special Congress of Soviets would refuse to ratify the treaty and would declare a "holy war" on Germany, provided there was "at least some semblance of support from the Allies." Trotsky had been at pains to point out that this did not involve friendly relations "because that would be hypocritical on both sides" but this did not preclude "some working arrangement." He had astutely suggested that if the Allies allowed Japan to enter Siberia, ratification of the treaty would be a foregone conclusion.

In transmitting this information, Lockhart pleaded with his government not to proceed with intervention. He held out hope that if they would only refrain from independent landings at Archangel and Murmansk and restrain the Japanese from landing at Vladivostok, it would not be impossible

. . . to obtain subsequently a direct invitation from the Russian Government to the English and American Governments to cooperate in the organization of Vladivostok, Archangel, etc. . . .

[19] *Cumming & Pettit, op.cit.,* pp. 81–82. This is plainly Gumberg's somewhat awkward translation from the Russian text. A first draft of this translation, in Gumberg's hand, is in the Gumberg MSS, *op.cit.* The Russian original appears to be nowhere available.

Secretary of State Robert Lansing (left) with the British Ambassador, Lord Reading

The notification to the American Embassy of John Reed's appointment as Consul at New York

Ambassador Francis and his staff in front of the clubhouse at Vologda

COURTESY OF EARL M. JOHNSTON

Third from left, Colonel Ruggles, the Military Attaché; fourth, Secretary of Embassy Norman Armour with his dog; Ambassador Francis in the center; to the extreme right, Philip Jordan

Pointing out that the Congress was scheduled to meet in Moscow March 12, he begged for support in a last-moment effort to keep Russia on the side of the Allies:

The Congress meets on March 12. Empower me to inform Lenin that the question of Japanese intervention has been shelved . . . that we are prepared to support the Bolsheviks in so far as they will oppose Germany and that we invite his suggestions as to the best way in which this help can be given. In return for this there is every chance that war will be declared (in fact, war between the Bolsheviks and Germany is in any case inevitable) and that it will arouse a certain amount of enthusiasm.[20]

Robins, with the help of Consul Tredwell and Captain Prince (who had returned to Petrograd with Robins), tried that evening to wire Trotsky's message to Francis. Unfortunately they were compelled to use the military code for its transmission; they had no other. But since Ruggles and Riggs, now on their way to Petrograd, had taken the military code books with them, the Embassy at Vologda had no means of decoding the message. When this fact became known to the Americans in Petrograd, later that day, they were confronted with a pretty problem. ("They left too soon to decipher the long code message of the day before! And no code communication between Petrograd and Vologda is possible! Oh la la!" Bullard expressively recorded.)

Tredwell, realizing the importance of the message, urged (in fact, practically ordered) Captain Prince of the Military Mission to despatch the message directly to the War Department in Washington, for transmission to the State Department "adding that we were endeavoring to get it to the Ambassador as soon as possible."[21] Together with one of the officers of the Military Mission, Tredwell worked all night encoding the message, with a view to despatching it to Washington on the morning of the 6th.[22] The message was evidently held, however, for clearance with Ruggles, who was arriving that night. Ruggles must have decided, for some reason, not to despatch it at that time. His decision was probably connected with the fact that he himself expected to see Trotsky almost at once, and he

[20] Francis MSS, *op.cit.*

[21] *Ibid.*, letter from Tredwell to Wright, March 6, 1918.

[22] Bullard wrote to Sisson on March 8: "Tredwell requisitioned Bukharski and the W.D. Code and they went off and stayed up all night. I learned the next day that long cables had gone to Washington and Vologda. . . ." (Bullard MSS, *op.cit.*)

no doubt wanted to send his own version of Trotsky's views; also with the fact that he (like the other Allied military attachés) was resentful of the free-wheeling negotiations of Robins and Lockhart. In any case, the records indicate that he did not actually despatch the message containing Trotsky's suggestions until nearly two weeks later. It did not reach Washington until March 22, by which time, of course, the Brest-Litovsk Treaty had long been ratified.[23]

Not only did Ruggles hold up despatch of this message, but he evidently failed to inform either Tredwell, Robins, or the Ambassador that he had done so.[24] Robins thus remained under the impression that Trotsky's query had gone forward to Washington. Believing that this would mean, in any case, a further delay in the Allied response (he had first hoped the Ambassador would take responsibility for a favorable reply without consulting Washington), Robins went to see Lenin again and pleaded for delay in ratification of the treaty, in order to give him time to get an answer from the United States government to Trotsky's questions. He did not name the date of this interview, but it could only have been on the 6th or 7th. "I want more time, Commissioner," he described himself as having said on this occasion.

It takes time to decode long cables like this and get an agreement. . . . America would take no policy that England and France do not agree to, and it will take time to get that agreement.[25]

He added that the day after he saw Lenin, either the 7th or 8th, the *Izvestiya* announced that the opening date of the Congress had been postponed from the 12th to the 14th, at Lenin's instance. He "thought" that the reason for the postponement "was to give us time to answer." This assumption gained considerable historical currency, and has been frequently—and not unnaturally—accepted as

[23] Department of the Army files in the National Archives reveal no record whatever of this telegram. Pentagon Records Section files (MB-879) do contain, however, a message from Ruggles, subsigned by Prince, despatched from Vologda as No. 5, March 20, 1918, transmitting paraphrased text of Trotsky document. The Office of the Chief of Staff received it March 22 at 4:57 a.m.

[24] Tredwell, a week later, made reference to "the question which I had Prince telegraph for me ten days ago when we discovered that our message to the Governor had not reached him." (Francis MSS, *op.cit.*, letter of March 15 from Tredwell to unknown addressee.) Francis later told the Department that Robins "came again Vologda much excited about Japanese invasion having previously cabled War College from Petrograd in . . . code. . . ." (National Archives, State Department File 123 Su 61/121.) Francis presumably had this from Robins.

[25] *Bolshevik Propaganda, Hearings . . . , op.cit.,* p. 805.

valid.[26] Actually, there is no evidence that this was so, other than Robins' own deduction which he based not on any specific statement of Lenin's but only on the coincidence of the postponement of the Congress soon after his talk with Lenin. On the contrary, there are serious grounds for doubt as to whether Robins' talk with Lenin had any important relation to the postponement of the Congress. A glance at Lenin's attitude toward the whole question of Allied aid, together with what is known about the timing of the postponement, will illustrate this.

When, on February 22, Trotsky told his colleagues in a meeting of the Central Committee about the receipt of the French offer of aid (Chapter XXIII), a debate ensued over the question as to whether it was permissible, in principle, for a government of the working people to accept aid from the "imperialists." Trotsky and a number of his comrades favored acceptance of aid; Bukharin and others opposed it. The opinion of Lenin, who was not at this session, was solicited in writing. It was on that occasion that he sent back his famous chit:

I request that my vote be added in favor of the acceptance of potatoes and arms from the bandits of Anglo-French imperialism.[27]

While Lenin was thus agreed in principle to the acceptance of Allied aid—if it could be had on favorable terms—two important reservations must be borne in mind.

First, Lenin was intensely suspicious of the motives of the Entente powers in offering this aid. He viewed the offer as a trap, designed to lure the Soviet government into resuming the struggle with the Germans in order to take military pressure off the Entente powers in the west and to destroy the Soviet government. He had stated this with characteristic pungency and irony, on the day prior to the incident just referred to, in his article "The Revolutionary Phrase":

Look at the *facts* with regard to the behavior of the Anglo-French bourgeoisie. They are now trying in every way to drag us into the war with

---

[26] See Carr, Vol. III, *op.cit.*, p. 48; also Williams, *Russian-American Relations*, *op.cit.*, p. 135; Wheeler-Bennett, *op.cit.*, p. 297.

[27] *Lenin*, Vol. XXII, *op.cit.*, footnote 119, p. 607. (Lenin's defense of this position was spelled out at greater length in his article "About Itching" published in *Pravda* that same evening. Here he drew the parallel of the acceptance by the American colonies of aid from Spain and France in the revolutionary war against England.)

Germany, promising us millions of blessings, shoes, potatoes, munitions, locomotives (on credit . . . nothing like "bondage," you understand—this is "only" on credit). They hope that we will fight Germany *now*.

It is understandable why they should want this: in the first place, because in that way we would divert a portion of the German forces; secondly, because Soviet power would most easily break down as a result of a premature military conflict with German imperialism.

The members of the Anglo-French bourgeoisie are laying a trap for us: "Just come along, my little dears, and go to war *right now*." They say, "We will profit magnificently from it. Germany will strip you bare, will make a good thing out of it in the east, and will give us better terms in the west, and incidentally Soviet power will go to the devil. . . . Come on and fight, dear 'allied' Bolsheviks, we will help you." [28]

Lenin obviously continued to adhere to this view of Allied motives throughout the entire period to which Robins referred. In his final statement at the Seventh Congress of the Party, on March 8, he emphasized that "in addition to the desire of the Germans to strangle the Bolsheviki, there is a similar desire on the part of the people in the west." [29] Similarly, in his statements to the Congress of Soviets, a few days later, he again spoke repeatedly of the "trap" of war with Germany into which the *bourgeoisie* (here he did not specifically mention the Entente governments) was attempting to lead Russia. [30] According to notes taken by one of the delegates to the Congress, Lenin ended his final speech at the Congress with the following words, which do not appear in the official stenographic account:

German imperialism will bog down in the Ukraine, in Finland, and in France. The Japanese imperialism is still more terrible. And here it will perhaps be necessary for us to conclude a series of the most shameful agreements with Anglo-French imperialism, with America, with Japan and others, in each case for the purpose of drawing breath and gaining time. [31]

---

[28] *Ibid.*, pp. 261–269, contains the entire article.

[29] *Ibid.*, p. 335.

[30] *Ibid.*, pp. 394 and 409.

[31] *Ibid.*, footnote 148, p. 614. This interpretation of Allied motives was to be perpetuated by Soviet historians in later decades. In his history of Soviet foreign policy Tikhomirov (*Vneshnaya Politika Sovetskogo Soyuza* [Foreign Policy of the Soviet Union], State Publishing Co., Moscow, 1940, p. 15) wrote: "When at the time of the negotiations [at Brest-Litovsk] disagreement appeared between the Soviet and German points of view about the peace, hopes immediately arose in Entente circles for the possibility of a conflict between Soviet Russia and Germany. The English 'representative,' the well known spy Lockhart, came to the Commissariat for Foreign Affairs daily, offering money, arms, and instructors in the hope of drawing Soviet

Secondly, Lenin was convinced, throughout, that delay in coming to terms with the Germans could result only in a deterioration of those terms from the Soviet standpoint and that it was necessary to ratify at once in order to gain a breathing space and build up some sort of Soviet armed force. This being the case, at no time did he view the distasteful possibility of Allied aid as an *alternative* to ratification of the treaty. How and why he contrived to give a contrary impression to Robins on the 5th must remain a matter of conjecture. Throughout the entire period to which Robins refers, Lenin continued, in the inner counsels of the Party, to take a strong and uncompromising stand in favor of immediate ratification. In the debates at the Seventh Party Congress on March 7th and 8th (and we must remember that it was on the 6th or 7th that Robins had asked him for "more time"), he urged ratification with fervor and eloquence. At no point in his lengthy statements to this party gathering did he ever mention the possibility of Allied aid at all, or deviate one jot from his insistence that the treaty be ratified forthwith. The Party Congress terminated its deliberations by passing a resolution recognizing it as necessary that this

. . . most onerous and most degrading peace treaty with Germany be ratified, in view of the extremely unhealthy state of the demoralized forces at the front, and in view of the necessity of taking advantage of even the tiniest possibility for a breathing space, before the advance of imperialism on the Soviet Socialist Republic.[32]

(The entry of the Japanese into Siberia was at that time regarded as a foregone conclusion. And Lenin did not believe that even ratification of the treaty would do more than to delay further German penetration into Russia.)

This resolution, drafted personally by Lenin and closely following his line of thought, made no mention whatsoever of Allied aid as a factor in the problem, and frankly placed the entire hope for the survival and further success of Soviet power on the spread of the revolution to the western countries generally. This was a secret reso-

---

Russia into war against Germany. For every Russian soldier who would remain on the German front, America cynically offered 100 rubles."

This last curious statement was repeated in his lectures on the Brest-Litovsk Treaty by the historian M. N. Pokrovski: *Vneshnaya Politika Rossii v XX Veke* (Russian Foreign Policy in the 20th Century), Publishing House of the Sverdlov Communist University, Moscow, 1926. The basis for the statement was not cited.

[32] *Lenin,* Vol. XXII, *op.cit.,* p. 339.

lution, not published until after the German collapse had led to the termination of the Brest-Litovsk Treaty; and there is no reason to suppose that it represented anything other than a frank and sincere statement of the opinion of the Central Committee.

In the light of the above, it seems most improbable that Lenin, unreservedly committed to ratification of the treaty not only by his personal views but also (after the 8th) by the formal resolution of the Party Congress, should have postponed the holding of the Congress of Soviets in the hope that Allied aid might obviate the need for immediate ratification. Such a position, if known to his comrades, could only have sown doubt as to the sincerity of his attachment to his hard-fought position, and would certainly have provided arguments for the opposition.[33]

At what time, and for what motives, the Congress was postponed, is not clear. The Germans had given the Russians fourteen days in which to ratify the treaty. This period expired on March 17. The Congress had to be held before this date. The original announcement, setting the 12th as the opening date, was published on March 5.[34] But it was then decided to move the government to Moscow prior to the holding of the Congress. This meant that a great deal had to be done in a short space of time. Most members of the Soviet of People's Commissars, including Lenin himself, proceeded to Moscow on Monday, March 11, which was plainly the earliest they could get away. Apparently, it became evident to them, at the time of the move, that they would need a day or two to install themselves in Moscow and to make adequate preparations, organizational and otherwise, before plunging into the actual work of the Congress. This was presumably the reason for the postponement from the 12th to the 14th.

The actual announcement of the postponement does not seem to have appeared either in the *Izvestiya,* where it would normally have been carried as an official item, or in the *Pravda.* The most plausible explanation of this fact is that the announcement was actually made on the 11th, when both papers were in process of moving to Moscow

[33] *Sezdy Sovetov v Postanovleniyakh i Rezolyutsiyakh* (Official History of the Soviet Congresses), Moscow, 1935 (p. 54), in discussing the background of the IV Special All-Russian Congress of Soviets, observes correctly that the Entente powers were interested, for military reasons, in preventing ratification, and mentions in this connection Wilson's message to the Congress, noting with satisfaction that this "maneuver" failed. It says nothing of any other attempt to prevent ratification.

[34] *Izvestiya,* No. 40, March 5, 1918.

and therefore skipped an edition. This is strongly borne out by the fact that on the preceding day, March 10, in its last Petrograd edition, the *Izvestiya* still referred to the Congress as scheduled for the 12th; and also by the fact that it was on the 11th that Consul General Summers, in Moscow, wired the news of the postponement to Washington.[35]

Thus the known circumstances do not bear out in any way Robins' impression that a decision was taken by March 6 or 7 to postpone the Congress in order to give the United States government time to answer Trotsky's questions. One can only conclude that here again either he was the victim of the sort of misinformation that so frequently dogged his path during the months of his activity in Russia, or that his memory failed him, or both.

After registering with Lenin his plea for more time, Robins, apparently convinced that he would need the Ambassador's help in obtaining a clarification of the American attitude, departed again for Vologda, with a view to discussing the matter with the Ambassador and then proceeding on to Moscow, where he intended to join the Soviet government and be present at the meeting of the Congress. He arrived in Vologda about midnight, March 8 to 9, and at once reported to the Ambassador on his interview with Trotsky and on the state of affairs in Petrograd generally. At two in the morning, after hearing Robins' story, Francis sent off a brief message to the State Department, telling of the confusion about the earlier telegram and adding:

. . . Since R. left Petrograd, Moscow and Petrograd Soviets have both instructed their delegates to the Conference of March 12th to support the ratification of the peace term. I fear that such action is the result of a threatened Japanese invasion of Siberia which I have anticipated by sending Wright eastward. Trotsky told Robins that he had heard that such invasion was countenanced by the Allies and especially by America, and it would not only force the Government to advocate the ratification of the humiliating peace but would so completely estrange all factions in Russia that further resistance to Germany would be absolutely impossible. Trotsky furthermore asserted that neither his government nor the Russian people would object to the supervision by America of all shipments from Vladi-

[35] National Archives, State Department File 861.00/1279. Francis wired on March 14 that he had learned from Robins, over private service wire from Moscow, that the Congress was opening that day. Had the announcement been made on the 6th or 7th, Francis would surely have known of this before.

vostok into Russia and a virtual control of the operations of the Siberian railway, but a Japanese invasion would result in non-resistance and eventually make Russia a German province. In my judgment a Japanese advance now would be exceedingly unwise and this midnight cable is sent for the purpose of asking that our influence may be exerted to prevent same. Please reply immediately. More tomorrow.[36]

It will be noted that Francis, while telling something of Robins' talks with Trotsky, apparently did not at that time wire anything of the content of the written statement of questions which Robins had procured from Trotsky.

Later that day, while Robins was still in Vologda, the Ambassador received Colonel Ruggles' telegraphic report of *his* interview with Trotsky and General Bonch-Bruyvich, which had taken place the preceding day. This, it seemed, had been inconclusive. The main thing, Ruggles emphasized, was to restrain the Allied governments from "reprisals and occupations." The Colonel added that he was in touch with the French Military Mission and would probably accompany the other Allied military representatives to Moscow.[37] It was plain that from this time on any negotiations he might have with the Soviet authorities about Allied military aid would be merged with those of the Entente military representatives. Francis also passed this news on to Washington, reinforcing with a powerful appeal of his own Ruggles' warning against any foreign intervention. "I cannot too strongly urge," he stated,

the folly of an invasion by the Japanese now. It is possible that the Congress at Moscow may ratify the peace, but if I receive assurance from you that the Japanese peril is baseless I am of the opinion that the Congress will reject this humiliating peace. . . .[38]

In the course of that same day, while Robins was in Vologda, Francis received from Chicherin what amounts to the first really bilateral diplomatic communication from the Soviet government on a political subject. This curious document[39] shows how predominantly the Soviet interest in the contacts with American representatives at that time was oriented to the hope of forestalling the

[36] Cumming & Pettit, *op.cit.*, pp. 84–85. Note that Francis, just after talking with Robins, still refers to March 12 as the opening date of the Congress.

[37] Francis MSS, *op.cit.*, Ruggles' telegram to Francis, March 8, 10 p.m.

[38] Cumming & Pettit, *op.cit.*, pp. 85–86.

[39] *Ibid.*, p. 87.

Japanese intervention rather than to any prospect of Allied material aid.

The message, it may be added, was occasioned partly by the fact that the first days of March had produced evidences of serious growing conflict between the Bolshevik authorities and the Allied consuls in Vladivostok. By this time Bolshevik authority was being asserted more or less openly in Vladivostok, as in the surrounding area, in ways that caused considerable alarm to the Allied consular authorities. Confiscatory taxes were beginning to be levied against foreign firms established in the area; political persecution of prominent businessmen in the port (some of whom were members of the Chamber of Commerce) was beginning to threaten the general pattern of commercial life. Conversely, the local communist press was becoming increasingly bitter in its attacks on the foreign consular officers, holding them responsible, in particular, for the embargo, just then in force, on movement of food supplies from Manchuria to the Maritime Province.[40] This growing tension did not particularly alarm the consuls, who were protected by the presence of their warships in the port. On February 28, the consuls issued a sharp public protest against the communist encroachments.[41] The receipt in Petrograd of the text of the consular protest naturally grated on the fears and sensibilities of the Soviet leaders, who were already convinced that Japanese intervention was just around the corner, and moved them to redouble their efforts to play off the United States against Japan by every means possible.

The communication to the American Embassy, signed by Chicherin, read as follows:

The People's Commissariat of Foreign Affairs warmly thanks the American Embassy for the friendly attitude which is being shown by it at the present critical time and for assistance being given by it in the complications which are arising now in the Far East. The People's Commissariat hopes that the American Government will act against this unpermissible interference in our internal affairs and in the very organization of the Soviet Republic which recently took place in Vladivostok by all the Allied consuls, including the American. According to information received by us from Khabarovsk, the consuls in Vladivostok presented an ultimatum protesting against the reorganization of local institutions on Soviet lines and the

[40] See Caldwell's telegram of March 6, 10 p.m., to the Department of State, *Foreign Relations, 1918, Russia,* Vol. II, *op.cit.,* pp. 70–71.
[41] *Izvestiya,* March 10, 1918.

creation of a local Red Guard. . . . The action of the Allied consuls is a step directed against the Soviet Government itself. The American Embassy will no doubt realize the adverse influence which this action will have. The People's Commissariat feels certain that the American Embassy will use all means to solve at its earliest convenience this new complication.

Assistant People's Commissary of Foreign Affairs,
TCHICHERIN.

The Ambassador and Robins pondered this message together, with the result that the former at once wired Washington to the effect that

. . . Trotsky complains that Allied consuls Vladivostok, including American, virtually oppose Soviet Government. . . .

and inquired whether Washington had instructed Caldwell to take this attitude.[42] The Ambassador failed to indicate, in his telegram, that Trotsky's complaint had been expressed in a formal written communication to the Embassy. (The Department replied some days later that it had given no instructions to the Consul at Vladivostok save to deal with the constituted authorities.[43])

Having completed his consultation with the Ambassador, Robins wired Trotsky, telling of Francis' intention to remain in Vologda, and reporting that the Ambassador had "telegraphed to Washington an energetic protest against all Japanese plans in Siberia" as well as a recommendation of support by the United States in case of a conflict with the Central Powers. "Your note," he added, "has been transmitted."

A footnote in the Cumming and Pettit volume says this last assertion relates to the sheet of questions handed to Robins on March 5. Just what Robins envisaged as the "transmission" of this document is uncertain. Ruggles had held up its transmission from Petrograd, and Francis, as we have seen, had not even described its content in his message to the Department of State.[44]

On the following day, Robins departed in his special car for Moscow, where he arrived on Monday, March 11, thus paralleling closely the movements of Lenin, who moved to Moscow from Petrograd on

---

[42] *Foreign Relations, 1918, Russia,* Vol. ii, *op.cit.,* p. 74; Telegram of March 10, 6 p.m.

[43] *Ibid.,* p. 79.

[44] Hard, *op.cit.,* p. 144, says Francis did wire the text of Trotsky's questions to Washington on the morning of the 9th. I can find no confirmation of this in the National Archives.

the same day. Trotsky, his nose out of joint at the rejection of his advocacy of a stronger front against the Germans, remained in Petrograd ("sulking," as Robins put it) until after the sessions of the Moscow Congress.

It is important to remember that Robins, when he arrived in Moscow on Monday, was still under the impression that the United States government had before it Trotsky's questions of March 5, and hoped that he would receive an encouraging answer to these questions prior to the opening of the Congress of Soviets, now scheduled for Thursday morning. He also had in mind the similar recommendations of Lockhart and Sadoul, and hoped that the reaction of the United States government would be part of a joint reply by all three Allied governments, assuring the Soviet leaders that there would be no Allied intervention without Soviet agreement and that Allied aid against the Germans would be forthcoming.

❖

Let us now turn, for a moment, to what was happening in Washington. The days immediately following the delivery to the Japanese of the President's note of March 5 continued to be agitated by a great flurry of communications of all sorts relating to the Siberian situation and to the possibility of Japanese intervention. The number of these communications was so great, and the variety of information, misinformation, urgings, warnings, and conjectures so profuse, that it is idle to attempt to summarize them here. Some were confusing in that they represented reactions to the first, rather than the second, of the two drafts the President had prepared for the communication to the Japanese government. Suffice it to note here that at no time during the week was the President permitted to forget the burning subject of Japanese intervention. It was clear that the French and British would continue to press the Japanese to intervene. And it was just at this time that a number of messages were received, from Francis and others, stressing the connection between the problem of intervention and the action to be taken by the Soviet Congress with respect to ratification of the Brest-Litovsk Treaty.

On Friday, March 9, Bullitt conceived the idea of the President's sending a message to the Soviet Congress, in the hope that it might strengthen the hands of the opponents of ratification of the Brest treaty. After getting suggestions from Miles and from Mr.

Lincoln Colcord (Washington corrsepondent for the Philadelphia *Public Ledger* and protagonist of substantially the Robins-Thompson line on Russian matters), he drafted a proposal for the wording of such a message and apparently sent it to the President the same day. Whether the proposal was cleared at higher levels in the Department is not apparent.[45]

The following morning, the President sent for House, who was in New York. The Colonel was more or less prepared for this summons. Thompson, in touch with Bullitt and Colcord at the Washington end, had been needling him along similar lines, through Mr. Norman Hapgood. As it happened, House was taken ill with "a first-class case of the grippe" on the day of the President's summons, and was therefore unable to go to Washington. But he had anticipated the call to Washington by sending to the President, the night before, a note on this very subject.[46] It read as follows:

What would you think of sending a reassuring message to Russia when the Soviet meets at Moscow on the 12th?

Our proverbial friendship for Russia could be reaffirmed and you could declare our purpose to help in her efforts to weld herself into a democracy. She should be left free from any sinister or selfish influence which might interfere with such development.

My thought is not so much about Russia as it is to seize this opportunity to clear up the Far-Eastern situation but without mentioning it or Japan in any way. What you would say about Russia and against Germany could be made to apply to Japan or any other power seeking to do what we know Germany is attempting.[47]

House, describing this note in his diary, says he advised that the President should "so word the message as to cover our position on Japanese intervention in Siberia." The President responded by producing what House described as "one of the most cleverly worded, three sentenced messages extant." It was designed for transmission to the "people of Russia through the Soviet Congress," and read as follows:

May I not take advantage of the meeting of the Congress of the Soviets to express the sincere sympathy which the people of the United States feel for the Russian people at this moment when the German power has been

[45] Gumberg MSS, *op.cit.,* letter from Colcord to Robins, February 5, 1919.
[46] House MSS, *op.cit.,* Diary, March 11, 1918.
[47] Seymour, Vol. III, *op.cit.,* p. 399.

thrust in to interrupt and turn back the whole struggle for freedom and substitute the wishes of Germany for the purposes of the people of Russia. Although the Government of the United States is unhappily not now in a position to render the direct and effective aid it would wish to render, I beg to assure the people of Russia through the Congress that it will avail itself of every opportunity to secure for Russia once more complete sovereignty and independence in her own affairs and full restoration to her great rôle in the life of Europe and the modern world. The whole heart of the people of the United States is with the people of Russia in the attempt to free themselves forever from autocratic government and become the masters of their own life. Woodrow Wilson.[48]

How much of this was the President's own draft and how much Bullitt's, the record does not indicate. The President called up Acting Secretary of State Polk on the 11th and read the draft message to him over the telephone. As read to Polk, the message spoke of German power being thrust in to interrupt and turn back the whole Revolution, thus implying American sympathy for the Revolution and indignation at German efforts to overthrow it. Polk suggested that the phrase "struggle for freedom" be substituted for the term "Revolution." The President agreed to the change. It seems doubtful that Polk had seen the message before.[49]

The message was handed over to the Department of State the same day for transmission. It was at once put on the wires to Summers at Moscow. He gave it to Robins, who handed it to Lenin personally, on the 12th. It was thus available before the Congress opened on the 14th.

The wording of the message is interesting as another reflection of Wilson's outlook on the Russian problem. Like other Wilsonian statements, it attributed to German diplomacy vis-à-vis the new Soviet state sweeping ideological motives—namely, the interruption and turning back of the whole "struggle for freedom" in which the Russian people were supposed to be engaged—which were scarcely present in the German mind. The German purpose at that time was to assure against any renewal of hostilities on the Russian side and to gain access to grain and other raw materials of the Ukrainian area. These motives were so overriding as to render any other thoughts decidedly secondary. The President continued, furthermore, to por-

---

[48] *Foreign Relations, 1918, Russia*, Vol. I, *op.cit.*, p. 395.
[49] Polk MSS, *op.cit.*, official desk diary, March 11.

tray the Russian Revolution, even in March 1918, as a struggle on the part of the Russian people to free themselves from autocratic government. He appears to have been disinclined to draw any clear line of distinction between the Soviet regime and the Russian people. Whether by conviction or for reasons of political expediency, he continued to appeal to an assumed community of aims between the United States and the political power dominant in Russia.

It is clear, today, that such an approach could hardly have evoked an enthusiastic response in Russia. Four years later, to be sure, the Moscow *Izvestiya* would refer to it in kindly words, as evidence for the assertion that "after the October Revolution the American Government was the only one of the Allied governments which did not immediately make any hostile move toward Soviet Russia." [50] But that was another day. In March 1918, the Soviet leaders were still carried away by the novel pleasure of hurling insults at the capitalist powers with impunity on any and all occasions. They were well aware, furthermore, that Wilson's kind words reflected no thought of recognition of their power by the United States government. Thus the message evoked in them primarily the characteristic desire to demonstrate that their ideological convictions were not so frivolous that they could be lulled into abandoning them by honeyed phrases from the other camp.

As for the real liberal elements in Russia: they were now in violent opposition to Soviet power. It could only have been irritating to them to see the President of the United States approaching the delegates to the Congress of Soviets, whom they themselves had come to view as the deadly enemies of true democracy, with professions of sympathy and appeals to an implied community of aims.

The response of the Congress to the President's communication reflected these realities. Wilson's message was read to the Congress on March 15 by the chairman, Sverdlov. An answering resolution was then proposed, the text of which had been drafted earlier in the Central Executive Committee. This resolution, adopted by acclamation, read:

The Congress expresses its appreciation to the American people, and in the first instance to the toiling and exploited classes of the United States of North America, for the expression by President Wilson, through the

[50] *Izvestiya*, September 19, 1922.

Congress of Soviets, of sympathy for the Russian people in these days when the Soviet Socialist Republic of Russia is undergoing heavy trials.

The Russian Socialist Soviet Federated Republic avails itself of this communication from President Wilson to express to all those peoples perishing and suffering under the horrors of the imperialist war its warm sympathy and its firm confidence that the happy time is not far distant when the toiling masses of all bourgeois countries will throw off the yoke of capitalism and will establish a socialist order of society, which alone is capable of assuring a firm and just peace as well as the cultural and material well being of all the toilers.[51]

This reaction, ignoring the President and the United States government (just as Wilson had ignored the Soviet government), addressing itself to the peoples of the warring countries, promising—and welcoming—an early overthrow of what, by implication, included the government of the United States, was meant to be offensive—and was. Zinoviev is said to have stated in a public speech, after his return to Petrograd following the Congress, that "we slapped the President of the United States in the face." [52]

It is hard to ascertain the effect of this reply on official Washington. House, ill in New York, seems to have left no record of his reaction. Wilson, also, remained silent. His papers throw no light on his feelings. The insulting overtones of the Soviet reply could hardly have escaped him, any more than they escaped a portion, at least, of the American press. The *New York Times,* in particular, which had theretofore warmly supported Wilson's policy of studied reiteration of sympathy for the Russian people, was greatly shocked by the reply—shocked, in fact, to a point where it finally abandoned hope of any sort of accommodation with the Bolsheviki. With people in their state, the paper concluded,

. . . no discussion is possible. They will have to be disregarded altogether. . . . No help is to be looked for from them, not because they may not desire to save themselves from the German hoof, but because all their measures are taken with the belief that the universal revolution must come first. Russia must be saved without them; saved in spite of them.[53]

[51] The above is my own translation of the resolution as given in the official Soviet publication of state documents, Klyuchnikov & Sabanin, Part II, *op.cit.,* p. 135. Consul General Summers' translation will be found in *Foreign Relations, 1918, Russia,* Vol. I, *op.cit.,* p. 399.
[52] Francis, *op. cit.,* p. 230.
[53] *New York Times,* editorial, Sunday, March 17, 1918.

In this way the exchange of messages with the Soviet Congress, conceived by House, if not the President, as a means of warning the Japanese against intervention, ended by strengthening the feeling among Americans themselves that some sort of intervention would sooner or later be necessary.

❖

The text of the President's message was sent both to Summers, in Moscow, and to Francis, in Vologda. Francis received it on March 12, two days after Robins' departure for Moscow. He thought it well framed and timely. Noting, however, the President's statement to the effect that the United States government was not then in a position to render effective aid to Russia, he apparently recalled that he had failed to communicate to Washington the substance of Trotsky's questions to Robins. He therefore at once despatched a telegram summarizing the Soviet document of March 5 (he still did not communicate the text), and inquiring whether the Department considered the President's message an adequate reply to Trotsky's questions. This message was not received in Washington until March 15, by which time the deliberations of the Congress of Soviets in Moscow were nearing their close.

On arrival in Moscow, Robins was, as will be recalled, still under the impression that Trotsky's questions were being carefully pondered in Washington. He had tea with Lenin and his sister the day the Congress opened. He found Lenin preparing to submit a resolution for ratification of the treaty. Lenin asked what Robins had heard from his government. The answer was "Nothing." Robins quotes Lenin as saying:

You will not hear. Neither the American Government nor any of the allied governments will cooperate, even against the Germans, with the workmen's and peasants' revolutionary government of Russia.

"I smiled," Robins added, "and said I thought differently." [54]

Lenin told Robins that Lockhart, too, had had no answer. This was not strictly correct. Lockhart was then still in Petrograd (he did not reach Moscow until the Congress was over). In a series of exchanges between Lockhart and his government in the days following March 5, it was made quite clear to him not only that the British

[54] *Bolshevik Propaganda, Hearings . . . , op.cit.,* p. 805.

government failed to see the logic of his warnings against Japanese intervention but that his representations along these lines were arousing irritation and disapproval in London.[55] These evidences were reinforced by veiled intimations from his wife, in England, that he was doing his career no good with his efforts to influence British policy.[56] Despite these evidences, he, too, continued to nurture hope that a favorable reply would be forthcoming to the questions Trotsky had placed to Robins. Lockhart felt, Tredwell reported on March 15,

> . . . that the whole situation now depends upon the question which I had Prince telegraph for me 10 days ago when we discovered that our message to the Governor had not reached him.[57]

In continuing to place such hopes on the reply to Trotsky's questions, Lockhart, like Robins, was overrating Soviet interest in the possibility of Allied aid, and underrating Soviet interest in spiking Japanese intervention, which was the main reason for the attention he was receiving at Soviet hands.

The Congress of Soviets was convened on March 14 and deliberated for two days. Lenin delivered a long report at the opening session, repeating the arguments for ratification he had advanced at the Party Congress, drawing the parallel of the Treaty of Tilsit imposed on Prussia by Napoleon, not deprecating the ignominy and weakness of Russia's position, but promising early relief and eventual triumph through the spread of revolution to other countries. After permitting intermediate debate by other speakers, he then delivered a final rebuttal and appeal for support, before bringing to a vote the resolution of ratification.

Robins subsequently gave the United States Senators a dramatic account of the moment preceding Lenin's final speech:

> About an hour before midnight on the second night of the conference Lenine was sitting on the platform; I was sitting on a step of the platform, and I looked around at this man, and he motioned to me. I went to him. He said, "What have you heard from your Government?" I said, "Noth-

[55] See Balfour's message of March 4 to Lockhart, *Foreign Relations, 1918, Russia,* Vol. I, *op.cit.,* pp. 390–391.

[56] Lockhart, *op.cit.,* p. 238.

[57] This is taken from a document in the Francis MSS, *op.cit.,* entitled: "Paraphrase of confidential information contained in Mr. Tredwell's letter of March 15, 1918, which he desired transmitted to the Ambassador and Colonel Ruggles only." Signed "L" (probably Lehrs).

ing." I said, "What has Lockhart heard?" He said, "Nothing." He said, "I am now going to the platform and the peace will be ratified"; and he went to the platform, and he made a speech of an hour and twenty-odd minutes or so, in which he outlined the economic condition, the military condition, the absolute necessity after the three years of economic waste and war for the Russian peasant and workingman to have the means, even by a shameful peace, for the reorganization of life in Russia and the protection of the revolution, as he said; and the peace was ratified by two and a half to one in that vote.[58]

These words conveyed, of course, the suggestion that had Robins been able to tell Lenin, at that moment, that his government had responded favorably to Trotsky's questions, the treaty might never have been ratified. Robins was surely sincere in his belief that this was so, and he must have left the steps of the platform sick with disappointment at the inexplicable silence of his government.

Actually, as we have seen, nothing in the available record supports such a suggestion in any way. All known evidence, in fact, would seem to controvert it. But the suggestion subsequently commended itself to many who were inclined to assign exclusively to the United States government the blame for an unhappy state of relations between the two governments. It became one more stone in the structure of belief that the United States government, swayed by the fear and prejudice of American capitalists, had rejected the hand of friendship proffered by the Soviet leaders in the days of the Brest-Litovsk crisis and had thus needlessly estranged them in the early days of their power, when they desperately needed sympathy and support.

❖

On that same day, it might be added, the Department of State finally received Francis' message of the 12th, giving it, for the first time, some real indication of the nature of Trotsky's questions, and asking whether they required any answer beyond the President's message. On March 19, four days after the treaty had been ratified, Washington despatched its reply:

Department considers President's message to Russian people . . . adequate answer.

By the time this message had been decoded in the club house in Vo-

[58] *Bolshevik Propaganda, Hearings* . . . , *op.cit.,* p. 807.

logda, and passed along to Robins in Moscow, life had moved on. Russia was out of the war. A new era had begun in the Russian capital. Once again, as so often in the course of these rapidly moving events, Washington—troubled, hesitant, and ill-informed—had spoken, reluctantly, into the past.

APPENDIX

ACKNOWLEDGMENTS

SELECTED BIBLIOGRAPHY

INDEX

APPENDIX

Suggested Communication to the Commissar for Foreign Affairs:

At the hour the Russian people shall require assistance from the United States to repel the actions of Germany and her allies, you may be assured that I will recommend to the American Government that it render them all aid and assistance within its power. If upon the termination of the present armistice Russia fails to conclude a democratic peace through the fault of the Central Powers and is compelled to continue the war I shall urge upon my government the fullest assistance to Russia possible, including the shipment of supplies and munitions for the Russian armies, the extension of credits and the giving of such advice and technical assistance as may be welcome to the Russian people in the service of the common purpose to obtain through the defeat of the German autocracy the effective guarantee of a lasting and democratic peace.

I am not authorized to speak for my Government on the question of recognition but that is a question which will of necessity be decided by actual future events. I may add, however, that if the Russian armies now under command of the people's commissaires commence and seriously conduct hostilities against the forces of Germany and her allies, I will recommend to my Government the formal recognition of the de facto government of the people's commissaires.

Respectfully,

[Note in lead-pencil at bottom: "O.K., D.R.F. Subject to change by Dept., of which Col. Robins will be promptly informed 1/2/18."]

[In the margin: "To Col. Robins."] [1]

[1] *Bolshevik Propaganda, Hearings* . . . , *op.cit.*, p. 1009; document identified as "Robins Document No. 1."

Appendix

Suggested Communication to the Department of State:

From sources which I regard as reliable I have received information to the effect that Bolshevik leaders fear complete failure of peace negotiations because of probable demands by Germany of impossible terms.

Desire for peace is so fundamental and widespread that it is impossible to foretell the results of the abrupt termination of these negotiations with only alternatives a disgraceful peace or continuance of war.

Bolshevik leaders will welcome information as to what assistance may be expected from our government if continuance of war is decided upon. Assurances of American support in such event may decidedly influence their decision.

Under these circumstances and notwithstanding previous cables I have considered it my duty to instruct Gen. Judson to informally communicate to the Bolshevik leaders the assurance that in case the present armistice is terminated and Russia continues the war against the Central Powers I will recommend to the American government that it render all aid and assistance possible. Have also told Robins of Red Cross to continue his relations with Bolshevik government, which are necessary for the present.

Present situation is so uncertain and liable to sudden change that immediate action upon my own responsibility is necessary otherwise the opportunity for all action may be lost.

Nothing that I shall do will in any event give formal recognition to the Bolshevik government until I have explicit instructions, but the necessity for informal intercourse in the present hour is so vital that I should be remiss if I failed to take responsibility of action.

[Note in lead-pencil in margin: "To Col. Robins: This is substance of cable I shall send to Dept. on being advised by you that peace negotiations terminated and soviet government decided to prosecute war against Germany and Austro-Hungary. D.R.F. 1/2/18."] [2]

[2] *Ibid.*, p. 1010; document identified as "Robins Document No. 2."

ACKNOWLEDGMENTS

The author wishes to acknowledge his indebtedness
to the following publishers:

To The Bobbs-Merrill Company, Inc., for permission to quote from *War Memoirs of Robert Lansing, Secretary of State,* 1935.

To Doubleday & Company, Inc., for permission to quote from *A Prisoner of Trotsky's,* by Andrew Kalpaschnikoff, 1920.

To Mr. Hermann Hagedorn, for permission to quote from his *The Magnate: William Boyce Thompson and His Time, 1869–1930,* published by The John Day Company. Copyright 1935 by Hermann Hagedorn.

To Harcourt, Brace & Company, Inc., for permission to quote from *Russian-American Relations, March 1917–March 1920,* compiled and edited by C. K. Cumming and W. W. Pettit, 1920.

To Harper & Brothers, for permission to quote from *Raymond Robins' Own Story,* by William Hard, 1920.

To Houghton Mifflin Company, for permission to quote from *The Letters and Friendships of Sir Cecil Spring Rice: A Record* (Volume II), edited by Stephen Gwynn, 1929, and from *The Intimate Papers of Colonel House* (Volume III: *Into the World War, April 1917–June 1918*), by Charles Seymour, 1928.

To the Librairie Plon, for permission to quote from *Mon Ambassade en Russie Soviétique, 1917–1919* (Volume I), by Joseph Noulens, 1933.

To Little, Brown & Company, for permission to quote from *My Mission to Russia and Other Diplomatic Memories,* by Sir George Buchanan, 1923.

To Oxford University Press, Inc., for permission to quote from *Soviet Documents on Foreign Policy* (Volume I: *1917–1924*), selected and edited by Jane Degras, issued under the auspices of the Royal Institute for International Affairs, 1951.

To G. P. Putnam's Sons, for permission to quote from *British Agent,* by R. H. Bruce Lockhart, 1933.

❖

Acknowledgments

The author wishes to acknowledge his indebtedness
to the following persons, for permission to quote
from hitherto unpublished material:

To Edward Goring Bliss, for General Tasker H. Bliss' telegram of February 19, 1918.

To George B. Creel, for George Creel's letter to President Wilson of December 27, 1917.

To Allen W. Dulles, for Secretary Lansing's memorandum covering the Cabinet meeting of March 20, 1917; and his note to Secretary Daniels of January 3, 1918.

To Thomas Francis, for Ambassador Francis' letters to Secretary Lansing of November 20, 1917, to General Judson of November 20, 1917, and his telegram to Secretary Lansing of December 15, 1917.

To Henry M. Fuller, Reference Librarian of the Yale University Library, for material from the personal papers of Edward M. House and Frank L. Polk.

To Herman H. Fussler, Director, University of Chicago Library, for Professor Samuel Harper's letters of October 19, 1918 to Jerome Landfield and of April 26, 1918 to Dr. Billings, and the passage from the draft manuscript.

To Hermann Hagedorn, for William Boyce Thompson's memorandum of about December 31, 1917.

To Clay Judson, for materials from the William V. Judson collection.

To Charles Seymour, for Colonel House's letter to President Wilson of February 2, 1918.

To Mrs. Woodrow Wilson, for President Wilson's letter to Secretary Lansing of February 15, 1918, as well as for permission to have access to the Wilson Collection for purposes of general research.

❖

The author wishes to acknowledge his indebtedness
to the following persons, for giving him the benefit of their valuable
memories and impressions of the events with which this study deals:

The Honorable Norman Armour

The Honorable William C. Bullitt

Peter I. Bukowski

John K. Caldwell

Fred M. Dearing

Frazier Hunt

William Chapin Huntington

Earl M. Johnston

Princess Alexandra Kropotkin

Sir Reginald Leeper

R. H. Bruce Lockhart

David B. Macgowan

Earl L. Packer

Livingston Phelps

Charles Stephenson Smith

Mrs. Maddin Summers

Mrs. William English Walling

Sheldon Whitehouse

SELECTED BIBLIOGRAPHY

MANUSCRIPTS

The following collections were used in the preparation of this volume:

In the Library of Congress:
Ray Stannard Baker Papers
Albert Sydney Burleson Papers
Hermann Hagedorn–W. B. Thompson Papers
Robert Lansing Papers
Breckinridge Long Papers
Roland S. Morris Papers
Woodrow Wilson Papers

In the Library of Princeton University:
Arthur Bullard Papers

In the Missouri Historical Society, St. Louis:
David R. Francis Papers

In the State Historical Society of Wisconsin, Madison:
George Gibbs Papers
Alexander Gumberg Papers
DeWitt C. Poole Papers
Raymond Robins Papers

In the Library of the University of Chicago:
Samuel N. Harper Papers

In the Library of Yale University:
Edward M. House Papers
Frank Polk Papers
Sir William Wiseman Papers

In the Newberry Library, Chicago:
William V. Judson Papers
Graham Taylor Papers

Bibliography

In the New York Public Library:
Thomas D. Thacher Papers

In the Archives of the American National Red Cross, Washington:
Various papers

PUBLIC DOCUMENTS

Publications of the United States Government consulted in the preparation of this volume included:

Bolshevik Propaganda, Hearings before a Subcommittee of the Committee on the Judiciary, United States Senate, 65th Congress, Third Session (1919).

The German-Bolshevik Conspiracy, War Information Series, No. 20-October, 1918 (Committee on Public Information, George Creel, Chairman).

Papers Relating to the Foreign Relations of the United States: The Lansing Papers, 1914–1920 (two volumes), (1939, 1940).

Papers Relating to the Foreign Relations of the United States: 1917 (1926) Supplement 1, *The World War* (1931) and Supplement 2, *The World War* (two volumes), (1932).

Papers Relating to the Foreign Relations of the United States: 1918, Russia (three volumes), (1931, 1932).

Papers Relating to the Foreign Relations of the United States: 1918, Supplement 1, Volume 1 (1933).

Papers Relating to the Foreign Relations of the United States: 1919, Russia (1937).

Proceedings of the Brest-Litovsk Peace Conference: The Peace Negotiations between Russia and the Central Powers, 21 November, 1917–3 March, 1918 (1918).

The National Archives of the United States Government:
Foreign Affairs Section
War Department Section
Microfilm Files of Captured German Foreign Office Documents (World War I period)
Justice and Executive Section

BOOKS

Non-periodical sources consulted in the preparation of this volume included:

Thomas A. Bailey, *America Faces Russia: Russian-American Relations from Early Times to Our Day,* Cornell University Press, Ithaca, 1950.

[526]

Bibliography

Ray Stannard Baker, *Woodrow Wilson, Life and Letters* (eight volumes), Doubleday, Doran & Co., Inc., New York, Volume VII, *War Leader, April 6, 1917–February 28, 1918* (1939) and Volume VIII, *Armistice, March 1–November 11, 1918* (1939).

Bessie Beatty, *The Red Heart of Russia*, The Century Co., New York, 1919.

Otto Becker, *Der Ferne Osten und das Schicksal Europas, 1907–1908*, Koehler & Amelang, Leipzig, 1940.

Samuel Flagg Bemis, Editor, *The American Secretaries of State and Their Diplomacy* (10 volumes), Volume X, Alfred A. Knopf, New York, 1929.

Edwyn Bevan, *German Social Democracy During the War*, George Allen & Unwin, Ltd., London, 1918.

Louise Bryant, *Six Red Months in Russia*, George H. Doran Co., New York, 1918.

George Buchanan, *My Mission to Russia and Other Diplomatic Memories* (two volumes), Little, Brown & Co., Boston, 1923.

Arthur Bullard, *The Russian Pendulum: Autocracy—Democracy—Bolshevism*, The Macmillan Co., New York, 1919.

James Bunyan, *Intervention, Civil War, and Communism in Russia, April–December 1918, Documents and Materials*, The Johns Hopkins Press, Baltimore, 1936.

James Bunyan and H. H. Fisher, *The Bolshevik Revolution, 1917–1918, Documents and Materials*, Stanford University Press, 1934.

Edward Hallett Carr, *A History of Soviet Russia: The Bolshevik Revolution, 1917–1923* (three volumes), The Macmillan Co., New York, 1950, 1952, 1953.

William Henry Chamberlin, *The Russian Revolution, 1917–1921* (two volumes), The Macmillan Co., New York, 1935.

Tao-hsing Chang, *International Controversies over the Chinese Eastern Railway*, The Commercial Press, Ltd., Shanghai, 1936.

V. M. Chernov, *Pered Burei* (Before the Storm), Chekhov Publishing House, New York, 1953.

George Chicherin, *Two Years of Foreign Policy: The Relations of R.S.F.S.R. with Foreign Nations, from November 7, 1917 to November 7, 1919*, Russian Government Bureau, New York, 1920.

Winston S. Churchill, *The Aftermath: The World Crisis, 1918–1928*, Charles Scribner's Sons, New York, 1929.

Grosvenor B. Clarkson, *Industrial America in the World War: The Strategy Behind the Line, 1917–1918*, Houghton Mifflin Co., Boston, 1923.

W. P. and Zelda K. Coates, *Armed Intervention in Russia, 1918–1922*, Victor Gollancz Ltd., London, 1935.

Bibliography

Frederic Coleman, *Japan Moves North: The Inside Story of the Struggle for Siberia,* Cassell & Co., Ltd., London, 1918.

George Creel, *How We Advertised America,* Harper & Bros., New York, 1920; *Rebel at Large: Recollections of Fifty Crowded Years,* G. P. Putnam's Sons, New York, 1947.

C. K. Cumming and Walter W. Pettit, Editors, *Russian-American Relations: March, 1917–March, 1920; Documents and Papers,* Harcourt, Brace & Howe, New York, 1920.

Henry Pomeroy Davison, *The American Red Cross in the Great War,* The Macmillan Co., New York, 1920.

Jane Degras, Compiler, *Calendar of Soviet Documents on Foreign Policy, 1917–1941,* Oxford University Press for Royal Institute of International Affairs, London, 1948.

Jane Degras, Editor, *Soviet Documents on Foreign Policy* (three volumes), Volume I, *1917–1924,* Oxford University Press for Royal Institute of International Affairs, 1951.

A. I. Denikin, *Ocherki Russkoi Smuty* (Sketches of the Time of Trouble in Russia) (two volumes), J. Povolozky & Cie, Éditeurs, Paris (1922?).

Blanche E. C. (Mrs. Edgar) Dugdale, *Arthur James Balfour, First Earl of Balfour, K.G., O.M., F.R.S.* (two volumes), Hutchinson & Co., Ltd., London, 1936.

Louis Fischer, *Men and Politics: An Autobiography,* Duell, Sloan & Pearce, New York, 1941; *The Soviets in World Affairs* (two volumes), Princeton University Press, 1951.

David R. Francis, *Russia from the American Embassy: April, 1916–November, 1918,* Charles Scribner's Sons, New York, 1921.

Olga Hess Gankin and H. H. Fisher, *The Bolsheviks and the World War: The Origin of the Third International,* Stanford University Press, 1940.

I. I. Genkin, *Soedinennye Shtaty Ameriki i SSSR—Ikh Politicheskie i Ekonomicheskie Vzaimootnosheniya* (The United States of America and the USSR—Political and Economic Relations between Them), State Social-Economic Publishing Co., Moscow-Leningrad, 1934.

Ellen Glasgow, *The Woman Within,* Harcourt, Brace & Co., New York, 1954.

G. P. Gooch and A. W. Ward, Editors, *The Cambridge History of British Foreign Policy: 1783-1919* (three volumes), Volume III, *1866–1919,* Cambridge University Press, 1923.

H. Graf, *La Marine Russe Dans La Guerre et Dans la Révolution 1914–1918,* Payot, Paris, 1928.

Stephen Gwynn, Editor, *The Letters and Friendships of Sir Cecil Spring Rice: A Record* (two volumes), Houghton Mifflin Co., Boston, 1929.

[528]

Bibliography

Hermann Hagedorn, *The Magnate: William Boyce Thompson and His Time, 1869–1930,* The John Day Co., New York, 1935.

William Hard, *Raymond Robins' Own Story,* Harper & Bros., New York, 1920.

Paul V. Harper, Editor, *The Russia I Believe In: The Memoirs of Samuel N. Harper, 1902–1941,* University of Chicago Press, 1945.

E. J. Harrison, *Peace or War East of Baikal?* Kelly & Walsh, Ltd., Yokohama, c. 1910.

Granville Hicks, *John Reed: The Making of a Revolutionary,* The Macmillan Co., New York, 1936.

Max Hoffmann, *Die Aufzeichnungen des Generalmajors Max Hoffman* (two volumes), Verlag für Kulturpolitik, Berlin, 1929.

Erwin Hölzle, *Der Osten im ersten Weltkrieg,* Koehler & Amelang, Leipzig, 1944.

Kikujiro Ishii, *Diplomatic Commentaries,* The Johns Hopkins Press, Baltimore, 1936.

Philip C. Jessup, *Elihu Root* (two volumes), Volume II, *1905–1937,* Dodd, Mead & Co., New York, 1938.

Andrew Kalpaschnikoff, *A Prisoner of Trotsky's,* Doubleday, Page & Co., Garden City, N.Y., 1920.

Alexander F. Kerensky, *The Catastrophe: Kerensky's Own Story of the Russian Revolution,* D. Appleton & Co., New York, 1927.

V. M. Khvostov and I. I. Mints, under editorial direction of V. P. Potemkin, *Istoriya Diplomatii* (The History of Diplomacy), Volume II, *Diplomacy in Recent Times (1872–1919),* State Publishing House for Political Literature, Moscow, 1945.

Yuri V. Klyuchnikov and Andrei Sabanin, Editors, *Mezhdunarodnaya Politika Noveishego Vremeni v Dogovorakh, Notakh, i Deklaratsiyakh* (International Politics of Recent Times in Treaties, Notes and Declarations), (three volumes), Literary Publishing House of the People's Commissariat for Foreign Affairs, Moscow, 1925, 1926, 1928–1929.

Alfred Knox, *With the Russian Army, 1914–1917: Being Chiefly Extracts from the Diary of a Military Attaché* (two volumes), Hutchinson & Co., London, 1921.

I. K. Koblyakov, *Ot Bresta do Rapallo* (From Brest to Rapallo), State Publishing Co. of Political Literature, Moscow, 1954.

A. Ye. Kunina, *Proval Amerikanskikh Planov Zavoevaniya Mirovogo Gospodstva v 1917–1920 gg* (Failure of the American Plans for World Domination 1917–1920), State Publishing House for Political Literature, Moscow, 1954.

Thomas W. Lamont, *Across World Frontiers,* Harcourt, Brace & Co., Inc., New York, 1951.

Bibliography

Robert Lansing, *War Memoirs of Robert Lansing, Secretary of State,* Bobbs-Merrill Co., New York, 1935.

V. I. Lenin, *Sochineniya* (Complete Works), (35 volumes), Volume XXII, *1917–1918,* State Publishing House, Moscow-Leningrad, 1930.

David Lloyd George, *War Memoirs of David Lloyd George* (six volumes), Volumes V and VI, Ivor Nicholson & Watson, London, 1936.

R. H. Bruce Lockhart, *British Agent,* G. P. Putnam's Sons, New York, 1933.

Judah L. Magnes, *Russia and Germany at Brest-Litovsk: A Documentary History of the Peace Negotiation,* Rand School of Social Science, New York, 1919.

Clarence A. Manning, *The Siberian Fiasco,* Library Publishers, Inc., New York, 1952.

G. Mannerheim, *Erinnerungen,* Atlantis Verlag, Zurich, 1952.

Arnold D. Margolin, *From a Political Diary: Russia, the Ukraine, and America, 1905–1945,* Columbia University Press, New York, 1946.

Marie, Queen of Roumania, *Ordeal: The Story of My Life,* Charles Scribner's Sons, New York, 1935.

George Thomas Marye, *Nearing the End in Imperial Russia,* Dorrance & Co., Philadelphia, 1929.

A. I. Melchin, *Amerikanskaya Interventsiya v 1918–1920 gg* (American Intervention 1918–1920), Military-Naval Publishing Co., Moscow, 1951.

Paul N. Milyukov, *Russia: To-Day and To-Morrow,* The Macmillan Co., New York, 1922; *Rossiya na Perelomye* (Russia at the Crossroads), (two volumes), Volume I, *Origin and Consolidation of the Bolshevik Dictatorship,* Imprimerie d'Art Voltaire, Paris, 1927.

James R. Mock and Cedric Larson, *Words that Won the War: The Story of the Committee on Public Information, 1917–1919,* Princeton University Press, 1939.

Constantin Nabokoff, *The Ordeal of a Diplomat,* Duckworth & Co., London, 1921.

Harley Notter, *The Origins of the Foreign Policy of Woodrow Wilson,* The Johns Hopkins Press, Baltimore, 1937.

Joseph Noulens, *Mon Ambassade en Russie Soviétique, 1917–1919* (two volumes), Librairie Plon, Paris, 1933.

O. Henry, *Seats of the Haughty,* Doubleday & Co., New York, 1916.

Ferdinand Ossendowski, *From President to Prison,* George Allen & Unwin Ltd., London, 1925.

Frederick Palmer, *Newton D. Baker: America at War* (two volumes), Dodd, Mead & Co., New York, 1931.

V. A. Panov, *Istoricheskaya Poddelka; Amerikanskie Poddelnye Dokumenty* (Historical Forgery; American Forged Documents), Vladivostok, 1920.

Bibliography

Albrecht Philipp, Editor, *Die Ursachen des Deutschen Zusammenbruchs im Jahre 1918*, Deutsche Verlagsgesellschaft für Politik und Geschichte, Berlin, 1925.

Richard Pipes, *The Formation of the Soviet Union: Communism and Nationalism, 1917–1923*, Harvard University Press, Cambridge, 1954.

M. N. Pokrovski, *Vneshnyaya Politika Rossii v XX Veke* (Russian Foreign Policy in the 20th Century), Publishing House of the Sverdlov Communist University, Moscow, 1926.

Stefan T. Possony, *A Century of Conflict: Communist Techniques of World Revolution*, Henry Regnery Co., Chicago, 1953.

Ernest Batson Price, *The Russo-Japanese Treaties of 1907–1916 concerning Manchuria and Mongolia*, The Johns Hopkins Press, Baltimore, 1933.

M. Philips Price, *My Reminiscences of the Russian Revolution*, George Allen & Unwin, Ltd., London, 1921; *War and Revolution in Asiatic Russia*, George Allen & Unwin, Ltd., London, 1918.

Oliver Henry Radkey, *The Election to the Russian Constituent Assembly of 1917*, Harvard University Press, Cambridge, 1950.

John Reed, *Ten Days that Shook the World*, Boni & Liveright, Inc., New York, 1919.

Jacques Sadoul, *Notes sur la Révolution Bolchevique*, Éditions de la Sirène, Paris, 1920.

Frederick Lewis Schuman, *American Policy Toward Russia Since 1917*, International Publishers, New York, 1928.

Charles Seymour, *The Intimate Papers of Colonel House* (Four volumes), Vol. III, *Into the World War, April 1917–June 1918*, Houghton Mifflin Co., New York, 1928.

Sezdy Sovetov v Postanovleniyakh i Rezolyutsiyakh (Official History of the Soviet Congresses), Moscow, 1935.

Leonard Shapiro, Editor, *Soviet Treaty Series* (two volumes), Vol. I, *1917–1928*, The Georgetown University Press, Washington, 1950.

Albert Shaw, Editor, *The Messages and Papers of Woodrow Wilson* (two volumes), Vol. I, *March 4, 1913 to January 6, 1919*, George H. Doran Co., New York, 1924.

Edgar Sisson, *One Hundred Red Days; A Personal Chronicle of the Bolshevik Revolution*, Yale University Press, New Haven, 1931.

George E. Sokolsky, *The Story of the Chinese Eastern Railway*, North-China Daily News & Herald, Ltd., Shanghai, 1929.

John Spargo, *Russia as an American Problem*, Harper & Bros., New York, 1920.

I. N. Steinberg, *In the Workshop of the Revolution*, Rinehart & Co., Inc., New York, 1953; *Souvenirs d'un Commissaire du Peuple, 1917–1918*, Librairie Gallimard, 1930.

Bibliography

Leonid I. Strakhovsky, *The Origins of American Intervention in North Russia*, Princeton University Press, 1937.

Nikolai Nikolaivich Sukhanov, *Zapiski o Revolyutsii* (Notes on Revolution) (7 volumes), Grzhebin Publishing House, Berlin-Petersburg, 1923.

H. W. V. Temperly, *A History of the Peace Conference of Paris* (six volumes), Vol. I; Vol. III, *Chronology, Notes & Documents*, Oxford University Press and Hodder & Stoughton, London, 1920.

M. Tikhomirov, *Vnezhnaya Politika Sovetskogo Soyuza* (Foreign Policy of the Soviet Union), State Publishing House, Moscow, 1940.

Leo Trotzki, *Mein Leben,* S. Fischer Verlag, Berlin, 1930.

Mark Vishnyak, *Dan Proshlomu* (Tribute to the Past), Chekhov Publishing House, New York, 1954; *Vserossiskoye Uchreditelnoye Sobranie* (The All-Russian Constituent Assembly), Paris, 1932.

Richard von Kühlmann, *Erinnerungen,* Verlag Lambert Schneider, Heidelberg, 1948.

Frederich von Rabenau, *Seeckt, Aus Seinem Leben 1918–1936,* Hase and Koehler Publishing House, Leipzig, 1940.

John Ward, *With the "Die-Hards" in Siberia,* George H. Doran Co., New York, 1920.

Robert D. Warth, *The Allies and the Russian Revolution*, Duke University Press, Durham, 1954.

Stanley Washburn, *Victory in Defeat: The Agony of Warsaw and the Russian Retreat,* Doubleday, Page & Co., Garden City, N.Y., 1916.

John W. Wheeler-Bennett, *The Forgotten Peace: Brest-Litovsk, March 1918,* William Morrow & Co., New York, 1939.

John Albert White, *The Siberian Intervention*, Princeton University Press, 1950.

Arthur Willert, *The Road to Safety: A Study in Anglo-American Relations,* Derek Verschoyle, London, 1952.

Albert Rhys Williams, *Lenin: The Man and His Work,* Scott and Seltzer, New York, 1919; *Through the Russian Revolution,* Boni & Liveright, New York, 1921; *The Soviets,* Harcourt, Brace & Co., New York, 1937.

William Appleman Williams, *American Russian Relations, 1781–1947,* Rinehart & Co., Inc., New York, 1952.

Chitoshi Yanaga, *Japan since Perry,* McGraw-Hill Book Co., Inc., New York, 1949.

A. Zaitsov, *1918 Godi; Ocherki po Istorii Russkoi Grazhdanskoi Voiny* (The Year 1918: Sketches in the History of the Russian Civil War), Paris, 1934.

Ye. M. Zhukov, Editor, *Mezhdunarodnye Otnosheniya na Dalnem Vostoke, 1870–1945* (International Relations in the Far East, 1870–1945), State Publishing House for Political Literature, Moscow, 1951.

INDEX

Index

Clark, Frank, Representative from Florida, 79

Clemenceau, Georges, French Prime Minister, declines to release Russia from obligations to Allies, 133; 151, 178, 300

Clemens, Samuel, and Friends of Russian Freedom, 12

Colcord, Lincoln, 510

Coleman, Frederic, 280

Committee on Public Information, establishment and nature, 45-46; personnel in Russia, 46-52; decides to undertake operations in Russia, 50; 78, 116, 126-27, 268, 271, 386; and Sisson documents, 445-51. *See also* Bullard, Arthur; Creel, George; Sisson, Edgar

Congress of Soviets, II Congress (November 7-9, 1917), 74-75; III Congress (January 23-31, 1918), 261, 347-49, 358-60, 401; IV Special All-Russian Congress (March 14-17, 1918), 371; Wilson's message to, 373-74, 509-14; 495, 498; postponement of, 500-05; 506, 509; ratification of Brest-Litovsk Treaty, 515-17. *See also* Lenin, V. I.; Trotsky, L. D.

Constituent Assembly, 204, 343-63, 398; Electoral Commission of, 344, 346-47

Constitutional-Democratic Party, 13 n., 163, 175-77, 347

Coolidge, Archibald, 450

Crane, Charles R., member of Root Mission, 20; visits Lansing, 176-77

Crane, Richard, 176

Creel, George, 30, 45; personal qualities, 46; effort to have Bullard assigned to Root Mission, 47-48; 50, 59, 77, 125-27; relays President's reprimand to Sisson, 128-29; 155, 245-46; controversy with Walling, 271-74; and Sisson documents, 445-48, 452

Crosby, Oscar T., Treasury Department delegate to Inter-Allied Council on War Purchases and Finance, 177-78, 180

Crosley, Captain Walter S., American Naval Attaché, Petrograd, 204

Crosley, Mrs. Walter S., 206

Czernin, Count Ottokar, Austro-Hungarian Foreign Minister, 221, 228, 366, 368, 372. *See also* Brest-Litovsk negotiations

Daniels, Josephus, Secretary of the Navy, 325

Davis, Jerome, Y.M.C.A. Secretary in Russia, 172 n. 11, 389

Davison, Henry P., Chairman of the War

Council of the American Red Cross, 52-53, 232, 388, 394

Declaration of London of September 1914, 87, 91-93, 132-33, 275

de Cram, Matilda, 38-40, 58, 114, 117, 126-28, 387-88, 416

Decree on Peace, 31, 74-77, 85, 142 n. 5, 220

Denikin, General A. I., 163

Department of State, Sisson papers in offices of, 453. *See also* United States

Diamandi, Count Constantine, Rumanian Minister, Petrograd, arrest, detention, and release, 331-342; 402

Don Cossack region, 160-65, map 162, 173, 179, 181-83, 188, 197, 200, 461

Dosch-Fleurot, Arno, 405

Drysdale, Major Walter S., American Military Attaché, Peking, 309 n. 34, 321-22, 468

Dukhonin, General N. N., 86; refusal to seek armistice, 89-90; dismissal, 91, 105 n. 11; 93, 95-96, 101, 104-06, 109-10, 149, 152, 154; murder of, 210

Dulles, John Foster, 149 n. 1

Duncan, James, member of Root Mission, 20; effect of inclusion on Root Mission, 22

Dunsterville, Major General, 186

Durnovo, Colonel, aide of Marushevski, 101-02

Dvinsk, 104; maps, 162, 436; 431

Dzerzhinski, head of Soviet political police, 215-16, 390

Ellis, William T., 386

Emerson, George, 286-87, 296-98

Estonia, 369, 371, 431

February Revolution, 8-10; American reaction to, 13-16; 280

Finland, 179, 341-42, 363, 412, 431, 433, 437, 444

Foch, Marshal Ferdinand, 300

Forster, Rudolph, 453

Fortress of St. Peter and St. Paul, map 37; Kalpashnikov in, 206, 209, 214-15; Diamandi in, 333, 341; 390

Foster, John W., 149

Fourteen Points speech, 139, 242-274

France, attitude on war aims problem, 131-39; 140; interest in Rumania and Ukraine, 170; talks and agreement with British at Paris, 178-81, 184, 186-87, 379; policy toward Ukraine, 184-85; 223; policy to-

Index

Index

Index

Niessel, General, Chief of French Military Mission in Russia, 308 n. 33, 493
Noulens, Joseph, French Ambassador to Russia, attitude toward Francis, 38; part in Diamandi incident, 332-36, 341; 355, 382-83; and question of Allied aid, 432-33; departure from Petrograd, 437; arrival in Vologda, 488
Novocherkassk, 161, map 162, 173, 181, 183
Novoye Vremye, 415 n. 5
Novy Mir, 31, 65

Omsk, 283, 286, 459
Oustinoff, Soviet Consul at New York, 405
Outlook, The, 361
Owen, Robert, United States Senator, 391-92

Page, Walter Hines, American Ambassador, London, 326, 445, 449, 468-69
Palestine, 187
Patchin, Philip, 446 n. 8
Peking, map 288, 472
Pereverzev, Minister of Justice in Provisional Government, 415
Perkins, Major Roger, member American Red Cross Commission to Rumania, 200, 202-07, 213
Persia, 187
Peters, Y. K., head of Military-Revolutionary Committee in Petrograd, 66, 390
Petrograd, map of, 37; threatened German occupation of, 371, 431-32, 437-38
Petrograd Soviet, 10-11, 22, 24, 79, 99 n. 1, 110, 115, 227, 344. *See also* Lenin, V. I.; Trotsky, L. D.
Petrov, P., 123, 402, 429 n. 28, 490
Phelps, Livingston, American Secretary of Embassy, Petrograd, 336
Phillips, William, Assistant Secretary of State, 124, 127 n. 55, 311, 319, 432
Pichon, Major, French Military Agent in Siberia, 308 n. 33
Pichon, Stéphane, French Foreign Minister, 309, 323, 326, 471
Platten, Fritz, 349
Poland, 221-23, 225, 238, 258, 261, 268
Polk, Frank L., Counselor of the Department of State, 153-54, 188, 271-72, 310, 325, 375, 387-88, 394; and Sisson documents, 445-46; and Wilson's communication of March 5, 1918 to Japanese on intervention, 479-82; and Wilson's message to Soviet Congress, 511
Poole, DeWitt C., American Consul at Moscow, 17 n. 6; commended for bravery, 74;

journeys to Cossack country, 180-83; and Sisson documents, 447-48; recommends joint occupation of Trans-Siberian Railway, 472
Poole, Ernest, 48 n. 19
Pornarède, Major de la, French Officer in China, 322
Pouren, 62
Pravda, 110, 224-25, 227, 229, 233; on Fourteen Points speech, 262-63; 332, 339, 348, 504
Pri-Amur, 280, 306
Pri-Azovski Krai, 415
Prince, Captain Eugene, aide to Military Attaché in Petrograd, 103, 437, 499
Prisoners-of-war (German-Austrian) in Siberia, 283-84, 321, 475, 477
Provisional Government, establishment and role of, 10-11; U.S. policy toward, 12, 16-26; supporters urge maintenance of U.S. agencies in Russia, 82-83; 94; view on war aims question, 143-44, 147-48; 290; and Constituent Assembly, 343-44. *See also* Kerensky, Alexander F.

Radek, Karl, 66, 234-35; wife in Foreign Office, 353; 496
Ramsay, Baron, 72
Ransome, Arthur (British correspondent), 261, 353, 490-91
Reading, Lord, British Ambassador, Washington, 317, 474-75, 477
Reed, John, personal qualities, 67-69; appearance at III Congress of Soviets, 359-60; 403 n. 14; appointment as Soviet Consul at New York, 405-411
Reinsch, Paul S., American Minister, Peking, 304, 472-73
Reinstein, remarks at III Congress of Soviets, 358-59; 407
Riggs, Captain E. Francis, Assistant American Military Attaché, Petrograd, 72, 437, 495-96, 499
Robins, Raymond, 52, 54-55, 57; encourages Thompson to leave Russia, 60; personal qualities, 62-65; 66; defends Gumberg, 67; 73 n. 2; initial call on Trotsky, 99-100; 107-08, 110, 112; part in Judson visit to Trotsky, 113-16; part in Sisson's effort to bring about Francis' removal, 126-29; permission to have contact with Soviet authorities, 129-30; opposes action on behalf of anti-Bolshevik centers, 170; interview with Trotsky on armistice conditions, 193; connection with Kalpashnikov incident, 200-17; and first Brest-